Mr. Acheson, Mr. Bevin and M. Schuman at Lancaster House for the opening of the London Conference of Foreign Ministers on 11 May 1950.

DOCUMENTS ON
BRITISH POLICY OVERSEAS

EDITED BY

ROGER BULLEN, Ph.D.

(London School of Economics)

AND

M.E. PELLY, M.A.

ASSISTED BY

H.J. YASAMEE, M.A. AND G. BENNETT, M.A.

SERIES II

Volume II

LONDON

HER MAJESTY'S STATIONERY OFFICE

ISBN 0 11 591693 8

Printed in the United Kingdom for Her Majesty's Stationery Office
(1243/87) Dd716939 6/87 C12 56-9531 10170

DOCUMENTS ON BRITISH POLICY OVERSEAS

Series II, Volume II

The London Conferences
Anglo – American Relations and Cold War Strategy
January – June 1950

PREFACE

This volume documents the London Conferences of May 1950. It begins with the extensive preparations within the Foreign Office for the various meetings of ministers and officials and then proceeds to document the discussions themselves. The London conferences provided for three separate series of talks, each of which was intended to review the problems and the progress of the western alliance in the period since the Washington conference of September 1949. The conference began with official and ministerial conversations (bipartite) between the British and the Americans. Simultaneously official and ministerial talks (tripartite) were held between the British, French and Americans and finally the conferences ended with a twelve power Atlantic Council. The timetabling and agenda of these various talks were elaborate and difficult and themselves became the subject of acute political and diplomatic sensitivities both between the British, French and Americans on the one hand and on the other between them and the remaining nine signatories of the North Atlantic Treaty.

In view of the extensive nature of all the discussions held in London in May 1950, this volume offers an unusually wide ranging global survey of British foreign policy at the height of the Cold War. Moreover the lengthy preparations within the Foreign Office for the conferences resulted in several important statements of basic policy objectives. As a consequence, many of the documents in this volume illustrate what Mr. Bevin and his officials thought were the aims, constraints and directions of policy. For the London conference of Foreign Ministers Mr. Bevin specifically elaborated the notions of the 'three main pillars' of British foreign policy: the United States, the Commonwealth and Western Europe (No. 74.i), thus anticipating Mr. Churchill's later formulation of the same idea in his phrase the 'three concentric circles'.

By 1950 Mr. Bevin, Mr. Acheson and M. Schuman, the Foreign Ministers of the United Kingdom, United States and France, were convinced of the importance and utility of conference diplomacy in consolidating the western alliance. They were agreed that it served many purposes. Conferences were regarded as the surest and most effective means of conducting what Mr. Attlee described as 'the higher direction of the Cold War'. It also enabled ministers and their advisers to exchange views on a wide range of questions, particularly on those extra-European questions where any one of the powers enjoyed a regional or local preponderance. Equally it enabled ministers to review the progress of important negotiations either at a preparatory stage or when brought by officials to the point of agreement and thus requiring ministerial authority for the final resolution of differences. This aspect of conference diplomacy was particularly important for German questions. It was considered essential that the Foreign Ministers of the three leading powers in the western alliance should give a sense of direction, purpose and unity both to their lesser allies and to public opinion throughout the western world. In advance of the ministerial discussions Mr. Bevin drew the attention of his Cabinet colleagues to the need for 'a strongly worded and convincing declaration of aims as a counter-weight to Soviet peace and other forms of propaganda' (No. 74.i). Consequently the London conferences issued a series of communiqués (e.g. Nos. 98.i and 113.i) which were intended to receive extensive publicity and boost public morale. Finally there was a widespread feeling in 1950 among all the Atlantic Pact states that this new organization needed to be strengthened and 'made into a living reality' (No. 74.i).

The immense problems involved in the co-ordination of the policies of twelve states certainly imposed strains on conference diplomacy but equally confirmed its importance. For the American, British and French governments there was a delicate balance to be struck in the Atlantic Council; on the one hand they were expected to give a lead, on the other they were anxious not to be accused of directing without consultation. The Foreign Office was well aware of the need not to admit the existence of an 'inner group', however composed, whose task it was to examine and establish both the economic and strategic priorities without reference to other allies (No. 41). The development of the North Atlantic Treaty organization was therefore a matter of prolonged bipartite, tripartite and twelve power discussion and in each case the forum of the discussion affected the tone and the content of the proceedings. Mr. Evelyn Shuckburgh, Head of Western Organizations department, warned on 6 April that 'our own cold warriors will probably not be ready to share their methods and secrets with representatives of the other eleven countries, and any general Atlantic cold war efforts would therefore be much more formal than real' (No. 17, note 3).

By its very nature conference diplomacy between allied powers has encouraged a constant jockeying for position. The creation and the operation of an informal hierarchy has always been a normal and natural feature of alliance diplomacy. The London Conferences of May 1950 were, however, unusual in the sense that the Foreign Office believed that the purpose of the bipartite Anglo-American talks, which were regarded as the most important, was to define the 'special relationship' between the two governments and place it at the centre of the Atlantic Pact. The United Kingdom would thus achieve a formal definition of its status as the principal ally of the United States. It expected to receive assurances about the rôle which it would play in defending and consolidating the affairs of the west which would confirm its position as a world power.

The first indications that Mr. Acheson and his officials thought it desirable to establish Anglo-American relations on a new basis came in a letter from Sir Leslie Rowan, Economic Minister at H.M. Embassy in Washington, to Mr. E.A. Hitchman in the Treasury in February 1950 (No.

2). He reported that the State Department had referred to 'the possibility of a working partnership' between the two countries. It was clear that American officials had no fixed ideas of what the definition of the special relationship would involve. It was however evident that it could not take an open and acknowledged form because of the effect it would have on other European allies, particularly France. It was, moreover, stressed that these overtures 'may be representing only one school of thought in the State Department'. Sir L. Rowan's letter was circulated in the Foreign Office and was the subject of high level discussion.

Further intimations of this new line in American thinking were conveyed in a personal letter from Sir Oliver Franks, H.M. Ambassador at Washington, to Mr. Bevin (No. 5). He believed that as a result of 'combined eagerness and frustration' the Americans were searching for new policies and that they realized that such policies could neither be 'formulated or made effective except in partnership with Britain'. In a more specific sense Mr. Acheson indicated that he expected the British government to take the lead in western Europe where there was an urgent need for measures which would link Germany to the western community of states. This was clearly an implied criticism of the reluctance of the British to give to their leadership the form which the Americans wished it to take. Mr. Acheson more openly criticized the British tendency to count the cost in foreign policy rather more than was necessary. Sir Oliver Franks believed that on the question of 'costs' the Americans should be made to see the British point of view; if they 'want our active partnership in the world, they must be prepared to make changes which will give us long term economic strength' (No. 11).

As result of these reports from Washington and the discussions held with the State Department concerning the agenda for the London conferences (No. 15, note 1), Sir Gladwyn Jebb, Deputy Under Secretary of State in the Foreign Office, recorded on 11 April 1950 that the Anglo-American talks, as defined by the Americans, 'should aim in the first place at establishing an understanding between the United States and the United Kingdom as to the basic relationship between the two countries and the rôle which each could play most effectively to ensure "world prosperity and progress"' (No. 15) and that all items in the tripartite and Atlantic Council discussions 'should be considered in the light of the general understanding reached' on Anglo-American relations. It was therefore with considerable optimism that Mr. Bevin and his officials began to prepare for these talks. 'It is the first time since the war', commented one Foreign Office official, that the Americans 'have approached us as a partner on the most general issues of policy' (No. 24). In the words of Sir Gladwyn Jebb, 'the favourable opportunity that we now have for establishing our own position in the world may not recur' (No. 15).

The Foreign Office was particularly anxious that French susceptibilities should not narrow the range of the discussions in London; M. Schuman had earlier informed Mr. Bevin that in his view a meeting of the North Atlantic Council 'might appear aggressive to the U.S.S.R.' (No. 3). Equally, it was considered essential that the French should be prevented from intruding upon the time set aside for the Anglo-American talks; M. Schuman had expressed his 'grave disquiet lest the initial bilateral Anglo-American talks should have an unfavourable effect in France' (No. 21, note 2). Eventually however, the French were persuaded, largely as a result of American insistence, to agree to a meeting of the North Atlantic Council and to the face-saving device, suggested by the Foreign Office, of a short tripartite procedural meeting with the American delegation immediately after its arrival in London. Moreover Mr. Acheson travelled to London via Paris where he had some preliminary talks with M. Schuman. With these difficulties resolved the Foreign Office and the State Department were able to agree on an agenda which constituted a global review of 'our current position in the Cold War' (No. 17). In the Foreign Office itself Mr. Bevin's advisers concentrated on the preparation of briefs both for the initial talks between officials which could be revised and amended in the light of these talks for the ministerial conversations.

The briefs prepared for the London conferences were mainly drafted within the Foreign Office. There was less inter-departmental consultation than was usual for such a major review of foreign policy. This was a subject of complaint from other departments after the conferences were over (No. 116). The Foreign Office briefs fell into two categories; those prepared within departments, sometimes after consultation with posts overseas, and those prepared by the Permanent Under-Secretary's Committee (P.U.S.C.). This Committee began to function on 1 February 1949 and it was established 'for the consideration of long-term problems' (Office Circular No. 3 of 17 January 1949). It met weekly and had its own secretariat. It was composed of senior Foreign Office officials and a junior minister, and was empowered to co-opt other officials as occasion required and to consult other departments of state and the Chiefs of Staff's organization. Its position within the Foreign Office was analogous to that of the Policy Planning Staff within the State Department. For the London conference of Foreign Ministers the P.U.S.C. revised and expanded some papers already drafted and under discussion, in the light of recent developments and of the stated aims of the Anglo-American talks, and prepared new drafts on matters arising from the agreed Anglo-American agenda. Additionally some assistance was given in the preparation of briefs by the Russia Committee acting under those terms of its instructions which emphasised the preparation of 'the forecast of Russian intentions' (Office Circular No. 3).

Within the Foreign Office it proved easier for the P.U.S.C. in its wide ranging surveys of Cold War diplomacy and of the opportunities and dangers implicit in the western community of states to stress the need for continuous Anglo-American consultation and the closer co-ordination of policies than it was for those who drafted briefs on specific issues actually to record either the existence of a satisfactory identity of outlook with the Americans or to see a way forward in the resolution of outstanding Anglo-American differences. On the level of general intentions the Foreign Office perceived few disagreements with the State Department, but on particular questions there was a long list of discord.

In mid-April 1950 when the preparation of briefs for the conference was just beginning, the P.U.S.C. revised its paper 'A Third World Power or Western Consolidation' and considered that 'the United Kingdom will have an increasingly important part to play in the consolidated West and must also seek to maintain its special relations with the United States' (No. 20). Two days earlier Sir Roger Makins, Deputy Under Secretary of State, had, however, recorded that in the field of atomic energy no effective Anglo-American co-operation existed and that 'our need for raw materials will be greater if cooperation is withheld by the United States' (No. 19). It was recognised that the resolution of technical problems was a matter of patient and detailed diplomacy conducted by experts. What was needed was an authoritative expression of the political will for cooperation. It was therefore essential that the search for a new and secure basis should be combined with the resolution of a number of outstanding differences.

From the outset of the preparations for the talks it was agreed with the Americans that one area of special difficulty, economic relations, should be dealt with in a general way rather than specifically and that no attempt should be made to conduct detailed bilateral economic negotiations at the conference. Mr. Bevin himself admitted that 'perhaps the greatest source of difficulty lies in mutual doubts and suspicions of each others economic policies' (No. 74.i) and he had also expressed the fear that as a result of American diplomacy the Soviet Union would be able in its propaganda to exploit 'the theme of Western Europe's subservience to the dollar' (No. 3, note 4). It was decided in London to sidestep rather than confront these problems; as these issues could not be resolved at the conference it was prudent not to raise them. In January 1950 the Foreign Office and the Treasury had together listed Anglo-American economic differences (No. 1.i) and Sir Leslie Rowan had already voiced his doubts as to whether the new partnership could be 'effective unless there was the possibility of frank discussion about the internal policies of each side' (No. 2). Mr. Bevin, however, insisted that he did not want to discuss these matters in detail and preferred that in the economic discussions the United Kingdom should stress firstly that the United Kingdom could only be an effective partner if she was economically strong, secondly that it was in the interests of both countries that the United Kingdom should stand on its own feet as soon as possible and finally that the two governments should discuss any differences on a 'basis of partnership' (No. 74.i). This was an easily agreed formula although not necessarily a successful one. Whether such a 'basis of partnership' could exist between a debtor nation and its major creditor was a question posed rather than answered (No. 34). The decision to exclude detailed economic negotiations from the conference agenda and the absence of any precise discussions on what Sir O. Franks had called the 'costing' of foreign policy therefore provided the basis for Mr. Bevin's statement that 'the Conferences are political' (No. 74.i).

The Treasury view of the economic background to the Anglo-American discussions was much bleaker than that of the Foreign Office. In his brief for the Chancellor of the Exchequer, Sir Stafford Cripps, on the P.U.S.C. paper 'British Overseas Obligations' (No. 43), Sir Edwin Plowden, Chief Planning Officer in the Treasury, who was invited to participate in Anglo-American discussions of economic policy, suggested that 'we should tell the Americans frankly that we are already overstrained and that it is only with the assistance of Marshall Aid that we can carry our present burdens' (No. 36). In his view British economic resources were not sufficient both to maintain her position as a world power and to maintain existing standards of living. The stark choices which such a statement implied, although appreciated within the Foreign Office, were not thought to require an airing in the Anglo-American discussions. Despite this difference in outlook between the Foreign Office and the Treasury, the underlying assumption of Treasury officials that if Great Britain was no longer able singlehandedly to sustain obligations overseas then she should seek to shift some of the burden on to the United States was a theme constantly reiterated in Foreign Office briefs. There was no dissent within the Foreign Office from the view of Sir Oliver Franks that the British government had 'two inter-connected priorities' (No. 11); effective action in foreign policy and the building of long term economic strength without which foreign commitments could not be supported. For a great power with limited resources these were aims which it was easier to formulate than to achieve.

The optimism evinced by Mr. Bevin and some of his senior advisers as to the opportunity for developing a new partnership with the United States of America was viewed with some scepticism both by some junior officials within the Office and more importantly by the Chancellor of the Exchequer. In a minute on the brief 'The general approach in bipartite conversations with the American delegation' (No. 24), Mr. Shuckburgh injected a strong note of caution. He doubted whether the Americans would be able to regard the establishment of a new partnership with the United Kingdom as the prime object of the talks and that their reluctance to do so would inevitably result in disappointment. Secondly he wondered whether the creation of an exclusive relationship with the United States would have the consequence of weakening the influence which the United Kingdom could exercise in Europe. This leadership had hitherto derived strength from the fact that the United Kingdom was not always willing to follow an American lead. Finally he believed that within such a relationship as it was proposed to establish, it would be extremely difficult to manage relations with the French and that they would come to feel that there was a 'sphere . . . from which they are excluded' (No. 24, note 9).

The effect of a new Anglo-American partnership on Anglo-French and Franco-American relations was, however, already under discussion. The P.U.S.C. had warned that in certain circumstances 'the possibility of a Franco-American partnership cannot be excluded' (No. 27). The French government had actively supported American ideas on western European unity and the announcement on 9 May, just before the ministerial talks began, of the Schuman Plan proposals (Volume I), came as a serious blow to Mr. Bevin and his officials. The new proposal and the wholehearted American support given to it highlighted the fear within the Foreign Office that a continental bias to United States policies in Europe would almost certainly be at the expense of British interests. This danger, however, only became apparent after the Anglo-American official talks were over. The sudden and dramatic shift in American policy was therefore unsuspected by Sir Gladwyn Jebb when he drew up his suggestions for handling the French in April 1950. In his view the real direction of the Atlantic Pact should be entrusted to an unofficial 'inner group' of the United Kingdom, the United States and Canada. It was, however, necessary to conceal the existence of this 'inner group' from 'the Latins': 'some façade' should be constructed which would enable 'France and, if possible, Italy' to be associated with the direction of the Atlantic Alliance (No. 41). From the British point of view therefore the ends which the new Anglo-American partnership should serve were to strengthen Great Britain's position as a world power and to emphasize the importance of the Atlantic framework for western consolidation.

The Foreign Office preparations for the London Conference represent the purest and the most complete expression of the 'Atlanticist' outlook in British foreign policy. There can be no doubt that Mr. Bevin regarded the signature of the North Atlantic Treaty as his greatest achievement. Thereafter he saw it as the starting point for all future developments. In its paper 'Western Organisations' the P.U.S.C. concluded that the advantage of building on the North Atlantic Treaty was considerable and listed eight reasons why the United Kingdom should seek to do so (No. 30). To a very great extent British enthusiasm for the Atlantic Community reflected its considered rejection of alternatives. The P.U.S.C. had concluded that the possibility of an even closer association than that which already existed between the United Kingdom and her Commonwealth partners was not practicable (No. 20) but more importantly had also reached the conclusion that it was not in Great Britain's interest either to encourage or to join a west European federation of states. The Foreign Office thought its policy towards western Europe should be enshrined in the principle of 'one foot in and one foot out' of Europe's affairs (No. 30) and in the notion that 'the United Kingdom must be regarded as a power with world interests and not merely as a potential unit of a Federated Europe' (No. 33). Antipathy to federalist tendencies in western Europe was balanced by a willingness to foster cooperation on the basis of inter-governmental organizations. This was not an abdication of British leadership in western Europe but merely a precise definition of its form and limits.

Officials in the Foreign Office were aware of the importance that Mr. Acheson and his officials attached to bold new policies which would bind Germany to the west, and to renewed efforts which would promote Franco-German reconciliation and they believed that the British government should take the lead in these endeavours. One of the tasks of the official bipartite talks was therefore to attempt to reconcile British and American differences about the nature and direction of British leadership in Europe (No. 34). Mr. Bevin was robustly defiant of any attempt to lead him at a pace and in a direction which did not accord with his own sense of priorities; he said 'he would like to get away from talk about Europe . . . The Americans were wrong to think in terms of Europe as a separate and self-contained unit' (No. 52). The aim of Atlanticist policies was both to include and to transcend Europe.

The chief ministerial critic of Mr. Bevin's Atlanticist emphasis for the London conferences was the Chancellor of the Exchequer, Sir Stafford Cripps. The briefs prepared by Foreign Office departments were not circulated to other departments in Whitehall, but the papers of the P.U.S.C. were circulated to selected ministers and their senior officials. In April, the Chancellor of the Exchequer made the common complaint of Cabinet ministers that he was not in a position to make detailed comments on Foreign Office papers and transact his own departmental business. He did however briefly minute on the P.U.S.C. paper on Anglo-American relations (No. 27) 'I am not sure I agree with the implications which seem to me to be much nearer permanent subservience to the U.S.A. than anything else'. He returned to this theme in May when Mr. Attlee held informal meetings of selected senior Cabinet ministers to discuss the British approach to the Conferences. This reflected the prime minister's preference for discussions of high policy with a small group of senior ministers rather than with his Cabinet colleagues as a whole. This was, as is well-known, a long established tradition of, rather than a departure in policy making.

The issues of high policy raised by the London conference, particularly for the future of Anglo-American relations, although presented to the Cabinet in the broad context of a general review of policy, were discussed in greater detail at two informal meetings of senior ministers, chaired by the prime minister (Nos. 57 and 63). It was at these meetings that the Chancellor of the Exchequer's misgivings about the aims of policy contained in the P.U.S.C. paper for the London conference were fully revealed. He raised a number of objections to aspects of Foreign Office policy; criticising both the direction and emphasis of measures for the development of N.A.T. organization, the possibility of switching economic discussions away from the O.E.E.C. towards N.A.T. and the general approach to Anglo-American economic discussions. The main thrust of his criticism was, however, a frontal attack on the Atlanticist assumptions of Mr. Bevin's policy. He regretted the absence of any 'reference to the policy of creating a "Third Force" by a combination of the United Kingdom, the Commonwealth and Western Europe'. He was convinced that the "Third Force" concept should not have been abandoned 'for he still looked forward to the day when this country could free herself from the hegemony, political and economic, of the United States' (No. 57).

In a memorandum for the Prime Minister before the second informal meeting of ministers, Sir N. Brook explained the manner and the reasons for the abandonment of the Third Force concept by senior ministers in the Economic Policy Committee in 1949 and reminded the prime minister that it was Mr. Bevin's belief that although the Cabinet had not discussed this policy change, it had nonetheless endorsed it (No. 62). At the second meeting of ministers, the Chancellor repeated his warnings about the 'hegemony of the United States over Europe' but contented himself with the position that ministers would, at some future date, discuss the fundamental issues involved. It was clear that the other ministers present at these meetings did not share either the Chancellor's misgivings or his belief that a wider review of policy by the entire Cabinet was necessary. Consequently there was no modification of Foreign Office aims for the talks and at the Cabinet meeting where Mr. Bevin outlined, generally rather than specifically, his objectives at the London conference, no reference was made to the differences which had arisen at the informal meetings of senior ministers.

This triumph was short-lived. Before his departure from Washington, Mr. Acheson in a conversation with Sir Oliver Franks indicated that he wished to shift the emphasis of the talks away from 'questions of organisation' to the search for new policies and in particular to concentrate on the urgent need for new measures to bind Germany to the west (No. 48). This volte-face clearly reflected the strong criticism by American diplomats in Europe of the idea of developing and extending Anglo-American co-operation and the fact that the United States government had been consulted by the French before they launched the Schuman Plan in advance of the tripartite ministerial talks in London (Volume I). Sir Leslie Rowan's suggestion (No. 2) that the idea of a strengthened Anglo-American partnership only represented one school of thought in the State Department was clearly correct. Not only had this line of thought come under attack, but an alternative, that of American support for France in western Europe, secured a greater advance towards the realisation of specific policy objectives. The danger of Franco-American co-operation in Europe at the expense of Great Britain which in its deliberations the P.U.S.C. had considered remote came in fact to dominate the London conferences.

In the wider context of Cold War strategy and particularly in their estimation of the position of the west in Europe, British and American policy makers had more common ground than differences. They were agreed that the next few years of the struggle would be crucial, that there was little likelihood of reaching a settlement of outstanding differences with the Soviet Union and that there were great dangers for the west in any proposal for a top level meeting with the Soviets. It was agreed that if such a meeting resulted in a spurious agreement with the Soviets, it would lull western public opinion into a false sense of security. If no agreement was reached, it would present communist propaganda with fresh ammunition for its peace campaigns, particularly in Germany. Finally if the western powers themselves proposed such a meeting then they would be preparing western public opinion for a 'let-up in the "cold war"' (No. 26). In these circumstances therefore it was safer to talk about the Russians rather than talk to them and western public opinion would be encouraged by a general declaration embodying western values and ideals in their most positive form (No. 26).

It was inevitable that German questions should loom large in any high level discussions between the three western occupying powers. It was not, however, an easy matter to draw up an agreed agenda on German issues. Each of the three Foreign Ministers had a different view of which German questions were the most pressing, on which it would be prudent to postpone decisions and how best to conduct delicate negotiations with the German government through the Allied High Commission. On the last questions there were two contrasting views: it was sometimes argued that the German government required timely concessions from the three occupying powers to persuade it to follow a particular course; equally it was argued that the allies must make no concessions and demand German compliance with the course they proposed. In any three power conference it was, however, essential to ensure that the great volume of German business did not overwhelm the conference agenda. There was therefore always a distinction to be drawn between high policy for Germany and more detailed administrative questions which could be left to expert discussions and decision.

In the context of the Cold War the future of Germany was regarded as the key issue of the European conflict. The western occupying powers had no doubt that they were engaged in a struggle with the Soviet Union for the allegiance of Germany. The great danger was that Germany would be tempted eastwards (No. 31). The aim of western policy therefore was to bind Germany to the west (No. 58). This demanded a careful presentation to German public opinion of aspects of western policy, for example, towards the question of German unification (No. 31) and an exposure of the reality of Soviet policy towards Germany and Germans, which partly accounted for the attention given to the German prisoners of war still held by the Soviet Union (No. 93). Although the three powers were agreed on the importance and urgency of binding Germany to the west, they held widely different views as to how this should be accomplished and what initiatives were required to ensure the success of such policy. At the London conferences Germany's proposed membership of the Council of Europe, of the Coal and Steel Pool and ultimately of the Atlantic Pact raised deep divisions. Foreign Office officials believed that the underlying French aim of wishing to keep Germany out of the Atlantic Alliance was assiduously pressed by all means at their disposal (No. 47). This much had been expected; what was a surprising development, however, was the change of direction in State Department policy towards Germany. It became apparent shortly before the London conference opened that the American delegation had changed its mind about the nature of discussions on Germany at the conference. It had initially proposed a review and consolidation of occupation policies. Subsequently it was indicated that a more urgent tone should be injected into the discussions on Germany and that they should be elevated to the level of high policy towards the future of Germany (No. 51). To the British experts on Germany in the bipartite official talks, this development was perplexing; it meant that the American delegation was not ready for the discussions they had proposed and indeed had to ask for a postponement (No. 58, note 1). In fact the Americans were unwilling to unfold their views on Germany until after the Schuman Plan had been communicated to the British government and were clearly seeking tripartite decisions on Germany's integration with her west European neighbours rather than bipartite discussions on less urgent questions of occupation controls.

At the departmental level within the Foreign Office the assessment of Anglo-American relations prepared for official and ministerial guidance necessarily drew attention to those issues where British and American policies diverged and which called for efforts either to reconcile differences or prevent even greater divergences. It was on Far Eastern affairs that the failure of co-operation was most marked. It was agreed by both governments that it was in the interests of the west to prevent China from passing into the Soviet orbit and that she was not yet irrevocably lost. China could still play an important role in Asian diplomacy and she had not yet severed all her valuable commercial links with the non-communist world. It was the British contention that America's policy towards China was 'defeatist' and negative (No. 56) and that the bankruptcy of American diplomacy in the Far East was adversely affecting both occupation policies in Japan and progress on a Japanese peace treaty (No. 50). British officials were alarmed by the drift of American Far Eastern policy and recommended that Mr. Bevin should ask Mr. Acheson where the United Kingdom would stand if the United States was not to have any Chinese policy for some years to come (No. 56).

In the Indian Sub-Continent and in Central Asia the British government wished to draw to the attention of the United States the aspirations it had for a settlement of the Kashmir dispute and was otherwise content to work on the principle that this was an area where Great Britain's Commonwealth relationships gave her in Western diplomacy a particular pre-eminence (No. 73). As far as French problems in Indo-China were concerned Mr. Bevin was anxious not to be placed in the position of being asked for further military aid which the British government would have to refuse (No. 32). Equally in South East Asia he was unwilling to be committed to a tripartite statement which 'would smack of "ganging-up" and would only lead to friction between the European and Asian Powers' (No. 69).

In the Middle East considerable common ground existed between the British and Americans on the broad issues of policy. The idea of a joint Anglo-American statement on arms supplies to Middle Eastern countries reflected a common interest of both powers to promote stability in the region (No. 10). The search for a concerted démarche on this issue involved a mutual willingness not to raise particular aspects of Middle Eastern problems on which the policies of the two powers diverged; the British tactfully relegated the problems of Israel and Palestine to a minor place and expected that the Americans would not press the British government to take decisions on the Saudi-Arabian territorial demands upon the British protectorates in the Gulf (cf. however No. 65.i). It was thought essential within the Foreign Office to avoid the situation 'of having Israel backed by the United States and the Arab countries by the United Kingdom' (No. 10, note 10). Throughout the negotiations on the Middle East statement, the Foreign Office was conscious that its position in the Middle East was weak and faced the twin dangers that 'the whole area will further disintegrate and become a ready prey for whichever power chooses to step in and take control' (No. 14). In view of these dangers, Anglo-American co-operation to provide stability for the region was designed to shore up British power and influence in the region. The Middle East statement provided a yet further example of Anglo-French conflict masked behind a procedural dispute. It was Mr. Bevin's decision that the French should not be excluded from the Middle Eastern statement (No. 65, note 5) but the late and apparently peremptory request for them to sign was a matter of both resentment and protest (No. 110).

On Persian questions the two Powers had established a basis of cooperation and were anxious both to strengthen the government against internal disruption and 'to give the Persians moral encouragement' (No. 86, note 3). There were some differences as to the means by which this end could be achieved, in particular on the effectiveness of dollar aid.

In the official tripartite talks Anglo-French differences surfaced in the procedural and organizational issues arising out of the development of the Atlantic Pact. The Foreign Office wanted to develop article 2 of the North Atlantic Treaty as a new and major initiative in western consolidation. The aim of such a policy was to ensure that the institutions of western co-operation were Atlantic rather than European. It was intended that at some stage this new body would assume some of the functions hitherto exercised by O.E.E.C., that it would attract to it some of those states, such as Sweden, who were members of the Council of Europe but had not signed the North Atlantic Treaty, that it would provide the means by which the discussion of economic questions could be integrated with the discussion of defence matters and that it would be in the first instance the body to which Germany would be associated as part of her gradual absorption into the Atlantic Community (Nos. 16 & 30). French opposition to these British schemes was manifested early in the tripartite discussions and the British noted with some alarm that American officials were disposed to support French arguments. Sir R. Makins was convinced that the French wanted to atrophy article 2 of the Pact, largely because they did not want Germany in any way associated with the North Atlantic Treaty. The French conception of the west as two zones, one Atlantic and one European, revealed a wide gulf between British and French policy, a gulf which could not be bridged by the hastily improvised compromises of conference diplomacy (No. 47).

The official bipartite discussions in April and early May were not as fruitful as Mr. Bevin and his advisers had hoped. In the Foreign Office it was felt that the American delegation was not fully prepared for the talks and that 'they had not developed very clear ideas on most of the subjects under discussion' (No. 117). As a consequence of American unprepared-ness and the reluctance of the British to give a lead in the tripartite talks, the American delegation was 'very susceptible to the active needling of the French'. Most importantly of all, however, it became 'quite clear early on in the official talks' that the Americans no longer regarded the redefinition of the special relationship as the main purpose of the London conferences. To the disappointment of the British at the inconclusive nature of the bipartite official talks was added a sense of frustration at the direction taken by the tripartite official discussions.

The public announcement by the French of the Schuman Plan on the evening of 9 May and the warm support given to it by the Americans yet further clouded the ministerial talks between Mr. Bevin and Mr. Acheson. It was becoming increasingly clear that the Americans had revised their strategy for the consolidation of the west. They abandoned the concept of a strengthened Anglo-American partnership for the French notion of 'two spheres', one Atlantic and one European, and were willing to accord to France the leadership in the European sphere, a leadership which had been offered to the British but which they had rejected in the form offered as incompatible with their world power status and with their Atlanticist outlook. In view of this entirely unexpected development it was obviously difficult for Mr. Bevin to attempt to salvage something from the wreck of his aspirations. Nevertheless he attempted to do so. There was no last minute realization in the Foreign Office that the ground which had been so carefully prepared had been swept away.

The Anglo-American ministerial talks opened in an atmosphere of marked cordiality. Mr. Acheson began the meetings with a stirring but vague tour d'horizon (No. 78). To Mr. Acheson himself Mr. Bevin commended this imaginative statesmanship but privately he informed some of his senior Cabinet colleagues that the talks were 'not very precise' and that Mr. Acheson had 'not studied' the papers which had been prepared during the official talks and that 'he did not want to have too many agreed documents' (Volume I, No. 3). This latter decision was most obviously manifested when it came to ministerial consideration of the officially agreed paper on Anglo-American consultation. This paper (No. 67) already reflected the fact that the American official delegation had neither wanted the precise definition which the British had hoped for, nor sought, as they had earlier suggested (No. 15), to place the agreement at the centre of the talks. Mr. Acheson's reaction to the paper was twofold; he 'entirely agreed with the general content of the paper in its exposition of the need for close and continued consultation' but considered that 'it was quite impossible to allow it to be known that any such paper had been drawn up or that it had been agreed to' (No. 84). Privately Mr. Acheson was intensely displeased by the existence of an agreed document on Anglo-American coordination and consultation and instructed his officials to burn all copies that could be found (No. 84, note 14). In his account of his meeting with Mr. Acheson to his senior Cabinet colleagues, Mr. Bevin stated that Mr. Acheson 'evidently preferred to aim at informal under-standings rather than formal declarations' (No. 88). In effect Mr. Bevin had to be content with much less than he was originally offered and much less than he had hoped for.

In the tripartite ministerial talks, it became clear that M. Schuman was anxious to play down references to the 'Cold War', the idea of which he described as 'distasteful' (No. 89), and in particular he doubted the usefulness of any strongly worded communiqué, embodying the positive ideas of the western powers, as a means of reassuring western public opinion as to the resolve of their governments only to negotiate from a position of strength. The French delegation conducted a successful campaign of attrition on the British draft of this proposed communiqué and eventually it was decided that this considerably weakened document should not be published (No. 113).

To the success of this exclusion, the French added a more significant success of inclusion. The British argument that after 1952 the functions of O.E.E.C. should be shifted towards the North Atlantic Treaty had found no favour with the American delegation in the official talks. Instead it had supported the French argument that the O.E.E.C. should continue to exist as the main forum for European economic discussions and that the United States and Canada should be associated with it. The British delegation felt that underlying French arguments in favour of retaining the O.E.E.C. as the main forum of economic discussion and negotiation was their determination not to let Germany be associated in any way with the North Atlantic Treaty 'which would lead to German rearmament' (No. 117). The American delegation supported the French proposals for O.E.E.C. at the expense of the British who were then forced effectively to abandon their attempt to make the Atlantic Pact 'the master association of the West and the umbrella under which all the various forms of cooperation should gradually be covered and even eventually merged' (No. 117). The French proposals were endorsed by the three ministers after protracted discussions by officials (No. 107). Mr. Bevin made no last minute attempt to re-open this question which was in itself an admission of a significant tactical defeat. Sir G. Jebb expressed British disappointment when he informed Mr. Jessup that he was 'rather sad that our main thesis on this subject had apparently had so little weight with the American Delegation' (No. 91).

In the event therefore the London conferences were far from satisfactory for Mr. Bevin and his officials; they represented a significant failure to implement Atlanticist ideas and failed to establish a secure and exclusive basis of Anglo-American co-operation within the western alliance. Moreover Anglo-French friction which had so marked the arrangements for and the proceedings of the conferences continued after the meetings had ended. The French ambassador in London, M. Massigli, complained to Sir William Strang, Permanent Under-Secretary of State, that on certain questions 'a greater regard might have been paid to the interests and susceptibilities of France' (No. 110).

In London the Foreign Office faced similar criticisms from both ministers and other departments of state. Sir Edward Bridges, Permanent Secretary to the Treasury, informed Sir William Strang that some ministers 'had expressed concern that policies appeared to be in process of formulation without adequate ministerial consideration' (No. 116). Equally, senior officials in Whitehall departments felt that the Foreign Office had both prepared for and conducted the conference of Foreign Ministers 'without any obvious signs that the views of departments concerned were being taken into account'. The role of the Foreign Office was defended by Sir W. Strang on the grounds that the purpose of the conference was not negotiations but 'a broad exchange of views' (No. 116). This was a more accurate assessment of what had actually happened at the conference than of what the Foreign Office had intended. It soon became apparent that dissatisfaction with the work and organization of the London conferences was common to both the Foreign Office and the State Department.

The post-mortem on the conference by British and American officials revealed a marked similarity of outlook. It was agreed that neither Mr. Acheson nor Mr. Bevin had mastered their briefs; the former because he was too preoccupied by other matters, the latter because he 'had come virtually straight from hospital to the meetings' (No. 117, note 3). Equally it was agreed that there were too many conference documents and that the work of both ministers and officials had been submerged in papers. It was also felt that it had proved extremely difficult simultaneously to hold bipartite and tripartite meetings in such a short space of time. Finally it was agreed that arrangements for future conferences would have to be simplified in the light of these criticisms. An account of the failures of policy at the London conferences and the implications for future policy was made by Mr. Shuckburgh in a letter to Mr. Gore-Booth (No. 117). A note of defiance was sounded in Washington telegram 2980 of 30 June

1950 after the outbreak of hostilities in Korea, which drew attention to the United Kingdom's capacity to act as a world power in support of the United States, a role which she would be unable to play if she 'were to be integrated with some form of Western European federation'. In the immediate aftermath of the London conferences the decision to reject the French invitation to participate in the creation of a Coal and Steel pool appeared entirely consistent with the objective which Mr. Bevin had sought to attain at the conferences themselves. It was clearly assumed that the short-term failure to secure a redefinition of the Anglo-American partnership did not undermine the validity of the policy of holding aloof from the federalist movement in western Europe.

The main sources for this volume have been the archives of the Foreign and Commonwealth Office, especially the Foreign Office political files (F.O. 371). Within this class extensive use has been made of papers from the Planning files of P.U.S.D. (ZP), on which the records of the London conference of Foreign Ministers are entered (see No. 29, note 1) and from the files of Western Organizations department (WU) which took the lead on Atlantic pact questions. Papers used from other F.O. departments classed in F.O. 371 include German—Political and Economic (C and CE); American—United States (AU); Economic (UE and UEE); European Recovery (UR); Far Eastern—General (F), China (FC), French Indo-China (FF), Indonesia (FH), Japan (FJ), Pakistan (FL), Miscellaneous (FZ); Eastern—General (E), Saudi Arabia (ES), Jordan (ET), Persia (EP), Palestine (EE); Southern—General (R), Trieste (RT), Turkey (RK); Northern—Soviet Union (NS); Western—Italy (WT), France (WF); United Nations (UP) and Africa—General (J). Additional documentation has been drawn from the Private Office papers of Mr. Bevin (F.O. 800) and also from the files of the Cabinet Office (CAB), Treasury (T) and Prime Minister (PREM).

I am most grateful to Sir Evelyn Shuckburgh for permission to use the letter printed as No. 117 and also to Associated Press for permission to reproduce the photograph in the frontispiece.

In accordance with the Parliamentary announcement, cited in the Introduction to the Series in Volume I, the Editors have had the customary freedom in the selection and arrangements of documents, including access to special categories of material such as records retained in the Department under Section 3(4) of the Public Records Act of 1958. They have followed customary practice in not consulting personnel files or specifically intelligence material. In the present volume there have been no exceptional cases, provided for in the parliamentary announcement, where it has been necessary on security grounds to restrict the availability of particular documents, editorially selected in accordance with regular practice.

I should like to thank the Head of Library and Records Department of the Foreign and Commonwealth Office, Dr. P.M. Barnes, and her staff for all facilities and help in the preparation of this volume. Kind assistance has also been received from the Records Branches of the Cabinet Office and Treasury, and from the staff of Her Majesty's Stationery Office and the Public Record Office. To members of Historical Branch, I am grateful for manifold assistance. I wish especially to thank Miss K.E. Crowe, B.A., for her valuable help at various stages in the preparation of this volume. Once again my greatest debt is to my Assistant Editor, Mrs Heather Yasamee, M.A., whose skill and judgement have been brought to bear on all stages in the editing of this volume.

ROGER BULLEN

April 1987

ABBREVIATIONS FOR PRINTED SOURCES

B.F.S.P.	*British and Foreign State Papers* (London, 1841–1977).
Cmd./Cmnd.	Command Paper to 1956/from 1956.
D.G.O.	*Documents on Germany under Occupation 1945–1954* edited by B.R. von Oppen (London, 1955).
F.R.U.S.	*Foreign Relations of the United States: Diplomatic Papers* (Washington, 1861f.).
Parl. Debs., 5th ser., H. of C.	*Parliamentary Debates (Hansard), Fifth Series, House of Commons, Official Report* (London, 1909f.).

ABBREVIATED DESIGNATIONS

A.B.C.	America, Britain, Canada	I.G.G.	Intergovernmental Study Group on Germany
A.H.C.	Allied High Commission		
ANCAM	Telegram series on atomic energy	I.L.O.	International Labour Organization
B.A.O.R.	British Army of the Rhine	MIN	Series of papers circulated to Ministers at London Conference
B.M.E.O.	British Middle East Office		
C.O.S.	British Chiefs of Staff	M.S.B.	Military Security Board
C.R.O.	Commonwealth Relations Office	N.A.C.	North Atlantic Council
		N.A.C.	American National Advisory Council on international monetary and general problems
DEC	Series of summary decisions of London Conference		
D.F.E.C.	Defence, Financial and Economic Committee (N.A.T.)	N.A.T.	North Atlantic Treaty
		O.E.E.C.	Organization for European Economic Cooperation
E.C.A.	American Economic Cooperation Administration	O.S.R.	Office of the U.S. Special Representative in Europe (Mr. Harriman)
E.C.A.F.E.	Economic Commission for Asia and the Far East (U.N.)		
E.C.E.	Economic Commission for Europe (U.N.)	P.U.S.C.	Permanent Under-Secretary's Committee
E.C.O.S.O.C.	Economic and Social Council (U.N.)	P.L.I.	Prohibited and Limited Industries
E.D.(W)	Official Committee on Economic Development (Working Group)	S.C.A.P.	Supreme Commander, Allied Powers, Japan (General MacArthur)
E.P.C.	Economic Policy Committee	S.P.D.	German Social Democratic Party
E.P.U.	European Payments Union		
E.R.P.	European Recovery Programme	TRI	Tripartite series of papers for officials (e.g. TRI/P/1) and Ministers (e.g. MIN/TRI/P/1) at London Conference
F.E.(O)	Official Committee on the Far East		
F.R.G.	Federal Republic of Germany	UKUS	United Kingdom/United States Bipartite series of papers for officials (e.g. UKUS/P/1) and Ministers (e.g. MIN/UKUS/P/1) at London Conference
G.A.T.T.	General Agreement on Tariffs and Trade		
G.D.R.	German Democratic Republic		
I.A.R.	International Authority for the Ruhr	U.N.R.W.A.	United Nations Relief and Works Agency

SUMMARY OF CONTENTS

The London Conferences

Anglo-American Relations and Cold War Strategy
25 January – 21 June 1950

	NAME	DATE	MAIN SUBJECT	PAGE
1	MR. BEVIN H.M.S. Birmingham Tel. No. 251655C	25 Jan.	Suggests meeting with Mr. Acheson and possibly M. Schuman in London. *Calendars*: **i–ii** Anglo-American differences.	1
2	SIR L. ROWAN Washington	14 Feb.	Letter to Mr. Hitchman (Treasury) reviewing progress of tripartite (A.B.C.) economic discussions in Washington and need for more fundamental talks with the U.S.	3
3	MR. BEVIN AND M. SCHUMAN: MEETING Foreign Office	7 Mar.	Discussion on arrangements and scope of projected 3-Power meeting in London.	7
4	MR. BEVIN AND MR. HARRIMAN: MEETING Foreign Office	8 Mar.	Conversation on E.P.U., European Integration, Dual Pricing, S.E. Asia and projected London meetings. *Calendars*: **i** E.P.U. **ii** Indo-China.	9
5	SIR O. FRANKS Washington	8 Mar.	Letter to Mr. Bevin reporting Mr. Acheson's concern at world situation.	13
6	SIR G. JEBB Foreign Office	10 Mar.	Minute of conversation with U.S. Minister, who transmits message from Mr. Acheson about London meetings. Need to improve effectiveness of N.A.C.	18
7	To SIR O. HARVEY Paris Tel. No. 277	14 Mar.	Instructions for consulting M. Schuman before replying to Mr. Acheson's proposal for tripartite and N.A.C. meetings in London.	20
8	MEETING WITH MR. BEVIN Foreign Office	15 Mar.	Problems of German economic situation, Income tax reform bill and Law 75. *Calendar*: **i**	21
9	MR. JACKLING Foreign Office	25 Mar.	Brief for Mr. Bevin on E.P.C. proposals for settlement of sterling balances and development of South East Asia. *Calendar*: **i** E.P.C. (50) 40.	26

NAME	DATE	MAIN SUBJECT	PAGE
10 To Mr. Burrows Washington	29 Mar.	Letter from Mr. Furlonge: the search for Middle East stability and possibility of Anglo-American statements. *Calendars*: **i–ii** C.P. (50) 78 and Briefs.	29
11 Sir O. Franks Washington Tel. No. 1031	30 Mar.	Importance of discussing economic problems with Mr. Acheson – difficulties of A.B.C. meeting in London.	33
12 Foreign Office Meeting	31 Mar.	Discussion of German and Austrian questions on agenda. *Calendars*: **i–ii** C.P. (50) 66 Austria.	35
13 Mr. Shuckburgh Foreign Office	6 Apr.	Minute on whether H.M. Opposition should be associated with London talks.	39
14 Sir K. Helm Tel Aviv	11 Apr.	Letter to Sir W. Strang representing need for a more positive British policy in the Middle East.	40
15 Sir G. Jebb Foreign Office	11 Apr.	Extract from brief on object of London bipartite talks: 'high issues' include Anglo-American relationship.	44
16 Foreign Office Meeting	13 Apr.	Discussion of U.K. proposals for development of Atlantic Pact organization. *Calendar*: **i**	45
17 Sir O. Franks Washington Tel. No. 217 Saving	14 Apr.	Texts of agendas for bipartite and tripartite meetings of Foreign Ministers in London. *Calendar*: **i** Spain and U.N.	48
18 Sir I. Kirkpatrick Foreign Office	15 Apr.	Record of conversation with French Ambassador to dispel rumour of British plans for early termination of state of war with Germany.	51
19 Sir R. Makins Foreign Office	17 Apr.	Minute to Mr. Bevin suggesting talks in London with Mr. Acheson and Mr. Pearson on atomic energy.	52
20 U.K. Brief Foreign Office No. 1	19 Apr.	P.U.S.C. memo: Third World Power or Western Consolidation. *Calendar*: **i** P.U.S.C. (50)4 United Nations.	54
21 To Sir O. Franks Washington Tel. No. 2014	19 Apr.	French disquiet at prospect of Anglo-American bilateral discussions before arrival of French delegation.	63
22 Sir O. Franks Washington	19 Apr.	Letter to Sir R. Makins on problem for U.K. of balancing Commonwealth and American consultation. *Calendar*: **i**	64

	NAME	DATE	MAIN SUBJECT	PAGE
23	Mr. Bevin Foreign Office C.P. (50) 73	20 Apr.	Extract from Cabinet memo. on China. *Calendars*: **i** Full text. **ii** Briefs on Lie proposal and Chinese rep. in U.N.	67
24	U.K. Brief Foreign Office No. 4	21 Apr.	General approach in bipartite talks with U.S. delegation.	69
25	Mr. Berthoud Foreign Office	21 Apr.	Minute on Anglo-American economic relations. *Calendar*: **i**	76
26	Russia Committee Foreign Office	21 Apr.	Memo. on relations with the Soviet Union.	78
27	P.U.S.C. Foreign Office	22 Apr.	Extract from memo. on Anglo-American relations: present and future. *Calendar:* **i** Remaining text.	81
28	Cabinet Conclusions 10 Downing St. C.M. (50) 24	24 Apr.	Extract: (5) China – discussion of No. 23.	88
29	Bipartite Officials 1st Meeting Foreign Office	24 Apr.	Procedures. Assessment of position worldwide in relation to the Soviet Union.	90
30	U.K. Brief Foreign Office No. 2	24 Apr.	P.U.S.C. memo. on Western Organizations. *Annex*: O.E.E.C. after 1952.	95
31	U.K. Brief Foreign Office No. 11	24 Apr.	Soviet intentions in Germany and possible Allied counter-measures. *Calendar*: **i** Status of F.R.G. and Berlin.	108
32	U.K. Brief Foreign Office No. 9	24 Apr.	Indo-China. *Calendar*: **i** S.E.A.	112
33	Bipartite Officials 2nd Meeting Foreign Office	25 Apr.	Western Europe and N.A.T. area. General attitude towards Soviet Union. *Calendar*: **i** North Atlantic Defence Committee report.	115
34	Bipartite Officials 3rd Meeting Foreign Office	25 Apr.	Commonwealth and sterling area. Anglo-American financial differences. Relations with Soviet satellites. *Calendars*: **i** Sub-committees. **ii** 4th bipartite official meeting.	121
35	Sir E. Plowden Treasury	25 Apr.	Brief for Sir S. Cripps. Treasury reservations on Western Organizations (No. 30).	129
36	Sir E. Plowden Treasury	25 Apr.	Brief for Sir S. Cripps on fundamental difference between Treasury and F.O. on British Overseas Obligations (No. 43).	131
37	Tripartite Officials 2nd Meeting Foreign Office	26 Apr.	Review of agreement on common world-wide objectives. General attitude towards Soviet Union.	133

NAME	DATE	MAIN SUBJECT	PAGE
38 U.K. Brief Foreign Office No. 15	26 Apr.	Re-establishment of German armed forces. *Calendar*: **i** C.O.S. views.	138
39 To Mr. Attlee 10 Downing St. P.M./K.Y./50/16	26 Apr.	Minute from Mr. Younger on the Arab States and Israel.	141
40 Tripartite Officials 3rd Meeting Foreign Office	27 Apr.	N.A.T.O., European integration and U.S., Germany, Migration. Tripartite coordination. *Calendar*: **i** German rearmament.	143
41 U.K. Brief Foreign Office No. 18	27 Apr.	Attitude towards French regarding talks with U.S. on major policy issues.	151
42 Sir S. Cripps Treasury E.P.C. (50) 44	27 Apr.	Memo. on fundamental economic discussion with U.S.A. *Calendars*: **i** *Annexes* A and B. **ii** Bipartite Sub-committee.	155
43 P.U.S.C. Foreign Office	27 Apr.	Memo. on British Overseas Obligations. *Calendar*: **i** *Annexes* I–III.	157
44 Sir O. Harvey Paris No. 272	27 Apr.	Review of French policy towards Germany.	172
45 Gen. Sir B. Robertson Wahnerheide Tel. No. 666	28 Apr.	German proposal for Federal Police Force. *Calendar*: **i**	176
46 Tripartite Officials 4th Meeting Foreign Office	28 Apr.	Atlantic Pact organisation, China and the U.N., Soviet Union, Yugoslavia, N.A.C. draft declaration.	178
47 To Sir E. Hall-Patch Paris	28 Apr.	Letter from Sir R. Makins on French proposals for O.E.E.C.: at variance with U.K. ideas for Atlantic Pact. *Calendar*: **i** meetings.	183
48 Sir O. Franks Washington	28 Apr.	Letter to Sir W. Strang reporting Mr. Acheson's hopes for discussion of high policy at London conference.	186
49 U.K. Brief Foreign Office No. 24	29 Apr.	Revision of Occupation Statute.	188
50 U.K. Brief Foreign Office No. 28	29 Apr.	Japan: Soviet threat and U.S. reluctance to proceed with Peace Treaty.	192
51 Mr. Penson Washington	29 Apr.	Letter to Mr. Allen: latest views of State Dept. on Germany.	196
52 Mr. Barclay Foreign Office	29 Apr.	Comments from Mr. Bevin on official talks and aims of conference: 'he would like to get away from talk about Europe'.	198

NAME	DATE	MAIN SUBJECT	PAGE
53 Gen. Sir B. Robertson Wahnerheide Tel. No. 673	1 May	Anglo-American differences on proposals for German unity and all-German elections. *Calendars*: **i–ii** Statement of conditions.	200
54 Mr. Bevin Foreign Office C.P. (50) 92	2 May	Cabinet memo. reviewing progress of official talks.	203
55 To Mr. Attlee 10 Downing Street P.M./50/18	2 May	Minute from Mr. Bevin expressing his concern at line of E.P.C. paper on fundamentals (No. 42) *Calendar*: **i**	207
56 Mr. Dening Foreign Office	3 May	Minute on lack of progress with Americans in official talks on China and Japan. *Calendars*: **i–iii** Sub-committees and papers.	208
57 Ministerial Meeting House of Commons	4 May	Disagreement over British policy on 'fundamentals', development of Atlantic Pact, P.U.S.C. papers on Germany and British Overseas Obligations.	210
58 Sir I. Kirkpatrick Foreign Office	4 May	General tripartite official discussion on Germany. *Calendar*: **i** Sub-committees.	215
59 Mr. Bevin Foreign Office C.P. (50) 93	4 May	Cabinet memo. on stalemate in Austrian treaty negotiations.	218
60 U.K. Brief Foreign Office No. 37	4 May	Request from Dr. Adenauer for security guarantee for F.R.G. *Annex* : draft reply (MIN/TRI/P/10).	221
61 Sir I. Kirkpatrick Foreign Office	5 May	General tripartite official discussions on policy towards Germany. *Calendars*: **i–ii** MIN/TRI/P/7 & 13. **iii** Benelux.	225
62 Sir N. Brook Cabinet Office	5 May	Brief for Mr. Attlee on position reached in ministerial discussion at No. 57.	227
63 Ministerial Meeting 10 Downing St.	5 May	Resumption of discussion at No. 57: Atlantic Pact organization; economic and defence questions.	230
64 U.K. Brief Foreign Office No. 38	5 May	Allied policy towards Germany. *Calendar*: **i** P.U.S.C. (49)62.	234
65 Mr. Furlonge Foreign Office	5 May	Brief for Mr. Bevin on Middle East statement. *Calendars*: **i–ii** MIN/UKUS/P/6 & 7.	239
66 Mr. Spender Canberra	5 May	Personal message to Mr. Bevin asking to be kept informed of London discussions affecting Australian interests.	241

NAME	DATE	MAIN SUBJECT	PAGE
67 BIPARTITE OFFICIALS Foreign Office	6 May	Report (MIN/UKUS/P/5) on Anglo-American relationship: recommends continued consultation and coordination of policy.	242
68 MR. WRIGHT Foreign Office	6 May	Brief for Mr. Bevin on Colonial Questions. *Calendar*: **i** MIN/UKUS/P/10. **ii** Africa.	244
69 TO MR. BOWKER Rangoon Tel. No. 357	7 May	Tripartite discussions on S.E. Asia: invites comment on proposed declaration.	246
70 SIR R. MAKINS Foreign Office	7 May	Brief for Mr. Bevin on bipartite economic papers MIN/UKUS/P/2 & 8. *Calendar*: **i** Sub-committees.	247
71 SIR R. MAKINS Foreign Office	7 May	Brief for Mr. Bevin on economic relations between U.S. and Europe: O.E.E.C. and French proposal.	249
72 SIR G. JEBB Foreign Office	8 May	Brief for Mr. Bevin on Atlantic Pact machinery. *Calendar*: **i** Davies memo.	251
73 BIPARTITE OFFICIALS Foreign Office MIN/UKUS/P/11	8 May	Heads of Agreement on Indo-Pakistan Sub-Continent and Burma. *Calendar*: **i**	255
74 CABINET CONCLUSIONS 10 Downing St. C.M. (50)29	8 May	Statement by Mr. Bevin of his objectives at London Conference. *Calendar*: **i**	257
75 MR. WRIGHT Foreign Office	8 May	Brief for Mr. Bevin on uncertainties over proposed Middle East statement.	261
76 MR. STEVENS Foreign Office	8 May	Brief for Mr. Bevin summarizing sub-committee discussion on German internal economic problems. *Calendars*: **i** MIN/TRI/P/15–18. **ii** Annex D.	264
77 LT. GEN. SIR G. MACREADY Wahnerheide Tel. No. 714	9 May	Text of Dr. Adenauer's letter of 6 May: Allied concessions on Germany at London Conference would help overcome SPD opposition to German entry to Council of Europe.	266
78 BIPARTITE MINISTERS 1st Meeting Foreign Office	9 May	Press relations. General assessment of world situation.	267
79 MR. ATTLEE, MR. BEVIN AND MR. ACHESON: MEETING 1 Carlton Gardens	9 May	Mr. Acheson's concern for 'a further major step forward'.	274
80 BIPARTITE MINISTERS 2nd Meeting Foreign Office	9 May	Anglo-American relations, China, N.A.T.O.	276
81 MR. BATEMAN Foreign Office	9 May	Brief for Mr. Bevin on Turkish security.	281

NAME	DATE	MAIN SUBJECT	PAGE
82 BIPARTITE MINISTERS 3rd Meeting Foreign Office	10 May	Extract: Anglo-American relations, Soviet Union, Middle East.	284
83 SIR E. HALL PATCH Paris Tel. No. 218	10 May	Concern of Dr. Stikker for O.E.E.C. in event of new economic machinery for Atlantic Pact.	286
84 BIPARTITE MINISTERS 4th Meeting Foreign Office	10 May	Middle East, Libya, Eritrea, Indian Sub-Continent, East–West trade, Schuman Plan, Coordination and consultation, Atlantic declaration. *Calendar*: **i** MIN/TRI/P/8.	288
85 MR. BEVIN AND MR. ACHESON: MEETING Foreign Office	10 May	Discussion of American ideas for progress with Japanese Peace Treaty. *Calendar*: **i** Commonwealth Working Party on Japan.	295
86 MR. FURLONGE Foreign Office	10 May	Summary of official discussion on Persia: question of statement. *Calendars*: **i–ii** Brief and Sub-committee.	297
87 SIR R. MAKINS Foreign Office	10 May	Brief for Mr. Bevin on atomic energy cooperation for discussion with Mr. Acheson and Mr. Pearson.	299
88 MINISTERIAL MEETING 1 Carlton Gardens	11 May	Summary by Mr. Bevin of his discussions with Mr. Acheson.	301
89 TRIPARTITE MINISTERS 1st Meeting Lancaster House	11 May	General assessment and common objectives. Soviet Union, Chinese representation at the U.N.	303
90 TRIPARTITE MINISTERS 2nd Meeting Lancaster House	11 May	U.N. matters (MIN/TRI/P/4), Consultation and coordination (MIN/TRI/P/6), N.A.T.O. (MIN/TRI/P/2–3), European Integration, Communiqué, Migration, Benelux.	309
91 SIR G. JEBB Foreign Office	11 May	Minute of conv. with Dr. Jessup on American support for French to strengthen O.E.E.C. rather than Atlantic Pact.	318
92 MR. YOUNGER Foreign Office	11 May	Minute to Mr. Bevin expressing his concern at so little progress in bipartite talks on Far East.	320
93 MR. ALLEN Foreign Office	11 May	Brief for Mr. Bevin on repatriation of German P.O.W.s from Soviet Union.	322
94 SIR A. RUMBOLD Foreign Office	11 May	Brief for Mr. Bevin on Trieste. *Calendars*: **i–ii** Brief and meetings. **iii** Eritrea.	323
95 TRIPARTITE MINISTERS 3rd Meeting Lancaster House	12 May	German problems (MIN/TRI/P/7, 12, 13, 26). Schuman Plan, peace treaty, P.O.W.s, reparations.	325

NAME	DATE	MAIN SUBJECT	PAGE

96 TRIPARTITE MINISTERS
4th Meeting
Lancaster House — 12 May — Germany (MIN/TRI/P/10, 11, 14–18, 23–4, 26–7). Migration (MIN/TRI/P/5, 25). Austria (MIN/TRI/P/20). — 334

97 TO MR. ATTLEE
10 Downing St.
P.M./50/19 — 12 May — Minute from Mr. Bevin on wording and timing of Middle East statement. Question of French association. — 342

98 TRIPARTITE MINISTERS
5th Meeting
Lancaster House — 13 May — South East Asia (MIN/TRI/P/9). Colonial questions (MIN/TRI/P/21). U.S. and Europe. N.A.T.O. (MIN/TRI/P/2, 3, 22, 28). Migration (MIN/TRI/P/5, 25). Declaration on Germany (MIN/TRI/P/13). *Calendars*: **i** Conference Statements. **ii–iii** Benelux. — 345

99 MINISTERIAL MEETING
1 Carlton Gardens — 15 May — Summary by Mr. Bevin of tripartite talks. — 352

100 SIR I. KIRKPATRICK
Foreign Office — 15 May — Emergency Planning in Germany. — 354

101 MR. BATEMAN
Foreign Office — 15 May — Memo. on progress towards statement on Turkey, Greece and Persia. — 356

102 ANGLO-AMERICAN-CANADIAN MINISTERIAL MEETING
1 Carlton Gardens — 16 May — Atomic Energy: technical cooperation and international control. — 357

103 GEN. SIR B. ROBERTSON
Wahnerheide
Tel. No. 757 — 17 May — Meeting of A.H.C. with Dr. Adenauer: decisions of London conference on Germany. — 361

104 GEN. SIR B. ROBERTSON
Wahnerheide
Tel. No. 752 — 17 May — Reply to Dr. Adenauer on security guarantee and Federal police force. *Calendar*: **i** MIN/TRI/P/10. — 363

105 MR. FURLONGE
Foreign Office — 17 May — Proposed statement on Middle East: approach to Israel. — 365

106 MR. FURLONGE
Foreign Office — 17 May — Approach to French on Middle East statement. — 367

107 TO SIR E. HALL-PATCH
Paris
Tel. No. 227 — 18 May — Agreement to associate U.S. and Canada with O.E.E.C. — 368

108 TO SIR H. CACCIA
Vienna
Tel. No. 211 — 18 May — London decisions on Austrian treaty negotiations. — 370

109 TRIPARTITE MINISTERIAL MEETING
Lancaster House — 18 May — Invitation to France to participate in Middle East statement. — 372

110 SIR W. STRANG
Foreign Office — 22 May — Records representations from French Ambassador at lack of prior consultation with the French on Middle and Near East statements. — 373

NAME	DATE	MAIN SUBJECT	PAGE
111 Lt. Gen. Sir G. Macready Wahnerheide Tel. No. 797	23 May	U.S. proposal for publication of London statement of conditions for German unity.	375
112 Mr. Jackling Foreign Office	24 May	Brief for Mr. Bevin on E.P.C. paper on sterling balances, revised in light of American attitude. *Calendars*: **i** E.P.C. (50) 58. **ii** Sydney Conference.	377
113 Mr. Bevin Foreign Office C.P. (50)118	26 May	Cabinet memo. giving account of meeting of North Atlantic Council, 15–18 May. *Calendars*: **i** N.A.C. statements. **ii** *Annexes* II–III.	379
114 To Sir O. Franks Washington Tel. No. 2771	16 June	Concern of Mr. Bevin at delay in setting up Committee of Deputies of N.A.C.	385
115 Mr. Wilson Treasury	16 June	Letter to Sir L. Rowan: records of London conference confirm that U.K. is still aiming for economic viability.	386
116 Inter-Departmental Meeting Foreign Office	17 June	Inadequacies of briefing coordination for London conference.	387
117 Mr. Shuckburgh Foreign Office	21 June	Letter to Mr. Gore-Booth (Washington) reviewing achievements of London conferences.	388

Microfiches

Fiche	Document Numbers	Fiche	Document Numbers
1	1.i–9.i	6	61.i–70.i
2	10.i–22.i	7	72.i–76.ii
3	23.i–32.i	8	84.i–104.i
4	33.i–47.i	9	112.i–113.i
5	53.i–58.i		

The London Conferences

Anglo-American Relations and Cold War Strategy

25 January – 21 June 1950

No. 1

Mr. Bevin (H.M.S. Birmingham)[1] to Foreign Office
(Received 25 January, 4.42 p.m.)

No. 251655C Telegraphic [AU 1053/3]

Immediate. Secret   H.M.S. BIRMINGHAM, 25 January 1950, 4.55 p.m.

Following personal for Strang[2] from Foreign Secretary.

Your letter to Franks of January 13th[3] about Anglo-American differences.

As you know I have been anxious to get Acheson[4] to London in the fairly near future and he himself seemed in principle quite keen to come. I believe such a visit would provide the best possible opportunity for clearing up some of the difficulties referred to in your letter and its enclosure. It would also make it possible to review, perhaps together with Schuman,[5] any outstanding European problems as well as those of the Far East and South East Asia. I should like too to be able to repay some of his hospitality and kindness to me in Washington.

2. I think, provided you see no objection, it would be desirable for Franks before his departure[6] to mention to Acheson that I am very keen on this project and that if I remain at the Foreign Office I will bring the

---

[1] Mr. Ernest Bevin, Secretary of State for Foreign Affairs, was on his return voyage from the Commonwealth Conference of Foreign Ministers held at Colombo from 9–14 January (British records on F.O.371/84817–9). After official visits to Cairo, Rome and Paris, Mr. Bevin returned to London on 3 February.

[2] Sir W. Strang was Permanent Under-Secretary of State for Foreign Affairs.

[3] This letter to Sir O. Franks, H.M. Ambassador at Washington, is reproduced at i below.

[4] Mr. D. Acheson was the American Secretary of State.

[5] M. R. Schuman was the French Minister for Foreign Affairs.

[6] Sir O. Franks was coming to London in February for a review of Anglo-American relations with senior officials.

matter up immediately after the election.[7] The visit might perhaps take place in March after that of the French President.[8]

CALENDARS TO NO. 1

i *6–13 Jan. 1950* *Anglo-American economic differences* listed in a Treasury note discussed with the Foreign Office on 6 Jan. Copy of note enclosed in letter from Sir W. Strang to Sir O. Franks of 13 Jan. Sir W. Strang comments that list includes not only sources of U.S. grievances against U.K. e.g. dual pricing of coal, substitution of sterling oil for dollar oil (see No. 2, note 3), liberalization of trade, facilities for U.S. air force in U.K. 'but also cases where the Americans appear to have let us down' e.g. rubber and tin. Considers that 'real sore points are dual prices, oil substitution and the International Wheat Agreement ... and the participation therein of Germany and Japan' (*B.F.S.P.*, vol. 154, pp. 446–475 for wheat agreement of 23 Mar. 1949 to which Germany and Japan acceded on 15 May 1950 and 23 July 1951 respectively). In order to prevent these differences from becoming a party political issue during the election campaign, Sir O. Franks is asked to suggest a truce to the Americans until after polling day. Cf. *F.R.U.S. 1950*, vol. iii, pp. 1599–1604 [UEE 59/1,2].

ii *14 Jan. 1950* *Anglo-American colonial differences* analysed by Sir O. Franks in Washington despatch No. 32. Anti-colonialism in U.S. is traditional, though most Americans now regard Communism as the greater danger to their civilization [UP 244/6].

[7] Following the British general election on 23 February in which the Labour Government of Mr. C.R. Attlee was returned to office with a reduced majority, Mr. Bevin remained Secretary of State for Foreign Affairs.

[8] President Auriol paid a state visit to the United Kingdom on 7–10 March.

On 26 January Mr. Bevin's telegram was repeated to Sir O. Franks in Washington with instructions from Sir W. Strang and Mr. H. McNeil, Minister of State at the Foreign Office, to 'broach the matter with Acheson before you leave'. Sir O. Franks saw Mr. Acheson that evening and reported in Washington telegram No. 324 of even date that Mr. Acheson intended to visit London in the spring once enough preparation had been completed to enable major decisions to be taken. On 11 February, with a view to a meeting in March, Mr. Bevin sent Mr. Acheson a personal message concerning the relation of German problems to negotiations for a European Payments Union, in progress since February under the auspices of the Organization for European Economic Cooperation, established in Paris under the Convention of 16 April 1948 (*B.F.S.P.*, vol. 151, pp. 278–96 and Volume I, No. 1, note 5). Mr. Bevin's message and Mr. Acheson's reply, transmitted on 23 February, are printed in *F.R.U.S. 1950*, vol. iii, pp. 627–9 and 632–3 respectively (British texts on CE 708 and 1061/45/181).

No. 2

Letter from Sir L. Rowan[1] (Washington) to Mr. Hitchman (Treasury)[2]

[*AU 1156/3*]

Secret   WASHINGTON, *14 February 1950*

My dear Hitch,

1. Since I have been back I have been thinking a good deal about where we are going in the Tripartite discussions. So far we have merely been dealing with a number of individual topics, most of them like oil[3] of the 'sore thumb' type. I had therefore felt that it would be desirable to have a talk among ourselves here about the position.

2. During the last week, and before I was able to have the talk, following which this letter is written, one or two things happened which all pointed in the same direction. In the first place, Allan Christelow[4] had a meeting with some members of the U.S. Treasury and it emerged that the N.A.C.[5] is concentrating its main discussions on the theme of *convertibility*. I see this question was also referred to in Snyder's letter of 3rd February to the Chancellor.[6] In the second place, Labouisse mentioned to me that the President was taking an interest personally in the problem of the dollar gap and that a pretty high level committee under possibly the Secretary of State would be set up which would examine it in all its aspects. In the third place, instead of our normal Wednesday meeting I had a long and quite informal talk with Labouisse at his request. It would be wrong to read too much into what follows because he was talking purely personally and may be representing only one school of thought in the State Department. But however this may be it does not seem to us to affect the conclusion we reach—namely that we should be prepared to respond—or, indeed, perhaps to take the initiative ourselves about talks on the more fundamental economic issues which face the U.S. and the U.K. From my talk with Labouisse I got the following impressions:

---

[1] Sir L. Rowan, Economic Minister at H.M. Embassy in Washington, deputized for Sir O. Franks on the 'continuing consultation' between America, Britain and Canada (A.B.C.) on economic problems. This form of consultation was agreed by the Foreign and Finance Ministers of the three countries in conference at Washington from 7–12 September 1949 and announced in their communiqué of 12 September (*B.F.S.P.*, vol. 154, pp. 688–694). For the records of weekly informal meetings of 'continuing consultation' held in Washington from 16 November, at which the United States and Canada were represented by Mr. H.R. Labouisse and Mr. W.D. Matthews respectively, see F.O. 371/75609 and 82936.

[2] Mr. E.A. Hitchman was a Third Secretary at the Treasury.

[3] For papers on the substitution of sterling oil for dollar oil in 1950, see F.O. 371/82983–82991.

[4] Mr. Christelow, Treasury Under Secretary and attaché at H.M. Embassy in Washington, was a member of Sir L. Rowan's delegation at the continuing talks in Washington.

[5] U.S. National Advisory Council on International Monetary and Financial Problems.

[6] This letter from Mr. J.W. Snyder, U.S. Secretary of the Treasury, to Sir S. Cripps, Chancellor of the Exchequer, is not printed.

(i) There is clearly a good deal of pretty deep thinking going on in the U.S. Government about relationships between the U.S. and the U.K.

(ii) Some elements in the U.S. Government clearly take a very serious view of the Russian danger which in turn makes them more anxious than ever to ensure that Western Germany is effectively brought into the western fold.

(iii) Labouisse kept on referring to the possibility of a working partnership between the U.S. and the U.K. and in view of (ii) the sooner the better.

(iv) They have not got any fixed ideas about what this will involve either on one side or the other. But they are clear that it could not take an open form because of the undesirable political reactions this would have on other European countries. But it must be a real partnership and if this were accomplished then we could hope that the sort of problems which currently give rise to tension between the Governments would be reduced to their proper proportions.

3. During the course of this talk Labouisse thought aloud about the steps which it would be necessary to take in order to establish such a working partnership. His ideas so far as they were formed seemed to be on the following lines:

(a) We should have to think out together what each would have to do. This would have to cover, of course, a wider field than purely economic, but here we are concerned only with the economic.

(b) On the economic side, we might consider together:
    (i) the steps required on both sides to get back to convertibility and full non-discrimination;
    (ii) insofar as this did not cover them, the following:
Sterling Balances
The righting of the U.S. import/export position;
    (iii) whether there are any other matters.

(c) We should have to consider whether such a partnership would be effective unless there was the possibility of frank discussion about the internal policies of each side. This would not be a question of either country having any right to impose any view on the other, but it would be, at the minimum, a question of seeing how far the appropriate external policies required modifications of internal policies in either country.

(d) We should also have to see how far anything agreed privately would need to be confirmed publicly. This is extraordinarily difficult remembering always the impossibility of setting anything approaching firm commitment on American policy without at least discussion in Congressional circles.

4. From all this it seems that at the moment there is in some quarters at

any rate a climate of opinion which, seeing the Russian danger, realises that purely on the basis of the material interests of U.S., to put it at its lowest, the U.S. must ensure that whatever else may happen the U.K. is kept strong and sound. It also means that they are anxious to establish some kind of general framework of objective against which such things as oil and other 'sore thumbs' would fall into their proper places and not give rise to the sort of tension which exists at the moment. At one stage in our talk, Labouisse said that if we could get some form of working partnership then we should have to place more reliance in future on the firm intention of the U.S. to see that we were properly supported and therefore we should not seek to follow policies which, even if they saved some dollars, gave rise to antagonisms between our countries over a wider field. He realises, as well as I did, what were the dangers and difficulties of such a position from our point of view.

5. The conclusions we draw are that we must be prepared to have talks with the Americans about fundamentals, that they may ask us to do so in the near future and that the climate of opinion is likely to be favourable.

6. The period after the Election may be a particularly appropriate time from our point of view to have such talks and I have no doubt that you have been thinking in London of our overall policies against the time when the next Government starts work. If the Americans approach us formally on these lines then I do not think that we can possibly refuse to talk. Indeed, I feel that there are some advantages in our taking the initiative even if the Americans do not. In the first place, we have in the tripartite arena a place where we can talk privately and entirely without commitment. If we find that the talks are leading nowhere well we can just stop and carry on as we are. On the other hand we can in this context put forward *any* proposals which we think proper in exactly the same way as we have been invited to do in connection with the sterling balances.[7] Furthermore, talks of this kind might enable us to get away from the creditor/debtor relationship which we now unfortunately have. We should not approach this in any cap-in-hand fashion; otherwise the working partnership will start on an unequal basis and that would be fatal. What we should have to say is that we can now see our way through; it is a difficult and a very long way but at any rate there is a light at the end; we believe that after 1952[8] we can be self-supporting at some sort of level, but whether it is a higher or a lower level, and what kind of trading arrangements it is based on depends mainly on the relationship between us and the U.S. Thus, the discussions must take place not on the basis of

[7] British proposals on sterling balances and South East Asia were in process of formulation: see further No. 9.

[8] 1 July 1952 was the date for the termination of Marshall Aid. Financial aid for the economic recovery of Europe was offered by General G.C. Marshall, U.S. Secretary of State, 1947–9, in a speech at Harvard on 5 June 1947 (*F.R.U.S. 1947*, vol. iii, pp. 237–9). This European Recovery Programme (E.R.P.) was administered through the Economic Co-operation Administration (E.C.A.).

one side thinking it is granting all the favours and the other side receiving but on the basis of an equal partnership.

7. But if we do get into such discussions, there are certain overriding points which we must make:

(*a*) It is not enough to consider the steps necessary to get back to convertibility and non-discrimination; we must also see what is necessary to *maintain* that position subsequently. This means that we cannot just have a fair-weather partnership. It must continue in good times and bad. This is clearly one of the crucial aspects of the matter and a most difficult one, especially in the light of the difficulties which an American Administration finds in committing itself for the future.

(*b*) On the economic side we must look at all the questions as a whole. It becomes more and more clear that one cannot pursue one single question without coming up very soon against all the others. Discussions of the sterling balances will obviously raise a number of other issues. And on oil, for example, one comes up against such fundamental points as convertibility and the necessity for keeping sterling strong.

(*c*) We must make, and ourselves be, quite clear that this is not merely a U.K. matter but a Commonwealth one; and that on general policies we shall certainly have to carry them with us. This is the same sort of problem that we are faced with in connection with the sterling balances, only, of course, on a much larger scale.

8. If you agree that we must be ready to talk fundamentals with the Americans or even ourselves propose this, then we shall want your authority so to proceed and your guidance. I should not ask for 'instructions' of the usual kind because I think we must be very tentative and free in discussion. We will ourselves here think out in more detail some of the problems but I am sure it is urgent that:

(*a*) We should make up our minds on the question of principle;

(*b*) if the answer is favourable, you should set the machine going at a pretty high level.

9. I have shown this to Hoyer Millar[9] and will of course show it to the Ambassador when he returns. I am leaving you to circulate it as you think best in London.[10]

Yours sincerely,

LESLIE

[9] Sir F. Hoyer Millar was H.M. Minister at Washington.

[10] A copy of this letter was circulated in the Foreign Office on 21 February for consideration with a draft reply from Mr. Hitchman. The letters were discussed in the Foreign Office by Sir R. Makins, Deputy Under-Secretary of State, Mr. M.R. Wright, Assistant Under-Secretary of State, and Sir W. Strang, who in view of strong Foreign Office interest in the issues raised asked for a fuller inter-departmental study. The correspondence was accordingly referred to the Working Group of the official committee on Economic Development (E.D. (W) records on CAB 134/203). On 11 March Mr. Hitchman replied to Sir L. Rowan that though the Economic Development Working Group agreed 'that we

ought to discuss the fundamental bases of our economic relationship with the United States in the fairly near future ... It seems to us better that these issues should arise out of discussions on specific subjects, rather than that we should have an abstract discussion on fundamentals with the Americans ... Our idea is that the discussions should start with the sterling balances and development in South-East Asia, but we expect that the issues involved in convertibility will also arise and we want to be in a position to deal with these as well. In short, before we start discussing specific issues, we want to formulate our views on the major points which are likely to arise out of such discussions' (UEE 59/4). The E.D. Working Group then began working on the draft of No. 42.

No. 3

Record of a Conversation between Mr. Bevin and M. Schuman at the Foreign Office on 7 March 1950[1]

[*WU 1071/26*]

Secret

Present: Mr. Bevin, Sir W. Strang, Sir O. Harvey, Sir I. Kirkpatrick, Mr. Dening, Mr. Barclay.[2]

M. Schuman, M. Baudet, M. Bourbon-Busset.[3]

Projected Three Power Meeting

Monsieur Schuman asked whether H.M. Government had reached any definite conclusion about the holding of a Three Power Meeting in the near future.[4]

Mr. Bevin replied that he had sent a message to Mr. Acheson at the end

---

[1] This conversation between Mr. Bevin and M. Schuman took place at 5.15 p.m. following M. Schuman's arrival in London with President Auriol that afternoon at the start of the French State visit. For separately recorded discussion at this meeting of E.P.U., Indo-China and South-East Asia, see note 5 below, No. 4.ii and No. 7, note 3.

[2] Sir O. Harvey was H.M. Ambassador at Paris. Sir I. Kirkpatrick was Permanent Under-Secretary of State for the German Section of the Foreign Office. Mr. M.E. Dening was an Assistant Under-Secretary of State in the Foreign Office with responsibility for Far Eastern, S.E. Asian and Commonwealth Affairs. Mr. R.E. Barclay was Private Secretary to Mr. Bevin.

[3] M. P. Baudet was Minister at the French Embassy in London. M. J.L. Bourbon-Busset was M. Schuman's *Directeur du cabinet*.

[4] During his visit to Paris in February (see No. 1, note 1) Mr. Bevin had informed French officials of his hopes for a tripartite meeting in the spring (record of conversation on UR 323/48). In response to an enquiry on 2 March from the French Ambassador in London, M. R. Massigli, as to progress towards such a meeting, Mr. Bevin cited Anglo-American differences, particularly over Anglo-German trade negotiations as causing delay. Mr. Bevin commented that it was 'very unsatisfactory that the Americans should allow the Germans to see that there were disagreements between the Occupying Powers. The Germans had always been adept at playing off one against the other. At the same time, American intervention in our negotiations with the Germans provided the Communists with an excellent propaganda point and made it possible for them to play up the theme of Western Europe's subservience to the dollar' (record of conversation on C 1644/20/18).

of January suggesting a meeting in London, but making it clear that a good deal of preparatory work would have to be done first. Mr. Acheson had indicated that he was in favour of such a meeting but he too was very anxious that it should be very well prepared, so that, when it took place, it should be possible to reach agreement on the policies to be followed in the next stage. Mr. Bevin said he thought it would be desirable if possible to get agreement on the European Payments Union proposals first[5] and he would also like to get the question of the admission of Germany to the Council of Europe settled.[6] As far as the Far East was concerned, he thought that Mr. Acheson would not be ready for talks until the U.S. Mission which had been touring that part of the world had got back to Washington and reported.[7] Mr. Bevin interjected that he had been put in a difficulty at the Colombo Conference because the Americans had not been able to make up their minds about a Japanese Peace Treaty. In any case he was, he said, most anxious not to create any difficulties for Mr. Acheson with Congress. He did not think it was yet possible to fix a date.

M. Schuman said that he had heard a report on the wireless that a spokesman of the State Department had announced the previous day that the U.S. Government was in favour of a meeting of the three Foreign Ministers and also of a meeting of the Atlantic Pact Council.[8] He was not

[5] Earlier on 7 March, Mr. Bevin had attended a meeting of the Economic Policy Committee of the Cabinet (for terms of reference, see Volume I, No. 26, note 1), at which British proposals for a European Payments Union were approved (E.P.C. (50) 31 of 3 March on CAB 134/225). This paper elaborated British objections to a report of 24 January by the O.E.E.C. Financial Experts (cf. Volume I, No. 4, note 8), on which subsequent negotiations for E.P.U. were based. The main features of the new British plan were: (*a*) special rules for sterling to protect its position as an international currency; (*b*) U.K. to lend to but not to borrow from the Payments Union, of which in all other respects the U.K. would be a full member; (*c*) U.K. to reserve the right to impose her own import restrictions, if necessary for the protection of U.K. balance of payments. In a separately recorded conversation on E.P.U. with M. Schuman on 7 March (F.O. 800/440: not printed), Mr. Bevin promised to let the French Government have a copy of these proposals. He explained that at this stage other copies were being transmitted only to Mr. W.A. Harriman, U.S. Special Representative in Europe of the E.C.A. at his office in Paris (O.S.R.), and to M. D. Stikker, Netherlands Minister for Foreign Affairs and recently appointed Political Conciliator 'Superman' of the O.E.E.C.

[6] The admission of the Federal Republic of Germany and the Saar as associate members of the Council of Europe (established in 1949: *B.F.S.P.*, vol. 154, pp. 509–20, and Volume I, No. 3, note 4) was on the agenda for a meeting of the Committee of Ministers of the Council of Europe held at Strasbourg from 30 March–1 April. Following agreement at this meeting, invitations for associate membership were extended on 1 April.

[7] For a report from Ambassador-at-Large Mr. P.C. Jessup on his fact-finding tour of fourteen countries in the Far East, December 1949–March 1950, see *F.R.U.S. 1950*, vol. vi, pp. 68–76: *ibid.*, pp. 87–91 for a report from Mr. R.A. Griffin, a former E.C.A. Deputy, on his mission to South-East Asia in March–April, 1950 to assess aid requirements.

[8] The North Atlantic Council was established as the principal body for the implementation of the North Atlantic Treaty, signed at Washington on 4 April 1949 by the Governments of the United Kingdom, Canada, Belgium, Denmark, France, Iceland, Italy, Luxembourg, the Netherlands, Norway, Portugal and the United States (*B.F.S.P.*, vol. 154, pp. 479–83). The Council, of which Mr. Acheson was the present chairman, was composed

sure that a meeting of the Atlantic Council was really desirable. He thought it might appear aggressive to the U.S.S.R. and in any case it would need careful preparation.

Mr. Bevin said that he had not had any official approach about a meeting of the Atlantic Council and he was inclined to agree that the time was not yet ripe for this.

In conclusion *M. Schuman* suggested that the meeting with Mr. Acheson might take place after the forthcoming meetings of O.E.E.C., the Council of Europe and the Brussels Powers.[9]

of the Foreign Ministers of the twelve N.A.T. signatories and served by a Working Group of officials in Washington of which Sir F. Hoyer Millar was the U.K. Representative. At the first Council meeting on 17 September 1949, decisions were taken for the establishment of a military structure based on (*a*) Defence Committee of N.A.T. Defence Ministers served by (*b*) Military Committee of N.A.T. Chiefs of Staff (*c*) Standing Group of British, American and French Chiefs of Staff in Washington for special policy and guidance (*d*) five Regional Planning Groups. This structure was expanded by the end of 1949 to include a Defence Financial and Economic Committee of N.A.T. Finance Ministers and a Military Production and Supply Board both with permanent working staffs in London: see further Lord Ismay, *N.A.T.O. the first five years 1949–1954* (Paris, 1954), pp. 24–7. Following Mr. Acheson's weekly press conferences on 1 and 8 March, it was reported that meetings of both the Atlantic Council and the Foreign Ministers of the United States, United Kingdom and France were being scheduled for the spring in London (WU 1071/13 and *The Times* of 9 March, p. 6).

[9] Following the meeting of the Committee of Ministers in Strasbourg (see note 6 above), the O.E.E.C. Council met in Paris on 4 April for the annual election of officers. New appointments included the election of M. Stikker as chairman, to be combined with his existing post of Political Conciliator. On 16–17 April the eighth meeting of the Consultative Council of the Brussels Treaty Powers was held in Brussels to discuss current defence projects. The treaty of economic, social and cultural collaboration and collective self-defence, signed at Brussels on 17 March 1948 by the Governments of the United Kingdom, Belgium, France, Luxembourg and the Netherlands, is printed in *B.F.S.P.*, vol. 150, pp. 672–77.

No. 4

Record of a Conversation between Mr. Bevin and Mr. Harriman at the Foreign Office on 8 March 1950 at 5.30 p.m.[1]

[*F.O. 800/517*]

Secret

Present: Mr. Bevin, Sir R. Makins.

Mr. Averell Harriman, Mr. Julius Holmes.[2]

Mr. Harriman began by saying that the United States Secretary of State

[1] Mr. Harriman was in London briefly while on his return to Paris from a visit to Washington. An American summary of this conversation is printed in *F.R.U.S. 1950*, vol. iii, pp. 643–4.

[2] Minister at the U.S. Embassy in London.

had been very glad to receive Mr. Bevin's message of 11th February about the European Payments Union and related questions.[3] This had come at a very opportune moment in the Congressional proceedings on E.R.P.

1. *European Payments Scheme*

Mr. Bevin said that Mr. Harriman now had the United Kingdom proposals for a payments agreement.[4] His Majesty's Government had a difficult task in reconciling their interests in the Commonwealth, in the maintenance of the sterling area, and in the stability of Western Europe. They had done their best to effect this reconciliation in the present payments proposals, and they could not go further. Mr. Bevin hoped that the United States authorities would look on this scheme objectively and without prejudice. It achieved the primary purpose, which was to keep Europe united and to bring Germany into the fold. The possibility that Europe might be divided into regional groups filled him with concern. Vested interests would be created which would subsequently be very hard to eradicate. *Mr. Harriman* replied that he was in complete agreement with this view. His experts were studying the United Kingdom scheme and were discussing it with United Kingdom experts. He had instructed them to look at our proposals with completely fresh eyes. He did not, however, know how far he would be in a position to express a definite opinion on the scheme before it had been studied by the other European countries principally concerned.[5]

2. *European Integration*

Mr. Harriman said that Mr. Hoffman[6] had asked him to tell the Secretary of State that, in spite of all that had been said in the press about Mr. Hoffman's views on European integration, the objective of E.C.A. for 1950 was limited to the fulfilment of the O.E.E.C. resolution of 2nd November, 1949, dealing with liberalisation of trade and payments.[7] On

---

[3] See No. 1, note 8.　　　　　　　　　　　　　　　[4] See No. 3, note 5.

[5] On 18 March Mr. Harriman and his deputy, Mr. M. Katz, informed Sir E. Hall-Patch, Permanent U.K. Representative on the O.E.E.C., that the U.K. proposals were not likely to be acceptable to the Payments Committee of the O.E.E.C., and if pressed would 'risk serious Anglo-American controversy' (*F.R.U.S. 1950*, vol. iii, p. 644: British record as reported by Sir E. Hall-Patch in his telegram No. 172 of 18 March is on UR 329/213). Similar reactions had been given to Mr. Bevin by M. Stikker in London on 15 March (record of conversation on UR 329/199). In deference to American concern, an abridged version of the British proposals was circulated to the O.E.E.C. on 20 March (text calendared at i below). That day Mr. Bevin told the American Ambassador in London, Mr. L.W. Douglas, that he hoped the E.P.U. question could be kept in proper perspective and publicity about Anglo-American differences over it kept to a minimum since 'every difference which cropped up between the United States and the United Kingdom brought smiles to the face of Stalin. We therefore needed to be doubly careful in the way we approached these problems' (UR 329/236).

[6] Mr. P.G. Hoffman was the Administrator of the E.C.A.

[7] Mr. Hoffman's frequent statements in favour of European economic integration and critical of British inaction were the subject of extensive comment in the Foreign Office; for which see F.O. 371/87137. The O.E.E.C. Council Resolution of 2 November 1949,

this objective and on this interpretation of integration, the State Department, the Treasury and E.C.A. were all agreed. Mr. Harriman said that there was no foundation for the reports of disagreement between the American Departments on this question. He added that, in his view, without British participation progress towards the objective would not be made.

Mr. Bevin, referring to the pressure which was being applied by the United States in the direction of the integration of Europe, asked what part the United States themselves could or would play in such integration. *Mr. Harriman* replied, speaking purely for himself, that he realised that the United Kingdom alone could not carry the burden of supporting an integrated Western Europe and that the United States Government must find some way to help. E.C.A. must be wound up at the end of 1952 but, no doubt, there were other ways in which the United States Government could play its part. Mr. Harriman referred to article 2 of the Atlantic Treaty,[8] which he thought, again as a personal opinion, could be developed with this end in view.

3. *Dual Pricing*

Mr. Bevin said that it would be necessary to concentrate on the European Payments Agreement. This would require very delicate handling in the United Kingdom, and it would not be easy to secure its willing acceptance in this country. For that reason, he requested Mr. Harriman to put aside the question of Dual Pricing, which he regarded as of considerably less importance. He understood that Mr. Hoffman was ready to do this. If it was pressed on the American side it might compromise the passage of the payments agreement. *Mr. Harriman* said that it was not correct to say that Mr. Hoffman was prepared to drop this question. It was a major issue between France and Germany, and it would be necessary to continue to press it if the Germans were to be kept up to their recent promises. He must, therefore, reserve the right to continue to discuss this question with His Majesty's Government. *Mr. Bevin* replied that the question could certainly continue to be discussed, but made it quite clear that he was not willing to agree to a change in the United Kingdom attitude before the payments agreement had been disposed of.

4. *South and South-East Asia*

Mr. Bevin gave Mr. Harriman some account of what had passed at the Colombo Conference, with special reference to the proposed Consultative

vigorously supported by Mr. Hoffman, contained measures aimed at the eventual creation of a single European market. These included in the first instance the removal of quantitative restrictions of 50% on specific imports between O.E.E.C. countries by the end of 1949 and the commissioning of a study by the O.E.E.C. Trade Committee for the elimination of dual pricing.

[8] In Article 2 of the North Atlantic Treaty the signatories resolved to eliminate conflict in their international economic policies and to encourage economic collaboration between any or all of them. The full text of article 2 is quoted in paragraph 22 of No. 30.

Committee at Canberra[9] and to the situation in Indo-China. *Mr. Harriman* said that the United States authorities had been interested and encouraged by the initiative taken at the Colombo Conference on the question of development in South-East Asia. As regards Indo-China, E.C.A. were interested in view of the effect of the Indo-Chinese war on the French economy. The United States Government was of course, interested from wider points of view, not least owing to the effect of further Communist penetration of the area on the position of Japan. But they considered that the French requests for aid would have to be reduced, and that before they could be entertained the French should take further steps to underline the independent status of the Emperor Bao Dai. *Mr. Bevin* gave Mr. Harriman an account of the reactions of the other members of the Commonwealth towards the Indo-Chinese question, and said that the attitude of Pandit Nehru,[10] in particular, would be influenced by the handling, on the French side, of the question of the French establishment in India.

5. *Mr. Acheson's Proposed Visit and Meeting of Atlantic Council*

Mr. Bevin said that he had discussed this with M. Schuman. They were both of the opinion that these meetings must be properly prepared. It might, therefore, be desirable not to fix the dates too early. He was having the matter studied and would be communicating with Mr. Acheson very shortly.

After some conversation on general topics, including the situation in Germany, Mr. Harriman took his leave.

CALENDARS TO No. 4

i *20 Mar. 1950 f. U.K. proposals for E.P.U.*: text of proposals, as circulated to O.E.E.C. with Treasury 'Child's guide' to special position claimed for sterling by U.K. and how this could be reconciled with a Payments Union in which U.K. would act as full member. Reactions to U.K. proposals, assessed by F.O. European Recovery Dept. on 3 April, vary from unequivocal opposition of U.S. to more cautious reservations of France, Italy and Benelux countries. [UR 329/231, 241, 309].

ii *7 Mar. 1950 Indo-China* discussed by Mr. Bevin and M. Schuman at meeting on 7 Mar. M. Schuman grateful for Mr. Bevin's efforts to encourage Commonwealth to support French policy in Indo-China. French measures for progressively increasing the powers of Emperor Bao-Dai explained by M. Schuman. With regard to French request for U.S. aid in Indo-China, M. Schuman referred to U.S. having 75 million dollars at their disposal, though not necessarily all for Indo-China [FF 1024/2].

[9] Though originally scheduled to take place in Canberra, the Commonwealth Consultative Committee met for the first time in Sydney from 15–19 May to work out plans for the development of South and South-East Asia, as agreed at the Colombo Conference. For a summary of proceedings, see No. 112.ii: full British records on F.O. 371/84539–84548.

[10] Indian Prime Minister and Minister for External Affairs.

No. 5

Letter from Sir O. Franks (Washington) to Mr. Bevin

[F.O. 800/517]

Secret and Personal   WASHINGTON, 8 March 1950

Dear Secretary of State,

Acheson and Lew Douglas came here to dinner on Monday evening (March 6th). Lew Douglas left early to catch a plane for New York and he is shortly sailing from there to London. He told me he was now fit again and that his holiday in Arizona had done him a great deal of good. On the other hand, the doctor had told him that he must lose 30 pounds and he had dieted very strictly to achieve this. I got the impression that this had imposed too severe and rapid a change and that it had affected his natural vitality and energy.

After dinner Acheson and I had a long talk.[1] Acheson particularly asked that his conversation should not be made the subject of official record or reported as he was talking very freely, with a mind that was far from clear or made up, and he was sure that most of the things he said would be changed as he and the State Department went on thinking in the next few weeks. At the same time the conversation left certain impressions on my mind and I think you may be interested to hear what these impressions are. In the course of the next two weeks I expect to dine again with Acheson alone and would then expect him to have rather clearer views which I could report. In the meantime I should be grateful if you would treat this as a purely private and personal communication to you of my impressions. At this stage it would be difficult and embarrassing if either of my guests had occasion to suppose their conversation had been reported to London.

Acheson gave me a strong impression that he was troubled about the course of events in the world in the last six months. He feels that there has been a deterioration in our common position and a corresponding increase of strength to the Russians. He is therefore searching for major new policies in the foreign field which will offset and indeed reverse this trend. Inevitably the areas in relation to which he is searching for policies are the European with the focus on Germany and that of South East Asia with the focus on Indo-China.

It was very clear to me that Acheson did not think that major policies of this kind could be formulated or made effective except in partnership with Britain. As regards Europe, he feels that unless we are able and willing to lead nothing whatever can happen. As regards South-East Asia, I think he feels that our long association with that part of the world and

[1] For a State Department briefing meeting with Mr. Acheson and Mr. Douglas to consider what line to take with Sir O. Franks at the discussion, reported below, see *F.R.U.S. 1950*, vol. iii, p. 638–42 and 1628–1632.

the countries round the Indian Ocean have given us an understanding of men and conditions there which the Americans cannot do without.

Acheson further gave me the impression that he would like to be able to move with us in formulating these policies pretty quickly, that is to say, during the Spring. He feels that there is urgency in the situation. Here, without in any way going against Acheson's view, I should like to make two comments.

First of all, I am sure it is true now, as so often, that the Americans are looking at time and events in smaller compartments than we naturally do. I should suppose that the results of the occupation of China by the Communists which now seems so threatening to the Americans were very fully foreseen by us some time ago and taken into account. Why else did we take the measures we took in Hong Kong and go to the limit in strengthening our position there?[2] Similarly, in Germany I should suspect that we are not so surprised by the weaknesses of the Adenauer Government[3] as the Americans are. I think they had brighter hopes at its inception than we had and did not foresee the probable consequences of certain policies of that government in terms of unemployment and dissatisfaction. This difference of temperament and perspective between us and the Americans is relevant to the way they are looking at the state of things in the world. Another factor which I think should be kept in mind is that the domestic political situation in Washington adds to the need for the President and Secretary of State to find new policies which are successful in the foreign field. There has been, as you know, a great volume of criticism, much of it unfair, directed against Acheson. He is held to have been too passive and too negative. This was so about China and Formosa where on the whole I should judge his views were clearly right and sensible. It has happened again in relation to his statements about the hydrogen bomb and the possibility of talks with the Russians about atomic energy.[4] There is very considerable body of vocal opinion

[2] Defence precautions taken in Hong Kong in 1949, as Communist advances were made in the civil war on the Chinese mainland, included the reinforcement of the British garrison at Hong Kong to some 25,000 troops.

[3] The coalition government of Dr. K. Adenauer, Chancellor of the Federal Republic of Germany, took office on 20 September 1949. This new postwar German Government was formed, together with an Allied High Commission which came into existence on the following day, in accordance with the Occupation Statute and the Agreement on Tripartite Controls (*B.F.S.P.*, vol. 155, pp. 490–5), approved by the Foreign Ministers of the United Kingdom, United States and France at their meeting in Washington on 6–8 April 1949 (Cmd. 7677 of 1949). The constitution of the Federal Government was set out in the Basic Law, promulgated on 23 May 1949 (*B.F.S.P.*, vol. 155, pp. 503–46; *op. cit.*, vol. 154, pp. 613–21 for the Charter of the Allied High Commission signed on 20 June 1949).

[4] The background to Mr. Acheson's press statements in January and February 1950 in which he defended U.S. plans to develop the hydrogen bomb and dismissed the immediate possibility of renewing negotiations with the Soviet Union for the international control of atomic energy is explained in Washington despatch No. 104 of 11 February 1950 on F.O. 371/88529: UP 233/11. See further UP 233/16 for an account by F.O. Research Department of negotiation in the United Nations for the control of atomic energy from 1946 to the

here, to which Democrats and Republicans alike have contributed, which calls for some positive move. In proportion as the President and Acheson do not wish to move along lines that have been publicly suggested here they feel it the more important to escape criticism for doing nothing by formulating different but positive policies.

These two factors are present in the Washington situation and in my view affect Acheson's thinking. I am sure however that they do not determine it. His view is far more objective than that. I mention them because they are factors in American thinking which are not likely to be shared in the same way by British thinking on the same subjects.

The next impression I received was that Acheson, given his view that major policies could only be formulated and carried out together with the British, was troubled about how to do this with us. I feel fairly sure about what was bothering him. It is the fact that when we embark with the Americans on discussion of matters of foreign policy whether large or small we have been compelled so often recently to bring in questions of cost and make it clear that what we could do and how far we could go along with the Americans turned on the question of expense. Acheson is, I think, a little inclined to treat the economic consequences of foreign policies in their effect on the national economies of America and Britain as secondary in importance and to say that, if only we could get satisfactory and effective policies in the foreign field agreed and applied, other matters would in a large measure look after themselves. Unless a successful foreign policy can secure a more peaceful world, counting the cost of particular operations has little point. Acheson clearly had in mind a number of occasions recently when we had introduced the question of the cost to us of suggested actions.

Because of the impressions formed in my mind by what Acheson said I pointed out that what was natural enough for an American could not be felt by me. My eyes were steadily fixed every week and every month on the 1st July 1952, the date at which we should no longer be in receipt of extraordinary assistance under the European Recovery Programme and when we had to be in a position to balance our international accounts. Our legitimate ambition to play our part as a world power was all that he could wish it to be, but to suggest that we could play it without continuous reference to our economic position in the middle of 1952 was absurd. Our actions before that date and after it had got to be such that it was possible for us to continue to exist. The power which we could exert in the world depended on the level at which we could exist. Therefore for Britain, as opposed to America which could look on the foreign scene with all the freedom that comes from the possession of a very strong and a very prosperous economy, there were always two equal and interconnected

deadlock reached in the U.N. Atomic Energy Commission on 19 January 1950 owing to the refusal of the Soviet Union to take part in further consultations until the representative of the Chinese Nationalist Government was withdrawn.

priorities, that of effective action in foreign policy and in the maintenance of our commitments throughout the world and that of creating and sustaining the conditions in which our economic existence could be assured and strengthened. Neither of these two great aims could be effectively pursued without the other. They went together step by step. Therefore we were bound to count the cost.

The feeling this part of the conversation left in my mind was that a good deal of misunderstanding might be removed if we were able to keep questions of what we and the Americans would like to see done in the foreign field in a separate phase of discussion from the equally important issues of what the cost should be and how it should be borne between us. I believe that the separate discussion of these matters, which I, of course, recognise to be essentially interconnected, would both help the Americans in their present state of mind and enable us to press harder than before for an apportionment of the burden which took full account of all that is implied by the date of 1st July 1952.

So far as Europe and the position of Germany were concerned, the conversation left no very distinct impressions on my mind except that Acheson was wondering whether the Atlantic Pact might be susceptible of some political development in which, of course, the Germans could not share. I also gained the impression that he might be toying momentarily with the idea that the United States as well as Germany might enter the Council of Europe and that between the Pact and the Council in their political aspects the problems of Germany might somehow be lessened and made more manageable. All this was very wide and vague and utterly inconclusive. Nevertheless it indicates the sort of attitude with which Acheson is approaching the problems of Germany and European integration. He said explicitly that he did not think that the correct approach to what was called the integration of Europe could be by documents or constitutions or definite political acts. It had to be by a much more gradual process, more on the lines of the British Commonwealth.

The last impression I received was that if really rapid action was taken by the French about the independence of Indo-China the Americans might do a good deal to strengthen that country. I should infer that Acheson will put great pressure on the French to act early and effectively. If this were done and the aspect of supporting colonialism completely removed from the picture so that Acheson would not run the risk of getting letters like the one he had received from Romulo of the Philippines[5] on this matter, I fancied that Acheson, no doubt momentarily and very vaguely, was looking at the possibility of straight military intervention by the Americans.

Yesterday I had a long conversation with Jack McCloy[6] who is over here

---

[5] This letter from M. C.P. Romulo, Philippine delegate to the United Nations, is untraced in Foreign Office archives: cf. *F.R.U.S. 1950*, vol. vi, pp. 752–3.

[6] U.S. High Commissioner in Germany.

to give evidence in connection with the third appropriation of the European Recovery Programme. He is clearly worried about the trend of affairs in Germany over the last six months. He holds that Russian propaganda is markedly increasing in quantity and quality and, while he does not think it is having much effect at present, fears that it may do quite soon. The Russians are offering the Germans a market from Poland to the Pacific. Many Germans have always believed that the natural market of Germany lay East and South East. The Russians have all this to offer and they are offering it. McCloy therefore feels there is urgency in the situation and is looking, like so many Americans here, for some imaginative and creative policy which will link Western Germany more firmly into the West and make the Germans believe their destiny lies that way. This conversation is relevant because I am sure that he will be saying all this and more to Acheson and will therefore reinforce the kind of attitude which I have indicated.

The only other point of interest was that Acheson appeared to be thinking of his trip to Europe as likely at the end of April or in early May. He was only talking[7] aloud but I think that the thought behind the words was that the necessary preparations would take at least that time.

The Americans seem to me to be groping desperately for ideas on foreign policy, both as regards Europe and South East Asia.[8] If we have ideas, their minds are wide open to them. I think in the next few weeks we have the opportunity to take advantage of this attitude of combined eagerness and frustration. If we were in a position to come forward with constructive policies and deal with the question of cost with equal vigour we might be able to get real progress in directions which we want. I believe this to be especially relevant in relation to problems in the Indian Ocean and South East Asia and to preoccupations with the sterling balances. What we might be able to do to give effect to a common policy in that part of the world might be very directly related to our financial burdens in the area of the Indian Ocean.

When I was in London in February the Prime Minister asked me to go and have a talk with him. He asked me a good many questions about the

---

[7] It was suggested in the margin of the filed copy that this word should read 'thinking'.

[8] In conversation with Sir O. Franks in November 1949 Mr. Acheson referred to the thought being given by the State Department to European integration and 'to a real French–German rapprochement, economic and political, & they & he would do all they could to press this forward. It afforded the only real chance of keeping Germany with the West & might give her an economic outlet in Western Europe. She had to have one somewhere. He did not reject the suggestion that he wanted the work of Charlemagne re-done after a 1000 years.' Mr. Acheson went on to speak 'of the American interest in the great underbelly of Asia as depending on two pillars, India and Japan. He hoped they in the S.D. would be able to think of the area including & between the two pillars as a whole in broad political & economic terms. He did not know whether the attempt to be so synoptic would come off but he would like it to be done like that (Indonesia included). His mind is clearly moving on the provision of dollar aid in this context' (letter from Sir O. Franks to Sir W. Strang of 27 November on F.O. 371/81637: AU 1053/1).

American attitude and I think he might be interested to see this letter. I enclose a second copy which might go to him, if you agree.[9]

Yours sincerely,
OLIVER FRANKS

[9] Further to this letter, Sir O. Franks wrote again to Mr. Bevin on 13 March to report a similar conversation with Mr. G.W. Perkins, Assistant Secretary for European Affairs in the State Department, 'Perkins and I went over almost exactly the same ground ... Perkins expressed himself as completely understanding why Britain had to count the cost and why therefore in any major attempt to agree on joint policies in Europe and Asia the question of what burdens Britain can or should carry and what effective help America is in a position to give is of equal priority with the political questions' (F.O. 800/517). Both letters were initialled by Mr. Bevin and copies sent to Mr. Attlee. On 12 April Sir O. Franks was informed by Mr. Barclay that the contents of the letters had been noted with great interest in the Foreign Office.

No. 6

Minute from Sir G. Jebb[1] to Sir W. Strang

[*WU 1071/18*]

FOREIGN OFFICE, *10 March 1950*

Mr. Acheson's Visit

Mr. Holmes left with me today the attached message to the Secretary of State from Mr. Acheson on the subject of his visit.[2] Mr. Holmes explained that Mr. Bevin had told him that I was trying to organise a timetable of Ministerial meetings and that, hearing that the Secretary of State was in hospital,[3] he had therefore thought it best to leave the message with me. We then had some talk about the timetable and I told him of the meeting which we had in view and of the provisional agenda. Mr. Holmes said that this seemed to fit in quite nicely with what Mr. Acheson obviously had in view. He added that it was a pity that the message had not come in 24 hours earlier since the Secretary of State could then have discussed it with Monsieur Schuman. But he hoped that the Secretary of State would be in favour of holding a meeting of the North Atlantic Treaty Council since he believed that Mr. Acheson wanted to transform the North Atlantic Treaty into something more approaching a living reality. I said that I would of course arrange for the Secretary of State to have Mr. Acheson's message as soon as possible, and that he would no doubt wish to get in touch with Monsieur Schuman before replying to it.

[1] Deputy Under-Secretary of State in the Foreign Office.
[2] Mr. Acheson's message, in which he proposed to come to Europe on 8 May for discussions with M. Schuman and Mr. Bevin and for a meeting of the North Atlantic Treaty Council, is printed in *F.R.U.S. 1950*, vol. iii, p. 828.
[3] On 10 March Mr. Bevin entered hospital for rest and heart treatment, returning to the Foreign Office on 14 March.

2. During the course of our discussion on the effectiveness or otherwise of the North Atlantic Treaty, Mr. Holmes said that, purely personally, he had been considering whether it might not after all be a good thing to set up something not unlike the Permanent Commission of the Brussels Treaty.[4] He had been much impressed by the way in which that Permanent Commission worked; the amount of material with which it dealt; and the quiet confidence which it inspired (I hasten to say that he did not derive these views from myself, but from my other colleagues!). He recognised that it would be more difficult to work such a body with twelve Ambassadors rather than with five, but he believed that the attempt might profitably be made, provided that the machine set up (Secretariat, etc.) was very small and was only developed when this was shown to be necessary. As for the place, he thought that it must be on the Continent of Europe if it was going to have any effect on French morale. He again emphasised, however, that all this was really entirely his own thinking and that he had no idea whether Mr. Acheson would agree. However, when I suggested that I should nevertheless record his personal thinking, he did not dissent.[5]

3. I must say I hope that there will be a meeting of the North Atlantic Council and I suggest that if it is held, it might be best to hold it in London, more especially in view of our own Parliamentary difficulties,[6] but it will be a pretty useless gathering unless some kind of intelligent agenda is prepared for discussion, and if this is to be done, then the absence of a Permanent Commission to prepare and elaborate various items for discussion becomes all the more marked. The sort of questions which I suppose might figure on the agenda are as follows:

(1) General approval of any strategical plans or concepts that may be submitted by the Military Committee.[7]

(2) General discussion on the North Atlantic Treaty Organisation as it

[4] The Permanent Commission, appointed by the Consultative Council of the Brussels treaty powers (see No. 3, note 9), met at ambassadorial level in London once a month as a forum for inter-governmental consultation and collaboration in social, cultural and civil defence matters. Sir G. Jebb was the U.K. representative on this commission.

[5] In a separate minute to Sir R. Makins of 11 March Sir G. Jebb endorsed Mr. Holmes' views: 'anything which binds America closer to Western Europe is to be encouraged, as such, and there therefore seems to be a case for adding somewhat to the existing North Atlantic machinery on the lines recently suggested by Mr. Julius Holmes' (WU 1075/14). Sir G. Jebb was commenting here on a long memorandum on Western Organizations by Mr. C.A.E. Shuckburgh, Head of F.O. Western Organizations Department, which recommended development of the Atlantic Pact organization in preference to those of the Council of Europe or Brussels treaty. This memorandum was circulated to the Permanent Under-Secretary's Committee of senior F.O. officials set up in 1949 to consider long term questions of foreign policy. Also circulated was Sir G. Jebb's minute of 11 March with supporting minute from Sir R. Makins and dissenting minute from Mr. W.I. Mallet, Assistant Under-Secretary of State superintending Western Organizations department. The memorandum itself subsequently formed the basis of No. 30.

[6] Cf. No. 1, note 7.

[7] See No. 3, note 8.

has now developed. Is the machinery adequate or should it be added to in any way, e.g., by establishing a small Permanent Commission?

(3) 'Cold War' questions. Is everything being done that can be done to resist the menace of Communism?

(4) Political questions. Would it be desirable for the North Atlantic Treaty Powers ever to try to reach common agreement on outstanding issues of policy in, e.g., the United Nations?[8]

GLADWYN JEBB

[8] On 14 March Sir O. Franks reported that the State Department in considering items for an N.A.C. agenda 'thought it important that at this stage something should be done to show that the North Atlantic Treaty Organisation was a live and constructive body and not interested simply in military questions.' An N.A.C. meeting would be useful if only for 'giving the various foreign ministers an opportunity of exchanging views as to what might be done to put more steam behind the North Atlantic Treaty Organisation' (Washington telegram No. 861 on WU 1071/15).

No. 7

Mr. Bevin to Sir O. Harvey (Paris)

No. 277 Telegraphic [WU 1071/26]

Immediate. Secret   FOREIGN OFFICE, 14 March 1950, 6.5 p.m.

Repeated to Washington No. 1397.

M. Schuman is no doubt now considering Mr. Acheson's reply to my invitation that he should come to London in the spring and his suggestion that he should spend a week or ten days beginning May 8th.[1] M. Schuman may, therefore, like to know my preliminary reaction to this proposal. I do not propose to send a definite reply until I hear M. Schuman's views.

2. In my view Mr. Acheson's visit would be opportune. We shall (we hope) have held important meetings of Committee of Ministers of Council of Europe, of Brussels Treaty Powers and of the Organisation for European Economic Cooperation, and shall hope to be able to report progress on all these fronts. It is in my view most important that our meeting with Acheson should be very well prepared, and there is a lot of work to be done on a number of subjects.

3. I am prepared to accept proposal for a meeting of the Atlantic Council, though the agenda will need further thought and must be prepared in good time. We should no doubt also take the opportunity for tripartite discussions on Germany which would be a sequel to our discussions in Paris at the beginning of November.[2] We should also review

[1] See No. 6, note 2.

[2] Mr. Bevin, Mr. Acheson and M. Schuman met in Paris on 9–10 November 1949 principally to discuss wider powers for the Federal Republic of Germany (British records on F.O. 800/448). The decisions on Germany reached at this meeting were embodied in the Protocol of Agreements relating to the incorporation of Germany into the European

the policies of the three Governments in Indo-China and South-East Asia generally, though, as I mentioned to M. Schuman last week, we shall have to consider carefully how to associate other Powers with special interests in that part of the world with our deliberations.[3]

4. There will be a number of purely Anglo-American questions which we shall discuss bilaterally.

5. As soon as I know M. Schuman's general reaction I will suggest a programme for the meetings.[4]

Community of Nations signed at the Petersberg Hotel (seat of the A.H.C.) on 22 November 1949 by the three Allied High Commissioners and Dr. Adenauer, printed in *B.F.S.P.*, vol. 156, pp. 584–8.

[3] When making this point at his meeting with M. Schuman on 7 March (see No. 3, note 1), Mr. Bevin observed that the Powers in Asia 'were rather sensitive to any suggestion that European Powers were trying to deal with problems with which they were vitally concerned. This applied not only to Asian Powers but also to Australia. The point to be aimed at was that publicity—and in this the French could help—should make it clear that any talks which might take place were not exclusive of other Powers, who should be kept informed . . . *M. Schuman* commented that it was necessary to take the same precautions in Asia as it was with Benelux over German questions. *Mr. Bevin* said that the Asian Powers were even more sensitive' (record of conversation on FZ 1106/6).

[4] On 17 March M. A. Parodi, Secretary-General at the French Ministry for Foreign Affairs, informed Sir O. Harvey that M. Schuman was in favour of a tripartite Foreign Ministers' meeting but had reservations about a meeting of the North Atlantic Council, since he did not see what questions were ripe for discussion by the Twelve. On 18 March Mr. Bevin replied to Mr. Acheson that both he and M. Schuman welcomed his visit to Europe. With regard to M. Schuman's doubts about an N.A.C. meeting, Mr. Bevin thought that 'provided we can show him that there are substantial subjects for discussion and that tangible results can be obtained from such a meeting, he will not oppose it' (F.O. telegram to Washington No. 1489 on WU 1071/18). In a reply transmitted to Mr. Bevin on 25 March (*F.R.U.S. 1950*, vol. iii, pp. 830–2), Mr. Acheson suggested various topics for the agendas of both meetings and informed Mr. Bevin of his message to M. Schuman, pressing for an N.A.C. meeting, to which M. Schuman eventually agreed. British suggestions for the agendas were transmitted to Washington on 24 March: see further No. 12, note 2.

No. 8

Record of a Conversation with the Secretary of State on Wednesday, 15 March 1950, at 10.15 a.m.

[C 1790/2/18]

There were present: Lord Henderson, General Robertson, Mr. Seal, Mr. Stevens,[1] Mr. Barclay.

German Economic Situation

The Secretary of State said that he had read General Robertson's despatch

[1] Lord Henderson was a Parliamentary Under-Secretary of State with responsibility for the German Section of the Foreign Office in which Mr. E.A. Seal and Mr. R.B. Stevens were respectively Deputy and Assistant Under-Secretaries of State. General Sir B. Robertson was U.K. High Commissioner in Germany.

on the German economic situation [i] with much interest. He enquired as to the prospects of obtaining a firm agreed Allied policy on the remedies to be applied.

General Robertson said that this was a pertinent question but difficult to answer. We on our side would probably be able to agree with any proposals put forward by the Americans though we might not regard them as going to the root of the problem. For example, Mr. McCloy was very keen on having the Germans float a national loan with the full fanfare of propaganda. General Robertson himself would be doubtful of the success of such a loan. The Americans again would like to see additional taxation measures, including purchase and luxury taxes, introduced. This would be a move in the right direction, but not a complete answer. If, on the other hand, the position were reversed and we were to propose for example the reintroduction of controls and rationing, the Americans would, in all probability, not agree unless such proposals were made by the Germans.

The Secretary of State said that he thought that the problem ought to be tackled on two planes. In the first place, we ought to be in a position at the tripartite Ministerial meeting on the 8th May, to reach agreement with the Americans and French on proposals which we could make to the Germans which should be very firm but not too strong. He would like to see some concrete ideas worked out for this purpose. In this connexion, he thought it was necessary to bear in mind that if there was to be an E.P.U. in which both the United Kingdom and Germany participated, which he thought was both desirable and necessary, we should have to make sure that the German economy was running on a satisfactory basis for such a purpose, otherwise the arrangements would not work. He did not want to see a conflict of ideas between the Americans, French and ourselves on this subject.

In the second place he could not help thinking that there might be a sudden change in the attitude of the American Government as regards free economy and controls. The requirements of U.S. policy in Japan might compel a reorientation of American thinking, and this might have its repercussions on American policy in Germany. To meet such an eventuality we ought to have more far-reaching proposals for the German economy up our sleeve in case there was a possibility later of applying them with American agreement.

As regards General Robertson's suggestion in his despatch that it would be desirable to build up a central economic advisory staff within the Federal Government, the Secretary of State enquired whether it would be possible to recruit some of our own economic planning experts to go to Germany in order to train the Germans for this purpose. He asked that this possibility should be examined. General Robertson said that he thought it might be difficult to make arrangements of this kind at this stage without appearing to impose Allied policy on the Germans and hence creating resistance to the measures which we wanted to see the

Germans take on their own responsibility.

The Secretary of State then referred to the two problems which General Robertson suggested in his despatch were susceptible of separate treatment, viz. the expellees[2] and the special position of Western Berlin. As regards Berlin, the Secretary of State said that he felt that the economic support of Western Berlin should be regarded in some measure as a problem separate from that of Western Germany as a whole, justifying the earmarking of special aid for Berlin which would, however, be channelled through the Federal Government which would be made responsible. General Robertson said that the idea had been mooted that a proportion of the aid earmarked to other O.E.E.C. countries should be given on condition that some part of the expenditure on these countries should be made in Berlin.

The Secretary of State said that he would like Memoranda prepared on the problem of financial support for Western Berlin and on the expellee question so that he could consider these problems together at the time of the Ministerial meeting in May.

The Secretary of State then enquired as to the present wage situation in Germany. *General Robertson* said that the efforts of the German trade unions had hitherto been directed to getting prices down rather than wages up, but the gap between the two was tending to increase and there were signs that the trade unions were becoming increasingly restive. *The Secretary of State* said that if there were an economic recession in the United States, or German competition with British goods became acute, and there were a big price discrepancy we might get quick reactions in this country and a demand that the trend towards liberalization should be reversed. He referred to the statement which had been made by the Minister of Health in the House on March 14th about the purchase of medical glassware in Germany;[3] and he asked that a report should be furnished to him on the present position as regards German wages, prices, and standard of living indicating comparisons with the United Kingdom.

Summing up this phase of the discussion *General Robertson* said, in reply to an enquiry from the Secretary of State, that, firstly, the High Commission would continue to watch the German economic situation and the economic policy of the Federal Government closely, and, secondly, that he would arrange for the preparation of a brief [i] for the forthcoming meeting of Ministers which would enable the Secretary of

[2] The expellees were the German populations of Poland, Czechoslovakia and Hungary whose transfer to Germany was agreed at the Potsdam Conference, 17 July–2 August 1945, (section XII of the Potsdam protocol, printed in Series I, Volume I, No. 603). By March 1950 there were some nine million expellees and refugees in Western Germany. That month the situation was aggravated by moves from the Polish government to expel remaining Germans in Poland (e.g. C 1715–1749/74/18). In his despatch at i below General Robertson referred to the problem of the absorption of those expellees already in Germany as 'an economic task of gigantic proportions'. For the London Conference brief on Refugees in Germany, see C 2905/436/18.

[3] *See Parl. Debs., 5th ser., H. of C.*, vol. 472, col. 1030.

State to put to Mr. Acheson concrete proposals for an agreed Allied policy on advice to be given to the Germans on measures to meet inflationary and other adverse consequences of an expansion of long-term credit.

Income Tax Reform Bill

General Robertson explained that the High Commission was not being asked to approve this Bill. It only had the power to disapprove it on grounds falling within the terms of the Occupation Statute; it could not be disapproved simply because we did not like it. The High Commission must substantiate a case that it would increase the need for foreign assistance; and this was difficult to prove. He was not convinced that Mr. McCloy would press the case for disapproval; he himself felt that, if the High Commission were to disapprove it, it would be acting *ultra vires*. It would also be putting itself in an impossible position *vis-à-vis* the Germans unless it were also prepared to tell the Germans what they should do instead. There was no half-way house between putting full responsibility on the Germans and taking over full responsibility ourselves. The Income Tax Reform Bill was, the Germans claimed, a linchpin in the German economic plan. Even the Land Ministers agreed that it would not reduce tax revenue. General Robertson also felt that he should not disapprove the Bill.

The Secretary of State expressed himself as entirely convinced by these arguments.[4]

Law 75[5]

General Robertson said that there were three things which mattered in

[4] When the Income Tax Law, passed by the Bundestag on 3 March and approved by the Bundesrat on 17 March, came before the Council of the Allied High Commission on 13 April, the American and French High Commissioners pressed for its disapproval on the grounds that the tax reductions would diminish the revenue of the Federal Government. General Robertson opposed the disapproval and the matter was postponed for further consideration. On 19 April he was instructed to restate British objections to the disapproval of the Law but not to press the issue to a vote and risk being outvoted (F.O. telegram to Wahnerheide No. 676 on CE 2106/45/181). On 20 April General Robertson reported that in A.H.C. discussion that day of the Income Tax Law, it was evident that Mr. McCloy and M. François-Poncet were determined to proceed with provisional disapproval. General Robertson, whilst dissociating himself from this decision, informed them that he 'would subscribe to their letter to the Federal Chancellor, and would not let it be known to the Germans that I was in disagreement' (Berlin telegram No. 456 on CE 2077/45/181). A letter of provisional disapproval was sent to Dr. Adenauer on 21 April which stated that the A.H.C. was not opposed to income tax reductions *per se* but that it must be convinced that the Federal Government would compensate for any loss of revenue by the introduction of other taxes. This action by the A.H.C. raised a storm of protest in Germany. Talks began on 24 April between the Federal Minister of Finance and the Financial Advisers of the A.H.C. to resolve these differences. Agreement was reached on the morning of 28 April and that afternoon the A.H.C. withdrew its provisional disapproval (Wahnerheide telegram No. 667 on C 2868/202/18).

[5] Anglo-American Military Government Law No. 75 for the deconcentration and reorganization of the coal, iron and steel industries in the western occupation zones of Germany, issued on 10 November, 1948, is printed in *D.G.O.* pp. 335–43. It was stated in

this Law which was due for consideration by the Council on March 16th. The first was that foreign, including U.K., interests should be adequately protected. This, he thought, was sufficiently looked after in the present redraft of the Law. Secondly, that there should be nothing in the Law which would upset the general political situation in Germany. In this respect, he thought that the situation was probably safeguarded. Thirdly, that the policy of H.M.G. in relation to the structure of ownership should not be prejudiced. In his view this was the only real point in dispute. As far as the preamble was concerned M. François Poncet had again suggested to him that the French would adopt the same attitude over this question as he himself had adopted over dual pricing, namely to abstain from voting but not to appeal to Governments. M. François Poncet said that this would enable the French to raise the issue at a later stage to which General Robertson replied that by that time they would be fully committed. From the point of view of ownership it was also important that the scope of the reorganisation scheme in the original Law should be maintained. Here an argument developed over the inclusion of certain firms, such as Stinnes. He himself could not see why these had to remain on the Schedule. Finally, he thought that it would be necessary to recall the Americans to their earlier commitments that the lines should be drawn horizontally so as not to allow vertical complexes and that the small combines should be included in the scope of the reorganisation.[6]

In conclusion, *The Secretary of State* said that he would like to have in advance of the meeting with Messrs. Acheson and Schuman on May 8th, a short appreciation of the position of Germany and of our policy in Germany, including a reference to Law 75, for the information of the Cabinet and Members of the Opposition.

CALENDAR TO NO. 8

i *6 Mar.–6 Apr. 1950 Economic situation in Germany* assessed by General Robertson in Wahnerheide despatches (*a*) *No. 19* problems outlined in detail: 'catastrophic developments of the last twenty years . . . cannot be put right within a few years'. Abnormal burdens of Western Berlin and expellees render German viability by 1952 an impossible target: impossibility of task is being used by Federal Govt. as alibi for not even moving in right direction. However, 'direct Allied intervention is politically impracticable'. Political aspects considered further in (*b*) *No. 25*. General Robertson's proposals for

the preamble to this law 'that the question of the eventual ownership of the Coal and Iron and Steel Industries should be left to the determination of a representative, freely elected German government'. The Allied High Commission was preparing a revision of Law 75 to provide the general framework and procedures for the reorganization. For the London conference brief on Law 75, see C 1933/49/181.

[6] After prolonged negotiation within the Council of the Allied High Commission, amendments to Law 75 were approved on 14 April, subject to an appeal to Governments by M. François-Poncet against the retention of the ownership clause in the preamble. Action was thereby suspended for thirty days: see further No. 96, note 13.

remedying situation, indicated in earlier despatch No. 19, are refined in (*c*) No. *37* and include (i) special aid for Berlin and expellees (rejected by Kirkpatrick on 27 Apr. as not likely to be agreed) (ii) measures for stimulating creation of long-term capital. For the Whitehall response to these proposals see No. 76.ii [C 1174, 1619/45/181; C 1846/9/18].

No. 9

Brief for Mr. Bevin[1]

[UEE 4/63]

FOREIGN OFFICE, *25 March 1950*

Sterling Balances and the Development of South-East Asia

Statement of Problem

The attached paper (E.P.C. (50) 40) [i] is to be considered by the Economic Policy Committee on Tuesday 28th March 11.00 a.m. It outlines a policy for dealing with the related problems of sterling balances and the development of South and South-East Asia and is intended as a basis for preliminary discussions with the United States Government next month and with the Commonwealth Governments at Canberra in May.[2]

Recommendation

2. That the Secretary of State should approve the proposals in this paper.

Arguments

3. On political and economic grounds South and South-East Asia has an urgent need for governmental assistance from the West for its economic development; such assistance must come almost entirely from the United States; a solution to the sterling balance problem must be an essential feature of any attempt to procure such aid from the United States, partially because its existence is a continued obstacle to progress towards convertibility—and this must be a major selling point in our approach to the Americans—and partially because until we have solved it we cannot reconcile our own debtor position to these countries with an active role in promoting their development. It is suggested that the above proposals offer the best chance of a resolution of this dilemma.

4. It will not be easy to persuade the Governments concerned to accept the proposals for funding part of their balances. Nevertheless, certain aspects of such an arrangement may well have some attraction for them. It

---

[1] This brief was prepared by Mr. R.W. Jackling of F.O. Economic Relations department to cover the paper for the Economic Policy Committee calendared at i below. Mr. Jackling's brief was submitted to Mr. Bevin by Sir R. Makins who added that the Foreign Office had taken part in all stages of the preparation of E.P.C. (50) 40 and 'apart from some questions of emphasis, I agree with it and its conclusions' (UEE 4/63).

[2] See No. 4, note 9.

will mean a strictly limited but steady and assured annual rate of release from the funded part of their balances, which in the meantime will earn a rate of interest appropriate to a government loan (perhaps 3 or 4%) as opposed to the present nominal rate of ½%.

5. There are certain specific points worthy of mention.

(i) Talks with the Americans before Canberra will be a delicate business in view of the susceptibilities of the new Dominions about their right to participate where their affairs are being discussed.[3] It is however essential that such talks should go into a certain amount of detail and that we should get a preliminary American reaction to our plans, particularly in the light of Sir Oliver Franks' views that the Americans are looking to us for an initiative in this matter. That the Americans are ready for a lead is demonstrated by Mr. Acheson's speech in San Francisco on March 15th (flag A) especially the marked passage on page 7.[4] In any case, without some indication that the U.S. support our objectives, an approach to the Commonwealth is almost certain to fail.

(ii) There are of course several non-Commonwealth sterling balance holders of which Egypt is the most important. The paper envisages that if the first round on sterling balances with Commonwealth countries is successful, the proposals for limited funding should be extended to non-Commonwealth holders. It may, however, be necessary for us to attempt a separate and earlier settlement with Egypt in the context of the current Anglo-Egyptian Financial Negotiations.[5] There is a general appreciation of this by other Departments but it might be worth specific mention in the Economic Policy Committee.

(iii) It should be remembered that any proposals connected with the economic development of India and Pakistan, and with a settlement of the sterling balances held by these two countries, are likely to be vitiated by an aggravation or even the continuance of the present economic dispute between them.[6] The effect of this dispute on their economies can hardly be exaggerated.

[3] The problem of whether to approach the Americans before the Commonwealth on sterling balances was considered in greater detail in paragraph 31 of E.P.C. (50) 40 e.g.: 'If we talk to the Americans first, we risk creating mistrust in the Commonwealth; if we talk to the Commonwealth first, we cannot say anything sensible because it may run completely counter to what the United States would be ready to assist.'

[4] Mr. Acheson's address to the Commonwealth Club of California on American policy in Asia is printed in the *Department of State Bulletin*, vol. xxii, p. 467–472 (cf. also *The Times* of 16 March 1950, p. 6). In the marked passage on the filed copy of this speech, Mr. Acheson indicated that American aid to South-East Asia would be forthcoming where appropriate.

[5] Negotiations were in progress for an extension of the Anglo-Egyptian Financial Agreement of 31 March 1949 (*B.F.S.P.*, vol. 154, pp. 95–113), resulting in an agreement of 10 September 1950 (*op. cit.*, vol. 156, pp. 532–4): F.O. correspondence on F.O. 371/80408–80416.

[6] The political and economic implications of the trade and payments dispute between India and Pakistan were considered in E.P.C. (50) 41 of 24 March (not printed from CAB 134/225) and discussed by the E.P.C. at their meeting on 28 March at i below.

(iv) The paper contemplates the possibility of some cancellation of Australian sterling balances. This will be further examined, but the bulk of these have been built up since the end of the war and thus have different origin to the other holdings. It would seem unlikely that either the Americans or Australians will be receptive to proposals to treat them similarly, but there is no serious objection to the attempt being made.

(v) Officials have not reached any final conclusion as to the association of the Colonies in South-East Asia with any scheme of American assistance. The Colonial Office fear that aid might be offered on terms incompatible with our administrative responsibilities but paragraph 23 leaves the matter open and further consideration is being given to this. The Foreign Office representatives have taken the view that this question of the Colonies needs very careful presentation to the Americans. On the one hand, an attempt by us to exclude the Colonies from a general plan for South-East Asia could excite suspicion, on the other hand if we are prepared to take the full responsibility for development of the Colonies in this area and link up our plans with the general scheme this would be represented as the principal United Kingdom contribution to the enterprise. But we must be prepared

(a) to make sufficient resources, including dollars, available to enable development e.g. in Malaya and Borneo to keep pace with development in other parts of the area, and

(b) to be frank and open about the policy.

6. To sum up, the paper recommends

(a) that we should attempt as soon as possible, to negotiate with the Commonwealth countries concerned (India, Australia, Ceylon and Pakistan), possibly at a conference of Commonwealth Finance Ministers in end June, a limited funding arrangement for part of their sterling balances.

(b) At Canberra, Commonwealth Governments should initiate the preparation of a detailed development programme which would form the basis of an approach to the United States for comprehensive American aid to the area. Tentative estimates suggest that in the early stages about $500 million annually might be required.

(c) The Canberra conference should also decide to invite non-Commonwealth countries in the area to associate themselves in this.

(d) If and when American aid is forthcoming we should attempt to link it with a settlement for the rest of the balances. As a condition of dollar aid, a further portion would be cancelled and/or funded and the remainder would be freed for use as currency backing and the finance of development schemes.

(*e*) Before Canberra, we should discuss the above proposals informally with the Americans.[7]

R.W. JACKLING

CALENDAR TO NO. 9

i *22 Mar. 1950 E.P.C. (50) 40*: British proposals for the settlement of sterling balances and development in S.E.A., approved at E.P.C. (50) 11th meeting on 28 Mar. [CAB 134/224, 225].

[7] Following approval by the E.P.C. of E.P.C. (50) 40 on 28 March (see i), Sir O. Franks was instructed on 6 April to approach Mr. Acheson for the opening of informal and exploratory A.B.C. talks on sterling balances. Commonwealth governments were informed of these instructions in a circular telegram of 8 April (UEE 4/39). Sir O. Franks spoke as instructed to Mr. Acheson on 13 April (see further No. 22, note 1) and arrangements were set in train for the opening of talks at the official level on 2 May and with Mr. Acheson on 5 May (UEE 4/40 and 42). In preparation for these talks, Sir O. Franks sent Mr. Acheson on 17 April an edited version of the proposals in E.P.C. (50) 40, for which see *F.R.U.S. 1950*, vol. iii, pp. 1632–9. When Sir L. Rowan saw Mr. Acheson on 5 May, Mr. Acheson gave his 'very much first thoughts' on these proposals. Mr. Acheson welcomed the British intention of proceeding with the settlement of sterling balances and agreed on the need for development in South and South-East Asia for which he indicated that limited American funds might be made available. However, 'he wished to emphasize that any proposals that might be made must be presented to the United States as related to the problems and needs of the various countries considered on their merits, and not as related to the objective of dealing with sterling balances' (Washington telegram No. 1380 of 5 May on UEE 4/42; cf. the American record in *F.R.U.S. 1950*, vol. iii, pp. 1639–1641).

No. 10

Letter from Mr. Furlonge to Mr. Burrows (Washington)[1]

[*EE 1017/23*]

Secret   FOREIGN OFFICE, *29 March 1950*

We were interested in Ray Hare's[2] initial reactions on the question of Middle East stability, as reported in your letter No. 1076/33/50 of March 10.[3] Owing to the forthcoming absence of the Secretary of

[1] Mr. G.W. Furlonge was Head of F.O. Eastern department. Mr. B.A. Burrows was a Counsellor at H.M. Embassy in Washington.

[2] Mr. R.A. Hare was U.S. Deputy Assistant Secretary of State for Near Eastern, South Asian and African Affairs.

[3] Mr. Burrows here reported reactions to F.O. suggestions that the State Department should issue a statement on the Middle East designed to ease tensions, particularly between the Arab states and Israel. In discussion, Mr. Hare 'pointed out the threat to the stability of the area occasioned by Hashemite-Saudi relations and wondered if some solution could not be found to take care of both this and the Arab-Israeli difficulties. He suggested "a regional tie-up" without being clear in his mind, we think, whether he meant agreements amongst all the states concerned or simply some action by the United States Government in the form of

29

State[4] and other preoccupations here, we shall not be able to formulate any authoritative view for some time to come, and the following paragraphs therefore represent only departmental thinking. As you will see, however, it is possible that decisions may be required by about the middle of April, and we should therefore like you to discuss these views with the State Department, on the understanding that they are being put forward primarily for the purpose of clearing our minds and must not be taken to commit us in any way.

2. We are glad to see that the State Department are inclined to agree that something more than reliance on United Nations processes is required if the conflicting forces in the Middle East are to settle down into anything approaching a stable relationship. While we have been considering the question primarily from the point of view of relations between the Israelis and the Arabs, we agree that the rivalry between the Hashemites and the other Arab States, and Saudi Arabia in particular, ranks second only to Palestine as a potential source of trouble. We doubt whether the State Department will wish to pursue the idea of a regional arrangement between all the Middle East States, which seems to us to be fraught with too many fundamental difficulties to be worth serious consideration. We are therefore beginning to think that the best, if not the only, step which could be envisaged in the near future may turn out to be some kind of pronouncements by both H.M. Government and the U.S. Government which would, by implication at least, cover all the Middle East frontiers.

3. As you will have seen from paragraph 5 of my letter No. ET/1024/9 of March 23 to Helm,[5] we are at present thinking on the lines that the formal incorporation of Arab Palestine in Jordan may provide the occasion for a step forward. In the first place we may have to make some sort of a public statement recognising this incorporation and announcing the extension of the Anglo-Jordan Treaty[6] to the incorporated area (We may well take this opportunity of recognising Israel *de jure* as a make-weight). But we are now thinking also that this statement could very well be extended to include a re-affirmation of our policy in the Middle East, on something like the lines of the attached draft.[7] If we were to decide to do this, there would seem to be great advantage in the U.S. Government following it up as soon as possible with a statement of their own which would (*a*) likewise recognise the extension of Jordan and of our

a statement or guarantee which would have regional application. Hare also enquired whether we had considered making some special move ourselves. He suggested for example a statement making it clear that we would not permit the enlarged kingdom of Jordan to act aggressively towards Israel' (EE 1017/23).

[4] On 29 March Mr. Bevin left London for a meeting of the Committee of Ministers of the Council of Europe at Strasbourg on 30 March–1 April. Mr. Bevin returned on 5 April after attending an O.E.E.C. Council meeting in Paris the previous day: cf. No. 3, note 9.

[5] This letter to Sir K. Helm, H.M. Minister at Tel Aviv, is not printed.

[6] The treaty of alliance between the United Kingdom and the Hashemite Kingdom of Jordan, signed at Amman on 15 March 1948 is printed in *B.F.S.P.*, vol. 151, pp. 90–100.

[7] Not printed. This draft statement was later overtaken by events: see No. 39.

Treaty thereto; (*b*) welcome and support our statement of opposition to the use of force as between any Middle Eastern countries.

4. So far as Israel and the Arab States are concerned, we think that the above is about as far as we could go. We should certainly not welcome any idea of stating publicly our intention of restraining Jordan from being aggressive towards Israel.

5. I am addressing you separately in regard to Saudi Arabia.[8]

6. I am sending copies of this letter to Troutbeck, Helm, Kirkbride and Trott.[9]

G.W. Furlonge

P.S. Since the above was drafted I have received your letter No. 1076/48/50 of March 27[10] (not copied to other posts). As you will see from paragraph 2 above, we agree, on the departmental level, with the remarks in your paragraph 3 about the difficulties of any sort of 'regional arrangement' in the Middle East whether under Article 51 [52] or otherwise. I understand, however, that the possibility cannot be entirely excluded that the idea of some form of 'regional arrangement' might come up again in future, in connection with the negotiations with Egypt,[11]

---

[8] Mr. Furlonge's letters to Mr. Burrows of 30 and 31 March on Saudi Arabia are not printed from ES 1051/6 and ES 1081/23 respectively.

[9] Sir J. Troutbeck was Head of the British Middle East Office in Cairo, with the rank of Ambassador. Sir A. Kirkbride was H.M. Minister at Amman. Mr. A.C. Trott was H.M. Ambassador at Jedda.

[10] In paragraph 3 of this letter Mr. Burrows reported further discussion with Mr. Hare. With reference to State Department's idea for a regional arrangement, Mr. Hare wondered if 'it might be possible to do something based on Article 51 [52] of the United Nations Charter' (*B.F.S.P.*, vol. 145, pp. 805–32). Mr. Burrows pointed out that in order to qualify as a regional agreement under Article 52, any agreement would have to be of a far reaching character providing for mutual assistance in the event of an external attack. He doubted that this would be possible since the best that could be hoped for was a non-aggression pact between Israel and Jordan, and possibly later between Israel and other neighbours. In paragraph 4 Mr. Hare referred to State Department's concern over the suggestion of a statement applying both to the possibility of an Israeli attack on Arab countries and to that of an Arab attack on Israel when British responsibilities were limited to the former possibility. Mr. Burrows recommended that there should be general U.S./U.K. statements to cover both possibilities in order to avoid the situation 'of having Israel backed by the United States and the Arab countries by the United Kingdom' (EE 1017/25).

[11] In response to an Egyptian initiative of 21 March, negotiations were in progress for the co-ordination of Anglo-Egyptian defence in the Middle East (F.O. 371/80376). At Strasbourg on 1 April, Mr. Bevin discussed the strategic importance of Egypt for Middle East defence with the Turkish Minister for Foreign Affairs, M. Sadak: 'Mr. Bevin said that he had been very satisfied by the attitude of the Commonwealth representatives at the Colombo Conference towards the Middle East, the importance of which was fully appreciated. In his view the United States were tending to become more engrossed with the problem of South-East Asia and, if they accepted the main responsibility for that area and the Atlantic, they would look to the United Kingdom together with some of the Commonwealth countries and the Middle Eastern Powers themselves to provide for the security of the Middle East' (record of conversation on JE 1024/9: see E 1028/1 for a further conversation on this subject between Mr. Bevin and M. Sadak in Paris on 5 April when the possibility of Turkish mediation in the Middle East, particularly in Egypt was discussed).

and while we should not wish you to mention this possibility to the Americans, it would be interesting if you could elicit from Ray Hare a rather more precise idea of what he has in mind, and in particular, how he meets the objections which you have put forward.

Your paragraph 4 is, I think, to some extent answered by paragraph 3 above. I now learn from Kirkbride that the Jordanians' present intention is for the 'union' (not the incorporation) of Jordan and Arab Palestine to be proclaimed by the new Assembly as soon as it meets, which will presumably be about the middle of April. It would therefore be useful to have the State Department's reactions on this point as regards the idea of statements by ourselves and them as soon as possible.[12]

G.W.F.

CALENDARS TO NO. 10

i *20 Apr. 1950 C.P. (50) 78: The Arab States and Israel* Cabinet memo. by Mr. Bevin recommending that on proclamation by King Abdullah of union of Arab Palestine with Jordan H.M.G. should (1) recognise this union and declare provisions of 1948 Anglo-Jordan treaty apply to areas united with Jordan with certain reservations regarding Arab Palestine/Israeli frontier and Jerusalem (2) accord Israel *de jure* recognition with similar provisos regarding Jerusalem and Israeli/Arab states frontiers (3) issue statement reaffirming H.M.G.'s desire for peace in Middle East and opposition to use of force between Middle Eastern States [CAB 129/39].

ii *28 Apr. 1950 U.K. Briefs on Middle East*: (*a*) Economic and Social Development (*b*) U.N. Relief and Works Agency for Palestine Refugees in the Middle East (*c*) Haifa Refinery [E 10210/1].

[12] In reply to this letter Sir O. Franks reported in Washington telegram No. 1114 of 7 April that the question had been discussed at length with the State Department. 'Our provisional estimate of the State Department's reaction is that if Jordan-Israel agreement could come about either by resumption of direct negotiations or, better still, with the help of the Palestine Conciliation Commission, at the same time as, or immediately after, the union of Arab Palestine and Jordan, they would be ready to go a long way in endorsing the agreement and making a general statement of the kind we would like, but that if the union comes about by itself, they would not do anything to oppose it but would hesitate to give it any very thoroughgoing or positive endorsement' (ET 1024/20). A resolution for the union of Arab Palestine with the Hashemite Kingdom of Jordan was adopted by both Houses of the Jordanian Parliament on 24 April and proclaimed that day.

No. 11

Sir O. Franks (Washington) to Foreign Office[1]
(Received 30 March, 7.49 p.m.)
No. 1031 Telegraphic [ZP 2/10]

Immediate. Secret   WASHINGTON, 30 March 1950, 1.41 p.m.

Repeated to Ottawa.

Your telegram 1706.[2]

I entirely agree with what you say in paragraph 2 about the difficulties of an A.B.C. meeting in London in May. But I think that the inclusion of economic problems in your talks with Acheson is of vital importance because it provides an opportunity to secure agreement with him on the inter-relation of political and economic problems. It can do so in a manner which will not cut across discussions which belong to the A.B.C. forum. If we secure such agreement with Acheson it will directly help future decisions, political and economic, with the Americans.

2. I also think that conversations about our economic situation can most effectively be initiated at the moment as high policy related to the political needs of the Americans for our assistance. My thought is therefore:

(a) The Americans feel that major policies in the foreign field can be formulated and carried out only with the aid of Britain;

(b) We want to play our full part in formulating and carrying out such policies with the Americans;

(c) But our ability to do so depends on our economic condition. We cannot adopt foreign policies without counting the cost.

(d) We must therefore always keep in mind the date 1st July 1952, when they have said and we must insist that we enter a new period when we receive no extraordinary outside assistance.

(e) Consequently, for us there are two interconnected priorities—that of effective action in foreign policy and that of building long term economic strength without which our foreign commitments cannot be supported.

[1] See No. 10, note 4.
[2] This telegram of 29 March (ZP 2/8) discussed the possibility of continuing the Washington A.B.C. talks at Ministerial level in London in May. The absence of Mr. Snyder and Mr. D.C. Abbott, Canadian Minister of Finance, from London in May was cited in paragraph 2 of telegram 1706 to Washington as one of two major difficulties about holding an A.B.C. meeting then. The other difficulty was the danger of reviving 'all the French suspicions which caused such trouble last September'. Following directly upon the A.B.C. talks in Washington, in which the French took no part, Mr. Acheson, Mr. Bevin and M. Schuman met for informal discussions on foreign affairs from 13–17 September. For an account of this Foreign Ministers' conference and subsequent French representations at the failure to inform them then of the impending devaluation of the pound announced on 18 September, of which the Americans had been earlier informed, see A. Bullock, *Ernest Bevin: Foreign Secretary 1945–1951* (London, 1983), pp. 716–723.

(*f*) We need a full recognition of this position and of its application in practice by the Americans, i.e. given they want our active partnership in the world, they must be prepared to make changes which will give us long term economic strength.

3. Many major matters in the political and economic field lie immediately ahead and the State Department sometimes regard the economic consequences of foreign policies on the national economies of the two countries as of secondary importance, whereas we must, in our case, take a different view. Unless therefore we can get the proper relationship established between the political and economic, we shall face continuing misunderstandings. Furthermore there are signs that the Americans are beginning to think of their (repeat their) economic problems and policies in the post-1952 period and anything which will help this on is good.

4. If your discussions proceed on these lines, there does not seem to me to be any risk of cutting across A.B.C. No doubt some of what you say will later become the subject of detailed discussions in A.B.C. But it would be mentioned as illustrative of the broad theme which you were seeking to establish. There would be no intention of reaching agreement on such matters or of formulating views, which would eventually involve legislative commitments in the financial field, and involve a number of other American agencies.

5. On the above basis, it seems to me that—(*a*) under 7(ii) of your telegram[3] the position would be rightly expressed as 'A general review' but not as an attempt to reach agreement on 'the plan of campaign and issues which require study'; (*b*) There should be no difficulty about the Canadians; they could expect to be kept informed but not to sit in.[4]

---

[3] Paragraph 7 of telegram No. 1706 to Washington (note 2) suggested a timetable for four separate sets of discussions featuring at '(ii) General review with Mr. Acheson in London of the plan of campaign and issues which require study.'

[4] Further correspondence on this subject is not here printed. Practical difficulties in arranging a meeting at which all A.B.C. Ministers could be present proved insurmountable. However A.B.C. officials met in London during the May conferences and concluded a brief review of developments since September 1949. Their recommendation for a future Ministerial meeting was agreed in principle by Mr. Bevin, Mr. Acheson and Mr. L.B. Pearson, Canadian Secretary of State for Foreign Affairs, while in London for the N.A.C. Meeting on 15–18 May. However no time was specified and in August it was decided to leave the matter temporarily in abeyance.

No. 12

Note of a meeting held in Sir I. Kirkpatrick's room on 31 March 1950 at 4.30 p.m. to discuss the Agenda for the Tripartite Talks to be held in London in May

[C 2514/2514/18]

Top secret

Present: Sir Ivone Kirkpatrick, Mr. E.A. Seal, Mr. R.B. Stevens, Mr. Mallet, Mr. Penson (British Embassy, Washington), Mr. Allen, Mr. Crawford, Mr. D. Wilson, Mr. D.D. Brown.[1]

Sir Ivone Kirkpatrick said that the plan was to prepare the ground for Ministerial talks by discussions at the official level beforehand. The Americans had said that they were clarifying their ideas and it therefore seemed likely that we should not have a firm Agenda even for the official talks until the American advance guard arrived on the 24th April.

2. In the official talks our aim should be to get a complete series of agreed recommendations, or agreed statements of unresolved differences, covering the whole of the Ministerial Agenda, which the three Ministers should then be invited to approve or decide. The best way to achieve this end would be for the British Delegation to have a complete series of papers which could be offered to the other two Delegations as a basis for discussion. Mr. Penson said that he thought the Americans too would be producing drafts with the same idea in mind. It was agreed that this was all to the good.

3. The meeting then discussed the Agenda outlined in paragraph B sub-section 1 of Foreign Office telegram No. 1591 to Washington of 24th March.[2]

1. *Germany*
  (*a*) Germany and the West
    (i) economic
    (ii) political

Sir Ivone Kirkpatrick said that he saw much merit in a proposal which had been put forward by Mr. Shuckburgh[3] to form an association of Nations in the 'Atlantic World' based on Article 2 of the Atlantic Pact. The

---

[1] Mr. J.H. Penson was Adviser on German Affairs, in H.M. Embassy, Washington. Mr. W.D. Allen, Mr. R.S. Crawford and Mr. A.D. Wilson were heads respectively of F.O. German Political, German Finance and German Commercial Relations and Industry departments. Mr. D.D. Brown, who prepared this record of the meeting, was Private Secretary to Sir I. Kirkpatrick.

[2] The topics for a trilateral agenda listed in paragraph B sub-sections 1 and 2 of this telegram, not printed from WU 1071/20, were the same as those listed in paragraphs 3 and 5 below.

[3] See No. 16.i.

underlying idea of this scheme would be to include the United States as a member of any association to be set up as the supreme co-ordinating body for Western Nations; and this was obviously prudent since the United States, as the most powerful nation in the West, would obviously have a considerable say in the policy of such a body. Mr. Stevens asked whether the proposed club was to be economic as well as political and pointed out that the measure of economic integration attainable at present was small as we could not allow it to lead to the convertibility of sterling. It was agreed that the proposal was for economic as well as political integration. The meeting decided that the draft P.U.S.C. paper on Western Organisations,[4] together with Mr. Stevens paper on Germany and the European Payment Union[5] could serve as a basis for the British draft on this aspect of the Agenda. Mr. Allen suggested that Germany's admission to International Organisations might also be discussed under this heading.

(b) *Soviet designs in Germany, and possible Western counter measures*

It was agreed that the material for a brief on this subject was contained in General Robertson's despatch No. 20 of 5th March, 1950 on Allied policy in the light of Soviet policy and that the brief should contain recommendations for a statement to be made by Ministers.[6]

(c) *Berlin*

It was suggested that the best sort of draft might be a statement of the problem of the remedies hitherto proposed, together with a Ministerial instruction to the High Commission to study this problem as a matter of urgency and submit further proposals. If the High Commission could produce tripartite recommendations before the meetings so much the better. It was suggested that more progress might be made if someone with imagination were given the time to review the Berlin problem as a whole and submit proposals for a more active policy.

---

[4] See No. 30 for the final version of this paper.

[5] This paper entitled 'Economic association of Western Germany with Western Europe and the Sterling Area', commissioned by Mr. Bevin in February and submitted in final form by Mr. Stevens on 28 April, is not here printed from CE 2121/45/181. This paper, prepared by a working party of representatives from the Treasury, Board of Trade and Bank of England with Mr. Stevens as Foreign Office chairman, concluded that on political grounds it was preferable for Western Germany to adhere to the West rather than enter the Soviet orbit or be a lone wolf. The countries of Western Europe would regard close association with Germany with misgiving unless the United Kingdom participated. Closer economic association involved risks of commercial rivalry and some degree of dependence upon an unstable economy: 'These risks are, however, less than those inherent in any alternative course and must be faced'. The rest of the conclusions were concerned with how closer economic association could be achieved, whether by a 'free' or 'rigid' method of expansion and the implications for sterling of Germany's dollar shortage.

[6] General Robertson's despatch No. 20, on which the brief at No. 31 is based, is not here printed from C 1709/20/18.

(d) German internal economic situation

The High Commissioner was understood to be working on a paper embodying his proposals to deal with unemployment and the lack of capital for investment.[7]

(e) Expellees

The Secretary of State had agreed with the High Commissioner at their recent Conference[8] that the problem of aid to Berlin and that of aid to German expellees from the East might be treated in isolation. A paper was being prepared to show how this could be done. Sir Ivone Kirkpatrick said that it would be dangerous to reduce such feeling of responsibility for these problems as the Federal Government might now have since the Federal authorities would then have no scruples about taking the measures which would intensify the present difficulties.

(f) Ruhr Authority[9]

Sir Ivone Kirkpatrick said that he did not think that a discussion of this detailed and technical subject would be the most fruitful use of the Ministers time. It was agreed that with this in mind a paper might be prepared.

(g) Defence of Germany

Sir Ivone Kirkpatrick said that discussion of this topic was academic until the military experts agreed that the physical resources for a successful defence were available to the Western Nations. This was not yet the case. It was suggested however that the question of a Federal Gendarmerie for Western Germany might be discussed under this head.

(h) Ending the state of war

Sir Ivone Kirkpatrick had been impressed by the United States argument against an immediate termination of the state of war.[10] He thought also that our policy on this matter must depend on the German response to the invitation to join the Council of Europe as an associate member. If the Federal Republic were to refuse this invitation, our reaction should be to leave the Occupation Statute more or less as it stood and there would then be no point in terminating the state of war. If, on the other hand, the Federal Republic accepted, then we might agree to revise the Occupation Statute as to bring the Federal Republic as nearly as

[7] See No. 8.i(*c*).　　　　　　　　　　　　　　　　　　[8] See No. 8.
[9] The International Authority for the Ruhr was established in Düsseldorf in 1949 under the agreement completed on 28 December 1948 (Cmd. 7677 of 1949, pp. 20–30), and signed in London on 28 April 1949 by the Governments of the United Kingdom, France, Belgium, the Netherlands, Luxembourg, and the United States of America to which the Federal Republic of Germany acceded on 16 August 1949: *B.F.S.P.*, vol. 154, pp. 483–99.
[10] These arguments were enumerated in an American note to the British government of 22 March, printed in *F.R.U.S. 1950*, vol. iv, pp. 612–5 (British copy on C 2215/148/18).

possible into the same position as Austria. This might involve the termination of the state of war but the question could best be decided at a later stage. Mr. Penson said that, formally at any rate, the Americans still took the position that no substantial relaxation of controls was called for when the Statute came under review next. It was agreed that the Benelux countries might be associated with the discussion of this subject.

4. The following additional subjects were mentioned which might arise under the heading of Germany and on which it would be useful to prepare drafts:

(i) *The Succession of the Federal Republic to the obligations of the German Reich*

Mr. Crawford said that he did not think the Foreign Ministers would wish to discuss the question of the repayment of Germany's foreign debts, but that it would be of great assistance in the technical discussions which there would have to be later if the Ministers could be asked for a ruling that these discussions should go forward on the basis that the Federal Government would succeed to the obligations of the Reich.

(ii) *The Curtailment of the Demilitarisation Programme*

Sir Ivone Kirkpatrick pointed out that our present programme of demolitions for the purposes of demilitarisation might very well look foolish in three or four years time as a result of the further development of our German policy. He thought therefore that a review of the present demolition programme should be undertaken urgently.

(iii) *Steel*

It was agreed that a paper was needed setting out what our policy should be if the Germans asked for an increase in their permitted level of steel production.[11] The paper should recommend that this question might be settled as part of the next general deal with the Federal Government on the lines of the Petersberg Protocol.

(iv) *Ship Building*

This also seemed a point for settlement in a general deal. We should refuse to relax present restrictions[12] and we would have to get American agreement to this attitude until the Federal Republic was more firmly associated with the West.

5. The meeting then turned to the Agenda proposed in paragraph B sub-section 2 of Foreign Office telegram 1591 to Washington.[2]

---

[11] The level of German steel production was fixed at an annual output of 11.1 million tons, as prescribed in article ix of the tripartite Prohibited and Limited Industries (P.L.I.) Agreement of 14 April 1949: *B.F.S.P.*, vol. 155, pp. 495–503.

[12] Allied restrictions on ship building in Germany were as prescribed in article xi of the P.L.I. agreement (note 11) and article vii of the Petersberg protocol (No. 7, note 2). For Allied differences over the liberal American interpretation of these restrictions in regard to German ships for export, see London brief No. 32 calendared at No. 76.i.

2. *Austria*

(a) *Treaty Policy*

It was agreed that the Secretary of State's recent telegram to Washington[13] might form the basis of the brief on this subject.

(b) *Alleviation of Occupation*

The meeting agreed that so soon as the Secretary of State had reached a decision on the submission [ii] that had been made, the Chiefs of Staff would have to be approached about the possibility of reducing the strength of British troops in Austria. We should then be in a position to inform the Americans and the French of the action H.M.G. proposed to take.

CALENDARS TO NO. 12

i *11 Apr. 1950   C.P. (50) 66: Austrian treaty.* Cabinet memo. by Mr. Bevin with summary at Annex A of outstanding articles 16 (displaced persons), 27 (prevention of German rearmament), 42 (U.N. property), 48 (debts), 48 bis (waiver of Allied claims) [CAB 129/39].

ii *3 Apr. 1950   Occupation in Austria*: proposals submitted by Mr. Mallet to Mr. Bevin for reducing burden of occupation costs on Austria include (a) reduction of British occupying forces and (b) civilianisation of British Element of High Commission. Recommendations for approaching Chiefs of Staff and discussion by officials at London conference approved by Mr. Bevin with instruction to 'Proceed urgently' [C 2549/942/3].

[13] This telegram No. 1416 to Washington of 28 March (C 2191/1/3) instructed that Mr. Acheson should be informed of Mr. Bevin's concern to secure quadripartite agreement on the five articles outstanding in the Austrian peace treaty, which was being negotiated in London by Deputies appointed by the Council of Foreign Ministers (*U.K.* Mr. W.I. Mallet, *U.S.A.* Mr. S. Reber, *France* M.M. Berthelot, *Soviet Union* M.G. Zarubin). Mr. Bevin's suggestions for concessions to the Soviet government which he hoped to discuss with Mr. Acheson in London in May were incorporated into a memorandum transmitted to Mr. Acheson on 6 April and printed in *F.R.U.S. 1950*, vol. iv. pp. 450–3: *ibid.*, pp. 453–4 for Mr. Acheson's reply of 24 April. Telegram No. 1416 was appended to a draft Cabinet paper reviewing the course of the Austrian treaty negotiations, which was submitted to Mr. Bevin for approval on 4 April (C 2441/1/3) and subsequently circulated to the Cabinet as C.P. (50) 66 on 11 April: text calendared at i.

No. 13

Minute from Mr. Shuckburgh to Sir G. Jebb

[ZP 2/71]

FOREIGN OFFICE, *6 April 1950*

No doubt this is outside a mere bureaucrat's proper sphere; but I wonder, having regard to the extraordinarily long-term and fundamental issues which Mr. Acheson wants to discuss with us,[1] thought should be

[1] i.e. items 1–5 of the bipartite agenda at No. 17.

given to the possibility of associating H.M. Opposition (? Mr. Eden)[2] with at any rate the most general of the bilateral talks.[3]

C.A.E. SHUCKBURGH

[2] Mr. R.A. Eden was deputy to Mr. W.S. Churchill, leader of H.M. Opposition.

[3] Sir G. Jebb minuted below that he doubted whether the association of Opposition leaders with the London Conference was 'really practical politics, but on the other hand, the Foreign Secretary may wish to have a word with them as regards major policy after this has been approved by H.M. Government and before the actual discussions start with Mr. Acheson'. Both minutes were referred to Mr. Barclay who minuted on 19 April: 'I had a word about this with the Secretary of State this morning. He said he did not believe it would be possible or desirable to have an officially bi-partisan foreign policy at the present time, and he therefore could not agree that any member of the Opposition should be brought in to any of the meetings. They could, of course, be invited to the social gatherings and he would also be quite prepared to let them know confidentially what line he was proposing to take in the talks as he had done on various occasions in the past, e.g. in the Atlantic Pact negotiations. I think that what he will want to do is to arrange for Sir W. Strang or Sir G. Jebb to go and see Mr. Eden, probably towards the end of the official talks and before the ministerial talks begin.'

No. 14

Letter from Sir K. Helm (Tel Aviv) to Sir W. Strang

[EE 1017/30]

Top secret and Personal   TEL AVIV, *11 April 1950*

Dear William,

In what follows I may stray rather outside what is strictly my province. But what I will say affects Israel and is therefore partly my concern. Also, I think you should have the general impressions I picked up in Cairo as well as the points more immediately affecting Israel which I have dealt with in a letter to Michael Wright.[1]

In a manuscript letter which I sent you just before I left, I said I had a feeling that one day we might need the Israelis.[2] My Cairo contacts have reinforced that feeling. Frankly, I have returned very depressed at what I picked up. Nowhere down there could I find the slightest spark of optimism—and my contacts were people who are by no means anti-Arab.

[1] In this letter of 10 April Sir K. Helm recorded the various conversations he had had while on a six day visit to Cairo. His principal meeting was with British Commanders in Chief of land and air forces in the Middle East on 5 April. When discussing the vulnerability of Arab Palestine to Israel, Sir K. Helm 'asked the Commanders in Chief whether from their point of view the strategic position would be seriously affected if the Israel frontiers should in fact reach the Jordan. Their reply was that it would make little difference. The really important factor was Israel's possession of the entire Negev and the blocking of direct access from the Canal base to Jordan. This fact in their view made the integration of Israel in our defence system second in importance only to the Egyptian base itself' (ER 1022/8).

[2] This letter of 27 March is not printed from ER 1904/13.

The best that I could hear was that the Egyptian machine was running down, the worst that the Arab world was heading for chaos. Everybody seemed agreed that things were slipping badly and expressions of disappointment and even disillusionment with the Arabs were general.

Everybody, of course, appreciated the difficulties due to our own weakness. But I seemed to find a general desire for a more positive approach on the part of H.M.G., and a feeling that there has been too much negation and appeasement and that a change of approach is overdue. The feeling, so far as I could make out, is that the Arab countries, led by us for so long, have lost all sense of direction since our positive leadership was withdrawn and that, unless it is restored in some modified form, the whole area will further disintegrate and become a ready prey for whichever power chooses to step in and take control.

These are rather startling statements and I never dreamt that I should have the temerity to make them in a letter to the Foreign Office, even in a personal one. But the impression left on me is such that I feel I have no choice. And let me say in parenthesis that I take no satisfaction from the fact that during our conference in London last July I happened to put in a paper which struck something like the same note.[3]

I see that in that paper I spoke of method rather than of policy. The policy, I fancy, is clear, namely to secure the Egyptian base and through integration to give it protection in depth. Obviously, the Egyptian base is fundamental. But I wonder whether we are going the right way about securing it and securing its defence in depth. Like my colleagues down there, I feel, as I have felt for the past year, that we need a more positive approach. I won't repeat what I wrote in last year's paper but I venture to suggest that the Middle East does need leadership, that we could give it, and that we should have more confidence in ourselves. If I may say so, we seem apt to see too many snags in any course of action and in the end to do nothing or, if anything, too late. Perhaps also we are too afraid of minor and temporary unpopularity.

To my mind it is the comparatively small things that matter as they together make up the big things and once we have given way over small things it becomes almost impossible to recover over the big ones. A case in point is, I think, our failure last year to put a tanker through the Canal at a time when the Egyptians more or less expected it.[4] Most people seemed to think we should easily have got away with it. But today it would be infinitely more difficult. Again, to illustrate my second point, was it necessary to be so defensive about the recent Anglo-Israel financial

[3] For this paper of 21 July 1949 circulated to a conference of H.M. Representatives in the Middle East, held in London on 21–28 July, see F.O. 371/75067:E 9108/1052/65 and F.O. 371/75072–3 for the records of the conference itself.

[4] For discussion of the possibility of sending British oil tankers through the Suez Canal in the summer and autumn of 1949 as part of an operation designed to secure the re-opening of the refinery at Haifa (cf. No. 10.ii): an idea revived by Sir K. Helm in December 1950, see correspondence on F.O. 371/73585–73586B, 80488.

agreement as I think the wording of paragraph 2 of Foreign Office telegram No. 173 to Amman suggests?[5]

I am not suggesting the big stick or bludgeoning, which would be fatal. But there are many stages short of that. Insofar as Israel is concerned, the dominating factor, so far as I can make out, is mutual fear. The Egyptians are afraid of the Israelis and the Israelis are afraid of the Egyptians. Israel wants peace with her neighbours and particularly with Egypt. I gathered in Cairo that at least certain elements in the Egyptian Government also want peace with Israel in spite of the trumpetings at the Arab League.[6] But with mutual fear prevailing there seems to be no hope of the two parties getting together by themselves or even under United Nations auspices. Is there not a part which we could play in bringing the two together and so preparing the way for the securing of the Egyptian base and its defence in depth? I think there is, and it is perhaps arguable that we might fare better with Egypt if she saw that were were not courting her alone.

I would, however, make a caveat in this connection. The only Arab state which Israel fears is Egypt, with whom she is desperately anxious to reach a settlement. Israel pursued the Jordan negotiations as a second best and I should rather expect that if she could sign up with Egypt she would become much more sticky with Jordan. Apart from the military base, our direct interest is, I assume, greater in Jordan than in Egypt. Even if it isn't, we do, I think, want Jordan to get the best possible terms from Israel and to get the two to settle down in peace. King Abdullah[7] would, I think, be out on a limb if Egypt were to sign with Israel before he does. For this and other reasons, therefore, it seems to me that our interest is to get the Jordan-Israel agreement concluded as soon as possible and then, if we can, to further the conclusion of an Egypt-Israel agreement. But the other way round would be risky. The point is, I think, of real importance if, as I have hinted above, some Egyptians are already nibbling at talks with Israel. I know that Kirkbride contemplates the possibility of resumed

[5] This telegram of 1 April reported the signature in London on 30 March of an agreement between the United Kingdom and Israel for the settlement of financial matters outstanding as a result of the termination of the Mandate for Palestine (text of agreement in *B.F.S.P.*, vol. 156, pp. 608–23). Paragraph 2 gave instructions for dealing with any hostile criticism on the lines of: 'In arriving at this settlement we had to take into account Israel's capacity to pay. Within the limits of that capacity we have driven as hard a bargain as we could. It was in fact a question of a settlement on the lines of the agreement or no settlement at all' (ER 1151/61).

[6] Members of the Arab League formed in 1945 were Egypt, Syria, Lebanon, Iraq, Jordan, Saudi Arabia and the Yemen. At the meeting of the Arab League Council on 25 March–1 April 1950, Egypt took the lead in censuring recent negotiations between Jordan and Israel for, *inter alia* a five-year non-aggression pact. These negotiations were suspended after the initialling of a 'basis for negotiation' on 24 February, pending elections in Jordan on 11 April. On 1 April the Arab League Council approved a resolution which stated that member countries should not enter into separate negotiations with Israel for any kind of agreement, on penalty of exclusion from the League.

[7] Abdullah I, King of the Hashemite Kingdom of Jordan.

Jordan-Israel negotiations after the formal union[8] about the beginning of May but possibly not immediately thereafter. I mentioned to him the possibility (in spite of the Arab League resolution) of Egypt getting ahead and he saw the danger. But the internal Jordan developments will take some weeks and my plea is that at the earliest possible moment we encourage King Abdullah and the Israelis to get going again. Unless and until the Egyptians move, the Israelis can be counted upon to make the running with King Abdullah, though if desired I could easily help to push them.

I am afraid that this letter has ended up by being rather woolly. It may also lay me open to the accusation of having stated the disease but of being extremely vague in my prescription of the cure. Actually, it would be presumptuous of me to prescribe the cure because, if the disease exists at all, that is essentially a matter for the Foreign Office. Unfortunately, my Cairo contacts leave me in no doubt about the disease even if I have described it rather crudely. I know it is easy from here or from Cairo to talk about the adoption of a more positive line and that you have to take into account all manner of factors and difficulties, many of them unknown to us. But it is saddening to be forced to the conclusion that, despite our expensive establishments, our position in this part of the world is going and to feel, as I do, that without any serious risk or additional expense, and without any very radical change of method, the position could even now be redressed. If what I have said should contribute in any small way to this, my visit to Cairo will have been well worth while.[9]

Yours ever,
KNOX HELM

[8] See No. 10, note 12.

[9] In his reply of 25 April Sir W. Strang commented: 'I do not think that anyone here would quarrel with your impression of the present state of affairs in the Arab countries, nor with your conclusion that these countries need the moral leadership which we could supply. As you know, our difficulty has all along been to attempt to improve our relations with Israel without at the same time prejudicing our vital stake in the Arab countries. In the continuing state of tension over Palestine, this has involved walking a difficult tight-rope between the two. A particular example of this arises over the question of arms: we should have liked to agree to make at least token supplies available to the Israelis, but, as you will have seen, this would, in the opinion of our representatives in the Arab countries, be likely to arouse a storm there which could hardly be of advantage to anyone' (EE 1017/30). After further discussion of the difficulties for British policy in the Middle East, Sir W. Strang concluded by drawing attention to the 'present incompatibility between friendship with Israel and friendship with the Arabs'.

No. 15

Extract from a Brief by Sir G. Jebb

[ZP 2/155]

Secret   FOREIGN OFFICE, 11 April 1950

Object of May Conversations

At the end of March the State Department submitted a memorandum to Mr. Acheson which stated that the proposed bipartite (United States–United Kingdom) talks 'should aim in the first place at establishing an understanding between the United States and the United Kingdom as to the basic relationship between the two countries and the rôle which each could play most effectively to ensure world prosperity and progress'.[1] State Department officials said at the same time that agreement on this point was 'the most important objective of the whole series of meetings'. All other items on the agenda of the bipartite, and all items on the agenda of the tripartite and Atlantic Council discussions 'should be considered in the light of the general understanding reached between [Mr. Bevin][2] and Mr. Acheson regarding the relationship between the two countries.'

2. We do not know that this memorandum was actually approved by Mr. Acheson, but we must presume it was. At any rate items 4 and 5 of the proposed tripartite[3] talks (which we are told were drafted by the Secretary himself) read as follows:

> 'What should United Kingdom–United States relationship be and what roles can each play most effectively in obtaining common world-wide objectives including the overcoming of present deficiencies?

> What is the best means of assuring as a corollary to the above questions the continuous survey of the world-wide commitments and capabilities of both partners to determine necessary adjustments.'

(The whole draft Agenda[4] is attached for convenience of reference.)

3. Though agreement on Anglo-American relations is thought by the Americans to be of fundamental importance, there are a number of other items on the agenda which can perhaps be resumed as follows:

(1) How can the Western World best be organised?

[1] Sir G. Jebb was here quoting from the summary of this memorandum given by Sir O. Franks in Washington telegram No. 1012 of 28 March (ZP 2/5). Sir O. Franks was shown this memorandum of 17 March, printed in *F.R.U.S. 1950*, vol. iii, pp. 828–30, when discussing with State Department on 28 March the agenda for the London Conference. The two further quotations in this paragraph are also from Washington telegram No. 1012.

[2] Square brackets as in filed copy.

[3] This is an error for bipartite: see No. 17.

[4] Not printed: see No. 17.

(2) How can Germany and Japan best be associated *with* the Western World?

(3 How can the menace of Communism best be resisted?

4. The Americans evidently expect some decision on the Anglo-American relationship, and they probably expect some decision on these three basic problems as well. If so it is evident that many high issues are involved and that the most careful preparatory work is essential. It seems also quite possible that, unless Mr. Acheson reaches agreements which both he and we can regard as satisfactory, his position in America may be still further weakened, and the favourable opportunity that we now have for establishing our own position in the world may not recur.[5]

[5] The remainder of this brief (paragraphs 5–27) was concerned with the projected organization of the conferences of which Sir G. Jebb was in charge. Foreign Office papers on the arrangements for the conferences are entered on FO 371/124918–124928:ZP 2. It was agreed that the United Kingdom should provide the secretariat, directed by Mr. Shuckburgh, for both the Foreign Ministers Conference and the N.A.C. meeting in London.

No. 16

Record of a meeting in the Foreign Office on 13 April 1950[1]

[WU 1071/145]

Secret

Development of the Atlantic Pact

A meeting was held on the 13th April to consider a paper [i] prepared by Mr. Shuckburgh on proposals for developing the Atlantic Pact on the political and economic side. The following were present:

Sir William Strang
Sir Roger Makins
Sir Gladwyn Jebb
Mr. Wright
Mr. Reilly
Mr. Shuckburgh

Sir William Strang said that the proposals in Mr. Shuckburgh's paper were directed to three main objectives:

(i) To emphasise the non-military character of any new structure under the Atlantic Pact.

(ii) To engage the United States as deeply as possible on the political and economic side.

[1] This record was prepared by Mr. D.P. Reilly, Assistant Under-Secretary of State in the Foreign Office, on 14 April and approved that day by Sir W. Strang.

45

(iii) To associate with the political and economic structure to be created, governments which were not parties to the Defence provisions of the Atlantic Pact.

The suggestions which Mr. Wright had criticised in his comments [i] on Mr. Shuckburgh's paper were aimed primarily at making it possible for non-signatories of the Atlantic Pact to be associated with the new economic and political Organisation.

Mr. Wright said that there seemed to be two alternative ways of tackling this problem. Either the signatories to be brought in could be associated with Sub-Commissions or Regional Groups under the Atlantic Pact; or we could drop for the moment the idea of associating non-signatories with the new structure and could concentrate for the present on developing the Atlantic Pact on the political and economic side. In discussion the following points were made:

(i) Our object is to build up the political and economic side of the Atlantic Pact before O.E.E.C. runs down completely, so that the residual functions of the O.E.E.C. may be drawn towards the Atlantic Pact Organisation rather than towards the Council of Europe.

(ii) We have a certain amount of time in which to work, since after 1952 there should still be enough for O.E.E.C to do to maintain its momentum for another year.

(iii) The countries which it is important to associate in some way with the Atlantic Pact are Western Germany, Sweden, Switzerland, and perhaps Austria. Some separate provision will have to be made for Turkey and Greece.

(iv) After 1952, Western Europe should be more or less in balance as regards dollar payments except for Western Germany, Austria, Greece, and possibly Turkey.

The Conclusions of the meeting were as follows:

(*a*) The first step is to obtain in the forthcoming Talks agreement in principle for the development of the Atlantic Pact on the political and economic side.

(*b*) The proposals in Mr. Shuckburgh's paper for keeping the political and economic side of the Atlantic Pact Organisation quite separate from the Defence side are sound.

(*c*) The meeting did not however agree with Mr. Shuckburgh's suggestion that the new economic and political structure should have no direct constitutional relationship with the existing Atlantic Pact organs and should be kept as loose and fluid as possible.

(*d*) As a start, there should be a Permanent Commission subordinate to the North Atlantic Council with a standing Secretariat. This Permanent Commission would deal with political and economic matters and would have nothing to do with Defence questions, for which it is not needed.

(*e*) On the political side, this Commission might be very useful for exchanges of views on such questions as the admission of the Chinese Peoples' Government to the United Nations, Colonial problems and so on. On the economic side, many of the subjects listed in paragraph 2 of Sir E. Hall Patch's paper on the Functions of O.E.E.C. after 1952, annexed to the latest draft of the P.U.S.C. paper on 'Western Organisations',[2] would fall very naturally to be dealt with by the new Permanent Commission. 'Harmonisation' for instance comes within the actual wording of Article II of the Atlantic Pact.

(*f*) We should not however attempt at this stage to list the subjects with which the new Permanent Commission might deal, as on Page 4 of Mr. Shuckburgh's paper. When the Permanent Commission was set up, we could discuss in it what exactly should be its field of action.

(*g*) The Defence side and the political and economic side of the Atlantic Pact Organisation would meet only in the North Atlantic Council.

(*h*) We should not attempt at this stage to devise arrangements by which non-signatories of the Atlantic Pact can be associated with its political and economic side only. (Any such association would need a revision of the Treaty). When the Permanent Commission met it could discuss how non-signatories might be associated with its work.

(*i*) It is essential that the seat of the Permanent Commission should be in London. We can point out that Washington is ruled out because of the importance of dissociating the new Permanent Commission from the Defence side of the Organisation. The French can be reminded that they have O.E.E.C. in Paris.

Mr. Shuckburgh was asked to submit a redraft [i] of his paper in the light of the above Conclusions.

CALENDAR TO NO. 16

i *3 Apr. 1950 f. Memo. by Mr. Shuckburgh.* Further to recommendations of draft of No. 30 Mr. Shuckburgh now makes specific proposals as to how Atlantic pact machinery could be developed. The main suggestion is for the establishment on fairly informal basis of an Atlantic Political Committee. Proposals criticized by Mr. Wright on 7 April for not going far enough. Revised paper of 20 April contains firmer proposals for a permanent political committee with headquarters in London and a permanent secretariat: this paper, later circulated as U.K. brief No. 17 of 27 April, was approved by Mr. Bevin as a guide without commitment [WU 1071/144, 145].

[2] See Annex to No. 30.

No. 17

Sir O. Franks (Washington) to Mr. Bevin[1] (Received 17 April)

No. 217 Saving Telegraphic [ZP 2/37]

Immediate. Secret　　　　　　　　　　　　WASHINGTON, *14 April 1950*

Repeated Saving to Paris.

My immediately preceding Saving telegram.[2]
Following is revised version of agenda agreed with the State Department:

(*Begins*).

Bilateral discussions between Mr. Acheson and Mr. Bevin.
General

1. Review and agreement on common world-wide objectives in the light of assessment of our current position in the Cold War.[3]

2. In the framework of the common objectives agreed to under 1, to determine what needs to be done and in general what each of us should undertake.

3. What are factors arising from United Kingdom–Commonwealth and sterling area ties and other United Kingdom obligations which need to be taken into account in considering the role the United Kingdom should play in Europe and other parts of the world?

4. What should United Kingdom–United States relationship be and what roles can each play most effectively in obtaining common world-wide objectives including the overcoming of present deficiencies?

5. What is the best means of assuring as a corollary to the above

---

[1] Mr. Bevin remained in nominal charge of the Foreign Office, dealing with all main papers, during his stay in the Manor House hospital in London from 11 April–4 May. Day to day business was handled by the Minister of State, Mr. K.G. Younger.

[2] In this telegram of even date Sir O. Franks reported discussion that day with officials of the State Department at which the texts of the agenda below were agreed. The State Department undertook to consult officials in the French Embassy in Washington about the tripartite agenda, 'but do not anticipate that they will disagree with it'. The texts of the bilateral and trilateral agendas below correspond to those printed under date of 17 April, as agreed by French and British Embassies, in *F.R.U.S. 1950*, vol. iii, pp. 836–7.

[3] When minuting on 6 April in favour of an American suggestion that the cold war should be discussed bilaterally at the London conference rather than by the North Atlantic Council of twelve as originally suggested by the British delegation, Mr. Shuckburgh commented: 'Neither we nor the Americans have yet thought out in detail a definite policy in relation to the cold war and the Atlantic Pact; and there is now very little time for us to do so and to coordinate our views before the Council meeting. The smaller Atlantic countries have probably little or nothing to contribute to the cold war and are, moreover, likely to be afraid of its political implications. This is particularly true of the Scandinavians. Finally, our own cold warriors will probably not be ready to share their methods and secrets with representatives of the other eleven countries, and any general Atlantic cold war efforts would therefore be much more formal than real' (WU 1071/52).

questions the continuous survey of the world-wide commitments and capabilities of both partners to determine necessary adjustments?

Specific

The following specific subjects should be discussed within the framework outlined in Points 1 through 5 above (depending on developments and the preparatory work some of the subjects listed may be dropped):

6. Western Europe and the North Atlantic area

(a) NATO

(b) Economic and Political Integration.

(c) Germany's relationship to above.

7. Eastern Europe

(a) General attitude towards Soviet Union, including questions of meetings, if any.

(b) Satellites

(c) Yugoslavia

(d) Trieste.

8. [9][4] Japan.

9. [10] South-East Asia, especially Indo-China.

10. [8] Near East,[5] including

(a) Arms shipments to Israel and Arabs.

(b) Egypt.

11. [12] Subcontinent of India, especially Kashmir.

12. [11] China.

13. The Colonial Question.[6]

(a) Brief discussion for the purpose of identifying the main problems on which later conversations might be conducted.

---

[4] Figure in square brackets denotes subsequent renumbering of items made at British request.

[5] In his telegram 216 Saving (see note 2) Sir O. Franks observed: 'The State Department asked us to remove Persia under the item dealing with the Near East. They are not yet absolutely certain whether they will want to raise it or not, but they see no need to put it on the agenda at this stage. They said that on present form they would wish to raise under this heading the subjects of Saudi Arabia and the Palestine Relief Agency.' On 19 April the Foreign Office replied in telegram No. 2016 to Washington 'We have no objection to the removal of Persia from the formal Agenda but shall ourselves wish to raise it. We should also wish to raise Saudi Arabia and note that State Department wish to discuss the United Nations Relief and Works Agency. We shall also probably wish to discuss Haifa oil and Arab/Israel relations but do not consider that it is necessary to put any of these subjects specifically on the Agenda' (ZP 2/36: cf. No. 10.ii for U.N.R.W.A. and Haifa oil).

[6] In his telegram No. 216 Saving, Sir O. Franks drew attention to the removal of New Guinea from this item since the State Department was 'nervous of Dutch reactions should fact of its inclusion on agenda leak out'. The Foreign Office agreed to the omission of New Guinea and saw 'no need even to discuss it unless the Americans particularly wish to do so.'

(b) Economic Development.
(c) Future of Africa.

14. Libya and Eritrea.

Tripartite discussions between Mr. Acheson, Mr. Bevin and Mr. Schuman.
General
  1. Review and agreement on common world-wide objectives, in the light of assessment of the current world-wide situation.

Specific
  In the framework of the common objectives agreed to under item 1, what needs to be done on the subjects listed below?
  2. Review and determination of what needs to be done to achieve closer association of European and North Atlantic areas.

(a) NATO
(b) European political and economic integration
        (i) long-term development of economic relationships with United States of America.
        (ii) Migration.
(c) Germany.[7]

  3. German problems.[7]
  4. Austrian Treaty problems.
  5. South-East Asia.[7]

(a) Indo-China.

  6. United Nations Developments

(a) Chinese representation—Soviet walkout.
(b) Lie's proposal [for] special meeting [of] Security Council.[8]

[7] The governments of the Netherlands, Belgium and Luxembourg were advised in Foreign Office notes of 21 April of arrangements for keeping them informed of tripartite discussions on Germany and for taking their views into account (texts on C 2731–3/2514/ 18). The Government of the Netherlands was advised in a further note of 21 April of similar arrangements with regard to tripartite discussions on South-East Asia (FZ 1106/9).

[8] With a view to ending the Soviet boycott of the Security Council and other bodies of the United Nations before the next session of the General Assembly opened in September, Mr. Trygve Lie, U.N. Secretary-General, proposed in March that, as provided for in article 28(2) of the U.N. Charter of 26 June 1945 (*B.F.S.P.*,vol. 145, pp. 805–32), a special meeting of the Security Council should be held not later than May 1950 at which member states would be represented by Foreign Ministers or Heads of Government: Mr. Lie proposed that this meeting should consider a six-point peace plan aimed at reducing East–West tensions: (1) the question of Chinese representation in the U.N.; (2) atomic energy and the hydrogen bomb; (3) the reduction of conventional armaments; (4) the admission of new members to the U.N.; (5) the creation of an international police force; (6) plans for periodic meetings of the Security Council. For the F.O. brief on these proposals for the London Conference, see No. 23.ii: and F.O. 371/88391, 88393, 88507–8, 88619–22, for further F.O. views and discussion with Mr. Lie in London, Paris and Moscow from 27 April–23 May. A further item on the U.N. relating to Spain was included by the Americans on an early draft agenda but later dropped: F.O. brief calendared at i.

7. The Colonial Question

(a) Brief discussion for the purpose of identifying the main problems on which later conversations might be conducted.
(b) Economic Development.
(c) Future of Africa.

8. General attitude towards Soviet Union. Should there be negotiations and, if so, in what forums?
9. Advisability of and means of continuously reviewing world-wide commitments and capabilities and most effective manner of conducting future discussions of this nature. (*Ends.*)[9]

CALENDAR TO No. 17

i *27 Mar. 1950 Spain and the U.N.* British policy towards the question of rescinding the 1946 U.N. Resolution on Spain, which *inter alia* debarred Spain from membership of the U.N., is considered in F.O. brief for London conference [WS 10345/19].

[9] The renumbered bipartite and tripartite agendas were circulated to the U.K. delegation on 21 April as D. Nos. 4 and 5 respectively (ZP 2/62 and 63).

No. 18

Record by Sir I. Kirkpatrick of a conversation with the French Ambassador

[*C 2591/148/18*]

FOREIGN OFFICE, *15 April 1950*

The French Ambassador called yesterday to have a general chat on his return from a short holiday in Paris.

He told me that he had been surprised to find at the French Ministry of Foreign Affairs a general idea that we intended, at the forthcoming Ministerial meeting, to press for the early termination of the state of war with Germany, to obtain recognition of Germany as a State and to favour the early end of the Occupation.

I told him that I was equally surprised to hear that this idea should be current in Paris and I assured him that it was without foundation. I said that the Americans, both on general political grounds and on the grounds of constitutional expediency, did not consider the present moment opportune for terminating the state of war. As regards the occupation, the Secretary of State had made a powerful statement at the Council of Ministers in reply to Mr. Vyshinsky,[1] and I had every reason to believe

[1] At the opening of the sixth session of the Council of Foreign Ministers which met in Paris from 23 May–20 June 1949, Soviet proposals for achieving economic and political

51

that Mr. Bevin's views remained unaltered. As regards his second point it was true that Mr. Bevin had used words in the Foreign Affairs Debate which might be interpreted as an expression of his view that provided Germany joined the Council of Europe and behaved properly in other respects we might consider allowing her to establish a Ministry of Foreign Affairs, subject of course to the retention of our reserve powers.[2] But even on this point I did not think that the Secretary of State had intended to express a definite view. I added that it was my personal opinion that provided the Germans entered the Council of Europe, and provided the three Western powers wished to relax the Occupation Statute, the safest course might be to give the Germans a Ministry of Foreign Affairs. It seemed to me more important to retain our other reserve powers. If we did so, the existence of a Ministry of Foreign Affairs, which would only be in relation with States friendly to us, since Russia and the satellites obviously would not receive Federal Diplomatic Missions, would in fact bring very little alteration to the existing state of affairs whilst adding to the internal prestige of the Federal Government. M. Massigli made no comment on this but remarked that he was glad to have my assurance that there was no ground for the apprehensions entertained in Paris.[3]

I.K.

unity of Germany were presented by M. A. Vyshinsky, Soviet Minister for Foreign Affairs. These were rejected on 28 May by Mr. Bevin when presenting counter-proposals on behalf of the three Western Foreign Ministers (*F.R.U.S. 1949*, vol. iii, p. 928 *et passim*): see further No. 58, note 3.

[2] These remarks, made by Mr. Bevin on 28 March in the course of a debate in the House of Commons on foreign affairs, are quoted in No. 49, paragraph 5, from *Parl. Debs., 5th ser., H. of C.*, vol. 473, col. 323: see also No. 38, note 1.

[3] Similar apprehensions, in regard to American policy, were the subject of press speculation in the United States at this time. According to the British Embassy in Washington some of these reports 'arose as a result of a garbled interpretation of some background briefing which Byroade gave selected correspondents before leaving for London' (C 3522/202/18). For further views on Germany from Colonel H.A. Byroade, Director of the Bureau of German Affairs in the State Department, see No. 51.

No. 19

Minute from Sir R. Makins to Mr. Bevin

[*UE 1245/53*]

Top secret   FOREIGN OFFICE, *17 April 1950*

We have deliberately refrained from putting the question of atomic energy on the agenda for the Acheson talks, but at the same time it will probably be a mistake not to mention the question while Mr. Acheson and Mr. Pearson are in London. The present position is that the negotiations for a comprehensive agreement on cooperation in this field[1] were well advanced at the time when the Fuchs case[2] broke and led to a suspension of the talks on the American side.

2. A hint was later given to us both by the Atomic Energy Commission and the State Department that it might be possible to pave the way for the resumption of the negotiations if preliminary tripartite talks on security standards in the atomic energy field could be held. This seemed to be a good idea on merits and we made proposals to the Americans accordingly. These, however, were cautiously received at the highest level in Washington and nothing so far has come of them. In the meantime, we are having to take decisions about the future of our atomic energy programme, particularly about our plans for developing weapons. These decisions may prejudice the most desirable solution, namely a combined Anglo-American-Canadian weapons production programme. We cannot hold back on our own production, but if we go ahead on our own it will mean additional expenditure for an inferior weapon.

3. It has always been anomalous that this field of atomic energy should be the one in which no effective Anglo-American-Canadian cooperation existed, and on any rational assessment of the issues it is absurd that the fact of one traitor having been found in our camp (there have been traitors also in the U.S.A.) should be allowed to wreck the policy of cooperation which is in the best interest of all three countries.

4. Time is running very short. It is now unlikely that acceptable arrangements could be agreed before Congress disperses unless the Administration are prepared to make a major effort. But in a year from now the two programmes must necessarily have developed and diverged further and the task of integration will have been made more difficult. Moreover, though we have succeeded in reaching a temporary agreement about the allocation of raw materials it will be more difficult as time goes on to make temporary arrangements and our need for raw materials will be greater if cooperation is withheld by the United States.

5. I therefore suggest that the opportunity should be taken of a confidential talk between the Secretary of State, Mr. Acheson and Mr. Pearson. The Prime Minister in view of his great and continuing interest in these atomic energy matters might wish to participate in this talk.[3]

ROGER MAKINS

[1] For an account of these negotiations in Washington between the United States, United Kingdom and Canada begun in September 1949 and continued intermittently until their suspension in February 1950, see M. Gowing, *Independence and Deterrence, Britain and Atomic Energy 1945–1952* (London, 1974), vol. i, pp. 282–98.

[2] On 2 February Dr. K. Fuchs, a British scientist working at the Atomic Energy Research Establishment at Harwell, was arrested on charges under the Official Secrets Act. For details of this case which resulted in his conviction on 1 March, see *ibid.*, vol. ii, pp. 144–150.

[3] This minute was submitted through Sir W. Strang. On 19 April Mr. Barclay minuted 'The S. of S. agrees with Sir R. Makins' proposal. He had been assuming that there would have to be an exchange of views on this subject.' Mr. Attlee was informed of Mr. Bevin's views and agreed that the proposed meeting should take place.

No. 20

Brief for the U.K. Delegation[1]

No. 1 [ZP 2/58]

Top secret   FOREIGN OFFICE, *19 April 1950*

A Third World Power or Western Consolidation

I

Introduction

Up to about the end of 1947, when the Great Power system known as the Council of Foreign Ministers broke down, it was assumed, with decreasing confidence, that the general structure of peace would be based essentially on co-operation between the United States, the Soviet Union, and the United Kingdom, which to some extent might be taken as representing the British Commonwealth and Empire. The breakdown on the question of Germany, however, destroyed this conception, perhaps temporarily, perhaps for ever. Although the United Nations was maintained as a kind of symbol of a real world system, and no doubt in the expectation that it would ultimately prove possible to revert to it, it was then clearly necessary to cast around for some alternative system of security which would be capable of maintaining peace for a long period to come.

2. This process of consolidating the non-Communist world really began in June 1947 with the announcement of the Marshall Plan and its acceptance by the Secretary of State. It passed from the economic to the political and military sphere early in 1948. At that time action in three stages was envisaged by the Secretary of State. The first stage was the conclusion of the Brussels Treaty, described as the hard core of the European system. The second stage was its reinforcement by the power and wealth of North America. The third stage was the extension of the European system. The first stage was completed by the signature of the Brussels Treaty on 17th March, 1948. The second stage was completed by the signature of the Atlantic Pact, which, for the first time, committed the United States and Canada to the defence of Western Europe. The third stage has now been initiated with the establishment of the Council of Europe. It therefore seems desirable to consider carefully what is to be the ultimate aim of this policy.

3. For the moment the Brussels Treaty and the Atlantic Pact provide a military alliance of those free democracies of the West which are threatened by the Soviet Government. But it has been suggested that this

---

[1] This brief was first prepared in 1949 for discussion by the Permanent Under-Secretary's Committee, emerging as P.U.S.C. (22) Final Approved of 9 May 1949. It was subsequently circulated to the Cabinet, though not discussed there, as C.P. (49) 208 on 18 October (see further No. 62).

should be a temporary phase, and that the real object should be to organise Western Europe into a 'Middle Power', co-equal with, and independent of, the United States and the Soviet Union alike. The supporters of this proposal admit that, for a considerable period of time, and notably for such period as Western Europe is dependent for its very existence on American economic support, the European political organisation, whatever it may be, will have to lean heavily towards America and away from the Soviet Union. At the same time it is suggested that the underlying aim of an organisation of Europe should be the eventual creation of a system which would enable Western Europe, plus the bulk of the African continent, and in some form of loose association with other members of the Commonwealth, to run an independent policy in world affairs which would not necessarily coincide with either Soviet or American wishes.

4. This concept of a Third World Power has had many advocates. In this country it has appealed particularly to those who find American capitalism little more attractive than Soviet communism, and to those who feel a natural dislike of seeing this country in a dependent position. But the policy is not without its advocates in the United States itself. These have included, at one time at any rate, the Planning Section of the State Department, who thought that the best way to consolidate the Western world was to build up another Power-unit with a strength equivalent to that of America and Russia. It has also found favour among the Isolationists, who feel that if this unit came into existence it would provide America with an excuse for retiring into her shell and leaving the task of containing Russia to the Third World Power.

5. Another school of thought, more common perhaps on the Continent of Europe than in the United States or the United Kingdom, has suggested that a Third World Power of this kind, even if its physical power were less than that of either of the other two Great Powers, would by remaining neutral develop an influence out of proportion to its strength, since it could hope to be courted by both sides. The ability of a weak State to exploit its neutrality in this manner is illustrated by the conduct of Bulgaria in 1914–15 and Italy in 1939–40, though the subsequent experiences of these two countries are not encouraging.

6. All these schools of thought, different as they are, have in common the assumption that it is possible to create a workable Third World Power, independent equally of Russia and of America. The object of this paper is to consider whether this assumption is justified; whether, if the creation of a Third World Power is possible, it is also desirable; and, if not, what the alternatives are.

II

Possible Composition of a Third World Power

7. The first question that requires consideration is what the composition of a Third World Power might be. The only serious suggestions that

have been made are that it should consist of the Commonwealth, or of Western Europe (including the United Kingdom) with its overseas territories, or of these groups combined. These suggested groupings may be examined under three headings, political, economic and military.

Commonwealth
(a) Political
8. There are no political tendencies in the Commonwealth to-day which suggest that it could successfully be consolidated as a single unit. The Commonwealth is not a unit in the same sense as the United States or the Soviet Union. It has no central authority and is unlikely to create one, and its members are increasingly framing their policies on grounds of regional or local interests. The only member of the Commonwealth which might assume a position of leadership within it is the United Kingdom, and it seems unlikely that any proposals originating in London for a closer co-ordination of Commonwealth policy would be welcomed at present. It should not be assumed that centrifugal forces are certain to increase and it remains true that concerted action may well be achieved in a crisis. The substantial identity of view among Commonwealth countries is undoubtedly an important influence for world peace. Nevertheless, there is no guarantee that a common policy will be followed.

(b) Economic
9. Since the creation of the O.E.E.C. (Organisation for European Economic Cooperation) machinery the economic planning of the United Kingdom is tending to become more closely tied in with Western Europe than with the Commonwealth. The general trend of O.E.E.C. planning has so far been satisfactory to the sterling Dominions. The United Kingdom, however, needs to be able to speak with greater authority in Paris as the representative of the whole sterling area. Moreover, a greater mutual exchange of economic information within the Commonwealth is needed if the central gold and dollar reserves of the sterling area are to be fully safeguarded. There is little sign that the Dominions would accept collective planning arrangements for the Commonwealth similar to O.E.E.C., but we may well hope to persuade them increasingly to discuss their long-term problems individually with the United Kingdom. Even so, Commonwealth countries are likely to take the view that their needs for investment capital for industrial development cannot be met by co-operation with the United Kingdom and Western Europe alone, but that dollar assistance will be needed. The Americans have shown reluctance in the past to use the United Kingdom as a channel for extending dollar aid to the rest of the Commonwealth.

(c) Military
10. The military picture is similar. As a result of the Brussels Treaty the United Kingdom has gone much further in military planning with Western Europe than it has with the Commonwealth. Moreover, the

Commonwealth is not a strategic unit, and here again it must be clear to the Dominions that their defence cannot be assured without United States support. For example, the Commonwealth, even with the help of Western Europe, will not in the foreseeable future be strong enough to hold the Middle East which is vital to its security.

(d) Conclusion

11. Despite the possibility of improved economic consultation, there seems little prospect of the United Kingdom being able to unite the Commonwealth as a single world power. The attraction exerted by the pound sterling and the Royal Navy is now less strong than that of the dollar and the atom bomb. An attempt to turn the Commonwealth into a Third World Power would only confront its members with a direct choice between London and Washington, and though sentiment might point one way interest would certainly lead the other.

Western Europe (including the United Kingdom) with its Overseas Territories
(a) Political

12. The progress so far made in such directions as Benelux and the Italo-French Customs Union[2] is primarily economic in character although there are political implications. These experiments have, however, not yet reached a sufficiently advanced stage to permit of optimistic conclusions regarding prospects of more far-reaching political unity. The new Council of Europe may gradually create in this old Continent a consciousness of European unity and a will to play an independent part in world affairs. But it must be recognised that centrifugal tendencies are still strong and there is a danger that the Council of Europe may seem to give Europe a greater cohesion and strength than it in fact possesses and so encourage the Americans to retire into an isolation dangerous both for themselves and for Europe. Whatever the tendencies may be, the fact remains that the military and economic situation of the Western European nations is now such that there can be no immediate prospect of welding them into a prosperous and secure entity without American help; and even with American help it is uncertain whether this can be achieved for some time to come.

13. The above has been written without special regard to the problem of Germany. The problem of including Germany, in whole or in part, in Western Europe and the effect which this would have on the possible constitution of a Third World Power, cannot be dealt with fully within the limits of this paper. There are many schools of thought on this topic. Some claim that Western Europe could only hope to achieve security and

[2] Full economic union of Benelux countries projected in March 1949 for July 1950 did not materialize. Similarly the Franco–Italian Customs Union treaty of March 1949 and Convention of June 1950 which superseded it remained unratified. For these and parallel developments in Scandinavia and the early work of the European Customs Union Study Group formed in November 1947 under O.E.E.C. auspices, see A.S. Milward, *The Reconstruction of Western Europe 1945–1951* (London, 1984), especially pp. 232–255.

independence if it included the whole of Germany. Others feel that the inclusion of all Germany in any Western European group would involve a serious risk of its eventual domination by a revived Reich, and moreover that Western Europe would thereby become involved in quarrels about Germany's eastern frontiers which it would be highly desirable to avoid. Others again say that the inclusion of Western Germany in the Western European group is now a foregone conclusion, that the addition of the Soviet Zone, if that ever became practicable, would not be of such weight as to alter the whole balance, and that ways can and must be found of integrating a united Germany into the European family of nations. In any event if Western Germany, or even a unified Germany, is, after a period of years, fully integrated in the economy of Western Europe, that would probably not in itself result in Western Europe becoming an independent Power of the same order of magnitude as the Soviet Union or the United States of America, unless indeed the *military* as well as the economic potential of Germany was fully developed—and it is difficult to see this being accepted by the Soviet Union or even by the Western democracies themselves.

(b) Economic

14. Western Europe, including its dependent overseas territories, is now patently dependent on American aid, although in the longer run it should be able to pay its way. It is, however, always likely to be dependent for the maintenance of a reasonable standard of living on a large exchange of goods and services with the Eastern *Bloc*, with the Commonwealth and with the United States. Although the O.E.E.C. countries and their dependent overseas territories now enjoy a preponderance of economic potential over the Soviet Orbit, this preponderance may well disappear within ten years if Soviet plans are fulfilled. Soviet plans may be particularly limited by commitments to the satellites and by high military expenditure, or even by technical shortcomings in Russia itself. But it is safest to assume that, even if the economy of Western Europe is closely linked with that of the United States, their present joint margin of superiority over the Soviet economic system will tend to shrink.

15. It is true that O.E.E.C. has shown the beginning of satisfactory economic co-operation but the impetus has been given by the United States in the conditions which they imposed as a price for dollar aid. There are already signs that as the individual countries become economically stronger and more self-sufficient the centrifugal tendencies are likely to increase, and it may well be that when American aid ceases altogether the present limited degree of European economic co-operation will not survive. We should in any case be wise not to place undue reliance on it at the expense of our relations with the Commonwealth and the United States.

16. Moreover, from the United Kingdom point of view, economic integration with Western Europe involves great risks which would only be

worth taking if we could be confident that economic integration would create a unit economically and militarily strong enough to be capable of resisting aggression. For the moment there seems little prospect of such a development and we might, if we went too far along this road, find Europe overrun and our own segment of the economy unable to function on its own.

(c) Military

17. From the military point of view, the situation is that even with American help there is nothing at present to stop the Russians occupying the entire Atlantic coast of Europe. In ten years' time Western Europe might possibly be able to hold out until full American assistance could be brought into play. Even this limited defensive rôle involves an expenditure which may well be too heavy for European national incomes. Unless, therefore, we are prepared to effect a drastic lowering of our present standards of living or to accept the remilitarisation of the Reich, any thought of a third World Power in Europe being militarily capable of resisting Russia by itself can be dismissed.

18. In actual military strength Russia is now, apart from weapons of mass destruction, vastly superior to the United States and Western Europe combined, and although as has been said our economic potential may for the time being be greater than that of the Russians the difference will lessen with time. Moreover, owing to the Soviet Union's present ability rapidly to overrun Western Europe there is a danger that American potential will be left with no area in which to deploy itself.

(d) Conclusion

19. Whereas in the case of the Commonwealth the principal difficulties in the way of consolidation as a Third World Power are political, in the case of Western Europe the difficulties lie mainly in the economic and military weakness of its members, though the political will to union must always be doubtful.

The Commonwealth and Western Europe Combined

20. Unfortunately, the objections to either group in isolation are not removed by their combination, and this alternative is therefore not examined in detail. Political cohesion of the Commonwealth countries with Western Europe is even less likely than with the United Kingdom, and the dangerous choice between London and Washington is not eliminated. Moreover, the economic and military weaknesses of Western Europe are not significantly diminished by the addition of the Commonwealth countries other than the United Kingdom, and the need for American support remains. Incidentally this need for American support underlines the danger of even trying to create a group which could give the United States an excuse for believing that a buffer state had been created and that accordingly America need not exert herself strenuously on behalf of Western civilisation.

21. The preceding paragraphs suggest that none of the possible combinations of Powers is likely in the near future to amount to a unit capable of pursuing a policy independent both of the Soviet Union and of the United States. There is moreover a further argument which is valid in regard to any possible combination of Powers. The belief in the ability of a Third Power to exploit its independence by a policy of neutrality and by playing off the other two Powers against each other is based on a total misconception of Marx–Leninist ideology. It is surely essential to take at their face value the frequent assertions by Soviet leaders that Marx–Leninism is the basis of their policy. This being so, they would not be prepared to establish any lasting agreement with a neutral, non-Communist Third World Power; at the most they might be prepared to make a show of reaching such an accommodation for tactical reasons. A policy of neutrality would in fact only encourage the Soviet Union to swallow its opponents one by one and, from the point of view of the United Kingdom especially, would afford no protection for our vital interests in the rest of the world, notably in the Near and Far East.

III

Consolidation of the West

22. The conclusion seems inescapable that for the present at any rate the closest association with the United States is essential, not only for the purpose of standing up to Soviet aggression but also in the interests of Commonwealth solidarity and of European unity. The form which such an association should take is a matter for another paper,[3] but it is perhaps worth recording the negative conclusion that the mobilisation of general collective security on the basis of Article 51 of the Charter does not seem a promising method. The probable result of such a process would be the establishment of a new United Nations organisation without the Soviet Union or its satellites, resulting in an unwieldy *bloc* of countries with no organised leadership, in which the special interests of single countries or groups of countries would be liable to paralyse action by the organisation as a whole.

23. The positive arguments in favour of the consolidation of the West, in which at first, at any rate, the United States would be the largest single unit, may be summarised as follows:

(*a*) As long as Russian policy continues to be based on the Marx–Leninist philosophy which regards all non-Communist Governments as enemies, these Governments will be forced to combine, and in this sense the consolidation of the West will come about as a natural process.

(*b*) The combination produced by this natural process, of which the Atlantic Pact is the first example, represents such a vast effort that once achieved it may in practice be very difficult to dissolve.

[3] See No. 30.

(*c*) The association of the United States, Western Europe and the Commonwealth, different though their cultural backgrounds and political philosophies may be, has at least in its favour a sufficient number of common traditions to make the group workable.

24. There are, of course, some arguments on the other side. It must be recognised that in a Western system the United States will be the most powerful member, will inevitably take the lead in a number of fields and will no doubt expect her views to prevail to a considerable extent. This, however, was already the case before the signature of the Atlantic Pact. In all fields in which the United States makes the major contribution, whether financial, military or otherwise, it is inevitable that proportionate (although not always determining) weight must be given to her views.

25. At the same time experience has shown that it is usually possible to reconcile British and American views. As United States policy evolves from isolation to the assumption of increasing responsibility in world affairs, her outlook (*e.g.* over colonial dependencies) is evolving also, and it has so far proved less arduous for us to find a common approach towards world problems with the Americans than with most other Powers. While, therefore, extremely difficult adjustments of policy, which are inevitable in any partnership, will have to be made under a Western system, there are not so far sufficient grounds for the fear that partnership with the United States in a Western system would involve the United Kingdom in dangerous dependence on the United States. There is sufficient kinship of ideas to make this unlikely. We are in fact more likely to find it difficult to reach a common approach with Western European countries, and most of all with Germany.

26. The fear is sometimes expressed that the United States might be tempted to indulge in adventurous policies, and that too close a partnership with them would add to the risk that the United Kingdom and its other partners might be involved against their will in the consequences of such policies. Although the possibility of their adopting ill-considered and therefore dangerous policies is always with us, the likelihood of the United States embarking on an aggressive policy is extremely remote. In spite of occasional violence of talk, American public opinion and the American Congress are both peace-loving and cautious, and more likely to err on the side of prudence than of rashness. Moreover, if the United States were nonetheless to embark on adventurous policies the United Kingdom would almost inevitably be involved in the consequences in any case, and it may reasonably be expected that partnership with the United States in a Western system would increase rather than diminish the opportunities for the United Kingdom to apply a brake to American policy if necessary.

27. The possibility must also be considered that a slump might occur in the United States which would have serious repercussions on the economies of the United Kingdom and of Western European countries.

This is true. But the effect would be much the same whether a Western system comes into being or not. Moreover, here again the existence of a Western system improves the outlook for fruitful discussion on economic policies between the members.

28. There is no necessary contradiction between the consolidation of a Western system and a much greater unification and strengthening of Europe. It is only the concept of Western Europe as a Third World Power acting independently both of the United States and of the Commonwealth, in other words as a Third World Power in the strict sense of the term, which is inconsistent with the consolidation of a Western system.

29. During the next ten to twenty years the economic dependence of Western European countries on the United States ought to disappear, and their ability to make a valid military contribution to a Western system ought to increase. Even to-day it is a mistake to regard the relationship of the Western European countries, and particularly of the United Kingdom with the United States as one of complete dependence. In fact, the United States has no desire to find herself confronted with a Western Europe under Communist domination, or a Western Europe which is completely neutral. On the contrary, the United States recognises that the United Kingdom and the Commonwealth, and to a lesser extent the Western Continental Europe, are essential to her defence and safety. Already it is, apart from the economic field, a case of partial interdependence rather than of complete dependence. As time goes by the elements of dependence ought to diminish and those of interdependence to increase. The United Kingdom in particular, by virtue of her leading position both in Western Europe and in the Commonwealth, ought to play a larger and larger part in a Western system.

30. It must, however, be appreciated that the Western system is coming into being under the pressure of Soviet policy. It is probably fair to say that it is a system desirable in itself, since had it been in existence at the time the wars of 1914 and 1939 might well have been avoided. But whether this is so or not, it might well prove that, if Soviet pressure were relaxed as a result of some major tactical deviation, the development of the system might be arrested in proportion as the compelling cause of the danger from the Soviet Union diminished. This aspect of the question will form the subject of another study.

31. There are two further points which require to be borne in mind in connexion with the consolidation of the West, though they cannot be fully developed within the limits of this paper. The first is that consolidation of the West cannot be solely a matter of agreement between Governments. It must also involve an internal consolidation of the peoples of the Western countries and a rejection of Communist influence.

32. Secondly, it may prove to be the case that the consolidation of the West in a passive sense will not prove to be enough, and that the only final hope for a settled world will be that the ideas it represents and the system which incorporates these ideas should spread eastwards.

Conclusions

33. The general conclusion of this paper may be summarised as follows:

(*a*) The Commonwealth alone cannot form a Third World Power equivalent to the United States or the Soviet Union.

(*b*) Commonwealth solidarity is more likely to be promoted by the consolidation of the West than by the formation of a Third World Power independent of America.

(*c*) A weak, neutral Western Europe is undesirable and a strong independent Western Europe is impracticable at present and could only come about, if at all, at the cost of the remilitarisation of Germany.

(*d*) The best hope of security for Western Europe lies in a consolidation of the West on the lines indicated by the Atlantic Pact.

(*e*) During the next 10–20 years, Western Europe, provided it continues on its policy of co-operation, should emerge from economic and even from military dependence on the United States but the two areas will remain interdependent.

(*f*) The United Kingdom will have an increasingly important part to play in the consolidated West, and must also seek to maintain its special relations with the United States.

CALENDAR TO NO. 20

i *25 Apr. 1950   P.U.S.C. memo. (50) 4 on the United Kingdom and the United Nations*: assesses the profit and loss accruing to the U.K. from membership of the U.N. and concludes that on balance the existence of the U.N. is an asset to British policy [ZP 3/1].

No. 21

Mr. Bevin to Sir O. Franks (Washington)

No. 2014 Telegraphic [ZP 2/39]

Immediate. Secret   FOREIGN OFFICE, *19 April 1950, 8.30 p.m.*

Repeated to Paris.

Your telegram No. 1210.[1] London Meetings.

The French reacted rather unfavourably towards our suggestion that their officials should not arrive in London until 27th April and it seemed that they were going to be touchy about bilateral discussions between ourselves and the Americans.

[1] This telegram of 18 April (ZP 2/39) is not printed.

2. We felt we should insist on having at least two days clear for such discussions and have today told the French Embassy that we are proposing to arrange the first tripartite discussions for Wednesday, April 26th, at 3.0 p.m. The Embassy's reaction was quite favourable and they thought that any criticism there might be in France could be allayed if M. Massigli (who will lead the French official party) could have a short meeting with Dr. Jessup[2] some time on the Monday or Tuesday. This can of course easily be arranged and we hope Dr. Jessup will agree. We made the point that we proposed to emphasise with the press the entirely preparatory and exploratory nature of the official talks, and that there would be no communiqués or announcements of policy of any kind during the first week. We shall in fact do our best to discourage press interest in these meetings, and we do not think the French need fear that their absence during the first two days will appear discriminatory.[3]

[2] Head of the American official delegation.

[3] Sir O. Franks was further informed in Foreign Office telegram to Washington No. 2026 of 20 April that 'we are now told by the American Ambassador that M. Massigli has expressed to him (though not to us) on behalf of M. Schuman "grave disquiet" lest the initial bilateral Anglo-American talks should have an unfavourable effect in France. He (M. Schuman) apparently now suggests that there should be at any rate an initial tripartite meeting on Monday the 24th . . . We view this development with grave misgivings and fear that even if the proposed tripartite meeeting on Monday next was in theory confined to procedural matters, in practice we should find ourselves in a position in which it would be barely possible for us to have bilateral talks with the Americans at all' (ZP 2/46). After some discussion with the State Department and the French Ambassador in London it was finally agreed that a tripartite meeting of officials on procedures should take place on 24 April. On the same day Anglo-American bilateral meetings began (see No. 29) with Franco-American meetings beginning on 27 April.

No. 22

Letter from Sir O. Franks (Washington) to Sir R. Makins

[UEE 4/31]

Secret   WASHINGTON, *19 April 1950*

Dear Roger,

Sterling Balances and South East Asia

I am sending some comments on Acheson's request to see what we were sending to the Commonwealth Governments[1] because I think the issue

[1] Following Sir O. Franks' approach to Mr. Acheson on 13 April for informal and exploratory A.B.C. talks on sterling balances (see No. 9, note 7), Mr. Acheson telephoned Sir O. Franks later that day to ask if he could see a draft of the circular telegram to the Commonwealth (*ibid.*) before its despatch (Washington telegram No. 1159 on FZ 1112/11). In reply on 15 April F.O. telegram to Washington No. 1951 stated: 'As the telegram to Commonwealth Governments has already been despatched there can be no question of letting Acheson have sight of it in draft. As, however, the Americans seem to have placed you in a position where it would be almost impossible not to let them have a sight of the text

raised is of a kind which will confront us in various ways in the coming period.

There can be no question of the right of the United Kingdom to communicate confidentially with other members of the Commonwealth. But as I see it what we are concerned with here is not so much a matter of rights as of tactics in a particular negotiation. We are in a particularly delicate position because in addition to being a primarily interested party in any new arrangement about sterling balances we are acting in the actual course of the negotiations in some sense as a broker between the two other groups, i.e. the Commonwealth holders of the sterling balances on the one side and the United States and Canada on the other, who have in one way or another an interest in the matter. Each of these other parties is afraid that we may appear to be acting as their representative and to be conveying impressions of their views and probable action to which they would not at present wish to be committed.

A 'broker' placed in such a position can do one of two things. He can either talk quite secretly to each of the other parties or he can let each know more or less fully what he says to the other. The alternative of really secret discussions seems to be ruled out by the publicity which has been given to the whole subject in recent months, if by no other considerations; and we are left therefore with the choice only of the precise degree of fullness with which we disclose to one side the substance of what we are saying to the other.

In these circumstances it seems to me that Acheson had in mind that the mere fact of United States participation in the conversations must have repercussions on the one side on the character of general United States policy towards the new nations of Asia and on the other of expectations or hopes which may exist of dollar assistance to those countries at some stage and in some form yet undetermined. Inevitably he is nervous that what we say to the Commonwealth countries concerned may create ideas about United States general foreign policy in the area and create expectations with regard to U.S. assistance which might go beyond what we would wish to be committed to at this very preliminary stage. I would repeat what I have already said that our position is such that, whether we like it or not, whatever we do say to either side in this negotiation is apt to be regarded as reflecting at least to some extent the views of the other side and just as

as despatched or to read it to them, you may at your discretion do so. If you do, it is most important that the Americans should not disclose to Commonwealth representatives other than the Canadians the fact that they have seen it . . . The proposal to hold a conference with Commonwealth Finance Ministers to discuss the funding idea is still in a tentative stage. You should not at present disclose to the Americans that we are thinking of holding it . . . You should know that we have no intention of ourselves raising the question of sterling balances at the Sydney Conference.' Foreign Office telegram No. 1968 of 17 April continued: 'We should have added that we do not wish the Americans to have the text on record, and we hope that you will be able to persuade them to refrain in future from tactless requests to see the actual text of confidential communications passing between the United Kingdom and other members of the Commonwealth' (FZ 1112/11).

the Commonwealth holders of balances have shown their anxiety that we should not appear to be committing them to action, so the Americans wish to be sure that we have not by mischance used words which might raise as yet unjustified hopes about their actions.

To sum up, I think that just as we are completely right when we say that we must be able to communicate confidentially with Commonwealth Governments the Americans are right when they say that if they are to be involved with the Canadians in bilateral talks with us in which their foreign policy to other members of the Commonwealth is involved, then they must know what is going on in the other set of bilateral conversations we hold with other Commonwealth members on the same topic.

It seems to me that we must edge our way through these difficulties but that we cannot expect the parallel series of talks to work out well if American requests for information about what is going on are to come up against a strict application of the privacy of our communications to Commonwealth Governments on these subjects. We cannot keep to one hundred percent. adherence to principle either way.

I am sending a copy of this letter to Liesching, Alec Clutterbuck and one to Harry Wilson Smith.[2]

Yours sincerely,
OLIVER FRANKS

CALENDAR TO No. 22

i *27 April 1950 Consultation with Commonwealth.* In letter to Sir R. Makins, Sir P. Liesching comments on No. 22, emphasizing the importance of safeguarding the confidentiality of U.K. communications with the Commonwealth. The difficulty for the U.K. in relations with the Commonwealth is 'to mark the distinction between our right to act and their right to be consulted.' Already strong pressure from India and Pakistan for more information on Anglo-American communications on sterling balances: —with some justification

---

[2] Sir P. Liesching was Permanent Under-Secretary of State at the Commonwealth Relations Office, Sir A. Clutterbuck was U.K. High Commissioner in Canada, Sir H. Wilson Smith was Second Secretary at the Treasury. In the Foreign Office this letter was circulated to Sir W. Strang, Mr. Dening, Mr. Wright and Mr. E.A. Berthoud, Assistant Under-Secretary of State, who commented on 25 April: 'The corollary of what Sir O. Franks says is that we must keep the Commonwealth Govts. more closely informed than at present of what we are saying to the Americans.' In reply to Sir O. Franks on 8 May, Sir R. Makins sent him a copy of Sir P. Liesching's comments, calendared at i, on which he commented: 'I fully agree with his view that our dilemma in this matter is full of danger to our good relations with the Commonwealth. Equally I recognise Acheson's concern about possible misrepresentation of the American position . . . But I think the principle remains that we cannot agree to show to the State Department the communications which we send to the Commonwealth. They are of a different order to the sort of communications that either the United States Government or ourselves make to other Governments and I hope you will do everything you can to persuade the State Department to be contented with an assurance that we are being most scrupulous in our communications with Commonwealth countries and that we will keep them fully informed in general terms of the information which we are giving them' (UEE/4/44).

since 'I cannot think of any occasion in peace-time on which we have gone so far towards representing other Commonwealth Governments without their authority or indeed without the fullest consultation.' To show the Americans communications with the Commonwealth would 'run the very real risk of giving the biggest holders of sterling the impression that we are playing against them and are hand in glove with the Americans'—an impression already fostered by 'recent outrageous leakages to the press in Washington' about possible cancellation of balances [UEE 4/44].

No. 23

Extract from a Memorandum by the Secretary of State for Foreign Affairs[1]

C.P. (50) 73 [CAB 129/39]

Secret   FOREIGN OFFICE, 20 April 1950

China

China will be one of the subjects to be discussed with the United States Secretary of State, Mr. Acheson, during his visit to this country in May. Preliminary talks at the official level are to take place in London upon the arrival on 24th April of a group of American officials led by Dr. Jessup, United States Ambassador-at-large, who has recently completed a tour of the Far East and South and South-East Asia. In these circumstances I consider it desirable to review the position in China, and to consider the line to be taken in the forthcoming talks with the United States.

Summary

2. Part I of this paper[1] contains a review of recent events relating to China, and reveals a profoundly unsatisfactory situation. Normal diplomatic relations between His Majesty's Government and the Chinese People's Government have not yet been established;[2] the condition of United Kingdom business interests in China has gravely deteriorated; the question of Chinese representation in the United Nations has led to a boycott by the Soviet and satellite states of all United Nations bodies in session, and the deadlock remains unresolved; the Hong Kong aircraft case[3] has given rise to many difficulties particularly with the United States;

[1] The preliminary summary and concluding recommendations only of this Cabinet paper are here printed. The full text of the paper, circulated to the U.K. delegation to the London Foreign Ministers' Conference on 25 April as brief No.13, is reproduced at i below.

[2] On 6 January 1950 His Majesty's Government accorded *de jure* recognition to the Central People's Government of China, formed in October 1949 under the Chairmanship of M. Mao Tse-tung with M. Chou En-lai as Prime Minister and Minister for Foreign Affairs. However little progress towards the establishment of normal diplomatic relations was made by H.M. Chargé d'Affaires, Mr. J.C. Hutchinson, who arrived in Peking in February for preliminary and procedural discussions : see further i below.

[3] The safekeeping and ultimate ownership of aircraft left in Hong Kong by the defeated Chinese Nationalist government was in dispute: see further i below.

and in recent weeks there has been growing evidence of Russian military aid to China. Part II of the paper examines the considerations affecting the policy of His Majesty's Government and reaches the conclusion that this policy should be continued, and that if there is to be a break in our relations with China, the initiative and responsibility for that break should be left to the Chinese. The policy of the United States towards China is examined in Part III and instances are given where the inconsistencies of that policy adversely affect United Kingdom interests and are harmful to our common aim of preventing the permanent alienation of China from the West. It is recommended that the whole field of our respective relations with China should be discussed in the course of the forthcoming bipartite talks with the United States Secretary of State. As regards United Kingdom business interests, it is not practicable at present to take any concrete measures for their assistance except to make representations to the Chinese People's Government on the basis of their immediate difficulties. Until normal diplomatic relations are established with the Chinese People's Government, the effectiveness of these representations is likely to be limited.
... 1

Recommendations

41. I invite my colleagues to agree to the following recommendations:

(*a*) That we should continue our present policy towards China.

(*b*) That I should discuss with the United States Secretary of State the whole field of the relations of both our Governments with China on the basis of this paper and seek to ensure that the United States do not adopt courses which are harmful to our common ultimate aim of preventing the permanent alienation of China from the West.

(*c*) That I should try to persuade the United States Government to modify their attitude towards Chinese representation in the United Nations to the extent of signifying to the four Powers represented in the Security Council their willingness to accept a change, even though they do not feel able to vote for it.

(*d*) That British firms should be informed that His Majesty's Government feel unable to give financial assistance, but will do what they can to help in any other way open to them.

(*e*) That His Majesty's Chargé d'Affaires in Peking should be instructed to make representations to the Chinese Government about the position of British economic interests in China.

E.B.

CALENDARS TO NO. 23

i   *20 Apr. 1950   Full text of C.P. (50)73 on China* covering recognition, Hong Kong aircraft case, military compound at Peking, British business interests, evacuation of British and other nationals from Shanghai, H.M. Consular establishments, internal situation, Chinese representation in the U.N. Draft of

Cabinet paper amended in discussion by Far East (official) committee on 17 Apr., when position of Chinese consuls in Malaya also considered [CAB 129/39; CAB 134/289].

ii *24 & 26 Apr. 1950   U.K.Briefs (a) No. 10 Mr. Trygve Lie's proposal for a special meeting of the Security Council* (see No. 17, note 8). Mr. Lie now agrees that meeting cannot be held unless question of Chinese representation is settled beforehand. British doubt that meeting would lead to agreement on any of the major issues [UP 219/20]. (*b*) *No. 14 Chinese representation in the U.N. & Soviet walkout.* British policy is to secure substitution of Chinese Nationalist delegate by representative of the People's Government in all organs and bodies of U.N. in which China is represented. Explains difficulties (e.g. voting procedures) in way of achieving this. In forthcoming London talks, U.K. delegation should try to persuade U.S. and/or France to recognise Peking Govt. or failing that at least to take a more active line regarding Chinese representation at the U.N. [UP 123/24].

No. 24

Brief for the U.K. Delegation[1]

No. 4 [AU 10512/2]

Top secret   FOREIGN OFFICE, *21 April 1950*

The general approach in bipartite conversations with the American delegation

I *Composition*

The American Advance Party will include Dr. Jessup (Senior Adviser to the Secretary of State), Mr. Perkins (Assistant Secretary for European Affairs), and Mr. Labouisse (Director of the Office of British Commonwealth and Northern European Affairs). Presumably Mr. Douglas and Mr. Julius Holmes, or both, will also take part.

2. Sir William Strang will be the leader of our official delegation and will take the Chair at the opening meeting, and whenever thereafter he can spare the time. When he is not in the Chair, his place will be taken by Sir Gladwyn Jebb, assisted by Mr. Michael Wright, who will be responsible for continuity. Sir Ivone Kirkpatrick, Sir Roger Makins and Sir Frederick Hoyer-Millar will also attend whenever they so desire. Other Under-Secretaries will attend as may be appropriate. Mr. Shuckburgh will normally attend as Secretary-General. Sir Edwin Plowden or Mr. R.L. Hall[2] will attend the opening meeting and any subsequent meetings at which their presence may be useful.

---

[1] The draft of this brief, prepared by Mr. Wright, was submitted to Mr. Bevin on 20 April by Sir W. Strang who explained that the draft 'is based generally upon the conclusions of papers prepared by the Permanent Under-Secretary's Committee' (ZP 2/61). The draft was approved by Mr. Bevin that day subject to modification of paragraph 29(3).

[2] Respectively Chief Planning Officer at the Treasury and Director of the Economic Section of the Cabinet Office.

II *The ground to be covered*

3. The State Department have suggested that the Bipartite Talks between the Secretary of State and Mr. Acheson, to take place on May 9th and 10th, should aim in the first place at establishing an understanding between the United States and the United Kingdom as to the basic relationship between our two countries and the role which each could play most effectively to ensure world prosperity and progress. The subsequent tripartite discussion with M. Schuman, and the proceedings of the Atlantic Council would be conducted in the light of the general understanding reached between the Secretary of State and Mr. Acheson regarding this basic relationship.

4. The Bipartite Talks beginning on April 24th ought to prepare the ground fully for the talks between the Secretary of State and Mr. Acheson. It should be our aim to reach provisional agreement over as wide a field as possible for their approval, and to narrow down points of disagreement for their consideration.

5. This might be done either by producing a single document containing a general statement and chapters on individual subjects for approval by both, or perhaps better by virtually identic documents produced by each side for approval by their own higher authority.

6. Attached (Paper D.1)[3] is the proposed agenda for the Bipartite Talks which suggests five general headings for discussion during the week beginning April 24th, and specific subjects to be discussed during the following week, when the second American Party will have arrived.

7. This brief is intended to cover only the first week.

III *General considerations*

8. The American suggestion that we should aim in the first place at establishing an understanding about the basic relationship between the two countries is an important development. It is the first time since the war that they have approached us as a partner on the most general issues of policy. But it is not an entirely sudden departure. It has been evident for some time past that as the United States moved out into world affairs, she was becoming increasingly conscious, first that the strength and prosperity of the United Kingdom, both in her own right and as the leading member both of the Commonwealth and of Western Europe, was an essential factor in the security of the United States; and second, that the United States cannot get the main lines of their foreign policy right, whether in Europe, the Middle East, or Asia, without our help.

9. This line of thought coincides with our own thinking. We may compare the analysis and conclusions contained in the paper on Western Consolidation produced by the Permanent Under-Secretary's Committee.[4]

10. There is therefore a good prospect that we shall find that our basic lines of thought are not far apart.

---

[3] Not printed: see No. 17. [4] No.20.

11. We accordingly have an unprecedented opportunity for discussing and perhaps reaching a wide measure of agreement with the Americans in the whole field of foreign policy. It is recommended that we should make the most that we can of this opportunity, and should not hesitate to discuss fundamental problems with complete frankness.

IV *Method of approach*

12. Experience has shown that in discussion with the Americans two rules are worth observing. First, complete and if necessary blunt frankness. Second, to avoid in the first stages a didactic approach or implying that we know all the answers and have cut and dried solutions ready. It is better to take the line that there is a common problem to which it is important that we should both find the right answer. We have certain ideas which we should like to look at together, without being sure that they are necessarily right. The Americans may have others, which we may not have thought of. The result of this joint approach to a problem is often that the Americans prepare themselves the solutions which we favour.

V *The first meeting*

13. With these points in mind, it is suggested that the first meeting or meetings should be devoted to a general discussion of Item 1 of the proposed agenda, on the basis of a joint approach as a group to a common problem. We might suggest that, subject to any later decision, there should be no formal notes kept and that all those participating should be free to express their views completely frankly and without formal commitment. The Americans could speak first if they wished.

VI *Our own general thesis*

14. Our own general thesis might be that we have to ask ourselves whether the Western World can survive the dangers which threaten it. We believe that it can, provided the problem is tackled courageously and in the right way. We have looked at the possibilities that the United States, the Commonwealth, Western Europe, or the Commonwealth and Western Europe together, could each as a single force provide for their own security. Our analysis so far indicates that none of them can do so. In particular, a weak neutral Western Europe is undesirable, and a strong independent Western Europe is impracticable at present. Our general conclusion is that the safety of all these countries or groups of countries lies in Western consolidation on the lines of, and largely within the framework of, the Atlantic Pact. Such a grouping alone can afford the industrial and strategic strength, and the political impact, necessary for survival. Our analysis further leads us to judge that closer cohesion within Europe can only be developed on a stable and lasting basis within this framework. Judging by M. Bidault's recent speech[5] French minds are working in a similar direction.

[5] In a speech at Lyons on 16 April M. G. Bidault, President of the French Council of Ministers, proposed the creation of an Atlantic High Council for Peace; see *The Times* of 17

15. So far, valuable progress has been made in developing strategic machinery under the Atlantic Pact. No comparable progress has been made in the development of the Pact for peaceful purposes, and in particular of political and economic machinery. Such development is provided for by Article II of the Pact, and we believe that it is important to make progress in this direction during the forthcoming meetings. If we agree on this principle at the outset, detailed work upon it can follow.

16. But the successful working of any machinery under the Atlantic Pact depends upon a working partnership between the United States and the United Kingdom (as the leading member, both of Western Europe and of the Commonwealth). If our two countries are working at cross purposes, paralysis of effort is bound to be the result.

17. We think that the conclusion to which this reasoning points is that both our Governments should work on the general principle that within a common approach to world affairs, and with full regard to their obligations as members of the United Nations and, in the case of the United Kingdom, as a member of the Commonwealth, they should endeavour to strengthen each other's position in the world on the basis of mutual respect and cooperation. It should be contrary to the policy of either Government to injure the other or to take advantage of the other. On the contrary, it should be their parallel and respective policy to strengthen and improve each other's position by lending each other all proper and possible support. (This is an adaptation of the principles already endorsed at the highest level on both sides in respect of the Middle East – circulated as Annex A)[6]

VII *Summary of general aim*

At the first meeting or meetings
18. We have been led to believe that the Americans will show us two papers regarding their general attitude on these talks. Subject to what may be said in these papers, and to what the Americans may have to say in discussion, our general aim at the first meeting or meetings might therefore be to establish three main principles:

April, p.4. On 19 April Sir O. Harvey reported in Paris telegram No.138 Saving that according to M. de la Tournelle, Political Director at the Quai d'Orsay, 'M. Bidault's proposals were personal to himself and did not represent any decision by the French Government . . . The Quai d'Orsay had been studying various proposals at the official level, but that nothing had yet been submitted to Ministers . . . The proposal at present in favour was for the institution of a Secretary-General for the Atlantic Organisation, with a small staff, who would be charged with the duty of co-ordination of all Atlantic Treaty activities, and who would be advised by a Committee of Ambassadors on which all the signatory Powers would be represented and which would not necessarily be in permanent session' (WU 1071/54).

[6] Appended to Annex A was the general statement of principles for British and American policies in the Middle East agreed in Anglo-American discussion at the Pentagon from 16 October – 7 November 1947: American text printed in *F.R.U.S. 1947*, vol. v, pp. 582–4: cf. also W.R. Louis, *The British Empire in the Middle East 1945–1951* (Oxford, 1984), pp. 109–112.

(1) That our common security lies in Western consolidation through the development of political and economic machinery under Article II of the Atlantic Pact.[7]

(2) That the successful development of the Atlantic Pact depends upon a working partnership between the United Kingdom and the United States.

(3) That both our Governments should work on the general principle outlined in paragraph 17, which should be further defined.

The Second Round

19. If we could agree on these three principles, or something like them, it would be logical next to examine what measures we can both take to help and strengthen each other (this would be in accordance with the thought behind Items 2, 3 and 4 of the Agenda, although not following them literally.)

20. It would perhaps be for the Americans to explain what help they wish from us. But we may bear in mind that in peacetime it is only we who can give a lead in Western Europe, which will be followed; it is only we who have the knowledge of South East Asia and the respect of the inhabitants, and it is we who bear the major responsibilities in the Middle East. In time of war, they need us as fighting partners, and they need bases in our territory.

21. On our side, our main thesis might be on the following lines.

22. We are already on the road to regaining strength. It is our determined aim to develop that strength and to maintain our position as a World Power. (It is extremely important that we should make such an affirmation of faith in ourselves, perhaps in expanded form. The American attitude may largely depend on their estimate of our confidence in our own future.)

23. We have our own ideas about the basis on which our internal strength can best be developed. The Americans may not always agree with them or like them. We ourselves have serious reserves about some aspects of American internal policy and in particular their unemployment policy and the apparent absence of means to counteract severe industrial recessions and slumps which may have a grave effect on Western economy as a whole. But so far as these are purely internal matters, they are for each of us our own affairs.

24. What is essential is that, in accordance with the principle outlined in paragraph 17 above, we should neither of us hinder the efforts of the other to build up their strength, but on the contrary help each other to do so.

25. For us it is vital, if we are to shoulder our share of the burdens of partnership, that we should be independent of continued American

[7] *Note in filed copy*: 'If the principle is agreed we could either discuss detailed proposals further during the first week, perhaps set up a small working party, or leave them to be worked out in the second week under item 6 (*a*) of the Agenda.'

financial aid by July 1st, 1952. We must measure our commitments against this overriding necessity.

26. We do not want any further grants or direct aid for ourselves. But we do want help on the following lines:

(a) Assistance in dealing with the problem of the sterling balances.

(b) Action on tariffs and administrative procedures connected with them, to enable us to sell a sufficient amount of goods in the American market. In other words, it is essential, both in our and in their own long term interests, that the Americans should really adapt policies consonant with their creditor positions. This is the economic counterpart and condition for the political and strategic burdens we are continuing to bear.

(c) That the Americans should refrain from weakening our general sources of strength. We have in mind particularly the position of sterling and the sterling area, and the position in our Colonies. These points will perhaps need separate consideration.

VIII *Item 5 of the agenda*

27. 'What is the best means of assuring, as a corollary to the above questions, the continuous survey of the world-wide commitments and capabilities of both partners to determine necessary adjustments.'

28. It might be of advantage to discuss next Item 5 of the Agenda, and to invite American views.

29. We might ourselves make the following points:

(1) There should be full and constant exchanges of information and views, and consultation between the two Governments about all common problems.

(2) It would be of advantage to try and work out, during the second week of the present discussions, statements (as far as this may prove possible) of common principles and objectives in the various areas and subjects under discussion. This would be subject to constant review and adaptation, and would not represent hard and fast commitments. This experiment has already been tried in the difficult area of the Middle East, and has, we feel, proved of considerable value. It is perhaps capable of wider application and of further development. Common principles and objectives in all or most fields of foreign policy would be an important step forward.

This suggestion might lead to a review of the topics for discussion during the second week.

(3) At the meeting at the State Department on the 14th September, 1949, Mr. Acheson, when informing Mr. Bevin that the United States would appoint representatives to play an active role in the work of the three European strategic planning groups, added that this statement would not in any way limit the 'ultra-secret global planning arrangements' which exist between the United States and the United Kingdom. We should not refer to this assertion in any talks with the United States

officials, not all of whom may be aware of it; but if possible, we should try to obtain endorsement of the principle during the Bipartite Ministerial talks.[8]

Since the United States and the United Kingdom have to consider defence arrangements for areas outside the Atlantic Region, these special bipartite strategic planning arrangements are of high importance. This should be continued and developed.

(4) It is essential that the spirit of partnership should be fully expressed in arrangements for the exchange of secret information and for atomic energy.

(5) It is extremely important that we should not work at cross purposes in the United Nations, and should find means of avoiding as far as possible the situation in which one country votes against the other on issues essential to either.

30. As regards the possibility of special bipartite machinery additional to the above, we should be wise to feel our way cautiously and to see whether the Americans have any suggestions to make. We must also bear in mind French reactions to any overt proposal for special Anglo-American machinery in the political field. One comparatively modest possibility would be to provide for a periodical review as a whole (not merely in particular areas) of the body of common principles and objectives which may have been worked out, as suggested in paragraph 29 above.

IX *Other points for discussion*

31. We should of course consider, after the opening meeting or meetings, what, if any, special points merit discussion during the first week – e.g., policy towards the Soviet Union, the relationship between European integration, the Council of Europe and the Atlantic Pact, and such economic matters as may emerge.

X *General*

32. The above is merely intended to suggest an outline of approach. The points included can be expanded or varied as we go along.

33. Finally, we should make it clear that in the first phase we are not speaking from a ministerial brief, or with commitment, but exploring

---

[8] The draft of this sentence read: 'We ought to try to get this statement specifically reaffirmed in any document that may be drawn up.' This was amended to the present text to take account of Mr. Bevin's view that 'to ask for reaffirmation might embarrass the Americans, particularly as some members of the present delegation would probably not be aware of what Mr. Acheson had said' (minute by Mr. Barclay on ZP 2/61). For the American record of the meeting in question in which Mr. Acheson is recorded as saying that matters of global strategy 'could be discussed bilaterally much better than in the regional groups', see *F.R.U.S. 1949*, vol. iv, pp. 325–8. The European regional planning groups as agreed in September 1949 (see No. 3, note 8) were Northern Europe (Denmark, Norway, U.K.); Western Europe (Belgium, France, Luxembourg, the Netherlands, U.K.), Southern European-Western Mediterranean (France, Italy, U.K.): cf. Lord Ismay, *N.A.T.O. The First Five Years 1949–1954*, p.25.

ideas which may be referred to higher authority when we see how the talks go.[9]

[9] When commenting on the draft of this paper in a minute of 20 April, Mr. Shuckburgh suggested that an early priority in the first week of talks with American officials should be to establish 'how to handle the French and to what extent we are going to be able to regard them as, so to speak, equal parties in the consideration of general problems. It is going to be very embarrassing if we arrive on Wednesday afternoon [26 April] and give the French the impression that there is a sphere in these general ideas from which they are excluded.' Furthermore Mr. Shuckburgh wondered whether 'despite what the State Department said in their memorandum to Mr. Acheson back in March [see No. 15, note 1] . . . it is really likely that the Americans will be able to regard the relationship with the United Kingdom as so exclusively the prime objective of the talks as a whole. Is it not the case that our importance to the Americans lies not only in our industrial, geographical and Common-wealth attributes, and in the influence which we carry in the Far East, etc., but also in the fact that we are the leading Power in Western Europe, and perhaps the only Power which can guide Western Europe out of Communism and collapse? Mr. Wright indeed refers to this in paragraph 20 of his paper, but I wonder whether he gives due consideration to the fact that, if we try to put ourselves into an exclusive relationship with the United States, we thereby cheapen our own value in the eyes of the Americans as well as weakening the influence which we possess in Europe. Is there not a danger that by adopting too much the line that we want to regard ourselves and the Americans as having a superior and special position, we may get the conversations into a false position and encounter the same sort of disappointment as we encountered (perhaps I am exaggerating) after the Washington talks last year, when I think we perhaps over-estimated the extent to which the Americans were really prepared to align their policy towards special relationships with the United Kingdom' (ZP 2/72).

No. 25

Minute from Mr. Berthoud to Sir R. Makins

[AU 1156/4]

Confidential   FOREIGN OFFICE, 21 April 1950

Anglo-American Economic Relationships

The attached paper [i] which E.R. Department have prepared in consultation with E.R.P. Department. started off as a review of outstand-ing points of friction between the Americans and ourselves, but has ended up by dealing with all the different questions on which we have fairly recently had differences of opinion.

The general picture is that our present relationships with the Amer-icans in the economic field are good and that we have nothing really to complain about. I do not think there are any specific economic points which call for special consideration at the forthcoming talks.

As regards the future, it is difficult to be confident as the Americans have so often in the past pressed us to go faster along the path of freeing trade and payments than we felt was justified by our economic circumstances. This pressure may well be renewed at any time in the

E.P.U. discussions in Paris, particularly in view of the material improvement in the position of our reserves. Indeed the most outstanding contribution which the forthcoming talks could make would be recognition by the Americans that our present level of gold and dollar reserves is inadequate and that our joint policy should be directed towards increasing them. This is all the more important because there are already pretty firm indications that the level of our reserves at the end of the *second* quarter will show a further bound forward.

The other quite general point is that the Americans should as far as possible maintain the spirit of the Marshall Plan as originally launched, namely to allow us to decide what is best for our own economic salvation and not to permit sectional interests in America which are hit by our increasing exports to or decreasing imports from that country, to press for legislation which would frustrate the purposes of the Recovery Programme. The most troublesome case in point is shipping.

A special word about oil. I think it would be well worth while as the price of important American concessions over a wider field (sterling balances and overseas commitments) to agree with the Americans to let-up on our oil substitution proposals[1] and to work out a settlement with them on a basis of full partnership. The Treasury would probably not agree with this but the idea would be likely to appeal to the Ministry of Fuel and Power.

I have not tried in these papers to cover differences of opinion between the Americans and ourselves as to our economic relations with Europe – integration and all that.[2]

E.A. BERTHOUD

CALENDAR TO NO. 25

i *21 Apr. 1950 Anglo-American economic relationship* reviewed by Mr. R.W. Jackling of Economic Relations dept. with a revise of the Anglo-American differences listed in the Treasury note in Jan. (No. 1.i). Most have now been resolved satisfactorily. 'In fact the Americans have shown latterly in many ways both their understanding of our difficulties and their desire to help us where they can in finding solutions to them . . . It is difficult to recall a calmer moment on the economic front in Anglo-U.S. affairs for a long time' However 'certain fundamental differences' remain. Potential difficulties include general trade and monetary policy, East-West trade and economic policy towards Germany [AU 1156/4]

[1] See No. 2, note 3.
[2] This paper, with enclosure (i), was submitted on 22 April to Sir W. Strang. Although not intended as a brief for the London Conference, copies were circulated to Sir G. Jebb, Mr. Wright, Mr. Shuckburgh, Sir E. Plowden and Mr. Hall.

No. 26

Memorandum for the Russia Committee[1]

[NS 1052/44]

Top secret   FOREIGN OFFICE, *21 April 1950*

Relations with the Soviet Union

This memorandum sets out to consider three questions:

(i) Are there any grounds for believing that the Soviet Government might be willing to acquiesce, either openly or tacitly, in an arrangement whereby the world would in effect be divided into two Western and Communist, spheres of influence?

(ii) Have the Western Powers anything to gain, or to fear, from an extra-ordinary high-level meeting with the Soviet leaders?

(iii) Is there any initiative the Western Powers can usefully take to improve their own position *vis á vis* the U.S.S.R.?

2. As regards question (1), it is hard to see, on the ideological plane, how the Politburo could ever accept or, if they accepted, fulfil one of the basic conditions of a division into spheres of influence, namely the cessation of subversive Communist activity in the Western sphere. As the *Times* leader of April 10th remarked: 'In a war of ideologies, the definition of strict spheres of interest is an anachronism'. On the practical plane, we may perhaps be entitled to believe that the Politburo are impressed by the increasing solidarity of the West. But it is improbable that they have so little faith in the efficacy of the means they are now using to check it that they feel obliged to agree to a genuine scheme for the division of the world into two spheres of influence. They have no reason yet to be convinced that the political and economic solidarity of the West is assured; the troubled waters of South-East Asia hold out the prospect of excellent fishing; and Africa offers a wide and almost untouched field for the exploitation of native grievances. In short, it is hard to believe that the Politburo feel the need for any new departure in foreign policy—least of all one such as a proposal for spheres of influence which, if observed, would require the abandonment of their forward policy in the Western and colonial spheres. (These arguments would seem to be equally valid against suggestions for 'neutralising' certain areas, e.g. Germany).

[1] The Russia Committee of Foreign Office officials and representatives from the Chiefs of Staff, C.R.O., C.O. and B.B.C., met at fortnightly intervals to review the development of Soviet policy, propaganda and activities. For papers and meetings in 1950 of this committee, which reported to the P.U.S.C., see F.O. 371/86750–62. The present memorandum was drafted by Mr. G.W. Harrison, Head of Northern department, as a brief for Mr. Bevin at the London Foreign Ministers' Conference. The draft was circulated to the Russia Committee on 17 April and revised after discussion there on 19 April (record on F.O. 371/86761: NS 1053/14). The present final text was circulated to the Russia Committee for information on 25 April as R.C./67/50.

3. As regards question (ii), the reaction of *Pravda* of March 19th to the seven points set out in Mr. Acheson's speech of March 16th[2] was entirely negative and there is no reason to doubt that *Pravda's* comments represent official Soviet thought. There are indeed no grounds for anticipating any such advance in Soviet thought as would enable agreement to be reached at a high level meeting on such practical questions as the future of Germany and Japan or control of arms production, whether atomic or 'conventional'. If a meeting took place (presumably on Western initiative) its primary object would thus be to satisfy the wishes of large sections of public opinion, especially in the U.S., where it is felt that a supreme effort must be made to come to terms with the Soviet Union and save world peace. While the proposal for a meeting might temporarily wrest from Soviet propaganda the initiative which it is gaining by its identification of the Soviet Union with the 'peace campaign', the failure of a top-level meeting—which, as far as we can see, would be bound to ensue unless the West 'sold out' to the Soviet Union—might well have a depressing effect on Western morale and leave the impression that no alleviation of the 'war of nerves' was to be hoped for. It must be borne in mind that it is extremely unlikely that the Soviet leaders would come to such a meeting with the object of reaching a genuine and lasting settlement. If they came at all, it would be with the sole purpose of unsettling those elements in the West who have resigned themselves to continuing tension, and of reinforcing those who believe that any settlement would be better than none. Thus a high-level meeting might do harm in either of two ways. If it resulted in some specious paper agreement, it might lull Western public opinion into a false sense of security and weaken our defence preparations and position in the 'cold war'. On the other hand, if no agreement resulted, it might present Communist propaganda with fresh ammunition for its attack on the Western 'warmongers'. A final argument against the Western Powers *proposing* a top-level meeting is that by doing so they would place themselves in a weak position by appearing anxious for a let-up in the 'cold war'. This would be particularly undesirable after a period of Communist success such as Mao's victory in China and the Sino-Soviet agreements.[3]

[2] In this address to the University of California at Berkeley, (printed in the *Department of State Bulletin*, vol. xxii, pp. 473–8: F.O. copy with *Pravda* commentary on NS 10345/9 and 11), Mr. Acheson suggested seven issues on which the Soviet Union could take steps to improve East/West relations: (1) the negotiation of peace treaties with Germany, Austria and Japan (2) the use of force in satellite countries (3) obstruction in the U.N. (4) the international control of atomic energy (5) attempts to undermine established governments (6) the treatment of diplomatic representatives (7) the distortion of the motives of other governments. These points, summarized in an annex to this brief (not printed), were developed in a series of speeches made by Mr. Acheson at this time: cf. No. 9, note 4 and D. Acheson, *Present at the Creation* (London, 1969), pp. 378–80.

[3] For the Sino-Soviet treaty of friendship, alliance and mutual assistance, signed in Moscow on 14 February, and related agreements of even date, see *B.F.S.P.*, vol. 157, pp. 633–642.

4. As regards question (iii), it should be noted that the above arguments, though still to some extent valid, apply with considerably less force to the idea of a special meeting (under Article 28(2) of the Charter) of the Security Council, attended by Foreign Ministers, e.g. at the beginning of the next General Assembly.[4] This possibility is already under consideration elsewhere and it is only necessary here to recall our attitude, which is that such a meeting (the pre-condition for which must be settlement of the question of Chinese representation) would be unlikely to do any good, but that we should not wish to be held responsible for preventing it. It may well be argued that an organ of the U.N. is intrinsically a more suitable forum for the discussion of world-wide issues than any meeting of three or four Powers.

5. A further possibility, which may be brought up by Mr. Acheson, would be the publication of a grand agreed declaration of the aims and terms of the Atlantic Pact Powers. This would require most careful consideration. Such a declaration could take the form *either* of a detailed statement of conditions in various parts of the world which would have to be fulfilled before we could accept a settlement with the Russians (i.e. an amplification of the 'seven points' in Mr. Acheson's Berkeley speech – see Annex): *or*, preferably, a restatement of basic Western principles – e.g. making the Western ideals of individual liberty and the rule of law (which figure in the preamble of the North Atlantic Treaty) our counter-challenge to the Soviet championship of a *Pax Sovietica*, and also emphasising our desire for free intercourse and trade among all peoples of the world.

6. For the reasons given in paragraph 3 above, it would be naive to think that the Politburo are yet thinking in terms of a genuine overall agreement. We have still very far to go in the process of what Mr. Acheson so rightly called 'building up situations of strength'. Until we have achieved this, there would seem to be more advantage in a resolute public statement of what we stand for than in a statement, which could only be unreal of 'appeasing' in present conditions, of what we would 'settle' for. If a broad statement of principles on the lines suggested above could be agreed by the parties to the North Atlantic Treaty, this might have the advantage of rallying Western opinion by a positive expression of our ideals which would counteract the Soviet 'peace' campaign. An alternative, but less spectacular objective, would be to work out formulations of Western ideals which would not be published as such but would be adopted as key themes of Western propaganda, to be used by each country in the manner and to the extent which it found desirable.

[4] See No. 17, note 8.

No. 27

Extract from a Memorandum for the Permanent Under-Secretary's Committee

P.U.S.C. (51) Final Second Revise [ZP 3/4]

Top secret   FOREIGN OFFICE, *22 April 1950*[1]

Anglo-American Relations: Present and Future

Summary

21. The preceding paragraphs [i] suggest the conclusion that there need be no fundamental conflict of interests between the U.S.A. and the United Kingdom in any part of the world, provided that the United Kingdom can achieve a position, closely related to the U.S.A., and yet sufficiently independent of her, to be able to influence American policy in the directions desired. If, on the other hand, the United Kingdom were forced to embark upon policies which entailed so sharp a contraction of British influence and responsibilities that it became clear that she was ceasing to exist as a leading world power, there would be a risk of a major divergence. The U.S.A. might then withdraw from any commitments in the Middle East, and even in the Mediterranean and Africa. She might also decline to accept any responsibility in South and South-East Asia and might limit her responsibilities in the Far East and the Pacific. Americans in many parts of the world might also seize the opportunity ruthlessly to squeeze out British interests which appeared to stand in their way.

Possible lines of United States Policy
(a) *Continued reliance on the United Kingdom*

22. For the time being, then, the United States is confirmed in its resolve to rely on the United Kingdom as its principal partner in world affairs. This policy implies close consultation on major international issues and a readiness to support British interests when they are compatible with fundamental American objectives and to the extent that American resources permit.

23. The policy of support for Britain is however part of a general policy of consolidation of democratic resistance to Russia. A major feature of the general policy is insistence on the need for greater unity in Europe. The State Department are known to have considered the development of their general policy in two phases:

---

[1] Date of submission by Sir. W. Strang to Mr. Bevin. In his covering minute Sir W. Strang explained: 'This paper was originally submitted to you in an earlier form on the 24th August, 1949 when you decided that you would not circulate it to any of your colleagues. The paper has been revised since you last saw it and it has been recently reconsidered by the Committee. In the light of developments in the last eight months it no longer seems so controversial as it did.' The earlier part of this paper, not here printed, is reproduced at i below.

(*a*) *Phase I*. While the Russian menace continues and the Iron Curtain remains in its present position, a system of Western consolidation based on an 'Atlantic community' would be maintained.

(*b*) *Phase II*. If the Soviet Union withdraws to approximately its 1939 boundaries, the objectives should be:

    (i) a close partnership between the U.S.A., the United Kingdom and Canada (and presumably with the rest of the Commonwealth in loose association).

    (ii) a European Union of all Europe outside the Soviet Union but excluding the United Kingdom.

24. This idea, however, has probably not yet been fully thought out and the policy for Phase II certainly does not command the same unanimity of support as that for Phase I. Although the tripartite financial talks have shown that an Anglo-American-Canadian nucleus is already coming into existence, it would be unwise on that account too confidently to hope that the Americans will at all times give privileged treatment to the United Kingdom over the other members of the North Atlantic Treaty or of the O.E.E.C. Although at present it is generally recognised, at any rate in the United States administration, that the United Kingdom cannot be expected to 'mesh' her economy fully into that of Western Europe, there are still powerful voices in the United States which are more ready to demand fuller British participation in the fortunes of Europe than a closer Anglo-American association.

25. So long, then, as the United Kingdom maintains her position as a world power and increases her economic strength and stability the United States may be expected to continue to welcome her as an intimate, but not exclusive, partner. But in the event of a disastrous weakening of the British position or of circumstances which, even unjustifiably, cause the U.S.A. to lose confidence in the United Kingdom as a reliable ally, the United States Government may be forced to consider possible alternative lines of policy. Indeed, it is not unlikely that they have already given some thought to what these alternatives might be. Americans do not hesitate to scrap ruthlessly something which is not working well, whether it be an automobile or a policy, and to try a new model.

26. The following seem to be the alternative courses which the United States Government might possibly follow in such circumstances:

(*a*) A retreat into isolationism:

(*b*) Reorientation of European Policy either towards:

    (i) Rearmament of Germany: or

    (ii) Reliance on France as principal European partner.

(*c*) An accommodation with Russia.

It is not suggested that any of these courses would be adopted by a single stroke of policy but rather by a series of decisions spread over some time. Such developments might well be deplored by large sections of American opinion; but it would be rash to assume that, if the notion that the United Kingdom was really down and out once caught hold, they would not take place with the support of the necessary majorities in Congress.

(a) A retreat into isolationism

27. The very fact that the U.S.A. has been thrust into a position of world leadership before she has developed fully the experience and political and economic philosophy necessary for the role, entails the danger of a retreat into isolationism should the general venture into world affairs appear to be a failure. There is no doubt that in the post war world American official circles have enjoyed the widespread support of public opinion in their policy of collaboration with like-minded countries in the ordering of world affairs. But isolationist sentiment is still latent in the U.S.A. and could be revived in many sections of the population if conditions were favourable. Individuals, groups, and in particular, newspapers which have supported and encouraged isolationist movements in the past (e.g. America First) still exist and are ready to go into action again. Indeed, a school of thought is already developing on the lines that the American tax-payer has supported Bretton Woods,[2] British loans, the United Nations, the European Recovery Programme, etc. and has subscribed billions to put the world right economically. In this way the United States Government has done all that should be expected of it, and more. The lack of success of these efforts must be due to the short-comings of the recipient countries, and the United States should therefore be slow in adding to its existing commitments until foreign countries have proved themselves worthy, by their own efforts, of further support. This new line of thought has a powerful attraction, since it allows for natural inclination, for an assumption of the inability to make mistakes and for a dislike of the acceptance of responsibility and the consequences of power. It would prove particularly attractive to American opinion if Russian pressure were to appear to relax at the same time as disappointment with Europe was growing.

28. Any retreat into isolationism has obvious dangers for the United Kingdom, which with Western Europe would be left on the Russian side of a dividing line drawn down the Atlantic and separating the world between the two great power blocs of the United States and the Soviet Union.

(b) Reorientation of European Policy
(i) Rearmament of Germany

29. But realisation that Russian Communism actively threatens the American way of life may be enough to prevent a retreat into isolationism.

---

[2] The agreements made at the United Nations Monetary and Financial Conference, held at Bretton Woods 1–22 July 1944, providing for the establishment of a International Monetary Fund and International Bank for Reconstruction and Development, are annexed to the Final Act printed as Cmd. 6546 of 1944.

If so, Western Europe will still be America's first line of defence against Russia and it will seem to American eyes, without the United Kingdom as a strengthening factor, to be a very weak line. If the United States Government wishes to find ways of building up Western Europe, one of the most obvious ways is to rearm Germany.

30. It is possible that a decision to rearm Germany would, in any case, not be unwelcome to American opinion. The revelation that Russia has the atomic bomb has already caused some professional military thinkers to seek some corresponding reinforcement to the Western ranks. The dominant 'Anglo-Saxon' strain among influential Americans which affects their thinking, and assists Anglo-American partnership, also extends to a genuine respect for German efficiency and leadership. The number of persons of German origin who have 'made good' in the U.S.A is remarkable. Moreover, since the end of the war, the United States Government has become deeply involved in the rehabilitation of Western Germany. Acceptance of German demands for the means of self-defence may come to be regarded as the only satisfactory way of binding a rehabilitated Germany to the Western world.

31. The rearmament of Germany might be combined with increased assistance to continental Europe, if the Americans assumed that the United Kingdom could not be regarded as a safe flank or even a firm base for an eventual campaign of liberation. Indeed, German rearmament would only be tolerable to the French and Benelux if they were given adequate reinsurance against misuse of German arms against themselves. Any change in the emphasis of American planning towards a firmer defence of the European continent will also undoubtedly involve help to Spain.

32. A policy of this kind would not only gravely jeopardise United Kingdom security in time of war but would also deprive her of any appreciable influence in European affairs in time of peace. The most likely result would be a Europe dominated politically and economically by German (apart from the even more unpleasant possibility of an agreement between Russia and Germany on 'spheres of influence' or other lines).

(ii) *Reliance on France as principal European Partner.*

33. France is perhaps less likely than Germany to be welcomed by the U.S.A. as her principal European partner. Although the French economy is more balanced than that of the United Kingdom, its industrial foundation is less solid for strategic purposes than that of Germany. The weakness of the French army has already forcibly struck influential American observers. The French, as a Latin race, would in any event fit less easily into the 'Anglo-Saxon' orientation of American policy. Finally, a country in which nearly a third of the electorate votes communist might seem a strange partner for the Americans in their present frame of mind.

34. Nevertheless, France has given ready support to American ideas

such as Western European unity; and the possibility of a Franco-American partnership cannot be excluded. The 'myth' of Lafayette colours the American emotional outlook in much the same way as the 'myth' of George III,[3] but with a rosy hue. From a more practical point of view the arrangements for Western European defence will certainly involve in any case much closer collaboration between the French and American armies, particularly if the Americans proceed with their plan for establishing the base for their European campaign in North Africa. The American administration has also emphasised to the French Government the leading rôle which, it is hoped, France will play not only as a check on German aggressive tendencies but as a partner with Germany, on a new basis of friendship, in Western Europe recovery and security.

35. If therefore the United Kingdom has to be abandoned as a principal ally, Germany is not the only possible substitute whom the Americans might consider. A specially close American partnership with France, though perhaps less damaging than one with Germany, would tend to give a continental bias to United States plans and policies in Europe, almost certainly at the expense of British interests.

(c) An accommodation with Russia

36. If the United Kingdom no longer seemed willing or able to maintain her position in the world and if alternative allies, as would be only too likely, proved unsatisfactory, the U.S.A. might feel bound to reach a *modus vivendi* with Soviet Russia. There has been in the past a good deal of support in the U.S.A. for the belief that the two most powerful countries in the world ought to be able to live together, and this might be revived in support of an accommodation.

37. Much would depend on the reaction of the Soviet Union to any difficulties which might arise between the U.S.A. and her European allies. The Soviet Government might make overtures to the U.S.A., accompanied by some concessions, in view of which the United States Government might be politically unable to maintain her present degree of readiness and vigilance. Alternatively the Soviet Union might try to take advantage of the situation to draw the United Kingdom and France more closely under her influence, as a counterweight both to American encroachment on Europe and to any resurgence of German power. In the latter event, the United States Government might feel that the path of prudence lay in an accommodation with the Soviet Union. The result would be to leave Western Europe exposed to Russian pressure, and this in its turn would be all too likely to entail the eventual communization of Europe.

38. It seems inherently unlikely, in view of the great weight of feeling against Russia which has been built up in the U.S.A., that the American

---

[3] The service of the Marquis de Lafayette on the side of the American revolutionary armies in the American War of Independence symbolized Franco-American friendship, whereas the policy of King George III was associated with Anglo-American hostility.

people would readily consent in the immediate future to a compromise with the Soviet Union. But Russian tactics on the lines described in the last paragraph might be successful. A severe economic depression in the U.S.A., if one were to occur, might have unforeseen consequences on the morale of her people and might perhaps force her to reduce overseas commitments and to enter into a premature settlement of difficulties with Soviet Russia.

(d) Summary

39. Any one of these alternative policies may, of course, be adopted for reasons not directly concerned with the British position. Isolationism, in particular, is a danger into which the Americans might without much temptation relapse. An accommodation with Russia on the other hand is only likely to be the last choice of a Government when other policies have failed. The most likely conditions, however, for the adoption of one of these lines of policy would be a marked decline in the political or economic strength of the United Kingdom, unsupported by any evidence of a vigorous intention to restore her position.

Effect on British policy

40. It is clear, from considerations of the alternatives open to the U.S.A., that the interests of the United Kingdom are likely to be best served by maintenance and consolidation of the present relations between the two countries.

41. It would be premature to consider now what action the United Kingdom should take if the U.S.A. were at any time to embark on an alternative course, since not only would much depend upon the circumstances in which the change took place but any British policy would then most probably be at the mercy of world forces outside her control. Any attempt at self-sufficiency – even if it was supported by some of the other Commonwealth countries – would mean a sharp contraction of political influence and material prosperity and might not succeed even on such reduced terms. If it failed the United Kingdom would probably be compelled to beg again for the benefits of association with the United States, not as an independent partner, but as a client existing on permanent doles from the American tax-payer. In either case, the Commonwealth connexions would be greatly strained and those with South Africa, India and Pakistan almost certainly severed.

42. These considerations point the need for the United Kingdom to continue, as she has done since the war, to shoulder the burdens— political, economic and military—of playing a leading part in world affairs, in close association with the United States but not necessarily dominated by her policies. The Anglo-American partnership will for some time inevitably be an unequal one. The inequality need not, however, be burdensome if the two countries are also working in close relationship with their fellow signatories of the Atlantic Treaty or with

members of the British Commonwealth in, for example, Asia and the Far East or with other like-minded countries at the United Nations. Only time and results will show the exact form in which the partnership will eventually develop and whether it will need some more formal expression.

Conclusions

43. (*a*) Although British and American political interests coincide in most parts of the world they rest on the assumption in American minds that the United Kingdom is the principal partner and ally on whom the U.S.A. can rely.

(*b*) Any change in this main assumption would have serious effects on the position of the United Kingdom in Europe and further afield. Such a change is most likely to occur if the United States loses faith in the power or will of the British people to restore and maintain their strength.

(*c*) The interests of the United Kingdom therefore demand that her present policy of close Anglo-American co-operation in world affairs should continue. Such co-operation will involve a sustained political, military and economic effort.[4]

CALENDAR TO No. 27

i   *22 Apr. 1950   Paragraphs 1–20 of P.U.S.C. (51) Final Second Revise* Historical review of Anglo-American relations [ZP 3/4].

[4] In a minute to Sir W. Strang of 23 April Mr. Bevin agreed that this paper could be used for the general guidance of officials at their preliminary bipartite and tripartite talks. However, 'I thought the paper was much too long-winded and unless shorter papers can be written and submitted to me I shall decline to do any more work while I am at Manor House' (ZP 3/4). With Mr. Bevin's agreement, the paper was given a limited ministerial circulation. Sir S. Cripps minuted on his copy on 2 May: 'There are a number of points here with which I do not wholly agree and although I agree with the [? actual] conclusions I am not sure I agree with the implications which seem to me to be much nearer permanent subservience to the U.S.A. than anything else. My trouble is I just haven't the time to write my views on all these papers + carry on with my work' (T 232/167).

No. 28

Extract from Conclusions of a Meeting of the Cabinet held at 10 Downing Street on Monday, 24 April 1950, at 10 a.m.[1]

C.M. (50) 24 [CAB 128/17]

Secret

China: general policy

(Previous Reference: C.M. (49)72nd Conclusions, Minute 3)[2]

5. The Cabinet had before them a memorandum by the Foreign Secretary (C.P. (50) 73)[3] reviewing the course of recent events in China and indicating the line which he proposed to take, in his forthcoming discussions with Mr. Dean Acheson, the United States Secretary of State, on the question of policy towards China.

The Minister of State said that the general policy which the Foreign Secretary had been pursuing, with Cabinet approval, had not so far evoked any satisfactory response from the Chinese People's Government. Though four months had passed since we formally recognised that Government, they had not yet agreed to an exchange of diplomatic representatives; their general attitude towards us continued to be unfriendly; and the prospects for British commercial interests in China seemed to be deteriorating. On the other hand, it could not be shown that this weakening of our position in China was the consequence of our policy of recognising the Chinese People's Government, or that it proved that policy to have been wrong. The Foreign Secretary therefore invited the Cabinet to agree that the present policy should be continued and that, in his forthcoming discussions with Mr. Acheson, he should seek to secure that the United States Government would not follow courses which were harmful to our common aim of preventing the permanent alienation of China from the West. He proposed, in particular, that we should seek to persuade the United States Government to modify their attitude towards China's representation in the United Nations to the extent of signifying to

---

[1] *Present* at this meeting were Mr. Attlee (*in the Chair*); Mr. H.S. Morrison, Lord President of the Council; Sir S. Cripps; Mr. H. Dalton, Minister of Town and Country Planning; Viscount Addison, Lord Privy Seal; Viscount Alexander of Hillsborough, Chancellor of the Duchy of Lancaster; Viscount Jowitt, Lord Chancellor; Mr. J. Chuter Ede, Secretary of State for the Home Department; Mr. E. Shinwell, Minister of Defence; Mr. G.A. Isaacs, Minister of Labour and National Service; Mr A. Bevan, Minister of Health; Mr. T. Williams, Minister of Agriculture and Fisheries; Mr. G. Tomlinson, Minister of Education; Mr. J.H. Wilson, President of the Board of Trade; Mr. J. Griffiths, Secretary of State for the Colonies; Mr. H. McNeil, Secretary of State for Scotland; Mr. P.C. Gordon-Walker, Secretary of State for Commonwealth Relations. *Also present* for items 5–7 were Mr. Younger and Sir H. Shawcross, Attorney-General. *Secretariat:* Sir N. Brook, Permanent Secretary and Secretary of the Cabinet; Mr. A. Johnston, Deputy Secretary (Civil) of the Cabinet and Joint Secretary of the Defence Committee.

[2] Not printed.

[3] See No.23.

the four Powers represented in the Security Council their willingness to agree that China should be represented in the Council by a delegate appointed by the Chinese People's Government, even though they did not feel able themselves to vote in favour of this charge. The Foreign Secretary also recommended that British firms in China should be told that the United Kingdom Government would be unable to give them any financial assistance, but would do what they could to help them in any other way; and that representations should be made to the Chinese Government about the position of British economic interests in China.

In discussion it was generally agreed that the delay in securing agreement on the exchange of diplomatic representatives was most unsatisfactory. It was recognised that the Chinese Government could find a plausible excuse for this delay in the fact that we had abstained from voting in favour of their representation in the Security Council. It would therefore be advantageous if the United States Government could be persuaded to modify their present attitude towards this question to the extent necessary to enable the existing deadlock to be resolved. At the same time some Ministers felt that the United States Government would find it politically difficult to go very far in this direction and that it would be inexpedient to press them to do so.

There was more general support for the view that, over the whole of this field, the forthcoming discussions with Mr. Acheson should be somewhat tentative and exploratory in character. It would be unwise to press him to proceed with the modification of United States policy towards China at a faster pace than that which he regarded as acceptable to American opinion. And we should certainly be slow to risk antagonising the United States Government over this for the sake of prospects—which had never been bright and now seemed to be even less promising—of establishing friendly relations with the Chinese People's Government.

Our relations with the Chinese Government were not likely to improve unless we could find some means of bringing pressure to bear upon them. There could be no question of threatening to withdraw our recognition from them. Nor had we any grounds for fixing a time-limit for the exchange of diplomatic representatives. But, in the representations which were to be made to them about the position of British economic interests in China, it should be possible to take a rather more forceful line. Thus, could it not be represented to them that, if they extinguished our commercial and financial interests in China we should have no interest in supporting their claims in the United Nations or in seeking to persuade the United States Government to adopt a more friendly policy towards them?

The Cabinet agreed that it must now be made clear to British firms that they should not expect the United Kingdom Government to give them any financial assistance in order to help them to maintain their establishments in China.

The Cabinet:
Approved the recommendations in paragraph 41 of C.P. (50) 73 on the understanding that, in his forthcoming talks with Mr. Acheson, the Foreign Secretary would not press the views of the United Kingdom Government on policy towards China to such an extent as to risk alienating the sympathy and support of the United States Government.[4]

[4] The Cabinet went on to discuss under item 6 Chinese civil aircraft in Hong Kong (see No. 23, note 3) and agreed that the question of their disposal should be settled in the Hong Kong court and that to this end the British government should obtain an Order-in-Council. Under item 7 on the question of whether or not Chinese Communist consuls should be accepted in Malaya (see No. 23.i) the Cabinet agreed to defer a decision until after Mr. Bevin's talks with Mr. Acheson at the London conference.

No. 29

Record of First Bipartite Official Meeting held in the Foreign Office on 24 April 1950 at 3 p.m.[1]

[ZP 2/193]

Top secret

Present:
United Kingdom: (Foreign Office) Sir W. Strang, Sir I. Kirkpatrick, Sir G. Jebb, Sir R. Makins, Sir F. Hoyer Millar, Mr. Wright, Mr. Shuckburgh, Mr. Hadow;[2] (Treasury) Sir E. Plowden, Mr. R. Hall.

United States: Dr. Jessup, Mr. Perkins, Mr. Holmes, Mr. Raynor, Mr. Labouisse, Mr. Stinebower, Mr. Trimble, Mr. Reber.[3]

[1] The British records of the Official meetings of the London Conference are printed from the Confidential Print text on ZP 2/193 which incorporated various corrigenda to the typescript draft records produced daily by the U.K. delegation. The London Conference opened with a tripartite meeting of officials held earlier on 24 April at 10.30 a.m. (British record not printed: cf. *F.R.U.S. 1950*, vol. iii, p. 838, note 2). At this meeting conference procedures and organization were discussed. It was agreed that each delegation would keep its own record of conversations and that the Secretary-General, Mr. Shuckburgh, in consultation with the Secretary of each delegation, would produce a summary joint record of agreements and disagreements as they emerged. These summary records of decisions (on ZP 2: F.O. 371/124918–28) were circulated in 'DEC' series e.g. UKUS/DEC/1. In this volume preference is normally given to the full records of meetings produced by the U.K. delegation, rather than the summary record.

[2] Mr. R.M. Hadow, Private Secretary to Mr. Younger, was the U.K. Delegation Secretary.

[3] In the State Department, Mr. G.H. Raynor was U.N. Adviser of the Bureau of European Affairs, Mr. L.D. Stinebower was Director of the Office of Financial and Development policy, Mr. J.Q. Reber was Chief of the Committee Secretariat Staff of the Executive Secretariat. Mr. W.C. Trimble was a First Secretary at the U.S. Embassy in London.

1. No points arose from the Tripartite talks of the morning and after Sir W. Strang had welcomed the American delegation on the occasion of these informal and confidential talks it was agreed that the best way to handle the work was:

(i) to have a general assessment of the world position. In the course of this certain weak spots would emerge which could later be considered in detail;

(ii) to reach a common interpretation of likely Soviet moves and capabilities;

(iii) to draw up a list of common objectives and suggestions how these should be attained.

2. The American general assessment was as follows:—

(i) Although the Soviets had gained no direct increase of power in the last two or three years, the situation was most serious. They had received a set-back in Yugoslavia but had made an advance in the atomic field and had gained a victory in China. This victory was probably more of a loss to the West than of direct advantage to the Soviets, and on the whole the set-back in Yugoslavia outweighed the victory in China.

(ii) On the military side, the Soviets had somewhat increased their lead on the West.

(iii) This might make them more provocative and bolder. Although it was unlikely they would embark on war against the West for the next two or three years, they might well pursue an adventurous policy in Berlin, Austria, Yugoslavia or Iran. As a result of their action in any of these places, the West would be faced with the choice of accepting the situation or of fighting. There was, therefore, a considerable risk of some incidents arising from a Soviet miscalculation of Western reactions, developing into a war. The development of atomic power in the U.S.S.R. had some influence on the Soviet attitude but would not be a major factor for another three years. On the whole the actualities of the power situation were unfavourable to the West

(iv) *Western Europe*—The Soviets had been held but not sufficient advance had been made by the West 'to give unclouded confidence' in its ability to balance the situation.

(v) *Germany*—This was the critical point in the world. Western Germany's orientation was of prime importance and would depend on the wisdom and daring of Western policy. Up till now, Western Europe had not developed a sufficiently strong organisation to attract Germany towards it. The Soviets regarded Germany as their prime objective and

[4] The agenda for this meeting circulated as UKUS/P/1, not printed, was (1) any procedural points arising from the tripartite meeting that morning (see note 1) and (2) general review of issues arising under items 1–5 of the bipartite agenda (see No.17).

accorded it top priority.

(vi) *Soviet orbit.*—It was important not to over-estimate Soviet invulnerability. There were four weaknesses in the Soviet system:

(*a*) the fundamental system of ruthlessness and fear which dominated the people inside each unit (the U.S.S.R. and each satellite)—this was possibly the greatest weakness;

(*b*) the actual relations between the U.S.S.R. and the satellites;

(*c*) the succession to Stalin;

(*d*) the dependence of communism on dynamic advance and victory. Any reverse might lead to a change of the system within Russia.

3. On the British side, general agreement was felt with this assessment, with the following reservations:—

(i) The gain to the Soviet in China was perhaps of greater potential value than the Americans considered and probably outweighed the set-back in Yugoslavia.

(ii) We had had the advantage of the Soviets in Western Germany up to last month.

(iii) The Atlantic Pact represented an initiative which had greatly lowered Soviet stock.

(iv) Although the Soviets might well be more provocative in the next two or three years, it was unlikely they would take serious risks. Russian history showed the extreme caution with which Russia moved, and the likelihood of a Soviet miscalculation leading to a war situation was not rated so high on the British side.

(v) On the whole, we believe that, while there was always a possibility of the Russians 'miscalculating,' a really serious risk of war would perhaps not arise for another five years or so.

(vi) Western Europe was less of a weak spot than it was a year ago and communism was held in check in France and Italy. The call for an all out Communist spring offensive was a sign of the seriousness with which the Russians viewed the present Communist set-back.

(vii) Germany was indeed a cardinal point in the struggle and the Russians realised it. If they lost Germany, they lost their dynamism and might have to fall back to Russia itself. It was, therefore, vital for us to improve the organisation of the West so as to attract Germany to it.

(viii) South-East Asia was the softest spot in the world picture and a review of the situation there was a first necessity.

(ix) Persia might well prove to be another weak spot.

4. It was agreed that the assessment of the situation did not differ on essentials. This situation had had a considerable effect on individual and joint policies and the whole purpose of the present conversations was to see what more could be done and what new lines should be pursued. Whatever the assessment of the possibility of a grave Soviet miscalculation leading to actual hostilities, it was essential to diminish the risk that the

Soviets should so miscalculate and a special effort should be made to consolidate the free world so as to give the Soviets no excuse for underestimating possible Western reactions.

5. The Americans felt there were two basic questions to be answered:

(1) On the basis of this common assessment of the situation, was it felt that we had reached a point when we could not afford to have any form of political defeat at the hands of the Russians?

(2) Was the political, military and economic progress of the Western system the first priority in meeting the present situation?

6. In answer to these questions, it was stressed on the British side that a very real sense of urgency was felt and Britain was determined to play her part. A large portion of the free world, however, lacked a sense of direction and it was therefore vital to have some framework on which the greatest strength could be developed. There could be no division of effort—Britain and the Commonwealth, Britain and Europe, the United States alone—what was wanted was a total organisation embracing all.

7. The Americans agreed that the Atlantic concept presented the strong point of the organisation of the free world. There were, however, many other groups in the free world and it was essential that the Atlantic Powers should not come to be looked upon as an exclusive club.

8. This was agreed to on the British side, who stressed that, while it might be impossible for the present to organise all parts of the world on the lines of the Atlantic community, one of the best ways of giving strength to the free world was to have a really united and powerful system of Western consolidation, which would give confidence in Western strength to countries not included in the Atlantic Treaty. It was therefore vital that the United States and the United Kingdom should work in concert and so far as possible avoid all rivalry or differences. The way had been shown by the Anglo-American agreement reached at the talks on the Middle East in 1947.[5] This agreement on Middle Eastern policy was still operative and working and was useful in demonstrating how Anglo-American co-operation could work in the rest of the world. We should proceed on three ideas which governed our relations:

(1) Anglo-American friction in any part of the world would lead to a paralysis of Western dynamism;

(2) It was essential to draw up common objectives; and

(3) Each side should do the utmost to help and strengthen the other in every sphere.

9. Britain was fully prepared to play a major part, but it was essential that she remained a world power if she were to be of the maximum use as a partner to the United States. Hence the preservation of the sterling area and Britain's special position in the colonies and under-developed areas was of the first importance. Some policies advocated by the Americans

[5] See No. 24, note 6.

93

might unconsciously encourage a break-up in the Commonwealth, which was not in the general interest.

10. To sum up the discussion, the British side felt that we both agreed on the extent and nearness of the Communist danger, and we both agreed that we could not afford any strengthening of the Russian position. Four questions were now relevant:

(1) Was it agreed that the best means of rallying the strength of the West lay in the further development of the Atlantic Pact?
(2) Did we agree that Western policy throughout the world would be ineffective if the United States and Britain were at cross-purposes?
(3) Should it be a common objective to help and strengthen each other?
(4) Should common objectives throughout the world be worked out in agreement over the next two weeks?

11. The Americans said that the answer was yes to all four questions, but each question must be viewed in the light of related circumstances. For instance, when strengthening each other, care must be taken not to weaken anybody else, and again, any strengthening of the Atlantic Pact should not be detrimental to the United Nations. The agreement reached about Middle Eastern policies formed a useful basis for a wider association between Britain and the United States.

12. The Americans then proceeded to a brief survey of special countries in the Far East and South-East Asia and invited information at a later stage, particularly on Burma, the Indian sub-continent, and Malaya.

13. It was agreed that special planning was necessary for Indo-China and Persia, that the forthcoming Soviet drive in Berlin should be fully discussed and planned for.

14. With regard to Germany, it was agreed that here lay a critical point and the two main problems to be faced were Berlin and the division of Germany. Secondly, we should plan how to win this battlefield. Russian stock had risen since last November and we must redress the situation.

15. The West must hold and take the initiative. Although much had been done by the West, public opinion was apt to consider the Russians as the only people with any initiative and the great strides taken forward by the West were often lost sight of. Communism did indeed have an ideological initiative which we could only counter by the offer of liberty. But a study was being made of the possibility of over-riding ideological message which could be presented on behalf of the West and this should be the object of urgent joint study and action. As well as any ideological message, however, it was essential to step up the power of the West, since this would be a major factor in restoring confidence to the rest of the world.

16. The meeting then decided that the talks should resume next day. It was agreed to take Items 6(a) and 7(a) of the Bipartite Agenda (United Kingdom Delegation Paper D.4)[6]—the latter item to include the question

[6] See No. 17, note 9.

of Mr.Lie's proposal for a special meeting of the Security Council and the question of Chinese representation—at 10.30 a.m. In the afternoon at 3.30 p.m. a further exposition of the United Kingdom's views on Items 2(3) and (4) of the Agenda would be given and discussed.

No. 30

Brief for the U.K. Delegation[1]

No. 2 [WU 1075/20]

Top secret   FOREIGN OFFICE, *24 April 1950*

Western Organisations

Introduction

The object of this paper is to consider the main organisations within which the countries of the West are working towards closer cooperation and how those organisations can be developed with most advantage to the United Kingdom.

2. The four main organisations are:

(*a*) the Organisation for European Economic Cooperation (O.E.E.C.);
(*b*) the Brussels Treaty organisation;
(*c*) the North Atlantic Treaty Organisation;
(*d*) the Council of Europe.

Recent lines of development

3. At the start of the Council of Europe and before its Assembly had met, it seemed possible that the best lines of further development might be:

(*a*) to merge the military functions of the Brussels Treaty organisation

[1] This brief was originally prepared for the P.U.S.C. (see No. 6, note 5) and circulated as P.U.S.C. (50) 9 on 25 April. As a draft P.U.S.C. paper it was sent to Sir E. Plowden on 14 April for circulation in the Treasury. Treasury objections that the proposal to develop Atlantic pact machinery was premature were discussed on 21 April by Sir R. Makins and Sir E. Plowden, when the latter evidently accepted F.O. arguments in favour of proceeding (see No. 35). The following day Sir R. Makins sent an advance copy of the present revised text to Sir E. Plowden and explained that it 'has been slightly revised to take account of the comments which we have received from the Secretary of State. The document is being re-copied and circulated to certain Ministers by the Secretary of State, including of course the Chancellor. None of the changes affect the main argument of the paper. The annex has been considerably shortened, mainly because the Secretary of State thought that too much speculation on the future of O.E.E.C. was premature and he wanted to look at any detailed proposals on his return to the Office. The Secretary of State has also reservations about the recommendation that the location of any additional machinery should be London. We are consulting him further on this and meanwhile the point has been left open. We are sticking by London' (T 232/166). Marginal comments by Sir S. Cripps on his copy filed on T 232/167 are not here noted: for his overall view see No. 35, note 4.

with those of the North Atlantic Treaty Organisation;

(*b*) to merge the social and cultural functions of the Brussels Treaty organisation with the Council of Europe;

(*c*) to establish a close working relationship on economic problems between the O.E.E.C. and the Council of Europe.

4. The merger of the military functions of the Brussels Treaty organisation with those of the North Atlantic Treaty organisation is already being successfully developed. The Brussels Treaty military machine, in fact, also serves as the Western European Regional Planning Group under the North Atlantic Treaty.

5. Very considerable progress towards greater unity has been made in the political, social and cultural spheres and progress is likely to be made towards defining the fields in which some of the Brussels Treaty work may be transferred to the Council of Europe. Nevertheless, some of the continental signatories of the Brussels Treaty, quite naturally, seem to fear that they would lose more than they would gain if political cooperation under the Treaty was transferred to what must necessarily be a looser association with a large number of powers.

6. In economic affairs, the O.E.E.C. and the Secretariat of the Council of Europe have so far been unable to agree either on the objectives of a common policy or on the division of labour between the two bodies.

7. These difficulties arise from fairly deep differences of opinion and are unlikely to be resolved quickly. As important decisions may have to be taken in the near future on the rôle of the United Kingdom in various Western Organisations, it is desirable to review again the objectives of British policy in this field and the most promising lines of approach to those objectives.

Basic objectives

8. The basic objectives, given the present relations of the Great Powers, are:

(*a*) to create a political, social and economic system in the non-Communist world stronger and more attractive than the Soviet system; this will have to be a broadly based association, including the United States and Canada, as Western Europe is not strong enough to stand alone;

(*b*) to ensure that this system is one to which the United Kingdom can belong, having regard to the special relationships of this country with the Commonwealth, the sterling area, Europe and the United States;

(*c*) to foster a greater degree of European unity as exemplified in existing organisations, viz. the Brussels Treaty Organisation, the O.E.E.C. and the Council of Europe;

(*d*) to avoid being led so far as Europe is concerned either to sacrifice the United Kingdom's national sovereignty in vital matters of defence or finance, or to being put in the position of appearing to be the one obstacle in the way of the idea of closer European cooperation;

(*e*) to facilitate the entry of the German Federal Republic into the organisation of the West.

Short-term policy

9. Any review of this policy must take account of long-term and short-term factors. The most convenient dividing line seems to be the end of 1952, when the European Recovery Programme is due to come to an end and the O.E.E.C. can hardly fail to lose momentum.

(*a*) *The Organisation for European Economic Cooperation*

10. Up to 1952 the O.E.E.C. will inevitably be the main forum for economic cooperation and, in view of the prime importance of economic recovery, its position must not be undermined by any of the other organisations. In particular, it will be undesirable if the Council of Europe, which contains in the Assembly a large element not subject to governmental control, is able to reach a position in which it can interfere with the work of the O.E.E.C.

(*b*) *The Council of Europe*

11. The Council of Europe must be steered away from seeking a federal system as the immediate solution to Western Europe's difficulties. There are several practical objections to any attempt to introduce a federal organisation of Europe at this stage;

(*a*) It would raise immediately and acutely the question of the United Kingdom's relations with the rest of the Commonwealth and indeed of the Sterling Area;
(*b*) If it is to be democratically constituted, it could only be introduced by putting the issues clearly to the national electorates and obtaining their approval;
(*c*) A constitution would have to be adopted and an independent judicial branch of the Government (like the United States Supreme Court) established;
(*d*) Fairly acute differences in economic structure and economic policy between the participating countries would have to be reconciled;
(*e*) Many long-established traditions of national independence would be affronted;
(*f*) Language barriers would have to be overcome.

12. To rush these fences would invite a failure. It would make continued British participation in the Council of Europe difficult, if not impossible. The gap between the national economic policies of the United Kingdom and her European partners is at present widening; a campaign for federation now would cause a complete split. In the event it might well break up the Council of Europe altogether—presumably the last thing its sponsors desire—since it is far from certain that there is any unanimous or sincere desire on the continent for federation in practice.

13. Perhaps a more immediate danger than that of pressure for

federation is pressure for some kind of compromise, whereby member states would be bound in certain circumstances to accept majority decisions of the Assembly or the Council of Ministers. This would mean a limitation of the independence of action of member states to which the United Kingdom, with her commitments and responsibilities outside Europe, could not agree. Moreover, many of the practical objections to federation would apply also to a compromise of this nature.

14. But to reject federation, or any compromise which would involve a restriction of the United Kingdom's freedom of action, is not to deny the usefulness of the Council of Europe altogether. The Council of Europe represents an ideal of closer unity which no one in Europe can afford to see publicly abandoned and it can do useful work in promoting better understanding and a greater degree of cooperation among the nations of Europe. If it is to be preserved, then the United Kingdom must be a member, as otherwise it would lose most of its meaning for the other member states. The Council of Europe is moreover the most suitable place for taking the next step in the closer association of the German Federal Republic with Western Europe. This association is very important to Western interests but it is only likely to be possible in a body in which the United Kingdom also participates, otherwise Germany would dominate the group and the United Kingdom would be powerless to hold her in check.

15. The major immediate object of British policy towards the Council of Europe should therefore be to bring Germany into it willingly and as an accepted partner (although for the time being, only as Associate Member). But the United Kingdom can also take part in other appropriate functions on the Council of Europe. This 'functional' approach means, in fact, developing as far as possible the principle of joint action between Governments in matters of common interest. It should not be allowed to involve any trespass on the existing functions of other organisations, or any surrender of the right of the United Kingdom Government to determine its own policy on vital matters.

16. The United Kingdom may not however be able to participate fully in all the activities of the Council. Indeed, it may not be appropriate for her to do so. The principle of 'one foot in and one foot out' of Europe's affairs is already foreshadowed in the British proposals for a European Payments Union, which take account of the special position of sterling as an international currency, and in defence planning, where the United Kingdom clearly cannot commit all her forces in the Western European theatre. This principle would also be consistent with the constant need for the United Kingdom to have regard to her relations with the Commonwealth and the United States of America.

17. European pressure on the United Kingdom to move in the direction of federation appears to arise largely from the fear of Germany and a desire to make the United Kingdom assume the main responsibility for controlling Germany. But this task is more than the United Kingdom

alone can undertake. To control Germany and to consolidate Western Europe, an association of states confined to Western Europe itself is not enough. It is therefore necessary to develop a more extensive 'Western Union', which must include the United States and Canada. It has already been recognised that the cost of the defence of Western Europe is beyond the resources of Western Europe itself. In the same way it should be recognised that the consolidation of Western Europe, including Germany, is not possible without a closer political and economic association of the United States of America and Canada with Western Europe.

(c) The Brussels Treaty

18. In the Brussels Treaty Organisation progress in the military field can continue on the present satisfactory lines, the military organisation being closely associated with the Western European Regional Planning Group under the North Atlantic Treaty, but yet preserving its separate identity.

19. The Brussels Powers are closely related to each other by tradition and geography and there should be a fairly wide scope for the further development of social and cultural cooperation between them, on the lines on which the present successful beginnings have been made. It may be possible to extend some forms of the present five-power cooperation to include the other countries represented on the Council of Europe, and the Brussels Powers have already submitted to the Council of Europe a list of the subjects which they think are suitable for treatment in the wider grouping. Development in this direction may not be very rapid, as the non-governmental character of the Assembly of the Council of Europe may present difficulties in some circumstances and social and cultural cooperation with so wide a range of countries naturally raises problems which do not arise among the five Brussels Powers. It is important that the relatively intimate cooperation between the five powers should not be sacrificed for a looser and less effective cooperation between a larger number of countries.

20. It remains to be seen whether it will be desirable to merge some of the functions of the Brussels Treaty Organisation in these fields with those of subordinate bodies under the North Atlantic Treaty, which may come into being if the non-military side of the North Atlantic Treaty Organisation is developed. Any such development of the North Atlantic Treaty Organisation should not be such as to lead to a duplication of functions or to prejudice the close degree of cooperation which already exists among the Brussels Powers.

(d) The North Atlantic Treaty

21. The North Atlantic Treaty Organisation still has a heavy task ahead of it on the military side of its work. The main outlines of its strategic planning have been agreed but there is much to be done before those plans can be effectively carried out.

22. Provision was made however that the North Atlantic Treaty should not necessarily be devoted exclusively to military purposes. Article 2 of the Treaty reads as follows:

'The Parties will contribute towards the further development of peaceful and friendly international relations by strengthening their free institutions, by bringing about a better understanding of the principles upon which these institutions are founded, and by promoting conditions of stability and wellbeing. They will seek to eliminate conflict in their international economic policies and will encourage collaboration between any or all of them.'

23. If such cooperation of a wider political nature is to be effective, it is clear that some machinery must be established, though it need not be very elaborate, at any rate in the early stages. All that is wanted, in fact, is for the Governments concerned to nominate their political representatives in one of the capitals to constitute a 'Permanent Commission' on the analogy of the Permanent Commission of the Treaty of Brussels. Once this machine has been established and a small Secretariat had been set up to look after it, it would probably be found that the work would have to be prepared by a smaller circle broadly similar to the Standing Group already set up on the military side. If it were possible to admit Italy to this 'inner circle', Italian *amour propre* would be gratified. It would also be for consideration whether, at a later stage, some kind of regional groupings might be formed within the Permanent Commission, since by such means it might be possible to associate non-members, such as Sweden, in political cooperation with a limited group of the Atlantic Powers. Specific objectives towards which cooperative action of this nature might be directed could include the coordination of steps to resist communism and closer cooperation in the United Nations.

24. The advantage of building on the North Atlantic Treaty are considerable:

(*a*) It is the most spectacular achievement of Western diplomacy since the war and is therefore attractive to public opinion;
(*b*) It has behind it the compulsive force of unity for collective self-defence and is therefore unlikely to wither away in the chill winds of political disagreement;
(*c*) Since it includes both the United States of America and Canada, as well as Western Europe it reflects in itself all the three main aspects of British foreign relations;
(*d*) It is the most satisfactory vehicle for a further positive gesture by the United States Government. It is likely that the United States Administration may soon be anxious to make some such gesture, in the face of criticism in the United States that American policy has been entirely negative;
(*e*) The present dependence of most nations of Western Europe on

United States military and economic resistance gives strength to the links binding the Atlantic community together;

(f) Problems are more likely to be fully considered in a world-wide context by the North Atlantic Treaty Organisation than by any purely European body; and it is in the interest of the United Kingdom that they should be so considered;

(g) It provides a grouping for the nations of Western Europe which is free from the disadvantages inherent in the non-governmental character of the Assembly of the Council of Europe;

(h) It might provide an ante-chamber for Germany's entry, in a non-military capacity, into the Atlantic community, of which the Federal Republic might eventually become a member.

25. The North Atlantic Treaty Organisation cannot, at this stage at least, take over the economic work which is at present done by the O.E.E.C. Moreover, it would be preferable that it should not grow so fast in the immediate future as to eclipse the Council of Europe, since such a development might diminish the attractions for Germany of membership of the Council. Some caution is therefore necessary at present in developing the non-military side of the North Atlantic Treaty Organisation. At the same time, the North Atlantic Treaty forms, from many points of view, the best basis for the future development of cooperation in the Western world. It is important that no useful opportunity should be missed of building up the non-military side of the Treaty Organisation and that other organisations should not be allowed to grow in such a way as to obstruct its further development.

Long-term Policy
(a) Economic Cooperation

26. At the present time all work on economic cooperation between the Western powers is, by common consent, concentrated in the O.E.E.C., subject to two exceptions, (a) the Customs Union Study Group[2] and (b) tripartite arrangements between the United Kingdom, Canada and the United States of America.

27. The position will change in 1952. A note on the work of the O.E.E.C. after this date is attached as Annex I. The Customs Union Study Group is of minor importance. The Economic Commission for Europe[3] is not included as it covers countries from the Soviet bloc. It is possible that the Board of Management of a European payments union may be in existence in 1952 and be able to carry on its functions after that year. The relationship of the Board to the International Monetary Fund should be a matter for consideration.

28. It will be observed from the annex that the members of the

[2] See No. 20, note 2.
[3] Established at Geneva in 1947 under the Economic and Social Council of the U.N. to facilitate economic reconstruction and development, and economic cooperation among European countries.

O.E.E.C. have resolved to continue the Organisation after 1952 and on paper the greater part of the work on which it is engaged, i.e. coordination of investment, harmonisation, overseas territories, etc. could go on as before. But the flow of American dollars under the European Recovery Programme provides the motive force of the Organisation and the 'friendly aid' which is afforded by the E.C.A. Mission is an important factor. It provides the focus for American policy in Europe. 1952 will be the last year of a Marshall Aid appropriation and the E.C.A. Mission will certainly be very much diminished. There will be a carry-over of Marshall Aid which will be expended in 1952/53 and to that extent the aid will taper off gradually, and the O.E.E.C. be encouraged to continue. But with the disbanding of E.C.A., O.E.E.C. is bound to lose momentum and the Council of Europe is likely to make a strong bid to take over the O.E.E.C. functions. In the circumstances, it must be assumed that a major effort will be needed if the O.E.E.C. is to be kept as the focus of economic cooperation in Western Europe.

29. If the list of O.E.E.C. functions in paragraph 1 of the Annex is examined, it will be seen that a large number of them could just as well be dealt with in the Atlantic Pact Organisation, if the difficulties inherent in the non-membership of Western Germany, Sweden and Switzerland (and in a lesser degree of Ireland, Turkey and Greece) could be solved. One or two of the functions end with Marshall Aid, and the work on liberalisation of trade should, by the end of 1952, be virtually completed. The importance of the so-called 'viability subjects' such as the export drive will depend on the size of the Western European dollar deficits in the 1952/53 and 1953/54 and whether separate arrangements are made to deal with certain segments of that deficit separately, e.g. Greece, Turkey and perhaps Western Germany. Certain subjects, such as harmonisation and coordination of investment which relate primarily to Intra-European questions could be transferred to the Council of Europe, though there would be certain risks involved in this course as 'harmonisation' in particular raises delicate questions affecting the internal policies of European countries which might not be very suitable for discussion in the Assembly. It would be necessary to endeavour to keep the handling of such questions firmly under the control of the Committee of Ministers. In fact under the wording of Article 2 of the Atlantic Pact, 'harmonisation' could be dealt with under the Atlantic Council.

30. It seems that the weight of advantage lies in developing an economic organisation under the Atlantic Pact to which the greater part of the subjects at present being handled by O.E.E.C. could be transferred after 1952. It is, in any case, hard to see how the question of the finance of defence and allocation of resources, with which the Atlantic Council will have to deal and which are excluded by the terms of the Statute of the Council of Europe, can be adequately handled without consideration and discussion of the economic policies of the countries concerned. Further, insofar as Europe's dollar problem will not be solved by 1952/53, some

further United States action will be required either by way of additional dollar aid or through the modification of United States economic policy to enable Europe to earn more dollars. Such questions are more satisfactorily discussed in a body of which the United States is an equal member with equal responsibilities than in an organisation like the O.E.E.C. in which the Americans occupy the equivocal and unsatisfactory position of patron. If this view is accepted, difficult legal and political questions would arise both as regards the position of the Convention for European Economic Cooperation and as regards membership. But these problems should not be insoluble.

(b) Military Cooperation

31. The North Atlantic Treaty is likely to remain for some time the main organ of the collective self-defence of the non-Communist world. As the area which it covers includes the metropolitan territories of the principal Western Powers, it will continue to have first claim on their loyalty, even if other regional defence schemes are developed later.

32. The Brussels Treaty military organisation will continue to exist at least as a regional planning group of the North Atlantic Treaty. It is reasonable to suppose that this and other regional planning groups will be continuously occupied in peace-time in keeping defence plans up-to-date and supervising the organisation of forces to implement those plans.

(c) Political Cooperation

33. In the political field the main scope for further progress would appear to lie in the development of whatever machinery had, by 1952, been set up under Article 2 of the North Atlantic Treaty as suggested in paragraph 22 above. In particular it might be possible to develop subsidiary regional or functional organisations, in which countries which were not signatories of the Treaty could participate.

34. An objection to action on these lines is that it would increase still further the number of international committees and other bodies which consume the time of Ministers and officials. This is a drawback which must be kept in mind, but it does not counter-balance the great advantages of such a development of the North Atlantic Treaty Organisation, in particular in bringing the United States into closer association, on a footing of equality, with the nations of Western Europe, and in making possible the association of such countries as Sweden with the Atlantic community. The difficulties caused by an additional growth of international bodies would be minimised if they were located so far as possible in one place so that the same officials could act in different capacities in different bodies.

35. The North Atlantic Treaty is, for the reasons given in paragraph 23 above, the most attractive organisation on which to build for the future. Nevertheless, any attempt to expand the North Atlantic Treaty on the political side will naturally raise problems of its relation to the Council of

Europe. The Council of Europe will not wither away. It commands a strong and vocal body of support. There is much useful work that it can do both in developing and in publicising cooperation between the countries of Europe. But its functions will always be limited by two factors:

(a) Owing to the non-governmental elements in its composition, there will always be a security limitation on its discussions;

(b) It is exclusively European in composition and by its very nature can never be anything else.

36. It seems likely that the political work of the two organisations will therefore develop along somewhat different lines. Major issues of policy affecting the United Kingdom as a World Power are more likely to arise within the North Atlantic Treaty organisation. If this development occurs, there will be in fact a fairly clear division of function between the North Atlantic Treaty political organisation and the Council of Europe. This division of function will also simplify problems arising from different membership and should avoid giving ground for complaint by countries which are members of the Council of Europe and not the North Atlantic Treaty Organisation. For example, Greece and Turkey are members of O.E.E.C. and of the Council of Europe; their interests are naturally somewhat different from those of the other members and they are therefore to some extent a distracting influence. If subjects with which they are not primarily concerned were dealt with within the North Atlantic Treaty framework, these distractions and consequent delays might be avoided.

(d) *Germany*

37. But the main problem of membership will concern Germany. The German Federal Republic should, if all goes well, become an associate member of the Council of Europe within a few months and may even be established as a full member by 1952. A more difficult question will be that of the association of Germany with other Western Organisations and in particular with the North Atlantic Treaty Organisation.

38. There would be many advantages in bringing Germany into the North Atlantic Treaty Organisation. The acceptance of Germany into such a body would encourage her to look to the West rather than to the East. At the same time it would ensure a continuing close American concern with German problems and it would make it possible for Germany's interests to be represented in an international forum in which there was no threat of German domination. There are however serious difficulties about the proposal to associate Germany with the North Atlantic Treaty under Article 10:[4]

---

[4] *B.F.S.P.*, vol. 154, pp. 481–2. It was here stated that 'The Parties may, by unanimous agreement, invite any other European State in a position to further the principles of this Treaty and to contribute to the security of the North Atlantic area to accede to this Treaty.'

(*a*) The North Atlantic Treaty is almost universally regarded as a military treaty of defence. The introduction of Germany therefore would at once pose the question of the contribution which she was to make on the defence side, which would certainly be awkward for the Western Powers now and might well be difficult after 1952;

(*b*) Russia and the satellites will believe, or affect to believe, that any association of Germany with the North Atlantic Treaty constitutes clear evidence that the Western Powers intend to rearm Germany. Consequently we may expect a violent reaction from Russia;

(*c*) The German Federal Government itself, whether or not it is asked for a contribution to Western defence, will no doubt wish to have some guarantee of its military security, whether or not the occupation still continues. It is very doubtful whether the Western Powers will be in a position to guarantee more than that part of Germany which lies west of the Rhine by 1952;

(*d*) There are also certain legal and constitutional problems. For example a decision has yet to be reached whether the German Federal Republic is a State, and, if so, whether it is the German State in succession to the Third Reich. Until such a decision has been reached there is doubt in law (and even after it is reached there may well be doubts in fact) whether the German Federal Republic is yet 'in a position to further the principles' of the Treaty as set out in its Preamble and 'to contribute to the security of the North Atlantic area';

(*e*) It is clear that any premature attempt to establish the German Federal Republic as a fully independent State in international law would sharpen the division of Germany into two halves. In view of the intense attraction for the Germans of German unity they might well regard such a step with misgiving.

39. These difficulties clearly cannot be solved at short notice. The first step should be to bring Germany into the Council of Europe, which has no responsibility of any kind for defence. It should then be possible to associate Germany gradually with subsidiary organisations which may be set up under the North Atlantic Treaty. These organisations may be arranged either geographically or functionally. If they were regional organisations, the introduction of Germany would perhaps arouse less comment; but, on the other hand, one of the main advantages of associating Germany with the Atlantic community as a whole would be to offset the preponderance of her population and industrial power in Europe alone. It may be therefore that the best hope lies in associating Germany with subsidiary and non-military functional bodies under the North Atlantic Treaty Organisation; in this way, the awkward questions connected with German adherence to the Treaty itself can perhaps be avoided, at least for some time.

Conclusions
(a) Short-term

40. Short-term policy up to 1952 should aim at:

(*a*) establishing Germany within the Council of Europe;
(*b*) retaining O.E.E.C. as the main economic forum;
(*c*) beginning to develop the non-military work of the North Atlantic Treaty, possibly by the constitution of a Permanent Commission, on the analogy of the Permanent Commission under the Treaty of Brussels;
(*d*) maintaining the present degree of cooperation among the Brussels Powers and extending it in the social and cultural fields to include, for certain functions, other countries represented on the Council of Europe.

(b) Long-term

41. In the longer term His Majesty's Government are likely to find the North Atlantic Treaty Organisation the most suitable basis for Western consolidation.

42. The North Atlantic Treaty Organisation can be used for political, military and economic cooperation in the following ways:

(*a*) In the economic sphere the greater part of the work which will be within the competence of O.E.E.C. after 1952 could be dealt with under the North Atlantic Treaty. The remainder of the work will either terminate with Marshall Aid, or might perhaps be dealt with in the Council of Europe. Difficult legal problems and questions of membership arise under this proposal, but if there is agreement on the general policy, these questions ought not to be insoluble;
(*b*) In the military sphere, the Brussels Treaty Organisation will continue as a regional subsidiary of the North Atlantic Treaty Organisation;
(*c*) In the political sphere, it may be possible to develop subsidiary bodies or groupings within the Permanent Commission on a regional and functional basis, the membership of which might include certain countries which are not signatories of the North Atlantic Treaty.

43. It is likely to be some time before Germany can accede to the North Atlantic Treaty. But in the meantime the German Federal Republic should, if possible, be associated with the work of any subsidiary bodies that may be established under the North Atlantic Treaty Organisation to deal with non-military questions.

ANNEX TO NO. 30

The work of O.E.E.C. after 1952

1. The principal functions of the O.E.E.C. at present are as follows:

(*a*) Establishment and administration of a European Payments Union.
(*b*) Liberalisation of trade.
(*c*) Coordination of investment (steel, oil, fertilisers and electricity).
(*d*) Harmonisation of economic, financial, social and tariff policies (including perhaps full employment policies).
(*e*) Manpower problems, in particular, emigration.
(*f*) Internal financial stability.
(*g*) Expansion of non-dollar sources of supply (e.g. agriculture, non-ferrous metals, textiles, and development in overseas territories).
(*h*) Other aspects of colonial development.
(*i*) Export drive for dollars.
(*j*) International investment, particularly dollar investments in the non-dollar world.
(*k*) Tourism.
(*l*) Technical assistance from the United States of America.
(*m*) Exchange of scientific and technical information.
(*n*) Administration of shipping provisions of Foreign Assistance Act.

2. Now that there is no longer any division of aid, the only items in this list which will automatically disappear in 1952 are the technical assistance schemes, such as work on projects (almost negligible) as is carried out by the Vertical Committees and the shipping work. There is at present a dollar element (i.e. possible access to a dollar pool) involved in the European Payments Union and the liberalisation of trade, but these activities may still be required, and the E.P.U. may still be workable if it has saved enough dollars out of the next two appropriations.

3. By 1952, there may be some change in emphasis on these activities. For instance, the studies on internal financial stability will either become decreasingly important or may be absorbed in the work on the harmonising of economic and financial policies. The present type of work now being done on liberalisation of trade may well have been completed, in so far as it can be confined to the purely European field. Whether the E.P.U. will be necessary in anything like its present proposed shape is anybody's guess. The work on agricultural expansion already important may be producing decisive results, though it will extend far beyond 1952. Apart from this, it seems that the remaining activities will be just about as necessary as they are now. It is not easy to know what new problems may have emerged by 1952 requiring similar treatment in a European framework.

4. However necessary they may be, will the European countries be willing to continue those activities without the incentive of dollar aid? It must first be said that even now, with the exception of the E.P.U. and the liberalisation of trade (as explained above), there is no direct dollar incentive. At the same time, the fact that the O.E.E.C. is fundamentally based on the receipt of dollar aid, does in fact provide a general spur to cooperation, in that the members are acutely sensitive to the effects on

public opinion in the United States if they fail to cooperate. Nevertheless, the idea of cooperation in these spheres has already become deeply ingrained in Europe, is likely to be enhanced by the work of the Council of Europe, and may be expected to be naturally stronger by 1952. Even, therefore, if the removal of incentives, which the end of American aid will imply, tempts certain countries to pursue a more individual line, we should expect the general desire to cooperate to be maintained, though at perhaps a slightly reduced tempo. It may be mentioned that the Convention of the O.E.E.C. contains no time limit, and that the members have indeed agreed to continue their association after 1952.

5. It seems almost certain, therefore, that most of this work will have to go on. The alternatives are:

(*a*) to maintain O.E.E.C. more or less as it is now.
(*b*) to retain some economic body, though distributing elsewhere part of the O.E.E.C.'s present functions.
(*c*) to re-distribute all the present functions of O.E.E.C.

If some economic body still remains, the question also arises as to whether it should come e.g. under the Committee of Ministers of the Council of Europe, or under some other organisation.

No. 31

Brief for the U.K. Delegation

No. 11 [C 2799/2514/18]

Secret   FOREIGN OFFICE, *24 April 1950*

Soviet Intentions in Germany and possible Allied Counter Measures

Recommendations

The three Foreign Ministers are invited to agree that:

1. The incorporation of a united Germany into a Western system remains the aim of the Western Powers. It is recognised that this involves an evolutionary process and that for the Allies to turn back or even to call a complete halt will bring about the collapse of their declared policy. What has to be determined is the timing and the extent of the advance at each stage.

2. No opportunity should be neglected of putting this policy before the German people and of inspiring them with confidence in the capacity and resolve of the Western Powers to achieve their aim.

3. For the moment Allied policy should be based upon the principle that the Government of the Federal Republic is the Government, and the only Government, of Germany.

4. A Statement should be embodied in any communique issued after the meeting, to place on record the main points of Allied policy affecting

Germany. This communique could be supported by a more detailed Press release on the militarised police of the Soviet Zone.[1]

5. The Allied High Commission in Germany should be invited to consider the establishment of a special liaison committee with the German Federal Government with the object of stimulating the Germans themselves to reply to Soviet propaganda while ensuring that the actions of the Federal Government in this field are consistent with the policy of the Western Occupying Powers.

6. There should be the closest co-operation and co-ordination of policy between the Western Occupying Powers and statements of policy and formal Press releases on conditions in the Soviet Zone should so far as possible be agreed beforehand between the three Occupying Powers.

Problem

According to the most recent indications the Soviet authorities now regard the Eastern Zone of Germany as sufficiently consolidated to serve as a base for more concentrated subversive action directed against the Western sectors of Berlin and the Federal Republic. A more active and coherent policy to counteract such Soviet plans has therefore become highly desirable.

Background

Although, when the Pieck Administration[2] was set up in October last, it appeared to be far more of an empty facade than advance publicity had suggested, the establishment of this Soviet-controlled administration on a firm footing has now been carried a long way as a result of intense propagandist pressure and political activity by the Soviet occupation authorities and the Socialist Unity Party (S.E.D.). The two bourgeois parties, the Christian Democratic Union and the Liberal Democratic Party, have been lured into co-operation in the Administration and the 'National Front' and have made a sorry showing of weakness and naïvete. The S.E.D. has thereby been enabled to consolidate its position and by engineering a drastic purge within the bourgeois parties to eliminate all potential opposition. The long promised elections in October 1950 are

---

[1] The draft communiqué and draft press release appended to this brief are not here printed. The background to these statements was a U.S. proposal of 27 March (C 2168/386/18) for a tripartite protest to the Soviet government against the creation of an armed police force (Bereitschaften) in the Soviet zone of Germany. This police force, already some 50,000 strong, and expected soon to double, was regarded as being, in effect, a covert army for East Germany. The British government declined to join with the proposed protest, while the French government expressed doubts as to timing. The Foreign Office view, put forward on 5 April and agreed by Mr. Bevin, was that the three Ministers should issue a general statement after their talks in May, designed to counteract Soviet policy in Germany on a broad front and including some reference to Soviet support for the police force in East Germany (cf. F.O. 371/85256–7 and *F.R.U.S. 1950*, vol. iv, pp. 948–951).

[2] On 11 October 1949 Herr W. Pieck, Joint Chairman with Herr O. Grotewohl of the Socialist Unity Party, was elected President of the newly proclaimed German Democratic Republic. The following day a government was formed under Herr Grotewohl.

clearly intended to set the seal on the programme to establish the S.E.D. as the monolithic party in the Soviet Zone.

Meanwhile the economic situation in the zone has improved, owing largely to the lifting of the counter blockade[3] and the consequent resumption of interzonal trade and also to increased imports from Soviet Russia and her satellites accompanied by a small reduction in reparation deliveries. The S.E.D. are exploiting this improvement to the full with the ever recurrent theme 'things are getting better here; things are getting worse in the West'. Although conditions generally in the Soviet Zone are still far behind those in the West, there are two things which the Soviet Zone can supply which at present the Federal Republic cannot—tolerable housing conditions for everyone and security against unemployment, although admittedly at a low standard of living.

The Soviet position is further strengthened by the fact that although the Federal German Government got away to a good start, there have since been sufficient developments, some unfortunate, some merely disagreeable to German minds, both in the political and economic spheres, to provide ample material for Soviet and Communist propaganda. All such developments have been worked up by the Soviet-licensed Press and radio, which has shown considerable skill in hammering home a few simple points designed to convince German opinion that it is only through the Soviet Union that unity will be attained and the withdrawal of the occupation forces secured, and to demonstrate the wickedness of Western Imperialism, the inevitability of impending economic crisis in the West and the advantage to the Germans of the Soviet way of life.

Information reaching the West from the Soviet Zone shows moreover that a perceptible change of mood is taking place in Eastern Germany. The Pieck Administration is tending to be accepted as the government of the Eastern Zone much as the Federal Government is accepted as the government of the Western Zones. Although Communism is no doubt as repugnant as ever to the mass of the population, a feeling of resignation and of isolation from the West is creeping in, together with a growing conviction that the Western Powers are becoming indifferent to their fate. The will of Eastern Germans to resist the weight of Communist pressure is on the wane. These who can resist it adapt themselves to totalitarianism as they have done before. Those who feel they cannot do so swell the flood of refugees to the West.

Objectives of Soviet Policy

Berlin still represents the immediate objective of Soviet policy in Germany. This problem is dealt with in a separate paper [*ib*].

Soviet subversive action in Western Germany is longer-term in

[3] Western restrictions on communications, transport and trade between Berlin and the Eastern Zone of Germany and between the Western and Eastern Zones imposed as counter measures to the Soviet blockade in 1948 were lifted together with Soviet restrictions on 12 May 1949.

character and the development of their plans would seem to depend on the success or failure attending their efforts against Berlin. The Russians believe that the 'inevitable' economic crisis and the desperate need for Western German industry to find new markets (which lie traditionally in the East) will at the same time undermine the position of the Bonn Government and strengthen the position of both extreme (and subversive) elements—the communists on the left and the nationalists on the right—and will force Western Germany to turn to the East.

The Russians probably reckon however, that the process is likely to be slow. Meanwhile, since the meeting of the Foreign Ministers in Paris,[4] they have quietly pursued their plans of encouraging interzonal trade and such intercourse between East and West as is in their interests. They have also pursued a more limited objective of trying to cause embarrassment to the Bonn Government by constantly sniping at it in their propaganda. At the same time they are pushing the idea of the National Front in the hope (already justified) of encouraging aspirations towards German unity on the part of the right-wing nationalists as the most promising element of disturbance in Western Germany. As regards the K.P.D.[5] (which has of late made no headway at all) they are biding their time in the hope that growing economic distress will provide a better breeding ground in the months to come.

Western Policy

The policy of the Western Occupying Powers towards Eastern Germany can only be a part and an aspect of their policy towards Germany as a whole. Such policy will only be successful if it is clear to the German people that the Western Occupying Powers are pursuing an all-German policy of their own and are not merely trying to counter Soviet policy in their zone. A positive policy must attack on both the political and economic fronts and must be primarily concerned with the main task of building up the stability and prosperity of Western Germany, under the necessary safeguards, of increasing the authority of the Federal Government and of fostering the confidence of the whole German people in the connexion with the West. It is of major importance that the Western Occupying Powers, both independently in their day-to-day propaganda and jointly, should re-emphasise their desire for German unity, their determination to remain in Berlin, and their recognition of the Federal Government as the only Government of Germany. They should aim at keeping constantly before the German public in as clear and simple a manner as possible the main aims of their policy for Germany.

A large part of the work of countering Soviet propaganda must however come from the Germans themselves. At present the Federal Government is not sufficiently active in this field and it is important that it should be encouraged to assume more responsibility and to co-ordinate its efforts with those of the Western Occupying Powers.

[4] See No. 18, note 1.   [5] Communist party.

i *24–29 Apr.   U.K. Briefs (a) No. 7 on the status of the German Federal Republic and its bearing upon the association of Germany with the Western World*: considers whether the Federal Government should be acknowledged by the Western Allies as the 'Government which speaks for the German State' or whether that State should be deemed to cease to exist in May 1945 and that it is now a question of creating a new German State. Balance of argument in favour of supporting claims of F.R.G. Western Allies will need to take up a formal position soon. 'Failure to assert that the Central Government of the three Western Zones is the *de jure* Government of the German State which has never ceased to exist will become increasingly embarrassing and adoption of the contrary view would have a seriously adverse effect on the future of Allied policy in Germany' [C 2797/2514/18]. (*b*) *No. 8 on Berlin*: recommends that western Powers must maintain their position in Berlin even though this will mean greater financial support [C 2798/2514/18]. (*c*) *No. 25 on Status of Berlin*: advantages of according Berlin status of a 12th Land in F.R.G. are outweighed by serious disadvantages e.g. likely Soviet retaliation [T 236/2483].

No. 32

Brief for the U.K. Delegation

No. 9 [FF 1025/2]

Secret   FOREIGN OFFICE, *24 April 1950*

Indo-China

The French object in the talks on Indo-China will probably be to get the United States and the United Kingdom to underwrite the French position without the French having to make any major political gestures or to promise complete independence. M. Schuman may therefore plead for more military (including some naval and air) supplies, for tripartite staff and defence talks, and for some kind of public guarantee by the United States and the United Kingdom of the frontiers of Indo-China.

2. The United States, who were for some time hesitant about supporting Bao Dai, are now keenly interested in Indo-China and anxious to prevent it falling under Communist control. The Americans are willing to supply arms (though not as much as the French first asked for), but believe that political action is as important as military action in Indo-China, and that the French must make political declarations leading up to complete independence. Mr. Acheson will therefore probably lay stress on a declaration by the French Government that they are planning to give the Associate States[1] independence by stages. He may also advocate that as much of the aid as possible is given direct to the three Associate States, for

---

[1] Viet Nam, Cambodia and Laos.

reasons of their prestige, and not through French channels. The French Commander-in-Chief is strongly against this owing to the bad effect on the morale of the French soldiery after doing all the fighting they would (he suggests) see the country bought up by dollar imperialism.

3. The position in Indo-China is serious. Though a quarter of the French armed forces are employed there (with a heavy consequent strain on French defences and on their ability to contribute to Western Union Defence), the military position is virtually a stalement. In the political field Bao Dai has not made as much progress as had been hoped. In our view a purely military solution is out of the question.

4. The French have gone a long way in handing over power, and it is expected that after an inter-State conference (starting on 9th May) a number of administrative functions, in economics, finance and communications, will be transferred to the three Associate States. But under the Agreements of 8th March, 1949[2] (beyond which the French do not intend to go) the French will retain permanent control of foreign affairs and defence.

5. The basic difficulty is the difference between the French and British theories about colonies. Whilst we regard it as a matter of course that colonies should be guided towards independence the French policy is to integrate and centralise, so that the overseas territories and France form a unit and colonials share in governing the whole. A French declaration that the Associate States were in time to become independent would have profound effects in France and in other French territories. Behind French reluctance to promise independence is also a feeling of exasperation that they should be asked to support the present drain on their budget and on their armed forces, with the prospect that if the Associate States are successfully set up the French will then have to withdraw.

6. Meanwhile, some other countries have followed the United Kingdom lead in granting recognition. Australia, New Zealand and South Africa have recognised the Associate States (Viet Nam, Laos and Cambodia), and Canada may follow suit. India, Pakistan and Ceylon have so far refrained, partly through suspicions of French policy and partly on account of doubts about the ability of the new States to establish themselves. Amongst foreign Asian countries, Siam is the only one to have given recognition, though several European states have done so.

Recommendations

7. The Secretary of State may wish to take up a middle position between the French and American standpoints.

[2] The exchange of notes of 8 March 1949 between France and Viet Nam regarding the unity and independence of Viet Nam within the French Union is printed in *B.F.S.P.*, vol. 155, pp. 472–87: *ibid.*, pp. 405–11 and 158–163 for similar French agreements with Laos and Cambodia on 19 July and 8 November 1949 respectively. For the inter-state conference between the Associated States and France held in Pau from 29 June–27 November, see F.O. 371/83613–7.

(*a*) We can of course agree on the importance of a stable and non-communist Indo-China, and that a French military withdrawal until the emergency is over would have grave repercussions elsewhere in South East Asia.

(*b*) As regards arms, we shall continue to supply what we can, but our resources are limited and other demands are heavy.

(*c*) Visits and informal staff talks are welcomed, but it is necessary to avoid publicity and to avoid giving the impression that there is any British commitment to intervene in Indo-China.

(*d*) As regards a French declaration of aims, whilst we recognise the difficulties on the French side, it must be realised by the French that a common United Kingdom/United States/French policy will be possible only in so far as the French follow a policy which will allay the suspicions of India and of other Asiatic countries. There are some practical steps which the French could take soon—for example, M. Schuman told the Secretary of State in March that Indo-Chinese affairs would be transferred away from the Ministry for Overseas France.[3] This has not yet been done.

(*e*) As regards the participation of the three Associate States in regional activities, it may be possible for them to play a part in the discussions on Economic Development which may develop as a result of the Sydney meeting.

8. The Secretary of State will recall that he decided earlier against the immediate establishment of a Legation in Saigon, where His Majesty's Government are at present represented by a Consul-General (Mr. Gibbs) with the personal rank of Minister. The Legal Adviser considers that there are precedents for the establishment of a Legation in countries which have not attained full independence, and if the Secretary of State so wishes he might care to take the opportunity of the talks to inform M. Schuman that he has decided to establish a Legation at Saigon. The United States and Italy have already done so. The forthcoming inter-state Conference (paragraph 4) would give a convenient justification for this action now, which would mark His Majesty's Government's approval of the French policy of transferring further powers to the Associate States.

CALENDAR TO NO. 32

i *29 Apr. 1950   U.K. Brief No. 23 on South-East Asia*: U.K. and U.S. largely agree on S.E. Asian questions. Assesses communist dangers in area and measures Western Powers should take to combat their spread. Action so far has been on piece-meal basis. Comprehensive plan for economic aid to foster political stability is now required: this may emerge from the Sydney Conference [FZ 1025/1].

[3] See No. 4.ii.

No. 33

Record of Second Bipartite Official Meeting held in the Foreign Office on 25 April 1950 at 10.30 a.m.

[ZP 2/193]

Top secret

Present:

United Kingdom Sir W. Strang, Sir I. Kirkpatrick, Sir R. Makins, Sir G. Jebb, Sir F. Hoyer-Millar, Mr. Dening, Mr. Wright, Mr. Shuckburgh, Mr. Harrison, Mr. Parrott,[1] Mr. Hadow.

United States Dr. Jessup, Mr. Perkins, Mr. Holmes, Mr. Raynor, Mr. Labouisse, Mr. Stinebower, Mr. Laukhuff, Mr. Sanders, Miss Camp.[2]

Agenda: UK/US/P/2[3]

Item 1 Western Europe and the North Atlantic Treaty Area

1. On the British side it was suggested that three points of agreement had emerged from yesterday's conversations:[4]

   (i) Since Germany was the critical point, both for the West and for the Russians it was essential that she should incline towards the former;
   (ii) The United Kingdom must be regarded as a power with world interests and not merely as a potential unit of a Federated Europe;
   (iii) The U.S.S.R. had the advantage in the propaganda field through the single simple idea conveyed by communism.

2. In considering what could be done to render more effective the machinery under the Atlantic Pact, it was therefore necessary to aim at something which would take account of these three points. If new machinery were to be set up it was necessary to see where it would lead and it was possible that Ministers during their talks in London might be able to point the direction.

3. M. Bidault had recently suggested some kind of central machinery for the Atlantic Treaty with certain powers in the political, military and economic field.[5] This central body would be, it was assumed, composed of

---

[1] Mr. G.W. Harrison and Mr. C.C. Parrott were Heads respectively of F.O. Northern and United Nations (Political) Departments.

[2] Mr. P. Laukhuff was Director of the Office of German Political Affairs in the State Department. Mr. W. Sanders was Special Assistant to the Assistant Secretary of State for U.N. Affairs. Miss M. Camp was a member of the Office of European Regional Affairs in the State Department.

[3] The two items on the agenda for this meeting, circulated as UKUS/P/2 (not printed), were: (1) Review of issues arising under items 6(a) and 7(a) of the bipartite agenda: see No. 17; (2) consideration of 7(a) to include Chinese representation in the U.N. and general attitude towards future meetings of the U.N.

[4] See No. 29.   [5] See No. 24, note 5.

officials and would report to the Atlantic Council. This proposal did not face certain difficulties such as the future of O.E.E.C., but at the same time would have great advantages in increasing French morale. From the British point of view such a proposal seemed very far-reaching. It might be an ultimate ideal but it did not appear to be immediately practicable. We favoured the idea of some closer United States–United Kingdom–United European organisation under the general Atlantic umbrella, for it was only with the emergence of such an organisation that European fears of German revival could be calmed and at the same time Germany drawn back into the Western system. Furthermore, any such arrangement allowed the United Kingdom to maintain its world position and also allowed for continuing United Kingdom and United States co-operation. Our ideas on the actual organisation were vague, but it was felt on the whole that the new machinery should be for the political and economic side and should be distinct from the military machine which was now working fairly satisfactorily. Further, if the new machine were political and to some extent economic there might be a chance of drawing in other countries which at present could not come into the Atlantic Treaty because it was purely military. On the purely military side the British suggestion was that the authority of the Standing Group and perhaps the Working Group should be increased.[6]

4. The new machinery to be set up on the political side might allow for the ultimate accession of Sweden, Switzerland, Austria and Western Germany. But it was vital to obtain Western Germany's participation in the Council of Europe first before any other organisations were thrown open to her. The new political machinery might have little economic work to do at first, but might consider the harmonisation programme, and perhaps investigate the scope for future economic work.

5. The new body might be under a Secretary-General who would be of sufficient status to command international respect but who would not have exceptional powers. The new body could either be of the representatives of the countries concerned in any given capital, or could be composed of special representatives. It would be responsible to the Atlantic Council but would differ from the Permanent Commission of the Brussels Treaty in having no control over military affairs. There remained the question of which countries would be represented. It seemed impossible to have any permanent body consisting solely of twelve national representatives from countries of varying sizes and power and some inner circle would be required. It might, however, be possible to have an organisation based on the regional principle as on the military side, or again the organisation might be on a functional basis with small groups set up for specific purposes.

6. The Americans argued that something needed to be done to set up machinery for considering the economic and financial side of the military

---

[6] See No. 3, note 8.

programme. There did not seem to be much that such a body could do on the political side, but it was possible that it might concern itself with the co-ordination of information. With regard to the organisation of such a body, the Americans preferred a Standing Group on functional lines with sub-committees. They also thought the Secretary-General should be of international status, but should not have the power to commit Governments to any line of action. The British proposal for a political and economic committee was not quite understood as it seemed to exclude the vital question of co-ordination of military and economic planning.

7. It was pointed out to the Americans that there seemed to be some confusion between two ideas. One question was the fusion of military and economic planning in so far as it concerned the specifically military effort of the Atlantic Powers; the other was new machinery which might be set up under Article 2 of the Atlantic Treaty, and that is what the British side had been suggesting.

8. In discussion it was agreed that any wide political organisation of the Atlantic Powers, which might ultimately draw in other Powers, was a very long-range project, but there was the germ of such an idea in Article 2 of the Atlantic Treaty. It might be possible, however, for a new central organ to be set up to co-ordinate the military and economic policies of the countries which could at the same time study the possibility of further political co-ordination. The stage had been reached when some sense of direction should be given to such organisations as the O.E.E.C. and the Council of Europe and at some stage this must come under a more comprehensive Atlantic system.

9. On Germany, it was agreed that the first objective was to bring her into the Council of Europe. This would not be sufficient for German aspirations, but Germany's progress towards full partnership in the Western system should be gradual and by stages. As Germany advanced along each step towards this ultimate objective, greater concessions could be made to her. If the aim was full partnership of Germany with the West, the question of her rearmament must at some stage be faced. Germany could only be rearmed when she was a full partner in the Atlantic system, for under this system she would be under the same measure of control and common planning as all the other members. It was impossible to rearm Germany until French strength had been greatly revived, and it was only after the French were in a strong position as powerful partners, in the Atlantic system that the Germans could be allowed in, under the overriding control of an Atlantic Chiefs of Staff organisation.

10. The ventilation of all these speculations about Germany's future was, however, extremely bad for the Germans and should be played down as much as possible.

11. It was tentatively agreed that there was a need for some new central permanent organisation in the Atlantic Treaty which could first of all act as a study group for the rationalisation of the Atlantic military and economic effort, but might also deal with political problems as well,

ultimately perhaps making progress along the lines of Article 2.

12. It was also agreed that precise examination of such items as the method of handling the Defence Committee's report[7] for the North Atlantic Council should be deferred for two or three days.

Item 2. General attitude towards the Soviet Union including:

(a) Negotiations;
(b) Mr. Lie's proposal for a special meeting of the Security Council; and
(c) Chinese representation.

(a) Negotiations

13. The Americans felt that there was very considerable pressure of public opinion in the United States in favour of opening negotiations with the Soviet Union. They themselves realised that broad negotiations would lead nowhere and might indeed have a bad effect on Western morale, if they were embarked upon and failed. Tactically, however, it might be necessary to negotiate, and it was therefore all the more important that any talks with the Russians should be put in a proper setting. They also assumed that the Soviets would think that any proposal to negotiate was a sign of weakness, would not enter upon talks with any sincere intention of trying to reach agreement, and would merely use the talks as a propaganda forum. If public pressure continued, it might be necessary to enter upon broad negotiations in which the fundamental issues between East and West could be discussed with the Soviets. If the Agenda for such discussions were framed in the right way, a failure of the talks need not necessarily have a bad effect on Western morale, but might serve to stiffen waverers into a conviction that it was hopeless to try and negotiate with Russia. The Agenda should therefore deal with:

(1) Soviet subversive activities outside their orbit;
(2) The treatment of peoples in the satellite countries;
(3) Atomic energy;
(4) Disarmament;
(5) Germany;
(6) The Far East;
(7) Implementation of the Yalta Agreement on liberated Europe;[8]
(8) Human Rights;

---

[7] The report of the North Atlantic Defence Committee was item 2 on the agenda for the N.A.C. meeting in London. The main feature of this report, agreed by the Defence Committee at its meeting in the Hague on 1 April and summarized at i below, was approval of the Medium Term Defence Plan. This plan was a statement of the ideal military requirements in men and material for the defence of the North Atlantic area. The Defence Committee's report comprised seven memoranda each with a covering note prepared for the N.A.C. by its working group in Washington: see further No. 72 and *F.R.U.S. 1950*, vol. iii, pp. 86–89.

[8] This declaration, issued as Section V of the Report of the Conference at Yalta on 11 February 1945, is printed in *B.F.S.P.*, vol. 151, pp. 225–7.

(9) The use of the United Nations machinery for settlement of disputes.

14. On their side the Soviets would obviously put up—

(1) The German Treaty and withdrawal of occupation troops;
(2) The Japanese Treaty;
(3) Chinese admission to U.N.O.;
(4) The withdrawal of the French from Indo-China;
(5) Korea;
(6) The North Atlantic Treaty;
(7) The abolition of the atom bomb;
(8) Agreement on conventional armaments;
(9) A universal Peace Pact.

15. It would be necessary for all these items to be discussed. There were also many forums in which such discussions could take place, but on the whole, the United States favoured the Security Council, though here it would be necessary to settle the question of Chinese participation first. The question was not one of urgency and on the whole, the United States were prepared to wait and see whether public pressure was maintained. It was desirable that the three Ministers should discuss the problem and if they felt there was advantage in negotiations with the Soviets, a considerable time would be necessary for work on the Agenda and on the positions to be adopted. No negotiations would be possible unless all three powers agreed on the necessity for them and on the Agenda, and until the question of Chinese participation in the United Nations had been settled.

(b) Special Meeting of the Security Council

16. The American attitude was that the Western powers should avoid returning a completely negative response, but this question too could best be studied in the light of public opinion. A special meeting would do nothing to diminish East–West tension. If, however, the British and the French felt that a positive response must be given, the Americans thought that a special meeting could best be held in New York before the autumn session of the Assembly.

(c) Chinese representation

17. The American attitude was unchanged. They were prepared to accept majority decisions on each body of the United Nations and would not campaign to influence votes against the admission of the People's Government.

18. In discussion of these three points it was agreed—

(a) That the only reason for opening negotiations with the Russians would be the force of public opinion, but if possible such negotiations should be avoided. If negotiations were necessary they should be in the Security Council;

(b) America and Britain did not wish to bear the onus of turning down

119

Mr. Lie's proposal. In any case a special meeting would be impossible until the question of Chinese representation was settled. In the meantime, however, it would be wise to continue study of the subjects to be discussed.

19. On the British side, it was stated that public opinion in favour of negotiations with the Russians appeared to be much less vocal than in the United States. So far as the British officials were concerned, they strongly deprecated any idea of entering into such negotiations if they could possibly be avoided, since there was no prospect of success and general disappointment was bound to result. They alluded, however, to the possibility of taking the initiative on the present occasion to make some grand declaration of the Atlantic Powers on their basic view of relations with Russia. This could be along the lines of Mr. Acheson's Berkeley speech[9] and might also contain a statement of basic Western principles. This might act as a counter to ill-informed proposals for negotiations or special talks. In the meantime, we would be well advised to go on building up our strength.

20. With regard to Chinese representation, the British attitude remained the same and it was felt we must continue to work for a solution. The problem would become acute before the next Assembly, as the question of new admissions would arise, and, if Russia were not sitting, might well lead to forcing Russia out of the United Nations altogether.

21. The Americans were unwilling to make any change in their basic attitude towards Chinese representation and suggested that the question of new admissions could either be shelved or solved by some form of general admission of both Soviet and Western candidates.

22. It was generally agreed that continued Soviet participation in the United Nations was in the interests of both the West and of the Soviet Union.

23. It was agreed that the question of an approach to the Soviets for the opening of negotiations might also be discussed with the French in the forthcoming tripartite talks.

24. It was agreed to meet again in the afternoon and to discuss Items 3 and 4 together with 6 (b) of the Bipartite Agenda (United Kingdom Delegation Paper D.4)[10] and if there was time to continue with Items 7 (b) and 7 (c).

25. The Meeting adjourned.

CALENDAR TO NO. 33

i *25 Apr. 1950 Defence questions on N.A.C. agenda* considered in a brief for F.O. meeting on 27 Apr. Brief summarizes seven memoranda comprising Defence Committee's report: (1–3) on cost and status of medium term defence plan; (4) coordination of N.A.T.O. agencies—suggests how this could be achieved through development of existing machinery especially the Standing Group; (5–7) strategic bases and security system [WU 1071/71].

[9] See No. 26, note 2.   [10] See No. 17, note 9.

No. 34

Record of Third Bipartite Official Meeting held in the Foreign Office on 25 April at 3.30 p.m.

[*ZP 2/193*]

Top secret

Present:

United Kingdom Sir G. Jebb, Sir R. Makins, Sir F. Hoyer-Millar, Mr. Wright, Mr. Shuckburgh, Mr. Marshall.[1] (For items II & III) Mr. Bateman, Mr. Harrison, Sir A. Rumbold, Mr. Sykes, Mr. Hadow.

United States Dr. Jessup, Mr. Perkins, Mr. Holmes, Mr. Labouisse, Mr. Stinebower, Mr. Laukhuff, Mr. Sanders, Mr. Raynor, Mr. Berger, Miss Willis,[2] Miss Camp.

Agenda

 I Items 3 and 4 of the Bipartite Agenda.[3]
 II Item 7 (*b*) of the Bipartite Agenda.
 III Item 7 (*c*) of the Bipartite Agenda.
 IV Future work.

I *Items 3 and 4 of Bipartite Agenda*

The meeting opened with a British statement identifying the factors arising from United Kingdom–Commonwealth and sterling area ties which had to be taken into account in considering the rôle of the United Kingdom in Europe and other parts of the world.

2. These were of two kinds. Political and economic, and ponderable and imponderable. The political factors were mainly imponderable. The Commonwealth was in a continual state of evolution and was always going through a further transformation.

3. The Colombo Conference had shown that there was substance in the ties between the members of the new Commonwealth.

4. The economic factors were mainly ponderable. The sterling area system was the largest area of free trade in the world. 50 per cent. of world trade was carried on in sterling and capital movements within the systems were free and efforts were continually being made to extend the system of payments through transferable account. The trade and payments of the sterling area, and especially the reserves, were measurable and known

---

[1] Mr. P.H.R. Marshall was a member of F.O. Economic Relations department with responsibility for economic and financial questions in the Commonwealth. Sir A. Rumbold and Mr. B.H.C. Sykes were respectively head and member of F.O. Southern department, superintended by Mr. C.H. Bateman, Assistant Under-Secretary of State.

[2] Mr. S.D. Berger and Miss F.E. Willis were First Secretaries at the U.S. Embassy in London.

[3] See No., 17.

facts. The strength of sterling was to some extent the index of confidence in the United Kingdom. Anything which weakened sterling threatened the stability and existence of the politico-economic system which it served and *vice versa*. The sterling area system was still vulnerable. The United Kingdom economy, the centre of the system, was itself over-loaded and we were, for example, carrying at least as heavy a proportionate defence burden as any other country. It was not the intention of this meeting to trespass on the preserves of the tripartite arrangements in Washington,[4] but the sterling balance question presented an example of the inter-action of the political and economic factors in the sterling area. We had not, until now, been fully able to tackle this problem owing to the development of the political situation in India and Pakistan.

5. The United Kingdom Government had had a long experience of operating the sterling system and felt that they knew what was best for it. They also felt that it was in the common interest of the Western world that this system should be nursed back to strength. Since the war, by our own efforts and with the assistance received first from Lease-Lend then from the American Loan[5] and finally through, Marshall Aid, very considerable progress had been made and it could be said that the sterling area had a prospect of becoming independent once again. On the other hand, we had had shocks. We had been subjected in some cases to pressure to adopt courses which we believed would endanger the stability of the sterling system particularly in relation to the freezing of trade and convertibility of sterling, and we had been badly bitten in 1947.[6] It might be that our policies often appeared to be unduly cautious and our insistence upon restoring viability might seem over great. The fact was, however, that we were operating on the margin of our resources; that the slightest additional strain was liable to have disproportionate consequences and that we were in fact obliged to look at every million pounds which we were asked to expend for any purpose. It was hoped it would be understood that in laying this emphasis on the stability of the sterling system, which was of course not co-terminous with the Commonwealth, we were not regarding our own Commonwealth position as an end in itself, but were taking the view that it was only through our leadership of a viable sterling system that we could play the part which was expected of us and which we ought to play in the general purposes of the non-Communist world.

6. On the American side it was pointed out that most of the difficulties which had arisen between the United States and the United Kingdom

[4] See No. 2, note 1.

[5] The ending of U.S. lease lend aid in August 1945 and negotiation of the Anglo-American Financial Agreement of 6 December 1945 (Cmd. 6708), which constituted an American loan, is documented in Series I, Volume III.

[6] For an account of the economic crisis leading to British suspension in August 1947 of the convertibility obligation imposed under the terms of the Anglo-American financial agreement (note 5), see R.N. Gardner, *Sterling Dollar Diplomacy In Current Perspective* (Revised ed. New York, 1980), pp. 306–336.

since the war had a financial basis. The United States Government recognised that the United Kingdom position was dependent on three prime factors:

(a) the dollar shortage;
(b) United Kingdom domestic expenditures;
(c) the implications of the sterling system.

The United States Government shared the British concern over these difficulties, though at times there had been differences as to the emphasis and priorities which should be placed on them. They felt that if the United Kingdom set viability as its transcendent objective it might have the effect (a) of weakening other parts of the Western system (e.g., in the case of E.P.U.) and (b) of causing repercussions on the domestic situation in the United States (as in the case of oil).

7. The United Kingdom Government naturally wanted to know what the United States Government was going to do. It was not possible to define precisely what might happen after 1952, but the British should judge the United States Government's intentions by what they had done in the past and should also realise that the Administration are fully aware that adjustments would be necessary when the European Recovery Programme came to an end. The appointment of Mr. Gordon Gray[7] was a sign of the importance which was attached by the United States Government to the steps to be taken after 1952. There was no full agreement yet within the Administration as to the next steps, but there was a sincere feeling that that the problem must be attacked vigorously, and they were prepared to examine every aspect of their internal and international economic policy. The recent case of the Japanese Government's taxation policy[8] was an example of a case where the United States had taken account of the impact of their policies on other countries.

8. As regards sterling, the United States Government certainly wanted to see sterling strong and convertible. They wanted to see it 'a world currency,' though not necessarily 'the world currency,' and it was assumed this was in line with British thought.

9. The leader of the American delegation said that he wanted to establish in the first place the principle that all the problems with which the Western countries were faced were common problems, and secondly that there must be some division of the responsibilities of each partner. United States Government would do their best to avoid damaging the British position in foreign political matters. They would recognise British leadership in the Commonwealth. They attached importance to the

[7] In March 1950 Mr. Gray was appointed Special Assistant to President Truman for the study of future aid policy after the termination of Marshall Aid in 1952.

[8] Following British representations to General D. MacArthur, Supreme Commander for the Allied Powers in Japan, and appeals from the foreign business community in Tokyo, the Japanese government announced on 12 April that proposals for increasing taxation on Allied Nationals in Japan would be modified: see further F.O. 371/83886 and 83847.

co-ordination of Western Europe with the United Kingdom playing its part. They would be willing to continue to support any steps which would further the attainment of balance in the international accounts of the United Kingdom and the sterling area at a reasonable level and the establishment of sterling as a sound currency. They would continue their effort to take such domestic steps in the United States as were necessary to further these common objectives. They would be receptive to any suggestions which the United Kingdom Government might wish to make on what might in the nineteenth century have been described as 'internal' American policies, if these were shown to affect the position of their Allies. They were ready to consider the post-1952 situation. They were prepared to establish and continue the practice of informal consultation between the two Governments as it had already been developed in such fields as joint military planning and the A.B.C. talks.

10. As a concomitant to the above, the United States Government would think themselves entitled from time to time to suggest courses of action for the United Kingdom to take, for example, to avoid injuring United States interests in our economic policy. They were prepared to regard the Commonwealth relationship as valid but not as an end in itself. A strong free world must include a strong Western European community developing on the basis of United States/United Kingdom collaboration.

11. If the United Kingdom accepted the idea of a strong Western European community, then, in cases where Commonwealth relations clashed with that idea, the United Kingdom and the Commonwealth ought to be ready to demonstrate the reasons for which the Commonwealth interest should have priority. The United Kingdom would need to accept greater participation and a position of stronger leadership in the organisation of Western Europe on the political, economic and military sides. In particular, they ought to support France.

12. It would from time to time be necessary for the United States Government to deal with European countries as 'Europe' (e.g. in the E.R.P.). The United Kingdom Government should not expect them in such cases to distinguish between the United Kingdom and other European countries in contexts in which they were dealing with the British *as Europeans*. The United Kingdom should recognise and accept that security and prosperity of the free world could not be reached through an insulated sterling or soft currency system protected from competition from the world at large.

13. The above required the United Kingdom Government to face the fact that the over-riding priority which they now gave to balancing their dollar accounts, might prejudice the achievement of wider world aims. This might mean that the attainment of self-support with the objective of reaching a position of economic independence would have to be re-examined and possibly some postponement of the present date (1952) accepted.

14. Just as the United States Government would accept suggestions

regarding their own internal economic policies so they would feel free to make comments on the internal economic policies of the United Kingdom. The United Kingdom should recognise that the United States Government had a particular concern, aside from the general point, with certain domestic issues. There should be a continuing and expanding consultation between the powers based on the general background of 'mutuality of interest'.[9]

15. It was felt on the British side that tribute should be paid to the steps already taken by the United States Administration in the internal field, following upon the tripartite talks in Washington in September.[4] All that the British side had put forward previously was based on the idea that the sterling system was not an end in itself but a means by which the United Kingdom could play its full part in obtaining the common objective. There were merely differences of emphasis between our view and that expounded by the Americans. We had tried to give a lead in Europe and we had tried to avoid any clash arising between our Commonwealth interest and our European position.

The British generally agreed that Dr. Jessup's statement was of the first importance and interest, and that it revealed, with perhaps some differences of emphasis, a basic identity of view between the United States and the United Kingdom position. They would like a little time to examine the statement and see whether there were any real differences of doctrine.

II *Relations with the Satellites*

17. The American side brought out the following points:

(i) Their general principle was to maintain diplomatic relations with the Satellites as long as the latter did not make intolerable conditions for their Missions. Their Missions were useful as listening posts and helped the morale of the inhabitants who might otherwise consider that they were abandoned by the West. They might moreover become invaluable

---

[9] In the Treasury, Mr. G.M. Wilson, Assistant Secretary, referred Mr. Hitchman to this record and that at i below: 'The American thesis is very clearly set out in paragraphs 9 to 14 of the record of the third Bipartite Meeting, and is the origin of what Mr. Berthoud was saying to you after London Committee [see Volume I, No. 9, note 2] yesterday morning. The argument is that there are wider considerations even than viability, and that we might have to postpone the achievement of viability in order to achieve these wider world aims. 2. All this may be perfectly valid in theory, but I doubt if it is much guide to action now. The question really is whether we are prepared to become perpetual pensioners and to go on living on charity indefinitely—with the limitation on our freedom of action which this involves. From the American point of view, it would no doubt be highly convenient for us to become mercenaries in this way and it would have certain advantages for us as well; but I am quite certain that no country could *voluntarily* accept this state of affairs if it saw the slightest chance of gaining financial independence. It is because we do see that chance that the arguments used by Mr. Jessup and Mr. Berthoud, plausible though they are, do not carry real conviction' (T 232/167).

in the case of new developments, *e.g.*, the spread of Titoism[10] to another country.

(ii) Action regarding relations with the Satellites should whenever possible be co-ordinated with the United Kingdom and France.

(iii) The propaganda offensive against the Satellite Governments should be stepped up and co-ordinated.

(iv) The United Nations remained a useful forum for the ventilation of disputes and for publicity.

In particular:

(*a*) The Human Rights issue should be presented.

(*b*) The question was under consideration whether the treatment of diplomatic representatives in the Satellites and the U.S.S.R. could be made a subject for debate.

(v) The Council of Europe might help to drive home the theme of the unification of Europe.

(vi) The usefulness of exile groups should be considered jointly.

(vii) The advantages of Titoism should be emphasised in our propaganda to the peoples of the Satellites, although the latter were not attracted to *any* brand of communism.

18. On the British side, general agreement was felt on the desirability of maintaining diplomatic relations with the Satellites and on the need of co-ordinating action towards them. The following reservations were made:

(i) We felt that our tactics regarding the Human Rights issue at the United Nations could best be decided nearer the time of the next session of the General Assembly.

(ii) It was questionable whether the ventilation of the treatment of diplomatic representatives in the Satellites and the U.S.S.R. would improve their lot. It might indeed exacerbate it.

(iii) We doubted the wisdom of 'labelling empty seats' at the Council of Europe.

(iv) Our view of exile groups was gloomier than that of the Americans; they were so divided amongst themselves. As most of the émigré committees were in the United States we agreed that the Americans should take the lead in relations with them but that we should try to co-ordinate our attitude towards them.

19. There was room for closer co-operation in cases where action on the part of the Satellites called for retaliation and that the best means of achieving this would be mutual consultation by telegraph. We did not think that reprisals need be reciprocal, but that they should usually be in kind (*e.g.*, in the recent Hungarian case we had expelled only one

---

[10] The pursuit of socialist objectives outside the Soviet orbit personified by Marshal J.B. Tito, Yugoslav Prime Minister and Minister of National Defence.

Hungarian diplomat when the Hungarians had expelled two Britons).[11] We were now considering the imposition of restrictions on travel and the issue of driving licences to Russian and Satellite diplomats in the United Kingdom in reply to similar restrictions in the U.S.S.R. and the Satellites. Regarding demands for the reduction of our staff in Satellite countries, we were in any case intending to make reductions for reasons of economy.

20. The American view was that retaliation in kind was not always appropriate, *e.g.*, when it implied the denial of a fundamental Human Right. The co-ordination of action was difficult in some cases, because of the time factor, but whenever possible, they agreed to exchange views. With regard to travel restrictions there were indications at present of relaxation in the Russian attitude, and the Americans did not wish to risk a further stiffening by imposing corresponding restrictions in the United States. They too, were cutting down their staffs in the Satellites for economy reasons and because large staffs now served no useful purpose. An indirect method of bringing pressure to bear on Russia and the Satellites would be to drop a hint at certain friendly capitals, *e.g.*, in Pakistan, Siam or Indonesia, that the Russians should be informed that the maintenance of their large staffs in those countries would be dependent on the granting of reciprocal rights to Western Missions in Moscow.

21. The British side then took up the American point about the co-ordination of propaganda. We felt that the best way of co-ordinating the services of the B.B.C. and the Voice of America would be for these organs to exchange representatives as they did during the war.

22. The Americans replied that a certain amount of co-operation took plact already, *e.g.*, regarding Soviet jamming, but agreed that further co-operation on the lines suggested was desirable and that this could be best achieved bilaterally without inviting the assistance of the French.

23. *It was agreed* that the general question of the East–West Trade and in particular the position of the Economic Council of Europe[12] and the economic situation in Germany could be considered separately.

III *Yugoslavia*

24. The British view was that there were only minor differences in emphasis between our policy towards Yugoslavia and that of the Americans. We believed that, although the economic situation in Yugoslavia was critical, the Tito régime would weather the next six months or so successfully. Our inability to be more generous towards

---

[11] On 18 April His Majesty's Government asked the Hungarian Government for the withdrawal of a press attaché from the Hungarian Legation in London as a reprisal for the Hungarian expulsion in March of the British Commercial Secretary and Assistant Military Attaché at H.M. Legation in Budapest in connection with the trial in Hungary in February of an American and a British businessman for espionage: cf. *Parl. Debs., 5th ser., H. of C.*, vol. 472, cols. *23–4* and vol. 475, cols. 24–5.

[12] See No. 30, note 3.

Yugoslavia at the time of the Anglo-Yugoslav Trade Agreement[13] was the result of our own economic position, but we should continue to do all we could to help. With regard to our propaganda policy towards Yugoslavia, we felt that it was important to attack the régime as a *Communist* one and to counter Russian insinuations that Tito was a lackey of the West.

25. The Americans agreed in general with our assessment. They wanted Tito's economic position to be secure but not to flourish, and to drive home the value of economic aid from the West. They had discouraged the Yugoslavs in January when they asked for a $6 million loan as this was totally inadequate to Yugoslav needs in the long run. The question of an International Bank loan was under consideration and the United Kingdom might be asked to contribute a share towards this later in the year.

IV *Future business*

It was agreed that the talks should be continued in three sub-committees next morning, 26th April. A plan for work during the rest of the week was sketched out and the Secretary-General was invited to circulate it next day. It was also agreed that the Secretaries of all three delegations should meet, when convenient, to arrange a programme for the second week of official talks. In principle, this programme should allow for meetings of special study groups in the earlier half of the week and for plenary sessions towards the end of the week.[14]

CALENDARS TO NO. 34

i *26 Apr. 1950   Records of Bipartite Sub-Committee Meetings*

(*a*) *No. 1.* further discussion of the economic problems raised in No. 34: officials agree that convertibility and end of trade discrimination is the ultimate objective. Joint memo. to be produced for Ministers reaffirming Anglo-American accord in principle but identifying current areas of tension [ZP 2/86].

(*b*) *No. 2 with draft report* (later withdrawn) on relationship between U.K. and Western Europe 'After reading the draft Mr. Perkins said that the Americans were not at present very sold on the idea of a United States of Europe, but would not oppose it if it came about. On the other hand they attached the greatest importance to the European problem and were determined not to let it go by the board' and felt the need for 'strong British participation and leadership' in solving problems of economic organization of Europe and Germany. Discussion of E.P.U. and Atlantic Pact [ZP 2/90; WU 1075/21].

(*c*) *No. 3. UK/US objectives worldwide* reviewed: In Middle East (Persia, Egypt, Eastern-Medit. Pact) UK/US policies are generally aligned. South Asia,

---

[13] This agreement of 26 December 1949 is printed in *B.F.S.P.*, vol. 154, pp. 324–329.

[14] For the sub-committee structure which emerged, see *F.R.U.S. 1950*, vol. iii, pp. 902–3. The British records of both bipartite and tripartite sub-committees were numbered in consecutive series i.e. bipartite sub-committees—Nos. 1–15, tripartite—Nos. 1–10.

Colonial Areas, Africa, Latin America. Afghanistan and Italian Colonies all referred for further discussion. Ways and means of Anglo-American cooperation and consultation considered though 'the Americans, while acknowledging the special relationships, between the United Kingdom and the United States, also emphasized the need to consider the problem of consultation with other allies in order to avoid suspicion and resentment'. Meeting concludes with agreement to produce 'a body of papers identifying common objectives in as many areas and fields as possible' [ZP 2/91].

ii *28 Apr. 1950 Record of Fourth Bipartite Official Meeting* at which discussion in Sub Committee's Nos. 1–3 above is reviewed [ZP 2/93].

No. 35

Brief by Sir E. Plowden for Sir S. Cripps (Treasury)

[*T 232/167*]

Top secret   TREASURY, *25 April 1950*[1]

Western Organisations
(P.U.S.C. (50) 9 (Final)

1. The main proposal in the Foreign Secretary's paper is that we should at once start to develop the non-military side of the North Atlantic Treaty machinery. The effect of this would probably be that, after 1952, most of the work which would then be within the competence of O.E.E.C. would be dealt with under the North Atlantic Treaty and the rest in the Council of Europe. It is proposed that, up to 1952, the O.E.E.C. should be retained as the main economic forum.

2. When we considered this proposal in the Treasury, our view was that there was no compelling reason for taking this step immediately and that it presented two major difficulties, first, the fact that certain countries, particularly Germany and Sweden, were not members of the Atlantic Pact; and secondly that, if economic relations between Europe and the Western Hemisphere were to come within the Atlantic Pact machinery, we could not properly continue our special tripartite arrangements in Washington.[2]

3. We discussed this at length with Sir Roger Makins and Sir Gladwyn Jebb and they put forward the following additional arguments in support of the Foreign Office proposal.

[1] Date derived from covering minute from Sir E. Plowden to Sir S. Cripps, not printed, submitting both the present brief on the P.U.S.C. paper on Western Organisations (No. 30) and the brief at No. 36 covering the P.U.S.C. paper on British Overseas Obligations (No. 43).

[2] These reservations were elaborated in a note of Treasury comments (not printed from T 236/2481) sent to Sir R. Makins on 19 April as briefing for the meeting with Sir. E. Plowden on 21 April (see No. 30, note 1 and further below), at which both No. 30 and No. 43 were discussed.

(*a*) The Americans have put an item on the agenda for the forthcoming talks which covers this point and they are themselves going to propose that some machinery should be set up under Article 2 of the Treaty. They attach real importance to the proposal. The Atlantic Pact is the one organisation in which we are equal partners with the Americans, at any rate formally, and this is of considerable importance.
(*b* The French are also thinking along the same lines—cf. the recent speech by M. Bidault.[3] They fear that, if the United Kingdom stands aloof from Europe, they will be dominated by Germany and they regard the Atlantic Pact as a safeguard against this. They are also anxious that the Atlantic Pact should not be regarded as a purely military organisation.
(*c*) If the Americans do make this proposal and we turn it down on the grounds that O.E.E.C. is adequate, we may be told that, in that case, we should really integrate with Europe.
(*d*) The ending of Marshall Aid is bound to weaken the O.E.E.C. and if, as we expect, the Council of Europe is at least as strong as it is now, a major effort of policy would be required to keep O.E.E.C. operating at its present level after 1952. We cannot therefore rely on O.E.E.C. being of major importance after 1952, and if we turn down the American proposal now, the chance of establishing some North Atlantic machinery for economic questions may not recur. We must therefore make up our minds now and cannot leave this for later decision.

4. As regards the particular difficulties mentioned in paragraph 2 above, the Foreign Office answers were:

(*a*) The difference in membership is a serious problem. Germany is the real difficulty. But she is already in O.E.E.C. which will go on till 1952, and we hope that she will come into the Council of Europe. Once the decision of principle is taken, ways can be found of associating the non-members of the Atlantic Pact with its economic work. In any case, a lot may happen in the two years that will elapse before the Article 2 machinery can take over from O.E.E.C.
(*b*) There is no reason why the tripartite arrangements in Washington should come to an end since our relations with the United States and Canada cover a much wider range of problems than those which will be covered by the Atlantic Pact machinery, e.g., the sterling/dollar relationship, the sterling balances, oil etc.

5. No change in the status of the O.E.E.C. is proposed so far as the next two years are concerned, and no radical change otherwise. When it was suggested that the economic clauses of the Brussels Treaty should be developed we turned the suggestion down and said flatly that this was not a suitable forum for discussion of economic matters. All that is involved here is our agreement that the Atlantic Pact machinery *may* provide a suitable forum for this purpose when Marshall Aid ends. No immediate

[3] See No. 24, note 5.

decision is involved as to the future of O.E.E.C. after 1952; but we shall then be in a position to choose between O.E.E.C. and the Atlantic Pact, which might not be the case if we reject the American proposal now.

6. We think that the arguments advanced by the Foreign Office are convincing, and we therefore recommend that you should agree to the proposals in the paper.[4]

[4] Sir S. Cripps minuted below on 28 April 'I don't agree, I am afraid. We can of course discuss the matter with the Americans but I am not convinced it is right or practicable.' On 1 May Sir S. Cripps' Private Secretary, Mr. W.A. Armstrong, informed Mr. Barclay that the Chancellor 'disagreed with our Western Organisations paper, but had subsequently said that he did not feel strongly about this, and was prepared to let it go' (minute by Mr. Barclay on F.O.800/481) see further No. 57.

No. 36

Brief by Sir E. Plowden for Sir S. Cripps (Treasury)

[*T 232/167*]

Top secret   TREASURY, *25 April 1950*

British Overseas Obligations
P.U.S.C. (79) Final [2nd] Revise[1]

The main argument of this paper is that any general withdrawal by the United Kingdom on the political and military fronts would have an adverse effect on our economic position; that some savings can be effected by sharing certain military responsibilities in the Middle East with other Commonwealth countries, by transferring certain economic obligations in South Asia to the United States (i.e. relieving ourselves of part of the burden of the sterling balances) and by arranging for some integration of research and development projects with the United States; and that if the claims which still remain upon the United Kingdom resources are found to be too heavy when related to the claims resulting from other policies of H.M.G. we shall either have to find the resources by sacrifices in other directions or risk the consequences of an uncontrolled decline in our standards and way of life.

2. We cannot see that the measures suggested by the Foreign Office would really afford any significant relief to the strain upon our resources.[2] The only measure that would afford relief in any significant way is the transfer to the United States of part of the burden of the sterling balances, but any saving that might be secured in this way is already needed if we are to manage our dollar position when E.R.P. ends. This saving cannot be counted twice. The Foreign Office do not suggest any further savings that

[1] Advance copy of No. 43. In his covering minute to Sir S. Cripps (see No. 35, note 1) Sir E. Plowden explained that this text took account of Treasury comments on the draft (see No. 35, note 2) but that there remained 'a fundamental difference of view between the Foreign Office and ourselves on the question of British Overseas Obligations.'
[2] Sir S. Cripps noted 'I agree' against this sentence in the margin.

might be made which would not imperil our position as a world power.

3. The problem raised by the paper, though not explicitly stated, is therefore whether our resources are adequate both to maintain our position as a world power and to maintain existing standards of living in the United Kingdom and, if they are not adequate for both these purposes, as we believe to be the case, which should be regarded as marginal. We cannot see any escape from this dilemma unless the Americans are prepared to play a larger part than they are at present doing, and this should determine the approach which we make to them in the forthcoming talks. We must at all costs avoid deluding either the Americans or ourselves into thinking that we can do things which in fact we cannot do. We are already severely overstrained. Any saving that would result from limiting our political and military obligations and from reducing the burden of the sterling balances is needed to relieve the general strain on our economy, and consequently would not be available to increase defence expenditure.

4. We therefore think that we should tell the Americans frankly that we are already overstrained and that it is only with the assistance of Marshall Aid that we can carry our present burdens. The United States has a national income more than six times as great as ours whereas her population is only three times as great. But the areas for which we are responsible are nearer to the cold war fronts and we do not see how these fronts can be held without further United States assistance. There are many ways in which that assistance can be given; it might take the form either of direct assistance to the United Kingdom economy or of the United States assuming greater direct responsibility in certain areas, e.g., the Middle East and South East Asia. But it is no use pretending, either to ourselves or to the Americans, that we can carry as much of the load as they can and they will be more ready to assist if we put before them frankly a realistic appreciation of the problem on these lines. We should also be less than candid if we did not tell them that, if war comes within the next five years or so, we should not be able to make a really worth while effort if there was any question of payment being made for services and supplies provided by one participant on our side to another.

5. If an approach to the Americans on these lines fails, Ministers will then have to consider whether any savings that we have to make should be at the expense of living standards in this country or of our position as a world power with the longer term risks to our living standards which, as we agree with the Foreign Office, this involves.

6. The objectives of United Kingdom foreign policy as set out in paragraph 6 of the paper read rather oddly. They were apparently designed to meet what were expected to be the views of the Treasury, but they do not affect the main issue.[3]

[3] Sir S. Cripps minuted below on 29 April 'I think this is an unsatisfactory paper. It tries to get the best of both worlds but fails. I agree with the Treasury comments very largely & we shall have to see what we can get out of it.'

No. 37

Record of Second Tripartite Official Meeting held in the Foreign Office on 26 April 1950 at 3.30 p.m.

[ZP 2/193]

Top secret

Present:

United Kingdom Sir W. Strang, Sir G. Jebb, Sir R. Makins, Sir F. Hoyer-Millar, Mr. Wright, Mr. Shuckburgh, Mr. Hadow, Mr. Harrison (for item II).

United States Mr. Jessup, Mr. Perkins, Mr. Bohlen, Mr. Labouisse, Mr. Stinebower, Mr. Wallner,[1] Mr. Raynor, Mr. J. Reber.

France M. Massigli, M. Alphand, M. de la Tournelle, M. Baudet, M. Lebel, M. André, M. Labouret, M. de Folin.[2]

Agenda:

I 'Review of the agreement on common world-wide objectives in the light of the assessment of the common world-wide situation.' (Item 2 of Tripartite Agenda—United Kingdom Paper, D.5.)[3]

II 'General attitude towards the Soviet Union. Should there be negotiations, and, if so, in what form?' (Item 8 of Tripartite Agenda—United Kingdom Paper, D.5.)[3]

The meeting opened with a discussion on the programme for the rest of the week (United Kingdom Secretariat Notice S.9).[4] This was agreed to, with the exception that it was felt a plenary tripartite meeting should take place on Thursday afternoon, April 27th.

2. The French suggested that at the end of the Ministerial meeting there should be some grand tripartite declaration by the three Ministers which would go beyond any mere communiqué on the work done. A special drafting committee might be set up to consider, as the official meetings went on, the material for such a declaration.

3. It was agreed that the setting up of such a committee might wait until the official talks had progressed a little further and more consideration had been given to the content of any such declaration as proposed by the French.

I

4. The discussion on Item I of the Agenda opened with an assessment

[1] Mr C.E. Bohlen and Mr. W. Wallner were respectively Minister and First Secretary at the U.S. Embassy in Paris.

[2] M. H. Alphand was Director of Economic Affairs at the French Ministry for Foreign Affairs. MM. C. Lebel and G. André were respectively First and Second Secretaries at the French Embassy in London. M. J. de Folin was Secretary to M. Parodi. M. V. Labouret was Second Secretary at the French Ministry of Foreign Affairs.

[3] See No. 17, note 9. 　　　　　　　　　　　　　　　　　[4] Not printed.

of the world-wide situation by the Americans. This followed closely the lines of the American assessment already given at the first United Kingdom/United States Bipartite official meeting (see paragraph 2 of the United Kingdom Record).[5] Two new points were made—

(i) A greater emphasis was placed on the immediate danger in the Middle East and South-East Asia, where urgent remedial steps were necessary; and

(ii) A further factor in the weakness of the Soviet orbit was seen to lie in the still great disparity between the Russian economy and that of the West.

5. The British assessment also followed the lines of the statement already made at the first Bipartite Meeting (paragraph 3 of the United Kingdom Record). Two further points were, however, made on the Soviet credit side—

(i) The Russian development of an atom bomb had undoubtedly had a great effect on Soviet and satellite morale and had increased the respect for the Soviet Union of many waverers.

(ii) The Communist campaign in the Colonies and dependent areas was a grave and developing threat.

6. On the credit side for the West, importance must (in addition to factors already mentioned) be attached to the fact that there had still been no slump, as predicted by the Soviet propagandists.

7. The French were in general agreement but felt there were certain additional points to be made—

(i) From the Continental point of view the Soviet peace campaign had a strong attraction. This reached down into the smallest villages and gave the Russians a very definite lead in propaganda over the West.

(ii) The unknown terrors of the atom bomb were responsible for much hesitation on the Continent. Here, too, the Soviet proposal for its complete abolition[6] had given the Russians a psychological advantage.

(iii) The French welcomed United States interest in the Middle East and were sorry that this area was not to be considered under the tripartite agenda.

(iv) The Americans and British were liable to look at the German problem in a purely 'cold war' setting. The French would like to remind them that for the Continent the German question had a significance all of its own, and the French felt that it was a mistake to regard Germany purely in the context of the struggle for power with Russia.

(v) The presentation of communism as a dynamic and moving force

[5] No.29.

[6] In 1947 the Soviet Union advanced a plan for the control of atomic energy within the framework of the United Nations based on the prior destruction of all existing stocks of atomic weapons and the public declaration of all atomic facilities. This plan, though rejected by the U.N. Atomic Energy Commission, was regularly revived by Soviet representatives.

for the future was an effective element in the Soviet campaign to undermine and disrupt certain sections of Western thinking. It was up to the West to present its ideals equally effectively.

(vi) While agreeing that the Atlantic Treaty was a major victory for the West, it must be remembered that unless it was effectively implemented and rendered efficacious as a military instrument in the very near future it might well prove a boomerang on the West. This might easily happen if the Russians were to provoke some crisis which the Atlantic Powers were too weak to cope with. If this happened the Atlantic Treaty would be exposed to the world as a hollow sham.

8. The Americans and British, commenting on the general theme underlying the French statement, agreed that it was unwise to minimise the powerful attraction of Soviet propaganda. In particular it was felt that the use of the term 'cold war' for public consumption was unwise, as it presented a false picture of the thinking of the West when compared to the Soviet 'peace campaign.'

9. Turning to the examination of common objectives the Americans suggested that, broadly speaking, there were three:

(i) Prevention of any extension of Soviet Communist domination by whatever means it was attempted.

(ii) Recapture and retention of the psychological initiative. The ultimate downfall of the Soviet system would be through the moral force of the West and to attain this objective we should press earnestly forward in building up the moral and material preponderance of the free world.

(iii) To convince the Russians that their present line of procedure was hopeless—and this objective was a matter of great urgency.

10. With regard to the specific lines of development of Western strength, the Americans felt that:

(i) It was necessary to build up the economic strength of the West so that it might support an increased defence effort and at the same time maintain the general high standard of living. To do this it would be necessary to subordinate narrow national interests to the general good, and all should combine in the maximum economic effort, the settlement of priorities, increase of production, common utilisation of man-power and the attempt to bring about individual economic adjustment without special assistance from outside.

(ii) It was vital to make faith in freedom a more dynamic force than any message which communism could supply. This was the answer to Communist ideology. Public understanding of the danger in which freedom stood and of the methods which were used to destroy it must be increased.

(iii) It was of importance to undertake a continuous review of problems of common concern. The United States, Britain and France had the primary responsibility for leadership, but they must secure the co-operation and participation of all other free nations and dependent territories. These others should be given the opportunity to share in the common effort and use should be made of all the available world agencies to make them feel they were playing their part.

11. In particular, Germany, the Middle East, South-East Asia and Africa must be convinced that their ultimate aspirations for freedom and a higher standard of living stood more chance of fulfilment in the Western camp than with the Russians. A vigorous united front must be maintained, based on common ideals which the Soviets could not accept without altering their whole conception of life, or reject without great damage to their reputation. The ideals of the West must be made to penetrate the Iron Curtain and stimulate the hope of the subjected peoples there that they, too, might one day be able to satisfy their aspirations for liberty and a better life.

12. The British strongly supported this American statement of objectives and defined the general British attitude towards Soviet expansion as set out in the Conclusion of P.U.S.C. Paper No. 31 ('British Policy towards Soviet communism').[7]

13. The French felt that to attain the prime objectives of the West the most urgent priority was to ensure the co-ordination of efficacious defence and to combine all available resources to this end. They also pointed out the dangers of overstressing the importance of freedom for dependent nations. Slogans were apt to run riot and the consequences of such slogans among semi-civilised peoples were apt to be different from those envisaged by their originators. In dealing with dependent peoples care should be taken not to weaken the whole material structure of Western strength. Finally, care must be taken in defining the objectives of the West so that they did not appear provocative, and it must be made apparent that the present building up of the defensive strength of the West in no way precluded a general reduction of armaments under the aegis of the United Nations.

14. The French finally returned to a plea for some form of 3-Power declaration which would be a sort of 'Free-World Charter' and in which the common worth objectives of the West should be set out. In answer to an enquiry from the British side they said that they were quite prepared to consider the desirability of such a declaration being made by all 12 Ministers rather than by 3 only. They felt, however, that a sub-committee should be established which could meet at intervals and try to pick up any useful ideas that emerged in the whole course of the discussions for embodiment in the proposed declaration.

15. It was agreed that this idea might be further examined and since instructions from Governments might be necessary the subject might be

[7] This paper of 28 July 1949 is not here printed. For a summary of its conclusions, as given at this meeting by Sir G. Jebb, see *F.R.U.S. 1950*, vol.iii, p.840.

further considered in two or three days' time.[8]

16. The Americans outlined their position towards negotiations with the Russians on the same lines as they had done at the 2nd Bipartite official meeting (paragraphs 13–15 of the United Kingdom Record).[9]

17. The British attitude still was that it would be highly undesirable to enter upon any broad and general negotiations with the Russians. On the other hand, negotiations on specific subjects were probably unavoidable and indeed might be of value at certain times. It was realised, however, that, should we be faced with a definite proposal such as that by M. Lie for a special meeting of the Security Council, it would be difficult to avoid embarking upon general discussions with the Russians. In that regrettable event the agenda would have to be very carefully drawn up. The British added that this general attitude probably reflected a smaller pressure of public opinion in the United Kingdom as compared with the United States and France.

18. The French entered a strong plea that the door to a general settlement with Russia should not be closed. Without running after the Russians the Western Powers should be constantly on the alert to see whether some opportunity did not present itself for general discussions which might lead to a *modus vivendi*. It must be remembered that negotiation was not an end in itself. It was one of the means of obtaining and maintaining peace. It would therefore be wrong to adopt an attitude that the Russians must give way completely, since they would never do this. The main interest of the West lay in the stabilisation of the position in Germany, the Middle East and South-East Asia. If this could be obtained it would be worth while making concessions to the Russians. A general truce in the cold war would be of great value, and French public opinion would certainly never acquiesce if an opportunity to bring about such a truce were neglected. We should, therefore, watch out for any symptoms of weakening or readiness to negotiate on the part of the Russians.

19. It was finally agreed—

(1) that the best basis for negotiating with Russia was Western strength, since the Russians always respected situations of fact;
(2) that no general negotiations with the U.S.S.R. should be entered into by one of the three Powers without the agreement of the others;
(3) that negotiations on specific subjects might be desirable and even profitable; and
(4) that whether general negotiations were necessary or not, the West should go on building up its strength.

20. The meeting adjourned after agreeing that another tripartite

[8] In a minute of 28 April to Mr. Bevin, Sir G. Jebb represented the value of making such a statement and recommended that a sub-committee should be set up to produce a draft either for issue as a tripartite or N.A.C. declaration. Mr. Bevin commented: 'I had in mind the Atlantic Organisation. It seems surprising for 3 Powers to do it. E.B.' (WU 1076/54).
[9] No. 33.

meeting should be arranged for 3.30 p.m. on Thursday, 27th April, to consider items 2 and 9 of the Tripartite Agenda.

No. 38

Brief for the U.K. Delegation
No. 15 [C 2837/2514/18]

Secret   FOREIGN OFFICE, 26 April 1950

Re-establishment of German Armed Forces

Recommendation

(*a*) The United Kingdom Delegation should not raise this subject.

(*b*) If the subject is raised by another Delegation, our attitude should be that there is no need to discuss the question in its short term aspect, since all three Powers are understood to be in agreement as to the impossibility of an early re-establishment of German Armed Forces, and that any discussion of the long-term aspect is premature.

(*c*) At the same time we should be honest and recognise in our minds although we need not say so, the full implications of our declared policy of bringing Germany into the Western system as an eventual partner with equal rights. This goal will take a long time to reach and we may not get there. But if we do, the end of the road means German participation in all Western organisations, including the North Atlantic Treaty, and a degree of German armament, of course under the direction and supervision of a common Western military machine. But this is over the horizon and we need not and indeed should not go into it now.

Background

The Governments of all three Western Powers have publicly declared themselves against the rearmament of Germany. The most recent occasion on which His Majesty's Government's attitude was stated was the Foreign Affairs Debate in the House of Commons on the 28th March, when the Secretary of State declared:

'. . . I must say to the right hon. Gentleman that we have set our face—the United States, France and ourselves—against the rearming of Germany, and that, I am afraid, we must adhere to.'[1] The French Government's

---

[1] See *Parl. Debs., 5th ser., H. of C.*, vol. 473, col. 324 and No. 18, note 2. Mr. Bevin was here addressing Mr. Churchill, who earlier in the debate had advocated German participation in the defence of Western Europe. When commenting on the P.U.S.C. paper on the future of Germany (No. 64.i.), Mr. Attlee referred to Mr. Churchill's suggestion for the integration of German forces in a Western Union force as a proposal which should be examined. Since 'I think it unlikely that Germany will settle down without some armed forces. One must consider the tradition of the German State. Without some armed forces, a gendarmerie

attitude was expressed by the French Foreign Minister in a speech to the National Assembly on the 24th February, when he said: 'The French Government, to the same extent that it is in favour of the progressive incorporation of Germany in a European whole and in favour of the admission of Germany to the organisations which will form the basis of peaceful cooperation between the countries of Europe, considers that it is quite impossible even to discuss the question of a restoration of Germany's military forces.' The United States view was expressed by the American High Commissioner in a speech at Stuttgart on the 6th February[2] after his return to Germany after consultation with his Government. On this occasion he said: 'the German people should take an increasingly active part themselves in the political and economic organisation of Europe. Germany cannot be allowed to develop political conditions or a military status which would threaten other nations or the peace of the world. That means there will be no German army or air force. German security will best be protected by German participation in a closely-knit Western European community.' The German Federal Government has also expressed general opposition to projects for German rearmament.

2. At the same time, the British Chiefs of Staff have examined the question,[3] and although they accept the view that immediate German rearmament would be imprudent on political grounds and is therefore impracticable for the time being, they have also stated that the successful defence of Western Europe against eventual Soviet attack can only be assured with the participation of Germany.

3. Even if this long-term view is accepted, all concerned are agreed that the creation of a German army now or in the near future is impracticable. The considerations on which this conclusion is based are as follows:

(a) In the present climate of opinion in France it is unlikely that any French Government could agree to the rearmament of Germany.

(b) The Russians are genuinely afraid of a revival of the military might of Germany. The rearmament of Western Germany might, therefore, provoke the Russians to a preventive war and so precipitate the catastrophe which it would be designed to prevent.

(c) In the present economic condition of Germany it would be impossible to organise German rearmament without American assist-

would be used to try to create clandestinely the framework of armed forces in the future. Is this not already being done in Eastern Germany by the Communists under Russian guidance? . . . I do not know how the French would view such a suggestion, but given the German Military tradition, it is worth considering whether it will be possible to sustain total prohibition indefinitely. Some such plan as is suggested might at some time give the best chance of diverting the German military instinct into a channel which would make for peace instead of war' (minute from Mr. Attlee to Mr. Bevin of 2 May on ZP 3/3).

[2] A text of Mr. McCloy's speech in which he announced a nine point programme for Germany is printed in *Department of State Bulletin*, vol. xxii, pp. 275–9 (F.O. copy on C 1364/10/18).

[3] See i below.

ance. The resources of America are not inexhaustible. If we assume, as we must, that in the distribution of American resources France and the Western European countries should have priority, there will in fact be nothing available for Germany for a considerable time to come.

(*d*) We have a major interest in keeping the American troops in Europe for as long as possible. At the moment the Germans are prepared to put up with the occupation because they realise that the occupation troops constitute the only protection against the Eastern German People's Police and the Russian Army. If the Germans were allowed to reconstitute the army this sense of dependence on the occupation troops would disappear and there would be strong pressure on the Western Allies to terminate the occupation. The Americans, under such pressure, would be only too inclined to withdraw their troops from Germany.

(*e*) Until Germany is far more involved with the West than she is at present we have no firm assurance that Germany will not throw in her lot with Russia. Until the Federal Republic is firmly in the Western camp it would be dangerous to allow it to rearm. Moreover, even if Germany does not ally herself to Russia, experience teaches us that an armed Germany soon develops a truculence and arrogance which makes it impossible to deal with. Experience also teaches us that plans for limiting German armed forces or for giving them only partial or defensive armament are unlikely to be successful. Total prohibition of German rearmament for a stated period with adequate measures for enforcement is the only safe solution.

4. The Chiefs of Staff, who have been consulted, have expressed the view that, apart from the establishment of a gendarmerie in Western Germany (which, they say, should be undertaken as a matter of urgency), 'there is no hurry about the formation of anything more, since we could not contemplate even the partial rearmament of Western Germany until the French Army has been built up'.

5. Thus, while it is by no means impossible that in the long term political considerations will develop which may outweigh the adverse factors listed above, the fact remains that as regards the short term the three Western Powers have independently reached the conclusion that the creation of a German army is undesirable at present. There would therefore appear to be no useful purpose in the Foreign Ministers discussing the matter at this stage, and it is accordingly recommended that it should not be raised by the Secretary of State during the forthcoming talks. If the question is opened by the French or United States representatives, it is recommended that discussion, if possible, should be limited to its short-term aspect, on which the three Powers are in agreement, and that discussion of its long-term aspects should be postponed.

i *4–18 April 1950   Correspondence on Chiefs of Staff views on military aspects of U.K. policy towards Germany* including record of C.O.S. discussion on 29 March and report C.O.S. (50) 108 of 3 April quoted in para. 4 above. At 29 Mar. meeting C.O.S. agree to instruct Joint Planning Staff to prepare further report on military problem of utilizing German resources for the defence of Western Europe. In response to F.O. request for views in time for discussion at London Conference, U.K. High Commissioner favours creation of gendarmerie but would prefer first overt step to be a request from Federal Govt: this would not be hard to elicit since 'we have indeed already had various hints' [C 2416/27/18].

No. 39

Minute from Mr. Younger to Mr. Attlee

P.M./K.Y./50/16 [ET 1081/45]

FOREIGN OFFICE, *26 April 1950*

The Arab States and Israel

The Cabinet were informed, in the course of their discussion on April 25th,[1] of the Foreign Secretary's memorandum C.P. (50) 78, that there was no reason to believe that the United States Government would take exception to our policy of welcoming the union between Jordan and Arab Palestine, though they would probably be unwilling, for reasons of domestic politics, themselves to make a similar declaration.

2. This forecast has now been confirmed by H.M. Ambassador at Washington, who has reported, in a telegram received on April 26th,[2] that the State Department regard the issue by H.M.G. of the statement referred to in paragraph 10 of C.P.(50) 78 as entirely a matter for us to decide and do not wish to suggest that its issue should be deferred.

3. As regards our proposed *de jure* recognition of Israel, the United States themselves have long since recognised Israel *de jure* and will no doubt welcome our action in doing so,[3] though they have not specifically commented on this point.

4. But as regards the further proposed statement referred to in paragraph 17 of C.P. (50) 78, the State Department have strongly urged that this should be deferred for the present, in order that opportunity

[1] At this discussion of No.10.i, Mr. Younger also informed the Cabinet that the Jordanian proclamation of union with Arab Palestine on 24 April gave some urgency to the recommendations at No.10.i. These recommendations were approved by the Cabinet. Instructions were also agreed for informing other Commonwealth Governments of these decisions and for a statement in Parliament.

[2] This telegram No. 1278, summarized below, is not printed from ET 1081/17.

[3] On his copy of this minute filed on F.O. 800/477, Mr. Bevin noted in the margin 'I agree'.

should be given for discussion during the forthcoming London meeting of a proposal that the United Kingdom and the United States, and possibly France, should at the outcome of these talks issue a joint statement on the following lines:

(*a*) An expression of deep interest in the establishment and maintenance of peace and stability in the Middle East;

(*b*) the reaffirmation of the principle of the political independence and territorial integrity of all the state[s] in the Middle East;

(*c*) an expression of opposition to the violation of frontiers by external force;

(*d*) an assurance that, on receipt of information that any Middle East state is preparing to violate the frontiers of another immediate action will be taken, both inside and outside the United Nations.

5. The State Department suggest that a statement on the above lines should be made either in London or as a result of a decision reached in London. They are confident that they could join in such a statement provided that it followed some clarification on the matter of arms supplies to the Middle East, e.g. the issue of a joint United Kingdom/United States statement regarding policy towards arms supplies for the Middle East and possibly the obtaining by us of some assurance that no party in the Middle East intends to use the arms supplied for any offensive purposes. It does not appear that the State Department intend to press H.M.G. either to supply arms to Israel or to restrict arms supplies to other Middle East countries.

6. This proposal by the State Department, which goes somewhat further than anything which they have hitherto seemed likely to be able to agree to,[4] would clearly have considerably greater advantages for the objects which we have in view than the proposed statement by H.M.G. alone on the lines of paragraph 17 of C.P. (50) 78.

7. In view of the urgency of the matter the Cabinet cannot be consulted, but I should like your approval to omit from the statement which I shall make in the House tomorrow the passage suggested in Recommendation (3) of C.F. (50) 78—and approved at yesterday's Cabinet Meeting—reaffirming H.M.G.'s. desire for peace in the Middle East and their opposition to the use of force between Middle Eastern states.

8. I am sending a copy of this minute to the Secretary of State for Commonwealth Relations.[5]

K.G. YOUNGER

[4] Cf. No.10 and note 12 *ibid.*

[5] Mr. Attlee minuted in reply on 26 April: 'I approve. It can be mentioned at Cabinet tomorrow.' For identic government statements in the House of Commons and House of Lords on 27 April, approved that morning by the Cabinet, announcing British recognition of the union of Arab Palestine with Jordan and *de jure* recognition of Israel, both subject to further explanations see *Parl. Debs., 5th ser., H. of C.,* vol. 474, cols. 1137–9 and *op.cit., H.of L.,* vol.166, cols.1211–3.

No. 40

Record of Third Tripartite Official Meeting held in the Foreign Office on 27 April 1950 at 3.30 p.m.

[ZP 2/193]

Top secret

Present:
United Kingdom Sir William Strang (Chairman), Sir Roger Makins, Sir Gladwyn Jebb, Sir Frederick Hoyer-Millar, Mr. Wright, Mr. Hadow.

U.S.A. Ambassador Jessup, Mr. Perkins, Mr. Holmes, Mr. Labouisse, Mr. Raynor, Mr. Stinebower, Mr. Laukhuff, Mr. Wallner, Mr. Sanders, Miss Camp.

France The French Ambassador, M. Alphand, M. de la Tournelle, M. Leroy, M. André.

Secretariat Mr. Shuckburgh.

Agenda

I 'Review and determination of what needs to be done to achieve closer association of European and North Atlantic Areas.
    (*a*) N.A.T.O.
    (*b*) European political and economic integration.
        (i) Long-term development of economic relationships with United States of America;
        (ii) migration.
    (*c*) Germany.'
    (Item 2 (*a*), (*b*) and (*c*) of Tripartite Agenda—United Kingdom Paper, No. D.5.)[1]
II 'Advisability of and means of continuously reviewing world-wide commitments and capabilities and most effective manner of conducting future discussions of this nature.'
(Item 9 of Tripartite Agenda—United Kingdom Paper, No. D.5.)

I (*a*) N.A.T.O.

The meeting opened with a short account of the work hitherto performed by the Working Group in Washington. So far a tentative draft Agenda had been drawn up (United Kingdom Paper No. D.8)[2] and, as far

---

[1] See No. 17, note 9.
[2] Not printed from WU 1071/57. Items on the provisional N.A.C. agenda were rearranged in the final agenda agreed by the North Atlantic Working Group on 3 May and printed in *F.R.U.S. 1950*, vol. iii, p.91. In particular items 2 and 3 of the provisional agenda were combined into item 4 of the final agenda: 'Review of progress in implementing the North Atlantic Treaty in the year since its signature, including reports of the Defence Committee and the D.F.E.C. Consideration of those steps, necessary to ensure increased self-help and mutual aid ...' etc. Provisional item 4 became final item 3: 'Review of and

as was known, agreed to by all the countries concerned. The Working Group was meeting on 28th April. It was possible that Items 2 and 3 on the agenda might be combined as one item. Material for Item 4 would emerge more clearly after the Tripartite Ministerial meeting in London and the Working Group were hoping that Ministers would be able to inform other Atlantic Powers direct rather than through the Working Group. In particular, however, the Working Group would welcome any indication from the official talks on the possible line which might be developed on Item 5. The Americans in particular stressed the importance, even at this stage, of letting the Working Group know the general line of thought, so that the other Atlantic countries would not come to the Council meeting totally unprepared to consider this item.

2. The Americans then gave their view on the general line which might be pursued. With regard to the work already being done by the Atlantic organisation, they felt that both the United Kingdom and the United States were agreed on the need for some central point at which the military and financial work could be co-ordinated. With regard to any new departure they thought there were three points which might be further co-ordinated—

(i) Foreign policy, at any rate in so far as it was relevant to Atlantic Treaty matters.
(ii) Information activities. It was important to get the emphasis of the Atlantic Pact off military matters and on to such other matters as could be developed.
(iii) Economic—particularly in the field of a co-ordination of the military and economic effort.

3. In order to procure this further development of co-ordination the Americans favoured the establishment of some body, working possibly through Deputies of the Ministers, which would meet far more often than the Council. It would be served by a permanent staff headed by a Secretary-General.

4. The French agreed that the improvement should be made in the present somewhat dispersed machinery under the Treaty—especially in the field of defence economics, e.g.—

(i) Supply—the joint standardisation of arms.
(ii) Rational division of production.
(iii) Financing and distribution of costs.

The French also felt that any new central organ should issue from the Council and should be composed of functionaries speaking for their Governments and meeting much more often than the Council. The subjects to be dealt with would be principally military and financial, but other tasks could be allotted to the body, and the whole to be served by a

exchange of views on world political developments . . .' etc. Item 5(a—d) remained the same: 'Promoting more vigorously the agreed objectives of the Treaty . . .' etc.

secretariat under a Secretary-General of high international status.

5. The French then enlarged on their ideas for a more general co-ordination of the economic effort of the West, which, they emphasised, was still unofficial and without any governmental authority. At the present there was no one dealing constantly with this problem. It was true that the E.C.A. was working with the O.E.E.C., but it would disappear in 1952. If development was foreseen along the lines of Article 2 of the Atlantic Treaty, certain European countries would be excluded. The French were against any disbandment of the O.E.E.C. effort. The solution seemed to lie in seeking some conventional link between the United States and Canada with Europe. It should be possible for the two American countries to sit in O.E.E.C. after 1952, not as members, but to consider any problems which might be of more than purely European interest. There were definite advantages in this scheme—

(i) There would be no duplication of organs.

(ii) The O.E.E.C. would retain its purely European calling.

(iii) At the same time the United States and Canada could be brought in for wider subjects, such as international exchange, investment and migration.

(iv) Such countries as Switzerland, who would not be prepared to come in under any Article 2 set-up, would remain in the European economic organisation. And, above all, Germany could play her part in the European economic scheme without being brought into the Atlantic Pact, to which the French (and this was a firm governmental view) were resolutely opposed.

6. The British view was that there was indeed a need for some new machinery. The purely military effort was not sufficiently geared to the economic-defence effort. On the whole the American scheme seemed sound. A co-ordinating body might be set up composed of representatives of Ministers which would sit in a given town with a permanent staff under some sort of first-class Secretary-General. There were organisational points which would have to be settled later, e.g.:

(i) Where it was to sit.

(ii) Practical functioning. It was unlikely that a body of 12 countries of widely differing size and interests could function satisfactorily. This difficulty, however, could be tackled later. The machine should be set up on a 12-Power basis and the exact return of smaller or working groups could, if necessary, be considered later.

7. The body suggested by the Americans would deal with political and possibly general problems. This would, however, lead to development along the lines of Article 2 and seemed to differ widely from the French proposals. The consequences of each proposal with regard to the German question might be considered. If the aim was to bring Germany into the Western world did the French think that the Council of Europe and

membership in a sort of enlarged O.E.E.C. would be enough to satisfy German ambition? If development along the lines of Article 2 took place it should be possible to take over much of the work of the O.E.E.C. and bring Germany into a wider Atlantic community *not* on the military side but for general political and economic purposes.

8. There seemed little point in having an Article 2 in the Atlantic Treaty unless it was used. The British and American proposal did not mean that O.E.E.C. would come to a stop in 1952, nor was it necessary at this stage to link the O.E.E.C. to the Atlantic Pact or the Council of Europe. It was almost impossible to separate general economic problems from those raised by the question of co-ordinating defence. There must be some connexion between the economics of defence and the more general economic questions being dealt with by O.E.E.C. There would obviously be increasing economic discussion in the Atlantic Pact and some sort of fusion would ultimately become necessary. In other words, the British solution favoured some sort of fusion inside the Atlantic Pact, but with some differentiation maintained between the military and non-military side.

9. The French again reiterated that they could never have Germany in any way associated with the Atlantic Pact. Their plan meant that:

(i) O.E.E.C. should continue, but could deal with certain wider issues together with the United States and Canada.

(ii) A body would be set up which would include Germany with the Western nations for economic purposes.

(iii) The Atlantic Pact would deal with problems arising from the impact on national economies of the military organisation, while the economic organisation would be dealt with by a sort of 'O.E.E.C. plus.'

They also pointed out that, while Western policy was to bring Germany into the Western system, if this was done by an 'Atlantic' rather than a 'European' approach, it would greatly widen the cleft between the West and the Soviet Union.

10. The Americans agreed with the British on the general difficulty of separating defence-finance problems from those of general economic import. It might be possible to deal with each in a separate group, but a link body for the two groups would be necessary.

11. The British suggested that the discussion had ranged into the field of long-term problems, and it might be better to confine the present review to what should be done immediately. There was no intention of bringing Germany into the Atlantic Pact, nor any proposal that Germany should be immediately brought into any subsidiary body relating to the Atlantic Treaty. The question was what organs should now grow up inside the Atlantic Pact—in time these organs might make a general link with the European side—and then the question of an association of Powers who had no military link with the Atlantic Pact would be considered. With regard to the French contention that any linking of Germany with the

Atlantic Pact would lead to a bigger cleft with the Russians, all were agreed that Germany should join the Council of Europe. This would lead to almost as big a cleft as if she was associated with some economic body in the Atlantic Pact, and it seemed immaterial how this cleft was brought about. If a really effective Western system was desired some means must be found of associating other countries with the general Atlantic bastion.

12. The Americans summing up said that it appeared that there was general agreement on the need for some immediate development inside the Atlantic organisation. The question of ultimate political and economic integration and the question of Germany were really separate problems with a much longer-term impact. It seemed that some indication could be given to the Working Group that all three Powers were agreed that some new machinery should be set up of a more continuing nature than the Council. All the members of the Treaty could be represented on it in the first place, and its general objectives would be—

(i) co-ordination of the military and economic aspects of defence into a programme of action;

(ii) co-ordination of policy in the political field with respect to common security problems;

(iii) co-ordination of information programmes referring to Pact matters.

13. There was a fourth possible term of reference which might be to consider how action under (i) above would lead to consideration of general economic matters.

14. It was agreed that a small sub-committee, consisting of Sir G. Jebb, Mr. Perkins and M. Alphand, should meet at 3.15 p.m. on 28th April to draft an agreed directive to the Working Group on the common line of progress which was to be advocated. The general line to be indicated would be the setting up of some central body with terms of reference along the lines of the first three American proposals, while the fourth point would have to be further considered. It might be that Ministers would wish to refer this point to the O.E.E.C. It might be possible after the tripartite meeting for some announcement to be made that the United States and Canada had agreed to meet the O.E.E.C. to discuss the future organisation which might be set up as a result of the Atlantic Council meeting. This would show that the North Atlantic Treaty was concerned with other matters besides the purely military aspect.

I (b) (i) *European Political and Economic Integration*

(1) *Relationship with the United States*

15. The leader of the American delegation made a statement on the American attitude. This closely followed the statement he had made at the Third Bipartite Official Meeting (United Kingdom Record Bipartite Official Third Meeting, paragraphs 9–14).[3] The United States approach

---

[3] No. 34

was based on the assumption that, provided the same trend in recovery went on, Europe would be able to continue after 1952 without external aid. But to this end progress must be made towards greater economic equilibrium subject to a reduction of quantitive restrictions and tariff barriers. The United States hoped to see an economic system based on a high level of expanding trade. There was a common need to strengthen the Western world. In order to meet this common need the United States would have to be prepared to make internal adjustments in order to fit in with common plans. The appointment of Mr. Gordon Gray was a step in this direction. It must, however, be borne in mind that Congressional agreement would be necessary for many of the steps proposed. Forward planning would be necessary if international accounts were to be balanced at a high level. Tariff barriers must be reduced in the United States and restrictions removed so as to allow other countries to earn dollars. It was possible that some countries might need further assistance after 1952 and the United States were prepared to face the need for continued active participation in order to secure common objectives. In return it was hoped that European countries would make a similar effort.

16. At any time the general relations of the West *vis-à-vis* the Soviet Union might reach certain crises, which would involve a general revision of Western plans. The United States were prepared to face the possibility of extraordinary economic needs arising out of such crises and, if necessary, were prepared to expand their commitment. They assumed that this was a common attitude with France and Britain.

17. The British welcomed this important and heartening statement and stressed the general wish to co-operate to the fullest possible extent through the European recovery programme and whatever organisation might be set up thereafter. They took note of the continuing United States interest and recognition that special crises might arise that would have to be met. Britain would co-operate in any action that was necessary, bearing in mind the fact that British economy was being nursed back to health and was bearing a load that it was only just able to bear.

18. The French also welcomed the United States statement which typified the generous attitude of the United States to the world problem. They were convinced of the need to organise Europe for the free movement of goods and men. Progress was being made along the lines of reduction of quantitive restrictions and it was hoped that more could be done in the way of lifting customs barriers. In particular, France could not add to the financial burden imposed by defence needs, especially in view of the heavy commitment in Indo-China. They knew that 1952 was the end of direct American aid, but the problem of the dollar gap would continue. It would be necessary to increase European exports to the United States and American investment in Europe.

I (b) (ii) *Migration*

19. The French were particularly interested in migration which they

considered a capital problem. The decongestion of the Western world, in particular of Germany and Italy, was vital. It was not proposed to discuss this item now, but the French thought that Ministers might agree to calling a conference to tackle this question. A list of the participants and the agenda could be drawn up first by a preparatory committee to be set up. There were already technical bodies dealing with the problem but they lacked political directive, and the conference which they proposed should serve to give political impetus to the various technical agencies. The French said they would put up a draft project along these lines for consideration by the Tripartite meeting on 28th April when agreement might be reached on whether their proposal should go before Ministers.[4]

I (c) *Germany*

20. It was generally agreed that the relationship of Germany with the European and Atlantic areas could best be considered after the specific talks on Germany had taken place.

21. The point was made from the British side that it was now time to consider where our policy towards Germany was leading. It was quite possible that this policy would be successful and the three Powers should now face the situation which would arise as a result of this success. All were agreed that the policy was to integrate Germany into the Western system. To assure this there must be first of all some definite Western system into which to integrate Germany. Secondly, we must consider what the situation would be if and when Germany became a full member of the Western club. These thoughts should be in the minds of the experts considering Germany in special committee next week.

II *Advisability of, and Means of, Continuous Reviewing World-Wide Commitments and Capabilities and most Effective Manner of Conducting Future Discussions of this Nature*

22. There were no doubts as to the advisability of close and continued co-operation.

23. The Americans proposed that the machinery might be improved. The three Ministers might agree in principle to meet several times a year. A public statement to this effect would allow them to meet as little or as often as they wished without drawing to their meeting undue public speculation as to the reason for it. In addition there should be the maximum exchange through the normal diplomatic channels. For instance, the Foreign Ministers of each country might have tripartite

[4] The French proposal on migration circulated as TRI/P/6 on 29 April, was further discussed in sub-committee on 4 May (No. 47.*ib.*) and at the fifth tripartite meeting of officials held on 5 May. All delegations were agreed on the vital importance of the question, but both British and American delegates thought a special conference would be premature and that the problem could be dealt with by existing organisations such as the I.L.O. The French dissented from this view. It was agreed that a paper incorporating these views should go before Ministers as MIN/TRI/P/5 of 6 May (not printed): see further No. 90, note 11.

meetings in their own capitals at frequent intervals with the Ambassadors of the two other countries. Such consultations would not, of course, interfere with the special channels already existing, such as the High Commissioners in Germany or the Austrian Deputies. Again, if a central Atlantic organisation got going the three representatives of the three Powers could develop some kind of special relationship and co-ordination. It was also necessary to improve consultation between the three of the United Nations. In reply to a British question the Americans agreed that one of the opportunities when the three Foreign Ministers might invariably meet and hold tripartite discussions was before the General Assembly of the United Nations. Similarly, if anything came of Mr. Lie's proposal for a special Security Council meeting the three Ministers should meet and consult beforehand.

24. It was generally agreed that a development on these lines would be welcomed and a recommendation might be made to the three Ministers to indicate their agreement to such plans at the end of their meeting.

25. It was agreed that there should be a further tripartite plenary meeting at 4 p.m. on 28th April, when the Agenda should be Item 6 and points arising out of Item 8 of the Tripartite Agenda (United Kingdom Paper No. D.5).[1]

CALENDAR TO NO. 40

i *19 Apr.–4 May 1950   Views of U.S. and Denmark on Germany and Atlantic Pact*
(*a*) Information from Mr. T. Achilles (State Dept.) of U.S. thinking on Germany and Atlantic Pact, reported in letters from Sir F. Hoyer-Millar (19 Apr.) and Washington Chancery (28 Apr.) State Department is convinced of urgency of bringing Germany closer to West, but is divided on whether this should be through expansion of N.A.T. machinery or greater use of Council of Europe. By 28 Apr., State Dept. doubts that German membership of O.E.E.C. or Council of Europe will be adequate, and is considering proposals to increase authority of Federal Govt. and to tie F.R.G. to Atlantic Pact, as reported by James Reston in *New York Times* on 26 April.
(*b*) *Denmark*: concern of Mr. G. Rasmussen, Danish Foreign Minister, for inclusion of Western Germany in Atlantic Pact, reported in letter from Mr. A.W.G. Randall, H.M. Ambassador at Copenhagen, to Mr. Harrison of 27 Apr. Mr. Rasmussen appreciates French objections but considers that a controlled measure of German re-armament is in interests of French defence as well as that of Belgium, Netherlands and Denmark.
(*c*) *Foreign Office* considers letters at (*a-b*) above on 4 May. Sir I. Kirkpatrick minutes on 6 May that his impression is that U.S. delegation in London are opposed to idea of German rearmament at present [ZP 2/64; WU 1071/74,77,98].

No. 41

Brief for the U.K. Delegation

No. 18 [ZP 2/88]

Top secret   FOREIGN OFFICE, *27 April 1950*

The general attitude to be adopted towards the French as regards our talks with the Americans on major policy issues[1]

The general line to be adopted in our talks with American officials on matters affecting relations between the United States and United Kingdom have been set forth in Mr. Wright's draft brief (United Kingdom Brief No. 4)[2]. The present paper is intended to analyse French feelings on such matters and to suggest a line which might be taken up with them in any bilateral discussions we may have with their officials if they should desire to raise the major issues involved.

2. It is clear that the French are now thinking more and more in terms of a development of the Atlantic Pact machinery. Unfortunately, the desired enthusiasm and determination to play a due part in the struggle against World Communism have not been created, so far as France as a whole is concerned, either by the signature of the Atlantic Pact or by the establishment of the Council of Europe. The French Communist Party itself may have lost some influence during the last year or so, but it still remains very strong, while nothing has alleviated the profound defeatism which seems to animate most sections of the French bourgeoisie.[3] Seeking desperately for some solution, therefore, which will enjoy the support of the majority of the French people, the minority M.R.P. Government have

---

[1] This brief was drafted by Sir G. Jebb and circulated with the covering note: 'The Secretary of State has agreed that this paper may be used as a guide during the official talks. He is anxious, however, that the subject should be handled with extreme care and the paper, the circulation of which is very limited, should not be considered at this stage as in any way representing Ministerial Policy. In particular, great caution must be exercised in handling any proposals for a surrender of sovereignty which might be unacceptable to the Commonwealth.' This note is based on Mr. Bevin's brief manuscript comments on the draft submitted by Sir W. Strang on 22 April after discussion with Sir G. Jebb, Sir I. Kirkpatrick, Sir R. Makins and Mr. Wright, and on a fuller minute by Mr. Barclay of 24 April in which Mr. Bevin's views were elaborated: 'He agrees that this paper can be accepted as a guide, but he considers that we must proceed with great care and he would like to be kept in constant touch with developments. He would also like to have a talk with Sir. W. Strang on this subject in the near future. The Secretary of State thinks that we must be extremely cautious about any surrender of sovereignty in fields which are not very clearly defined. Otherwise he thinks that there will be trouble with members of the Commonwealth. He thinks that the Commonwealth countries would be prepared to accept arrangements under which there was some surrender of sovereignty in limited fields, such as transport or even customs, but if the position was left vague the Commonwealth countries might find themselves forced into a position of closer association with Western Europe than they would wish.'

[2] No. 24.

[3] For a major Foreign Office review on France in June 1950, see Volume I, No. 136.i.

clearly come to the conclusion that they must point to the possibility of some real organisation of the entire Western world. This thesis was eloquently canvassed in an article in *Le Monde* of about a month ago, and it has now found expression in a speech by M. Bidault at Lyons.[4] It is true that this particular speech now seems to have been repudiated by the Quai d'Orsay, but M. Bidault is after all the Prime Minister, and in any case has been known to fly kites of this description before. The basic idea behind a project which, official or not, undoubtedly commands support in France, is briefly as follows:

(*a*) the Council of Europe cannot fulfil the original hopes of its French sponsors owing to the reluctance of the United Kingdom to become involved in any federal plan, thereby leaving France at the mercy of Germany if France, for her part, came into such a federation; and

(*b*) up to now at any rate, the Atlantic Pact machinery has proved too slow, while the relations between the military programme and the economic problems now dealt with in O.E.E.C., have not been fully appreciated. Thus

(*c*) the real power should be attributed to a machine to be established under the Atlantic Pact and notably to some 3 (or 4) Power 'Standing Group' which might be able to impose its strategic and economic will on the weaker brethren with a resulting economy of effort and wider efficiency. Needless to say, any suggestion that this no doubt essential function should be performed by some Anglo-American or Anglo-American-Canadian group would be strongly resisted by all Frenchmen.

3. The official French plan[4] (of which we have now had an advance indication from the Quai d'Orsay) does not go as far as M. Bidault's speech, but is far-reaching enough. It consists essentially in appointing a Secretary-General to the Atlantic Pact Organisation of the 'Superman' type who would be 'advised' by the diplomatic representatives of the Atlantic Pact nations in the capital concerned. It seems that very considerable powers should be attributed to such a Secretary-General and the French clearly hope, by this means, to establish a machine which, to some extent at any rate, might work independently of Governments.

4. A common feature of any French plan in this connexion, therefore, is likely to be a suggestion that wide powers should be conferred on some body to be established under the Atlantic Pact which would concern itself with both military and economic matters. The general criticism of this conception is, of course, that—like many French ideas—it is both too logical, too far-reaching and inopportune. The French are no doubt right in thinking that some kind of machinery which would coordinate military and economic effort is a desirable thing to aim at, but they are almost certainly wrong in thinking that such a body could be constituted now, or even within a year or two.

[4] See No. 24, note 5.

5. On the other hand, the last thing we want to do is to discourage the French in their new-found enthusiasm for the Atlantic Pact and indeed our own major brief[5] suggests that our chief objective should, in fact, be to establish certain machinery under the Atlantic Pact which would deal with political and economic matters. Our views, moreover, would of course be profoundly affected by whatever the Americans have got to say under this heading. Moreover, it may be that only by the development of some such machinery can the French—and indeed other Continental Governments—be placed in the position which they probably really wish to be placed in, namely of being forced to reform their military machine, collect more taxes, and generally place themselves from the strategic and economic point of view, in a more healthy position. After all we are constantly told that unless the French are in a position to fight effectively in the event of war, our own position is practically untenable, and it may well be argued, therefore, that we should, in principle, be prepared to make concessions provided that these would really result in an early reform of the French system, even if this might mean taking certain risks as regards the acceptance of what may be unpalatable advice regarding our own system as well. Essentially what we want to do, therefore, is to encourage a sense of confidence in the French.

6. The real trouble of course is fundamental and can only be solved by time and by an increased sense of security following on the reconstitution of the French army with American aid. At the moment indeed, the real core of the anti-Communist coalition consists (if we ignore the Scandinavian States) of the metropolitan territories of the United States and Canada, together with Great Britain. In all these countries Communism is a negligible quantity; the existing régime is both respected and popular; and in none of them is there the slightest apprehension that the country would be likely to be over-run by the Russians in a few days or weeks after the outbreak of a war. The Continental countries of Western Europe are still in a very different position from this. Nearly all were over-run during the last war and the profound lack of confidence which this produced is still reflected in their policies, and notably in the policy of France. It must be recognised, therefore, from the start that the real direction of the Atlantic Pact effort must lie in Anglo-American-Canadian cooperation and, if possible, in some unofficial 'inner group' whose duty it might be to examine both economic and strategical necessities.

7. However, if this should be the line indicated by the logic of events, it is essential that there should be some facade perhaps by way of an 'inner group' with which France and, if possible, Italy should be associated, and that the existence of any unofficial Anglo-Canadian-American Consultative Group should be kept entirely from the Latins—to say nothing of the journalists! Though it would be difficult, it might well not be impossible, to achieve all this *desiderata* in the long run by constructing some new

[5] See No. 16.i and No. 30.

153

Atlantic Pact machinery. For the time being, however, such machinery should be limited to political and economic matters.

8. The general objective behind such specific proposals as these would be the constitution, over a period of years, of a machine established under the Atlantic Pact, which would act as an 'umbrella' for three main groupings—the United States and the dollar area, the United Kingdom with the British Commonwealth and the sterling area and the Council of Europe. The development of the 'umbrella' is, in fact, probably the only means whereby the French could agree to further European 'integration' without the full participation of the United Kingdom, since only the fact that they would be represented in some central coordinating Atlantic machinery would, in such circumstances, quiet their apprehensions of being dominated by Germany. Equally, only by the establishment of such central machinery could we continue our Tripartite talks with the Americans and Canadians on common economic problems without incurring the wrath and suspicions of the French and the other Continentals.

9. The conclusions as to our general attitude to be adopted towards the French on these sort of problems would, therefore, seem to be as follows:

(1) Subject to what the Americans may have to say, we should not accept anything so far-reaching as M. Bidault's scheme, or even as the scheme which was likely to be put forward officially by the French Foreign Office.

(2) We should, however, on no account damp down French enthusiasm and should indicate that we, as well as they, are absolutely in favour of developing some machinery under the Atlantic Pact.

(3) Subject again to American thinking, we should hold out to the French the *ultimate* prospect of developing such machinery so as to coordinate the activities—political, economic and military—of the three main constituent pillars of the system, namely the United States, the United Kingdom and British Commonwealth and Western Europe.

(4) In holding out this prospect, however, we should not, at present at any rate, do anything which would expose us to any attack on the part of the French or anybody else, that we are proposing to abandon the Council of Europe, or, at this stage, to determine the future of the O.E.E.C., after 1952.

No. 42

Memorandum by the Chancellor of the Exchequer[1]
E.P.C. (50) 44 [CAB 134/225]

Top secret   TREASURY CHAMBERS, *27 April 1950*

Fundamental discussions with the United States

1. Evidence is accumulating that the United States Administration is engaged in a stock-taking of its basic financial and economic policy. There have been references in the American Press to a high level Committee established for this purpose and to consultations with outside advisers. One or two hints have been dropped to our own representatives in Washington whose recent reports suggest that the time is fast approaching when we should be ready once more to discuss 'fundamentals' with the United States. I share this view. Experience shows the wisdom of discussion with the United States while their minds are still flexible and while they are still searching for conclusions. Moreover,

(*a*) it was always the intention in the September Tripartite discussions that there should be continuing examination of fundamental financial and economic policy; through nobody's fault, the Tripartite discussions since September have been occupied mainly with *ad hoc* difficulties; e.g. on oil.

(*b*) we have in fact reached a stage in our own affairs (e.g. improvement in our dollar position and in our overall balance of payments) when it is most desirable to engage in stocktaking with the United States on future policy; and

(*c*) whether we like it or not, this kind of fundamental discussion will arise once we open conversations on such far-reaching topics as sterling balances and economic development in South East Asia.

(*d*) The disagreements which we have had and are having with E.C.A. on O.E.E.C. matters are in part due to fundamental differences which can only be resolved through frank talks at the highest level.

(*e*) I have received a letter from Mr. Snyder (reproduced at Annex B [i] to this paper) asking 'for a full statement of the trade and payments policies which your Government expects to pursue in the coming period.' Certainly we should not miss any opportunity for fundamental discussion with the United States. Our future is so closely linked with theirs that we have everything to gain from such discussions.

2. It is essential to us that we should be able to discuss United States internal policy (particularly full employment and all the various implications of United States depressions) and we should not get very far if we refused to discuss our own internal policy. It is now becoming increasingly

---

[1] Cf. No.2 and note 10 *ibid.*, for the origins of the present paper.

appreciated that one cannot separate internal financial policy from external financial policy. We should welcome the opportunity to explain our internal policy and to clarify the part which it must play in the handling of our external problems. It would of course be essential to maintain

(a) Budget secrecy in the narrower sense, and
(b) the principle that there is to be no *interference*[2] with each others decisions on internal policy.

3. Apart from internal policy, we should want to discuss in the next round of conversations:

(i) the righting of the United States balance of payments;
(ii) sterling balances and the strengthening of the United Kingdom capital position;
(iii) South East Asia development, including its effect on our Colonies in that area;
(iv) the related questions of non-discrimination and convertibility;
(v) the maintenance of sterling as an 'international' currency.

A separate memorandum (E.P.C.(50)40)[3] has been circulated on (ii) and (iii), and conversations in Washington have already begun. Annex A [i] to this paper sets out in summarised form certain basic considerations of external financial policy. To some extent these are a restatement or an extension of policy decisions already taken; if they are generally agreed they can contribute to the briefs which will need to be prepared for our representatives in the forthcoming discussions.

4. If discussions between Ministers are to be successful, it is essential that there should be preparation of the ground by officials in Washington. The main forum for exchanges of views between ourselves and the United States on such matters ought to be found for the time being within the arrangements for continuing tripartite consultation, i.e. ought, in the circumstances, to include Canada as well as the United States and the United Kingdom. It would be useful if there could be some suitably arranged visits by senior officials to Washington in order that the United Kingdom point of view may be presented not only in the tripartite talks there but also in other appropriate quarters, e.g. to the United States Treasury, E.C.A., Council of Economic Advisers, Federal Reserve Board and Bank, etc. *Special arrangements will be required to keep in touch with the rest of the Commonwealth.*[2]

5. The tentative programme might be

(a) Immediate instructions to Sir Leslie Rowan and other officials to exchange views with American and Canadian representatives in Washington in a preliminary and informal manner;
(b) On the occasion of Mr. Acheson's forthcoming visit to London, a

---

[2] Italics denote underlining in original.　　　　　　　　　　　　[3] No. 9.i.

general review of the plan of campaign and of the issues requiring study;

(c) Tripartite meetings at the Ministerial level later in the year;

(d) If, as already proposed in (E.P.C.(50)40), a meeting of Commonwealth Finance Ministers is held this summer that would provide the opportunity for full discussion and consultation within the Commonwealth.

6. A copy of the reply that I should propose to send to Mr. Snyder's letter is contained in Annex C.[4]

R.S.C.

CALENDARS TO NO. 42

i *Annex A:* summary of fundamentals of external financial policy.
Annex B: letter from Mr. Snyder to Sir S. Cripps of 11 April with reply of 17 May suggesting Anglo-American informal talks in Washington on fundamentals as supplement to continuing A.B.C. talks [CAB 134/225; T 232/262].

ii *27 Apr. 1950 Bipartite sub-committee No. 4* record of discussion following on from that in sub-committee No. 1 (No.34.i.) on Anglo-American economic strategy and problems: U.K. doubt stability of U.S. economy while U.S. doubt sincerity of U.K. motives. U.K. economy 'healthier than it had been for some time.' However inflation in next 2 years likely to outstrip production [ZP 2/92].

[4] Not printed: see Calendar i for the revised reply of 17 May.

No. 43

Memorandum for the Permanent Under-Secretary's Committee

P.U.S.C. (*50*) *79 Final 2nd Revise* [ZP 3/5]

Top secret   FOREIGN OFFICE, *27 April 1950*[1]

British Overseas Obligations

The object of this paper is to consider the tasks to which the United Kingdom is now committed overseas and to assess their importance in the light of the existing economic and military factors affecting the relations of the United Kingdom with foreign powers, other members of the

[1] Date of circulation. The general lines of this paper were approved by Mr. Bevin on 9 March and modified in the light of Treasury views (see No. 36, note 1). Following discussion of the final draft on 21 April (see No. 35, note 2) the present text was submitted on 22 April to Mr. Bevin, who approved it for a limited Ministerial circulation. Extensive underlining and critical comments in the margin by Sir S. Cripps are not here noted from the text of his advance copy filed on T 232/167. For his views on this paper, see No. 36, notes 2 and 3.

Commonwealth and its own colonial territories. These relations have therefore been surveyed regionally; the survey, although an integral part of the paper, has been attached as Annex I [i] in order not to break the thread of the main argument. The broad conclusions to be drawn from this regional survey are summarised in paragraphs 22–23 of the main paper.

2. The word 'obligation', unless otherwise specifically defined, has been used throughout this paper to denote any British undertaking, which requires the expenditure by His Majesty's Government either of money or of military or administrative effort outside the United Kingdom, irrespective of whether the material result of such expenditure is a net profit or loss to the country.

3. Where reference is made in this paper to 'the West' or 'the Western world', these phrases are intended to mean those countries which are associated with the United Kingdom and the United States of America in the world-wide struggle against Stalinist communism.

Basic Factors

4. United Kingdom foreign policy is determined by certain fundamental factors.

(a) The United Kingdom has world responsibilities inherited from four hundred years as an Imperial Power.
(b) The United Kingdom is not a self-sufficient economic unit.
(c) No world security system exists, and the United Kingdom, with the rest of the non-Communist world, is faced with an external threat.

5. Of these factors (a) and (b) are long-standing and likely to remain so; (c) reflects the present political situation in the world and although, it is hoped, it will not be a permanent factor, it is at present superimposed on (a) and (b) and cannot be disregarded.

Main objectives of United Kingdom Foreign Policy

6. Taking these factors into account, the United Kingdom is at present pursuing the following major objectives:

(a) To maintain the United Kingdom's position as a world power while keeping the highest possible general standard of living in the United Kingdom.
(b) To maintain the Commonwealth structure.
(c) To maintain a special relationship with the United States of America.
(d) To consolidate the whole 'Western' democratic system.
(e) To resist Soviet Communism.
(f) To ensure that the Middle East and Asia are stable, prosperous and friendly.

Obligations resulting from these objectives

7. These objectives involve for the United Kingdom a number of major

requirements and obligations, to each of which it must devote a substantial part of its total resources.

(a) Maintenance of a relatively high rate of imports and of consumption and capital investment at home while balancing foreign payments, and closing the dollar gap.

(b) Defence of the United Kingdom.

(c) Maintenance, development and defence of the British Colonies.

(d) A major contribution to the maintenance of sea and air communication across the world in peace and war.

(e) Participation in the occupation of Germany, Austria and Trieste in peace, and in the 'defence of the West' in war.

(f) Economic and military backing for the Middle East.

(g) Economic assistance for countries in Asia (especially the Commonwealth countries in South Asia) and military backing in South-West Asia and Hong Kong.

Consequent strain on the United Kingdom

8. The effort to meet all these requirements is putting a very heavy strain on the United Kingdom's present resources. Maintenance of its world position absorbs a much higher proportion both of the national income and of Government expenditure than it did between the wars. (Annex III [i] to this paper contains a summary of United Kingdom Defence and Foreign Imperial expenditure in 1929–30, 1938–9, 1948–9 and 1949–50). Owing mainly to the state of undeclared war with the U.S.S.R. the United Kingdom is obliged to support larger forces, which must be equipped with far more costly armaments. The Government is now responsible for much expenditure (e.g. development of economic resources) previously left to private individuals, and moreover a wider realisation of the United Kingdom's obligations to its colonies, and of the danger of neglecting them, has led it to spend more on promoting their welfare. All this is a heavy load for a country struggling to balance its foreign payments and to meet the special problem of the dollar gap. It is aggravated by the accumulation of war-time debt represented by the 'sterling balances' which can now be used to buy exports from the United Kingdom. Among the largest and most insistent holders of the balances are countries in key positions in the struggle with Soviet Communism – India, Egypt and Pakistan – so that there are very strong political and strategic grounds for meeting their demands for releases. These unrequited exports however absorb important resources which might be used for consumption or investment at home, or for paying for imports from elsewhere, particularly dollar imports. (A summary of the main features of the present position affecting the sterling balances is at Annex II [i]). The result is to increase inflation and the difficulty of closing the dollar gap and thus generally to weaken the United Kingdom's economic reserves.

9. The resultant strain can be seen most clearly in the problem of

defence expenditure. Even with the defence expenditure now approved the position is far from satisfactory. To meet present requirements a large proportion of the total forces available must be kept in exposed positions in Germany, Austria, Trieste, Malaya and Hong Kong, so that there are now practically no reserves against any intensification of Russian pressure at any point. The Army must sacrifice re-equipment if it is to be ready to meet all the current calls upon it, and while the Navy and R.A.F. are more fortunate in this respect, all three Services can only make adequate preparations for war in the long term if they receive more money in future years. The United Kingdom's initial contribution to the defence of the West will thus in any case be smaller than is militarily and politically desirable; its forces available for the defence of the Middle East will scarcely be adequate; and it can make no allowance at all for the defence of South and South-East Asia and the Far East in war.

10. Proposals have been made to reduce the defence budget on purely financial grounds to a figure compatible with other existing rates of Government expenditure. The Chiefs of Staff consider that any such reduction, although comparatively small in terms of the total budget, would have most serious consequences. It would involve the withdrawal in peace of British forces from the western hemisphere, South-East Asia and the Far East and the abandonment of the Indian Ocean area, and would make it impossible for the United Kingdom to contribute in war to the defence of both the Middle East and Western Europe.

11. If this is so, a comparatively small reduction in the defence budget would mean a severe contraction of influence. A limited contraction of obligations, although it might entail a considerable loss of influence, would probably not of itself lead to any appreciable reduction in defence costs. The budget cannot in any case be apportioned between regions. Decisions on the size of military expenditure in the immediate future will have implications on the whole structure of the United Kingdom's forces over the next few years. Their ability to give backing to its policy, and hence to its world economic and political positions, is at stake.

The problem

12. The essence of a sound foreign policy is to ensure that a country's strength is equal to its obligations. If this is not the case, then either the obligations must be reduced to the level at which resources are available to maintain them, or a greater share of the country's resources must be devoted to their support. It is clear that the claims on the economic resources of the United Kingdom resulting from the sum of the policies, internal and external, at present being pursued by His Majesty's Government impose a strain on the United Kingdom economy which is heavier than it can bear and that these claims must be diminished if the country is to remain stable and healthy in the future. The problem, as far as the external obligations of the country are concerned, is to determine how far, if at all, these can be reduced or transferred to other shoulders

without impairing the world position of the United Kingdom and sacrificing the vital advantages which flow from it.

Possible solutions
(a) *General Withdrawal*

13. One suggestion sometimes advanced is that the United Kingdom should withdraw from as many onerous overseas obligations as possible. Advocates of this course maintain that the United Kingdom cannot, in its present economic position, support the status of a World Power, with obligations not only to hold many exposed positions of the present state of undeclared war but also to make heavy unrequited payments in order to sustain its political influence. They argue that neither political prestige nor military influence is essential to the maintenance of satisfactory trade relations with areas producing essential supplies. They say, in effect, that the sterling area should continue to exist, even if the British Commonwealth and Empire ceased to be, and that the reduction of defence expenditure made possible by the abandonment of Britain's imperial and world position would not impair but would rather actually improve the standard of living in the United Kingdom.

14. These arguments neglect important factors. They rest essentially on the assumption that this country can support its population and balance its payments by commercial means alone, unsupported by political prestige or influence. Although the main factor in the United Kingdom's ability to procure the imports it needs must remain its ability to produce and export efficiently, nevertheless it is undeniable that its trade relations with other nations are much assisted by the goodwill established over many years as the world's leading mercantile power and by the knowledge that the United Kingdom can if necessary call on the resources of world-wide possessions to fulfil its obligations. The United Kingdom's economic and political position must be regarded as a whole in terms of world confidence and credit. Broadly speaking economic relations become progressively more difficult through the political range from colonies, other members of the Commonwealth, friendly foreign countries, and less friendly countries like Argentina, to countries in the Soviet orbit.

15. The sterling area in particular could never have come into being in its present form if its members had not been long accustomed to regard London as their natural source of credit and reserves and if the United Kingdom had not been indisputably the leading political and military power within the association. Now that New York has in many respects succeeded to London's old financial position, it can hardly be doubted that if the United Kingdom were to abdicate as a World Power the continued existence of a sterling area based on London would be impossible. If the sterling area fell apart in this way, those of its members which now earn foreign exchange for the United Kingdom, would become either its customers or its competitors. The effect of such a development would be cumulative. The realisation that the United Kingdom no longer enjoyed

the advantages conferred on it by the existence of the sterling area would gravely undermine its credit and would therefore still further reduce its overseas earnings, particularly from invisible exports. The outcome would inevitably be a heavy fall in the standard of living.

16. This situation is very much aggravated by present relations with the Soviet Union. The Russians would be only too ready to fill any vacuum created by a British withdrawal. It is obvious that when an area falls into Communist hands, its economic and trading value to the Western world becomes greatly reduced, while Western capital assets are liquidated with little or no compensation. A withdrawal such as that from India may cause relatively little loss of economic assets. But where there is a vacuum left for Communism to fill, little or nothing can be salvaged.

17. Finally a general withdrawal from the status of a World Power would greatly reduce the support which the United Kingdom received from its membership of the Commonwealth, from its special relationship with the United States and from its Western European and other alliances, all of which form essential parts of its present world position. It would certainly lead to a radical change of the whole Commonwealth relationship. It would also greatly affect the present close-Anglo-American partnership, which rests on the assumption in American minds that the United Kingdom is the principal partner and ally on whom the United States can rely. If the United States lost faith in the United Kingdom's ability and will to maintain its world position, as they would if it carried out a general withdrawal from its overseas obligations, the partnership might well be broken, with grave effects, especially on the priority accorded to the United Kingdom in the field of economic help. Similarly the United Kingdom's influence on its European partners and other allies and their willingness to continue as such depend largely upon its status as a World Power and upon their belief that it is ready and willing to support them.

18. The picture of splendid isolation on a peaceful and prosperous island is therefore illusory. The grim reality would be a progressive descent into weakness and a severe fall in the standard of living which it would be impossible to arrest even by the most ingenious economic expedients.

(b) No withdrawal

19. To attempt to maintain all its existing obligations would no doubt be less dangerous for the United Kingdom than a general withdrawal, but it has already been seen that there are objections to this course also. While it would avoid the loss of economic advantages involved in a general withdrawal, it could only be achieved with safety if other claims on the United Kingdom economy were diminished by a voluntary reduction in the standard of living. Any such voluntary reduction would no doubt be less than the forced reduction which would follow a general withdrawal. But it could not be negligible if it was to solve the problem successfully and to provide sufficient reserves of economic and military strength. Without

a general review of all the claims upon the United Kingdom resources, no estimate can be made of the extent to which the standard of living would have to be reduced to give the necessary reserves of strength. Moreover it must be remembered that if the standard of living is reduced too far, this would in turn, by depressing morale and reducing production, diminish the country's ability to fulfil its obligations. Some reduction in the standard of living may be inevitable but it is clearly desirable to limit it as far as possible.

(c) Partial Shedding of obligations

20. It is, therefore, desirable to examine the extent to which the present strain on the United Kingdom could be relieved by a partial shedding of obligations without compromising the basic objectives of the United Kingdom and bringing about a general decline in our world position.

Regional factors

21. The survey of British responsibilities in various parts of the world contained in Annex I suggests the following general conclusions:

(a) There is a wide degree of interdependence between the United Kingdom's various obligations. The abandonment of any one obligation may start a crumbling process which may destroy the whole fabric, and this is even more likely in present than in normal times. Further, the effects of abandoning any vital position in the East-West struggle may be cumulative and might actually in the long run force the United Kingdom to increase its defence expenditure, rather than to reduce it.

(b) It is therefore impossible for the United Kingdom to withdraw safely from any major obligation if it leaves a vacuum. It must ensure that any major obligations which it gives up are taken over by its friends. Moreover, reduction of direct British responsibilities should be as gradual and undramatic as possible.

(c) The special problem of the dollar deficit of the sterling area means that a given responsibility must often be assessed largely in terms of its dollar earning or dollar saving aspect, rather than on grounds of its economic advantage as a whole. At the same time, most British commitments are in parts of the sterling area. Assessment of the dollar profit or loss must be regarded in the wider setting of the sterling area, the maintenance of which brings substantial benefits to the United Kingdom.

(d) Detailed examination of the United Kingdom's regional obligations suggests that some are more important to it than others, and that their relative importance may vary as between war and peace and indeed at different periods in time of peace. Since the United Kingdom has inadequate reserves, it is essential to establish what is the true relative importance of its various responsibilities.

22. In the light of the above, the consequence for the United Kingdom of its main obligations may be summarised as follows:

(*a*) Some British colonies are of great economic value, but others are a considerable liability. But if the United Kingdom withdrew from any of them its prestige in friendly and hostile eyes alike would suffer, with serious results for its world position, and moreover it would be abandoning its responsibility for the welfare of its colonial peoples.

(*b*) Western Europe is, within the Atlantic Pact, the nucleus of any Western system of defence. The Chiefs of Staff have emphasised its very great importance for the air defence of the United Kingdom in war. They consider that to hold the enemy east of the Rhine is vital to the defence of the United Kingdom, which is the first 'pillar' of British strategy, and that the defence of the United Kingdom and of Western Europe must therefore be considered together. In order to strengthen French morale and will to resist, and on the recommendation of the Chiefs of Staff, His Majesty's Government have given an undertaking to reinforce the British Army of the Rhine with a Corps of two divisions in the event of war with Russia. These would however be territorial divisions and the undertaking to send them does not involve any addition to the size of the Army. The obligations which Western Europe's importance in war forces the United Kingdom to assume in peace-time are therefore still limited.

(*c*) The Chiefs of Staff consider that the Middle East is crucially important to Allied strategy and that it must be held if humanly possible, although the allocation of resources to it must not be allowed to compromise our ability to sustain the first 'pillar' of our strategy.[2] The strategic value of the Middle East in war depends on its importance as a base for a strategic air offensive, on its oil reserves, whose importance is likely to increase as time passes, on its position as a barrier for the defence of Africa and on the need to hold it if the United Kingdom position in South and South-East Asia is to be maintained. In peace, too, the Middle East is of great value, both as a centre of firmly established British influence and also as a source of oil, which is an essential dollar-saver and a potential dollar-earner. The maintenance of Western influence generally in the Middle East is as important in the present world-wide struggle against Communist expansion as it would be in war.

[2] This view was embodied in a paper by the Chiefs of Staff on defence policy and global strategy considered by the C.O.S. committee on 11 May as representing 'a most important change in the emphasis to be placed on the relative importance of Western Europe and the Middle East. . . . If we lost the Middle East we would still survive: if we lost Western Europe, we might well be defeated . . . *The Minister of Defence* said that a logical deducation from the conclusion that the defence of Western Europe should have first priority was that everything possible should be done to build up the Western Union Defence Organisation' (C.O.S. (50) 74th meeting on DEFE 4/31: see further Volume III).

(*d*) South-East Asia is very important in peace, as a dollar-earner and as a sterling source of essential raw materials. These raw materials are however not essential in war. Moreover the United Kingdom alone could not now defend South-East Asia in war. Its loss before a war starts would be a grave disaster.

(*e*) South Asia, though at present politically disturbed, is of great potential importance in resistance to Communism throughout Asia as a whole, and in particular is the main bastion of defence against Communist penetration westwards into the Middle East. The three Asian members of the Commonwealth have a special relationship with the United Kingdom which should not be weakened if this bastion is to be maintained. Strategically it is important to us that South Asia should not be occupied by our enemy in war, but on the other hand its value to us in war would not be sufficient to justify our assuming additional and specific military obligations towards it. If friendly relations were established between India and Pakistan, it is possible that they might be able and willing to furnish some assistance to the United Kingdom in war if she wished to call upon them. Economically South Asia contains important United Kingdom investments, but at present it represents a heavy drain on the United Kingdom because of the sterling balances.

(*f*) Africa is economically important to the West in peace and, particularly if South-East Asia were lost, in war; but the Western position in Africa depends largely on the continuation of Western (at present British) influence in the Middle East.

23. It appears from the above survey that, of the main areas containing major United Kingdom interests, the three in which United Kingdom and indeed all Western influence is at present particularly vulnerable, should be put in the following order of importance to the United Kingdom:

The Middle East
South-East Asia
South Asia

This is the order of importance to the United Kingdom assessed with reference to British interests only. But the British stake in these regions means, in the present international situation, that Western prestige, including that of the United States of America and the Commonwealth, is deeply involved. From the point of view of the Western world as a whole, it is harder to make a distinction between these three regions. The intrusion of Soviet control into any one of these would be a grave disaster. But in view of the desirability of shedding some obligations, it is necessary to examine what steps can be taken to this end.

Possible Relief
(*a*) *Financial Relief*

24. South Asia is not an area in which the United Kingdom now has any heavy military obligations in peace. The main obligation to this area arises

from unrequited exports in the shape of sterling balances. If the drain in this direction could be reduced without endangering any vital interest, it should be possible to build up some reserves of economic strength without any fall in the United Kingdom's standard of living.

25. Any proposal to reduce or postpone releases to India or Pakistan (by a funding operation or other means) must however be handled with the greatest care. Otherwise they might suspect that it is the first step in a unilateral repudiation of liabilities and the delicate fabric of friendly confidence which has been so laboriously built up might be irremediably destroyed. The reaction might be violent, leading to irretrievable steps such as leaving the Commonwealth and the sterling area, or seeking to reinsure with Russia, or an attempt to rely wholly on their own devices and resources which, at the present state of their development, are inadequate to prevent chaos. The repercussions of such steps throughout Asia might be disastrous. It is therefore essential that the leaders of India and Pakistan should be brought to accept a course of action agreeable to debtor and creditors alike and should be persuaded that action to reduce the strain of sterling releases is not a part of a general withdrawal of Western support.

26. Similarly, action to lighten the burden of debt to Egypt cannot be considered in isolation from the wider question of defence arrangements in the Middle East. While these arrangements must not on any account be jeopardised, it may nevertheless be possible to reach some satisfactory agreement on the problem of Egypt's sterling balance. An essential feature may however have to be an assurance of increased Western support in other forms.

27. These measures, if successful, would afford some financial relief. Some slight additional relief might be derived from an extension of American investment in the Colonies, although the political and moral grounds for maintaining United Kingdom expenditure on welfare and development projects in the colonies are too strong for any large reduction to be possible here.

28. Two points arise on these proposals. The extent of the sterling balances is shown in the statement attached at Annex II [i] to this paper. The total obligations of the United Kingdom in this regard amount to some £3,000 million, of which the three most urgent cases, India, Pakistan and Egypt, amount to just over £1,000 million. The problem of sterling balances, therefore, though large, is not overwhelming. A solution of it, coupled with other reductions in unrequited exports, might allow an increase in defence expenditure, which could perhaps be devoted to necessary tasks, such as modernisation of equipment or more research and development; but they do not of themselves make possible the withdrawal, into a much needed reserve, of forces already deployed to fulfil existing obligations. Secondly, although the United Kingdom may shed obligations in this way, the Western world as a whole, while Soviet hostility lasts, cannot do so. All these proposals, therefore, involve the

assumption of new obligations by friendly powers.

29. It is therefore still necessary to look for some way of lightening the United Kingdom's direct defence burdens and to consider how other countries may be expected to help.

(b) Relief of defence burdens

30. The only formal defence obligation of the United Kingdom in South Asia is the defence agreement with Ceylon.[3] Under this agreement both parties are committed to give each other such military assistance as it may be in their mutual interest to provide; Ceylon has agreed to provide the United Kingdom with such naval and air base facilities as it needs and the United Kingdom has agreed to help in the training and development of the Ceylonese forces. British troops are shortly to be withdrawn from the Island, except for Signal detachments. In South-East Asia, existing obligations in Malaya and Hong Kong arise from the need to resist the extension of Soviet power into focal points of Asia; if a general war broke out, it is out of the question that any attempt could be made by the Western Powers to hold the region as a whole. All troops not needed for the defence of essential bases would have to be withdrawn to other more vital areas, principally the Middle East. Some troops must be kept in readiness in the Middle East even in peace but reinforcements will be needed in war; at present it is doubtful whether the forces upon which the area can rely at the start of a war will be adequate to stop a Russian advance to the Suez Canal. It is in the Middle East then, and in the lanes of sea communications surrounding it, that assistance will be most important and to which first priority should be given.

31. It is admittedly unlikely that other friendly powers would be willing to send troops to the Middle East in peace, even if the countries of the area were prepared to receive them. The most that can be expected at present is that they should undertake to send forces of a stated size to the area immediately on the outbreak of war and meanwhile take their part in planning the allied strategy there. This promise of co-operation might perhaps in due course be embodied in a wider and more formal regional defence agreement, including both the countries of the region and their supporters from outside.

32. Co-operation even to this extent would strengthen the hand of the United Kingdom in making dispositions against the risk of war. It would make possible a review of the policy for reinforcing the two major theatres of operations—Western Europe and the Middle East—on the outbreak of war. In peace in the immediate future little more can be expected than some thinning out of garrisons at exposed points—Hong Kong, Malaya, Germany, Austria and Trieste.

33. Some economies might be achieved if arrangements could be made

[3] This agreement of 11 November 1947 is printed in *United Nations Treaty Series*, vol. 86, pp. 25–9.

for integrating research and development projects to some extent with those of the United States.

34. It would not follow however that any major reduction in defence expenditure could safely be made. Any relief obtained through thinning down garrisons or by integrating defence research projects would need to be used for assembling reserves against any intensification of Soviet pressure and for making better preparations for war.

(c) *Countries which may afford relief*
(i) *Western Europe*

35. It remains to consider which friendly nations may be expected to take over financial obligations or to share in the burden of defence obligations. Clearly, it is not yet possible to ask the United Kingdom's Western European allies to help with this problem, although, if closer political or economic unity can be achieved in Western Europe, a general review of strategic and economic responsibilities may be possible.

(ii) *Commonwealth*

36. It is unlikely that other members of the Commonwealth will be able to contribute to any great extent financially. In respect of the sterling balances of India and Pakistan, moreover, a transfer of financial obligations within the Commonwealth would very largely only involve a shift of liabilities from one part of the sterling area to another. The sterling area as a whole would derive little, if any, benefit nor would the United Kingdom as the central banker of the sterling area.

37. It has also been suggested that the Governments of the Commonwealth should be asked to contribute to the cost of the defence obligations, which the United Kingdom has assumed but from which the whole Commonwealth benefits. This idea is very attractive. It would, for example, be possible for contributions to be made in the shape of reductions in the United Kingdom's sterling debt to other Commonwealth countries. (The idea might even be extended to Egypt, another large holder of sterling balances which stands to gain from United Kingdom defence undertakings.) But it needs very careful consideration, since contributing countries would presumably demand a voice in deciding how their money was spent and, if so, the freedom of action of His Majesty's Government in the United Kingdom would be severely restricted. It might indeed lead to a demand for a full-scale Imperial Defence Committee and such a wide issue requires full and separate consideration.

38. No such objections would apply to any undertaking by other Commonwealth Governments to share in the defence of the Middle East in war and in preliminary planning. Particularly, the co-operation of Australia, New Zealand and South Africa would be valuable. New Zealand has already agreed in principle to send troops to the Middle East in war. But the Australian Government have so far been unwilling to associate themselves publicly even with the making of plans and there have only

been exploratory discussions of such a possibility with the South Africans. Progress towards any formal agreement may therefore have to be slow and to be confined in the first instance to separate approaches to the governments concerned, although there is no reason to doubt that all these governments would be ready to help if war with Russia broke out.

(iii) *United States*

39. The United States Government may be even more reluctant to participate in the near future in any political pact for the Middle East and the Indian Ocean area. At the same time, they have recognised the importance of the Middle East (including Greece, Turkey and Persia), to the security of the United States. They also maintain air bases in Tripoli and at Dhahran in the Persian Gulf. They readily discuss with us the strategic problems of the Middle East, but their suggestions for their own contribution to its defence have varied. In the immediate future they would probably be unable to contribute land forces, at least at the outset, but indicate that they might possibly be prepared to do more later on. In any case, there may be advantages in consolidating British Commonwealth influence under United Kingdom leadership in the Middle East to the extent that this may be possible.

40. Different arguments however apply to the desirability of arousing American interest in the problem of sterling balances, and indeed the subject is already being considered in the Tripartite discussions in Washington.

41. The United States Government are heavily committed to the East-West struggle, where their efforts are perhaps not even yet proportionate to their resources, in comparison with those of their partners. They have interests in the Far East in the light of which they cannot ignore developments in South and South-East Asia. They are interested in the development of backward areas as a prophylactic against Communism. Finally they have already expressed willingness to examine the whole question of sterling balances. They might therefore be prepared to accept, as a first move, a plan by which a proposal to reduce or postpone the use of sterling balances by India and Pakistan would be linked with an offer of compensating United States assistance, which might make it acceptable to the Indian and Pakistani Governments. It would of course be essential that the negotiations should not lead to the withdrawal of India and Pakistan from the Commonwealth, and every effort should be made to keep them in the sterling area.

42. If this plan could be launched successfully, the United States Government might later be ready to consider a similar operation in the Middle East (in support of the important American investments in the area and in acknowledgment of the greater British military effort there) and perhaps also economic support of developments in British colonies.

(iv) *Collective defence by countries of the Atlantic Community*

43. The possibility of effecting economy of effort through the integration of United States and United Kingdom research and development work has been mentioned in paragraph 33 above. It might be argued that the rationalisation of the defence effort under the Atlantic Pact and the division of labour which may be agreed upon will lighten the burden upon the United Kingdom. This hope is likely to be illusory. The collective effort should result in greater efficiency and increased returns from the same expenditure of resources. But this is not likely to enable the United Kingdom to relax its effort in this field. If it did so, there would be consequences in terms of the decline of the position and influence of the United Kingdom in the world, similar though not necessarily equal to those which would result from a relaxation of effort in other circumstances.

The problem restated

44. This examination of British overseas obligations suggests that, while it would be desirable on political and strategic grounds to maintain the existing obligations of the United Kingdom in full, they could be lightened or transferred to some extent without undue risk to the vital interests and position of the United Kingdom. But though some alleviation would result from a partial shedding of obligations to the extent shown, the burden will remain and must remain a heavy one so long as the present state of international tension continues. It is, in fact, probable that in themselves these alleviations would be insufficient to relieve the strain. However, it is also clear that if these obligations had for any reason to be further reduced, a rot would set in which would involve far more serious effects on the United Kingdom economy than the effort to maintain the overseas obligations at a safety level. The consequences to a Great Power of a failure of will and a relaxation of grip in its overseas commitments are incalculable. This paper has estimated as carefully as possible what is necessary to sustain a foreign policy adequate to uphold the position of the United Kingdom and the extent of the alleviation of existing burdens which can be achieved, and the next step may be to relate the claims which then fall upon the United Kingdom economy to the claims which result from the internal and other policies of His Majesty's Government. On the assumption that these policies have been reviewed in the same manner as foreign policy, it may be found that the total effort required is within the capacity of the national resources. If so, the problem is solved. But if, as may well be the case, the claims are still excessive, then a choice of the utmost difficulty lies before the British people, for they must either give up, for a time, some of the advantages which a high standard of living confers upon them, or, by relaxing their grip in the outside world, see their country sink to the level of a third-class power with injury to their essential interests and way of life of which they can have little conception.

Conclusions

45. (*a*) The United Kingdom cannot divest herself of her position as a World Power, because:

(i) many of the United Kingdom's overseas obligations carry with them contributions to her standard of living in peace and would provide her with essential supplies in war;

(ii) in present conditions, if the United Kingdom were voluntarily to abandon her position of political influence in selected areas, she would probably find herself not only without economic access to those areas but unable, through loss of prestige, to prevent a further involuntary decline in her influence elsewhere and consequently a general decline in the strength of the Western Powers;

(iii) in war, some present areas of British influence would be important to the Western Powers not only economically but strategically as well.

(*b*) The ability of the United Kingdom to sustain her overseas obligations must therefore be considered not in the light of their impact on the budget but of their effects on the whole economic and political strength of the country.

(*c*) Retention of all existing obligations would sustain British prestige in world affairs and Britain's contribution to the Western cause and is therefore preferable to any general withdrawal; but it would involve some reduction, at all events temporary, in her standard of living and would not remove the present risks inherent in operating without reserves.

(*d*) All overseas obligations cannot be said to be of equal value to the United Kingdom and it would in her interests alone, be wise to shed any obligations where the advantages gained do not balance the effort and resources expended.

(*e*) But such a question must in present conditions be considered not in Britain's interests alone but in those of all the Western Powers and Commonwealth. The United Kingdom cannot safely relinquish her responsibilities unilaterally but should seek to transfer to her allies any burdens in the common cause which she can no longer carry.

(*f*) The most hopeful lines of approach in the first instance seem to be:

(i) to share certain military responsibilities in the Middle East with other Commonwealth countries;

(ii) to transfer certain economic obligations in South Asia to the United States;

(iii) to arrange for some integration of research and development projects with the United States.

(*g*) The alleviations which might result from these policies would be appreciable but they would of themselves not greatly lighten the load upon United Kingdom resources since, in present international conditions, the burden must remain heavy.

(*h*) Any further withdrawal from overseas obligations would involve risks to the United Kingdom position in the world which could not be accepted. If the claims which still remain upon the United Kingdom resources are found to be too heavy when related to claims upon these resources resulting from the other policies of His Majesty's Government, a choice of the utmost gravity has to be made. Either the resources must be found, if necessary by sacrifices in other directions, to uphold a foreign policy adequate to maintain the United Kingdom position in the world at a safety level, or the consequences of an uncontrolled decline in this position upon the standards and way of life of the British people must be accepted.

CALENDAR TO NO. 43

i *Annex I* Regional survey.
Annex II Sterling Balances.
Annex III Tabulation of U.K. defence and foreign and imperial expenditure [ZP 3/5].

No. 44

Sir O. Harvey (Paris) to Mr. Younger[1]

No. 272 [C 2848/96/18]

Confidential   PARIS, *27 April 1950*

Sir,

On the eve of the Secretary of State's discussions with Mr. Acheson and M. Schuman on tripartite world policy, it may be useful if I summarise, even though they have for the most part been reported to you separately, recent developments in French policy towards Germany in the two months which have elapsed since I wrote my despatch No. 127 of 22nd February.[2] The conclusion of that despatch was that the French Government and people were prepared to accept the need for a reconciliation with Germany and for maintaining the Western German Government sufficiently for it to withstand pressure from the East, but that the implications of this policy caused them some alarm and the pursuit of the ultimate objective was thus liable to show hesitation and inconsistency. The developments of the last two months have not led me to change that opinion.

2. When the question of the entry of Germany into the Council of Europe as an Associate Member came up again in the days immediately before the last meeting of the Committee of Ministers of the Council, one might have expected that the quibbling and bargaining attitude adopted

[1] This despatch was addressed to Mr. Younger who was in day to day charge of the Foreign Office while Mr. Bevin was in hospital, see No. 17, note 1.
[2] Not here printed from C 1476/96/18.

172

by the Federal Chancellor would have resuscitated those French fears which were so freely expressed last autumn, when the French hesitated even to discuss the entry of Germany into the Council. In fact, so far as Governmental action was concerned, the contrary was the case. M. Schuman considered that the best method of stopping German bargaining was to take the bold initiative of suggesting that the Committee of Ministers should issue a formal invitation without further ado to the German Government on a 'take it or leave it' basis.[3]

3. The next major event in this connection was Dr. Adenauer's proposal for a Franco-German union.[4] This German initiative was considered by French public opinion, with the exception of the Gaullists, as both out of place and premature. It implied the failure of the French policy of 'making Europe'[5] before it had been given a fair trial, and the fact that it was at first coupled with the question of the Saar made it unpalatable. When dealing with the matter in an important speech at the quarterly meeting of the National Committee of the M.R.P. on 26th March the Minister for Foreign Affairs emphasised the importance of not taking short cuts in matters of this kind and pointed out that the realisation of union was in fact a long and laborious process, at the very start of which it was necessary to measure the difficulties. He then reiterated the French official policy, described in my despatch under reference, that although the French did not reject the idea of an agreement, a rapprochement with Germany must come within the framework of a European solution.

4. Shortly after Dr. Adenauer's proposal, French interest in Germany was again aroused by the Foreign Affairs debate in the House of Commons at the end of March, when Mr. Churchill advocated German participation in the defence of Western Europe. Not a single French newspaper, even those of Gaullist sympathies, commented favourably on Mr. Churchill's suggestion, and all welcomed the Secretary of State's firm reply.[6] This public reaction was entirely shared by the French Government, and the President of the Council went out of his way to tell me how much he appreciated the attitude of His Majesty's Government. Nevertheless, one may detect on this occasion a slight lessening in the rigidity of the French attitude compared to that adopted last autumn when the same question was raised in American circles, and when it proved almost impossible to induce French opinion to accept at their face value the official denials that any rearmament of Germany was contemplated. Although French opinion still considers that it is far too early to raise this

[3] See No. 3, note 6.

[4] On 7 and 21 March 1950 Dr. Adenauer suggested in interviews with Mr. Kingsbury Smith, Chief European correspondent of the American International News Service, the formation of a Franco-German union as a foundation for a United States of Europe: see K. Adenauer, *Memoirs 1945–53* (trans. B.R. von Oppen—London, 1966), pp. 244–8.

[5] For Sir O. Harvey's despatch No. 271 of even date on 'making Europe', see Volume I, No. 98.i.

[6] See No. 38, note 1.

question, that in any case France must herself be rearmed effectively before Germany, and that rearmament of Germany now might well precipitate war with Russia, it now seems possible that many Frenchmen already feel in their heart of hearts that German rearmament of some kind is inevitable sooner or later.

5. If, on this issue, there are some small signs of a slightly less rigid attitude in the comparatively distant future, there are equally signs that the recent statements of Dr. Adenauer in Berlin and Bad Ems[7] have hardened some French hearts. These statements, and the singing of a verse—comparatively harmless—of 'Deutschland über Alles', have been taken more in sorrow than in anger. But they will not be lost on those Frenchmen who are convinced that no good will ever come out of Germany. Although I doubt whether they will deter M. Schuman in any way from his policy, they are bound to be added to the list of small incidents which confirm him in his opinion that Dr. Adenauer is not a man to be trusted, and in a speech on April 26th he took the occasion to point out to the Germans that an accumulation of claims and grievances was no way to make progress.

6. There have been indications recently of French official policy on two minor questions within the major problem of Allied policy in Germany. The first is on the subject of Berlin. Earlier this month a spokesman of the Ministry of Foreign Affairs reiterated that the French Government was opposed to the idea of incorporating Western Berlin in the Bonn Republic so long as that city remained divided and under two different administrations. He emphasised that the Berlin problem could not be solved except as part of that concerning the unity of Germany as a whole; the French Government remained favourable to the unification of Germany provided that it was preceded by truly free elections and followed by the establishment of a sincerely democratic régime, which at the moment was prevented by the Soviet Union.

7. The second concerns the French wish to see both the Military Security Board[8] and the International Authority for the Ruhr strength-

[7] In a speech at Berlin on 18 April Dr. Adenauer 'advocated a review of the Occupation Statute immediately instead of in the autumn. He also deplored the small role which Germany was at present permitted to play in foreign affairs. He denied that a strong German economy was a potential danger and criticised economic controls which were not simple and which created the impression that they were dictated by fears of German competition. He also made a plea for stronger police powers' (Wahnerheide telegram No. 147 Saving on C 2771/54/18). Dr. Adenauer further criticized Allied policies in Germany in a party rally speech at Bad Ems on 23 April, reported the following day in Wahnerheide telegram No. 633: 'One of the reasons for the deterioration in Allied-German relations was to be attributed, he [Dr. Adenauer] thought, to the fact that the public abroad could not understand that "nation feelings" were developing again in Germany ... The Allies, Dr. Adenauer said, should apply more common sense and less sentiment to the handling of German questions' (C 2757/202/18). At Dr. Adenauer's request both speeches were followed by the singing of a verse of the German national anthem; see reports in *The Times* of 19 April, p. 8 and 24 April, p. 4.

[8] The Military Security Board for the Western Zones of Germany was established under

ened. The Foreign Affairs Commission of the National Assembly recently passed a resolution emphasising that it was high time the latter body assumed the full powers laid down for it. Shortly thereafter a Quai d'Orsay spokesman set out publicly the exact position regarding the powers of the Authority under the various different articles of the London Agreements[9] and explained that, when representatives of the countries concerned met in June 1950 to discuss the matter, the French Government would be in favour of a rapid transfer of the administrative powers which under the London Agreement belonged to the Authority. There can be little doubt that the French Government sincerely wish to see these two bodies strengthened. In their view these two organisations, together with the Allied occupation of Germany and the hope that German nationalism may be rendered harmless in a Western European system, are the main pillars of the consistent French policy of ensuring security from German aggression.

8. I should also mention a series of articles which have appeared recently on the German problem in the newspaper *Figaro* under the signature of M. Raymond Aron.[10] These articles, a brief summary[11] of which I enclose, recommend that at their forthcoming meeting the Foreign Ministers of the three Western powers ought to take a radical decision between the alternatives of trying once again to negotiate with the Soviet Union for the unification of Germany and of recognising that no faith can be placed in such negotiations and consequently taking the lead themselves in adopting a thoroughly liberal policy towards Western Germany. The writer strongly favours this second alternative which, as he acknowledges, is indeed already the policy of the three western Allies but which their hesitation and lack of drive fails to put across effectively. These articles have so far made little or no impression on French public opinion but they are, I think, significant in that for the first time in recent years the French Government are urged to go both further and faster towards reconciliation with Germany than they are at present doing.[12] I doubt however whether this lead will be followed by many Frenchmen, and I still believe that M. Schuman's present policy is if anything ahead of French public opinion in general.

9. The President of the Republic, when I saw him after his visit to London, spoke of the importance of convincing French opinion that it was not for lack of offers to discuss with the Soviet Government that the Western Powers had fallen back on the permanent division of Germany.

---

the tripartite directive of 17 January 1949 (*D.G.O.* pp. 350–5), for the disarmament and demilitarization of Germany.

[9] See No. 12, note 9.   [10] French journalist and political scientist.

[11] Not printed.

[12] *Marginal annotation* in the Foreign Office: '*Le Monde* has been doing this for a long time.' On 8 May Sir I. Kirkpatrick observed that 'M. Aron in the Figaro is very far in advance of the French delegation here.'

President Auriol, inspired in this by the late Léon Blum,[13] has always felt uneasy at the division of Europe. On this occasion he favoured one more formal invitation being addressed to the Soviet Government by the three Western Powers to a Four-Power Conference, two conditions being attached, the abolition of the Cominform[14] and consent to control of atomic research. Supposing, as he undoubtedly did, that the Soviet Government would reject these conditions he felt that French opinion would be much more firmly wedded to the policy of integration with the Western half of Germany only. I do not think for a moment that M. Schuman would agree with such a proposal which would appear somewhat naive and more likely to confuse than clarify the issue.

10. I am sending copies of this despatch to His Majesty's representatives at Washington, Rome, Brussels, The Hague, Luxembourg and Wahnerheide.

I have, &c.,

OLIVER HARVEY

[13] French President of the Council of Ministers (1936–7, 1938 and 1946–7), who died on 30 March 1950.

[14] Communist Information Bureau, established in 1947.

No. 45

General Sir B. Robertson (Wahnerheide) to Mr. Bevin
(Received 29 April, 5.24 a.m.)

No. 666 Telegraphic [C 3333/3333/18]

Priority. Top secret   WAHNERHEIDE, 28 April 1950, 11.25 p.m.

Repeated to Washington, Paris.

At the private session today referred to in my immediately preceding telegram,[1] the Chancellor presented us with a written proposal for the

[1] In this telegram of even date General Robertson reported a meeting between the three High Commissioners and Dr. Adenauer at which the Chancellor discussed tactics for securing the entry of Germany into the Council of Europe. 'He himself felt that the best course would be for him to obtain a Cabinet decision on the matter before the meeting of the Ministers in London, but to defer putting the matter before the Bundestag until after that meeting. He felt that it would be difficult to avoid a controversial debate in the Bundestag. This might create a bad impression before the Ministers' meeting.' General Robertson and M. François Poncet favoured securing an immediate Cabinet decision but 'McCloy, somewhat to my alarm, said that the London Conference could not be expected to produce any result of special concern to Germany. It would discuss the world situation and only deal with Germany in that framework. Was it therefore, worthwhile taking a Cabinet decision and announcing it before the meeting of Ministers since that meeting could have no effect on the issue?' (C 2859/85/18). With reference to these remarks by Mr. McCloy, General Robertson commented in a letter to Sir I. Kirkpatrick the following day: 'The American tendency to swing from one extreme to another like a pendulum appears to be much in evidence at the moment. Not long ago they wanted to make every conceivable concession to the Germans and generally to keep the pace as hot as possible. Today McCloy is saying that we shall never get a proper answer so long as Adenauer is Chancellor, no

authorisation of a Federal Police Force 25,000 strong as a general reserve for the enforcement of the will of the Federal Government and as a local police for the Federal Capital. With reference to the former, his proposal is for an armed force housed in barracks and he remarked that an examination would be required as to whether, and under what conditions this force should have powers of arrest.

2. I am now having a translation made of the Chancellor's written proposal and will telegraph it later.[2]

3. From the chair I replied that the Military Governors in approving the Basic Law had stipulated that if the Federal Government should require any additional police forces it should obtain the authority of the Military Governors or High Commissioners. The Chancellor had acted correctly in putting this proposal before us. However, it was an important proposal which we should have to consider carefully and on which we should probably have to seek instructions from our Governments. My colleagues nodded assent. After the meeting Francois-Poncet remarked to me privately that it would be difficult to get this proposal approved by Governments. However, he did not say that he was against it himself.

Foreign Office please pass to Washington and Paris as my telegram Nos. 98 and 117 respectively.[3]

CALENDAR TO No. 45

i *28 Apr. 1950 U.K. Brief No. 22 (without annex): Establishment of a German Gendarmerie.* Recommends (*a*) that Foreign Ministers should agree not to oppose formation of Federal gendarmerie (*b*) initiative should be left to Federal Govt., and Foreign Ministers' agreement should be kept secret (*c*) High Commissioners should discuss secretly size and character of body required [C 3335/3333/18].

amendment to the Occupation Statute can be considered for the present, and it is time that we showed the Germans where they get off' (C 2960/20/18).

[2] A translated text of Dr. Adenauer's letter (reference Geh.40/50) was transmitted to the Foreign Office in Wahnerheide telegram No. 669 of 29 April and subsequently appended (though not here reproduced) to the brief at i below: for a printed text see *F.R.U.S. 1950*, vol. iv, pp. 684–5.

[3] On 4 May General Robertson reported in his telegram No. 695 discussion that day in private session by the High Commissioners of the Chancellor's request. Mr. McCloy and M. François Poncet 'recognised the inevitability and indeed the desirability of the creation of such a force. However, they laid great stress on the need for very careful handling of this issue. François Poncet in particular said that French public opinion was not yet ready to swallow a proposal for the establishment of a German force of 25,000 men.' Both Mr. McCloy and M. François Poncet 'thought that it would be advisable to proceed by steps and to grant permission for a much smaller figure than that proposed by the Germans . . . I said that I would not commit my government as to the attitude which it would take on this matter. Personally, I thought that the Chancellor had an excellent case and I was surprised at the modesty of its figure rather than by its size. It would of course take some time for the Germans to recruit and organise a force of 25,000. It might therefore be possible to give permission initially for a somewhat smaller figure provided that the intention was clearly stated that this figure would be reviewed again at a fixed date in the near future' (C 3336/3333/18).

No. 46

Record of Fourth Tripartite Official Meeting held in the Foreign Office on 28 April 1950 at 4 p.m.

[*ZP 2/193*]

Top secret

Present:

United Kingdom Sir W. Strang, Sir G. Jebb, Sir R. Makins, Sir F. Hoyer-Millar, Mr. Wright, Mr. Rose,[1] Mr. Shuckburgh, Mr. Hadow, Mr. Maclean.[2]

United States Mr. Jessup, Mr. Perkins, Mr. Bohlen, Mr. Raynor, Mr. Wallner, Mr. Sanders, Miss Willis.

France M. Massigli, M. Alphand, M. de la Tournelle, M. Baudet, M. Leroy, M. Labouret, M. de Folin.

Agenda:

I Report of the Sub-Committee set up by the Third Tripartite Official Meeting to consider the terms of a communication to be made to the Working Group. (Paragraph 13, United Kingdom Record Tripartite Official Third Meeting.)[3]

II Item 6 of Tripartite Agenda. (United Kingdom Paper, No. D.5.)[4]

III Items arising from Item 8 of the Tripartite Agenda, namely—

    (a) Common attitude to the Soviet Union and satellite countries, with particular reference to Diplomatic Missions.

    (b) Yugoslavia. In particular measures of financial assistance.

IV Question of appointing a Sub-Committee to draft a declaration.

I

The Sub-Committee reported that their task had proved more contentious than had at first seemed likely. There was some difference of opinion between the French and the British whether a new body should be set up, or whether the organisation would merely be an extension of the Council by means of permanent Deputies. There was also disagreement on the status of the Secretary-General. The Americans announced that they had already informed their representative on the Working Group of the line they favoured (*i.e.*, that already recorded in paragraphs 2 and 3 of the United Kingdom Record of the Third Tripartite Official

[1] It is not clear from this record whether this was Mr. E.M. Rose, assistant head of Western Organisations Department, or Mr. C.M. Rose, who was attached to the U.K. Delegation.

[2] Mr. A.D. Maclean of News Department was attached to the Secretariat of the U.K. delegation.

[3] No. 40. No record of the meeting of the sub-committee on 28 April has been traced in Foreign Office archives.

[4] See No. 17, note 9.

Meeting). They then circulated a draft[5] indicating their instructions to their representative in Washington and it was agreed that, subject to certain drafting amendments, this draft should be sent by Mr. Perkins, as President of the Working Group, to the Working Group as an indication of tripartite line of thought. It was obvious that each country viewed the actual functions of the organisation in a different light and each country might further clarify its own thoughts on the subject and send its interpretation to its own representative in Washington. The Sub-committee under Sir G. Jebb should meet again and try and reach agreement on the exact terms of reference of any Committee of Deputies.[6]

II

(a) Chinese Representation

2. The Americans outlined their view with regard to Chinese representation along similar lines to those they had adopted at the Second Bipartite Official Meeting. (See United Kingdom Record, paragraph 17.)[7]

3. The British position was explained and the importance of the Ecuadorean, Egyptian and French votes in the Security Council was stressed. Since the Egyptian position had not been finally established the importance of the French attitude was stressed. We assumed that the Americans were being completely neutral and were bringing no pressure to bear on countries one way or the other. We also appreciated the difficulties in which the French found themselves as a result of Chinese recognition of Ho Chi Minh.[8] It was, however, urgent to reach some

---

[5] Not printed.

[6] Separate French and British draft terms of reference were circulated to delegations on 29 April and 1 May as TRI/P/8 and 9 respectively (*F.R.U.S. 1950*, vol. iii, pp. 904, note 4 and pp. 905–6, notes 3–4). Following discussion of both drafts in sub-committee on 2 May (*ibid.*, pp. 903–5), a new text based on the British, more general draft was circulated as TRI/P/10 on 2 May (*ibid.*, pp. 905–6). This text, as amended by U.K. delegation (TRI/P/17 of 3 May), was further discussed in sub-committee on 4 May (*ibid.*, pp. 906–8: agreed text circulated as TRI/P/19 *ibid.*, p. 1023, note 3). At the fifth tripartite meeting of officials on 5 May it was agreed that TRI/P/19 should go to Ministers with some verbal variation and with reserves from all three delegations. The paper was accordingly circulated as MIN/TRI/P/3 on 6 May (*ibid.*). When agreeing to accept the British draft at the sub-committee on 2 May, the French delegation stipulated the condition that the detailed points in their own draft which specified defence tasks should be embodied in a separate directive from the Council. A draft directive was accordingly circulated as TRI/P/11 on 2 May (not printed) and discussed in sub-committee on 4 May (*F.R.U.S. 1950*, vol. iii, pp. 908–10) together with a British redraft, TRI/P/16 of 3 May (also not printed). The text, there agreed as a draft resolution (TRI/P/20 of 4 May, printed *ibid.*, pp. 909) was approved at the fifth tripartite meeting of officials on 5 May for submission to Ministers with some verbal amendment and with British and American reserves. The paper was accordingly circulated as MIN/TRI/P/2 on 6 May *ibid.*

[7] No. 33.

[8] The recognition of the Viet Minh government of M. Ho Chi Minh was announced by the Central People's government of China on 19 January 1950: followed by Soviet recognition on 30 January.

solution before the next Assembly as the question of new membership would present an ugly dilemma and we might indeed be faced with the alternatives of voting in our own candidates and not those of the Slavs, of voting against all candidates including our own, or of voting in favour of everybody, all of which courses would seem to be equally undesirable.

4. The French felt regret at the present state of affairs in the United Nations, especially since the Six-Power talks on atomic energy had been halted. If things were allowed to remain as they were there might well be a move by the small Powers, convinced of the inability of the great Powers to run the machine, which might be directed against our interests. The Russians would be quick to harness any such move and possibly get some resolution passed on the abolition of the atom bomb. The French agreed that the new membership question might well lead to the break-up of the United Nations, and they would not be prepared to accept any action in this matter, which would lead to a greater split between East and West coming about. The French were attracted by the Secretary-General's point on the difference between a vote for admission of the People's Government and recognition of that Government, but they had not yet taken up a definite position in the matter. But some solution might lie along these lines. (They were assured by the British representatives that although the United Kingdom attitude was that any State prepared to vote in favour of the Peking Government's admission to the United Nations should have the courage of its convictions and recognise too, a solution along the lines suggested by the French would not be illegal though it might be illogical.) At the same time, French public opinion would find it hard to understand how France could vote for Mao when he had recognised Ho Chi Minh.

5. The British suggested that although the French were not prepared to take a firm position they might at least indicate to Ecuador and Egypt how valuable their votes in favour of the People's Government might be in the general interest.

6. It was agreed that the question of Chinese representation, although there was a divergence of view, should be discussed by Ministers, who should be forewarned of the serious situation in which we might find ourselves before the next Assembly.

(b) *Mr. Lie's Proposal for a Special Meeting of the Security Council*

7. The British and American representatives outlined their attitude as already set forth in the Second Bipartite Meeting (United Kingdom Record Bipartite Official Second Meeting).[7] The British, in particular, drew the attention of the French to the likelihood of being faced with a more clear-cut proposal from Mr. Lie once the question of Chinese representation had been settled. This would almost certainly entail a debate with the Russians on all outstanding points of disagreement. If there could be no agreement (and this seemed likely) the results might well be disastrous. But if faced with this situation it would be better to have the discussions in the Security Council under the ægis of the United

Nations. The Americans were in agreement that it would be difficult not to respond favourably, and that if a meeting must take place it should be in the Security Council before the General Assembly this autumn.

8. The French were unable to predict what their governmental attitude would be since Mr. Lie would only be seeing M. Schuman next day. They thought, however, it would be generally in line with British and American thought.

III

(a) Common Attitude to the Soviet Union and Satellites

9. The British and American representatives said that this item had been raised in tripartite meetings as it was felt that there should be general tripartite consultation on action to be taken *vis-à-vis* the satellites and Russia over the restrictions and expulsions now being practised. The general idea would be joint consultation before retaliation.

10. The French agreed that if it was a question of applying similar methods in similar cases they saw advantage in some form of co-operation. It was very difficult, however, if the idea was that all three should act together if one out of the three were attacked. In particular, there should be no fixed rules as to what should be done and each case would have to be judged on its merits, since each Government must weigh up the factors applying to any individual case in the light of consideration such as current economic negotiations, relevant at the time. On the other hand, they seemed to agree, when pressed, that general proposals for retaliation might possibly be concerted after preliminary discussion.

11. The Americans stressed that they did not advocate any rigid approach. They felt that this was a common problem which must be faced, since it was obvious that the Soviets were out to eliminate Western centres behind the Iron Curtain. What was wanted was common consultation so that our actions could be more closely geared. There were certain points which the Americans felt could be held in common:

(i) Despite provocation and difficulties we should maintain our Missions in the satellite countries unless the position became intolerable. Our Missions were useful for collecting information, for encouraging the satellite peoples to believe they were not forgotten by the West and for watching and exploiting any developments along the lines of Titoism which might emerge.

(ii) Each of our three countries should inform the others on any retaliatory steps they proposed to take.

(iii) It would be useful to co-ordinate propaganda to the Iron Curtain which would show the peoples of the area that they were not forgotten.

(iv) The three countries should consult on use being made of the United Nations as a forum in which to hold up the satellites for Treaty violations, in particular the Human Rights clauses.

(v) It would be valuable if the Council of Europe could serve to remind satellites that there was a place for them in the European community one day.

(vi) Consultation on the effective use of exiles would be valuable. The French pointed out the dangers of dealing with exiles and the Americans reassured them that all they wished for was consultation, so that exiled groups could not play off the three Powers one against the other.

(vii) The three Powers should be alert to consult on any Titoist developments. Their Missions in Iron Curtain countries might be instructed to consult and collaborate on any new developments in this field.

12. With regard to a query where joint consultation could take place in a centralised form the Americans suggested that this was a possible subject for treatment by the new political machinery in the Atlantic Pact.

(b) Yugoslavia

13. The French position with regard to financial assistance to Yugoslavia was conditioned by the fact that France was a major creditor. It was therefore felt that until these old credits had been worked off and the creditors satisfied, not necessarily 100 per cent., France was not prepared to scale down or abandon the debts due to her, or to examine the question of fresh credits.

14. The Americans stressed the political importance of the economic approach to the Yugoslav problem. All were agreed that developments in Yugoslavia had been a serious set-back for the Soviet Union and it was vital to keep Tito afloat and the breach between him and Moscow open. The Export/Import Bank had already granted a 20 million dollar credit and were considering another credit of 15 million dollars. This was in addition to the International Bank loan based on the currencies of six countries which amounted to 25 million dollars. There was a further question whether military supplies should be made available to Yugoslavia in the event of more overt action by the Soviets. The Americans had circulated a questionnaire to France and the United Kingdom on the subject and had received a reply from the French to the effect that light materials only should be supplied and that any arming of Yugoslavia should not be detrimental to the Western effort as a whole. The question of military supplies, in the French view, also depended considerably in the way developments shaped in Yugoslavia. The Americans understood that the United Kingdom reply was under draft and would be received shortly.

15. The likelihood of a Soviet attack on Yugoslavia now appeared considerably less than six months ago, but the Americans considered that the situation should be constantly kept in mind and reverted to if necessary.

16. The British representatives pointed out that while we had no precise information on the general Balance of Payments situation in Yugoslavia, we had an indication that the sterling position was not at all

bad. Despite slow deliveries by the Yugoslavs their sterling position was still strong, and they had taken up considerably less of the British loan than we had anticipated. They had not been ordering capital equipment to the extent which they had at first indicated they might find necessary, or to the extent which we had thought they would. The necessity for a sterling *tranche* in any International Bank loan did not therefore appear to be very considerable.[9]

IV

Draft Declaration

17. The French representatives circulated a French draft[10] giving their ideas on the form which a declaration might take. It was agreed that the British and American representatives should have this translated and circulated to all concerned for study, and the question could be reverted to next week when ideas had clarified themselves to a greater extent.

18. The Meeting adjourned.

[9] Discussion at this meeting under II and III above (Chinese representation, Mr. Lie's proposal, common attitude towards Soviet Union, Yugoslavia) formed the basis of a report to Ministers circulated as TRI/P/13 on 3 May. This paper was amended in discussion at the fifth bipartite and sixth tripartite meetings on 4 and 6 May and circulated to Ministers as MIN/TRI/P/4 of 6 May, printed in *F.R.U.S. 1950*, vol. iii, pp. 1078–81.

[10] This draft, circulated as TRI/P/7 on 29 April (not printed from ZP 2/105) was in response to discussion at the second tripartite meeting of officials (No. 37, paragraphs 2–3, 14–15) on the French proposal for a grand declaration of Western objectives. This draft was overtaken by discussion in sub-committee from which emerged American draft (*a*), and (*b*) a longer Anglo-French draft, described by Mr. Shuckburgh as a 'watered-down version' of a British paper (for which see No. 84.i). Both texts were circulated as TRI/P/23 on 5 May for discussion on 6 May: see further No. 84, note 5.

No. 47

Letter from Sir R. Makins to Sir E. Hall-Patch (Paris)

[WU 1071/78]

Confidential   FOREIGN OFFICE, *28 April 1950*

We had got on very well with the Americans about the proposed development of the Atlantic Pact Organisation. We had it pretty well agreed,[1] in principle, that there should be a permanent committee at a high level with a secretary-general with medium powers, which would deal with the co-ordination of the defence, economic and military activities of the organisation, co-ordinate foreign policies and collaborate on information and propaganda policies. It was clear that this body should deal with economic problems which have a direct relationship to the pact and which do not come within the competence of the O.E.E.C. It was recognised that

[1] See No. 33.

apart from joining the Council of Europe there was no immediate step which could be taken to bring Germany into closer association with the west, but the terms of reference of the proposed standing body should be drafted with the possibility in mind of associating with its work at some later stage, countries such as Western Germany, Sweden, Switzerland, etc.

When this question was considered at a tripartite meeting,[2] however, up bobs Alphand with an entirely new idea. This is that the Atlantic Pact organisation should deal only with the limited economic problems which might arise in connexion with the finance of defence and that all general economic problems should continue to be dealt with in the O.E.E.C. with which would be associated in some way for particular problems with the United States, Canada and perhaps other countries. The French position was that they could not agree that Germany could ever join the Atlantic Pact and they were therefore afraid of any association of Germany with the Atlantic Pact organisation in the future since this might well lead on to membership. They were anxious to see established a system of collaboration between European countries and North America which could develop in a non-military framework and which would include Western Germany, Switzerland and Sweden. Apart from these quite respectable reasons, the scheme had other obvious advantages from the French point of view which Alphand did not mention. We replied in effect, that Alphand's proposal would atrophy Article 2 of the Atlantic Pact, whereas we were anxious to develop it. Secondly, we said that the economic problems raised by the necessity to increase expenditure on defence, were of such magnitude that we did not believe that it would be possible, in practice, to differentiate between the economic problems concerned with re-armament and general economic problems. We did not think it was necessary to specify at this stage that the proposed standing group should deal with problems other than those specified above though as time went on the organisation would, no doubt, develop and it might be possible to differentiate it, at that stage, so as to associate with it other countries not signatories of the pact for non-military purposes.

The Americans showed some signs of being attracted to the French proposal since they are somewhat barren of ideas and are reluctant to adopt our step by step approach, specially as regards Germany. The issue, therefore, remains undecided. Various compromises are already in the air, namely that some body should study the form of relationship between North America and Western Europe in general economic, and non-military problems after 1952. I should welcome any comments which you may have to make on this latest bright idea of Alphand's.

More generally there are signs of a considerable gulf between the French and ourselves. They seem to want to restrict the operation of the Atlantic Pact to the minimum and seek other avenues of co-operation with North America outside the pact, and to think in terms of 'two zones' the

[2] No. 40.

184

Atlantic and the European whereas we want to work towards the 'larger lunacy'.[3]

We are having a bilateral discussion with the French tonight in which, no doubt, they will press their views further but I will get this letter off without delay.

Incidentally, at yesterday's tripartite meeting,[2] Jessup made a very encouraging speech affirming the willingness of the United States Government, to support Western Europe after 1952 even though the European Recovery programme itself had to terminate. The Americans have told us that this is settled policy but that they have not yet decided how they can operate. They are, no doubt, looking to Mr. Gordon Gray for the answer to this.[4]

Yours sincerely,
ROGER MAKINS

CALENDAR TO NO. 47

i *28 Apr.–5 May 1950 French ideas for Atlantic Pact and O.E.E.C.* further discussed without reaching agreement at (a) Anglo-French meeting in French Embassy on 28 Apr. (b) tripartite sub-committee on 4 May where French proposal for U.S./Canadian membership of O.E.E.C. (TRI/P/15, for which see No. 71, note 1) is discussed (also migration cf. No. 40, note 4) (c) Anglo-American bipartite sub-committee on 5 May. Americans in state of

---

[3] A phrase used by the Canadian humorist, Stephen Leacock.

[4] In reply on 1 May Sir E. Hall-Patch was unable to throw much light on M. Alphand's proposals for O.E.E.C.: 'The line he took does not seem to square at all with what we understood French views to be.' Sir E. Hall-Patch speculated that M. Alphand's ideas sprang from French fears of finding themselves '"in the queue" with the other European countries' in an Anglo-American dominated Atlantic Pact organization. 'If, on the other hand, the O.E.E.C. was maintained, perhaps with only a rather slender link with the United States, France might be able to build up an economic system in Europe which would be more in line with her desires. This might particularly be in Alphand's mind at present when, on financial policy at least, France seems to be lining up with Benelux and Italy against us for the moment.' In a letter to Sir W. Strang on 5 May, Sir O. Harvey agreed with Sir E. Hall-Patch's views and referred to doubts expressed by M. Schuman as to the suitability of the North Atlantic treaty as a basis for constructing a general organization. On 3 May M. Schuman had informed Sir O. Harvey that when he and M. Bidault had come to examine the details of M. Bidault's own proposal for developing the North Atlantic Council (see No. 24, note 5), 'they felt that this would not work. There were eight nations outside the Atlantic Pact who were inside the O.E.E.C. They included countries such as Sweden and Switzerland who would not wish to join the Atlantic Pact because of its military aspect, as well as Germany whose admission would cause difficulty for other nations. On the other hand, it was generally agreed that the O.E.E.C. must continue after 1952 in some modified form and that the United States and Canada should be associated with it as members and not as monitors as at present.' By maintaining separation between O.E.E.C. and N.A.C., 'it would be possible to retain the eight nations within the fold of the O.E.E.C. The latter would continue to deal with purely European economic questions but the United States and Canada should take part as Associates when questions extending beyond Europe were raised' (Paris telegram No. 162 Saving of 4 May on WU 1071/87).

'bewilderment'. U.S. dislike French proposal for building up O.E.E.C. yet do not want to set up new organization and see extreme difficulty of achieving anything through N.A.T. British delegation suggest doing nothing for time being since French likely to come round on association of Germany with N.A.T. Already at meeting on 28 Apr. Alphand a little swayed by argument that exclusion of Germany could lead to 'a Western system undergoing heavy burdens on its economy in order to build a secure defence, while the Germans, guaranteed against aggression by the Western powers with no obligations to bear their share in the defence burden, were free to develop an unrivalled economic progress'. See further No. 71 [WU 1071/79; ZP 2/193; UR 1017/4].

No. 48

Letter from Sir O. Franks (Washington) to Sir W. Strang[1]

[ZP 2/118]

Secret   WASHINGTON, 28 April 1950

Dear William,

I had a long talk with Acheson yesterday evening during which he discoursed on his hopes and intention in London. He knew there were many particular things that would have to be mentioned or talked about and there were also, in the view of his State Department officials, many questions of organisation to be considered. He had been considering the latter all the week, and while his mind was not closed at all to new organisations if they were necessary, what really interested him was the objective he wished to pursue and the policies and acts to be selected to pursue it. Questions of organisation were subsidiary to these considerations and should flow from them. He hoped that not a great deal of new organisation might be wanted.

All this was a preliminary to a general statement that he hoped there would be a good deal of time in London for reflective discussion on high policy. He himself had views: they might be right or they might be wrong. If they were wrong he would be glad to see them corrected. His desire was to achieve agreement and real understanding of the main issues.

There was first the objective of action. As he saw it, the objective was to deal, satisfactorily to us all, with Russia. We had not very long in which to lay our plans and act, perhaps three or four years.

If there were agreement on the objective, then very important policies should follow on four main topics. The main topics were – defense, Germany, Asia, and the general maximisation of international trade and the removal of hindrances to the freer movement of men, goods and currencies. On the first of these he thought the defensive effort called for

---

[1] This letter, initialled by Sir W. Strang on 1 May, was seen by Mr. Bevin and Mr. Younger.

was very great. On the part of Western European countries it might well involve a diversion of effort in manpower and materials which they could not afford. Yet it had to be done. What actions must the United States be prepared to take in order that what should be done was in fact done! Similarly, as regards Germany, while it would be completely wrong to begin thinking in terms of a German army it was important to tie her in to the West in all sorts of relations and by all sorts of ties so that whether she wanted to or not Germany could not look East. This had to be done quickly and therefore major changes must be discussed with a view to their rapid accomplishment. This would clearly involve adequate protection for Germany as the Germans could not be expected to come West if their fate was simply to be that of a battlefield or a no-man's land. Then again, as regards the countries of the girdle of Asia, it was essential that their level of prosperity should be sustained, that they should grow more and better food and be able to participate more largely in world trade. Here, too, we could not wait very long. As regards trade and prosperity he was obviously thinking of some relationship which included the United States and Canada with some or all of the Western European countries now in O.E.E.C. He was fluid in his mind about how this should be done but I think has reached the conclusion that whatever integration may or should mean it only becomes real in a context which includes North America as well as Western Europe and Britain.

This is not a very clear account, but Acheson himself was not much clearer. The points left in my mind were that he obviously attaches the greatest importance to such a discussion of high policy. I very much hope that it will be possible to allot generous time for this. Secondly, I think he is very far from crystallised in the views which he holds about most of these things with the exception of his belief in the reality and pressing importance of the ever present Russian menace. Thirdly, I do not think he distinguishes at all adequately between things which America might do in one way or another on a temporary basis to help us or other countries on defense or on economic matters and long-term changes in American policy which would enable us and other countries to know what sort of world we were living in and rely upon a normal and stable course of events to enable us to do what we needed to do. It is from this point of view that I still think that Acheson does not fully recognise the importance of July 1, 1952. He, of course, sees that it is a very important date but as he told a group of journalists the other evening the important thing is to stop talking about 1952 as the time when aid ends. In my opinion this is not the important thing. Aid must end. What we want are new American policies which will enable us with the United States to play our part as a world power in a condition of world affairs which permits us to take a longer view than temporary help and yearly Congressional approval can ever permit.

Yours sincerely
OLIVER FRANKS

No. 49

Brief for the U.K. Delegation

No. 24 [C 2903/20/18]

Secret   FOREIGN OFFICE, 29 April 1950

Revision of the Occupation Statute

1. It is recommended that if the question of the revision of the Occupation Statute is raised in the forthcoming Ministerial meetings, the Secretary of State should express the following views:

(1) it is premature to review the Occupation Statute or to set up a three-Power Committee for this purpose at the present time,

(2) the programme for revision between September 1950 and March 1951 laid down in the Statute should be adhered to and the three Governments will maintain contact with a view to the establishment of a three-Power Committee for this purpose in September 1950,

(3) if, when the review of the Statute is made Germany has already given evidence of her desire to associate with the West the three Governments of the Occupying Powers should bear in mind the importance of furthering their declared intention to facilitate the integration of the Federal Republic into Western Europe, and should in this context therefore be ready to examine the question of modifying the present system of control in the field of foreign relations.

Argument

2. The existing Occupation Statute defining the respective powers and responsibilities of the German Federal Government and the Allied High Commission came into force on the 21st September, 1949. It stated that it was the desire and intention of the three Occupying Powers that, so long as the occupation continued, the German people should enjoy self-government to the maximum possible degree consistent with the occupation. The limitations imposed on this self-government were defined by setting out certain broad fields in which powers were specifically reserved to the occupation authorities. The list of these fields as set out in the Occupation Statute is annexed.[1] While the Statute stated that the occupation authorities reserved the right to resume the exercise of full authority, it also expressed the hope and expectation of the three Occupying Powers that the occupation authorities would not have occasion to take action in fields other than those specifically reserved. The Statute contained a provision that after twelve months, and in any event within eighteen months of its entry into force the Occupying Powers would undertake a review of its provisions in the light of experience of its

[1] This extract from article 2 of the Occupation Statute (see No. 5, note 3) is not here printed.

operation and with a view to extending the jurisdiction of the German authorities in the legislative, executive and judicial fields.

3. The German Federal Chancellor has recently been showing increasing signs of irritation over the working of the Occupation Statute and now appears to have embarked upon a public campaign for its early revision, partly no doubt in the hope of thereby limiting still further Allied interference in internal German affairs but probably also in the expectation of facilitating full German participation on a basis of equality in international organisations such as the Council of Europe. In his speech in Berlin on the 18th April[2] he expressed hope that the forthcoming ministerial talks in London would deal extensively with the German question and advocated an immediate review of the Occupation Statute instead of waiting until the autumn, in view of the rapidity of developments since it was drawn up.

4. General Robertson has recently expressed the view that, while the time has not yet come to review the Occupation Statute, it is important to resist any tendency to argue that no changes of consequence should be made when the time for revision arrives. He considers that revision of the Statute in a sense favourable to the German Federal Government is essential to progress on the road towards the integration of Germany into Western Europe; and that she cannot be so integrated so long as her foreign affairs are conducted by the Occupying Powers and her foreign trade is under their tutelage. He has recommended that when the Foreign Ministers meet they might authorise the initiation of a study of the extent to which, at an appropriate time, the Occupation Statute should be revised in order to facilitate further progress towards the Allied objective.

5. The Secretary of State in his speech in the Foreign Affairs debate on the 28th March[3] spoke as follows:

'On the basis of the Occupation Statute, I do not think it is right for a nation like Germany to begin arguing with us about the terms on which she will come in to the Council of Europe. What I do say is that if they come in and whole-heartedly accept, we on our part will accept them as an act of faith and not delay too long in getting to the next stage. What is the next stage? Under the Occupation Statute, one of the problems is dealing with foreign policy. We shall have at some time, I presume, to take a decision, the Occupying Powers I mean, as to whether we will hand the conduct of foreign policy back to Germany. It is only at that stage that she can act as an equal in the Committee of Ministers. I am not prepared, and I do not think the Cabinet would be prepared, to violate that by hybrid arrangements. We think it is too dangerous.'

6. There are cogent arguments in favour of deciding, when the time comes to review the Occupation Statute, to remove the item reading

---

[2] See No. 44, note 7.   [3] See No. 18, note 2 and No. 38, note 1.

'Foreign affairs, including agreements made by or on behalf of Germany' from the reserved field, thereby allowing the German Federal Government to establish a Ministry for Foreign Affairs and enter into normal diplomatic relations with foreign Governments. Under the Petersberg Agreement[4] of last November the German Federal Government was authorised to exchange commercial and consular representation with other countries and to participate as fully as practicable in international organisations. The authorising of normal diplomatic representation would be a natural next step. It is indeed difficult to see how Germany could participate as a full and equal member in organisations such as the Council of Europe unless this step were taken. Moreover, so long as the Federal Government is denied control over its foreign relations, there is a tendency, from which relations between the Occupying Powers and the Federal Government are already suffering, for a sense of isolation and frustration to develop in Germany. In addition, so long as no Government Department dealing with foreign affairs can be established, the handling of foreign affairs tends to become excessively concentrated in the hands of the Chancellor himself. Further it is not in our power to prevent the Chancellor from developing his own informal contacts with foreign countries on an unofficial and somewhat furtive basis, and there would be considerable advantage in forestalling the unhealthy growth of this tendency by allowing the Federal Government to conduct its relations openly and through properly established channels. The Germans have been largely isolated from contact with the Western world for over ten years and the speeches of their statesmen reveal a lamentable ignorance of that world. It would be all to the good that this ignorance should be lessened by the reports which would be made to the Federal Government by their diplomatic representatives abroad. It would be for consideration whether the Occupying Powers should retain any controls, such as those which the Allied Council in Vienna enjoy under the Control Agreement of June, 1946,[5] in regard to the conduct of foreign affairs by the Austrian Government. It would also be necessary before control over foreign affairs was relinquished for steps to be taken to ensure that the German Federal Government assumed responsibility for carrying out the obligations, such as those in the Safehaven Agreement,[6] entered into on behalf of Germany by the Allied Occupying Powers.

7. The control of foreign trade and exchange is closely linked with the

[4] See No. 7, note 2.

[5] The quadripartite agreement on controls in Austria signed at Vienna on 28 June 1946, in which the respective powers of the Austrian government and the Allied Commission in Austria were defined, is printed in *B.F.S.P.*, vol. 146, pp. 504–511.

[6] Safehaven was the codename for the Allied programme to forestall any German attempts to conceal assets and looted property in neutral countries, adopted under resolution VI of the Final Act at Bretton Woods in 1944 and pursued through separate agreements e.g. with Switzerland and Sweden (1946), Italy (1947) and Spain (1948). Cf. W.N. Medlicott, *The Economic Blockade* (H.M.S.O., 1952 f.) vol. ii, pp. 622–9 and *Germany 1947–1949: The Story in Documents* (Washington, 1950), pp. 385–409.

control of foreign affairs and it would be logical for both to be exercised by the same authority. Before these particular powers were handed over we should, however, require certain safeguards: we should wish the Federal Republic to have undertaken the obligations of the General Agreement on Trade and Tariffs[7] and to have become a member of the International Trade Organisation which will not be set up until the autumn. We should also require to have reached an understanding with the Federal Republic concerning the various classes of financial claim against Germany. It would also be necessary on the relinquishment of this particular power for His Majesty's Government to be released by the United States Government from their contingent financial liability under the Revised Fusion Agreement.[8] It is of course by no means certain that the United States Government will be willing to forego this control, and it must in any case be assumed that they will wish to continue to exercise control over German economic policy though the Economic Cooperation Agreement,[9] and probably also to retain the powers of control over internal action under paragraph 2(h) of the Occupation Statute. We should favour the retention of the latter if during the next six months the Germans show an attitude of irresponsibility towards their economic problems, and perhaps also if United States behaviour suggests that, were E.C.A. to be the only remaining control, they would tend to give the Germans bad advice. Otherwise, however, there would be something to be said for relinquishing the reserved powers under Article 2(h) so that the Germans have to assume full responsibility in the economic field before the cessation of E.R.P. aid.

8. A number of the other reserved powers are of a transitional character and are required only until the completion of specific Allied programmes, e.g. those relating to reparations, restitution and Displaced Persons. Other relating, for example, to non-discrimination in trade matters, foreign interests in Germany and claims against Germany need to be retained until such time as it is considered suitable to exchange them for specific undertakings by the Germans. All those in 2(a) and also Ruhr control, decartelisation and deconcentration in 2(b) would on present showing have to be retained.

9. In any event it would not seem desirable that the Occupying Powers should yield to Dr. Adenauer's pressure for revision of the Occupation Statute in advance of the due date. The Chancellor told General

[7] The text of the G.A.T.T. agreement at Geneva on 30 October 1947 with signatures and protocol is printed in *B.F.S.P.*, vol. 148, pp. 759–820: *ibid.*, vol. 151, pp. 243–278, 522–47, vol. 154, pp. 673–7 and 700–6 for subsequent modifications and amendments following the establishment of the International Trade Organization under the Havana Charter of 24 March 1948. Cmd. 7375.

[8] For the Anglo-American agreement providing for the economic fusion of their zones of Occupation in Germany of 2 December 1946, as revised by agreement on 17 December 1947, see *B.F.S.P.*, vol. 146, pp. 484–8 and vol. 147, Part I, pp. 1191–1202.

[9] i.e. the O.E.E.C. Convention: see No. 1, note 8.

Robertson that the establishment by the three Foreign Ministers of a committee for this purpose would have an immensely favourable effect on German public opinion and ease many of his difficulties. But there do not seem to have been any important enough developments in the international field to justify a departure from the programme laid down in September 1949 and the Occupying Powers are entitled to claim that the German Federal Government must first prove its goodwill and earn their confidence by carrying out fully the provisions of the Petersberg Agreement before any departure from the programme could be agreed to. While a decision by the three Foreign Ministers to advance the date of the review of the Statute might help Dr. Adenauer and possibly be useful to him in his dealings with the Bundestag, there is also the risk that it might raise exaggerated hopes and lead him to decide finally against taking in the interim any further step towards the West, such as a decision to join the Council of Europe as an associate member, until revision of the Occupation Statute had actually taken place. Apart from these arguments against early revision of the Occupation Statute, there is the practical consideration that the German Federal authorities are experiencing great difficulty in finding properly trained men for their new Foreign Service. Judging by the delay that has occurred since the Petersberg Agreement over the appointment of German Consuls-General to London, Paris and New York, it would seem most unlikely that they would in any case be in a position to establish a Ministry for Foreign Affairs and a Foreign Service before several months had elapsed.

10. In the light of the foregoing considerations it appears that the furthest that we should go at present is to agree to examine revision of the Statute as soon as the twelve months period expires next September.

No. 50

Brief for the U.K. Delegation

No. 28 [FJ 1021/62]

Secret   FOREIGN OFFICE, *29 April 1950*

Japan

If the Soviet Union were to obtain control over Japan's reserves of trained manpower and industrial capacity, the world strategic balance would be altered to the grave detriment of the democratic powers. Japan remains the only highly industrialised country in Asia, and the attraction of Japan into the Soviet orbit must rank high on the Soviet list of priorities. The position is to some extent safeguarded while Japan remains under United States military occupation, but not entirely, since the occupation does not of itself provide complete security against a change in Japanese ideology. The Japanese people are known to be eager for a

Peace Treaty. They were aware that, for a number of years, the attitude of the Soviet Government prevented the convening of a Peace Conference. Now, however, Communist propaganda is able to contend, with a degree of plausibility, that there is still no Peace Treaty and the Japanese remain unfree because the United States wishes to retain her hold over Japan. The prolongation of the occupation lends colour to this propaganda, and it is conceivable that the time may come when the Japanese will adopt an attitude of non-cooperation towards the occupation authorities. It is true that there are as yet no signs of such a development. The fact, however, remains that resentment among the Japanese at the prolongation of Japan's inferior status, marked by the continuance of the occupation and the absence of a Treaty of Peace, is bound to grow. The longer the occupation lasts, therefore, the harder it will be to reach an eventual solution. The United States points to the dangers of making any change in the present régime of control in Japan. The answer is that the occupation cannot last for ever, and there is every reason to believe the dangers will grow rather than diminish with the passage of time.

2. The essential Japanese problem is how to arrange the transition of Japan from her present status as an occupied ex-enemy to the status of a fully sovereign member of international society in such a manner as to ensure that she remains outside the Soviet orbit and in voluntary association with the democratic powers. The United States would, it is believed, accept this assessment of the problem. Hitherto, however, they have attempted no solution. They have contented themselves with a number of palliative measures which they have usually introduced on a unilateral basis, thus causing unnecessary friction with friendly powers. The Supreme Commander for the Allied Powers in Japan has, for example, given a steadily increasing measure of autonomy to the Japanese Government, and the United States Government have urged other Governments to treat Japan in various important respects as though a state of war no longer existed. Thus, His Majesty's Government have been pressed to deal directly with the agents of the Japanese Government abroad in various international bodies, although His Majesty's Government's own representative continues to be deprived of direct access to the Japanese Government in Tokyo. United States policy has appeared in effect to be trying to drift into a state of peace with Japan while leaving unresolved a whole series of problems which demand final solution on an international basis.

3. In September 1949 Mr. Acheson told the Secretary of State that the United States Government had reached the view that the time had come to endeavour to negotiate a Treaty of Peace with Japan. It later emerged, however, that the United States Department of Defence did not share this view, and, indeed, actively opposed a Peace Treaty, on the grounds that United States strategic interests were bound to be seriously jeopardised. There have been recent reports that the deadlock within the United States Administration has now been resolved. It is possible that the United States

delegates to the London talks will bring with them proposals for an important forward move relating to Japan.[1] It is known that United States officials have been studying a proposal that the state of war should be declared at an end. It may well be that the United States Government have decided to sponsor this proposal as an interim solution of the Japanese problem. The proposal is discussed in FE(O) (50) 23[2] attached, in which the conclusion is reached that a declaration terminating the state of war has many disadvantages, and that His Majesty's Government should continue to press for a full Treaty of Peace. It is necessary, therefore, to examine the nature of the United States objections to a Treaty of Peace.

4. It has been suggested that the conclusion of a Peace Treaty could be reconciled with the adequate securing of United States strategic interests (and hence the strategic interests of like-minded powers also), if the United States were to conclude a bi-lateral Defence Pact with Japan which would permit the United States to retain forces in Japan and give her access to Japanese bases. The principal United States objections to this proposal appear to be:

(a) It would be necessary to specify the period of validity of the Pact and possibly also the size of the forces retained in Japan. The present situation in the Far East is so uncertain that the time limit would have to be long and the size of the forces large. The psychological reactions in Japan and in other Asian countries might be unfortunate.

(b) At present United States forces are in Japan on the basis of agreed international instruments to which the Soviet Union and China are parties. To sign a new bilateral Agreement to which these two countries were not parties might mean that the international legal basis for retaining United States forces in Japan was less secure.

5. It is considered that the first of these two objections would apply with at least equal force to the declaration of the termination of the state of war. The primary purpose of such a declaration would be to permit the United States to continue to retain substantial forces in Japan for an unspecified period of years, whilst at the same time giving a gesture of encouragement to the Japanese. But whereas under a bilateral Defence Pact United States forces would remain in Japan by arrangement with the Japanese, under the alternative proposal the Japanese would have no voice in the decision. It is in any case doubtful whether the reactions in

---

[1] On 25 April Mr. Dening suggested to Sir W. Strang that it would be helpful if Dr. Jessup could give some indication of current U.S. thinking on a Japanese peace treaty which could be passed on to the Commonwealth Working Party of officials who were meeting in London from 1 May under the direction of Commonwealth High Commissioners in London and the Secretary of State for Commonwealth Relations, to consider details of a peace settlement for Japan, as agreed at the Colombo Conference (see No. 85.i for their report). Sir W. Strang replied that day 'I have spoken to Dr. Jessup. He will enquire. But he thinks that Mr. Acheson will want to give the first indications himself on his arrival' (FJ 1021/59).

[2] This note of 25 April prepared by the Foreign Office for the Cabinet Far East (Official) Committee is not printed from CAB 134/290.

other Asian countries would be so adverse as the Americans appear to think. Such a move would probably be welcomed in the Philippines. There are no grounds for believing that India would be sharply critical, since the proposal has already been discussed with Pandit Nehru, who did not react adversely. Indeed, the only Asian country which it can be confidently prophesied would react adversely is China; and under her present Government, China would react adversely to any arrangements whatsoever designed to ensure the interests of the democratic powers.

6. The exact nature of the second objection is obscure, but it appears to imply a doubt as to the wisdom of making peace with Japan on a partial basis, i.e. without the participation of the Soviet Union and China. The United States have hitherto raised no objection on this latter score, and indeed Mr. Acheson told the Secretary of State last September that it was clear that the Soviet Union and China would never agree to a Peace Treaty which would be acceptable to the democratic powers, and that it would finally be necessary to go ahead without them. If a partial Peace Treaty of the kind described is considered to be acceptable it follows that Japan would thereby regain the right to exercise the attributes of full sovereignty. It would therefore follow that she would be free to conclude whatever arrangements she chose (provided of course that they did not conflict with any provisions that might be included in the Peace Treaty) with any state with whom she was at peace. It is hard, therefore, to see on what substantial grounds the legal basis of a Defence Pact could be attacked. It can, of course, be assumed that the Soviet Union and China would question the legal validity of a Defence Pact. There seems no reason why this should be permitted to prevent the taking of a step which seems otherwise justified, since no practical consequences could follow from whatever objections the Soviet Union and China might raise.

7. The question of the possible resurgence of Japan's military strength and the re-emergence of Japan as a potential aggressor is not discussed in this paper. In the brief prepared for the Colombo Conference (SAC(49)18)[3] it was stated 'The view that Japan by her own unaided efforts is unlikely again to present a serious threat to security cannot be disputed in so far as it relates to the short term. In the long run, that is to say a generation or more ahead, the position will depend on a variety of factors which cannot at present be foreseen.' It is considered that the real threat from Japan lies in the possibility of some form of association between Japan and the Soviet Union, and that it is not therefore necessary at present to discuss the possibility of the re-emergence of Japan as an aggressor in her own right.[4]

[3] Not printed.
[4] A copy of this brief drafted in Far Eastern department was sent to Mr. R.S. Milward of Research department for information. Mr. Milward wondered in a minute of 23 May 'whether the point of view of the U.S. War Department is not dismissed rather too lightly'. Mr. Milward pointed to U.S. War Department's fears that 'the Japanese, if politically free, will flirt dangerously with China & the Soviet Union . . . The War Department also are

aware of the hopeless economic mismanagement of the "liberated" Philippines & South Korea (perhaps also Burma) and are particularly disgusted by the collapse of Nationalist China. The[y] must increasingly feel that—although they may avoid the word "colonial"—a quasi-colonial status alone can protect any part of Asia. They would therefore prefer to retain legal control and the right of political & economic intervention in Japan, even at the cost of considerable resentment and unrest . . . Our view & that of the State Department is more considerate and is, I believe, the right one, but I would not care to bet on which course will, in fact, succeed in denying Japan to communism' (FJ 1021/62).

No. 51

Letter from Mr. Penson (Washington) to Mr. Allen

[C 3011/2514/18]

Secret   WASHINGTON, *29 April 1950*

My dear Denis,

I think I should report recent developments here, since my letter of April 19th,[1] in the thinking preparatory to the forthcoming Conference of Ministers. When I last wrote, the suggestions which I was instructed to make on returning from London were being considered by the State Department. Perry Laukhuff is now with you and you have doubtless spoken to him, so it may be that you are already well up to date. On the other hand, further developments have taken place here since he left, and they may be of interest in case you have not already had them from the Americans direct.

It is evident that much hard thinking has taken place in the State Department during the last three weeks, and on the whole the German problem now looms larger among the subjects for the Ministers' Conference than before. Even three weeks ago, some State Department officials were saying that Germany was not of course the main dish on the menu.[2] They are beginning to see, however, that it will hardly be possible for Acheson to return without at least some indication that the policy which the Three Powers have been pursuing with regard to Germany has

[1] In this letter (not printed from C 2738/148/18) Mr. Penson reported discussion with State Department further to some of the German questions discussed in No. 12. 'As regards the termination of the State of War, the State Department's views are likely to be in accordance with their memorandum of 22 March, which I believe is not unacceptable to you, apart from the question of putting the Occupation Statute on a contractual basis.' However, Mr. Penson explained that the State Department was unlikely to press very strongly the contractual proposal, first made in the U.S. memorandum of 22 March (see No. 12, note 10). 'As regards any other relaxations, the State Department's attitude appears to be one of great caution . . . I believe that their general view will be that the position in Germany, should, broadly speaking, be kept stabilised for some little time further. The only things they have mentioned as needing attention are the scope of the Ruhr Authority; Berlin, from a long range point of view; and ship building for export.'

[2] Cf. No. 45, note 1.

been further elaborated and strengthened as a result of the Conference. It is pretty clear that public opinion looks for this, and that it will not be satisfied with a few minor discussions on economic or other points of difficulty, such as shipbuilding. The above does not mean, however, that the Americans contemplate that striking decisions will necessarily be taken which could be announced immediately after the Conference.

Byroade is still of the opinion that the extent of German association with Western Europe indicated in the Petersberg Agreement[3] is insufficient to hold that country as a useful member of the West. The 'primary objective' is clearly stated in the Agreement, but the specific proposals, including Germany's admission as an associate member to the Council of Europe, are in fact only partial, placing Germany as they do in a somewhat inferior position—necessarily so no doubt—in the European community. It is worrying Byroade a good deal, and he told me yesterday that Acheson, who had started with the idea that Germany could, to some extent be left alone at the forthcoming discussions, is now agreed that some further elaboration of the Petersberg policy should be attempted if possible. They share, however, the Foreign Office view that steps cannot immediately be taken to bring Germany into the Council of Europe as a full member. Byroade, I think, also fears that, even were full membership possible, it might not be all that was needed in the circumstances. Membership of the Atlantic Pact, the State Department believes, is unsuitable for Germany because of the Pact's strong defense orientation, quite apart from other constitutional difficulties. Therefore, Byroade says, he would like to see another organisation into which Germany could be brought. For this reason he is inclined to look favourably on Bidault's suggestion of a 'High Council'.[4] According to the press, the State Department has asked the French for further particulars, and doubtless they will be bringing the matter up any way at the forthcoming Conference. I said that there had been little enthusiasm for Bidault's suggestion either in the press in the United States, or, as far as I knew, in London. To this he replied by reiterating that something more was wanted and that Bidault's suggestion had seemed to offer a solution. He went on to say that in this he was definitely not expressing Acheson's present views. Acheson was keeping his mind open on this subject, and probably it would still be open when he arrived in London.

I asked Byroade about recognition of Germany as a 'State' and the Federal Republic's successorship to the Reich. To this he replied that all these matters hung together, in his view. It would make it much simpler to agree to our views as to the Federal Republic's statehood if we could all see more clearly where we were going in the major question of securing for Germany an appropriate place in the community of Western Europe. He referred in similar terms to the revision of the Occupation Statute from

[3] See No. 7, note 2.
[4] See No. 24, note 5 and No. 47, note 4.

the point of view of giving the Federal Republic powers in foreign affairs and diplomatic representation.

He then went on to the subject of defense, and the uncertainty felt in Germany as to our intentions. It was true, he said, that the Germans ought to recognise that the occupation forces were Western Germany's defense guarantee, that they were larger than those which would be required merely for occupation if there were not a threat from the East; no doubt they did recognise this to some extent, but the uncertainty persisted. If we could visualise a place into which Germany might step in the Western European community in the course of the next few months or so, it would make it easier for the United States to offer some specific defense guarantees. At the end of the conversation he emphasised again that all these matters, in his view, hung together. He said he thought Acheson was convinced of this and believed that it was 'all or nothing'. I expressed some doubt whether, in view of what he had said and of the expectations which had been aroused in the United States and elsewhere, he could be satisfied with 'nothing'. Byroade agreed and I think admitted that he might have to be satisfied with something less than 'all'.

I have quoted this conversation at some length as indicating the course of Byroade's thinking. We believe that Acheson is relying increasingly upon him and on his judgment of what is wanted in Germany. Accordingly these developments will doubtless be of interest to you.

Byroade has put off his departure from Washington until Tuesday, May 2nd, or perhaps Wednesday. Reinstein[5] is leaving today. I also hope to leave on Wednesday. I judge that the postponement of Byroade's departure signifies that ideas are still developing here, especially in Acheson's mind, and that he wants Byroade with him a little longer. I hope to see you Thursday, all being well.[6]

Yours ever,
J. HUBERT PENSON

[5] Mr. J.J. Reinstein was Director of the Office of German Economic Affairs in the State Department.
[6] This letter was circulated to Western Organizations Department, Mr. Mallet, Sir I. Kirkpatrick, Sir G. Jebb and Sir R. Makins.

No. 52

Note by Mr. Barclay of a discussion with the Secretary of State at the Manor House Hospital on 29 April 1950

[ZP 2/98]

Secret

The Secretary of State said that he noted in the records of the official talks that a good deal of attention was being given to the question of negotiations with the U.S.S.R. He quite agreed that sooner or later we should have to have negotiations, but in his view the time was not yet ripe for these, since the organisation of the West was not yet sufficiently firm. He thought that the purpose of the forthcoming talks should be to strengthen this organisation by developing the Atlantic Pact or in other ways so that in due course the Western Powers might be in a position to talk.

The Secretary of State said he hoped to get agreement that the Americans, the French and ourselves should be, as it were, the foster-parents of Germany in the Council of Europe. Europe's nervousness about the possibility of Germany ultimately acquiring a dominant position on the Continent, of which there was plenty of evidence, could be overcome if there was some American commitment, and he would like to see the U.S. Government accept some obligation with regard to Germany. Any such involvement of the United States on the Continent could be supported by some sort of declaration on the part of the twelve Atlantic Powers on the lines proposed.[1]

Sir W. Strang explained that it had been the Americans who had first raised the issue of talks with the Russians, saying that there was some pressure for this in the United States. This led Dr. Jessup to suggest that it would be wrong to rule out the possibility of negotiations. The French were, of course, subject to similar pressure.

The Secretary of State said he thought that the line to take was that the forthcoming conversations were in the nature of a preparatory strengthening of our position which would make talks with the Russians a possibility in due course.

The Secretary of State said that he would like to get away from talk about Europe. We must think in terms of the West, the Free Nations or the Free World. We must aim at bringing in all the non-communist countries, including those of South and South-East Asia. The Americans were wrong to think in terms of Europe as a separate and self-contained unit.

The Secretary of State thought that in the final communique or declaration we should try to bring out the grim determination of the free nations to defend themselves. He wished to develop the idea of the common pooling of resources which had under-lain the Atlantic Pact. There should be no more talk of the United States coming to the help of Europe.

The Secretary of State said that he accepted the view that we should aim at getting London adopted as the seat for any new machinery set up under the Atlantic Pact.

In further discussion the Secretary of State made it clear that he was not in favour of the Alphand conception of the development of O.E.E.C. with which the United States and Canada would somehow be brought into relation.

[1] See No. 46, note 10.

No. 53

General Sir B. Robertson (Wahnerheide) to Mr. Bevin
(Received 1 May, 9 p.m.)

No. 673 Telegraphic [C 2922/9/18]

Immediate. Secret   WAHNERHEIDE, *1 May 1950, 6.30 p.m.*

Repeated Saving to Paris, Washington.

Your telegram No. 731[i].

German unity and all-German elections.

My own hope, as I made clear in para 2 of my telegram No. 657,[1] is that the Ministers at their London meeting will produce a comprehensive statement of Allied policy on the whole question of German unity. As I indicated there and in para 3 of my telegram No. 575,[1] it seems to me that an offer of all-German elections made immediately thereafter to the Russians would add much significance to the Ministerial pronouncement, which itself might well indicate that such an offer would be made in the near future by the High Commission.

2. My proposal is thus the exact contrary of that made by the Americans in the first sentence of para 5(*j*) of their paper on all German elections (my telegram No. 576).[1] They wanted a proposal on elections by the High Commission first, and a statement on unity by the Ministers afterwards. I dare say they would now be prepared to come round to the other view.[2]

---

[1] In Wahnerheide telegram No. 657 of 27 April General Robertson reported a private session that day of the Allied High Commission at which American and German proposals for German unity and all-German elections were discussed. In response to a statement by Mr. McCloy on 28 February in which he declared that 'the political unification of Germany on the basis of free all-German elections is a major objective of United States policy' (*F.R.U.S. 1950*, vol. iv, pp. 604–5), Dr. Adenauer had submitted proposals to the A.H.C. on 22 March for all-German elections (Cmnd. 1552 of 1961: *Selected Documents on Germany and the Question of Berlin 1944–1961*, pp. 128–9). These were endorsed in a proposal of 15 April from Mr. McCloy for an approach to the Soviet government for quadripartite negotiation of an Electoral Law (text transmitted in Wahnerheide telegram No. 576 of even date, not here printed from C 2543/9/18). General Robertson commented in Wahnerheide telegram No. 575, also of 15 April, that the American proposal was based on the assumption that the Soviet government would not accept the offer: 'I must admit that as with the Berlin Election project I find this proposal specious rather than brilliant. At the same time with all the talk that has been going on and with the Federal Government's initiative facing us it seems to me that we should be wrong to turn it down now. The essential point is clearly to ensure that our conditions for the Electoral Law are so water-tight as to avoid any risk of their being accepted by the Soviets . . . I have however, some doubt as to the timing of the offer to the Soviets' (C 2542/9/18). On 27 April the High Commission agreed that the question required consideration by the three Foreign Ministers and approved a recommendation to this effect. This recommendation, transmitted in Wahnerheide telegram No. 658 of 27 April (not printed), also referred to a study being made by the A.H.C.'s Political Affairs Committee of the necessary conditions for all-German elections.

[2] The French view as put forward by M. A. Bérard, French Deputy High Commissioner,

3. In deciding what conditions should be attached to our advocacy of German unity or all-German elections we should also consider how and when these conditions should be stated. Whether our proposal is strictly serious or only propaganda, in either case it must appear to be seriously meant. If it is strictly serious, the less said about conditions initially the better. On the other hand, if it is really only propaganda and if we are most anxious to insure ourselves against the possibility of its acceptance or even of having to negotiate with the Soviet, then our conditions must be sufficiently stated for this purpose. Even in this case, however, we must realise that a laborious catalogue including every conceivable condition will completely spoil the propaganda effect which we desire to achieve by making it apparent to everybody that we are carefully fortifying ourselves against any practical result coming out of our proposal. Therefore in giving my comments on the various conditions which you have proposed in your telegram No. 731 I do not necessarily imply that all these conditions should be made public simultaneously with the comprehensive statement of policy referred to in para 1 above.

4. In the light of the above my comments on the conditions set out in your telegram No. 731 are as follows:

(a) *Condition 1.* While, of course, the French will not like the idea of an all-German government in Berlin, I think we should stick to this and try and make them swallow it. But to propose the establishment of such a government in accordance with the Basic Law is in complete contradiction to the American proposal, which endorses Adenauer's proposal, which in turn was for elections to an all-German Constituent Assembly to draw up a new all-German Constitution. I am sure there would be no prospect whatever of advance on the basis of the Basic Law, and therefore I prefer the American and German proposal.

(b) *Condition 3.* As drafted might be taken to mean that the S.E.D. and K.P.D. should be illegal. Adenauer's proposal was 'freedom of action for all parties throughout Germany'. I think this is preferable. We cannot put the S.E.D. out of court before the case starts. Our only hope is to induce the Russians to let it enter a fair fight with the democratic parties one day, in which it would be decisively defeated.

(c) *Condition 5.* Is so drafted as to suggest that our main objection to the *Volkspolizei* is that they indulge in political activity. I should like to see our real objections to the *Volkspolizei* as a semi-military force brought out more clearly. Here again. if our proposal about elections is to be a real one, it will probably be vain to insist on the dissolution of the *Volkspolizei* in advance. We should have to hope that their presence would be neutralised by that of the 'commissions composed of representatives of the four Occupation Powers or of representatives of

at the meeting on 27 April and reported in Wahnerheide telegram No. 657 was that the offer of all-German elections to the Soviet government should be included in a statement of policy from the Foreign Ministers at the London Conference.

the United Nations' proposed by Adenauer.

(*d*) *Condition 6.* (If used at all in the statement on unity and I consider it would be more appropriate in a future proposal about elections) should clearly answer the question: 'Elections to what?'. I suggest also that the second sentence of Condition 6 should be dropped, as going beyond the German/American proposal and demanding an ideal we should be unlikely ever to attain.

(*e*) *Condition 9.* I suggest that, for propaganda reasons, the word 'Control' in the title of the Commission should be dropped.

5. As reported in para 3 of my telegram No. 658 the Political Affairs Committee is meeting, probably on Wednesday,[3] to study the conditions which must be observed if all-German elections should take place. The U.S. paper was deliberately designed to leave out, as conditions for elections, those conditions for unity which would be most unacceptable, leaving them to be put forward at a later stage if the Russians should unexpectedly agree to embark on the course proposed. The only conditions for elections proposed in the American paper were in effect those proposed by Adenauer, which in addition to those I have already mentioned were:

(*a*) the draft Constitution prepared by the Constituent Assembly should be submitted to the German people for ratification.

(*b*) All Occupation Powers should desist from influencing the activity of any political party.

(*c*) Personal safety of everyone working for any party should be guaranteed by all Occupation Powers and by the German authorities both before and after the elections.

(*d*) Freedom of circulation and distribution for all newspapers throughout Germany.

(*e*) Freedom of personal movement throughout Germany.

6. I am instructing my representative on the Political Affairs Committee to take the line that it would be useful for the High Commission to recommend conditions for unity as well as for elections. As for elections, he will agree unless you instruct me to the contrary that those proposed by Adenauer and supported by the Americans are sufficient. As for conditions for unity, he will put forward those contained in your telegram No. 731 as modified by my remarks above.[4]

---

[3] 3 May.

[4] On 2 May the Foreign Office replied in telegram to Wahnerheide No. 751: 'We agree generally with the arguments set forth in paragraphs 1–3 of your telegram . . . Since the elections would constitute only a first step towards the achievement of German unity, we rather deprecate treating them as an isolated issue, and consider it essential to set forth at least the fundamental principles without which German unity would not be acceptable to us. In this way we would make it clear from the outset that we intend to guarantee a way of life for a united Germany which would be as free as that already enjoyed by the Germans of the Federal Republic. Otherwise we might appear to be weakening and prepared to

Foreign Office please pass to Washington and Paris as my telegrams Nos. 164 and 153 respectively.

CALENDARS TO No. 53

i *28 Apr. 1950   Draft conditions for German unity* proposed by F.O. in tel. to Wahnerheide No. 731 for circulation at London conference (1) all-German government in Berlin (2) freedom of individual (3) political freedom (4) independent judiciary (5) abolition of militarised and political police (6) free elections (7) cessation of reparations from current production (8) cessation of industrial exploitation (9) quadripartite control by majority vote [C 2838/9/18].

ii *4 May 1950   A.H.C. recommendation on conditions for German unity* agreed at meeting on 4 May, reported in Wahnerheide tel. No. 693 (text in tel. No. 694). French succeed in dropping Berlin as the capital from condition 1 in [i] above [C 3010, 3013/9/18].

compromise with the Russians at the expense of the Germans themselves' (C 2922/9/18): see further calendar ii. A brief was accordingly prepared for the London Conference (not printed from C 3367/9/18) which recommended the issue of a Ministerial statement on German unity and instructions to the Allied High Commission for the preparation of a draft electoral law as the basis for an approach to the Soviet government for all-German elections.

No. 54

Memorandum by the Secretary of State for Foreign Affairs

C.P. (50) 92 [CAB 129/39]

Secret   FOREIGN OFFICE, 2 *May 1950*

Conversations with United States and French Officials

My colleagues will wish to have a broad outline of the progress of the current talks between United Kingdom, United States and French officials, the object of which is to prepare the way for my meeting next week with the United States Secretary of State and the French Foreign Minister, and for the ensuing session of the Atlantic Council.

2. Both in the bipartite talks between officials of the United Kingdom and the United States and in the tripartite talks with the Americans and the French the agenda this week has been confined to broad and general topics. From to-day, the discussions will break down into sub-committees and will begin to deal with such specific subjects as Germany, South-East Asia, Colonial questions, &c.

3. The first object in both bipartite and tripartite meetings was to establish a *general agreed estimate of the present situation*.[1] The outcome of this discussion was a broad agreement that the trend of power in the last

---

[1] Italics as in original.

twelve months has been, on balance, unfavourable to the West, and that the present situation is one of danger; that, on the other hand, there were certain weaknesses in the Soviet position; and that it was not likely that they would be prepared to run a serious risk of war for several years. They might well, however, adopt a more forward policy than hitherto in the 'cold war', and it was therefore necessary to examine very carefully the various points in the world where they were looking for weak spots in the Western system, of which Germany was clearly the most important.

4. There was general agreement that the Western Powers cannot permit further Soviet advances in the world which would materially strengthen the Soviet position; that they must therefore build up, while preserving their economic progress and development, a framework in which the maximum industrial and military strength can be deployed; that this can only be done by the combined resources of the Atlantic Pact Powers acting in the interests of the whole of the free world; and that within the Atlantic Pact Organisation there must be specially close understanding and co-operation between the United States, the United Kingdom and France.

5. In the bipartite talks with the Americans there has been a close review of the *relationship between the United Kingdom and the United States*[1] and of the rôle which each should play in the world. The Americans have expressed themselves as anxious to regard the United Kingdom as a country with which they must have the most intimate possible relations; and methods have been suggested for improving the machinery of consultation at all levels and at all times. On the other hand, the Americans have made it clear that so far as European affairs are concerned we must not expect them to regard us as entirely different from the other European Powers. On the economic side, they have said that they believe the United Kingdom ought to give more of a lead in Europe, particularly in such matters as the European Payments Union (E.P.U.), but they have definitely stated that they do not think we should accept any form of organic union with Europe. Their thinking on this is clearly not very far advanced, and the matter will be discussed further with them.

6. *The leader of the United States team of officials, Dr. Jessup, has made important statements,*[1] both in the bipartite and in the tripartite meetings, about the intention of the United States Administration to find a means of supporting European countries after the end of the European Recovery Programme.[2] At the same time the United States Delegation have raised the question whether the United Kingdom, by concentrating on the attainment of viability at all costs in 1952, is prejudicing the development of desirable wider European interests and in some cases American policy, owing to the hostility which some of the United Kingdom's actions arouse in the United States. We have, of course, strongly pressed our own point

[2] See Nos. 34 and 40.

of view on this and the Americans have shown an understanding of the need for changes in their own economic policy. The Americans have also drawn attention to doubts which are felt in some American minds whether we are wholeheartedly devoted to the objectives of the Tripartite Declaration of September 1949.[3]

7. Perhaps the main subject that has been dealt with in detail has been *the question of developing the machinery of the North Atlantic Pact.*[1] There is complete agreement that something must be done to co-ordinate and give impetus to the various committees responsible for the elaboration of common defence plans. There is also agreement that some new step forward in the political field is necessary within the Atlantic Pact. Out of these two points of agreement has emerged a suggestion that the Atlantic Council when it meets in May should set up a committee of Deputies of the Foreign Ministers, charged with the duty of co-ordinating all the activities of the Atlantic Treaty. There are, however, differences of opinion both on the status and the character of this committee and on the exact field which it should cover. The French, supported apparently by the Americans, feel very strongly that if any real defence is to be provided for the Western Powers, this committee must be influential and effective and that it must have a Secretary-General of high standing and great energy who will give drive and impetus to its work. Secondly, the French have expressed a strong view that the North Atlantic Treaty is not a proper forum in which the general economic problems of the area can be considered. Their main reason is unwillingness to see Germany associated with the Atlantic Pact in any shape or form now or, apparently, at any time in the future. They therefore suggested that the O.E.E.C., while continuing to deal in its present form with purely European economic questions, should be expanded in some way by the association of the United States and Canada for the purpose of dealing with economic problems common to Europe and the Western hemisphere. We have pointed out that this system both atrophies Article 2 of the Pact and involves separation between the economics of defence and the general economic life of the countries concerned, which is unrealistic; and that in our view there is no need at present to take any decisions which would prejudge the possibility of the Atlantic Pact's eventually becoming a forum in which broad economic questions are handled. The French attitude (which may or may not represent the final views of the French Government) seems to be dictated partly by reluctance to conceive of Germany's joining fully in the life of the Atlantic community, and partly by a desire to make sure that any new machinery on the non-military side shall be firmly established in Paris.[4]

[3] See No. 2, note 1.

[4] The position reached in tripartite official talks on Atlantic pact machinery (see Nos. 40 and 46) was reviewed in more detail in U.K. delegation brief No. 33 of 1 May (not printed). Sir G. Jebb recorded that Mr. Bevin when approving the general lines of this brief was 'quite clear that he wants to aim at the eventual construction of one machine for coordinating the

8. As regards *relations with the Soviet Union*, there has been discussion of the question whether the time is ripe for any attempt to reach a settlement by negotiation with the Soviets. All three delegations have admitted that they see no prospect whatever of such negotiations being successful and have declared, with varying degrees of emphasis, that they have no intention of being drawn into them if they can help it. On the other hand, the French have laid great stress on the need to show that the Western Powers still place peace and disarmament in the forefront of their basic objectives and that they are not ruling out the possibility of a settlement. The Americans also thought that we should be prepared to consider the possibility of talks with the Russians if opportunity should arise at a later stage or if there were a really strong movement of opinion in favour of making a last attempt to get agreement. They stated, however, that it was not the intention of the United States Government to negotiate with the Soviet Union unless the United Kingdom and French Governments agree on the need for such a step, and unless agreed positions are worked out in advance. It has been made entirely clear that in our view general negotiations are unlikely to succeed until such a time as we have built up a 'situation of strength' in the West, towards which the conclusion of the Atlantic Pact itself has made a great, but only initial, contribution.

9. There have also been exchanges of view on common policy towards the satellite States in the matter of diplomatic representatives,&c., and on a common attitude towards Yugoslavia.

10. The French have suggested a *Joint Declaration* to be issued by the three Powers, or perhaps by the Atlantic Council itself. The chief object of this declaration would be to set forth the aims and ideals of the Western Powers; to introduce the theme of peace and prosperity; to draw attention (as it were incidentally, however) to the sacrifices which must be made if peace is to be secured; and generally to wrest the propaganda initiative from the Soviet Union.

11. I would emphasise that these conversations are entirely without commitment on either side. There has been free and open discussion of basic questions, but no decisions have been taken in the name of Governments.[5]

E.B.

affairs of the Western world and not two' (WU 1071/92). The question of location of any new Atlantic Pact machinery was examined in U.K. delegation brief No. 30 circulated on 1 May (not printed), to which was appended a minute of 28 April by Sir G. Jebb suggesting that if London was secured as the location for new machinery, the British could afford to be more flexible towards meeting the French as to the form of the organization. 'Seeing that, in practice, everything will depend on the way the new machinery is stage-managed, there would appear to be a strong argument in favour of London, since we are, in effect, the only people who can do such stage managing.' Sir W. Strang recorded below on 29 April: 'The Secretary of State agrees that we can propose London' (WU 1071/78).

[5] Mr. Younger drew upon this Cabinet paper in preparing a summary brief of 4 May (not printed from CAB 21/1761) for the ministerial meetings that day: see No. 57.

No. 55

Minute from Mr. Bevin to Mr. Attlee

P.M./50/18 [F.O.800/517]

Top secret   FOREIGN OFFICE, 2 May 1950

E.P.C. (50) 44[1]

Fundamental discussions with the United States

I have read this E.P.C. paper and I hope it will be possible for me to be present when it is taken by the Committee.[2]

2. I would, however, like you to know at once that I am much disturbed by the approach and general tone of the Annex of this paper, which does not seem to me to be in line with our general relationship with the United States, or the understandings which were reached with the United States and Canada at the Tripartite meeting in Washington last September. My feeling is that at the Washington talks the Americans did what they could to help at the time, and since then have been carrying out their undertakings to the best of their ability. But it was also understood that we should make contributions on our side.

3. Now this paper seems to me to suggest that we can arrange our own affairs as we please, in our own little circle, and that the Americans can adapt themselves to our ideas if they so wish. I do not think that it is right that we should take this line or indeed that we are in a position to do so. I want to stick to the intention and the spirit of what we agreed last September, since it is in the same spirit that I am proposing to discuss the whole range of our policy with Mr. Acheson when he arrives later on in the month.

4. I am sending a copy of this minute to the Chancellor of the Exchequer.[3]

ERNEST BEVIN

CALENDAR TO NO. 55

i 3 May 1950 Further criticisms of E.P.C. (50) 44 from (a) Mr. Hall (Economic

[1] No. 42.
[2] The Economic Policy Committee was due to discuss No. 42 at a meeting on 5 May. However the meeting was cancelled since Mr. Bevin, who was still largely confined to bed after leaving hospital on 4 May, was unable to attend.
[3] When submitting this minute to the Prime Minister, Mr. D.H.F. Rickett, Principal Private Secretary to Mr. Attlee, suggested in a covering minute of 2 May that a small meeting of Ministers, at which Mr. Bevin could be present, should be held to clear up outstanding points of difference on No. 42 and various P.U.S.C. papers, in particular British Overseas Obligations (No. 43) and Germany (No. 64.i) before talks with Mr. Acheson began. Arrangements were subsequently made for the meetings recorded in Nos. 57 and 63.

Section, Cabinet Office) who while acknowledging that there is 'sharp difference of opinion between ourselves and the Americans about the rate of progress which we ought to make, and the risks we ought to take' considers line proposed in E.P.C. (50) 44 of telling Americans that 'we cannot modify our present policies at all until our reserves are much larger than they are today, and until the rest of the world is, and is likely to remain, in balance with the dollar area' is 'much too rigid a line, and if persisted in, will be likely to have a bad effect on our relations with the United States' and feed existing U.S. suspicions that 'what we really wanted to do was to build up an independent currency area'. (*b*) reservations from Sir L. Rowan in Washington telegram No.1356 about tactics: if substance of E.P.C. (50)44 'represents the limit to which we can go in discussion rather than the basis from which we are to start it is liable to cause considerable disappointment in American minds and to render discussions much less fruitful than we had hoped' [CAB 21/2247; PREM 8/1204; T 232/199].

No. 56

Minute from Mr. Dening to Sir W. Strang

[F 1022/15]

FOREIGN OFFICE, *3 May 1950*

South-East Asia and Far East talks

I think you should know that our talks with the Americans, while mildly (but only mildly) encouraging as regards South-East Asia, have led to nothing at all on China or Japan. We had of course expected that their lips would be sealed on Japan, and I gained no impression that Mr. Acheson will have very much to add to this position when he talks with the Secretary of State.

On China, it is crystal clear that the Americans have devoted no thought to this subject at all, and their attitude is completely negative and defeatist. We got them to agree that it is a common aim that China should not pass irrevocably into the Soviet orbit. We also got them to agree that China is not yet irrevocably lost. But as for doing anything about it, they did not have a thought. In reply to questions, Mr. Merchant[1] thought that the United States might withdraw recognition from the Nationalist Government when Formosa was captured, though even this is by no means certain. This would not of course mean recognition of the People's Government; recognition is not in sight and may not happen for ten or twelve years. What is likely to happen in the meantime has been given no thought, but there is a faint hope that Manchuria, Inner Mongolia and Sinkiang may sow the seeds of friction with the Soviet Union. Apart from that, the United States will keep their face firmly averted from China in

[1] Mr. L.T. Merchant was U.S. Deputy Assistant Secretary of State for Far Eastern Affairs.

the hope that while it is in that position some miracle will occur to change the situation in their and our favour.

As a counter to this, I asked whether they would agree that the danger is acute and that time is not on our side. They found themselves in complete agreement as to this, but did not apparently propose to do anything about it.

To the suggestion that there is no consultation on Far Eastern matters comparable to that which takes place over Europe and the Middle East, Mr. Merchant said—I believe quite truthfully—that this did not arise from any desire not to consult, but merely because of developments in China and the fact that the United States had been unable to resolve their difficulties over Japan; which had led to silence on this subject since the two Secretaries of State last met in Washington in September. The Americans agreed that consultation on policy at a higher level (i.e. between the respective Secretaries of State and the respective Ambassadors) during the intervals between Ministerial meetings was desirable, and agreed recommendations to this effect will be made.

But as regards policy on China and Japan, the Americans have not got one, and as regards China they do not even appear to have thought about it. At the end of the meeting I indicated that the Secretary of State might wish to ask Mr. Acheson where we and other Western Powers would stand if in fact it was the determination of the United States to have no policy in regard to China for a number of years.

The fact of the matter is that the United States have neglected and are neglecting the Far East, and that unless and until they can be moved from their inertia, the rest of us will all be in very acute danger.[2]

ESLER DENING

CALENDARS TO NO. 56

i *1–3 May 1950 Bipartite sub-committee meetings (a) No. 5 on Indo-China* U.K. and U.S. against French idea for issue of declaration on Indo-China and S.E. Asia: require further information on French policy in Indo-China. Qualified recognition of Associate States by U.K. explained [FF 1025/3]. *(b) No. 10 China* and *(c) No.11 Far East* mainly Japan—as summarized in No.56. Agreed report on China later circulated as UKUS/P/8 of 5 May, not here reproduced [FC 1022/314; F.O. 800/449].

ii *1–4 May 1950 Tripartite sub-committee Meetings Nos. 2, 4, 6, on South East Asia and Indo-China:* French proposal for 3-Power declaration against communism in S.E.A. countered by U.K. proposal for declaration by S.E. govts. themselves.

[2] Sir W. Strang minuted below on 4 May to Mr. Bevin: 'This is the black spot in the talks. In other spheres we seem to be getting somewhere.' Mr. Bevin replied 'I had better get Acheson aside for this rather more secret enquiries E.B.' Sir W. Strang further commented on Mr. Dening's brief at iii below: 'This is a very serious position and the Secretary of State will wish to bring it home to Mr. Acheson. U.S. policy in the Far East—or lack of policy—is a gift to the Russians. W. Strang, 6/5.'

Texts (not here reproduced) of (*a*) agreed U.K./U.S. minute on tripartite objectives in S.E.A. on which French reserve position and (*b*) agreed tripartite minute on fields of common endeavour, circulated with covering minute as TRI/P/21 of 4 May are printed in *F.R.U.S. 1950*, vol. iii, pp. 943–5 and 947–8. [FZ 1025/3, 6, 8].

iii *6 May 1950 Brief from Mr. Dening to Mr. Bevin* covering final papers on (*a*) *S.E.A. and Indo-China* (MIN/TRI/P/9) a revision of TRI/P/21 still with French reservation as discussed at 6th tripartite meeting on 6 May. (*b*) *China* (MIN/UKUS/P/1) a revision of UKUS/P/8 as approved at 6th bipartite meeting on 5 May (*c*) *Japan* (MIN/UKUS/P/4). Mr. Dening discusses in detail 'serious divergences' with U.S. over China and Japan [F 1022/15; FZ 1025/7].

No. 57

Note of an informal meeting of Ministers held in the Prime Minister's Room at the House of Commons on Thursday, 4 May 1950, at 5.30 p.m.[1]

[*CAB 21/1761*]

Top secret

Present:
The Rt. Hon. C.R. Attlee, M.P., Prime Minister (*In the Chair*); the Rt. Hon. Herbert Morrison, M.P., Lord President of the Council; the Rt. Hon. Sir Stafford Cripps, K.C., M.P., Chancellor of the Exchequer; the Rt. Hon. E. Shinwell, M.P., Minister of Defence; the Hon. K.G. Younger, M.P., Minister of State.

Also present:
Sir Edward Bridges, Treasury; Sir William Strang, Sir Roger Makins, Foreign Office.

Secretary:
Sir Norman Brook.

The meeting had been called to consider various questions of policy which were likely to arise in the forthcoming discussions with the United States Secretary of State.

---

[1] See No.55, note 3. This note was prepared by Sir N. Brook on 4 May as a provisional draft. Item 1 was circulated to Sir E. Bridges, Permanent Secretary to the Treasury, and Sir R. Makins on 5 May for comment. In his covering minute to Sir E. Bridges, Sir N. Brook observed 'I am not at all sure that I have got the technicalities right—and I am somewhat concerned about the inconsistency between the opening and concluding remarks of the Chancellor.' In reply on 5 May Sir E. Bridges doubted whether records of this meeting and the second meeting at No. 63 should be kept at all: 'Indeed, I think that much of the record of the discussion yesterday is probably too explosive for anything except your purely personal records.' This was endorsed by Sir S. Cripps: 'On the whole I agree with Sir E. Bridges.' In the Foreign Office Sir R. Makins showed a copy of item 1 to Mr. Bevin and Mr. Younger before returning it to Sir N. Brook without comment. On 23 May Sir N. Brook sent copies of No. 57 and No. 63 to Sir E. Bridges and Sir W. Strang as his own private records of the meetings which were not for circulation.

1. Economic Questions

Discussion turned first on the general question of Anglo-American economic relations.

The Chancellor of the Exchequer said that he had seen the joint memorandum on this subject which had been prepared by United Kingdom and United States officials in preparation for discussions on Items 3 and 4 of the Agenda for the talks (U.K.U.S./P/6).[2] This, being the work of officials, ignored the fundamental difficulty of the different political attitude of the two Governments. The views of the Labour Government of the United Kingdom on economic methods and objectives were widely different from the bi-partisan approach of the United States Government. The former believed in a planned economy, for which discrimination and non-convertibility were essential instruments: the latter, believing in a free economy, were constantly pressing the former to pursue economic policies which they would not and could not accept. Moreover, the tone of the memorandum was one of apology for the failure of the United Kingdom Government to carry out all that the United States Government desired. It had nothing to say about the failure of the United States Government to reduce their tariff barriers. If this was to be the keynote of the economic discussions with Mr. Acheson, the whole approach to the problem would be misjudged. It would be quite unprofitable to seek to patch up compromises on matters of less importance, without facing the main political difficulty. If we and the Americans were to work together in economic affairs, we must each be tolerant of the other's political views; and the Americans, in particular, must accept the fact that the United Kingdom Government were committed to a planned economy and resolved to retain all the essential instruments of economic planning.

The Prime Minister said that he was not sure that it would be good tactics to open these conversations by stresssing the differences between the two Governments in matters of political theory. He saw no practical advantage in beginning by insisting that, politically, the two Governments were poles apart. He would prefer to make a more practical approach—seeking a basis on which the two Governments could co-operate, but losing no opportunity of pointing out that the United States Government were quite ready to adopt the methods of the controlled economy when it suited their domestic purposes, e.g. in their policy of supporting farm-prices.

The Chancellor of the Exchequer said that the Americans were pressing us to embark prematurely on a second experiment in convertibility. When the Organisation for European Economic Co-operation had first been established they had recognised that the convertibility of sterling could only be achieved after a prolonged period of discrimination against the dollar, and they had urged us to base our policies on the aim of attaining

[2] This paper of 3 May on important factors affecting Anglo-American relations is printed in *F.R.U.S. 1950*, vol. iii, pp. 957–60: see further No. 70.

viability by 1952. Now they were suggesting that we should enlarge the area of convertibility of sterling progressively, and accept risks at the cost of postponing until after 1952 our attainment of viability. If we were ready to experiment now in the liberalisation of trade, they would be ready to give us continued dollar aid beyond 1952. The Chancellor deprecated these suggestions on two grounds. First, he was convinced that any such progressive approach to convertibility would undermine the strength of sterling: for as soon as any such channel was opened all the currencies of the world would seek conversion to dollars via sterling. Convertibility, in his view, could be attained only at a single stroke when the strength of sterling had been made unassailable. Secondly, he did not wish to be put in the position of having to continue to accept dollar aid after 1952. It was essential to our future as a nation that we should achieve independence of United States financial aid as quickly as possible.

In further discussion the Chancellor said that he agreed that our economic problems could only be solved on the basis of a close partnership to be founded on a frank recognition of the different political outlook of the two Governments. So long as these political differences were not glozed over, he favoured the closest possible co-operation: indeed, he would wish to go further than anything proposed in the joint memorandum and set up a combined team of United Kingdom and United States officials working together continuously on problems of common concern, both political and economic, and submitting their joint recommendations to the two Governments.

The meeting were informed that the Foreign Secretary had been similarly alarmed at the approach indicated in the Chancellor's paper E.P.C.(50) 44 on Fundamental Discussions with the United States.[3] This had seemed to him to strike much too rigid and uncompromising a note as a basis for discussion with Mr. Acheson. Thus, the conditions proposed in paragraph 5 of the Annex[4] for sterling-dollar convertibility seemed somewhat extreme. And the later paragraphs of the Annex seemed to suggest that the United Kingdom Government had done all that they could be expected to do: any further contribution must come wholly from the United States. While the Foreign Secretary had no intention of using apologetic language in these discussions, he saw no practical advantage in adopting a hectoring tone.

The Chancellor of the Exchequer said that the stipulations set out in the Annex to E.P.C. (50) 44 were no more strict—indeed, in many respects they were less strict—than those which Ministers had approved as a basis for the Washington talks in September (paragraphs 19–22 of E.P.C. (49)73).[5] The Chancellor admitted that in the Washington talks he and the

---

[3] No. 42. [4] No. 42.i.

[5] E.P.C. (49) 73 of 4 July 1949 on the dollar situation (CAB 134/222) was approved by the Economic Policy Committee on 7 July (E.P.C. (49) 27th meeting on CAB 134/220) as a general guide for the U.K. delegation at the Washington financial talks: see No. 2, note 1 and further No. 62, note 3.

Foreign Secretary had not found it possible to insist upon all the conditions set out in E.P.C. (49)73; and he recognised that in the forthcoming discussions it might be necessary to forego some of the points made in the Annex to E.P.C. (50)44. It was, however, important that negotiators should set out clearly, before they embarked on their discussions, the aims which they wished to achieve. This was the object of the Annex to E.P.C. (50)44.

In conclusion *The Chancellor of the Exchequer* said that he did not think there was any difference of substance between his views and those of the Foreign Secretary. He was, however, concerned to ensure that our case should be put clearly and fearlessly to the Americans. In particular, he wished to impress on them the importance which we attached to building up the strength of sterling. *The Prime Minister* said that it would be useful to make it clear that a change of Government in this country would not involve any change of policy in this respect; a Conservative Government would be equally concerned to establish the strength of sterling and to achieve at the earliest possible moment complete independence of United States financial aid.

2. *North Atlantic Treaty Organisation*

Discussion then turned on the proposal, put forward by officials of the United States, the United Kingdom and France for consideration in the Tripartite talks (TRI/P/17),[6] that the North Atlantic Treaty Organisation should be strengthened by the creation of a body of 'Deputies' to Council members which could meet more frequently than the Council itself, and by the establishment of a permanent organisation including a general Secretariat.

The Chancellor of the Exchequer said that he saw no need for this development of the Organisation. And he could not agree that Deputies to Foreign Ministers should exercise the powers of the Council itself and be able to 'co-ordinate' the financial work of the organisation and commit Finance Ministers.

Sir William Strang said that it had been suggested from various quarters that there was need for some more permanent machinery to help in co-ordinating the work of the various branches of the Organisation. It was not merely the financial and economic work which was in question. There was also need to develop the work of the Organisation in the direction of building up what the Foreign Secretary called 'the Atlantic community'. The Council itself could meet only at rare intervals; and the need had been felt for some machinery which would ensure that work was carried on continuously between their meetings.

The Minister of Defence agreed that there was urgent need for some permanent machinery of this kind. There was also need to rationalise the relations between the North Atlantic Treaty Organisation and the Western Union Organisation. Finance was not the most urgent of the

[6] See No. 46, note 6.

problems confronting these Organisations. The more urgent need was for some body which could undertake intensive study of the military and production problems—e.g. how best to build up forces which would be internationally balanced, how best to rationalise the production of equipment in the various Allied countries, etc. These were not merely, or mainly, financial questions. The proposed meetings of Deputies would frame recommendations for decision by the Council or by the constituent Governments. Each of the Deputies would act within the limits of instructions given to him by his Government: none of them would be able to commit his Finance Minister outside the limits of those instructions.

The Chancellor of the Exchequer feared that the decisions of such a body of Deputies, even though framed in terms of recommendations, would in fact go far to commit Governments. When a project had been agreed in an international body of this kind, it was difficult for any particular Government to decline to carry out its part in the plan. Thus, he saw from the report which the Minister of Defence had made on the recent meetings at Brussels and The Hague (D.O. (50) 31)[7] that the North Atlantic Defence Committee had invited the Defence Financial and Economic Committee to 'recognise that additional finance would be required to meet the requirements of the medium-term plan over and above anything envisaged by current defence budgets'. This recommendation was bound to cause some embarrassment to the United Kingdom Government, which had hitherto held the view that any further contribution towards the requirements of Western Union or North Atlantic Treaty planning must be found within the limits of the Defence Estimates already approved.

The Prime Minister said that he would wish to have some further discussion of the proposals in TRI/P/17[6] before these were brought forward in the forthcoming talks with Mr. Acheson.

3. *General*

The Chancellor of the Exchequer said that he had various other criticisms to offer on the papers which had been recently circulated in the P.U.S.C. series. Thus, he was by no means satisfied with the paper on the Future of Germany (P.U.S.C. (49) 62)[8] and found himself in disagreement with various points in the paper on British Overseas Obligations (P.U.S.C. 79).[9]

His main difficulty, however, was that in all these papers he found no reference to the policy of creating a 'Third Force' by a combination of the United Kingdom, the Commonwealth and Western Europe. These papers seemed to imply that this conception had been finally abandoned. He found difficulty in accepting that conclusion; for he still looked forward to the day when this country could free herself from the hegemony, political and economic, of the United States.

The Lord President expressed surprise at this statement by the Chancellor. He himself had never found any great attraction in the conception of

[7] Not printed: cf. No. 33, note 7.   [8] No. 64.i.   [9] No. 43.

a 'Third Force'. In any event, that conception had always been put forward as an alternative to a policy of Anglo-American co-operation. And he had been under the impression that, as such an alternative policy, it had been deliberately rejected by Ministers in their discussion of the line to be taken by the Foreign Secretary and the Chancellor of the Exchequer in the Washington talks of September, 1949.

The Prime Minister said that this point must be discussed further at a later meeting.

No. 58

Memorandum from Sir I. Kirkpatrick to Mr. Bevin

[C 3063/2514/18]

FOREIGN OFFICE, 4 May 1950

Germany

The first official discussion on the German problem took place to-day[1] and was conducted by M. Massigli and French Deputy Commissioner in Germany, Dr. Jessup and Colonel Byroade, Head of the German Department in Washington, and myself with Mr. Steel.[2]

There was general agreement on the following principles:

(i) We are committed to a policy of associating Germany with the West and must persevere with this without paying too much attention to fluctuations of climate in Germany.

(ii) Success can only be attained by a process of evolution in the course of which Germany on the one hand and the Western powers on the other have respectively to take progressive steps in advance.

(iii) For the moment it is for the Germans to take the next step, namely, to join the Council of Europe. Until they do so we are not called upon to make any further advance. And indeed we should be ill-advised to do so.

(iv) As soon as the Germans have joined the Council of Europe (and

[1] General tripartite discussions on Germany were originally scheduled to begin on 1 May (cf. No. 40, paragraphs 20–21). Owing to delay in receiving their instructions, the American delegation, though prepared to discuss certain topics in sub-committee, asked that the more general discussion of high policy for Germany be postponed. At the first sub-committee meeting on German problems, held on 1 May (not printed from C 2998/2514/18), it was agreed that sub-committee discussions would be divided into two groups: A (economic) and B (political). It was further agreed on 1 May that Benelux representatives should be given the German agenda for the Foreign Ministers' conference, when it was drawn up, and should also be informed of those subjects discussed in sub-committee which were considered of interest to them: see further No. 61.iii. Responsibility for preparing Austrian problems for the Foreign Ministers agenda was transferred to the Deputies for Austria working in London on a draft peace treaty (cf. No. 12, note 13).

[2] Mr. C.E. Steel was Deputy High Commissioner for Germany.

there was general agreement that they were likely to do so), the Allies would be well-advised not to allow too long to elapse before proceeding to the next stage.

(v) The next stage should be the elimination of certain obstacles to German association with the West. The basis of the transaction would not be that we are making concessions to the Germans but that in view of their closer association with us we would be justified in removing certain security limitations which we had imposed on Germany in different circumstances.

(vi) The main obstacles to further association of Germany with the West lie in:

(a) the circumstance that Germany cannot be a full member of many Western organisations so long as she has no direct access to Governments, and her foreign affairs are solely controlled by the High Commission.

(b) The maintenance of all the existing restrictions on German industry including shipbuilding.

(c) The failure of the Allies to carry out their undertaking to interpret the Occupation Statute liberally, and the unsatisfactory working of the High Commission machinery owing to the fact that the High Commissioners had been reluctant to use that system of majority voting which we pressed so eloquently on the Russians last summer.[3]

(vii) Ministers should be invited to consider modifications in the above three fields if and when the Germans joined the Council of Europe.

It was agreed that a paper on the above lines should be drafted for submission to Ministers and that we should also attempt to draft a much broader statement of our general policy towards Germany which Ministers might wish to issue at the end of the London Conference. Drafts of both papers will be considered at a further Tripartite meeting of officials tomorrow.

The Americans then returned to their proposal that there should be a declaration of Western attachment to the principle of German unity; and that we should make a proposal for all-German elections.

I told the Americans that the three Ministers had agreed in Paris last June to proclaim their attachment to German unity. I did not therefore think that if Mr. Acheson pressed it, you would demur to doing this again.

[3] Western tripartite proposals for quadripartite agreement on controls in Germany and Berlin based on decisions by majority vote with right of veto reserved for exceptional cases only, were rejected by the Soviet delegation at the meeting of the Council of Foreign Ministers held in Paris from 23 May – 20 June 1949 (see No. 18, note 1). Tripartite agreement for majority vote procedure in Germany was contained in the tripartite agreement on controls of 8 April 1949 later appended to the Charter of the Allied High Commission of 20 June 1949 (see No. 5, note 3). Similar arrangements for Berlin were made in the tripartite agreement on revised internal procedure for the Allied (Western) Kommandatura of Berlin signed on 7 June 1949 and printed in *D.G.O.*, pp. 397–8.

On the other hand I was more doubtful about the suggestion that we should propose all-German elections. I said that if the Americans were very anxious to press this also I thought you would prefer a statement by Ministers that they favoured unity and considered elections an essential first step, to any idea of addressing a communication to the Russians inviting them, under certain conditions, to hold all-German elections. The first seemed to me a rational statement of fact which Ministers could very properly make, whereas the second was a mere propaganda move. It was agreed that a Tripartite Drafting Committee would attempt to produce for the consideration of Ministers a draft statement on German unity.

Other subjects being discussed in Tripartite working parties are:

   (i) *Economic*
     The economic situation in Germany.
     The International Ruhr Authority.
     The economic position in Berlin.
     Steel: level of production.
  (ii) *Political*
     The German proposal for a Federal Police force.
     Adenauer's request for a security guarantee.
     Berlin.
     The American proposal to protest against the militarised police in
       the Soviet Zone.
     The cessation of the state of war and the connected question of
       Germany's pre-war obligations.

I am doing my best to reduce the agenda for the Ministers to manageable proportions and I hope that, apart from the general question of our overall policy towards Germany, we may be able to restrict the field of argument to:

   (i) Federal Police.
  (ii) The International Ruhr Authority.
 (iii) Berlin.[4]

I. KIRKPATRICK

CALENDAR TO NO. 58

i *2 & 5 May 1950*   *Tripartite Meetings (Nos. 3, 7, 8) of Sub-Committee on German political problems*: on *Berlin* agree (1) no modification of status (cf. No. 31.ic) and (2) that Western position should be maintained (cf. No.31.i.b): statement on (2) agreed, (cf. *F.R.U.S. 1950*, vol. iii, p. 927). *Protest against police in Soviet zone* to be further considered. *German unity and all German elections*: agreement for (*a*) general declaration on Germany (*b*) more detailed statement of Three Power conditions for German unity based on recommendation from High Commission (No. 53.ii, see further No. 61.ii). *Status of F.R.G.* Recommendations in No. 31.i(*a*) withdrawn by U.K. delegation in view of U.S. recommendation to Ministers for establishment of special study group [C 3022, 3184, 3185/2514/18].

[4] Mr.Bevin minuted below 'I agree steps taken and will await the next paper': see No. 61.

No. 59

Memorandum by the Secretary of State for Foreign Affairs

C.P.(50) 93 [CAB 129/39]

Secret   FOREIGN OFFICE, 4 May 1950

Austrian Treaty

With reference to C.P. (50) 66 of 11th April,[1] I now set out, for the information of my colleagues, the position of the Austrian Treaty negotiations as it emerges from the last meeting of the Deputies and from discussions with United States and French officials.

2. At the last Deputies' meeting on 26th April,[2] the Soviet representative adopted a particularly discouraging attitude. My colleagues will recall that the Soviet Government had made the settlement of certain of the outstanding articles[1] dependent on the settlement of their own claims against Austria in Article 48 *bis*, in regard to which separate Austro-Soviet negotiations were begun in Vienna last autumn. On 26th April the Soviet Deputy not only refused to discuss Article 48 *bis* or to give information about the Austro-Soviet negotiations, but declined to give any assurance that if the other four outstanding articles were settled, 48 *bis* would also be settled, or to renew the assurances he had given in the past regarding the settlement of Articles 42 and 48 once Soviet interests had been met in the other articles (as they have been). Furthermore, the Soviet Deputy read a long statement accusing the Austrian Government of failure to carry out the laws and regulations regarding the denazification and demilitarisation of Austria, and accusing the Western Powers of blocking Soviet attempts to ventilate these matters in the Allied Council in Vienna. He then tabled an addition to the already agreed Article 9 of the Treaty, which deals with the dissolution of Nazi organisations.

3. This action by the Soviet Deputy, and the attitude of the Soviet Government which it represents, makes it difficult for me any longer to nourish the hope that agreement on the Austrian Treaty can now be won by further concessions from the Western Powers. We must, I fear, conclude that the Soviet Government have no intention of completing the Austrian Treaty until wider political developments make it in their interest to do so. This means that, whatever concessions we now make, there is not merely no guarantee but little likelihood that we shall get a Treaty.

4. The present position may therefore be summarised as follows:

(1) The Russians are not at present ready to conclude the Treaty unless we have first given way on Articles 16, 27, 42 and 48.

[1] See No. 12.i.

[2] For the American report of this meeting of the Deputies for Austria (No. 12, note 13) and text of the Soviet amendment to article 9 referred to in paragraph 4(3) below, see *F.R.U.S. 1950*, vol. iv, pp. 454–5.

(2) There is no guarantee whatsoever that when we have given way they will conclude the Treaty.

(3) It is quite possible that they will then either decline to settle Article 48 *bis*, or will raise fresh difficulties such as the addition that they have now tabled to Article 9.

(4) Discussion of the outstanding articles at the Deputies' Conference will almost certainly lead to the abandonment of our position, and the French and Americans agree with us that there should be no settlement of these articles one by one without any return.

(5) The French are ready to ask the Soviet Deputy whether acceptance of Articles 16, 27, 42 and 48 will bring about a settlement of Article 48 *bis*. The Americans and we feel that any such specific offer would irretrievably prejudice our position on those articles.

(6) The Americans are prepared to settle Articles 42 and 48 provided this brings with it a settlement of Article 48 *bis*, and in the last resort would seek authority to accept also the Soviet texts for Articles 16 and 27 if this would then complete the Treaty.

(7) His Majesty's Government would hope that a new settlement can be reached with the bondholders before the Soviet text for Article 48 is accepted.

(8) The three Western Delegations agree that if the Russians were to consent to settle Article 48 *bis* and to conclude the Treaty, we should have to be prepared to settle the four other articles on the best terms possible.

5. What is to be our attitude in the forthcoming discussions with the French and United States Foreign Ministers? There are two alternative courses:

(*a*) To settle Articles 16, 27, 42 and 48 (and the new Soviet Article 9) on the best terms we can get;

(*b*) to decline to settle any of these articles except on our terms unless the Russians agree to settle Article 48 *bis* and to complete the Treaty.

6. In favour of the first course are the following arguments:

(1) So long as the articles protecting our claims against Austria (42 and 48) remain unsettled, the Russians can represent themselves as championing Austrian interests against the claims of the Western Powers. They have already been taking this line in their propaganda.

(2) So long as the Russians are able to point to the existence of other unagreed articles besides 48 *bis*, especially those involving Western claims on Austria, it is impossible to make it crystal clear to public opinion, especially in Austria, that the Western Powers are not, partly at least, responsible for holding up the Treaty.

(3) Until we have settled Articles 16, 27, 42 and 48, which it is within our power to settle by accepting the Soviet text, we shall not have done all we can to complete the Treaty.

(4) If we settle these four articles the responsibility for holding up the Treaty will be placed openly and squarely on the Russians so long as they hold up the settlement of Article 48 *bis* or raise new difficulties.

(5) Until we have settled these four articles the Russians are most unlikely at present to settle 48 *bis* and to complete the Treaty.

(6) If we settle the four articles the Russians might settle Article 48 *bis* and complete the Treaty.

7. In favour of course (*b*):

(1) There is no guarantee, or even likelihood, so long as Soviet policy towards Austria remains unchanged, that the settlement of these four articles will bring about the settlement of the whole Treaty.

(2) If there were no agreement on the Treaty as a whole the Western Powers would for no purpose have accepted texts which are objectionable to them or prejudicial to their interests.

(3) By accepting these four articles we should have abandoned our last bargaining cards without getting anything in return except some propaganda value. If and when negotiations are then resumed and the Soviet raise new demands, as they did on 26th April in regard to Article 9, we shall have nothing left to bargain with, though it is only fair to admit that bargaining counters have not proved of much value in the past when it has been our desire to get the Treaty concluded.

(4) The propaganda point may have some importance, but what the Austrians want is to get the four occupying Powers out of the country, and a settlement of the four articles which does not bring this about will have only temporary propaganda value.

(5) Until a new agreement has been concluded between Austria and the bond-holders and the guarantor Powers it would be difficult for His Majesty's Government to settle Article 48 on the Russian terms without laying themselves open to the accusation of having surrendered other people's interests, which it is our duty to maintain, in order to accommodate the Russians.

(6) We should have made a further concession to the Soviet for which we get no return, and this might not be without its influence on our general position in the cold war.

Conclusions

8. My opinion is that we should adopt the second course and stick fast to our present position unless and until the Russians are prepared to settle Article 48 *bis* and to agree the whole Treaty. This is the line that I propose to take in the forthcoming discussions with Mr. Acheson and M. Schuman. It is a pity that the French and the Americans should have agreed to make the concessions necessary to get the Treaty only after the Russians have ceased to want a Treaty. The fact that the Russians have ceased to want a Treaty has altered the whole position, and I do not now advocate the making of concessions which are unlikely to serve any useful purpose.[3]

E.B.

[3] No progress was made by the Deputies at their meeting on 4 May and discussion was

adjourned until 22 May: *F.R.U.S. 1950*, vol. iv, pp. 456–7. Meanwhile, as requested (No. 58, note 1) the Western Deputies prepared a report on the Austrian treaty negotiations for Ministers at the London conference, which was circulated as MIN/TRI/P/20 on 9 May: *ibid.*, pp. 457–8. In a covering brief to Mr. Bevin on 11 May, Mr. Mallet explained that the recommendations of Part I of MIN/TRI/P/20 followed the lines of No. 59. The Foreign Office was largely in agreement with the recommendations of Part II *viz*: *A*(i) to treat Austria as far as possible as a free and independent country (ii) to reduce occupation costs borne by Austria; *B* appointment of civilian High Commissioners (position reserved by French delegation); *C* each occupying government to assume costs of its occupation in Austria; *D* issue of declaration, as requested by Austrian government.

No. 60

Brief for the U.K. Delegation[1]

No.37 [C 3136/27/18]

Top secret   FOREIGN OFFICE, *4 May 1950*

Security guarantee for the Federal Republic

Recommendation

The United Kingdom Delegation should endeavour to secure the approval of the United States and French delegates for the draft reply to Dr. Adenauer which is annexed to this brief.

Background

At a Meeting with the Allied High Commissioners on the 8th December, 1949, the German Federal Chancellor raised the question of the defence

---

[1] The draft of this brief, cleared at the official level with the Ministry of Defence, was submitted on 28 April to Mr. Bevin who referred it to the Defence Committee for approval. The Defence Committee of the Cabinet was reconstituted in 1947 '(a) To handle current defence problems. (b) To coordinate departmental action and plans in preparation for war' (terms of reference on CAB 131/3). The Defence Committee was chaired by the Prime Minister with the Minister of Defence as his Deputy. The other members of the committee were the Lord President of the Council, Secretary of State for Foreign Affairs, Chancellor of the Exchequer, Minister of Labour and National Service, First Lord of the Admiralty, Secretaries of State for War and Air and Minister of Supply. On 2 May copies of the brief were sent to Mr. Attlee and Mr. Shinwell, who both agreed with the line proposed. The brief was evidently not circulated to the rest of the Defence Committee. When telephoning Mr. Attlee's approval of the lines of the brief to Mr. K.M. Wilford, Assistant Private Secretary to Mr. Bevin, Mr. Rickett 'said that he himself was not entirely happy at decisions on such a matter as this being taken by the P.M. and S. of S. alone and wondered if it was not a matter for other Ministers as well. He is, I believe, thinking of the Chancellor in particular who, I am told, feels that he is not being brought sufficiently into the picture of the forthcoming discussions' (minute by Mr. Wilford of 3 May). Mr. Barclay explained to Mr. Rickett on 4 May that 'in our view the paper did not raise any new point of policy. It was rather a question of tactics as to how we should answer a somewhat embarrassing question. The proposed answer was a statement of fact and it hardly seemed necessary to worry any more Ministers about the exact terms of the reply. In the light of this explanation Mr. Rickett agreed. R.E.B. 4th May 1950' (C 3136/27/18).

of the Federal Republic against possible Soviet aggression. He said that rumours that the North Atlantic Treaty Powers were hesitating between defending the Rhine or defending the Elbe were raising profound disquiet in Germany. He further stated that he had definite information that the armed gendarmerie in the Eastern Zone was nothing less than an army, and that, moreover, it would become a good army and would obey the Russians.

2. The Federal Chancellor expressed the view that the Western Allies were in duty bound to maintain the security of the Federal Republic and that, in any case, unless the Russians were halted in their present position, Western Europe would be finished. He asked for an Allied declaration that 'the territory of the Federal Republic would be defended against attack'.

3. The Federal Chancellor subsequently published his views on the necessity for a guarantee of the Federal Republic's security and he has since restated them on several occasions. In a speech at Koenigswinter on the 25th February Dr. Adenauer confirmed that he was absolutely opposed to any form of German remilitarisation. On account of Germany's precarious geographical position, however, and of the disarming of Germany, he added that he had asked the High Commissioners to request their Governments to make a declaration to the effect that they will assume responsibility for German security. He said that he must insist on this demand, as in his opinion international tension was sure to increase. He realised of course that such an Allied guarantee did not in itself bring security with it, but it did imply an obligation. Dr. Adenauer has recently taken the line that unless the Federal Republic obtained a security guarantee it would be rash for it to commit itself to a policy of integration with Western Europe. It is likely that he will persist in his request for a specific guarantee and will raise the matter again with the Allied High Commission.

4. His Majesty's Government recognise that a certain degree of uneasiness exists among the population of the German Federal Republic arising out of fears that plans for the defence of Western Europe envisage the abandonment of German territory between the Elbe and the Rhine in the event of Soviet aggression. They accordingly recognise that the Federal Chancellor's preoccupation with the defence of the Federal Republic is to some extent legitimate, but they are not in a position to give any assurance that the Federal Republic will be defended on its Eastern frontiers. No Power can safely give even its ally an assurance that its entire territory will rest inviolate. The most effective defence of the territory of the Federal Republic lies in the creation of a Western security system so effective that the Soviet are discouraged from aggression.

5. Until Western Germany can be trusted politically and be permitted to rearm, her security must depend on (a) the presence of allied troops in Western Germany (b) the existence of the North Atlantic Treaty, Article 6 of which covers the occupation forces in Europe of any Party to the

Treaty. This state of affairs is likely to continue until Western Germany has shown conclusively by her actions that she is prepared to cooperate with the West and has been accepted into the North Atlantic Treaty Organisation.

Suggested Reply to Dr. Adenauer

6. In considering how to deal with Dr. Adenauer's approach, the Western Powers can choose between three courses of action:

(*a*) they can continue to ignore the request for a security guarantee on the grounds that matters of defence are beyond the scope of the Federal Chancellor's responsibility under the Occupation Statute;

(*b*) they can answer the request for a security guarantee by making a public statement of their own views on the matter, including a reference to the North Atlantic Treaty;

(*c*) they can instruct the High Commission to discuss the matter privately and orally with the Federal Chancellor.

7. Course (*a*) is unlikely to prove satisfactory since Adenauer will merely persist in his request and play upon public opinion in Germany with damaging effect.

Course (*b*) involves a degree of publicity which, on the whole, the subject had better do without.

8. It is recommended therefore that the approval of the French and United States Governments should be sought for Course (*c*).

9. A draft text of the reply to be given to the Federal Chancellor is annexed, together with certain supplementary oral explanation which the High Commissioners might be authorised to give.

10. In the event of the Federal Chancellor asking whether there is any objection to the publication of the statement made to him by the High Commission, it is suggested that the High Commission should tell him that it is confidential and that any publicity is to be avoided.

Annex to No. 60

Draft Reply[2]

The three High Commissioners, having consulted their Governments on the request made by the Federal Chancellor for a declaration that the territory of the Federal Republic would be defended against attack, have been authorised to make the following reply.

Dr. Adenauer's request was sympathetically considered by the Foreign Ministers of the three Powers in the course of an examination of questions relating to the security of Germany during their recent meeting in London.

[2] This draft reply, to Dr. Adenauer, was considered by a sub-committee on German problems and emerged as MIN/TRI/P/10 of 6 May subject to the amendments recorded in notes 3, 5 and 6 below.

The Federal Republic does not lie alone and unprotected in Europe. Under Articles 5 and 6 of the North Atlantic Treaty, an armed attack upon the occupation forces of the Western Allies in Germany will be considered as an armed attack against all the parties to the Treaty, and will at once bring into play the provisions of Article 5 of the Treaty. So long, therefore, as the Western occupation forces remain in Germany the Federal Republic enjoys in effect the same measure of protection under the North Atlantic Treaty as is enjoyed by any of the parties to that Treaty.

The three Allied Powers have no present intention[3] of withdrawing their occupation forces from Germany.

Oral explanation

The defence for Germany at present, as for the rest of Western Europe, will be assured by further consolidating the system expressed in the North Atlantic Treaty and so deterring the Russians from launching a war. The build-up of this system is proceeding steadily under the combined efforts of all the members of the North Atlantic and Brussels Treaty organisations.

In so far as Dr. Adenauer is seeking a guarantee that any given line will be defended or that the territory of the Federal Republic will remain inviolable[4] he is asking for a guarantee of an unprecedented nature, and one which it is in the nature of things impossible for one Power ever to give to another. The Western Occupying Powers are unable to give him such a guarantee just as they are unable to give it even to one another.[5]

Furthermore, the High Commissioners wish to point out that the common object of deterring the Russians from attacking the West is most likely to be secured not by an attempt to hold a particular line of defence but by convincing the Russians[6] (*a*) that such an attack will involve them in a world war, and (*b*) that the defence of the West will be effectively conducted. Point (*a*) is ensured by the presence of Allied troops in Germany; (*b*) is the responsibility of the Atlantic Pact and Brussels Treaty Powers and is being resolutely undertaken.

[3] Inserted here in MIN/TRI/P/10 was 'in the present European situation'.

[4] In the original draft this sentence began 'In so far as Dr. Adenauer is seeking a guarantee of the territorial inviolability of the Federal Republic he is ...' This was expanded to the present text by Sir I. Kirkpatrick in the light of doubts from both Mr. Attlee and Mr. Shinwell that the requested guarantee was unprecedented in view of the nature of the guarantee to Belgium before 1914.

[5] This paragraph was replaced in MIN/TRI/P/10 by 'If Dr. Adenauer seeks a guarantee that the territory of the Federal Republic will remain inviolable he is asking for a guarantee of an unprecedented nature, and one which it is in the nature of things impossible for one Power ever to give to another.'

[6] The preceding passage from 'is most likely ...' was replaced in MIN/TRI/P/10 by 'through Germany will most effectively be secured by convincing the Russians.'

No. 61

Memorandum from Sir I. Kirkpatrick to Mr. Bevin

[C 3062/2514/18]

FOREIGN OFFICE, 5 May 1950

Germany

As a result of a further meeting of experts today[1] it was agreed to submit the attached paper[2] for consideration by Ministers.

The paper is not ideal because as usual we found the French basically resisting the idea that when the Germans had entered the Council of Europe as associate members we must—as you said in your House of Commons speech[3]—proceed to the next stage without undue delay. As an example of their attitude I would refer you to the addition in ink on the first page.[4] I induced the French with great difficulty to agree to this, but could not bring them to accept the words 'full membership of the Council'.

Nevertheless the paper in its present form does not seem to me to be too inadequate. And you and Mr. Acheson will no doubt persuade M. Schuman to accept the view that Germany's associate membership of the Council of Europe does not represent 'the incorporation of Germany in a Western system' and that consequently when the first stage is completed we must bend our minds to organising the next stage in the process of evolution.

Preliminary consideration has also been given to draft statements to be submitted to Ministers regarding their general policy towards Germany and also the question of Germany unity. We hope to complete these papers [ii] tomorrow.

There was also some discussion on Adenauer's request for a security guarantee and we hope to have an agreed draft paper for you tomorrow.[5] As regards Adenauer's request for a Federal police force both the French and the Americans wish to await the arrival of their High Commissioners before committing themselves. The discussion showed that we and the Americans appreciated that the Germans had good grounds for asking for a Federal police. But the French were naturally very sticky. M. Massigli said that it might be possible to start with a Federal police force in the Bonn area and then to extend it subsequently. But he could not commit

---

[1] For the first general tripartite discussion on Germany, see No. 58.

[2] This paper, the earlier version of i below, was circulated as TRI/P/22 of 5 May (C 3096/2514/18) and was the same as the text printed in *F.R.U.S. 1950*, vol. iii, pp. 932–3, with the addition of the preamble: 'As a result of general discussion, the following agreed points are submitted to the Ministers.'

[3] See No. 18, note 2.

[4] This addition to the sentence at 4(c) read 'but desire to facilitate the full participation of Germany in the Council of Europe' (*op. cit.*, p. 932).

[5] See No. 60, note 2.

himself at this stage. In view of the insistence of the Americans and the French that they must consult their High Commissioners it was agreed that we should organise a meeting of the three High Commissioners early next week and prepare a suitable paper for the Tripartite discussions.[6]

The economic and political sub-committees hope to complete most of their work today and I have arranged that my committee should run through their work tomorrow. In this way you should have most of the material papers in your hands before Monday.[7]

I. KIRKPATRICK

CALENDARS TO NO. 61

i *6 May 1950 MIN/TRI/P/7, Policy towards Germany* Lists next moves in drawing F.R.G. closer to the west: e.g. German entry into Council of Europe and progressive relaxation of controls. Recommends establishment of study group to work out programme and to report by 30 September 1950 (terms of ref. for study group circulated as MIN/TRI/P/12, printed *F.R.U.S. 1950*, vol. iii, p. 1050, n. 7) [C 3098/2514/18].

ii *7 May 1950 MIN/TRI/P/13 Declaration on Germany* with annexed statement of conditions for German unity. Agreed principles (drafts at No. 53.i. and 58.i.)

[6] At a meeting on the morning of 11 May the three High Commissioners reached agreement on a recommendation to Ministers (MIN/TRI/P/27, not printed from C 3337/3333/18) for the creation of a Federal police force of up to 5,000 men, rather than the 25,000 requested by Dr. Adenauer (cf. No. 45, note 3). This force was to include the policing of Bonn. At the same time, however, the High Commissioners suggested that they should study requirements in more detail with the federal authorities. In a minute to Sir I. Kirkpatrick of 11 May, General Robertson explained the background to MIN/TRI/P/27: 'M. François-Poncet informed me that M. Schuman was prepared to accept the formation of a force not exceeding 5,000 but that he would not agree to any larger force. Mr. McCloy supported the French position. Under the circumstances it seemed to me to be better to take what we can for the moment. I hope that the Chiefs of Staff will feel comforted by the instruction to the High Commissioners to study this matter further as obviously the results of this examination would only be to recommend an increase in the size of the force'.

[7] 8 May. At the sixth tripartite meeting of officials held on 6 May at 11.15 a.m., 'The Americans entered a reservation on their position on paper TRI/P/22 since the policy laid down in it was really subject to agreement in the wider context of the future of Germany in a Western setting. It was pointed out that not all the papers going to Ministers were intended to be dogmatic or in any way commit countries to specific policy, and it was finally agreed that the paper should go forward subject to amendment to its introductory phrase' (as cited in *F.R.U.S. 1950*, vol. iii, p. 933, note 2). The paper was accordingly circulated as MIN/TRI/P/7 on 6 May (text at calendar i). Also circulated to delegations at their sixth meeting was a revision of the statement on Berlin agreed in sub-committee on 5 May (see No. 58.i.) circulated as TRI/P/24 which went forward to Ministers as MIN/TRI/P/14 on 6 May, (*op.cit.*, pp. 1091–2, notes 2–3). It was further agreed at the sixth meeting that German papers still being prepared in sub-committee should go forward without consideration in the plenary session. These papers included MIN/TRI/P/12, 13 (see calendars i and ii) and MIN/TRI/P/11 of 6 May in which the U.S. delegation proposed a protest to the Soviet government at the formation of militarised police in the Eastern zone (see No. 31, note 1 and No. 58.i). This proposal was supported in principle by the French delegation but not by the U.K. delegation which reserved its position.

are (*a*) freely elected all-German government (*b*) individual freedom (*c*) political freedom (*d*) independence of judiciary (*e*) prohibition of political secret police and formations (*f*) assurance of economic unity e.g. by unified currency and customs (*g*) surrender and disposal of industry in Germany acquired by foreign powers since 8 May 1945 (*h*) establishment of quadripartite supervision. First step towards German unity is holding of free elections. Formation of all-German government to be followed by peace settlement: *ibid.*, pp. 1086–9 [C 3102/2514/18].

iii *9 May 1950 Tripartite official meeting with Benelux representatives* to discuss German items on Ministerial agenda [C 3250/2514/18].

No. 62

Memorandum from Sir N. Brook to Mr. Attlee

[*PREM 8/1204*]

CABINET OFFICE, *5 May 1950*

Anglo-American Conversations

The following notes may be of some help to you in connection with the further meeting which you are holding at 4.15 p.m. this afternoon.

1. *Economic Questions*

You will not wish to traverse again the detail which was covered in the discussion yesterday evening.[1] At the end of the first part of that discussion the Chancellor said that he accepted the need for a close partnership with the United States in economic matters, that on this there was no substantial difference between him and the Foreign Secretary, and that the conditions set out in the Annex to E.P.C. (50) 44[2] were not put forward as 'breaking points' in the discussions.

What does call for further discussion is the apparent inconsistency between this attitude towards economic co-operation with the United States and the Chancellor's reference, at the end of yesterday's meeting, to a policy of creating a 'Third Force' of the United Kingdom, the Commonwealth and Western Europe. In the earlier part of yesterday's discussion the Chancellor fully accepted a policy of active economic co-operation with the United States. He even spoke of a 'joint Anglo-American Foreign Office' – a combined team of United Kingdom and United States officials working together continuously on problems of common concern, both political and economic, and submitting their joint recommendations to the two Governments. Yet, at the end of the discussion, he said that we should aim at freeing ourselves from the political and economic hegemony of the United States, and look forward

[1] See No. 57.

[2] No. 42.i.

to the day when we could lead a 'Third Force' which would stand mid-way between American capitalism and Russian Communism.

I think his colleagues will wish to know tonight how the Chancellor reconciles these two views. This 'Third Force' conception was advocated, previously, as an alternative to the policy of Anglo-American co-operation, but it was definitely rejected by Ministers before the Washington talks of last autumn. It was discussed and discarded at an important meeting of the Economic Policy Committee on 7th July, 1949—see, in particular, page 2 of the Minutes E.P.C. (49) 27th Meeting.[3] From this meeting onwards preparations for the Washington talks went forward on the basis that we were definitely going in for a policy of active co-operation with the United States—and the talks were, successfully, conducted on that basis. Later, the Foreign Secretary circulated to the Cabinet a paper containing detailed arguments in support of his policy for 'the consolidation of the western world', as compared with a policy for building up a 'Third World Power' (C.P. (49) 208).[4] The Foreign Secretary said at the time that this was circulated for information and that he did not wish it to be placed on the Cabinet's agenda: it is clear that he assumed that the 'Third Force' conception was rejected and that he had full Cabinet support for his policy of working towards 'the Atlantic community'.

2. *Atlantic Treaty Organisation*

You will wish to resume yesterday's discussion about the proposal to establish a standing body of 'Deputies' under the North Atlantic Treaty Organisation. This proposal is set out in the joint paper by U.S./U.K./French officials—TRI/P/17,[5] reproduced as Annex VI in the collection of papers headed 'The London Conferences, May 1950'.

The Chancellor's main objection is that this proposed body of Deputies is to have the powers of the Council and, by paragraph (*a*), is 'to co-ordinate the work of the Defence Committee, the Defence Financial and Economic Committee and all other bodies established under the Organisation'. The Chancellor claims that no Deputy, whether an official or a Junior Minister, should be empowered to amend or override the work done by, or on behalf of, the Finance Minister in the Financial and Economic Committee.

On the other hand, it is clear that there is urgent need for more

---

[3] See No. 57, note 5. On page 2 of the minutes of this meeting 'It was pointed out that the policy of insulating ourselves completely from the dollar world had some popular appeal and might in some ways be tempting ... It might be better to avoid discussion [in Washington] of any long-term solution and merely attempt to find temporary remedies for the immediate difficulties of the non-dollar world. After full discussion, however, it was agreed that we should enter into negotiations with a view to finding some compromise solution to the long-term problem which would be acceptable to American and Canadian opinion as well as to ourselves. Political and economic chaos would result if we tried to cut ourselves off entirely from the dollar world, and a satisfactory agreement would avoid a great deal of hardship' (CAB 134/220).

[4] See No. 20, note 1.   [5] See No. 46, note 6.

continuous co-ordination of the work of the various parts of the Organisation, and that the Council itself cannot meet sufficiently often to provide this co-ordination. Experience in Western Union has shown that it is useless to have Defence Ministers meeting to work out requirements, and Finance Ministers meeting to agree that the money for those requirements cannot be found. What is needed is some body on which the national representatives are speaking, not merely on behalf of Defence Ministers or Finance Ministers, but on behalf of Governments; and this is what the new proposal is designed to provide.

It is clear that, in this new meeting of 'Deputies', the United Kingdom 'Deputy' would have to represent—not merely the Foreign Secretary or the Chancellor of the Exchequer or the Minister of Defence—but the United Kingdom Government. He would have to speak in accordance with instructions given to him on behalf of the Government as a whole. There would have to be in Whitehall a stable interdepartmental organisation, comprising representatives of the Departments mainly concerned, to which he would report and from which he would receive his instructions. And this interdepartmental committee of officials would have to work under the aegis of the Defence Committee and the Cabinet and obtain instructions from them from time to time, as required. This machinery would be closely parallel to that which has been operated, very smoothly and efficiently, for E.R.P. questions. Sir Edmund Hall-Patch, as the United Kingdom representative on O.E.E.C., has received his instructions through the London Committee (a committee of officials comprising representatives of the Departments mainly concerned) which, on matters of important policy, has worked under the direction of the Economic Policy Committee. This new 'Deputy' would not be merely a representative of the Foreign Secretary, any more than Sir Edmund Hall-Patch has been merely a representative of the Chancellor.

If it is understood that some machinery on these lines will be established—and it is certainly the desire of the Foreign Office that it should be—the Chancellor's main objection to this proposal may be met. It might also help him, however, if some slight adjustments could be made in the proposed terms of reference of the Deputies. The trouble with the existing draft[5] is that, in the two lines preceding paragraph (a), it identifies the tasks of the Council and those of the permanent 'Organisation' which is to be established under it; and, as a result, it confers on the permanent Organisation the full powers of the Council itself. It might be better if this part of the draft could be altered so as to read:

'The main tasks of the proposed Organisation shall be:

(a) To assist in co-ordinating the work of the Defence Committee . . .
(b) To recommend to the Council or to Governments the steps necessary to ensure that effect is given to plans . . .

3. *Western Organisations*

The Chancellor of the Exchequer was also disturbed at some of the statements in the paper on Western Organisations (P.U.S.C. (50) 9).[6] This comtemplated that, when Marshall Aid comes to an end, the continuing work of O.E.E.C. might be transferred to an appropriate body established under the North Atlantic Treaty. The Chancellor construed this as a proposal that the Foreign Office should take over all the work of international economic co-ordination in which the Treasury have interested themselves through O.E.E.C.

It might be helpful if you would ask Sir Roger Makins to make a statement this evening about this paper. I believe that he will say that it represents only some preliminary thinking on very long-term issues, that it commits no one, and that the Foreign Office are certainly keeping an open mind on the various alternative possibilities which it discusses. He will probably be able to say also that there is no danger of any commitment on this during the forthcoming talks with Mr. Acheson. He will certainly be able to reassure the Chancellor that the Foreign Office have no intention of trying to take over the international work of the Treasury in economic affairs.

4. *Germany*

I understand that the Chancellor also wishes to raise some points on the paper about the Future of Germany (P.U.S.C. (49) 62).[7]

I believe that this paper also is something in the nature of a cockshy. You have raised some points on it. And, in any final paper on this subject, the Foreign Office will need to take account of the points raised in the Chiefs of Staff paper on global strategy, which is coming up to the Defence Committee in the week after next. (C.O.S. (50) 139).[8]

Here again the immediate point is to ascertain how far these questions are likely to be discussed, and to what extent the Foreign Secretary may enter into commitments, in his forthcoming talks with Mr. Acheson.

NORMAN BROOK

[6] See No. 30.   [7] See No. 64.i.   [8] See No. 43, note 2.

No. 63

Note of an informal meeting of Ministers held at 10 Downing Street on Friday, 5 May 1950, at 4.15 p.m.[1]

[*CAB 21/1761*]

Top secret

Present:
The Rt. Hon. C.R. Attlee, M.P. Prime Minister (*In the Chair*); the Rt. Hon. Herbert Morrison, M.P., Lord President of the Council; the Rt. Hon. Sir Stafford Cripps, K.C. M.P., Chancellor of the Exchequer; the Rt. Hon. E.

[1] The note was prepared by Sir N. Brook as a private record; (See No. 57, note 1).

Shinwell, M.P., Minister of Defence; the Hon. K.G. Younger, M.P., Minister of State.

Also present:
Sir Edward Bridges, Treasury; Sir William Strang, Sir Roger Makins, Foreign Office.

Secretary:
Sir Norman Brook.

1. *North Atlantic Treaty Organisation*

The Meeting resumed the discussion, which they had opened on 4th May,[2] of the proposal that the North Atlantic Treaty organisation should be strengthened by the creation of a body of 'Deputies' to Council members and by the establishment of a permanent Secretariat.

The Chancellor of the Exchequer repeated his objections to this proposal. Under the constitution proposed in TRI/P/17[3] the Deputies would be empowered to co-ordinate the work of Defence Ministers and Finance Ministers; and the language used in the paper seemed to imply that they would have power to override recommendations made by those Ministers.

The Prime Minister said that, so far as the United Kingdom was concerned, the Deputy would not be merely a representative of the Foreign Secretary: he must be answerable to the Government as a whole and be able to put forward views approved by all the United Kingdom Ministers concerned. It would have to be arranged that he should receive his instructions through a committee of officials comprising representatives of all the Departments directly concerned and acting under the authority of the appropriate Ministerial Committee, presumably the Defence Committee. He would therefore be in a position comparable to that of our permanent representative on the Organisation for European Economic Co-operation in Paris, who reported to, and received his instructions from, the 'London' Committee acting under the directions of the Economic Policy Committee.

In discussion there was general agreement with the views expressed by the Prime Minister. At the same time it was thought that some adjustment might usefully be made in the terms of reference proposed in TRI/P/17. Thus, it would be preferable that the Deputies should be empowered 'to ensure co-ordination', rather than 'to co-ordinate', the work of the Defence Committee of the Council and its Defence Financial and Economic Committee. It might also be preferable to express the task of the Deputies as primarily one of co-ordinating the preparation of material for the Council itself and dealing with minor matters between meetings of the Council.

Sir William Strang thought that there should be no difficulty in securing agreement to the first of these suggested amendments. The second suggestion would not, however, meet the wishes of the United States and

[2] See No. 57.   [3] See No. 46, note 6.

231

French Governments, who were anxious that the Deputies should play a more important part in the continuing work of the Organisation.

The Prime Minister, in conclusion, said that the apprehensions voiced by the Chancellor of the Exchequer should be met if arrangements were made to ensure that the United Kingdom representative on the proposed body of Deputies acted under instructions from the United Kingdom Government conveyed to him through a suitably constituted interdepartmental committee of officials acting under the direction of the Defence Committee.

2. *Economic Co-ordination*

The Chancellor of the Exchequer said that he had been concerned to see the suggestion in paragraph 30 of P.U.S.C. 9[4] that, after the end of the European Recovery Programme in 1952, the work now being done by the Organisation for European Economic Co-operation (O.E.E.C.) might be transferred to some organisation established under the North Atlantic Treaty Organisation (N.A.T.O.). Although no such transfer could take place until after 1952, this paragraph seemed to contemplate that some economic organisation would be established now under N.A.T.O. so that it could be ready to take over the functions of O.E.E.C. in 1952. He would be strongly opposed to any such development. For none of the countries of Western Europe was prepared to stand up to the United States; and if Europe's economic problems were to be discussed in an organisation of which the United States was the leading member, the result would be to perpetuate a hegemony of the United States over Europe and the United States way of life would be imposed on all the countries of Europe. The O.E.E.C., on the other hand, provided a forum in which Europe's economic problems could be discussed by Europeans. If this organisation were continued after 1952 it might not be necessary to have Americans present even as observers.

Sir Roger Makins said that it was not proposed to put forward, in the forthcoming discussions, the suggestion thrown out in paragraph 30 of P.U.S.C. 9.[4] The Foreign Office were in no way committed to that suggestion. The question of future arrangements for European economic co-ordination after 1952 was a long-term question which, in their view, should remain open for the time being. The only positive suggestion which was to be made in the forthcoming discussions was that the proposed body of Deputies should be invited to consider what further action should be taken under Article 2 of the North Atlantic Treaty (which was concerned with economic questions) taking into account the work of the existing agencies in this field. It should, however, be recognised that the French might wish to have the substance of this question considered in the forthcoming discussions. Their objective was to ensure that Germany should in no circumstances be brought into the North Atlantic Treaty Organisation. They therefore desired that all

---

[4] See No. 30.

questions of economic co-ordination should continue to be handled by O.E.E.C.; and it was their suggestion that North American interests in these matters should be met by associating representatives of the United States and Canada with the O.E.E.C. in some informal way.

The Chancellor of the Exchequer, in conclusion, said that he hoped that the suggestion thrown out in paragraph 30 of P.U.S.C. 9 would not be pursued without full Ministerial discussion.

3. *North Atlantic Defence Committee: Hague Meeting of 1st April, 1950*[5]

The Chancellor of the Exchequer developed the objections which he had raised, at the previous meeting on 4th May, to the procedure followed at the meeting of the North Atlantic Defence Committee at The Hague on 1st April in recommending to the North Atlantic Council an increase in the 'value of the present military commitments' of the Treaty Powers. In his view the fact that the Minister of Defence had been a party to this recommendation went a long way towards committing the United Kingdom Government to providing fresh money for defence, and also encouraged the North Atlantic Council to enquire into the financial and economic capacity of the United Kingdom.

The Minister of Defence said that the North Atlantic Defence Committee was not itself competent to commit Governments to expenditure; and its recommendations could not commit Governments.

The Prime Minister said that he did not regard the United Kingdom Government as committed by the terms of the recommendation to which the Minister of Defence had assented. In his view such a recommendation from the North Atlantic Defence Committee was comparable to a recommendation from the United Kingdom Defence Committee to the Cabinet. Nor did he think that the prestige of the Minister of Defence would be in any way affected if the United Kingdom Government felt unable to accept this recommendation.

The Chancellor of the Exchequer said that he hoped that, when this matter came before the North Atlantic Council, the Foreign Secretary would make it clear that the United Kingdom Government did not regard themselves as committed by this recommendation. He also hoped that the Foreign Secretary would discourage the idea that any organisation of the Council could properly make independent enquiries into the financial capacity of the United Kingdom to make any particular contribution towards Atlantic defence.

[5] See No. 33, note 7.

No. 64

Brief for the U.K. Delegation[1]

No. 38 [C 3138/2514/18]

Secret   FOREIGN OFFICE, 5 May 1950

Allied Policy towards Germany

Conclusions

1. The Western Powers should continue to proclaim their desire to create a unified democratic Germany, free to enter into political and economic relations with the West.

2. The conception of a so-called 'neutral' Germany is impracticable, since Germany is certain sooner or later to gravitate to East or West.

3. Consequently the Western Powers must give her the necessary impulse to turn towards the West.

4. So long as Germany remains divided, this can only be done by sustaining the prestige of the Federal Government and reiterating that our aim is the eventual association of the Federal Republic as a full member of a Western system.

5. This affirmation should be backed by deeds. In particular the Western Powers must begin to treat Germany as a future partner and restrict their interference in German affairs as much as possible.

6. Germany must be required to fulfil her obligations under the Petersberg agreement and join the Council of Europe. Until she does so no further advance can be made.

7. But the Western Powers must recognise that when Germany has entered the Council of Europe they cannot safely delay too long with the next stage and that so long as the conduct of foreign affairs is vested solely in the High Commission, Germany can make no further progress towards association with the West.

Argument

Leaving out of account the possibility of a united Germany dominated by or exclusively allied with the Soviet Union, as being completely unacceptable to the Western Powers, it is possible to envisage three other solutions of the German problem:

(i) a united Germany free to associate with the West;

(ii) a neutral Germany associated neither with the East nor with the West;

---

[1] In accordance with instructions from Mr. Bevin this brief combined the substance of three papers (*a*) P.U.S.C. (49) 62 at i below; (*b*) Cabinet memorandum, C.P. (50)80 of 26 April on policy towards Germany (CAB 129/39, not printed); (*c*) memorandum by General Robertson of 18 April on progress and prospects of the Western Allies' German programme (not printed from C 2765/2514/18). The draft of this brief, submitted to Mr. Bevin on 3 May, was approved by him as guidance for the U.K. delegation.

(iii) a divided Germany.

A United Germany

2. It has been the aim of the Western Allies since 1945 to see created a unified Germany, administered by a democratic central German Government, free from foreign domination, independent of external economic help and incapable of renewed aggression. Such a Germany would be able to sign a Peace Treaty and to enter into close political and economic relations with the West.

3. Such a solution must remain the firm long-term objective of the Western Powers. But the present division of Germany, which has been brought about by the Soviet Government's failure to cooperate in four-Power control of Germany and which reflects the deadlock in relations between the Western world and the Soviet *bloc*, makes this objective impossible of attainment in the foreseeable future.

4. German unity would have to be brought about by the free election of a German Government, committed to the preservation of human rights and civil liberties, free to enter international organisations and subject to a workable four-Power system of occupation and controls pending the conclusion of a peace treaty. Though such a solution might have its attractions for the Russians, it is most unlikely that they would propose it or agree to it unless they were forced to conclude that, owing to the success of Western policy in Germany and the failure of their own in the Soviet Zone, a united Germany under four-Power control was less objectionable than the continuance of the existing situation. They have clearly not yet reached that position.

5. Even if they did and made proposals for a unified Germany under four-Power control the Western Allies would have to scrutinise any such proposals very carefully before accepting them as a basis for negotiation. For, though the present division of Germany with a highly vulnerable Western outpost in Berlin constitutes a potential threat to the peace, any agreement to restore the unity of Germany would introduce fresh drawbacks and dangers of its own. The Western Powers would have to insist that any such agreement contained adequate political, military and economic safeguards against the dangers of both Russian Communist expansion and resurgent German nationalism. It would clearly be extremely difficult at any time, and impossible at present, to secure four-Power agreement on such safeguards.

A Neutral Germany

6. This solution would involve the creation of a German buffer state associated neither with the East nor with the West and perhaps forbidden by treaty to enter into such associations. It would carry with it most of the risks and dangers attendant upon the first solution (a united Germany) as well as certain further disadvantages of its own.

7. The creation of an officially neutralised Germany would probably

involve the immediate withdrawal of occupation troops; but, whereas Russian troops would be likely to withdraw only to the Polish-German frontier, American and British troops might have to withdraw from the Continent altogether. A neutral Germany would be unable to participate in Western organisations such as the O.E.E.C., Council of Europe and North Atlantic Treaty. Finally, all experience shows that Germany would not be content for long to play a purely static role and that her restless ambition would sooner or later drive her to gravitate either to the West or to the East, and, in the absence of the necessary impulse towards association with the West, it is unlikely that she would long resist the inevitable Russian pressure and penetration designed to associate her permanently with the East. Such an outcome would clearly be disastrous for the Western Powers.

A divided Germany

8. Since therefore a united Germany under adequate safeguards, though desirable is at present unattainable, and a neutral Germany highly dangerous so long as aggressive Russian Communism remains an active potential threat, the Western Powers must for the time being base their policy on the continued but temporary division of Germany. Only by increasing the prestige and authority of a Western German Government and by simultaneously associating Western Germany more and more closely with a consolidated Western world, thereby making possible the progressive relaxation of present security safeguards and controls, can the Western Powers hope to bring about German unity on terms acceptable to themselves and to the German people.

9. Such a policy was initiated with the decision taken by the Western Powers in 1948 and carried into effect in April–September 1949 with the establishment of the German Federal Government and the enactment of a separate Occupation Statute for Western Germany. Its main principles were embodied in the Petersberg Protocol signed by the German Federal Chancellor and the three Allied High Commissioners on the 22nd November, 1949. That agreement was designed to provide a programme of action for the period until the Occupation Statute was due for review after September 1950 and before March 1951. The programme comprised on the one hand the progressive association of Germany with the West, through participation in international organisations and the exchange of consular and commercial representatives, and on the other the gradual relaxation of security controls, beginning with shipbuilding and dismantling.

10. Some progress has been made in carrying out this programme. The German Federal Government has joined the O.E.E.C., the International Authority for the Ruhr, the International Wheat Council and the Central Rhine Commission. A German Consul-General is being appointed in London. The Federal Government is gradually building up its authority and its administrative efficiency in the face of serious difficulties. The

West Germans both in the Republic and in Berlin have maintained a solid resistance to Communism and right-wing nationalism is not yet a serious danger as an organised political force. As the Germans steadily acquire political experience and grow in self-reliance, Allied controls are being gradually relaxed and the Control Commission reduced in so far as is consistent with the need to complete the tasks in the economic and security fields to which the Allies are committed.

11. But the rate of progress towards a more normal association between Germany and the West has nevertheless been disappointing. In the economic field unemployment has increased, the prospect of German viability is as remote as ever and the German administration's tendency to irresponsibility and its attachment to the theory of the free market economy have not been diminished by Allied criticism and interference. In the political sphere, despite the Federal Chancellor's sincere desire for Western European unity and reconciliation, his own behaviour and utterances, as well as those of less responsible politicians of all parties, have too often been intemperate and ill calculated to inspire confidence abroad. Germany's failure so far to join the Council of Europe is a symptom of her continued sense of isolation and grievance and of her lack as yet of a sufficiently urgent conviction of mutual understanding and common interest to make rapid progress possible. Differences, delays and difficulties on the Allied side in matters such as the deconcentration of industry, demilitarisation, the Saar and the Income Tax Law have aggravated the situation.

12. Meanwhile the Russians have profited by the relatively slow advance towards consolidation in the West to bring about a very considerable improvement of conditions in the Eastern Zone. The Pieck Administration has firmly established its position under Communist control, economic conditions, though still bad, have improved and a new aggressive self-confidence has shown itself in the National Front campaign of propaganda against the Western Allies, particularly in Berlin. The West Berliners and West Germans have so far been proof against this propaganda but its constant reiteration, coupled with the menace of Soviet military strength, will inevitably make an impression in time unless matched by clear evidence of steady progress in the West by which it can be refuted.

Allied Policy

13. In this situation it is essential that all three Western Powers should refuse to be discouraged but should steadfastly adhere to their declared policy. The alternative is to admit failure. They must insist on the full implementation by the Germans of the Petersberg Protocol and of any other engagements they enter into and should decline to review the Occupation Statute before the due date. But they should continue to show that they have an all-German policy of their own, that they are working for a free and united Germany with its capital in Berlin, and that they

regard the Federal Government as the Government, and the only Government, of Germany. They should reaffirm that their objective is the eventual association of Germany with the West and an equal partner. Their affirmations should be reflected in their deeds. As the Federal Republic is able by its policy to allay Allied anxieties about security and to convince the allies of its determination to cooperate with the West by progressively carrying out the Petersberg policy, the Allies should be prepared to make an advance towards the association of the Republic with the western world. The Allies should take care that the High Commission reflects in its actions the agreed allied policy towards Germany, that it restricts interference in German affairs as much as possible and that it operates expeditiously and effectively by allowing the majority vote to function as intended and by interpreting the Occupation Statute liberally. The Allies should recognise that the complete association of Germany with the West as a partner is impossible so long as the Federal Republic cannot become a full member of the Council of Europe or join many international organisations because her foreign affairs are conducted solely by the Occupying Powers; and that consequently changes in this respect should be considered when the time comes to review the Occupation Statute, always provided that the Federal Government has joined the Council of Europe. In the meantime, whilst avoiding any impression that they are soliciting or depending on German help, they should lose no opportunity of convincing the Germans of the strength and unity of the Western community and of the dependence of German security and prosperity upon close association with the West.

CALENDAR TO NO. 64

i *19 Apr. 1950 P.U.S.C. (49) 62 Final Revise on the future of Germany* with doubts from Air Ministry on 8 May that the conclusion that Germany should remain disarmed is really in British interest. Stronger criticism of this conclusion from General Robertson on 6 May (for Mr. Attlee's comments, see No. 38, note 1). Sir S. Cripps minuted on his copy (not reproduced from T 232/167): 'Are we to risk Germany helping us agst. Russia or are we to continue to regard her as a potential enemy??' On 5 May, Sir O. Harvey commented that P.U.S.C. (49) 62 illustrated the difference between British and French attitudes to Germany: Britain tended to treat Germany 'as pawn in the contest between the Great Powers. To the French on the other hand Germany has an intrinsic importance which more than outweighs its rôle in the cold war' [ZP 3/3].

No. 65

Brief by Mr. Furlonge for Mr. Bevin

[*E 1023/89*]

FOREIGN OFFICE, *5 May 1950*

Proposed Anglo-American Statement on the Middle East

Ever since the beginning of the Palestine conflict we have inclined to the view, which is strongly held by our Representatives in the Middle East, that some form of Anglo-American guarantee of the frontiers between Israel and the Arab States provides the best, and perhaps the only, prospect of a lasting settlement. We have on occasion discussed this question with the State Department, who while not dissenting from our view, have hitherto indicated that it would be difficult, if not impossible, for them to undertake any such guarantee. Recently, however, they have indicated willingness in principle to participate with us in a joint statement on policy in the Middle East which, while not constituting a guarantee of the frontiers between Israel and the Arab States, would go as far as possible in that direction. They have indicated at the same time that they attach importance to any such statement also covering the frontiers between Saudi Arabia and the Hashemite countries, with which view we agree.[1]

2. A related question is that of arms supplies to the Middle East. The State Department, and Mr. Acheson personally, have loyally defended our deliveries of arms to the Arab States in the face of strong Zionist pressure in Congress and outside. We have of course to meet similar criticism in this country. The Americans have indicated their desire to find some formula which could be included in a joint statement on Middle East policy and which could assist both of us to meet such criticisms.

3. In view of the State Department's expressed willingness to consider participating in a joint statement, it was agreed by the Cabinet of April 26 to omit a general policy declaration from the Commons statement on April 27 on our recognition of Greater Jordan and Israel.[2]

4. We have now considered with the Americans, on the official level and without commitment, the possibility of issuing a statement to cover the above points, and both sides have made a number of suggestions.[3] One point discussed was whether the proposed statement should preferably be bipartite or tripartite. We agree with the Americans that

---

[1] See No. 10.   [2] See No. 39, notes 1 and 5.

[3] The British records of bipartite sub-committee meetings on the Middle and Near East on 1, 2 and 5 May are not printed from E 1023/26, 33, 43 and J 1022/1: see, however, *F.R.U.S. 1950*, vol. iii, pp. 975–988 for the American records, calendars i–ii for the reports to Ministers on the discussions and No. 84, note 9 further to discussion on Persia on 5 May. The draft statements on the Middle East and American redraft, cited in paragraph 5 below, are annexed to MIN/UKUS/P/6 at calendar i.

French arms supplies to the Levant States and French membership of various Middle East bodies such as the Palestine Conciliation Commission, tend to suggest that French participation is desirable, and that the French might well take amiss their exclusion. Against this, we feel that the effect of the statement in the Middle East might be weakened by French participation in view of the lack of influence of the French in many parts of the area and the suspicion with which they are regarded in others.

5. As a result of these discussions the attached alternative outline drafts, bipartite and tripartite, have emerged. The Americans have since suggested a redraft of paragraph 3 of their draft. We understand that the drafts, with this amendment, have been submitted by the State Department to the President who is understood to approve in principle of their general lines. We have also telegraphed them, as working party papers, to our Middle East posts for their comments, which are awaited.[4]

6. We feel that this is a question which the Secretary of State will wish to discuss with Mr. Acheson, but for the purpose of our further discussions with the Americans (which are of course on the official level and without commitment) it would be helpful for us to have his guidance on the following points which are still in doubt.

(*a*) Whether a joint statement covering arms supplies and general policy would be helpful.

(*b*) Whether in that event it should be tripartite or bipartite. (If tripartite it could be issued at the conclusion of the present London talks; if bipartite at some suitable time later.)

(*c*) Whether we may pursue discussions on the basis of the attached drafts.

(*d*) Whether the last paragraph of the statement should be on our lines or the Americans'. (The latter has the advantage of coming nearer to a guarantee of a territorial settlement between Israel and the Arabs, but in its present form might appear to commit us to supporting the territorial *status quo* throughout the Middle East in all the unpredictable circumstances of that area. This point might be met by redrafting.)[5]

G. W. FURLONGE

CALENDARS TO NO. 65

i *7 May 1950 MIN/UKUS/P/6* Report of sub-committee discussions 1–5 May

---

[4] Comments received on 4–8 May from H.M. Representatives in the Middle East on the text telegraphed to them on 3 May were on the whole cautious and followed on from their replies a few days earlier to the question of whether there should be a statement at all. The balance of opinion, led by Tel Aviv and Jedda, was then in favour of a statement, though Beirut was firmly against with Baghdad and Jerusalem doubtful as to timing. In the second set of replies H.M. Representatives were more evenly divided as to the value of a statement on the lines proposed, but were unanimous in approving French participation.

[5] Mr. Bevin minuted below: 'I do not see how I can settle the question of arms until I have an agreement regarding Egypt. The arms to them must be for wider purposes. If we do it, I prefer tripartite.'

(note 3) with covering brief for Mr. Bevin. *N.A.T. and Middle East*: N.A.T. not an 'exclusive club' but with regard to British suggestion for some form of regional arrangement to tie up with N.A.T., U.S. too heavily committed to extend Atlantic Pact to Middle East. *Arms Supply*: statements annexed. *U.N.R.W.A.* U.S. hope for more contributions from U.K. and France for Palestine Refugees. *Saudi Arabia*: U.S. press for settlement of Saudi frontier dispute with Persian Gulf States (U.S. suggestion for direct Saudi-Gulf negotiations resisted by U.K. as explained in F.O. tel. to Jedda No. 259 of 19 May). *Persia*: regarded as a 'critical sore spot'. *Egypt*: U.S. agree on importance of U.K. maintaining defence base in Egypt [E 1023/42; ES 1081/36].

ii *6 May 1950   MIN/UKUS/P/7* Report of sub-committee discussion on Libya, Eritrea, Suez Canal and Haifa Pipeline on 2 May, with covering brief for Mr. Bevin: general agreement on policy [J 1022/2].

No. 66

Personal Message from Mr. Spender (Canberra) to Mr. Bevin[1]

[*FZ 1025/18*]

5 May 1950

We have received from Gordon-Walker the agenda for the talks you will be having with Acheson and Schuman from 11th to 13th of this month.

I was most interested to note that you will be seeking to reach agreement on common world-wide objectives and the course of action which should be followed (*inter alia*) in South East Asia. As you know from our conversations at Colombo, we attached the highest importance to the situation in that area, and to the attitude of the United States towards both immediate and long-range developments which may vitally affect our interests, indeed our very existence. It is for this reason that we suggested the holding in Australia of the Consultative Committee which will begin its work in Sydney on 15th May, and I know you share our determination that the British Commonwealth shall make a constructive contribution in South East Asia.

Clearly your talks with Acheson and Schuman will have an important bearing on the outcome of the Sydney meeting and I trust you will keep us informed both generally as to the progress of your conversations and in detail on those questions which are of immediate and direct concern to us.

I am sure you will agree that in any global planning due weight must be given to South East Asia and the Pacific. While we welcome the recent

[1] This message from Mr. P.C. Spender, Australian Minister for External Affairs, was handed to Mr. Bevin at his flat on the morning of 6 May by the Australian Resident Minister in London, Mr. E.J. Harrison. Copies were subsequently circulated in the Foreign Office to Mr. Younger, Sir W. Strang, Sir R. Makins, Mr. Dening, South East Asia and Far Eastern departments and in the Commonwealth Relations Office to Mr. Gordon-Walker.

evidence that the United States is paying increased attention to this area, we cannot help but recall a tendency during the war to regard South East Asia and the Pacific as unimportant or secondary in the first instance. It would be a matter of grave concern to us if, in the present critical situation, a similar 'strategic decision' were to be made which might involve major risks to Australia.[2]

[2] At their meeting on 6 May (note 1) Mr. Bevin assured Mr. Harrison that representatives of Commonwealth governments in London would be kept informed of the progress and outcome of the tripartite talks. In addition the Commonwealth Relations Office telegraphed regular reports of the talks directly to Commonwealth governments. Mr. Bevin supplemented this information by giving a personal account of the conference to Commonwealth High Commissioners in London on 23 May. On 26 May Mr. Bevin replied to Mr. Spender that he hoped these arrangements had been helpful. On 1 June Mr. Harrison handed to Mr. Younger a second message from Mr. Spender requesting further elucidation on tripartite decisions on S.E. Asia. With regard to tripartite discussions with Dr. Stikker on 13 May on Indonesia (see No. 98.iii) Mr. Spender observed: 'We should have thought that this would have been an appropriate opportunity for Mr. Bevin to raise the question of whether Australian views on the future of Netherlands New Guinea should be heard, or at least to point out the main arguments for the Australian case' (FZ 1025/23). On 12 June Mr. Younger sent Mr. Harrison a memorandum which gave further details on S.E.A. talks and explained that in regard to discussions with Dr. Stikker on Indonesia, Australian 'interests were not in any way overlooked' (FZ 1025/24).

No. 67

Agreed Anglo-American Report[1]

MIN/UKUS/P/5 [AU 10512/2]

Top secret   FOREIGN OFFICE, *6 May 1950*

Continued Consultation on and Coordination of Policy

1. It is the common purpose of the two countries to build up the strength and closer unity of the non-Communist world.

2. In working towards this purpose special burdens and responsibilities fall upon the United States and the United Kingdom. They would bear the principal brunt of action in the event of war, and they have common interests not only in the Atlantic area but throughout the world.

3. If they work at cross purposes the effort to build up the strength of

[1] This paper, printed in *F.R.U.S. 1950*, vol. iii, pp. 1072–4, emerged from the decision at the fourth bipartite meeting of officials (No. 34. ii) to produce joint papers identifying common objectives in specific areas. A British draft (UKUS/P/5, printed *op. cit.*, pp. 890–2) was revised at the fifth bipartite official meeting on 4 May to become a more general paper. This revise (*ibid.*, p. 1072, note 3), was further amended after brief discussions at the sixth and seventh bipartite official meetings on 5–6 May (*ibid.*, pp. 964–5, 970), when it was agreed to circulate the amended text (MIN/UKUS/P/5) to Ministers, but without commitment. For the concern of Mr. D. Bruce, U.S. Ambassador in Paris, at the 'possible dangerous consequences' of the draft paper, UKUS/P/5, and countervailing arguments from Mr. Douglas in London, see *op. cit.*, pp. 960–1 and 972–4. For Mr. Acheson's reactions, see No. 84.

the non-Communist world will be endangered, if not paralysed.

4. In the light of these special responsibilities it is particularly desirable that, in the light of their obligations as members of the United Nations and of their other associations, there should be continuous consultation and close co-ordination of policy between them.

5. It is of course recognised that the development of closer consultation with other like-minded Governments is desirable, and that opportunity should be taken to develop the practice, which already takes place in a wide field.

6. It is further recognized that the close relationship between the United States and the United Kingdom should assist closer United Kingdom relations with Western Europe, and foster the development of closer relations between all members of the Atlantic Community.

7. It will be of advantage if as a result of the present discussions common objectives can be identified both in geographical areas and in functional fields. An attempt should be made to bridge such divergencies of view as may be found to exist. If there are points on which it is impossible for the time being to reach agreement, it should be the aim to limit as far as possible both the area of disagreement and the effect of such disagreement on other questions.

8. If such a body of common objectives can be worked out, it would be of advantage to arrange for periodical reviews of them as a whole. One suggestion is that this might be done in one of the two capitals between the Foreign Secretary and the Ambassador of the other at intervals of perhaps two months.

9. It should be an essential principle in the co-ordination of policy that it is contrary to the policy of either Government to injure the other or take advantage of the other. On the contrary, it should be their parallel and respective aim, within their agreed objectives, to strengthen and improve each other's position by lending each other all proper and possible support. This principle has already been recognized on both sides in a particular area, namely, the Middle East, and therefore would not constitute a new departure.

10. One field in which divergent attitudes might result in weakening of each other's position in face of communist attacks is the approach to colonial questions. Further discussion and consultation is desirable with the aim of avoiding misunderstandings and divergencies both in general approach and in discussions in the United Nations. In this general category of questions the problem of Africa should receive special consideration.

11. As regards the United Nations, it is highly desirable to avoid divergencies at Lake Success and in general (subject always to special cases) to avoid situations arising in which one country finds itself in the position of opposing or voting against the other. There might be advantage in extending the practice of consultation prior to important meetings of the United Nations.

12. Consultation in the specialised agencies of the United Nations might be further developed, and delegations attending technical conferences, e.g. on radio frequencies, might be briefed more fully in the light of general common objectives.

13. In the strategic field it is noted with approval by both sides that the principle of close direct consultation is already established and is being put into effect.

14. United Kingdom representatives suggest that the question of exchanges of security information, and certain questions concerning Atomic Energy, may require discussion later in the talks.

15. Increased co-ordination on information policies is desirable and should be further discussed. There may be scope for some additional machinery for this purpose.

16. In the co-ordination of policy constant day by day exchanges of view play an important part. This is particularly valuable before policies are finally formulated. Constant contact between officials at appropriate levels is an important factor.

17. The appointment of officers specially qualified in particular fields to the respective Embassies has proved a valuable experiment which might be continued or developed with advantage.

18. Consultation and co-ordination between American and British representatives in the field, as well as in Washington and London, is important and might be further developed where appropriate. In some areas representatives in the field have already been given a general directive in this sense. This might be further developed.

19. Consideration should be given to the question of assuring that appropriate procedures exist in each government for bringing to the attention of other departments and agencies the practice of consultation and the general policy considerations which should be kept in mind even in technical matters.

20. The economic aspects of co-operation are dealt with in other papers.[2]

[2] See No. 70.

No. 68

Brief by Mr. Wright for Mr. Bevin

[ZP 2/131]

Top secret   FOREIGN OFFICE, *6 May 1950*

Item 13 of the Bipartite Talks: Colonial Questions

The Secretary of State may wish to note that there is basic agreement on the long term objectives of colonial policy as conceived by the United Kingdom and United States, and that the two Powers have expressed the desire to work in harmony in the United Nations.[1] It has been agreed that there should be further meetings (perhaps bipartite) on the United Nations aspect of these questions, and agreement has been reached on the main points to be discussed. Meanwhile, the Secretary of State may wish to stress to Mr. Acheson the following points:

(a) Since the United States agrees with the basic aims of British colonial policy, it should be possible for them to afford the United Kingdom a greater measure of support on colonial questions in the United Nations. It is of the first importance that the two Powers should not appear in opposite camps on any United Nations issues. The United Kingdom is anxious to review with the United States the question of tactics in the United Nations in an endeavour to reach a meeting of minds.

(b) The dangers of United Nations interference in the colonial empire are very great. The United Kingdom accepts United Nations supervision of her trust territories, but cannot agree that it should be extended to her other colonies, since this would seriously prejudice the success of the United Kingdom policy of leading her colonies to healthy and stable self-government within the British Commonwealth. The present is a critical period in the development of the colonial empire and ignorant or prejudiced outside interference could do untold harm. Unless some means can be found to curb it the anti-colonial drive in the United Nations could lead to an undermining of the United Kingdom's position as a world power.

(c) It is very desirable that the later bilateral talks should cover much wider aspects of colonial questions than just the position in the United Nations, since the United Kingdom attitude cannot be properly understood except against a background of general colonial aims and achievements. It is also desirable that these talks should be held in London rather than Washington, since experts in all aspects of colonial administration could then attend and explain exactly what the United Kingdom is aiming at and achieving.

2. The Secretary of State may also wish to note that the United Kingdom and United States are basically agreed on long term objectives in Africa. The United Kingdom would welcome the chance of reviewing her whole policy in Africa at the later bilateral talks.[2]

---

[1] Bilateral and trilateral sub-committee meetings on colonial questions, 3–5 May, are not here printed: cf. *F.R.U.S. 1950*, vol. iii, pp. 948–55. For the bipartite report as agreed at the seventh bipartite meeting of officials on 6 May, see i below and *F.R.U.S.*, *op. cit.*, pp. 1093–1103 for the tripartite report MIN/TRI/P/21 of 9 May, described by Mr. Wright in a covering brief of 12 May as 'encouraging' (UP 244/38).

[2] In tripartite discussion on 5 May the French delegation's line on Africa was broadly similar to the U.K./U.S. position and it was agreed that the questions raised in the policy statements by each delegation appended to MIN/TRI/P/21 (see note 1) should be considered in detail at a later date. In his short covering brief of 12 May, Mr. Wright observed that 'considerable progress towards agreement on the approach to African problems emerged from the conversations of our three delegations. This progress towards

3. As regards economic development, the Secretary of State may wish to note that the problems which this involves are being dealt with separately and therefore have not been discussed in any detail during the present series of talks.[3]

M.R. WRIGHT

CALENDARS TO NO. 68

i *8 May 1950 MIN/UKUS/P/10*: bipartite report on colonial question (*a*) main problems (*b*) economic development (*c*) future of Africa. [ZP 2/138].

ii *1 May 1950 Communism in Africa*: aims, strategy and procedure of Communists in Africa examined in U.K. brief No. 31: communism in Africa still in early stages [J 1017/7].

agreement covered both general policy in Africa and practical collaboration between the Colonial Powers.'

[3] Sir W. Strang minuted below on 6 May: 'I wish I could be sure that there was much more than mere words in some of these American asseverations.' Mr. Bevin commented: 'This is difficult so I must deal with when I deal with China' (cf. No. 56, note 2 and No. 85).

No. 69

Mr. Bevin to Mr. Bowker (Rangoon)[1]

No.357 Telegraphic [FZ 1025/5]

Secret   FOREIGN OFFICE, *7 May 1950, 5.5. a.m.*

My immediately preceding telegram.

London Three Power Conference

In the course of the discussions on South East Asia at the official level,[2] the French Delegation proposed that at the end of the Conference the three Foreign Ministers should issue a declaration on South East Asia emphasising the solidarity of the three Powers on the problem of containing communism there. They set great store by such a declaration. The American Delegation opposed in principle any such declaration since it would smack of 'ganging-up' and would only lead to friction between the European and Asian Powers. The United Kingdom Delegation emphasised that the principle of Commonwealth consultation made it impossible for them to consider any declaration without first consulting

[1] This telegram to Mr. R.J. Bowker, H.M. Ambassador at Rangoon, was also addressed to H.M. Representatives at Bangkok No. 236, and Djakarta (Batavia) No. 175, repeated to Saigon and Saving to Singapore, Washington, The Hague and Paris. Preceding Foreign Office telegram No. 356 explained that this telegram, on which H.M. Representatives were invited to comment, constituted the text of a C.R.O. telegram to U.K. High Commissioners in Canada, Australia, New Zealand, South Africa, India, Pakistan and Ceylon.

[2] See No. 56.ii.

with the Commonwealth countries, but that in view of known feelings of certain Commonwealth countries on the subject and of the fact that the 3 Asian members of the Commonwealth were directly involved in the area, it would not be practicable to seek Commonwealth views on or concurrence in the kind of declaration proposed, however unexceptionable its terms. They therefore put forward the alternative suggestion that independent states in South East Asia might be persuaded to make suitable declarations themselves which the Western Powers and perhaps other friendly countries would endorse.

2. My immediately following telegram contains our draft of such a declaration.[3]

3. While we are by no means certain that this proposal will find favour with Ministers, it would be very helpful to have for our own information your opinion whether the Commonwealth Government concerned (who should not at present be informed of the existence of this proposal):

(a) would welcome the publication of such a declaration by one or more of the independent states of South East Asia, and either

(b) would be prepared to issue a similar statement, or

(c) would be prepared to join the United Kingdom, United States (and presumably also France) in endorsing such a statement.[4]

[3] Not printed.

[4] The replies from U.K. High Commissioners, apart from in Australia, were generally unenthusiastic. On 13 May High Commissioners were informed in C.R.O. telegram Y. No. 119 that it was agreed at the tripartite ministerial meeting that day (No. 98) not to press at this stage either for a general tripartite declaration on South-East Asia or statements by independent states of S.E.A. themselves.

No. 70

Brief by Sir R. Makins for Mr. Bevin[1]

[UEE 139/4]

FOREIGN OFFICE, 7 *May 1950*

Anglo-American Papers produced by Economic Sub-Committee

'Some factors affecting U.S./U.K. economic relations' (MIN/UKUS/P/2).[1]

This is a short background paper which was written on our side in consultation with Sir E. Plowden and Mr. R. Hall. It reflects a useful discussion. It does not ask for any decision, but recommends the intensification and extension of Anglo-American discussion of economic policy under the continuing Tripartite arrangements.

[1] This joint paper of 6 May, prepared in draft by the U.K. delegation, emerged from the sub-committee discussions at i*a* below. Originally designated UKUS/P/6 (see No. 57, note 2) it was approved with some slight modification (*F.R.U.S. 1950*, vol. iii, p. 960, note 3) at the fifth bipartite meeting of officials on 4 May for circulation to Ministers as MIN/UKUS/P/2.

2. The paper picks out some important differences of outlook and emphasis and represents a useful exchange of views.

3. This paper has been criticised by the Chancellor because it leaves out what he considers an important factor, namely that Socialist planned England and capitalist unplanned America can never meet on the same ground.

4. This antithesis is quite misleading; it was discussed last summer and it was agreed that the U.S. had made quite long strides, in its own way, towards forms of the Welfare State. It is also an unprofitable conception, and the Chancellor formally agreed that Anglo-American partnership on a give and take basis was the right course.

5. The paper has also been criticised by Treasury Ministers for being too weak a statement of our position. It is, however, obvious that when we

(a) are in receipt of aid

(b) are in receipt of war material under the military assistance programme

(c) have asked for U.S. help in the sterling balance problem

(d) have asked for help over development in South and South East Asia

(e) need U.S. support in other parts of the world,

we cannot take up a completely intransigent attitude.

'*U.K. Relationship to Western Europe*' (MIN/UKUS/P/8).[2]

This is also a background paper. It sets out quite usefully what the U.S. mean by 'integration' and our reaction to it, and notes one or two points of difference. On the whole the two points of view are not really far apart.

ROGER MAKINS

CALENDAR TO No. 70

i *1–17 May 1950 Bipartite sub-committee meetings on Anglo-American economic issues* further to discussion at No. 34.i and No. 42.ii. (*a*) Criticism from U.S. delegation, at meetings on 1 and 3 May, of reluctance displayed by U.K. to move towards full convertibility and trade non-discrimination even in the more limited European field e.g. difficulties made by U.K. over E.P.U. (*b*) U.K. concern for an International Tin Agreement, in view of consequences for Malaya and sterling balances of likely drop in world demand for tin, received non-committally by U.S. at meeting on 8 May. (*c*) Sterling balances raised at separate meeting on 8 May when U.K. press for a more positive response to proposals of 17 April than the rather negative preliminary reactions given by Mr. Acheson on 5 May (No. 9, note 7). This response not forthcoming at further meeting on 17 May [UEE 139/1, 3, 5, 6].

[2] This joint paper of 6 May prepared in draft by the U.S. delegation emerged from the sub-committee discussions at calendar i. Originally designated UKUS/P/9 (printed in *F.R.U.S. 1950*, vol. iii, pp. 967–70) it was approved with some slight modification (*ibid.*, p. 970, note 2) at the seventh bipartite meeting of officials on 6 May, for circulation to Ministers as MIN/UKUS/P/8.

No. 71

Brief by Sir R. Makins for Mr. Bevin

[*UR 1017/4*]

FOREIGN OFFICE, *7 May 1950*

Anglo-American–French talks
Long term Economic Relationship between U.S.A. and Western Europe

There is an item on the Tripartite Agenda (No. 2(*b*)(i)) called 'Long term development of economic relationships with the United States of America'. This item was put on by the French.

2. The French circulated a proposal that the representatives of the United States and Canada should 'enter into relations with the competent organs of the O.E.E.C., with a view to examining the best methods of ensuring regular economic co-operation between the various countries concerned.'[1]

3. The attached telegram from Paris[2] shows that the French were first thinking of dealing with this matter under the North Atlantic Pact Organisation but later changed their minds. Cross examination of M. Alphand has disclosed that the fundamental reason for this change is that the French are unalterably opposed to any association of Germany with the Atlantic Pact organisation in any form, now or in the future. They wish, therefore, to divert from the North Atlantic organisation any discussions involving Germany. We have also found out that the French consider that European economic problems should continue to be discussed in the purely European context in the O.E.E.C. which should be strengthened and brought into closer relationship with the Council of Europe, and that the United States and Canada should merely be associated with the O.E.E.C. for certain purposes. The relationship would therefore be purely external and would emphasise the distinction in the general economic field between North America on the one hand and Europe on the other.

4. We have recognised that the problem will arise of associating those countries of Western Europe which are not signatories of the Atlantic Pact, including Germany, with the activities of the Atlantic organisation.[3] But that problem does not arise immediately, since the Pact organisation is still in the early stage of development, while the O.E.E.C. and the Council of Europe are functioning satisfactorily and fulfil present needs. We have said that we do not wish to put on one side Article 2 of the Atlantic Pact; that we wish to deal in one place and not in two with all the problems

---

[1] This quotation formed the substance of TRI/P/15 circulated on 3 May. For discussion of French ideas for Atlantic Pact and O.E.E.C. summarized below see Nos. 40, 47 and 47.i.

[2] Paris telegram No. 162 Saving, for which see No. 47, note 3.

[3] Marginal note by Sir R. Makins: 'This para. shows the line we have taken in the talks.'

concerning the consolidation of the West; and that we doubt whether in the long run it will be easy to make a clear distinction between many of the economic questions arising out of re-armament and other general economic questions. Finally we have said that we do not want to pre-judge now the question of the relationship of Germany with the Atlantic Pact organisation. For these reasons we have proposed that in studying the implementation of Article 2, the Atlantic Council should take into full account the attributes and functions of the O.E.E.C., that is to say, that they should seek to avoid duplication of effort or treading on the O.E.E.C. toes. This proposal has been rejected by the French up to the present time.

5. The Americans would be prepared to accept our proposal but they do not think it goes quite far enough. They agree with us that it is too early to take any decisions on this matter. They do not want to interfere with the working of the O.E.E.C., they do not want to pre-judge the question of the relationship of Germany with the Atlantic Pact and they do not like the French proposal. On the other hand, they are very reluctant to do nothing. They have toyed with the idea of having a special study made of the question of the long-term economic relationship of North America and Europe, separately from either the O.E.E.C. or the North Atlantic Treaty organisation but they recognise that this would be setting up yet another study group. The suggestion has also been made that the nature of the problem should be recognised and should continue to be discussed in the tripartite context. This is also open to objections.

6. The Americans admit that just as we sometimes 'drag our feet' in relation to Europe they are likely to drag their feet ten times more if any question of 'integration' is raised. This is natural and understandable. Finally, the Americans have said that they do not intend to make any proposal on this question. The position is, therefore, that the French and British proposals would remain un-reconciled and that unless the French withdraw, the question will go to Ministers. The proposal which we have put forward is in line with the Secretary of State's general instructions and it ought to be possible to insist on it, particularly as the real reason for the French attitude is not one which we, or the Americans, can accept. It leaves the question entirely open and does not compromise the French position. On the other hand, more especially as the statement by Dr. Jessup,[4] which will presumably be repeated by Mr. Acheson, of the United States' continued interest in Western Europe and its intention to support it after 1952 is fully satisfactory from our point of view, all that is strictly necessary under this item of the Agenda is that we and other countries should take note of this declaration with satisfaction and promise our support.

8. In a word, this is a matter which is not ripe for solution now, but which will find its solution as time goes on. It is better to leave it alone

---

[4] See No. 40, paragraphs 15–16.

rather than to embark on a course of action which may be the wrong one.[5]

ROGER MAKINS

[5] Sir W. Strang minuted below: 'The S. of S. should know that the Chancellor of the Exchequer does not agree that the Atlantic Pact Organisation should deal with general economic affairs, apart from the aspect related to defence expenditure. W.S. 6/5.'

No. 72

Brief by Sir G. Jebb for Mr. Bevin[1]

[WU 1071/117]

FOREIGN OFFICE, *8 May 1950*

Atlantic Pact Machinery

I have already, in Cabinet Paper (50)92,[2] given the Cabinet some account of the progress of the talks between officials which have been taking place during the last week or so, for the purpose of preparing for the important series of Bipartite, Tripartite and Atlantic Council discussions which start on May 9th. In the present paper I wish to examine in further detail, the central question of developing the Atlantic Pact Machinery in order to give greater effect to the common intention of the signatories of the Pact. Before approaching this specific question, however, I should like to say a word by way of background.

2. The joint survey of the present international situation by the officials of the three Governments, acting on instructions from their respective Foreign Ministers, comes to the broad conclusion that though the danger of war is not very great at the present time, or indeed (short of some major miscalculation on the part of the Russians) for the next few years, there will then be a very real risk of the Soviet Union endeavouring to achieve world domination by force of arms unless it is apparent to their Government that a world war, if started, would both be long and not necessarily successful from the point of view of the Soviet Union. By 1955 or 1956, however, the Soviet Union are likely to have a stock of atomic bombs, and sufficient defensive weapons to counter an air attack, and it may appear to them that such a war, if started, might be both short and successful unless indeed the Western world had, by that date, produced not only sufficient defensive weapons for countering an air attack, but also sufficient defensive weapons of the most modern type for countering any advance by the Soviet armies on the Continent of Europe. If, therefore, this survey is broadly speaking correct, and if the necessary preparations by the Western world are going to be ready in order to prevent a war from

[1] This paper was originally drafted as a Cabinet Paper but was used instead as a brief for Mr. Bevin at the bipartite meetings of the London Conference.

[2] No. 54.

breaking out in 1955 or 1956, they must be started now. This was clearly the broad conception which the North Atlantic Defence Committee had in mind at its meeting in The Hague last month[3] when it recommended *inter alia* as follows:

'That the North Atlantic Council issue instructions that will provide for full coordination and closest liaison between the permanent agencies of the North Atlantic Treaty Organisation and their respective Staffs.

'2(*a*) That the North Atlantic Council agree to the immediate need for urgent regional and allied action to ensure the progressive build up of the forces estimated as being required to support the Medium Term Defence plan; and

(*b*) That the North Atlantic Council agree that an immediate determination should be made as to the financial and economic potentialities of the members to increase their present expenditure for military purposes, particularly for the implementation of an agreed armament programme.'

3. I suggest that, in the circumstances, we cannot disregard the recommendations of the North Atlantic Defence Committee and according to my information this is the general view of the Foreign Ministers of the 12 countries who will meet in London in just over a week's time. In a remarkable series of speeches,[4] Mr. Acheson has recently developed the thesis that the free world, of which the North Atlantic Treaty countries represent the nucleus, must combine if freedom is not to be extinguished and democracy to die. Hopes have been aroused by this strong and welcome American lead and it is no exaggeration to say that all the free nations, and not least those in Western Europe are now looking to the London Conference for a sign that their common defence is being powerfully organised and that the so-called 'Atlantic Community' is destined to become a real factor in world affairs, with an appeal greater than that of the Soviet Union and the satellite countries which it has enslaved. These expectations must not, indeed cannot, be disappointed.

4. In their examination of the best machinery which should now be established to transform the Atlantic Pact into a living reality, the officials of the three countries have provisionally (though of course without any commitment) approved two papers which form Annexes A and B.[5] The first paper deals with the nature of the proposed new machinery; the second with the draft resolution by the Council which, in effect, lays down the lines which should govern the activities of the new machine. As regards the first, my colleagues will wish to have the following explanations.

5. Article 9 of the North Atlantic Treaty reads as follows:

[3] See No. 33, note 7.   [4] See No. 26, note 2.
[5] Not attached to filed copy. Annex A was evidently MIN/TRI/P/3 and Annex B, MIN/TRI/P/2 (see No. 46, note 6).

'The Parties hereby establish a Council, on which each of them shall be represented, to consider matters concerning the implementation of this Treaty. The Council shall be so organised as to be able to meet promptly at any time. The Council shall set up such subsidiary bodies as may be necessary; in particular it shall establish immediately a Defence Committee which shall recommend measures for the implementation of Articles 3 and 5.'

It is entirely clear from this Article that the Council is the supreme body so far as the North Atlantic Treaty itself is concerned, and that such bodies as the Defence Committee and the Defence Economic and Financial Committee are subsidiary to it. This does not of course mean that the Ministers who sit on the North Atlantic Council can issue directions to their colleagues in their Governments who sit on the Defence Committee or on the Defence Economic and Financial Committee. Nevertheless, there must be a point at which the work of the various Committees must be brought together and reviewed in the light of the situation as a whole, and this can only be the Council. Further, there is less likelihood of difficulties arising between the subsidiary bodies of the Pact machinery if there is a central body representing the Council keeping the whole structure continuously under review.

6. Now if there is so, it follows that the North Atlantic Council has a most important rôle to play in coordinating the activities of all the bodies established under the Treaty: but it is equally plain that the Council would be quite unable to fulfil such a coordinating rôle if it only met once or twice a year and possessed no permanent secretarial staff. It might, of course, be suggested that the Brussels Treaty system should, broadly speaking, be applied in the sphere of the North Atlantic Treaty, namely that a 'Permanent Commission' of regular diplomats should serve the Council and its Committees attempting, under the Council's general authority, to do something in the way of coordinating the work of other bodies—not of course at the Ministerial level—and that when crucial decisions are to be taken a special meeting of Ministers would be held, consisting of the Foreign Secretaries together with their colleagues of Finance and Defence. But if this system were, in fact, applied to 12 nations instead of to 5, it seems clear that the final court of appeal would be a body consisting of no less than 36 Ministers, together with the necessary attendant advisers, which really does present a rather disturbing picture. On the other hand, the Brussels Treaty Permanent Commission does at least possess a small permanent staff, which is not yet the case with the Atlantic Treaty Organisation.

7. It is now suggested that the North Atlantic Council should be enabled to meet frequently and regularly by each Foreign Minister appointing a 'Deputy'. This Deputy might be either the diplomatic representative in the State concerned at the place selected, or a special Deputy. Persons of Ministerial rank could of course be appointed, and

253

indeed some States would be likely to appoint Ministers. If such Ministers were appointed, they would naturally be directly responsible to their own Foreign Ministers though the attitude which they adopted would be that of the Government as a whole established by appropriate interdepartmental and ministerial consultation. Acting under the control and direction of the Council thus re-organised, would be a small group which would probably consist of 4 or 5 able men of different nationality, the leader of whom might, or might not, be called 'Secretary-General'. The principal function of this group would be to see to it that the Council's directives were translated into action and that there was no duplication or waste of effort on the part of the subsidiary bodies established under the Treaty. The Secretary-General (or whatever he is called) would in his turn have the right to report to the Council (or to the Deputies) and it is hoped that if he were a man of real intelligence and ability, he would be able to play an important and beneficent rôle. My colleagues will observe that in describing this group in the paper at Annex A[5] the word 'executive' has been put in brackets. The French—and probably also the Americans— hold strongly that the retention of this adjective is necessary to give an indication of the kind of work which the new group will do, but the British officials, on my instructions, have so far maintained that, in English at any rate, the word 'executive' gives the impression that the group concerned would be able to take some kind of independent action which of course, in practice, everybody agrees should be reserved for Governments. Generally speaking, I believe that if something on the lines of the machinery described in the paper at Annex A is approved, the exact way in which the proposed new machine would operate could be elaborated in the light of experience; nor is it of course certain that the actual machine now suggested is the best; that can be further examined by Foreign Ministers at the coming Conference. All that I would say at this point is that I am certain that some kind of machinery on the lines suggested is a necessity at the present time.

8. The paper at Annex B[5] attempts to set out what the general considerations should be which would guide the Council—and hence also the Deputies—in carrying out their new tasks. I should hope that the draft now prepared would meet with the broad approval of my colleagues. As will be seen, the three main considerations have been set down in the beginning of the paper and the two perhaps more contentious considerations have been put in the form of questions which it will be for the Council and its subordinate bodies to answer as soon as they can. The main point is that unless the Western world can somehow or other rationalise its production and at the same time, by manufacturing in large quantity the latest weapons, prepare for a future war rather than for a past one, not only will the total cost for all the countries concerned be considerably greater, but also the necessary military efficiency that is required for resisting Russian aggression at the critical time will not be achieved.

9. For all these reasons I would ask my colleague[s] to give me authority to negotiate on the basis of the two draft documents now prepared. Naturally I would, before entering into any commitment, consult them again. Here I am only concerned to repeat that unless some forward move of an important and even dramatic character is made during the forthcoming meetings, we shall be in serious danger of witnessing the collapse of the Atlantic system and a revival of 'Third Force' neutrality policies on the Continent of Europe. As to what would then happen, I can only ask my colleagues to accept my considered view that, far from preserving Western Europe, including the United Kingdom, from eventual Communist rule, such a development would be best calculated to ensure it.

CALENDAR TO NO. 72

i 4 May 1950 Memo. by Mr. E. Davies (Parliamentary Under-Secretary of State) on the need to 'sell the idea of the Atlantic Community in a far more positive and vigorous way than we have done hitherto': recommends (a) issue of statement showing fundamental differences between East and West for which Soviet Union is to blame (b) positive declaration on Western objectives (c) establishment of more machinery for inter-governmental cooperation. Copy of memo. sent to Sir G. Jebb who refers Mr. Davies to his own paper at No. 72 above and draft Atlantic declaration for which see No. 46, note 10 and No. 84.i [WU 1076/65].

No. 73

Joint Anglo-United States Record of Heads of Agreement reached at Bipartite Meeting on 4 May 1950[1]

MIN/UKUS/P/11[FL 10118/106]

Top secret   FOREIGN OFFICE, *8 May 1950*

Indo-Pakistan Sub-Continent and Burma

The problems of the Indo-Pakistan sub-continent (including Afghanistan) and of Burma have been discussed by officials of the United Kingdom and the United States of America, who have recorded jointly the following heads of agreement.

Indo-Pakistan Relations

2. It was agreed:

(a) That close liaison between the United States and the United

---

[1] The British record of bipartite sub-committee meeting No. 12 on 4 May (F.O. 800/449), at which representatives from the Commonwealth Relations Office joined the Foreign Office delegation led by Mr. Dening, is not printed: see *F.R.U.S. 1950*, vol. iii, pp. 996–1000. In a covering note to No. 73, Mr. Shuckburgh stated that the plenary meeting of officials did not have the opportunity of examining it.

Kingdom had shown close agreement to exist regarding their aims in the sub-continent.

(*b*) That the United States' rôle should be to supplement, not to supplant, the endeavours of the United Kingdom and Commonwealth which, from past experience, present economic relationships and the Commonwealth link, had a primary interest in India and Pakistan, though no longer any responsibility there.

(*c*) That for the future, each situation of difficulty arising in Indo-Pakistan affairs should be discussed between the United Kingdom and United States Governments as it arose and ways and means of profitable intervention or assistance then assessed.

Kashmir

3. It was agreed:

(*a*) That full support should be given to the United Nations Representative (Sir Owen Dixon), who would shortly be leaving Lake Success for Kashmir; and

(*b*) That, although it would be inadvisable for either the United Kingdom or the United States to propose partition, a solution involving some form of partition would be considered sympathetically provided it was proposed by the Representative or the parties and was subject to agreement by both parties.

French and Portuguese Settlements in India

4. It was agreed that there was little to be done save to see how Indian negotiations with the French and Portuguese developed, and if necessary to counsel moderation and realism.

Afghanistan

5. It was agreed that one of the reasons for lack of Soviet activity in Afghanistan might be their appreciation that Russian activity in Afghanistan would frighten India and Pakistan into making up their quarrels; and another that, since affairs were in any event progressing unhappily in Afghanistan, the Soviet Union could afford merely to wait until disintegration began. Russian activity in Afghanistan, when it occurred, would spell danger to the rest of the sub-continent.

Afghan/Pakistan Dispute over the N.W.F.P. Tribal Areas ('Pathanistan')

6. It was agreed that the close consultation between the United States and United Kingdom Governments which had hitherto been maintained, and as a result of which the United States Ambassador, following the United Kingdom suggestion, had been instructed to warn the Afghan Government of the dangers of their agitation about the tribal areas, should continue.

Burma

7. It was agreed that consultation should be close and constant and that, in general, United States aid should be complementary to that given to Burma by the United Kingdom and Commonwealth, which were

regarded as having the major interest in assisting Burma to achieve political and economic stability and to resist communist pressure.

CALENDAR TO NO. 73

i (a) *Kashmir*: origins of Kashmir dispute, a major cause of tension in Indo-Pakistan relations, examined in F.O. memo. of 16 May. Further memo. of 30 Aug. reports failure of Dixon mission [FL 1015/235, 403]. (b) *French and Portuguese territories in India*: recent history of French (Chandernagore, Pondicherry, Yanaon, Karikal, Mahé) and Portuguese (Goa, Daman, Diu) reviewed in Research dept. memo. of 6 Mar. [D.O.35/2973]. (c) *Afghanistan*: London brief of 1 May on internal developments and earlier despatch on U.K. policy towards North West Frontier Province dispute with Pakistan [FA 1061/61, 112].

No. 74

Extract from Conclusions of a Meeting of the Cabinet held at 10 Downing Street on Monday, 8 May 1950, at 11 a.m.[1]

C.M. (50) 29 [*CAB 128/17*]

Secret

London Meeting of Foreign Ministers

3. The Cabinet had before them a memorandum by the Foreign Secretary (C.P. (50) 92)[2] reporting the progress made in the early stages of the discussions between officials of the United Kingdom, the United States and France in preparation for the forthcoming meeting of Foreign Ministers.

The Foreign Secretary said that the Ministerial discussions, which were to open on the following day, would be developed in three stages. First, there would be Anglo-American conversations: secondly, there would be tripartite discussions between the United Kingdom, the United States and France: and, finally, there would be the meeting of the North Atlantic Council. Concurrently, opportunity would be taken to discuss matters of common concern to the United Kingdom, the United States and Canada, including certain questions relating to atomic energy research.

The Foreign Secretary said that throughout these talks his primary objective would be to secure a closer understanding with the United States Government on major questions of policy in relation to Europe and the Atlantic area, the Middle East and the Far East. In all matters of foreign

[1] *Present* at this meeting were Mr. Attlee (*in the Chair*), Mr. Bevin, Sir S. Cripps, Mr. Dalton, Viscount Addison, Viscount Alexander of Hillsborough, Viscount Jowitt, Mr. Chuter Ede, Mr. Shinwell, Mr. Isaacs, Mr. Bevan, Mr.Williams, Mr. Tomlinson, Mr. Wilson, Mr. Griffiths, Mr. McNeil, Mr. Gordon-Walker. *Also present* for item 3 was Mr. Younger. *Secretariat*: Sir N. Brook and Mr. Johnston.

[2] No. 54.

policy and defence policy there could be no doubt that our interests would best be served by the closest co-operation with the United States and Canada. It was clear that, even with the support of the Commonwealth, Western Europe was not strong enough to contend with the military dangers confronting it from the East. To withstand the great concentration of power now stretching from China to the Oder, the United Kingdom and Western Europe must be able to rely on the full support of the English-speaking democracies of the Western Hemisphere; and for the original conception of Western Union we must now begin to substitute the wider conception of the Atlantic community.

One of the problems which we should have to face in the forthcoming discussions was how our financial and economic policies could best be related to this general conception of political and defence policy. It was clearly desirable that the objectives which we were pursuing in our relations with the United States Government on matters of foreign policy and defence should be in harmony with the aims of our financial and economic relations with the United States. The United States authorities had recently seemed disposed to press us to adopt a greater measure of economic integration with Europe than we thought wise; and there was some risk that the United States might join with the countries of Western Europe in accusing us of lack of co-operation in economic policy. One possible solution of this difficulty would be to obtain from the United States Government a further declaration of their determination to support the stability of sterling, and an assurance that in the context of collaboration in foreign policy and defence no pressure would be put on us which might impair the strength of our economic and financial position.

Another grave problem to be faced was the position of Western Germany in relation to this new conception of the Atlantic community. The Foreign Secretary had circulated a separate memorandum (C.P. (50) 80)[3] on policy towards Germany. Western Germany now contained a formidable industrial community of about 40 million people which, having been cut off from its former sources of food supply in Eastern Germany, must now live largely upon its exports. It was a challenging task for statesmanship to bring this community into association with the Western world, in a peaceful and constructive spirit, by means acceptable to public opinion in France. The first instinct of the French people had been to insulate Western Germany from the Atlantic community, and to limit her association with Western Europe to the economic questions handled in the Organisation for European Economic Co-operation (O.E.E.C.). The President of the French Republic had, however, adopted a rather more conciliatory attitude in his remarks about French policy towards Germany in a speech which he had made on the previous day on the occasion of the fifth anniversary of the German surrender at Rheims. If Western Germany were allowed to evolve as part of a European

[3] See No. 64, note 1.

organism, through association first with the O.E.E.C. and with the Council of Europe, France might in time be persuaded to modify her present insistence that Germany should be insulated from the North Atlantic Treaty Organisation. This, however, was not a process which could be rushed; for it must not be forgotten that both France and Italy were genuinely apprehensive about a resurgence of German militarism.

The forthcoming talks with the United States Secretary of State would also provide an opportunity for a frank exchange of views on policy towards China and Japan. There were as yet no indications that the United States Government had been able to formulate any fresh policy towards China; and the continuing uncertainty about American policy was undoubtedly embarrassing to a number of the other countries of the Commonwealth. Nor were there any signs that the United States Government were yet ready to consider the conclusion of a peace treaty with Japan. Although the conclusion of such a treaty would be greatly to our advantage, it was difficult to see what pressure we could effectively bring to bear to induce the United States Government to face these issues.

In the third phase of these discussions, when the meeting of the North Atlantic Council opened, the Foreign Secretary hoped that it might prove possible to frame a formal declaration of policy to be made on behalf of all the North Atlantic Treaty Powers. The Cabinet would, of course, be given an opportunity of seeing the draft of any such declaration before it was finally adopted.

In conclusion the Foreign Secretary said that in the forthcoming discussions various economic and defence questions were likely to be raised which were of close concern to other Ministers. He would be glad if he could have his colleagues' assistance on these matters, as they arose; and he proposed that, as the discussions developed, he should keep in close touch with the Ministers most directly concerned.

Discussion showed that the Cabinet fully endorsed the Foreign Secretary's ultimate objective of merging the original conception of Western Union into the wider conception of the Atlantic community, and thereby ranging the United States and Canada in support of the countries of Western Europe in their resistance of any Communist encroachment from the East. There was general support for the Foreign Secretary's view that the strength of the Soviet Union and her satellites could not be matched by the Commonwealth and Western Europe without the full support of North America; and that, from the point of view of foreign policy and defence, reliance must be placed on the greater strength of the Atlantic community.

In discussion the following points were also made:

(a) In paragraph 8 of C.P. (50) 92 it was stated that, in the official discussions preceding the Ministerial talks, the United States and French delegations had been prepared to consider the possibility of further negotiations with the Soviet Government, but that United

259

Kingdom officials had taken the line that general negotiations with the Soviet Union were unlikely to succeed until the Western Powers were able to negotiate from a position of strength. It was suggested that the Government would be placed in a difficult political position if any report were circulated that the United States and French Governments had been in favour of making an approach to Moscow and that this had been prevented only by the unwillingness of the United Kingdom Government to associate themselves with such an approach.

The Foreign Secretary explained that these were preliminary discussions only, and it was not yet known what view would be taken by United States and French Ministers on this point. His own attitude was clear. No good would come of negotiations with the Soviet Government unless the Western Powers knew precisely what their objectives would be in such negotiations and had some grounds for believing that they could secure them. If the Russians gave any indication that they were ready to discontinue the cold war and genuinely anxious to negotiate a general settlement, he would be quick to seize any opportunity for full and frank discussion of all outstanding issues. But experience had shown that, in dealings with the Soviet Union, it was useless to negotiate from weakness.

The Cabinet fully endorsed the Foreign Secretary's view on this question. They considered, however, that there was force in the point that the attitude of the United Kingdom Government might be misrepresented if reports became current that the Americans and the French had favoured a final attempt to secure a peaceful settlement with the Soviet Union by negotiation. *The Foreign Secretary* undertook to bear in mind the importance of ensuring that the United Kingdom Government could not be misrepresented as having been alone in placing obstacles in the way of any such negotiations with Moscow. In this connection it was suggested that, if the Americans showed any disposition to favour general negotiations with the Soviet Government, we might suggest that we should be prepared to enter into such negotiations on the basis of an agreed agenda including the question of atomic energy. This, it was thought, would induce the Americans to adopt a more realistic attitude towards such a proposal.

(b) With reference to paragraph 6 of C.P. (50) 92 it was urged that in the discussion on economic questions we should make it clear that we were not prepared to adopt policies which would prejudice our prospects of attaining economic viability by the end of 1952. There was general support for this view.

(c) The Cabinet endorsed the Foreign Secretary's statement on future policy towards Germany. It was essential that Western Germany should be brought into closer association with Western Europe, and that France should be persuaded to adopt a realistic view of the future place of Western Germany in Europe. The first experiment in this direction could be taken in the Council of Europe. But, before long, it would be necessary to consider how Germany could best contribute towards the defence of Western Europe—though this raised grave questions which would require most careful consideration. French and Italian anxieties about a resurgence of German militarism were among the reasons for substituting, for the original conception of Western Union, the wider conception of the Atlantic community. For, in the wider context of the North Atlantic Treaty, France and Italy could feel greater assurance of security against German aggression and would therefore be more justified in taking the risk of agreeing to some measure of German rearmament.

(*d*) In connection with the defence of Western Europe, reference was made to the importance of building up the great potential military strength of France. Importance was also attached to the need for a more complete integration of the machinery established under the Brussels Treaty and under the North Atlantic Treaty.

(*e*) It was agreed that the Commonwealth Relations Office should arrange to be kept informed of all matters arising in the course of the forthcoming discussions which would be of direct concern to any of the other self-governing members of the Commonwealth.

The Cabinet:

Endorsed the Foreign Secretary's statement; and took note of C.P. (50) 80 and 92 and of the points raised in the discussion.

CALENDAR TO NO. 74

i *7 May 1950 Mr. Bevin's brief for Cabinet Meeting* objectives at London Conference: U.S. likely to accept 'special relationship' in return for U.K. taking lead in Europe: 'I will accept this, but I want to get the Americans away from drawing a hard line between North America and Europe. We must move on to the conception of the Atlantic community . . . In this wider grouping it will be easier for us to cooperate effectively over Western European and other matters, since it brings together the three main pillars of our policy, the Commonwealth in some degree, Western Europe and the United States' [ZP 2/137].

No. 75

Brief by Mr. Wright for Mr. Bevin

[*E 1023/91*]

FOREIGN OFFICE, *8 May 1950*

Possibility of a statement by the Americans and ourselves, and perhaps the French, about the Middle East: and arms for Israel

We have had a further talk with the Americans since the brief submitted to the Secretary of State last week.[1]

[1] No. 65.

2. Both they and we are in considerable uncertainty about the best line to take. But the following represents a further clarification of ideas as far as we have been able to take them.

3. At the time of the conclusion of the Atlantic Pact both the Americans and ourselves made separate but virtually identic statements about the Middle East, referring specially to the importance of supporting the integrity and independence of Greece, Turkey and Persia. Copies are attached at Annex A.[2]

4. It might be of advantage to reaffirm these statements at or soon after the conclusion of the present meeting of the Atlantic Council.

5. Further, we have felt for a long time past that the best assurance of a lasting settlement between Israel and her neighbours would be some form of Anglo-American guarantee. The Americans say that it is practically impossible for them to give an actual guarantee, but they are now inclined to agree to make a joint statement, or identic statement going further than they have done before. The text they are now thinking of is at Annex B.[3] Apparently they might like to make it still stronger.

6. The suggestion has emerged from our talks that a statement on these lines might be drafted which would refer to the Middle East as a whole, including Greece, Turkey and Persia as well as the Israel-Arab situation. This would have a number of advantages if a suitable form of wording could be found.

7. As regards arms for Israel, the Americans would like a statement on the following lines:

(a) The two governments are agreed that the shipment of arms or war material from the United Kingdom or the United States to any country of the Near East will be permitted only on the understanding that the purchasing country has given formal assurances of its intention not to undertake any act of aggression against any other state of the Near East.

(b) The two governments recognise that all the states in question need to maintain a certain level of armed forces for the purposes of assuring their internal security and their legitimate self-defence and to permit them to play their part in the defence of the area as a whole. All applications for arms or war material from these countries will be considered in the light of this principle. The two governments wish, however, to reaffirm their opposition to the development of an arms race between any of these countries.

[2] The annexes to this brief are not attached to the filed copy. When informing the House of Commons on 18 March 1949 of agreement for a North Atlantic Pact, Mr. Bevin stated: 'Here I should like to make a special reference to our relations with our ally Turkey and with our old and faithful friend, Greece, both of whom, with our active assistance, are making the most strenuous efforts to defend their independence and integrity. Our actions in supporting that independence and integrity are clear expressions of our interest in the security of those countries and, represent a policy which we shall continue to pursue (*Parl. Debs.*, 5th ser., *H. of C.*, vol. 462, col. 2535).

[3] See Annexes in No. 65.i.

8. (*a*) presents difficulties for us. Since we supply arms to Egypt, Jordan and Iraq under Treaty obligation, there is objection to our making such supplies dependent on a new condition. On the other hand Egypt has already given assurances on these lines both in public and to the Americans. We are trying to find a way round this either by obtaining further assurances, or by re-wording the paragraph, or both.

9. The Americans point out that Mr. Acheson has publicly supported our delivery of arms to the Arab States in the face of pressure from Congress which is increasing. They feel it is most desirable that something should be done to relieve this pressure. There is also pressure in the House here.

10. The wording in paragraph 7 would, it is hoped, show that we and the Americans are not at cross purposes, and help to relieve the pressure. But it would not commit us to giving arms to Israel.

11. The best solution to this problem might be that the Americans should agree to supply some arms to Israel (and to Arab countries if they wish), and that we should do so a little later on. The Americans are reluctant that we should get in the position in which we supply arms to Arab States, and they supply arms to Israel. But for the time being this might be the best solution.

12. The Secretary of State may however wish to go further and to agree to the supply of some arms to Israel now. The main objections are that this might have a bad effect on our prospects of agreement with Egypt, and that Abdullah might regard it as a stab in the back, at least so long as he has not negotiated an agreement with Israel. It would certainly have some degree of bad effect on our relations with all the Arab States. But if it were done after an American statement coming nearer to guaranteeing frontiers, the disadvantages might be less.

Possible association with the French

13. It might be best for the Americans and ourselves to make separate but virtually identic statements, leaving it for the French to make a similar statement if they so desire.

Recommendations

14. It is recommended that the Secretary of State should discuss these suggestions with Mr. Acheson, and to try to reach agreement in principle that:

(*a*) The Americans and ourselves might issue separate but virtually identic statements about the whole Middle East. It would be for the French to decide whether they wished to make a statement on similar lines.

(*b*) The wording should be further considered during the coming week.

(*c*) The present forms of wording under consideration would not commit us to supply arms to Israel immediately. This question should

263

be discussed with Mr. Acheson with special reference to the possibility of the United States supplying some arms now, and we ourselves somewhat later if not at present.

Mr. Bateman agrees as regards Greece and Turkey.[4]

M.R. WRIGHT

[4] This brief was seen on 9 May by Sir W. Strang who noted 'seen by S. of S.'

No. 76

Brief by Mr. Stevens for Mr. Bevin

[*CE 2207/45/181*]

FOREIGN OFFICE, *8 May 1950*

You may like to know that the German internal economic situation and the economic policy of the Federal Government were discussed at some length in the official working party on German economic problems (Tripartite) which met last week.[1]

There was general agreement between ourselves, the French and the Americans

(i) that the two great objectives in Germany today must be to reduce unemployment and improve the balance of payments position, and that of the two the first was probably the more urgent. It would also facilitate the integration into the Western Germany economy the refugees from the Eastern areas.

(ii) The best way of achieving either was by expansion of the German economy, for which purpose an increase in the funds available for long term investment particularly in the basic industries and housing was required.

(iii) There were various ways in which such funds might be provided and used to best advantage, among them the application of conditions for release of counterpart funds[2] and the release of certain funds which were still notionally in existence since currency reform. By either method it should be possible to steer the funds concerned into those channels in which they could be most usefully employed for the long term benefit of the economy.

(iv) The precise method to be used and the best means of securing German cooperation should be worked out in the High Commission.

[1] The British records of tripartite working party A (economic questions) of the sub-committee on German problems (see Nos. 58 and 61) which met from 2–6 May are not here printed: cf. *F.R.U.S. 1950*, vol. iii, pp. 918–23 and i below for the main papers produced.

[2] Counterpart funds derived from receipts in local currency generated by the sale of American goods received under Marshall Aid.

(v) Efforts were already being made unilaterally and might be considered tripartitely in Germany for providing the German Government with technical assistance designed to improve their statistical and accounting procedure. (Details of what the United Kingdom is doing are given in Annex at Flag A.)[3]

(vi) The Allies cannot hope to impose an economic policy on the Germans and it would be undesirable for them to try to do so. They must proceeed mainly by advice and example, with only sparing use of the reserved powers.

The suggestion was made at one stage that some of these ideas might be set out in writing together with a recommendation that if the High Commissioners saw no objection a message from the three Foreign Ministers indicating that they were watching the situation closely should be conveyed to Dr. Adenauer. In the end, however, it was found difficult to find a form of words which put our precise views in agreed terms on such matters as the relative importance of solving unemployment and the balance of exchange deficits, the form of the proposed remedies and the role of the High Commission with respect to German economic policy. A much watered down version of the proposed message to Adenauer was produced (Flag B)[3] but the Sub-Committee on German questions decided, and I think rightly, that it was scarcely worth while putting forward to Ministers.

Other matters touched on in connexion with the German internal economic situation were Berlin (which is the subject of a paper to the Foreign Ministers),[4] East West Trade (covered by an Anglo-French paper) [ic] and Obstacles to Trade—travel, visas, etc. This last was also the subject of a paper (Flag C)[3] which was agreed in the Economic Working Party; but the Sub-Committee decided to remit it direct to the High Commissioners rather than encumber Ministers with more papers than was strictly necessary.

As a result of lengthy inter-governmental discussions in London prior to the Tripartite meetings, the tripartite conversations reported above and various exchanges of view which we have had with the British Element in the High Commission, I think it can be said that there is no basic divergence of view on the Allied side with respect to the requirements of the German economy; and active steps are being taken in Germany to consider how an economic expansion can best be put into effect. In the circumstances, I do not think that there is any need for any specific resolution or other action by the three Foreign Ministers.

By way of background you may like to see the attached Memorandum (Flag D) [ii] which was prepared in London after very careful consultation with all the departmental experts concerned.[5]

R.B. STEVENS

---

[3] Not printed. [4] See No. 58.i.
[5] A copy of this brief with annexes was sent to General Robertson on 9 May.

i *6 May 1950   German economic papers: with covering brief from Mr. Stevens to Mr. Bevin* on (a)   *level of steel production* (MIN/TRI/P/15: U.S. amendment subsequently circulated as MIN/TRI/P/24)—position reached in sub-committee is satisfactory (for London brief on steel level see Volume I, No. 7.i) (b) *International Authority for the Ruhr* (MIN/TRI/P/18) French concern for early transfer of powers to I.A.R. not shared by U.K./U.S. (c) *East/West Trade* (MIN/TRI/P/16) U.S. not associated with Anglo-French proposal for facilitating W. German trade with Eastern Europe. (d) *Nationalisation of Allied Property* (MIN/TRI/P/17) U.K./U.S. not in favour of French proposal for exemption from nationalisation of allied property in German coal and steel industries. But agree compensation should be sought. U.K. position elaborated in subsequent brief from Mr. Stevens to Mr. Bevin on 11 May. *Ship building* (MIN/TRI/P/23) U.S. proposal for increase in number of German ships built for export also circulated on 11 May. U.K. brief No. 32 explains long-standing Anglo-American differences [CE 2151/34/181; C 3103–6/2514/18; CJ 2316–7/92/182].

ii *8 May 1950   Annex D to No. 76*: Whitehall view of Germany's internal economic position: main problems are unemployment and balance of payments, but remedies lie in hands of Federal Govt. Allies should only act in advisory capacity. Concern of General Robertson (letter of 3 May on draft of memo.) that Allies should not opt out [CE 2207, 2063/45/181].

No. 77

Lieut-General Sir G. Macready[1] *(Wahnerheide) to Mr. Bevin*
 (Received 9 May, 11.55 a.m.)

No. 714 Telegraphic [C 3119/2514/18]

Priority. Secret   WAHNERHEIDE, *9 May 1950, 11 a.m.*

Repeated Washington, Paris, Berlin (Saving).

Following is translation of a letter addressed to High Commissioner by Federal Chancellor dated 6th May and just received.

Begins.

Dear General Robertson, according to various utterances by leading social democrats, the SPD will do its utmost to delay as long as possible the Bundestag debate on the Council of Europe. In doing so it is obviously guided by the intention of exploiting a none-too-positive result of the London Conference as regards the question of Germany in order to influence public opinion against Germany's accession to the Council of Europe and, if possible, to prevent it altogether.

It would, therefore, be desirable, if some tangible results could be

[1] General Macready, Economic Adviser to U.K. High Commissioner in Germany, was Acting High Commissioner in the absence of General Robertson and his Deputy, Mr. Steel, who were both attending the London Conference.

achieved at the London Conference. First and foremost I am thinking in this connection of Allied concessions in the field of shipbuilding and of the admission of foreign capital investments in Germany. It would also be useful if the Conference, in a communique, were to express a sympathetic view on the question of raising the steel quota at a future date. Furthermore, it would be very desirable if the Conference would decide to charge an Allied committee with the task of reviewing the Occupation Statute.

With kind regards, yours very sincerely, Adenauer.[2]

Foreign Office please pass to Washington and Paris as telegrams Nos. 107 and 128 respectively.

[2] In the German Political department of the Foreign Office, Dr. Adenauer's requests were regarded as attempts to gain concessions in return for Germany's entry to the Council of Europe on which the Federal Cabinet had taken a favourable decision that morning (see Volume I, No. 5). It was therefore suggested that no reply should be sent to Dr. Adenauer for the present but that he should be given advance notice of any statement on Germany issued by the London Conference. Sir I. Kirkpatrick referred the department's suggestions to General Robertson who commented on 11 May 'This letter is addressed to me and was not intended, I believe, to be more than a personal, and rather understandable, appeal to me to do my best for him. McCloy received a similar, but not identical, approach [F.R.U.S. 1950, vol. iv, pp. 636–7] Poncet, significantly, did not. There is therefore no need to regard this as a further attempt to sell the horse. I shall not answer this letter unless instructed to do so, but I propose to see A. I should then make a renewed attempt to convince him that he goes about things the wrong way. I am told that on being informed of the latest Schuman proposal, he remarked "There! you see I was right to treat them (the French) rough"' (C 3119/2514/18).

No. 78

Record of First Bipartite Ministerial Meeting held in the Foreign Office on 9 May 1950 at 11.30 a.m.[1]

[ZP 2/192]

Top secret

Present:

United Kingdom Mr. Ernest Bevin, Mr. Kenneth Younger, Sir William Strang, Mr. Ernest Davies, Sir Roger Makins, Sir Gladwyn Jebb, Mr. Wright, Mr. Barclay, Mr. Hadow.

United States Mr. Dean Acheson, Mr. Lewis Douglas, Mr. Cooper,[2] Dr. Jessup, Mr. Harriman, Mr. Perkins, Mr. Bohlen, Mr. Labouisse.

Secretary-General Mr. Shuckburgh.

[1] The British records of the Ministerial meetings of the London Conference are printed from the Confidential Print text on ZP 2/192—further copy on F.O. 800/449. This text incorporated various corrigenda to the typescript draft records produced daily by the U.K. delegation.

[2] Mr. J.S. Cooper, Special Adviser to Mr. Acheson.

I Relations with the Press.
II General Assessment.

Item I Relations with the Press

1. After the usual courtesies had been exchanged the SECRETARY OF STATE suggested that the first item to be considered was how to deal with the press, which would be very anxious to know what had happened. He thought it better if nothing in the nature of a general communiqué were issued until the end of the Tripartite Ministerial talks.

2. MR. ACHESON agreed with this, but said that if anything specific arose in the Bipartite Talks it might be worth while giving some agreed line to the press as had been done over Indo-China in Paris.[3] He thought that at the end of each day's work it might be advisable to consider whether any such item had arisen and whether any special press guidance should be issued.

Item II Assessment of the Situation

3. At Mr. Bevin's invitation, MR. ACHESON gave a general outline of the thinking which had been taking place in the State Department. He said that to the Americans it seemed that the next three or four years were the most critical. The West was falling behind in preparedness while the Soviets were going ahead with an armaments programme which placed them almost on a war-time footing. This meant that the gap between the Russian war potential and the Western had widened considerably and unless something urgent were done to narrow this gap we might see the Soviets entering upon more and more provocative and risky policies, which would culminate in a very dangerous situation between the end of 1952 and 1954.

4. Against this general setting it was necessary to see what had been done by the West. There was The Hague report of the Atlantic Defence Ministers,[4] which had stressed the need for a more rational and scientific approach to the whole problem of defence which must be taken out of the rut of independent national defence forces armed along old lines. This problem would demand a very large effort by all the Atlantic countries—greater perhaps than the economy of Western Europe could stand. It was therefore necessary to strengthen the economies of each European country and specific steps in this direction might be examined later in the agenda.

5. With regard to Germany the Americans felt that unless she were quickly integrated in the Western community a very difficult situation would arise, and if by any chance she went into the Eastern Camp the problem of a settlement with Russia might well be insoluble.

6. In South-East Asia, if Communist expansion were not contained, any

[3] For the text of a statement on Indo-China, issued by Mr. Acheson after talks with M. Schuman in Paris on 8 May, see *F.R.U.S. 1950*, vol. vi, p. 812, and vol. iii, pp. 1010–3 for the talks.
[4] See No. 33, note 7.

hope that China might one day defect or become a liability to the Soviet orbit would disappear. There were urgent steps to be taken in South-East Asia, but talking in military terms the Americans felt that here was a secondary theatre where a holding operation was necessary while the main effort was directed to Western Europe. There was also the need for a settlement in Japan.

7. Another item over which the Americans were concerned was that of propaganda. It was vital that the Information Services and themes of the West should be co-ordinated and made more effective. In this field it was felt that the Soviets with their peace campaign had scored a very considerable success.

8. Finally, there was the question of organisation. What was wanted was action rather than fresh organisation for its own sake. When it had been decided what was to be done, then an organisation would be charged with carrying out the task. One of the suggestions now being looked at was the formation of a continuing group in the North Atlantic Treaty Organisation. The present Council only met twice a year and was, therefore, not in a position to give the vigorous co-ordination and drive necessary. Tasks often fell between the various committees. What was needed was a group—not necessarily giving orders—but finding out what was not being done or what should be done and acting as a spur on the bodies responsible for any specific action. The precise form of this group would be considered later in the agenda, but even at this stage Mr. Acheson would like to mention that any permanent secretariat to serve the group should be headed by a person of stature who could talk as an equal and not as a subordinate to the Council or its Deputies, although, of course, he would take orders from the Council. Further, the group might be charged with the consideration of economic problems relating to the common defence effort.[5]

9. There was also the question of how to get wider co-ordination in the general economic field. It might be possible to associate the United States

---

[5] In a brief of 9 May for Mr. Bevin at this meeting, Sir G. Jebb explained that 'one of the reasons why the Americans and French are keen on having what is vaguely called a "Secretarial Group" to assist the proposed Foreign Ministers' Deputies is because they think that by this means they may be able to avoid the establishment of any "Standing Committee" or "Working Group" or whatever it might be called, within the Council itself. They believe (rightly, I think) that something on the lines of the latter is essential if the new machine is going to work properly, but they also think that the nomination of certain countries to serve on the Committee would present insuperable difficulties. From this way of thinking has proceeded the idea that some high-powered person ... might be appointed—not necessarily as Secretary-General so much as "Chief Coordinator"—who would be assisted by four or five able men, one of whom would certainly be an Englishman and another a Frenchman. This person and his staff would of course be subordinate to the Council and only act on its directives. The French have so far insisted on referring to such a "Secretarial Group" as an "Executive Organ"; but as you know we have reserved our position on this, and I must say I do not think this title is at all desirable. The general idea on the other hand has a good deal to recommend it, even though it may represent a new departure in international practice' (WU 1071/141).

and Canada in some way with the O.E.E.C. so that this task could be carried on after 1952.

10. A study of these items was necessary and when it had been decided on the major objectives to be pursued it should be possible, as a result of these talks, to draw up some kind of major criterion of what should be done and how to promote the general strength of the West.

11. MR. BEVIN said that he agreed generally with Mr. Acheson's analysis. England, being a little nearer Europe that the United States, was even more alert to the growing pressure of the military strength of any one Continental Power.

12. In particular, he felt that Russian policy would in the immediate future concentrate on two particular spots—Germany and South-East Asia. He thought that the form which Russian action would take in these two areas would be the promotion of civil war. This was entirely in line with Russian policy, which liked to strike at points as far apart as possible and in a form in which Russia was not directly involved. The immediate recognition of Ho Chi Minh[6] and the development of para-military formations in Eastern Germany,[7] together with the general Russian Berlin policy, were pointers to Russian action in the two areas mentioned. A similar policy had been carried out in Greece, which might have turned out to be a central point of Russian disruption in the Balkans and the Middle East had the Russians not failed there.

13. Whatever the precise assessment of the maximum time of danger, it was clear that the issue between communism and the West must come to a head in the next few years. It was, therefore, vital for the Western Defence Organisation to be ready to carry the weight of a great programme of preparedness concurrently with a maintenance of the high standard of living, which was the keynote of Western civilisation. It should be possible to carry out both these tasks if the problem was looked at as a whole and dealt with rationally rather than in a piecemeal and chaotic way. If the West did not build up its strength in the near future the Russians would proceed to more and more provocative and risky policies until, finally, we were faced with the situation (such as that over Poland in 1939) when we must fight or submit.

14. The task of building up a system strong enough to deter the Russians from such a course was, however, beyond the strength of Western Europe alone, although Western Europe could be a major contributor to the whole. The only hope lay in the building up of a whole Atlantic Community, whose productive capacity, fighting ability, inventive power and morale was greater than that of Russia. Nor would the badly shattered morale of Europe be restored until the European nations felt that they, along with the United Kingdom, were a part of a unified Atlantic Community. This meant that there must be a dual approach to the problem so that not only was Europe organised as effectively as

[6] See No. 46, note 8.   [7] See No. 31, note 1.

possible, but a kind of 'Atlantic umbrella' must be erected, in the shadow of which Europe could undertake this task of its own reorganisation.

15. When considering the system we wished to see as a whole. Mr. Bevin felt that some of the major issues were of an economic and financial nature which must be smoothed out before each member could play its most effective part. For instance, the United Kingdom could only carry the major burden she bore on behalf of the West if the continued and successful operation of the sterling area could be assured.

16. With regard to Germany, Mr. Bevin thought there was hope that Dr. Adenauer would follow the line desired by the West. It was first of all necessary that Germany should come into the Council of Europe. There might not be much in the practicable possibilities of this body, but by taking this step, which showed that the Germans were willing not only to join the Western club but prepared to accept its rules, they would have gone some way to blotting out the legacy of distrust they had built up for themselves. Then, once the Germans showed that they were willing to co-operate peacefully in the development of a healthy Western European community by their actions in the O.E.E.C., and the Council of Europe, the Western Powers should be prepared to move fast and generously as a response. For instance, a great deal more freedom might be allowed the Germans in their foreign relations. If the Germans joined the Council of Europe, Mr. Bevin felt, the Soviets would have received a major setback and the West would have done much to catch up leeway in redressing the balance of power.

17. Turning to the question of organisation, MR. BEVIN agreed that what was wanted was an effective organisation which would indicate to the world that the Western system was an active and operative one rather than a mere paper plan. He thought, however, that care should be taken in examining along what channels development should flow. The O.E.E.C. channel was one which, officially, fell in 1952. The Atlantic Treaty, on the other hand, went on for a long time. It might be that the O.E.E.C. was at the moment the most useful line to be pursued in order to bring France and Germany together. We had tried to get the Council of Europe to use the O.E.E.C. for its economic side so as to avoid duplication of organisation and so as to pave the way for ultimate fusion in perhaps an even bigger organisation. But the whole question should not be rushed.

18. To sum up, MR. BEVIN said that we all agreed that Russia was a predatory expansionist Power, for whom time was no object and who was prepared to use any method to achieve its end of world domination. The only way to halt this power was to build up the strength and determination of the West. When the West was on an equal or a superior footing to the Russians it might be possible to enter upon successful negotiations. Until that time Soviet proposals for negotiations would be put forward merely to destroy us. With specific reference to South-East Asia, Britain had played a major rôle. Faced with a critical situation at the end of the war she had left India, and though the position might have been considerably

weakened by this act in the initial stages there was now great hope that the Indian Sub-Continent would begin to work together. If India and Pakistan could be held to the West, the position in the whole of South-East Asia could be stabilised, but if they followed the path of disruption the whole of South-East Asia was lost. Stalin realised this, hence his intensive campaign in the area. The French position in Indo-China was a weak spot and while helping the French to the best of our ability, we should persuade them that the major hope lay in a generous spirit of co-operation with Asian nationalist aspirations.

19. MR. ACHESON said he would like to add a few details to the general picture:

(1) *The Defence Plan*

He thought it was vital to make some immediate increase in the armed forces as an earnest of future Western expansion. The American Defence Secretary had called on his department to see what more they could do to bring their organisation up to the level required by The Hague Ministers' report. There is also the question of what further military aid could be given to the other Atlantic nations.

(2) *Economic*

There was need to find some broad economic basis which would allow the diversion of man-power to the military effort without harming the economic life of a country. In America it was realised that economic interest in Europe must continue after 1952 and an examination was going on as to what rôle America could best fulfil in this direction. Mr. Gordon Gray had been appointed to examine what could be done in all departments so that American internal economic policies could be adjusted to the wider needs of the Western system. He was also examining how the investment programme should be directed not only to serve the general objective of strengthening the European economy but to strengthen other subsidiary areas of importance to that economy. It was hoped that by the summer a body could be set up to co-ordinate these policies which could put them before the public as a necessary step in the general Western interest. American public opinion would, however, only be prepared to accept these internal policies if they felt that all this was merely a part of a wider programme designed to improve Atlantic defence and that similar action was being taken in European countries. The American people would want to feel that people in Europe were doing the same thing. It was not possible now to go to the American people and persuade them to adopt lower tariffs on purely intellectual grounds. Action in Europe now needed to increase both production and productivity. If this action was taken it might be possible to maintain the standard of living and increase the defence effort.

(3) *Germany*

Germany would only be attracted to the West if she felt that her security and her ability to earn a living were best served by adherence to a

Western partnership. A major increase in the strength of the West would give the Germans confidence and dissuade them from wavering. For the meanwhile, however, talk of rearming the Germans was to be avoided. Germany had her contribution to make towards the general effort of the West and if she showed willingness to be a law-abiding member of the Western Community the first step might be to bring about a change in the conception of the occupation forces. These could become to be looked upon less as a police force to ensure good behaviour and more as outposts of the general Western defence system. The Germans might be more ready to contribute to occupation costs if this concept could be achieved.

(4) *German Economy*

German economy was in a bad way and as a result Germany was looking to the East for trade. It was necessary to open the markets of the West to Germany and to allow the Germans to enter into and compete in the economic life of the whole Western system. In this way the great productive machine of Germany could be utilised in the interests of the West.

(5) *South-East Asia*

In South-East Asia the United States also had its troubles. Conditions in the Philippines were bad due to maladministration. In Indo-China the primary objective was to win support for Bao Dai and unless something could be done to bolster his position the situation might become very critical in the next few months. It was for this reason that the Americans had agreed to send military aid and to embark on some small schemes of economic help which might have an immediate effect. The major effort must, however, come from the French. In Indonesia there were doubts as to whether the Dutch were really pulling their weight. In Malaya and Burma the United Kingdom bore the major burden, but the United States would be glad to see what they could do to help. The Canberra Conference[8] might lead to concrete schemes in which the Dominions and America might contribute.

20. Mr. Bevin said that with regard to the first two points just made by Mr. Acheson, Britain was faced by a serious dilemma. Before Western Union, our defence budget had been £660 million a year. The defence organisations of our European partners were in a hopeless condition and as an act of faith we had taken the risk of promoting greater Western European military preparedness by contributing a further £100 million a year to this end. The present Defence Budget of £780 million a year was about all the country could stand. Our ability to spend more on defence depended on the balance of payments situation. Britain was not a self-supporting country and must constantly be thinking of the heavy sums to be spent overseas in order to maintain her livelihood. It was essential to couple the defence problem with the economic one. If Britain could earn more it might be possible to spend more on defence, but it was

[8] See No. 4, note 9.

273

impossible to find more money merely by demanding further sacrifices from the people of the country. The Americans must be aware of the need for constant adjustments in the day-to-day regulation of the lives of all the people of this country which arose from this balance of payments problem. The extra amount that had to be earned by exports to solve Britain's problem was comparatively small, but until this extra amount could be assured we were hampered in our efforts to do more for common Atlantic defence. Subject to this, the Cabinet were at one in believing that whatever sacrifices were necessary in order to combat communism they would have to be made.

21. Another item which might weaken us in our ability to attain the common objectives set out was the colonial question. Any undermining of our position in the colonial field meant that Britain was called upon to make a greater effort to maintain this position. For if Britain were to fail in the colonies a vacuum would be left which would be exploited by Russia. Britain was making a big contribution to the common cause in Malaya, the Gold Coast and elsewhere. MR. BEVIN hoped that the Americans realised the burden we were bearing and agreed that it would be fatal if these colonies were lost to the West, since they were an essential part of the foundations of Europe's economic existence.

22.The Meeting adjourned until the afternoon.

No. 79

Notes on a Conversation after Lunch at 1 Carlton Gardens on 9 May 1950[1]

[*AU 1027/14*]

Top secret

Present:
Prime Minister, Mr. Bevin, Mr. Barclay, Mr. Acheson, Mr. Douglas.

The atmosphere at lunch and throughout was extremely warm and

[1] These notes were prepared by Mr. Barclay, as explained in his letter to Mr. Rickett of 10 May: 'The Foreign Secretary asked me to be present at the private lunch which he gave yesterday for Mr. Acheson, the Prime Minister and Mr. Douglas, which I think was a great success. Certainly the atmosphere could not have been more friendly and all concerned seemed thoroughly to enjoy themselves, though towards the end the Foreign Secretary began to tire a bit and had to leave it to the Prime Minister to do most of the talking for the U.K. side. It was not, of course, possible for me to take any notes at the time and, as I had to go on to other meetings, I could not do any sort of a record until late in the evening. I then tried my hand at a short note on some of the points which arose, and of this I enclose a copy. It is not, I fear, very complete, and does not by any means cover the whole ground. I leave it to you to decide whether it is worth showing to the Prime Minister. Apart from Oliver Franks, I am not giving the record any other circulation outside the Foreign Office' (PREM 8/1204). Mr. Rickett replied on 11 May that he would certainly show the record of conversation to Mr. Attlee.

friendly and the Ministers talked very freely and without any apparent restraint. By the time we got to coffee Mr. Acheson showed signs of wishing to get down to business and after references had been made to the Marshall Plan and to Mr. Acheson's share in inspiring General Marshall's famous speech,[2] he said that he felt that the time had come for a further major step forward. There was general agreement that without the Marshall Plan, Italy (most certainly) and France (probably) would have been lost. What was needed now was a determined effort by the Western Powers to show that they were not prepared to give way under the pressure of Russian communism; on the contrary that they were determined to strengthen and consolidate their position. In the old days the British fleet by a show of force had been enough to maintain the peace of the world. It was just as essential now to be able to demonstrate to the peoples of Asia, as also to the Satellite Powers, that the West was strong, organised, and determined to maintain its way of life. *Mr. Acheson* elaborated somewhat on his thesis of the 'positions of strength' and spoke with particular reference to South-East Asia.

Mr. Acheson urged that it was essential that the U.S. and U.K. Governments should themselves accept, and somehow get their peoples to realize, that resistance to the Russian danger must have absolute priority and furthermore that we had only got a few years in which to organise and strengthen ourselves. There were many things the U.S. Government would like to do in the domestic field and others which they would be strongly pressed to do (e.g. make various concessions to the Veterans)[3] which were just not possible if Defence was to be given first priority. Only new schemes which were going to lead to an immediate increase in productivity should be allowed to go forward. He made a similar point with reference to South-East Asia, saying that in his opinion the provision of tractors or other equipment to increase food production immediately in a given area was more valuable than any long term scheme of development.

Mr. Acheson emphasised that it was going to be very difficult to get the U.S. Administration or the American people to make the necessary sacrifices unless they saw that it was part of a general organised effort of the Western nations to enable them to stand up to the Communist threat. He thought, however, that they could be brought to take on greatly increased responsibilities provided that they were satisfied that the U.K. and other Western Powers were also contributing to the utmost of their ability. The American people must be made to feel that they were part of a general scheme. *Mr. Bevin* said that he believed that a relatively small additional expenditure on defence—say an additional 5% or 10% would make all the difference. But this would only be possible if there was increased productivity.

[2] See No. 2, note 8.

[3] Such as the granting of larger budget allocations for pensions, hospitals and educational facilities, for which the U.S. Army Veterans Associations frequently lobbied.

The Prime Minister and *Mr. Bevin*, who had expressed agreement with many of the points made by Mr. Acheson, referred to the effects of the U.K. geographical position on the defence and general policy of H.M. Government. They spoke also of the importance of the U.K.'s Commonwealth ties and of their effect on U.K. policy towards Europe. Mr. Bevin emphasised the great desire of the British people to reach the stage when they were no longer receiving aid, but were fully independent economically and financially. *Mr. Acheson* said that he accepted this, and only asked that the attainment of such independence should not be made the highest priority where steps which were necessary to achieve it ran counter to the general good of the Western world.

The Prime Minister and Mr. Bevin emphasised their wish to work in harmony and on a basis of partnership with the U.S.

No. 80

Record of Second Bipartite Ministerial Meeting held in the Foreign Office on 9 May 1950 at 4 p.m.

[*ZP 2/192*]

Top secret

Present:

United Kingdom Mr. Ernest Bevin, Sir William Strang, Mr. Ernest Davies, Sir Ivone Kirkpatrick, Sir Roger Makins, Sir Gladwyn Jebb, Mr. Dening, Mr. Wright, Mr. Barclay, Mr. Hadow.

United States Mr. Dean Acheson, Mr. Lewis Douglas, Mr. Cooper, Dr. Jessup, Mr. Harriman, Mr. McCloy, Mr. Perkins, Mr. Bohlen, Col. Byroade, Mr. Martin.[1]

Secretary-General Mr. Shuckburgh.

    I Anglo-American Relations (Items 3, 4 and 5 of Agenda).
    II China.
    III North Atlantic Treaty Organisation.

Item I Anglo-American Relations

1. THE SECRETARY OF STATE opened by saying that the three items of the Agenda could really be discussed as one, given a general assessment of the situation based on:

    (*a*) the realisation of Russian aggressiveness, and
    (*b*) the need to build up the strength to deter Russia.

---

[1] Mr. E.M. Martin was Director of the Office of European Regional Affairs in the State Department.

What was needed was common agreement on the rôle that each of our two countries should play in order to further common objectives.

2. Mr. Acheson said that the papers before the Ministers for consideration (MIN/UKUS/P/2,5 and 8)[2] were very general. He thought there was no argument on the general thesis that America and the United Kingdom should work in the closest possible co-operation in every field and should have constant consultation to ensure common action. It had always been the policy of the United States Administration to support sterling and the stability of the sterling system, although he admitted occasionally the Americans had seemed to throw some doubt on this. This was the most positive statement he could make. He did not think that there could be much discussion here of specific questions. There was the European Payments Union which could not be discussed in detail, and on which the main point was that there must be a payments union. There were the sterling balances which were under discussion in Washington. There might, however, be other immediate problems which it would be of value to discuss. What were these specific problems?

3. Mr. Bevin said that he had, in the morning session, touched on our differences over the colonial question. It was vital to avoid conflict in this field. What was needed was a constant exchange of views and opportunities for the Colonial Office to explain its policies for the sympathetic consideration of the Americans, so that we were not all dragged along in the wake of vociferous but irresponsible smaller members of the United Nations.

4. Mr. Acheson said that he entirely agreed and he understood that the principle had now been accepted that we should have the closest consultation before United Nations meetings so as to be able to present a united front.

5. Mr. Bevin said that his second difficulty was the question of American defence plans in the Pacific. Until more was known about the broad American concept for this area it was difficult for the Dominions such as Australia and New Zealand, who were only too willing to play a part, to know exactly where they stood and what they should do.

6. Mr. Acheson replied that if the difficulty arose over strategic plans he was afraid he did not know what the position was. If, on the other hand, it was connected with the Japanese settlement he thought he could supply some information, but he would prefer to do this more privately with Mr. Bevin, and he hoped that the information he gave would not be passed on to anyone for the present.

Item II China

7. Mr. Bevin said he thought one of our major difficulties was that of differing views on China. It was essential that our differences here should not be allowed to affect our general agreement in other areas. We

[2] See No. 70, notes 1 and 2 for MIN/UKUS/P/2 and 8 and No. 67 for MIN/UKUS/P/5.

ourselves felt that it was essential to keep a foot in the door in case things should ultimately work out favourably. All we could do for the time being was to keep in constant touch with the Americans and tell them of our views and moves. There was no reason why we should not follow different lines and agree not to let this prejudice Anglo-American co-operation elsewhere.

8. MR. ACHESON repeated the reasons which had led the United States to adopt the policy with regard to China they at present followed. Nothing had happened to change the situation. The question of Chinese recognition in the United Nations was a dangerous and serious one. The Americans also had their difficulties over the blockade (which was partially successful), nationalist bombing (which was pointless) and pressure to guarantee the integrity of Formosa. The solutions to all these questions were not clear. He wondered if the British attitude was still entirely the same.

9. MR. BEVIN replied that we were assailed by as many doubts as to the possible outcome as the Americans. It was still a question whether we should get anywhere in our negotiations with the Communists. A communication from the People's Government had just been received questioning our sincerity over such items as Chinese representation in the United Nations and the Aircraft in Hong Kong, but on the whole we felt we must still pursue the course we had decided upon.

10. MR. DENING explained that there were four possible developments, all of which would be very slow to take shape:

(1) China might become a Soviet satellite.
(2) Mao Tse-Tung might break away on Titoist lines.
(3) Traditional trends might lead to a general break up of Central authority in China.
(4) China might become a great Communist power in her own right.

11. There followed some discussion on the possibility of things going the way of (2) or (3) above. MR. ACHESON explained that American policy was based on the hope of one of these two things happening and they, therefore, thought it would pay to convince the Chinese that communism was another name for Russian imperialism. Similarly over trade their policy was to make this as unimportant as possible without taking steps which might amount to economic warfare. MR. BEVIN on the other hand thought that Communist technique knew too well how to deal with dissidents or defaulters for it to allow any internal break-up in China. The strong Central régime now set up offered the Chinese peace, which they all longed for.

12. MR. ACHESON asked whether, if the United States and United Kingdom both entered into relations with Communist China this would not lower morale generally in South-East Asia.

13. MR. BEVIN replied that originally it had been the British representatives in South-East Asian countries who had pressed the United Kingdom

to recognise the Chinese Government. They were now becoming more doubtful themselves. There was the problem of how the South-East Asian countries could cope with large Communist Chinese missions, bent on disruption in their midst and how they were to deal with large Chinese minorities.

14. Summing up MR. BEVIN said he thought the position could be left as it was. The United Kingdom would not press the United States to change its policy but at the same time the United States must realise that we could not go back. The United States and the United Kingdom must keep in close touch and not allow differences in China to affect any other of their policies.

15. MR. ACHESON agreed and said he thought that the force of events might ultimately bring both of our China policies much closer together. With regard to Chinese representation in the United Nations the American attitude as explained in the official talks had not changed. It was a very difficult problem for the United States, but he agreed that a review of the situation would be necessary before the next United Nations Assembly.

Item III North Atlantic Treaty Organisation

16. MR. ACHESON said that it had been agreed in the morning that some new machinery was necessary. There had been agreement also on the purpose of this machinery, but it had not yet been agreed how this purpose was to be achieved. In general the idea seemed to be for some kind of Continuing Group who could co-ordinate all activities and for some kind of outstanding figure at its head to give a lead. British ideas hitherto had seemed to favour a small committee of not too many members, but this would lead to great difficulties with the twelve countries involved. The Americans thought that the Group might consist of all twelve, but would in effect work on functional lines with many fewer involved in specific items. The Group should have a Chairman of stature, who would ensure that only a small body of countries was in fact engaged in doing the work. The members of the Group should be of sufficient standing to be able to carry their Governments in support of resolutions made by the North Atlantic Council.

17. The locality of the new organisation, the Americans felt, should be in Europe rather than in Washington, so that the majority of members would be in close touch with their Governments and it was hoped that if there was any argument over the various sites which might be suitable in Europe, it would not be necessary to come to a compromise by falling back on Washington.

18. The leading figure the Americans had in mind would have a small staff, but would not be 'executive' except in so far as he was free to follow things up once he had received direction from the Council.

19. At present matters were referred from the Defence to the Supply and Finance Committees and months of delay and inaction followed. The

leading figure who would be at the head of the new Group, would stop this sort of thing happening.

20. MR. BEVIN said that the United Kingdom accepted much of this, but in particular we felt that the 'leading figure' referred to should be an American. He would be appointed by the Council and his power to take action would flow from the Council. The machinery proposed by the officials (MIN/TRI/P/3)[3] seemed satisfactory, but the document had not been drafted sufficiently clearly to point out that the organisation proposed was merely acting for the Council all through. He accepted the idea of a Continuing Body, and of an active administrative group which would work under this body. It would, however, of course, be necessary to get acceptance from all the other North Atlantic Treaty Powers, and it was therefore vital to be clear in our minds as to what we wanted set up.

21. SIR WILLIAM STRANG said that there appeared to be two ideas: the Americans thought of a Continuing Group consisting of Deputies drawing their powers from the Council with a leading figure who would be Chairman of the Group at the same time as being a national representative. This Chairman would be served by a secretariat. The British view was the same except that the leading figure would be a Secretary-General, served by a secretariat, under the Deputies.

22. There was some discussion on the precise form the new organisation should take, in which it was pointed out that if the 'leading figure' was a representative of his Government he would have access to a great deal more information through his Government than if he was merely an international figure with no particular governmental organisation to feed him. It was also generally agreed that the work of the 'leading figure' would be a full-time task which would not allow the appointment of anyone charged with other duties.

23. MR. BEVIN thought that the officials might go back to consider the matter again and redraft the document MIN/TRI/P/3 to bring out more clearly the overriding authority of the Council in relation to the new mechanism.[4]

---

[3] See No. 46, note 6.

[4] Following this discussion British and American officials produced a redraft of MIN/TRI/P/3 circulated as an American paper (MIN/TRI/P/22, not printed) on 11 May. This was countered by a French revise of both MIN/TRI/P/2 and 3, circulated as MIN/TRI/P/28 on 12 May, printed in *F.R.U.S. 1950*, vol. iii. pp. 1103–5. A second French revise of MIN/TRI/P/3 was circulated as MIN/TRI/P/29 on 13 May (*ibid.*, pp. 103–5) which was substantially the same as the final resolution at No. 113.i. In notes prepared in the Foreign Office for Mr. Bevin on 12 May it was explained that 'the main point of the French draft is to make it clear that the "Executive Officer" (who it is assumed would be American), whether or not he is also Chairman of the Council of Deputies and therefore leader of one of the national delegations on this Council, should in his coordinating functions be helped by a small number of highly competent assistants, who would be drawn from the non-American Governments; or in other words the "Executive Officer" would have a small international staff. This is our idea of the way the machinery should be set up and we should, therefore, support the French amendment to the American redraft which we can otherwise accept as it stands' (WU 1071/89).

24. The Meeting then turned to consideration of the draft Directive for the new organisation set out in MIN/TRI/P/2.[3] MR. ACHESON said he was not clear what relation this document bore to the Defence Ministers' report. It seemed to him that the document under consideration had been drafted without sufficient study being made of the terms of the Defence Ministers' report and it was not clear whether the proposed Directive approved of or censured this report.

25. MR. BEVIN agreed and said he thought that if it was felt that any item of the Defence Ministers' report was not satisfactory the proper way to deal with it was to consider it at the Council Meeting and then refer it back to the Defence Ministers for revised action.

26. SIR GLADWYN JEBB thought that it would be undesirable merely to refer the whole Defence Ministers' report to the new Atlantic organ for action. The draft Directive was, in a way, a digest of the report which called for action on certain lines by the new body.

27. MR. BEVIN and MR. ACHESON were in agreement that the best way to deal with the matter was to consider the various reports by the Defence, Finance, &c., Committees in the Atlantic Council. The resolutions in these reports could then be accepted or rejected and when this had been done the salient points could be picked out and drafted into a Directive of action for the new body.

28. It was agreed to meet at 10.15 a.m. on 10th May, and the Meeting adjourned.[5]

[5] For Mr. Bevin's summary to ministers of his meetings with Mr. Acheson on 9 May, which he described as 'a little disappointing', see Volume I, No. 3.

No. 81

Brief by Mr. Bateman for Mr. Bevin

[RK 1071/9]

FOREIGN OFFICE, 9 May 1950

Turkish Security

There are two aspects of this question, the first of which may call for Tripartite consideration and the second of which affects only H.M. Government and the U.S. Government. They are:

(a) The Turkish Government have formally requested His Majesty's Government 'to bear in mind the question of Turkish security at the London Conference.'[1] It is understood that similar requests have been made to the U.S. and French Governments.

[1] This request was made in an aide-mémoire handed to Mr. Younger by the Turkish Ambassador, Mr. C. Açikalin, on 3 May (not printed from RK 1071/7) and followed up by the Ambassador with Mr. Bateman on 5 May (RK 1071/8).

(*b*) The Head of the United States Military Mission in Ankara—General McBride—is known to be advising the Turkish General Staff on operations and war planning, but is not divulging details either to H.M. Ambassador or the British Military Attaché, although he has been reminded by the Commander-in-Chief, Middle East Land Forces, that the defence of Turkey is primarily a British commitment.

Recommendations

As regards (*a*), it is recommended that the three Foreign Ministers should reiterate the substance of the statement made by each at the time of the signing of the North Atlantic Treaty in May, 1949 (copy attached).[2]

As regards (*b*), the Secretary of State may find an opportunity of discussing General McBride's activities with Mr. Acheson.

Background

(*a*) The Turkish Government regard the Anglo-French-Turkish Treaty of 1939[3] as the keystone of their foreign policy. They realise, however, that, in practice, the Treaty affords them little more than paper security and for the past six months they have been pressing for some political arrangement by which the United States Government would at least associate themselves with the 1939 Treaty. It should also be said that the Turks felt themselves affronted at the inclusion of Italy in the North Atlantic Treaty and their exclusion from it. They have been repeatedly told that, for the present, it is not feasible that the United State Government should undertake any further commitments in the Eastern Mediterranean and that it is regarded as essential that the strength of the West (including the Western half of the Mediterranean) should first be built up. They contend, however, that the arrangements contemplated under the Atlantic Treaty leave the security of the Eastern Mediterranean and the Middle East wide open, and that it is unsafe for the West to prepare its own defence while leaving Turkey in the air. The Turks were alarmed at the speech made by Malenkov[4] last November in which Turkey was indicated as one of the principal countries hostile to Russia lying along the Russian borders. The Turkish Government have convinced themselves from this and other signs that the Kremlin intend sooner or later to pick a quarrel with Turkey and that unless some statement is published at the end of the Conference dealing with Turkey, her position will become actually worse since the Kremlin may conclude that the West is indifferent to Turkey's fate.

Within the past week the Turkish Government has tried to establish yet another point. When the Secretary of State saw M. Sadak in Paris at

[2] Attached to this brief was the extract from Mr. Bevin's statement in the House of Commons on 18 March 1949 cited in No. 75, note 2.

[3] This treaty of 19 October 1939 is printed with protocols in *B.F.S.P.*, vol.151, pp. 213–7.

[4] M. G.M. Malenkov was Deputy Chairman of the Soviet Council of Ministers.

the beginning of April, he suggested that it might be possible for Turkey to help iron out some of Britain's difficulties in the Middle East and especially in Egypt.[5] The Turkish Ambassador now argues that, as the Egyptians, Arabs and Israelis know that Turkey is the Ally of Great Britain, she will be less able to act effectively in accordance with the Secretary of State's suggestion than if she were a member of some larger political arrangement. All these points have some plausibility, but they are, to say the least, arguable. It is sufficient to say, however, that the Turkish Government are not content with the indications already given of the interest of the three Powers in Turkey's defence.

(b) Under existing arrangements the defence of the Eastern Mediterranean is primarily and initially a British obligation. It appears, however, that the Head of the United States Military Mission to Turkey is acting on instructions from General Collins, the Chief of the U.S. General Staff, in advising the Turks on defence planning. There is no *prima facie* reason why General McBride should not collaborate in this matter with his British colleagues and it may well be that a word in season to Mr. Acheson will have the desired effect. It is possible that the Americans will not be more forthcoming about planning for Turkey until the British and United States Chiefs of Staff have reached agreement on the new set-up for theatres of command in the Mediterranean and the Middle East. It is also possible that Lord Tedder[6] may help to clarify matters on his arrival in Washington. Meanwhile, it appears that General Collins, during his recent visit to Turkey, disclosed to the Turks that they might anticipate some advantages from American strategic air operations.[7]

There is nothing to show that the British and American Military Missions to Turkey are at cross purposes—rather to the contrary. All that is required appears to be a little more close collaboration between the Heads of the two Missions.[8]

[5] See No. 10, note 11.

[6] Marshal of the Royal Air Force, Lord Tedder, was shortly to take up his appointment, announced in March, as Chairman of the British Joint Services Mission in Washington and U.K. representative on the Standing Group of the Military Committee of the North Atlantic Treaty Organization.

[7] For General Collins' discussions in Turkey on 26–27 March and report of 10 April on his return from a tour of Greece, Turkey, Iran, Saudi Arabia and Egypt, see *F.R.U.S. 1950*, vol. v., pp. 1241–7, 1248–50. With regard to General Collins' visit to Turkey, the British Chiefs of Staff asked that H.M. Ambassador in Ankara should 'emphasise to General Collins the importance we attach to reaching an agreed assessment with the Americans of the military capabilities of Turkey. At present the Americans hold the opinion that the Turks should be able to stand on their own feet in about 12 months time, while we take the view that it will be a long time yet before Turkey can manage without outside assistance ... Our view, as you are well aware, is that Turkey is of the greatest strategic importance in relation to the defence of the Middle East, and that it is, therefore, essential that the Americans should not withdraw assistance from Turkey at too early a date' (letter to Mr. Wright of 22 March on JE 10345/8).

[8] When submitting this brief initially to Sir W. Strang, Mr. Bateman commented on his

recommendations at (*a*) and (*b*) above: 'Probably the Turks will not be satisfied with what is suggested, but as we cannot satisfy them anyway, the recommendation is about as much as we can do ... The Greek Ambassador has also been enquiring about the Eastern Mediterranean defence arrangements, but it was easier to fob him off.' Sir W. Strang recorded below on 11 May 'Point (*a*) in the annexed memo. was raised by Mr. Wright and myself with the two Ministers, but neither of them was inclined to pursue it [see No. 84, note 7]. We must raise it again. Point (*b*) is being discussed with the U.S. Delegation by Mr. Wright.'

No. 82

Extract from Record of Third Bipartite Ministerial Meeting held in the Foreign Office on 10 May 1950 at 11 a.m.

[*ZP 2/192*]

Top secret

Present:

United Kingdom Mr. Ernest Bevin, Mr. Kenneth Younger, Sir William Strang, Sir Ivone Kirkpatrick, Mr. Ernest Davies, Lord Henderson, Sir Brian Robertson, Sir Roger Makins, Sir Gladwyn Jebb, Sir Frederick Hoyer-Millar, Mr. Wright, Mr. Barclay, Mr. Hadow.

United States Mr. Dean Acheson, Mr. Lewis Douglas, Mr. Cooper, Dr. Jessup, Mr. Harriman, Mr. McCloy, Mr. Perkins, Mr. Bohlen, Col. Byroade, Mr. Hare, Mr. Martin.

Secretary-General Mr. Shuckburgh.

I Anglo-American Relations (MIN/UKUS/P/2 and 8).[1]
II European Economic and Political Integration.[2]
III Germany.[2]
IV Soviet Union, &c. (MIN/TRI/P/4)[3]
V Middle East (MIN/UKUS/P/6)[4]

Item I Anglo-American Relations

MR. BEVIN said that he understood that Mr. Acheson did not want to stick too rigidly to an examination and adoption of the many papers prepared by the Officials, but in order that the various Departments in America and the United Kingdom might have something to work on as a result of the Conference he suggested that papers MIN/UKUS/P/5,[5] 2 & 8 might receive the general approval of Ministers. MIN/UKUS/P/5 was for consideration in the afternoon, and he therefore suggested that the other two papers might now be looked at.

2. MR. ACHESON, after summarising the points raised in the two papers,

[1] See No. 70, notes 1 and 2.
[2] For items II and III, not here printed, see Volume I, No. 4.   [3] See No. 46, note 9.
[4] No. 65.i.   [5] No. 67.

said they were in general line with American thinking and at Mr. Bevin's suggestion the papers were adopted as working documents which set forth the broad basis for conduct by the two countries.
. . .[2]

Item IV Soviet Union, &c. (MIN/TRI/P/4)[3]

25. MR. ACHESON said that the paper before the meeting generally expressed the agreement between the United States and the United Kingdom on action to be taken with regard to possible negotiations.

The paper (MIN/TRI/P/4) was accepted as a guiding document for action in the fields it covered.

Item V Middle East (MIN/UKUS/P/6)[4]

26. MR. ACHESON said that four points of agreement emerged:

(1) Both America and Britain thought that the security of the Middle East was vital.
(2) They were agreed that they must work together in the area, and
(3) They thought that the Atlantic Organisation should show its interest in the security of the area.
(4) A Middle Eastern Pact was not immediately practicable though the British seemed to be more sympathetic towards such a development than the Americans. The possibility of informal defence talks with countries of the area had been suggested and the Americans would study the possibility of entering into such talks.

27. In particular he wished to raise one point—the supply of arms for Middle Eastern countries. The United States recognised the importance of the steps taken in the military field by the United Kingdom with regard to such countries as Egypt and the United States Chiefs of Staff thought that Britain's Treaty relations with the Middle Eastern countries were of value. At the same time there was much public excitement in the United States on the question of armaments for the Arabs, and it was necessary to try and do something to calm this down. This question might be discussed and then it might be seen whether it was possible to issue a series of declarations both by the United States and the United Kingdom on the one hand and the recipients of arms on the other that the arms supplied were not to be used for any kind of aggression against other Middle Eastern countries. The United States and the United Kingdom might say that they were against armaments races and point out the action that they would be prepared to take should the arms supplied be used for aggression in the area.

28. The conflict to be resolved was that between the need for security in the Middle East against external aggression and the likelihood of internal conflict between the countries of the Middle East. The solution seemed to lie along the lines of making a series of declarations of the nature he had indicated.

29. MR. BEVIN said he appreciated the American attitude and he realised that there was pressure in America with regard to this very complicated situation. A major factor which must be taken into account was Arab fear of Jewish aggression. He did not know if this was justified and he himself felt that the Jews could probably be more successful along the lines of commercial infiltration of the Arab States. If arms were not supplied to the Arabs they would get them from the Soviet satellites, and if we did supply arms but made this supply dependent upon a series of declarations, as Mr. Acheson had suggested, the Arabs might still get supplies of arms on the side from the Soviet satellites. Who could then say that the Arabs were going back on any declaration they had made?

30. Mr. Acheson then had to leave the meeting which was adjourned until 3.30 in the afternoon.

No. 83

Sir E. Hall-Patch (Paris) to Mr. Bevin
(Received 10 May, 1.51 p.m.)

No. 218 Telegraphic [WU 10723/7]

Immediate. Secret   PARIS, *10 May 1950, 1.51 p.m.*
Repeated Saving to The Hague, Washington.

My telegram No.215 paragraph 2 (*c*).[1]
Article 2 of the North Atlantic Pact.
M. Stikker said he understood there had been discussions in London about the setting up of some economic organisation under Article 2 of the Atlantic Pact. He was apprehensive about the turn events might take. It was obvious that the economic effects of re-armament would be most serious. Issues of fundamental financial and economic policy would have to be faced by all the parties to the Atlantic Pact. Many of these issues were being handled in O.E.E.C. and they could not be dealt with unless the impact of re-armament was taken fully into account. The O.E.E.C. could probably assemble the best body of experts to deal with the whole problem but there were obvious difficulties in O.E.E.C. undertaking work in connexion with the Atlantic Pact. The trouble was there was not enough expert manpower for the work to be split between two bodies. He did not see clearly how to proceed, but he was most anxious not to withdraw expert manpower from O.E.E.C. and so handicap it in the last two years of the European Recovery Programme when so many important issues for the future were coming before it for decision.

2. I said that as far as I knew your views you felt that O.E.E.C. should

[1] In this telegram of even date, not printed, Sir E. Hall-Patch listed topics discussed with M. Stikker on the evening of 9 May.

be allowed to continue its work unhampered until 1952. He maintained however that there was unrelenting pressure on both sides of the Atlantic for speedy re-armament and also some agitation for a separate organisation to deal with it. He felt there was danger in this course as rehabilitation of the shattered economy in Europe and re-armament both made heavy calls on a limited European productive capacity. The two would have to be considered as a whole and kept under constant review as a whole or there would be serious trouble. For example he would have to make it clear that Holland could not assume the military burdens allotted to her without serious risks of inflation which the Netherlands Finance Minister[2] declined to accept. If the military burden was to be shouldered essential rehabilitation work would have to be shelved and 'viability by 1952' become a dream. From the point of view of efficiency he thought the work of assessing the total economic burden and keeping it under constant review should be entrusted to O.E.E.C. He realised the difficulties but he saw no other solution with the dearth of expert manpower. Moreover, it was in his view dangerous to defer a decision on this important issue until 1952. It was work which would have to be started immediately and developed assiduously in the coming two years if serious trouble were to be avoided. This was one of his main preoccupations and he would have views which he would have to express at the North Atlantic Pact discussions. If possible he would like an opportunity of going over the ground with British Ministers in the first instance. He seemed to be particularly worried about the position of Canada. There have apparently been some exchanges between the Netherlands and Canada in the context of the North Atlantic Pact and M. Stikker seems rather concerned as to the Canadian attitude.

3. I pointed out that it would be extremely difficult for O.E.E.C. to discuss the economic aspects of the North Atlantic Pact because the economic implications of the Pact were worldwide and O.E.E.C. normally concerned itself only with Europe. There was also the position of Switzerland and Sweden to be considered. Above all there was the crucial question of security.

4. As regards Switzerland and Sweden, M. Stikker said he had given some thought to these particular difficulties and did not think they were insurmountable. As regards security, he realised this was a most important point. What were my views about security in O.E.E.C.? I said that security in O.E.E.C. was non-existent: it was as leaky as a sieve. I felt that this would be a major obstacle in having any really confidential work done in O.E.E.C. He took the point but again expressed the view that manpower was so short that duplication must be avoided at all costs. If necessary, we might have to apply stringent security measures in O.E.E.C. if it proved to be the most convenient place for the general economic problem to be studied. I confined myself to saying that I thought our security people

[2] Professor Pieter Lieftinck.

would be most reluctant to entrust any confidential information to O.E.E.C. in present circumstances.[3]

[3] In an undated minute, Mr. C.O.I. Ramsden of F.O. Western Department, commented on this telegram: 'I suspect that in voicing his apprehensions over the impact of rearmament on the economic future of Europe, Dr. Stikker was speaking more in his capacity of the Netherlands Foreign Minister, than as "Superman" of O.E.E.C. The Dutch have been as vocal as any of the N.A.T. powers in expressing their desire to eat their cake and have it, i.e., to have full security without the attendant expense ... this telegram is a useful warning of what we may expect when the question of more money for N.A.T.O. comes up' (WU 10723/7).

No. 84

Record of Fourth Bipartite Ministerial Meeting held in the Foreign Office on 10 May 1950 at 3.30 p.m.

[ZP 2/192]

Top secret

Present:
United Kingdom Mr. Ernest Bevin, Mr. Kenneth Younger, Sir William Strang, Mr. Ernest Davies, Sir Roger Makins, Sir Gladwyn Jebb, Sir Frederick Hoyer-Millar, Mr. Dening, Mr. Wright, Mr. Barclay, Mr. Hadow.

United States Mr. Dean Acheson, Mr. Lewis Douglas, Mr. Cooper, Dr. Jessup, Mr. Bruce, Mr. Harriman, Mr. McCloy, Mr. Perkins, Mr. Bohlen, Mr. Hare, Mr. Stinebower.

Secretary-General Mr. Shuckburgh.

    I Public session of Atlantic Council.
   II Middle East (MIN/UKUS/P/6).[1]
  III Libya and Eritrea.
  IV Indian Sub-continent (MIN/UKUS/P/11)[2]
   V East-West Trade.
  VI French proposal of 10th May.[3]
 VII Co-ordination and Consultation (MIN/UKUS/P/5).[4]
VIII Atlantic Declaration (MIN/TRI/P/8).[5]

[1] No. 65.i. [2] No. 73.
[3] For the French proposal of 9 May for the creation of a European coal and steel community, elaborated in *The Times* on 10 May, p.6, see Volume I, chapter I *passim*.
[4] No. 67.
[5] MIN/TRI/P/8 (text at i below) contained the same alternative draft declarations circulated in TRI/P/23 (see No. 46, note 10). When TRI/P/23 was discussed at the sixth tripartite meeting of officials of 6 May it was the *American* view that the two drafts 'showed a major difference in philosophy between the Americans on the one hand and the British and French on the other. Some vigorous and forthright statement was needed, and the

Item I Public Session of Atlantic Council

1. There was some discussion as how best to handle this problem. MR. BEVIN suggested that the photographers must be allowed in to the first session at Lancaster House and that there then might be a public session at the end of the Council meetings when the press would be present and the Ministers of all twelve Atlantic members might make short speeches. It was agreed that Mr. Bevin's proposal should go forward from Mr. Acheson as a suggestion by the chairman. If the other countries did not agree and wished for a public session at the very beginning then this would have to be catered for.

Item II Middle East (MIN/UKUS/P/6)[1]
(a) Arms Shipments to the Middle East

2. MR. BEVIN said that he had been considering the suggestion for a declaration to be made by the United States and British Governments, and perhaps the French Government about internal stability in the Middle East and the supply of arms and he would like to pursue this matter. We could not avoid sending arms to Jordan, Iraq and Egypt under our Treaty obligations. Presumably we should also have to supply certain arms to Israel. He took it that the suggestion was the supply of arms to these and neighbouring countries should be coupled with assurances on their part that these arms would not be used for an attack on any neighbouring country. There would also be a strong statement against aggression by either side.

3. He was, however, faced with the problem of supplying the Egyptians with sufficient arms to build up an army which could fulfil a rôle in the general interests of Middle Eastern security. Similarly, the Iraq Government were continually faced with the Kurdish question and must have forces capable of maintaining internal security. When he asked these two countries for a declaration along the lines suggested, they might well ask whether it was intended only to supply sufficient arms to maintain their defence establishments at a level which would not give them preponderance over Israel. This would be difficult situation as clearly Iraq and Egypt needed a bigger defence establishment for purely internal purposes than did Israel. Moreover there was a difficulty over treaty obligations.

4. MR. ACHESON said that as he understood it nothing in the declaration

Anglo-French [draft B] went nowhere near fulfilling what the Americans thought should be said ... In particular the *Americans* felt that paragraph 6 of the Anglo-French draft amounted to an acceptance of the Russian thesis and showed a willingness to meet the Russians on their own ground. There were four or five other items which the Americans did not find in any way acceptable, such as the reference to general disarmament and atomic energy. 3. On the *British* side it was pointed out that the Anglo-French draft represented the lowest common denominator of agreement which could be reached with the French and in fact considerably watered down the original United Kingdom draft [i] which we much preferred ... The *French* thought that the ideas in both drafts were very similar' (British record on ZP 2/193). It was agreed to present both drafts to Ministers with brackets round the passages in version B on which reservations had been made.

would apply any limit to which any specific country would be held if the armament programme of that country at a certain level was necessary for general security purposes. The main purpose of the declarations would be to allow the Western Powers to go ahead and do what they thought necessary to bring the armaments of the Middle Eastern countries up to an efficient standard without the Israeli Government or its sympathisers elsewhere in the world being able to accuse the West of building up the aggressive potential of the Arab States. If assurances were given by the various countries in the area these would, in a way, sum up to a Middle East non-aggression pact and this, together with a strong statement by the United States, Britain and perhaps France, would do much to quieten public comment and disquietude on the whole question.[6]

5. MR. ACHESON handed Mr. Bevin the latest American draft suggestion for the declaration[7] and suggested that the two delegations should get to work on this and put forward recommendations both as to the content of the declaration and the procedure to be followed. If this work could be completed while the London Conference was still in session it might be possible to take action from London. MR. BEVIN agreed and directed that the outcome of the official deliberations should be made available for consideration by the Prime Minister who was closely interest in the subject. He thought that the declaration need not necessarily be a joint one, and there was always the difficulty of associating France with Middle Eastern matters, but he thought the three Powers might individually issue identical declarations.

(b) *Relief for Palestine Refugees*

6. MR. ACHESON asked what the position was with regard to the British contribution.

7. MR. BEVIN said that our position at present was that we had agreed to put up the equivalent of $7 million for the next 18 months.

8. MR. ACHESON said that he noted this statement with sorrow.

9. MR. BEVIN thought that it might be useful to get some clear commitment from the French and the Canadians and MR. YOUNGER said that if we could get some firm offer by these other countries it might be possible to see whether the United Kingdom might not do more.

10. MR. BEVIN suggested that opportunity might be taken for a

[6] Following this discussion it was agreed in the Foreign Office that assurances of non-aggression towards any other state in the Middle East should be sought initially from Egypt, Jordan and Iraq. Instructions were sent accordingly while H.M. representatives at Beirut, Damascus, Jedda and Tel Aviv were alerted to the possibility of seeking similar assurances from the government to which each was accredited:see further No. 97, note 6 and No. 105.

[7] The text of this re-draft is printed in *F.R.U.S. 1950*, vol. iii. p. 1029, note 4. According to the American record (*ibid.*, p. 1029) Mr. Wright suggested at this point the possibility of widening the scope of the declaration to include Greece, Turkey and Iran. This idea was rejected by Mr. Acheson and Mr. Bevin: see further No. 101.

[8] See further No. 88.

discussion with Mr. Pearson and M. Schuman, at which the Chancellor of the Exchequer might be present to discuss the whole situation.[8]

(c) *Saudi Arabia*

11. MR. WRIGHT said that the principal question was the frontier problem. The two delegations were at present working on the matter and hoped to produce an agreed line. We hoped that it could be agreed that both countries should make it clear to [King] Ibn Saud that we wished for a settlement and were not working at cross purposes. This might facilitate a quicker and more satisfactory outcome with the Saudi Arabians.

12. MR. BEVIN thought that it would be useful if the officials could produce some kind of progress report on the matter before the London Conference broke up.

MR. ACHESON noted that there was general agreement between us over the line to be taken in Persia.

(d) *Persia*

13. MR. WRIGHT pointed out that delay in reaching agreement with the Persians over the Anglo-Iranian Oil Company was holding up prospects for progress in the general field of Persian economic development. The United States and the United Kingdom were in close accord and our representatives in Tehran were pursuing a common line of persuasion and explanation with the Persians to the effect that it was really in their best interests to ratify the supplemental oil agreement[9] which would greatly benefit Persia.

(e) *Economic Development*

14. The Ministers took note of the official recommendation in the paper before them.[1]

Item III Libya and Eritrea

15. MR. BEVIN and MR. ACHESON thought that it was hardly necessary to go into this matter in any detail. We were both in full agreement over policy towards Libya and Eritrea.[10] But it was for consideration whether Eritrea should be discussed with Count Sforza while he was in London.[11]

16. MR. WRIGHT said that the only item which really arose over Libya was with regard to American strategic facilities in Tripolitania. The American view on their requirements and how those requirements could

[9] This agreement, signed on 17 July 1949 between the Iranian Government and the Anglo-Iranian Oil Company (A.I.O.C.) but still not ratified by the Majlis, provided for an increase in oil royalties and various fixed payments from the A.I.O.C. to the Iranian Government. In the context of economic aid for Iran, the U.S. delegation suggested at a sub-committee meeting on 5 May (see No. 65, note 3) that the British government might take some action to expedite ratification, since 'such a step might in itself settle the whole problem, in view of the additional royalties which would then accrue to the Persian Government' (British record on E 1023/43).

[10] See No. 65.ii.

[11] See No. 94.iii for Mr. Bevin's discussion on Eritrea with Count Sforza, Italian Minister for Foreign Affairs, on 13 May.

be regarded as providing some revenue for the future state of Libya would be of value to us as the administering power so that we could plan accordingly. It was also of importance to the United Nations Commissioner for Libya. Mr. Acheson took note of the desirability of clarifying the American attitude on the financial aspect of the question.

Item IV Indian Sub-Continent (UKUS/P/11)[2]

17. MR. BEVIN and MR. ACHESON agreed that there was no problem to be discussed here. There was a close harmony of view, but the situation was one which should be constantly watched.

Item V East-West Trade

18. MR. ACHESON said that he had been particularly asked to raise the question of Lists 1 (*a*) and 1 (*b*),[12] since the National Security Council in Washington was seriously disturbed over the security aspect of East-West Trade, which was at the moment being dealt with by experts in Paris. He thought the matter should receive Ministerial attention. List 1 (*a*) was of materials which it was dangerous for the Russians to have: List 1 (*b*) of subsidiary materials which, if supplied in sufficient quantity, would add to the Russian war potential. There was a large difference of opinion over the items under 1 (*b*), which he understood provided one-third of all the items included in East-West Trade. It was not proposed that these articles should be prohibited but they should be controlled. He realised the connexion of this question with the European balance of payments situation. He thought the whole problem should really be lifted out of the technical context and political decisions made upon it. Naturally, the United States would like agreement on the 1 (*b*) List as near to their own view as possible, since the United States could only act in accordance with the level of trade agreed upon by the European countries. MR. BEVIN said that he had understood that the United Kingdom position was very close to that of the United States, and asked Sir Roger Makins to explain what was happening. SIR ROGER MAKINS said that there was in fact a difference of opinion, since we were being asked to transfer a number of items from List 1 (*b*) to List 1 (*a*) to an extent which we thought amounted to a change in policy.

19. MR. ACHESON said it really amounted to a decision between the security risk involved and the value to Western Europe of East-West Trade. The bare bones of the problem should be presented to Ministers who could be asked to weigh whether the good done to European economy outweighed the harm done by supplying the Soviets with war material.

[12] For the items on and the distinction between lists IA and IB of the American security export control programme and International Lists I-III, agreed in Paris in November 1949, see *F.R.U.S. 1950*, vol. iv, pp.87–93 and *F.R.U.S. 1949*, vol. v, pp. 173–6 for the 1949 conference between Belgium, France, Italy, the Netherlands, the United Kingdom and United States and the subsequent establishment there of a Consultative Group on strategic export control, (later joined by Canada, Norway and Denmark).

20. MR. BEVIN agreed that the matter should be presented to Ministers and instructed that a paper should be prepared setting out the problem so that a political decision might be reached.

Item VI French Proposal of 10th May for International Control of Steel and Coal

21. MR. ACHESON and MR. BEVIN exchanged drafts of the line they proposed to take with the press on this matter.[13] It was felt that the position adopted by both the Americans and the British was very similar. The British line had already been given to the News Department for use by the press, and MR. ACHESON said that now he had satisfied himself that Mr. Bevin had no objection to his proposed line he was prepared to take similar action.

Item VII Co-ordination and Consultation (MIN/UKUS/P/5)[4]

22. MR. ACHESON said that he had read the paper before him and had been struck by two thoughts. The first was that he entirely agreed with the general content of the paper in its exposition of the need for close and continued consultation on all the parallel interests of the United States and United Kingdom. The second was that it was quite impossible to allow it to be known that any such paper had been drawn up or that it had been agreed to. He was in complete agreement that it was vital that our policies should be aligned as closely as possible. He also thought that our interests were either the same or very close in all parts of the world. Our policies were not always in accord, but it was necessary to do the utmost to bring them into either complete alignment or as close alignment as possible. He could not for obvious reasons admit any knowledge of a paper of the kind before him, but he would always be prepared to say quite openly that America must have the closest possible relations with Britain: both countries bore the greatest responsibility in the world and both should therefore maintain the greatest and most effective contact.[11]

---

[13] The text of these draft statements for the press on the Schuman Plan are printed in *F.R.U.S. 1950*, vol. iii, pp. 1032–3.

[14] In his memoirs Mr. Acheson referred to his 'immediate and intense displeasure' at the existence of No. 67 and to his instruction that 'all copies of the paper that could be found were collected and burned': *Present at the Creation* – London, 1970 – pp. 387–8; cf. also No. 67, note 1. The discussion between Mr. Acheson and Mr. Bevin recorded above overtook discussion in F.O. American department for the implementation of paragraph 19 of No. 67. On 16 June Mr. E.J. Barnes of P.U.S.D. drew the department's attention to Mr. Acheson's views as expressed at the ministerial meeting above and warned against the circulation of a guidance paper to Whitehall departments based on MIN/UKUS/P/5 since '(a) We should not wish even by implication to suggest openly that Ministers had approved such a paper. (b) The Americans already take all their commercial opportunities without them being handed to them on a plate (c) The Foreign Office should not appear to be advising other Departments to give in to the Americans against their better judgement (I think we are already suspect on these grounds)' (AU 10512/2). A suggestion from Mr. Barnes for circulation of a paper concerned only with cooperation between international organizations was not pursued.

Item VIII   Atlantic Declaration (MIN/TRI/P/8)[5]

23. MR. ACHESON said he thought the idea of a declaration was a good one, and those charged with our propaganda activities should get to work and produce some agreed draft. There was no point, however, in making a grand declaration unless it was really a good one. It should not try and cover every conceivable point but should be something pithy which would stick in the mind and be used with the greatest effect in the propaganda field.

24. SIR WILLIAM STRANG explained that the British delegation had produced a draft which they thought extremely satisfactory. We had tried to reach agreement with the French on this draft and as a result had had to produce an Anglo-French draft now before the meeting which did not really at all fill the bill. The Americans had also produced a draft which we infinitely preferred to the Anglo-French draft.

25. MR. ACHESON said that his Information experts would shortly be arriving and he thought that they and the British experts should consult and try and produce a satisfactory document.

26. MR. BEVIN said that if we liked the American draft, this should be the basis on which to go to work. The French line, with its emphasis on agreement with Russia, might be pursued in the communiqué at the end of the Council meeting, but it had no place in a declaration of faith. When the experts had produced a document it might go before the Atlantic Council, not as a United Kingdom/United States draft, but as a paper prepared in the Secretariat as a working basis for general agreement.[15]

27. The Meeting adjourned.

CALENDAR TO NO. 84

i *6 May 1950   MIN/TRI/P/8* U.S. and Anglo-French versions of declaration for issue by North Atlantic Council on Western objectives with original British draft [WU 1076/54].

[15] As a result of this discussion Anglo-American officials were instructed to produce a further draft based on the American draft in MIN/TRI/P/8 and including some points of the original British draft (calendar i). On 13 May Mr. Hadow informed Mr. Bevin: 'Our experts met last night and are in the process of producing a paper. *The French of course do not know anything about this.* When the Anglo-American experts have produced a satisfactory draft they will be ready to meet the French early next week' (minute on WU 1076/54).

No. 85

Record of an Anglo-American Meeting in the Foreign Office on 10 May 1950[1]

[*FJ 1021/73*]

Top secret

Present:

U.K. Mr. Ernest Bevin, Sir W. Strang, Mr. Dening.

U.S. Mr. Dean Acheson, Mr. Merchant.

Japan

The Secretary of State said that his position in regard to the question of a Japanese peace treaty was growing more and more awkward. He was constantly being approached by various interests who asked what the position was, and everyone knew that we were in very close touch with the United States. While it was possible to say that Russia was responsible for the hold-up, it was the view in the United Kingdom that the Americans were the masters of Japan and that they could therefore make the pace. The absence of any communication from Mr. Acheson about a peace treaty had made the situation very difficult at Colombo, and in order to tide over this situation the Secretary of State had proposed the setting up of a Commonwealth Working Party. We were now in a difficulty that the Working Party was meeting[2] but still had no United States view.

Mr. *Acheson* said that he had handed a memorandum to Sir O. Franks in December last which set out the dilemma in which the United States Government found themselves.[3] This dilemma still existed and remained unresolved. The difficulty was one of security. The Service representatives felt that a situation in which Russia and China participated in a peace treaty would mean that there was no security in the Pacific. This would be too dangerous and they were not prepared to contemplate it. A treaty without Russia would, however, create other difficulties. The Service Departments thought that as a non-signatory Russia might feel that the situation offered them opportunities to interfere with Japan in a manner which would create dangerous possibilities. Mr. Acheson said that Mr. Johnson, the Defence Secretary, and General Omar Bradley[4] were leaving for Japan towards the end of May. They were due back on the 12th June, by which date it was hoped they would be in a position to clarify the situation.

---

[1] This meeting evidently took place immediately after the bipartite ministerial meeting at No. 84: cf. *F.R.U.S. 1950*, vol. vi, pp. 1198–1200.

[2] See No. 50, note 1 and i below.

[3] For this American memorandum and meeting between Mr. Acheson and Sir O. Franks on 24 December 1949, see *F.R.U.S. 1949*, vol. vii, pp. 927–30.

[4] Chairman of the U.S. Joint Chiefs of Staff.

Mr. Acheson said that the State Department had been thinking of two possible alternatives:

(1) a treaty containing the fewest possible enforcement provisions accompanied by a separate instrument in which on the one hand as many of the Far Eastern Commission countries[5] as possible would enter into a treaty with one another and also with Japan, in the first instance to prevent aggression and in the second to protect Japan against aggression. In the latter case Japan would undertake to give military facilities in her territories in return for protection.

(2) an intermediate stage in which the controls of occupation would be removed and sovereignty returned to Japan, who would have international relations with other Powers. But SCAP and the occupation would remain in order to protect Japan.

Mr. Acheson said the Service representatives preferred the second alternative.

In response to an enquiry by Mr. Acheson as to whether the Commonwealth Working Party had considered this problem, *Mr. Dening* said that, by a coincidence, the officials of the Working Party had already that morning discussed the two alternatives mentioned by Mr. Acheson. They had considered the possibility, if Russia and China participated in a peace treaty, of a security arrangement in which these two countries would offer to participate. This would be unlikely, and also unsatisfactory. The Working Party had envisaged two possibilities, either that the other Powers would enter into some arrangement such as that mentioned by Mr. Acheson, or that there should be a bilateral treaty between the United States and Japan which would provide security for the latter.[6] As to this,

---

[5] Member countries of the Far Eastern Commission, established in December 1945 (terms of reference printed in Series I, Volume II, pp. 906–8) were the Soviet Union, United Kingdom, United States, China, France, the Netherlands, Canada, Australia, New Zealand, India and the Philippine Commonwealth.

[6] On 11 May Mr. Dening recorded that when the multilateral option was discussed by the Commonwealth Working Party: 'I tried to pour cold water on it by saying that such a multilateral treaty might involve commitments for Commonwealth powers which they might find themselves unwilling or unable to undertake. My impression was that while Canada, Australia and New Zealand were on the whole in favour of a bilateral pact, the idea of a multilateral pact for some reason or another appealed to India and Ceylon (Pakistan has remained dumb throughout virtually the whole proceedings). If anything of this sort came to pass, we might find that Australia and New Zealand were unwilling to commit any forces to the Middle East in the event of war because of their commitments towards Japan.' This point was brought up at a meeting of the British Chiefs of Staff Committee on 17 May when Mr. Wright reported that at the bipartite ministerial talks: 'Mr. Bevin had pointed out to Mr. Acheson the undesirable effect on our own planning and on the planning of New Zealand, Australia and South Africa of continuing ignorance of United States plans for the defence of the Pacific area. Mr. Bevin had pointed out that theatres could not be regarded strategically as self-sufficient areas and it was not possible, for example, to plan the contribution which New Zealand or Australia might make to the Middle East until United States intentions in the Far East were made clear. Mr. Dean Acheson had appreciated the

Mr. Acheson said that United States thinking tended to favour having as many Powers as possible. *Mr. Dening* said that the second alternative mentioned by Mr. Acheson had also been considered by the Working Party, and had been generally disliked, first because it would not satisfy the Japanese that their sovereignty was completely restored and would place a propaganda weapon in the hands of Russia and China, and secondly because it was felt that the Japanese would tend to play the other Powers off against SCAP.[7]

CALENDAR TO NO. 85

i *17 May 1950 Report of Commonwealth Working Party on Japanese peace treaty* (*C.M.J.(50)8*): summary of discussion and consensus towards early conclusion of peace treaty at meetings from 1–17 May. Covering minute by Mr. Dening on 17 May discusses question of communicating perhaps bowdlerised version of report to U.S. government and concludes that despite bad start (explained by Mr. Dening in minute of 2 May) Working Party meeting had been a success. Note by Mr. Bevin—'Good' [FJ 1021/68, 75].

importance of this matter and had undertaken to follow it up on his return to Washington ... *The Committee*: took note of the above statements' (extract from C.O.S. (50) 77th meeting on ZP 2/183).
[7] This conversation coincided with an article in the *New York Times* on 12 May by James Reston, apparently inspired by the State Department, which stated that Mr. Acheson would not as had been hoped be able to make progress in London towards arrangements for a Japanese peace treaty since neither President Truman nor the Joint Chiefs of Staff were yet in favour. When drawing this article to the attention of the Foreign Office in a letter of 13 May, Washington Chancery commented: 'This seems to make it even more likely that, as we have already suggested, the United States will begin to advocate openly that the Western Powers should slide into a state of peace with Japan' (FJ 1021/74).

No. 86

Memorandum by Mr. Furlonge[1]

[*E 1023/72*]

FOREIGN OFFICE, *10 May 1950*

Persia

Persia was discussed at a meeting of the Anglo-American Bipartite Sub-Committee on May 6[5], during which we and the Americans agreed that our diagnoses of the present situation there virtually coincided and we both put forward suggestions for remedying this situation. The

[1] This memorandum, summarizing the position reached after bipartite sub-committee discussion on 5 May (see No. 65, note 3 and No. 84, note 9) and receipt of comments from Sir F. Shepherd, H.M. Ambassador in Tehran, on 9 May (Tehran telegram No. 207: not printed from EP 1022/3), was evidently prepared as a brief for the further sub-committee meeting on 16 May reported in ii below.

comments of H.M. Ambassador at Tehran have since been obtained on the American suggestions. The following summarises the present position.

2. *U.S. suggestions.*

For action by U.S. Government

(a) the despatch to Persia of an economic mission which would study the situation and recommend a loan from the Export-Import Bank to finance certain specific projects within the Seven Year Plan, this loan to be dependent on the Persians executing certain reforms and controls.

(b) Increase in the U.S. information activities.

For action by H.M. Government

(c) A modification of the Supplemental Oil Agreement[2] to make it more palatable to the Persians.

3. *U.K. suggestions.*

(a) The issue of a joint Anglo-American statement expressing continuing interest in Persia.[3]

(b) A subsequent approach to the Shah urging him to carry out certain short-term reforms.

4. It has been recommended to the Secretary of State and Mr. Acheson, respectively, that they should take note of the points put forward and authorise their pursuance on the official level.

Our criticisms of U.S. suggestions

5. (a) Persia has already been over-surveyed and all relevant information is available. Sir F. Shepherd confirms that the Persians are beginning to scoff at survey missions.

(b) Sir F. Shepherd doubts if this would help.

(c) On present information we expect the Supplemental Agreement to come before the Majlis[4] for ratification shortly. It would be bad tactics to suggest any modification before the Persians have specifically asked for them.

U.S. comments on U.K. suggestions

6. While agreeing generally with the U.K. suggestions, the Americans would prefer that the proposed joint statement should be linked with some positive measure of assistance to Persia, e.g. that at (a) above.

Recommendations

7. That in further official discussions with the Americans we should take the following line.

(1) We accept their suggestion that the proposed joint statement, and

---

[2] See No. 84, note 9.

[3] The suggestion for a statement to 'give the Persians moral encouragement' emanated from Sir F. Shepherd in Tehran telegram No. 182 of 22 April (EP 1016/33).

[4] Iranian Legislative Assembly.

subsequent joint approach to the Shah by our representatives in Tehran, should be linked to some positive measure designed to help Persia.

(2) In view of the importance of the Supplement Oil Agreement to Persia's economy, it is essential to concentrate in the first place in getting this ratified.

(3) The U.S. suggestion for an economic Survey Mission should be held over for the present, and the U.S. Ambassador in Tehran should be instructed to inform the Persian Government that the United States attaches as much importance as we do to seeing the Agreement ratified; but that if and when this is done it may be possible to consider some further measure of economic assistance to Persia.

(4) The State Department should in the meantime also examine the possibility of an Export-Import Bank loan on the basis of information already available, with the idea of this loan being proposed to the Persian Government directly after the Supplemental Oil Agreement has been ratified.

(5) We should pursue the idea of a joint statement, to be made soon after the ratification of the Supplemental Agreement and of a subsequent joint approach to the Shah.

G.W. Furlonge

Calendars to No. 86

i *26 Apr. 1950* U.K. *Brief No. 16 on* (a) *Persia* 'political and economic condition of Persia has gravely deteriorated in recent months' (b) *Persian/Soviet relations* lull in Soviet pressure on Persian govt. regarding interpretation of Persian/Soviet treaty of friendship of 1921 [EP 1021/1].

ii *16 May 1950 Bipartite sub-committee meeting* on Middle East statement, Refugees, Persia and Saudi Arabia. On Persia, U.K. point out fairness of supplemental oil agreement and ask for U.S. support in pressing for ratification without modification. General agreement for a joint declaration on Persia at some future date [E 1023/72].

No. 87

Brief by Sir. R. Makins for Mr. Bevin for talk with Mr. Acheson and Mr. Pearson on cooperation in Atomic Energy

[UE 1245/70]

Top secret   FOREIGN OFFICE, *10 May 1950*

I attach a copy of my minute of 17th April[1] which was approved by the Secretary of State and the Prime Minister suggesting that the question of

---

[1] No. 19.

technical co-operation on atomic energy should be raised with Mr. Acheson and Mr. Pearson while they were in London. Since this paper was written there have been further developments.

(a) The Americans have agreed to call a tripartite meeting in Washington to discuss the establishment of common security standards in the atomic energy field.

(b) The American Ministers concerned have considered the position and apparently come to the conclusion that it will not be possible to seek Congressional agreement of proposals for technical co-operation with Canada and ourselves until the new session in January 1951. This means in practice that since business is always difficult to transact with a new Congress, a year must elapse before new arrangements for co-operation could come into effect.

2. But the U.S. Administration seem to be thinking in terms of possible renewal of the negotiations before the end of the present year with the object of presenting proposals to Congress as soon as possible after it re-assembles in January, 1951.

3. If Mr. Acheson confirms this judgment, the delay involved is very unfortunate. We understand that the Fuchs case[2] made an interruption of the negotiations inevitable. But we do attach the highest importance to reaching an agreement for full exchange of information on atomic energy and on an integrated weapons programme, which we believe to be in the interests of all three countries.

4. It is clear that in present circumstances there can be no assurance that an agreement will be reached, and in the absence of such an assurance, the U.K. has no alternative to progressing as fast as possible with a programme which includes all facilities for the manufacture of atomic weapons. It had been our hope that following upon the adoption of an integrated weapons programme it would be possible for the U.K. to slow down or to suspend certain parts of our programme with resultant economy and efficiency, and for example to share facilities for testing atomic weapons. It is obviously undesirable that the programmes of the three countries should diverge more than is essential, and the question of raw material is likely to become more difficult to settle as time goes on.

5. Mr. Acheson might be asked whether there is any way in which the timetable could be accelerated, e.g., by securing from Congress before it rises a general authority to negotiate an agreement on the lines which were under discussion before the Fuchs case, or whether he has any other suggestion to make.

6. In the meantime, Mr. Acheson should be told that we wished on our side to proceed, as far as possible, as if a tripartite agreement were in existence, but that there were one or two points of difficulty for us arising out of the delay in reaching an agreement, on which we would have to

[2] See No. 19, note 2.

consult the U.S. Government and in which we relied upon their collaboration.[3]

[3] This brief was initialled by Mr. Bevin, who added on the short covering minute from Sir. R. Makins 'Fix a meeting for this E.B.': see further No. 102.

No. 88

Note of an informal meeting of Ministers held at 1 Carlton Gardens on Thursday, 11 May 1950, at 9.30 a.m.

[PREM 8/1204]

Secret

Present:
The Prime Minister, the Lord President of the Council, the Secretary of State for Foreign Affairs, the Chancellor of the Exchequer, the Minister of Defence.

Sir William Strang, Sir Norman Brook, Mr R.E. Barclay.

The Foreign Secretary reported the main features of his discussions with the United States Secretary of State on the previous day.[1]

Mr. Acheson seemed, in general, to be disinclined to commit himself to formal documents embodying statements of agreed policy. He evidently preferred to aim at informal understandings rather than formal declarations. He had, however, expressed his broad agreement with the general lines of the document (MIN/UKUS/P/8)[2] on the relationship of the United Kingdom to Western Europe.

Mr. Acheson had said that general co-operation between the United Kingdom and United States Governments would be greatly assisted if early agreement could be reached on the *oil* question and on the *European payments* scheme.[3] He evidently attached great importance to securing an early solution of these two problems. *The Chancellor of the Exchequer* said that fresh proposals on the European Payments Union had now been circulated to the Economic Policy Committee (E.P.C. (50) 51)[4]: these went

[1] A full summary of Mr. Bevin's conversations with Mr. Acheson on 9 and 10 May (Nos. 78, 80, 82, 84, 85 and Volume I, No. 4) was circulated to the whole Cabinet in C.P. (50)114 on 19 May (not printed from CAB 129/40).
[2] See No. 70, note 2.
[3] For these remarks by Mr. Acheson under item II of the third bipartite ministerial meeting on 10 May, see Volume I, No. 4.
[4] This paper of 10 May (not printed from CAB 134/225) contained proposals (in substantial modification of earlier ones at No. 4.i) which would serve as a basis for further negotiation within O.E.E.C. for a European Payments Union, with the U.K. as a full member. These proposals, printed in *F.R.U.S. 1950*, vol. iii, pp. 658–9, were approved by the Cabinet at a meeting immediately following the present meeting and were subsequently discussed with Mr. Harriman and Mr. Katz in London before submission to the O.E.E.C.

some way towards meeting the views of other European countries and, if they were approved by his Cabinet colleagues, would enable us to take in Paris before the end of the week a fresh initiative which might go a long way towards securing a solution of this problem. He also understood that there had been a favourable turn in the current negotiations with the United States oil companies. He would go into this matter at once: he might well find that there was a basis for securing a solution of this problem while Mr. Acheson was in London.

The Foreign Secretary said that, on *economic questions* generally, Mr. Acheson favoured a continuing exchange of views as contemplated when the tripartite machinery was established in Washington following the financial discussions there in the autumn of 1949. *The Chancellor of the Exchequer* said that he hoped that the tripartite machinery in Washington would not be made the main focus for our economic discussions with the United States Government. At the time when this machinery had been established many of the important economic questions which we wished to discuss with the United States authorities were of close concern to Canada. But Canadian participation in these discussions was now less necessary, and might on occasion be inconvenient. In his view, France was now a more important candidate than Canada for the third place in any tripartite economic discussions including ourselves and the Americans. He therefore hoped that we should place decreasing emphasis on the use of the existing tripartite machinery in Washington. *The Foreign Secretary* said that Mr. Acheson was not likely to favour the establishment of another 'continuing organisation': in general, he was inclined to prefer informal and *ad hoc* arrangements for consultation.

In a discussion on the *Middle East*, Mr. Acheson had referred to our sale of arms to Arab countries, and had suggested that both Israel and the Arab States might be invited to make a public declaration that they had no intention of using force against their neighbours. *The Foreign Secretary* said that he was inclined to favour such a declaration as a step towards a final settlement in this area. He was strongly of the opinion that it would also help to secure a final settlement there if the United Kingdom could increase their contribution to the United Nations fund for the relief of Arab refugees. The United States Government were inclined to support us in the Middle East, though their support would take a less definite form than that which they were giving in the Atlantic area; and it would be of great assistance in securing their support if we could be a little more forth-coming over the Arab refugee fund and get that issue out of the way. *The Chancellor of the Exchequer* said that he was reluctant to increase the already heavy burden on our total expenditure in the Middle East. After some further discussion, however, it was agreed that some further expenditure would be warranted for the sake of securing a general settlement in this area; and it was decided that the Foreign Secretary

Payments Committee on 16 May. For further correspondence leading to the establishment of E.P.U. on 19 September 1950, see F.O. 371/87100–87133.

might offer to increase our contribution to this fund from the sterling equivalent of 7 million dollars to the sterling equivalent of 9 million dollars.

No. 89

Record of First Tripartite Ministerial Meeting held in Lancaster House on Thursday, 11 May 1950, at 11.30 a.m.

[*ZP 2/192*]

Top secret

Present:

United Kingdom Mr. Ernest Bevin, Mr. Kenneth Younger, Sir William Strang, Mr. Ernest Davies, Sir Gladwyn Jebb and other Advisers.

United States Mr. Dean Acheson, Mr. Lewis Douglas, Mr. Cooper, Dr. Jessup, Mr. Bruce, Mr. Harriman, Mr. Perkins, and other Advisers.

France M. Schuman, M. Parodi, M. Massigli, M. Alphand, M. de Margerie,[1] M. Lebel, and other Advisers.

Secretary-General Mr. Shuckburgh.

    I Relations with the Press (MIN/TRI/P/19).[2]
    II Assessment of situation and common objectives (MIN/TRI/P/1).[3]
    III The attitude towards negotiations with Soviet Union-Chinese Representation; Mr. Lie's proposal (MIN/TRI/P/4).[4]

1. MR. BEVIN opened the meeting by welcoming the assembled delegates. He said that all were acutely aware of the difficulties ahead and the need for direction and wise judgment. In the United Kingdom in particular, the public were conscious of the importance of the decisions which would be taken at the present meeting. For that reason the British public particularly welcomed the London Conferences.

2. MR. ACHESON said he was delighted to be here. The problems to be faced were possibly more serious than any which had been tackled in the past. But the record of past achievements gave hope that future efforts would be equally successful.

[1] M. R.J. de Margerie was Assistant Director of Political and Economic Affairs at the French Ministry for Foreign Affairs.
[2] Not printed.
[3] MIN/TRI/P/1, agreed in final form on 6 May at the sixth tripartite meeting of officials, is printed in *F.R.U.S. 1950*, vol. iii, pp. 1075–8 (British copy on WU 1071/116). This paper was based on the substance of discussion at the first bipartite (No. 29) and second tripartite (No. 37, paragraphs 4–13) meetings of officials and emerged from a first draft by Mr. Shuckburgh circulated as TRI/P/12 on 3 May (ZP 2/119: cf. *F.R.U.S. op. cit.*, p. 1075, note 1).
[4] See No. 46, note 9, also notes 9 and 12 below.

3. M. Schuman confirmed in the name of France the importance which was attached to these meetings and the desire to associate fully in the common effort.

4. Mr. Bevin then raised the question of Chairmanship and Mr. Acheson and M. Schuman agreed in proposing that Mr. Bevin should be the Chairman.

Item I Relations with the Press

5. The Secretary-General asked for a decision on press relations and referred the meeting to Document MIN/TRI/P/19.[2]

6. The document was agreed by all and Mr. Acheson pointed out that it should be interpreted as meaning that press guidance should be given at the end of each day. The form of this guidance might be a communiqué or briefings for the press or both. On the whole he felt it would be a good thing to give out as much as possible. He would also like to point out that if the bulk of the information to be imparted was reserved until Saturday it would probably not receive satisfactory coverage.

Item II Assessment of Situation and Common Objectives

7. At Mr. Bevin's invitation M. Schuman opened the discussion. He said that there was no doubt of the general agreement on the document[3] before the meeting. He would, however, like to make an introductory remark. He thought it relevant to ask his two colleagues to take into account the state of mind on the Continent. This was important when considering how to present the ideas contained in the document. We were all agreed on the matter but the way in which this matter was presented to the masses and Parliaments of Europe was of importance psychologically.

8. The Russians with their peace propaganda and their proposals to ban the atom bomb[5] were beginning to have some success even in non-Communist circles. While we were all agreed that we must be firm and go on building up the common effort for the defence of liberty, it was essential to underline the attachment of the West to the ideal of peace and to point out how the building of strength was intended to serve peace.

9. Tension and anxiety were growing and we must realise that the climate was not a propitious one in which to put across our ideas. Propaganda was going on in all our countries which said that the world was being split into two *blocs*, conflict between which was inevitable. It must be one of our preoccupations to calm the fear and disquietude caused by this propaganda.

10. At the same time we should not lull our people and Parliaments into a sense of false security. The message must be one of watchfulness and of pooling of effort to meet the common danger. The best way in which the public could be reassured was not only by building up our strength and cohesion but by letting the truth be known.

11. He thought there were six points which should be constantly made:

[5] See No. 37, note 6.

(i) The inevitability of war should not be accepted.

(ii) War could only be avoided if the West were strong.

(iii) The two systems could co-exist without a conflict (as Stalin had already said).

(iv) It was not the fault of the West that the two ideologies were growing more and more hostile. The situation was due to the actions of Russia and the satellites, the Cominform[6] and the preaching of subversion within our own territories.

(v) There was, therefore, reason for anxiety and we should bear in mind the need to plan and act for our own defence.

(vi) The idea of the 'Cold War' was as distasteful as the idea of a real war, and we should avoid giving the public the impression that we were engaged in any sort of war at all.

12. There were other points to be taken into account. There was a certain amount of anti-American propaganda on the Continent which played on national pride. The national Governments could not stamp out this sort of thing, though naturally, they would do their best to counter such propaganda. It was therefore essential not to say anything in communiqués which could be twisted for the use of anti-American elements.

13. Then there was the widespread though erroneous belief that safety was to be found in a position of neutrality between the two *blocs*. The Governments of the West naturally had no such thoughts, but their task of removing this demoralising idea from the public mind must be rendered easier, otherwise there would be a reduction in the effort and sacrifices necessary from all of us.

14. Texts which issued from the Conference, which were to be made public, should take these ideas into account, and not all these ideas were based on any sympathy for communism. To sum up, the general line should be of greater cohesion, more agreement, determination to pool our resources and energy, while at the same time calming the psychological and peculiar fears which were prevalent and which might undermine the whole position of the West.

15. In particular, if the document before the meeting were to be accepted by all the three Governments he thought that the point made in paragraph 13 (*h*),[7] which seemed to have been added rather as an afterthought, should be brought into more prominence and discussed in the text, possibly at the beginning.

16. MR. ACHESON said that he would like to point out to M. Schuman that, as far as he understood, there was no question of adopting the

[6] See No. 44, note 14.

[7] Sub-paragraph 13 (*h*) of MIN/TRI/P/1, added by the French delegation at the last official discussion of the paper on 6 May, read: 'The efforts of the Western Nations should be directed towards reducing the risks of war and establishing the conditions of a lasting peaceful settlement. This requires the development of adequate strength and consequently the combination of their efforts for building up that strength'.

document formally and there was certainly no idea that it should be publicised. He understood that the only action necessary was to take note of it as a good analysis of the situation and as containing common objectives on which all were agreed. How the contents of the document might be presented in any public communiqué was a matter which would naturally be discussed outside the meeting before any agreed line was issued.

17. Turning to the contents of the document itself, he said he agreed with the objectives. If anything, he felt more stress should be laid on the need for quick and effective action not only in the military field but also in the economic since this both supported the military effort and provided for the standard of living on which our way of life was based. We should recognise the dangers of the situation confronting us. The Soviets had to put so much effort into military preparedness over the last years that they had widened the gap with Western defence capabilities considerably. If the gap were further widened, dangerous consequences would flow from the disparity. Certain steps were therefore urgent. The first was to adopt the Medium Term Plan[8] and to take immediate steps towards its execution. Secondly, it was vital to build the economic foundation on which a satisfactory military programme and high standards of living could be maintained. This demanded both internal and international action to increase production.

18. It followed from all this that how to make full use of the German economic potential should be studied. German productivity should not be allowed to languish or to fall into the hands of others.

19. Then there was the question of priorities. The heart of the Western system depended on the development of European relations with the Western hemisphere and with the countries of Asia. The strengthening of the Atlantic relationship and the economic machinery of the Atlantic Powers was therefore of first importance. Secondly, came the question of Asia. Here, he felt, the task was one of a holding operation, until the strength of the West had been built up. He did not mean to say that Asia should be allowed to slip, but the West was not at present strong enough to conduct major operations in two widely separated parts of the world.

20. How to present our actions to the world, he agreed, was a matter of great importance. Our main objective was an increase in strength, but this increase must not be presented so that it could be interpreted as intended for aggression. It was rather a guarantee against war. He agreed with M. Schuman that national susceptibilities must be taken into account and that the best way of countering Communist propaganda was by pointing out the truth.

21. Finally, he thought the question of organisation should be considered and here he would only say that organisation was not an end in itself but a tool to accomplish action.

---

[8] See No. 33, note 7.

22. To sum up he felt there were seven points which must be borne in mind

(i) We must appreciate the danger confronting us.

(ii) We must be prepared in the military field.

(iii) We must try to build the economic underpinning for this military preparedness together with the maintenance of a high standard of living.

(iv) We must make use of Germany's productive capacity.

(v) We should endeavour not to lose the East while we were trying to win in West.

(vi) We must bear in mind the importance of the presentation to the world of our actions.

(vii) We must have an effective organisation through which to act.

23. Mr. Bevin, summing up, said that there was clearly no divergence of view. He thought the objectives set out in the paper served to concentrate our minds on what we wanted to achieve. The paper was not, however, a formal agreement to be rigidly observed between us.

24. With regard to what M. Schuman had said about presentation, he thought that the answer was that it was necessary to present our actions in different ways in different places. There was the Continent, where the peoples were nearer to the Communist menace and where there were bigger internal Communist parties than in the United States or the United Kingdom. Then there was the large neutral area the adherence of whose peoples to our principles we hoped to win. Finally, there was the area of uncertainty where extreme Communist pressure was being brought to bear in every way. He did not mean to say that we should follow the Communist practice of being entirely opportunist in our propaganda line according to the locality. We should adhere to our fundamental principles, but the way these principles were put forward must be considered in the light of the susceptibilities of people to whom we were speaking.

25. He had particularly liked Mr. Acheson's summary of seven points at the end of his speech. He suggested that the principles set out in the paper under consideration should be taken as a general guide. The three countries could study the best method of handling the presentation of these principles and in this study, he thought, the seven points made by Mr. Acheson should serve as a working basis.

26. It was agreed to make this the general conclusion of the meeting.

Item III Attitude towards Negotiations with Soviet Union—Chinese Representation—Mr. Lie's Proposal, &c. (MIN/TRI/P/4)[4]

27. Mr. Bevin said that in particular he thought the question of negotiations must be tackled. A lot of people seemed to think that all one had to do was to go to Moscow and conduct negotiations which would be a success. These people did not realise the fundamental difference between

the Soviet concept of life and that of the rest of the world. He invited his colleagues to open the discussion.

28. M. SCHUMAN said that he had two points to make. Firstly, he assumed that the document was confidential and not for publication, otherwise he would have to make reservations with regard to the first paragraph which he thought could easily be misunderstood.[9]

29. Secondly, there was the concrete problem to be faced. All three Powers were sceptical as to the value of any negotiations with the Soviet Union, though they bore in mind the possibility that favourable opportunities might occur. They knew what effort had been expended in negotiating with the Soviets last year.[10] There had been very small results but the fact that negotiations had been held had served to reduce tension considerably. There was now a complete deadlock, and it appeared as if the Soviet Union had no desire to enter into normal relations with the West. Indeed, they had now cut off the satellites to a large extent and the process was going on in China.

30. The situation was particularly serious because of the impasse reached in the Security Council which meant that the whole field of action through the United Nations was being restricted. If the situation went on the prospects were very dangerous. The question was how to get the United Nations working effectively again.

31. On the question of China he felt he could speak freely since the French Government had not yet recognised the People's Government or taken a firm position over the matter of Chinese representation. It was in essence a psychological and political problem for France because of the Indo–China situation.

32. He would like to put forward as an idea the impression he had gained (largely as a result of Great Britain's experience) that Mao Tse Tung did not really want recognition from the West or wish to take up the normal contacts of everyday relations. The problem of recognition was therefore not particularly acute.

33. On the other hand the situation in the Security Council was very serious. It was not a question of Chinese membership, since China was already a full member under the Charter. It was really a question of a verification of who was in fact in control and who should therefore represent China. It might be possible to seek a solution along such clear-cut lines and it was important not to allow the problem to extend to cover fields which were really not related to it. Territorially the Nationalist representative on the Security Council represented very little—in fact the Nationalist Government only controlled territory which was not legally Chinese. The Communists on the other hand did control the whole of

[9] The first paragraph of MIN/TRI/P/4 stated: 'It is agreed that there is no prospect that negotiations with the Soviets at present would lead to any general settlement. The right course for the West is therefore to continue to build up situations of strength' (*F.R.U.S. 1950*, vol. iii, p. 1078).

[10] See No. 58, note 3.

China. But, he would repeat, they did not seem very anxious to press for their candidature at the Security Council and seemed rather to concentrate on the unseating of the Nationalist representative. Unless the Security Council could be got working again the situation might become acute even before the General Assembly. There was not only the question of new members but all sorts of situations might arise in which a paralysis of the Council might be dangerous. There was also the question of the election of a Secretary-General.[11] Was it wise therefore to close our eyes to the situation until August, as was suggested in paragraph 11 of the document under consideration? It might be possible that no progress could be made until then. At the same time should an occasion arise it might be valuable to review the situation earlier.

34. Finally, he would like to make a reservation on paragraph 4 of the document.[12] The Security Council might indeed serve as the forum in which discussions with the Soviets might be started. But since the Security Council meetings were open, if real negotiations were to be conducted it would be necessary to move from the Security Council to some other venue so that the meeting did not develop into an airing of propaganda themes but get down to the real facts it must face.

35. MR. BEVIN then adjourned the meeting until 3.30 p.m.

[11] Mr. Lie's term as Secretary-General of the U.N. was due to expire in February 1951. In November the Assembly voted to extend this term for a further three years.

[12] This paragraph stated that 'The Security Council would probably be the only practicable forum for general discussions, though the Council of Foreign Ministers offers a possible alternative' (*op. cit.*, p. 1079).

No. 90

Record of Second Tripartite Ministerial Meeting held in Lancaster House on Thursday, 11 May 1950, at 3.30 p.m.

[ZP 2/192]

Top secret

Present:

United Kingdom Mr. Ernest Bevin, Mr. Kenneth Younger, Sir William Strang, Mr. Ernest Davies, Sir Roger Makins, Sir Gladwyn Jebb, and other Advisers.

United States Mr. Dean Acheson, Mr. Lewis Douglas, Mr. Cooper, Dr. Jessup, Mr. McCloy, Mr. Bruce, Mr. Harriman, Mr. Perkins, and other Advisers.

France M. Schuman, M. Massigli, M. Parodi, M. Alphand, M. de Margerie, M. Lebel, and other Advisers.

Secretary-General Mr. Shuckburgh.

I Continuation of Discussion on MIN/TRI/P/4[1]
  (a) United Nations matters and Chinese representation.
  (b) Mr. Lie's proposal.
  (c) Yugoslavia.
  (d) Exiles
II Future Consultation and Co-ordination (MIN/TRI/P/6).[2]
III North Atlantic Treaty Organisation (MIN/TRI/P/2 and 3)[3]
IV European Political and Economical Integration.
V Communiqué.
VI Migration.
VII Benelux Ministers.

Item I Continuation of Discussion on MIN/TRI/P/4[1]
(a) United Nations matters and Chinese representation

1. At Mr. Bevin's invitation MR. ACHESON resumed the discussion. He said, as he understood it, M. Schuman had largely applied himself to the recommendation in paragraph 11 of MIN/TRI/P/4 that the three Governments should have further consultation through their representatives in New York in August. There was no reason why these representatives should not start a study of certain problems immediately. They might consider now:

(i) Whether the Security Council could function in the absence of two permanent members;

(ii) What should be done about the appointment of a Secretary-General;

(iii) Whether it was wise in the absence of the Soviets to proceed to the election of new members.

2. There were possibly many other points they might usefully debate. But on the question of China, while he did not wish to impose any taboo on discussion of this subject, he thought that there was little likelihood of any good being done in this field at the moment.

3. As he understood it, the Russians were promoting the nomination of a Communist representative by asking for the Nationalist representative's expulsion. Their behaviour raised the question whether the West must accept the Russian point of view in order to get them to play their part in the United Nations. In short we were being coerced to take a step which might not necessarily be right, in order to try and achieve some sort of Russian co-operation. On this he felt it was a bad principle to let the Russians think they could get what they wanted merely by refusing to take

[1] See No. 89, note 4.
[2] MIN/TRI/P/6, agreed, at the sixth tripartite meeting of officials on 6 May, is printed in *F.R.U.S. 1950*, vol. iii, p.1039, note 7. This paper, drafted by Mr. Shuckburgh on 3 May, incorporated the substance of discussion at the third tripartite meeting of officials on 27 April (No. 40, paragraphs 22–4) and concluded with a recommendation that the three Ministers should meet again soon, possibly in New York before the next session of the U.N. General Assembly due to open on 19 September.
[3] See No. 46, note 6 and No. 80., note 4.

part in United Nations activities. It was clear that the heart of the Russian interest was not in the United Nations aspect of the question. They were merely using the United Nations angle in order to reduce the standing of the West in other parts of the world. That was to say, they thought, if they could get the West to give way over China, this would have a damaging effect on morale in South-East Asia.

4. M. Schuman had suggested that Mao Tse Tung was not really anxious to take his place in the Security Council. If this were true, we might find ourselves in the position where we gave way by agreeing to the expulsion of one Chinese representative, and then discover that no Communist representative was coming forward.

5. If the matter had been differently handled by the Soviets and there had been no threats or build-up of tension it might have been possible to examine the matter on the lines of who was actually in power in China. But this was not so, and it was therefore impossible to separate the question of Chinese representation from that of recognition of the Chinese People's Government, and indeed of the whole Western position in South-East Asia. It might be that the passage of time would help and the situation move in one way or the other – for instance, Anglo-Chinese relations might clarify or the position in Formosa change.

6. MR. BEVIN said that two points seemed to have been discussed. One was that of opening negotiations with the Soviet Government. On this he thought he could reassure M. Schuman on the subject of paragraph 1.[4] This was to be interpreted as meaning that not only military strength should be built up but economic strength as well. This was necessary so that the West could help other nations. A sound economic position was the best basis for dealing with the Russians in that it proved that the Western economic system was preferable to the Communist one.

7. The other point was the general question of China. The latest position in our negotiations was that the People's Government had put forward two tests of sincerity for the British Government. The first was a vote against the Nationalist representative in New York and the second was our handling of the question of the aircraft in Hong Kong.[5] Both these were very vexed questions and the outcome of our negotiations was still far from clear.

8. With regard to Chinese representation in the Security Council, he had always felt that this was a most difficult problem to handle; it seemed clear that the People's Government, in that they controlled the large proportion of China, had a sound case for being regarded as the legal representatives of China in the Security Council. It was on the grounds of their control of China that we had decided to recognise them. But there were still two more votes needed before their representative could be seated, and it seemed as if everyone were hanging back and waiting for someone else to take the first step.

[4] See No. 89, note 9.   [5] See No. 23, note 3.

9. He agreed with the three points which Mr. Acheson had suggested for discussion by our representatives in New York, but the question of Chinese representation was equally urgent, and we were in favour of trying to clear the whole matter up as soon as possible.

10. As he understood it, the representatives in New York should be instructed to go ahead on the three points mentioned by Mr. Acheson. He had also understood that M. Schuman favoured an examination in New York of the question of Chinese representation. Was it intended that this question should be taken up as well, or did Mr. Acheson wish it still confined to Governments?

11. MR. ACHESON said that if there was a technical deuce[6] which the experts could produce to solve the difficulty he would be delighted. But he doubted whether such a trick could be found. The question of Chinese representation was a major point in United States foreign policy and, though he was prepared to talk about it here or in New York, neither he nor his representatives would have any authority to come to definite conclusions. For the United States public the whole question was not a legal argument, but one of whether we should give way to Russian pressure. It was felt that the Russians were using the Chinese problem in order to undermine the whole Western position in Malaya and Indo-China (as the British and French well knew) in the Philippines and lately in Indonesia too. If we gave way, we set back the whole cause of the West in Asia, and it was more dangerous to do this than to allow the admittedly dangerous situation in the United Nations to continue. The United States was bringing no pressure to bear on the members of the Security Council to abstain from voting for the People's Government, and it seemed that the fact that such countries as Ecuador, Cuba and Egypt had not yet taken a position meant that they were, as a result of their own thinking, unwilling to do so. It therefore seemed that exploration of the matter in the technical field would not really get our three countries anywhere until one or other of them was prepared to change its fundamental position.

12. M. SCHUMAN said that he felt that it was important to have a continuous exchange of views on the matter. It was not necessary to reach a decision to-day, and if there had been no change in the situation before August there would be no need for our representatives in New York to discuss it before then. But events might take place which would make it desirable for our representatives to discuss it earlier.

13. MR. BEVIN, summing up, said that he thought the conclusion generally reached was that the three points mentioned by Mr. Acheson might be referred for study to our representatives in New York and that the question of Chinese representation should be left open until August unless one of the Governments saw reason to raise it before then.

14. *This was agreed.*

---

[6] In the typescript record on ZP 2/160, it was suggested that this word should be 'device'.

(b) Mr. Lie's proposal for a Special Meeting of the Security Council

15. Mr. Bevin then referred to Mr. Lie's proposal for a special meeting. It seemed premature to discuss this until the result of Mr. Lie's travels[7] were known. Furthermore, it seemed impossible to pursue Mr. Lie's idea until the problem of Chinese representation had been settled.

16. Mr. Acheson, who thought the point had been well covered by the paper under consideration, and M. Schuman agreed that the question should be left over for the time being.

(c) Yugoslavia

17. Mr. Acheson said he would like to make special reference to the paragraphs in MIN/TRI/P/4 on Yugoslavia. The latest information was that the Yugoslav economic situation was not responding as hopefully as it might have and the International Bank was now not going forward with a loan. He appreciated the French position, but it was not unique, and both the United States and the United Kingdom were creditors of Yugoslavia, but had proceeded to give economic help. The question of further help might now become urgent and he hoped the French could associate themselves with it.

18. M. Schuman said that the French Government were ready to make a contribution towards an agreement on the subject. At the same time, they could not abandon the French interests involved. They were, however, prepared to take account of the political need for dealing with the Yugoslav economy.

19. Mr. Bevin said that it appeared that all were agreed that the question of help should be examined.

(d) Exiles

20. M. Schuman said that before passing on to other items he would like to call attention to paragraph 16 of the paper. It was the view in France and Britain that the employment of exiles should be extremely cautiously approached. It was vital to pick the right individuals who were not swayed by their personal grievances. However, he was glad that there was agreement on the judicious use of such people and thought they might be of value especially in the propaganda field. In this connexion he had a suggestion to put forward. Might it not be possible to use some funds from Marshall Aid for the employment of exiles in propaganda programmes? They would serve to interpret Marshall Aid to the satellite countries and give a true picture of the situation in the Western countries.

21. Mr. Bevin thought that this suggestion might well be passed on to the appropriate body, and Mr. Acheson said that he thought Mr. Harriman might well examine the proposal and report on it.

[7] See No. 17, note 8. On 2 June, Mr. C. Parrott commented on Sir G. Jebb's account of a conversation with M. Lie in London on 24 May on his return from Moscow: 'The Soviet reactions to Mr. Lie's proposals seem to be much the same as our own. They see no advantage in holding a periodic meeting of the Security Council at a high level, but are anxious not to give the impression that they are against it' (UP 106/9).

Item II   Consultation and Co-ordination (MIN/TRI/P/6)[2]

22.   MR. BEVIN said that the paper before the meeting was more a rough code of conduct than a rigid set of rules to be formally adopted. In general the principle was that we should have fuller consultation on all matters and attempt to agree. M. SCHUMAN, while agreeing fully with the paper, thought that the special contacts between the three countries should be as unspectacular as possible, so as not to offend the susceptibilities of other countries. MR. ACHESON said he was fully in agreement with the recommendation and thought that Point (*e*) of the paper might be included in a communiqué of the meetings so that when the Ministers met in the autumn there would not be undue speculation as to why they were doing so.

23.   MR. BEVIN said that it appeared that all were in full agreement with the principles set forth in the paper.

Item III   North Atlantic Treaty Organisation Machinery (MIN/TRI/P/2 and MIN/TRI/P/3)[3]

24.   M. SCHUMAN said that the French had no objection to MIN/TRI/P/ 2, but there now seemed to be more than one version of MIN/TRI/P/3 current.

25.   MR. BEVIN said that a new version of MIN/TRI/P/3 had just been circulated by the Americans and might be considered.[8] With regard to MIN/TRI/P/2, he thought consideration of it would be premature as it depended to some extent on other decisions. It might be looked at later.

26.   M. SCHUMAN said that with regard to the new draft he would have to refer it to his Government as it impinged on the military field. He would, however, be prepared to exchange views later. MR. BEVIN and MR. ACHESON said they were in the same position and it was agreed to give more precise examination to the draft at the end of the discussion on German and Austrian problems the next day.

Item IV   European Political and Economic Integration

27.   At Mr. Bevin's suggestion M. SCHUMAN expounded the French idea of future development of the O.E.E.C. by the association of the United States and Canada with the work. He said that the essence of the French proposal was contained in paper TRI/P/15[9] which had been circulated at the official meetings. The problem was a very important one for Europe. On the defence side the situation was taken care of by the Atlantic Treaty. It was now necessary to see how the organisation of European economy could be related to that of the Western Hemisphere. At first it had been thought that this might be done by a development of Article II of the Atlantic Treaty. But the French had soon seen that the major obstacle to this lay in the difference of membership between the Atlantic Treaty and the O.E.E.C. To proceed under the Atlantic Treaty organisation would mean the exclusion of certain members of the O.E.E.C., such as

---

[8] For this paper MIN/TRI/P/22, see No. 80, note 4.   [9] See No. 71, note 1.

Switzerland (who played an important part in the European economic scene) Austria, Turkey, Sweden and Greece.

28. Furthermore, the O.E.E.C. had rendered great service to Europe and had built up an efficient and experienced structure which had not yet finished its task. It would be unwise to make any radical changes which might check the development already achieved.

29. The French did not therefore want the Atlantic Treaty organisation to cover the entire field of economic relations between Europe and the Western Hemisphere. Nor did they want the O.E.E.C. to stay purely European. The solution seemed to be to plan for an association after 1952 between the O.E.E.C. and the United States and Canada. There was no need to rush consideration of the problem, but it would be useful for the Western nations to know now that the problem of future development after 1952 was under consideration. In making this proposal, moreover, the French had in mind M. Bidault's proposal for a High Council for peace under the Atlantic Treaty[10] which would stress the peaceful needs of the Treaty in the economic, social and cultural fields.

30. MR. ACHESON agreed that the time to consider the problem was now and not in 1952. We had to look at both the substance of the matters on which to concert our efforts and at the means of best ensuring common action.

31. With regard to the substance, he thought the efforts of the West should be concentrated firstly in the economic field, which in turn was connected with the military, and to make co-operation in both these fields possible there must be concertation [*sic*] of effort in the political field. In the economic field we were half-way through the Marshall Plan. This Plan was based on the assumption that, barring contingencies Western Europe would be free of the need for extraordinary outside help after 1952. It looked as if this assumption might be broadly proved correct. There were, of course, some countries which would not be free of this need, for example Austria, but on the whole it looked as if the Marshall Plan would have fulfilled its purpose by 1952.

32. Two situations made it clear that there was need for further co-operation of effort between the Western hemisphere and Europe. The first was that still greater adjustments would be necessary between Europe and the Western hemisphere if Europe was to be viable after 1952. The second was the need for a great military effort, which placed considerable strain on the European economies. To meet these two situations it was necessary for a great increase in productive plant, production and productivity in Europe. There must be a firm basis for the acquisition of raw materials and an opportunity for Europe to export. It would be thus that Europe would have the economic strength to sustain the military effort required together with a high standard of living. All this required great progress towards (*a*) the convertibility of currencies; (*b*) the removal

[10] See No. 47, note 4.

of quantitative restrictions; (c) the reduction of tariffs; and (d) the freer movement of peoples. He would also like to draw attention to the value of the German economy to the West. This economy could only be made full use of if raw materials and markets were available to the Germans. The Americans considered that a constructive investment programme was necessary, not only in the metropolitan countries, but in areas where investment would be of value in bringing aid to the economies of those metropolitan countries.

33. All this required a parallel effort in both Europe and the United States If this effort could be co-ordinated, so that American action could be taken against a background of a parallel effort in Europe, the peoples of the West would see that the total economic and military strength of the Western world which was being built up guaranteed their ultimate security.

34. In the military field it was essential to make a start with the Medium-Term Plan, since time was short. Out of this plan could be created balanced and rationalised forces which the economies of the individual countries could afford to pay for.

35. Returning to the French proposal MR. ACHESON said that the Americans felt that no one organ could deal adequately with all problems. The North Atlantic Treaty Organisation took care of the military side. The kind of meeting now in progress dealt with the political aspects of co-operation. On the economic side, the need was to build on some practical organisation which was already in being. In the O.E.E.C. there was assembled a body of experts, backed by a mass of information and experience, who could go to work and put forward not paper resolutions but practical programmes of action.

36. In the United States the need for an alignment of economic effort with that of Europe had been felt and the problem was now under study. The President had recently appointed Mr. Gordon Gray to examine the whole question, and it was hoped that he could report by mid-summer. A commission could then be set up to make agreed proposals which could be examined by Congress in the following January. The task of the United States would be made easier if parallel action was going on in Europe. There would be a definite connexion between the two efforts and American public opinion could be told that both the United States and Europe were studying what adjustments could be made on each side so that the economic programme of the Western world could carry on after 1952 with vigour and success. Any sacrifices that the American public were called upon to make could then be viewed in the light of a general contribution towards the furtherance of this programme.

37. He was therefore attracted by M. Schuman's suggestion. The O.E.E.C. had the staff and experience and was not scheduled to come to an end in 1952. He thought that the action going on in the United States could be closely associated with the many bodies carrying on the O.E.E.C. work.

38. On the other hand economic problems which had a direct bearing on the military effort should be retained in the North Atlantic Treaty Organisation, and he thought that similar development in the Western Union Organisation might gradually be brought into line with North Atlantic Planning.

39. It was not desirable at the moment to reduce to any specific form the type of association which might be set up. The technical experts of all three countries might meet and discuss how the association between the American effort and the O.E.E.C. could best be brought about. Time was pressing and it would be a pity not to use such an organisation as the O.E.E.C., and set up some new organisation which would take time to settle down. It was clearly impossible to come to a conclusion since the Canadians were not present, and he suggested that we might clarify our thoughts and before leaving London have a conversation with the Canadians on the matter.

40. MR. BEVIN said that for the time being he could not make a contribution to the discussion. Wide economic issues were involved and he would like time to think the matter over. One of the questions which arose was Germany's place in the future Western system. He suggested that the meeting might revert to this subject later on.

Item V Communiqué

41. A draft communiqué was circulated to the meeting and MR. YOUNGER said that although it did not seem to contain much, the general opinion was that it was better to have some communiqué than none at all.

42. MR. ACHESON said that he would like to stress that the press offices of the various delegations should be asked not to stray outside the communiqué and, for instance, give a detailed account of the Agenda.

43. The communiqué, subject to minor amendments, was agreed.

Item VI Migration

44. MR. YOUNGER asked whether this item should be discussed at this stage.

45. M. SCHUMAN said that it had a direct connexion with the German question and might be discussed next day. MR. ACHESON agreed, and said that the American delegation would be circulating a suggestion which might be considered overnight.[11]

Item VII Benelux Ministers

46. The SECRETARY-GENERAL said a request had been received from the Benelux Ministers for a meeting with the three Foreign Ministers present

---

[11] This paper MIN/TRI/P/25 (see *F.R.U.S. 1950*, vol.iii, p. 1043, note 7) was a revision of MIN/TRI/P/5 (see No. 40, note 4) and represented a shift of position from the American delegation towards the French proposal for an international conference, though now watered down to a recommendation for the conferring of experts after the London Conference.

in order to receive information about what had been decided with regard to Germany.

47. M. SCHUMAN said that this was the usual practice and *it was agreed* that the Benelux Ministers might be received sometime on Saturday afternoon.

48. MR. YOUNGER proposed that the meeting should be resumed at 10.30 a.m. on the next day and that the Agenda should be:

(i) Germany and Austria;
(ii) Further consideration of Atlantic Pact machinery (American Revise on TRI/P/3).[8]

No. 91

Minute from Sir G. Jebb to Sir W. Strang

[UR 1019/1]

FOREIGN OFFICE, *11 May 1950*

During the tea interval this afternoon I spoke to Mr. Jessup about Mr. Acheson's statement on the French proposal that America and Canada should enter into negotiations with O.E.E.C. regarding long-term economic matters,[1] and said that I was rather sad that our main thesis on this subject had apparently had so little weight with the American Delegation. I added, of course, that this thesis did not in any way represent an official view, but we had hoped that in the light of it Mr. Acheson would at least have not come down so firmly in favour of the French proposal. The main reasons why we did not like the latter proposal were as follows:

(a) If long-term economic matters affecting the Atlantic Community were centred in the O.E.E.C., the tendency might well be to perpetuate indefinitely the conception of the 'Two Zones' within the Atlantic Community itself—the American and the European. This distinction was inherent not only in the present proposal but also in the whole set-up of O.E.E.C., which had a purely external relationship with the North American continent.[2]

[1] See No. 90, paragraphs 30–39.
[2] In a minute of 15 May to Mr. Bevin and Sir W. Strang, Sir R. Makins warned of the 'very real danger of the situation crystallising into a permanent division between the two zones in the North Atlantic community, North America and Western Europe', since the general trend of French policy was to avoid much involvement in the Atlantic pact whereas the Americans 'have reservations of their own as regards becoming too involved in an Atlantic organisation on the economic side'. In view of this 'the site of the new organisation becomes of more than usual importance . . . It is quite essential that we should obtain a decision in favour of London' (WU 1071/121). Sir W. Strang agreed, observing 'we have always known that the French have never been absolutely whole-hearted about the Atlantic Pact. The line they have been taking at the present conferences is consistent with this'.

318

(*b*) Were such a tendency to manifest itself, it would be clear that the United Kingdom would be regarded more and more as a purely European country. She would thus be under pressure more and more to 'integrate' herself with Western Europe, and to the extent to which such 'integration' took place her position as leader of the Commonwealth and manager of the Sterling Area would be prejudiced. Indeed, it might well be that over a few years this position would disappear and the United Kingdom would then become a purely Continental country, forming part of some wider Western European grouping.

(*c*) Even if this were thought to be too alarmist and pessimistic a view, the fact remained that any weakening of the position of the United Kingdom would take much of the cement out of what was now one of the main props of the Atlantic system outside the purely Atlantic area, and if this prop began to weaken it was not at all clear that its place could be taken either by some new Western Europe organised on 'Third Force' lines, or indeed by the U.S.A.

(*d*) In addition, the development of O.E.E.C. on the lines suggested would tend over the next few years to make the Atlantic Community have two centres and not one. One centre would be dealing with military and military-economic problems: the other centre would be dealing with general economic problems. In the one system America would be a full member: in the other she would only be a part member. One system would exclude Germany altogether: the other would include her. Seeing that the French had now taken a step which might well result in some fusion of the German and French economy it was not clear how such a system could be maintained on political, economic, or even purely logical grounds.[3]

Mr. Jessup did not seem, however, to be entirely convinced by these arguments. He agreed that the position of the United Kingdom as leader of the Commonwealth and manager of the Sterling Area was essential to the Atlantic Community as such, but he did not feel that it would, in fact, be materially weakened by the steps now suggested.

GLADWYN JEBB

[3] In a separate minute of 11 May on the French proposal for a coal and steel community (see Volume I) Sir G. Jebb raised the following points for consideration ' (*a*) the extent to which we should positively encourage the new development would seem to depend to a large degree on whether the French will accept what I suggest should be our main thesis—namely that some European Economic Union, – the United Kingdom, Commonwealth and the Sterling area, and the United States—should be regarded as the three main pillars on which the "Atlantic Community" should rest; (*b*) that they should therefore abandon their resistance to our own proposal gradually to develop Article 2 of the Atlantic Pact, so as to deal with economic problems affecting the "Atlantic Community" as a whole—more especially since, under their own new proposal, the joint economies of France and Germany can no longer be entirely dissociated from the general armaments programme that it is the intention of the Atlantic Pact Powers to develop' (CE 2446/2141/181).

No. 92

Minute from Mr. Younger to Mr. Bevin

[UP 123/83]

FOREIGN OFFICE, 11 May 1950

I am worried that there seems to have been so little clarification of the Far Eastern question in the course of the Bipartite Talks. I had understood that the long and short-term implications of the divergent policies of the U.S. and U.K. were to have been thrashed out, but as far as I can gather there seems to have been a minimum of discussion ending merely in an agreement to differ. Presumably that means that for the next few months at least we are to pursue our present line of policy with the object of 'keeping the door open' in China without paying too much attention to American susceptibilities, while they will feel free to carry on their relations with the Nationalists in Formosa without much regard to its effect on our position.

It seems to me there is a danger that in this way we will get the worst of both worlds.

It seems clear that in the short run we are not going to get much change out of the Peking Government. British interests in China are likely to have a very thin time and we will probably not get an exchange of Ambassadors. The decision over the Chinese aircraft in Hong Kong and the decision not to allow Chinese Consuls to go to Malaya,[1] both of which seem to me correct decisions, will no doubt be used by the Peking Government as an excuse for prolonged stone-walling. Nevertheless, it seems to me far too early to assume that Peking will not eventually want relations with us and will not be prepared to do trade with us, and I think we should therefore do everything that is practicable to improve our relations. Almost the only thing we can do in this way at the present moment is to assist the Chinese in the United Nations, a point to which they apparently attach importance, and I am not myself satisfied that our policy of abstention is the right one. It is possible to justify it on rather technical grounds where subordinate bodies are concerned, but I find it very hard to justify when it comes to any of the senior organs. I understand that our Delegation is instructed to abstain when the question comes up in ECAFE,[2] and it is probably too late to alter these instructions, but I think we should reconsider the policy before the issue arises at ECOSOC[3] or elsewhere. I cannot myself see what we gain by refusing to vote for the Peking Government. It does not appear to give us any bargaining lever with them. It seems to be little more than an attempt to ride two horses at once.

---

[1] See No. 28, note 4.
[2] Economic Commission for Asia and the Far East.
[3] Economic and Social Council of the U.N.

I would hope that before Mr. Acheson leaves we could take some opportunity of impressing upon him our view that the People's Government should be accepted in the United Nations. From the general point of view of the functioning and prestige of the United Nations it will be damaging if the Russians boycott the Security Council and the General Assembly in September. Quite apart from this I feel that our weak position in Hong Kong gives us a very real motive for wanting to see the People's Government inside the United Nations. A new government like the Peking Government is likely to attach great importance to its position as the one permanent Asian member of the Council, and it seems to me a good deal less likely that they will allow themselves to be used by the Russians for a direct or indirect attack on Hong Kong if by so doing they endanger their position in the United Nations. Such a situation is unlikely to arise this year but might well arise fairly quickly once they have settled with Formosa.

I realise that the American difficulty about altering their policy in China arises almost wholly from domestic political causes and from the coming elections.[4] No doubt we must accept it as a fact that Mr. Acheson cannot do much till the elections are over. That, however, seems to me no reason why we should not present our own policy to him much more fully than seems to have been done in the Bipartite Talks.[5]

K.G. YOUNGER

[4] Mid-term elections to Congress of 7 November 1950.

[5] Mr. Bevin minuted below: 'I will talk to Acheson'. However on 31 May Mr. Hadow recorded: 'This has just come down from the S/S office. Apparently Mr. Bevin was unable to have a further word with Mr. Acheson as indicated in his minute. Mr. Younger feels we should now, at any rate, consider on what occasion we could, if it were decided to change policy, vote for the People's Government.' In a minute also of 31 May Sir W. Strang commented: 'We should have done better to vote for the admission of the representative of the People's Government once we had conveyed *de jure* recognition. Sir G. Jebb and I were inclined to think so at the time. We do not seem to have gained anything by our subsequent attempt to ride two horses (this is what the Peking press calls our "double-faced policy"). The Minister of State's memorandum of the 11th May, with which I agree, puts a strong case in favour of a change of policy now, that is to say, a decision to vote for the representative of the People's Government. If I understood him aright, the Secretary of State's view now is that we should so vote at the meeting of the Economic and Social Council on the 2nd July next, though without disclosing this to the Chinese People's Government, at any rate at this stage.' This change of policy was subsequently agreed but not implemented at the E.C.O.S.O.C. meeting on 3 July in deference to American sensitivities over the Korean crisis.

No. 93

Memorandum by Mr. Allen[1]

[C 3320/74/18]

FOREIGN OFFICE, 11 May 1950

Repatriation of German Prisoners-of-War from the Soviet Union

On the 4th May Tass announced that the repatriation of German prisoners-of-war from the Soviet Union to Germany had been completed. The announcement stated that altogether 1,939,063 German prisoners-of-war had been repatriated from the Soviet Union to Germany since Germany's surrender. It added that 13,546 German prisoners-of-war held on war crimes charges remained in the Soviet Union.

Owing to the lack of any authoritative figures of the total number of German prisoners-of-war repatriated by the Russians it is difficult to contest the Soviet announcement on the basis of detailed figures. On the other hand Soviet statements issued some years ago put the figure of German prisoners-of-war held in the Soviet Union at higher than the recent Tass announcement: the German Federal Chancellor has recently drawn public attention to a Tass statement issued in 1945 immediately after the capitulation which claimed that three and a half million prisoners-of-war were in Russian hands. Moreover, the Allied High Commission are satisfied that a very large number of German families are still awaiting the return of relatives from Russia: a recent German Red Cross statement claimed that there are still about 100,000 German prisoners in Russia who had been in contact with their families in Germany but had not returned.

The United States delegation have proposed that it would be useful from the propaganda point of view if the three Foreign Ministers could issue some statement indicating that they have taken note of this situation and will do what they can to help. The matter has been discussed with the U.S. and French delegations and tripartite agreement has been reached among officials on the annexed draft of a statement.[2]

It is suggested that this draft be considered by Ministers when they discuss German problems tomorrow, 12th May, as an additional item on the agenda.

It is likely that Mr. Acheson will raise the matter. His delegation, who have agreed to advise him to do so, are anxious that the statement should

---

[1] This paper was evidently prepared as a brief for Mr. Bevin in tripartite Ministerial talks (Nos. 95 and 96). For earlier correspondence on German concern for the repatriation of prisoners-of-war from the Soviet Union and Dr. Adenauer's request for an Allied protest to the Soviet Government, resisted by the High Commission in April, see F.O.371/85109–85120.

[2] This draft statement circulated as MIN/TRI/P/26 on 11 May is not printed: final text at No. 98.i.

be issued as soon as possible and preferably in advance of any general communiqué on German questions that may be published by the Conference. The U.S. delegation consider that advance publication of the attached statement would ensure that it got better publicity and would be useful both from the point of view of reassuring German opinion and for answering Soviet propaganda.

D. ALLEN

No. 94

Brief by Sir A. Rumbold on Trieste for the Secretary of State's talks with Count Sforza

[*RT 1015/154*]

FOREIGN OFFICE, 11 May 1950

It has been arranged in principle that the Secretary of State should receive Count Sforza on Saturday, May 13th.[1] We know that Mr. Acheson has also agreed to have a private talk with him sometime during the next week and it can be assumed that he will have a private talk with M. Schuman too.

Count Sforza will of course raise the question of Trieste. The line upon which we, the Americans, and the French all agree, and to which we can count on Mr. Acheson and M.Schuman to conform, may be summarised as follows:— (*a*) we still adhere to our statement of March 1948 declaring that the Free Territory solution contemplated in the peace treaty[2] had been proved impracticable and mentioning our proposal that the territory in question should be returned to Italy, and we shall probably say so when we reply to the recent Soviet note;[3] (*b*) we have, however, no means of compelling the Yugoslavs to accept this proposal without qualification and the more the Italians harp on it in public the less likely they are to reach an

[1] This meeting (records at i – ii below) was arranged at Count Sforza's request following American and French rejection of an Italian suggestion for a Four Power meeting in London. However, both Mr. Acheson and M. Schuman agreed to see Count Sforza separately. When pressing for a meeting with Mr. Bevin, the Italian Ambassador in London observed to Sir W. Strang on 8 May that 'there were plenty of people who were only to anxious to pretend that Great Britain was less well disposed towards Italy than was either the United States or France. That was why he was anxious that it should not be said that Mr. Bevin alone of the three Foreign Ministers had not been able to see Count Sforza' (WT 1056/2).

[2] The tripartite statement on Trieste of 20 March 1948, published in *The Times* on 22 March is appended to the brief at i below. For a text of the Italian Peace Treaty of 10 February 1947, see *B.F.S.P.*, vol. 148, pp. 394–439.

[3] An extract from this nine-page note of 20 April 1950, in which the Soviet government alleged that the Western Powers had prevented the implementation of the Italian Peace Treaty with particular reference to Trieste, is printed in *Documents on International Affairs 1949–1950* (R.I.I.A., 1953), pp. 515–19: *ibid.*, p.519 for the Western reply of 16 June.

agreement with the Yugoslavs; (c) it ought not to be so difficult to reach agreement with the Yugoslavs on a future Yugoslav-Italian boundary provided the negotiations are conducted in private and both sides stop taking up fixed positions in public; (d) we do not wish to be involved in the details of the negotiations, although it seems to us that ethnic considerations might play an important part in deciding the boundary and that the agreement should probably be fortified by economic arrangements involving Austria as well.[4]

The Secretary of State should know that the Italian Ambassador, who thinks on the same lines as we do, has promised Sir William Strang to do his best to influence Count Sforza in the desired sense; moreover he says that he thinks that Count Sforza's innermost thoughts are not far removed from our own ideas. Sir William Strang undertook to report this to the Secretary of State as also the Ambassador's thought that if Count Sforza could be convinced that Italy would get a special place in the Atlantic Pact Organisation he might feel more inclined to make a sacrifice over Trieste for the sake of western consolidation.[5]

The Italian press has been much calmer about Trieste lately and Signor de Gasperi's speech in the Senate was a considerable improvement on those of Count Sforza.[6]

A. RUMBOLD

CALENDARS TO NO. 94

i *28 Apr. 1950 U.K. Brief No. 20 on Trieste*: British policy remains the encouragement of a direct settlement between Italy and Yugoslavia. Tentative Yugoslav moves for a compromise settlement on Trieste rebuffed by Count Sforza in a series of 'intransigent' speeches in April. [RT 1015/130].

ii *1–30 May 1950 Anglo-Italian conversations on Trieste* Convs. between Sir W. Strang and Italian Ambassador on 1 and 8 May are followed by Bevin-Sforza conversations on 13 and 19 May and personal letter from Count Sforza to Mr. Bevin of 18 May. Count Sforza receptive to encouragement from Mr. Bevin

---

[4] Sir A. Rumbold was here drawing on comments by Mr. Bevin made to Sir W. Strang on 2 May: 'He said that what he was aiming at was the opening of negotiations between Italy and Yugoslavia. He had reluctantly agreed to associate himself with the Three Power declaration, but he had never thought that it would be possible for Italy to obtain the whole of zone B. Broadly speaking, the best solution would be for Italy to have zone A and Yugoslavia zone B. The basis of agreement would be both territorial and economic . . . If only conversations on this subject could be set going quietly, it might be possible at the same time to encourage a new economic connection to grow up, not only between Italy and Yugoslavia, but in a wider field including Austria and Greece' (RT 1015/138).

[5] The Italian Ambassador suggested this possibility in conversation with Sir W. Strang on 1 May, for which see calendar ii below.

[6] Speaking in the Italian Senate on 3 May, Signor A. de Gasperi, Italian Prime Minister, reiterated his own confidence in the tripartite declaration of 1948 and the Atlantic Pact as providing the basis on which the Italian government hoped to reach a settlement on Trieste by direct negotiation with Yugoslavia (cf. *The Times* of 4 May 1950, p. 3 and calendar i for recent speeches by Count Sforza).

for negotiations with Tito on Trieste. On 30 May Italian Ambassador informs Sir W. Strang that Count Sforza had been 'very well pleased' with his talks with Mr. Bevin, though he was delaying negotiations with Tito until the atmosphere improved [WT 10535/6; RT 1015/148, 152, 162, 164, 189].

iii   *13 May 1950   Anglo-Italian conversations on Eritrea* Following some discussion of Eritrea between the Italian Ambassador and Sir W. Strang on 1 May (ii above), the future of Eritrea is discussed between Count Sforza and Mr. Bevin on 13 May. Count Sforza unable to support publicly the policy of partition with Abyssinia as favoured by H.M.G., yet agrees that Eritrea unlikely to survive as an independent economic unit. Both Italian and British governments to accept eventual decision of U.N. [JT 1512/211].

No. 95

Record of Third Tripartite Ministerial Meeting held in Lancaster House on Friday, 12 May 1950, at 10.30 a.m.[1]

[ZP 2/192]

Top secret

Present:

United Kingdom Mr. Ernest Bevin, Mr. Kenneth Younger, Sir Ivone Kirkpatrick, Lord Henderson, Mr. Ernest Davies, Gen. Sir Brian Robertson, and other Advisers.

United States Mr. Dean Acheson, Mr. Lewis Douglas, Mr. McCloy, Mr. Cooper, Dr. Jessup, Mr. Bruce, Col. Byroade, and other Advisers.

France M. Schuman, M. Massigli, M. Parodi, M. Poncet, M. Alphand, M. Lebel, and other Advisers.

Secretary-General Mr. Shuckburgh.

German Problems
(*a*) Policy towards Germany (MIN/TRI/P/7),[2] paragraphs 1–27, 46–49.
(*b*) Declaration by Ministers on Germany (MIN/TRI/P/13),[3] paragraphs 28, 34–45.
(*c*) Statement on Prisoners of War (MIN/TRI/P/26),[4] paragraph 36.
(*d*) Terms of Reference of Working Party on Germany (MIN/TRI/P/12),[2] paragraphs 31–33.

MIN/TRI/P/7[2]

THE SECRETARY OF STATE declared the meeting open and proposed to take document MIN/TRI/P/7 on Policy towards Germany.

2. M. SCHUMAN, in his opening statement, touched on the difficulties

---

[1] An extract from the summary of conclusions of this meeting (see No. 29, note 1) is printed in Volume I, as No. 19.
[2] No. 61.i.   [3] No. 61.ii.   [4] See No. 93, note 2.

with the Soviet Union which had led the three Western occupying Powers to set up a separate régime. He stated that the Western Powers might have found recently that gratitude was rare in Germany. Nevertheless, they desired to maintain their policy which had been chosen not only in the interest of Germany but in the interest of Europe and of peace. This policy consisted in restoring progressively to the Germans responsibility for their own affairs and the rights of an independent State.

Aims of Immediate Policy

3. What were the short-term aims of the Western Occupying Powers? They were awaiting Germany's entry into the Council of Europe and did not propose to bargain about it; it had been virtually promised by the German Government in the Petersberg Agreement. At the same time they should give study to certain questions of long-term interest, particularly to the revision of the Occupation Statute. While awaiting a revised and alleviated occupation statute they should apply more liberally the present controls. They should take steps to activate organisations designed to last beyond the present stage—i.e., the Military Security Board and the International Authority for the Ruhr. The principle of their policy should be to maintain in Germany the supreme authority of the High Commission, but to limit control to the essentials, i.e., to maintaining Allied security and to preserving and fostering a democratic system in Germany. He would personally suggest reducing controls on the Länder and thus reducing the number of Control Commission staffs which needed to be employed and he would further suggest fostering closer direct relations between the Western German Government and other Governments; this would be better than improvised press interviews and would strengthen Germany's position in the Council of Europe.

Reservation about anticipating Peace Treaty

4. He wished to make a general remark on the agenda which almost amounted to a reservation. Several questions had been proposed for study by a working party, for example, the succession of the Federal Republic to the pre-war obligations and rights of the German Reich. He thought it important in handling these questions not to do so in such a way as to give the appearance of concluding a separate Peace Treaty with the German Federal Government.

Economic Policy

5. The economic connexions between Western Germany and the rest of Western Europe were already highly developed. It was important to co-ordinate the use of E.C.A. Funds with the general political aims of the Western Occupying Powers.

French Proposal for Integration of Western European Coal and Steel Industries

6. He would like to say, in conclusion, a word on the French plan.[5] This

[5] See Volume I, No. 2.

plan applied in the first place to Europe and only secondarily to France and Germany. The German aspect was, however, particularly important. The proposal, he thought, could only have been made by France. A proposal from any other Government could scarcely have been accepted by French opinion and would not have produced the requisite change in the psychological atmosphere. The French Government did not underestimate the technical and political difficulties of the plan but were firmly resolved to overcome them. The French offer was neither a *fait accompli* nor a bright idea thrown out at random. As regards Germany it was quite understood that Germany could only act under the control of the High Commissioners whose rights on this point as on all others remain intact.

Proposal for High Commissioners to Study French Plan in London

7. He would like to propose that the High Commissioners take advantage of their presence together in London to study, with the help of the French Delegation, the principles which might form the basis of an agreement on the lines of a French proposal.

Other Preliminary Studies

8. There would also have to be a study of how far the proposed contractual authority for the coal and steel industries could co-exist with authorities like the Military Security Board and the International Authority for the Ruhr imposed by the sovereign will of the Occupying Powers. The French Government would like to associate with the preliminary studies of their proposal all interested European countries.

9. MR. ACHESON said that document MIN/TRI/P/7 might be handled in two ways. The Ministers might try to amend it in the course of their present meeting or might give instructions for its redrafting by officials after the meeting. He preferred the latter course.

Guiding Principles for the Activity of the High Commission

10. During the next eighteen to twenty-four months the influence of the High Commission in Germany would be greater than thereafter. He was not suggesting that the High Commission could be wound up at the end of that period, but its influence on German affairs would, in his view, thereafter decline because of various factors, for example, the cessation of E.C.A. payments. The High Commission should use its influence in order to bring Germany into the Western camp and the policy of the Western Occupying Powers on controls should be determined by the consideration whether or not a proposed course of action would maintain and increase the prestige of the High Commission. With this end in view the High Commissioners should according to circumstances either use their powers or leave them unused.

11. Here he thought there was perhaps a point of difference between him and M. Schuman. M. Schuman had suggested relaxing Allied controls in the Länder and increasing the German Government's control of their foreign relations in the West. But legislation by the Länder had a most

important influence on the state of affairs throughout Germany. The same was true of legislation by the separate States in the United States. If the High Commission were to limit its activities in the Länder then it would be giving up most of its really productive authority. It should rather use its prestige and powers to direct the Germans along a line which was new to them, but which would in the end lead to a free society. This policy promised better results than the application of purely restrictive controls such as those exercised by the Military Security Board. The best possible control was to create the kind of society which would not choose to act against the long-term interests of the non-Communist world. The Western Occupying Powers should try to inspire the Germans with a desire to identify themselves with the West. For example, the Germans should come to look on the Occupying Forces not as a prison guard, but as a protection. It was to be hoped that they would then be willing to contribute towards the maintenance of those forces. In the economic field the Germans should adopt the idea of an expanding European economy and not return to the pre-war ideal of self-sufficiency. All this, in his view, required vigorous exercise of the High Commission's functions; but this was not inconsistent with giving the Germans more freedom. The Germans could be encouraged to act under the guidance and help and sometimes the direction of the High Commission.

12. The policy outlined above pre-supposed that Germany's true interests were with the West or should be made so. It was futile to believe that Germany would whole-heartedly join the West if she had no security and no economic future there. This was the reason for pressing on with the European Payments Union, the relaxation of trade barriers and for giving the Federal Republic effective help to deal with unemployment and the refugees.

M. Schuman's Reservation about a Peace Treaty

13. He agreed with M. Schuman that there should be no appearance of a separate Peace Treaty, but the points to which M. Schuman had referred were important and if left unsettled would retard German economic recovery. They should be settled, but in such a way as to take account of M. Schuman's reservation.

French Plan for Coal and Steel

14. The United States had welcomed the French proposal for the integration of the Western European Coal and Steel Industries. It was impossible yet to judge the final result of the plan, which would affect almost everything under discussion. He hoped that all the Western Powers would be given an opportunity to comment as the proposal was worked out. He approved and accepted M. Schuman's suggestion that the High Commissioners should meet.

15. MR. BEVIN said that in his view the prestige and powers of the High Commission should not be the first object of the Western Occupying

Powers. Their main object was to get the Federal Government respected by the German people. They wanted the Germans to make their own Government work. This raised the question of how far the Federal Government should be kept in leading strings. The Allies should be very clear and in complete agreement about what they wanted to do in Germany. For this reason he favoured the idea of setting out the kind of democratic methods which the Germans should follow. This would give a criterion for intervention. If the Germans themselves resented something done by their Government that would lead to one situation, but if the High Commission objected and disallowed it, that would lead to quite a different situation. Unless the Germans respected their Government they might slip back into extreme nationalism, and that would give rise to a very difficult situation. He felt, therefore, that the Germans must be allowed to learn by trial and error.

Exercise of Control in the Länder

16. He would not object to a reduction of the control exercised by the Allies in the Länder provided that there was no danger to the prestige and security of the Occupation Forces. He attached importance to this point, and he agreed with Mr. Acheson that all fundamental controls must be maintained.

Documents MIN/TRI/P/7[2] and MIN/TRI/P/13[3]

17. He thought that MIN/TRI/P/13, the draft declaration, should be redrafted so as to include the fuller statement of the fundamental principles set out in MIN/TRI/P/7.

Differences of Policy within the High Commission

18. He was concerned about the conflict of policies which he had observed from time to time within the High Commission. His Majesty's Government in the United Kingdom, having adopted a policy of planned economy and of full employment, had an outlook which sometimes gave rise to a conflict of views within the High Commission, for example, about Military Government Law 75.[6]

French Proposal for the Integration of Western Europe Coal and Steel Industries

19. In this connexion he thought it important that when the French proposal came to be applied the Germans should be able to exercise proper democratic control. There must be no danger of a return to the system of privately-owned cartels which had been among the causes of the last war. They must therefore be careful how the plan developed, but he wished to make it clear that he was not against the basic conception. Indeed, he had always considered that the divisions caused by national frontiers made it impossible for European heavy industry to function

[6] See No. 8, note 6.

economically, and he therefore wished to give the French proposal not only a welcome but a helping hand.

Upshot of Discussion

20. He saw some difficulty in redrafting the documents under consideration, i.e., MIN/TRI/P/7 and MIN/TRI/P/13, seeing that the American delegation apparently wished to retain a large measure of control, whereas the United Kingdom and French delegations were ready in certain cases to relax controls. It was important to ensure that the three Governments interpreted alike any statement made to the Germans on their behalf.

21. M. SCHUMAN said that he wished to add to his remarks on two points:

Reduction of Controls in the Länder

He had emphasised that his suggestion about the Länder was a purely personal one. He had not intended to suggest that the Allies should relinquish control of Länder legislation which was in any case exercised by the High Commission. His idea had been that perhaps in 6 months' time when the Occupation Statute came up for revision it might be found possible to reduce the numerous allied staffs at present maintained in the Länder. He agreed with Mr. Acheson that the main aim should be to bring about a change of heart in Germany. He thought there were no serious difficulties between him and his colleagues and he had not proposed any amendment to the documents submitted.

French Plan for Coal and Steel

22. He had said in his statement to the press that there was no question of establishing a cartel, but the real guarantee would be in the wording of the agreement which he hoped would be made shortly. This agreement, moreover, would be between Governments whereas a cartel was by definition the result of an understanding between industries. He would not like to miss the opportunity of thanking Mr. Attlee for his statement made in the House of Commons yesterday,[7] and he had seen nothing in Mr. Bevin's remarks which conflicted with Mr. Attlee's statement. France could not carry out this scheme unaided and would welcome help from all interested countries.

23. MR. BEVIN asked whether there would be close consultation with trade unions about this proposal.

24. M. SCHUMAN replied that the French Government was constitutionally obliged to consult the Economic Council, on which trade unions were represented, before taking a final decision. In addition there would be further direct consultation with the trade unions on technical points. Other countries concerned would no doubt take steps to keep their own trade unions informed.

[7] See *Parl. Debs., 5th ser., H. of C.*, vol. 475, col. 587.

25. MR. ACHESON said that there was no difference between him and his colleagues about whether or not to relax controls. There might be a difference as to whether the control exercised should be positive or negative. Mr. Bevin had spoken about the provisional veto imposed by the High Commission on the German Income Tax Law.[8] He had said that if in such a case the High Commission did not interfere and conflict therefore arose between the people and the Government in Germany, such a conflict would make the Government responsive to public opinion and therefore be a good thing. He (Mr. Acheson) replied that in Germany there would be no conflict. In similar circumstances in Great Britain, the United States or in France, he agreed that public opinion would be aroused, but in Germany he thought there would be no protest. Democracy was a very tender plant in Germany and the High Commission should make it their business to foster the growth of that plant. If the High Commissioner vetoed an objectionable law the Germans would then learn how democratic public opinion regarded this kind of law. Otherwise they would never learn.

26. The issue was not whether to retain or abolish the controls, but whether, having retained them, to exercise them or not. The United States delegation thought that the Western Occupying Powers could move away from a régime of restriction faster in the industrial and economic fields, than in the political. The presence of the power to intervene and its occasional use in the political field seemed to him desirable and important.

27. MR. BEVIN said that it was perhaps a question of degree, but he felt that the High Commission should not intervene in things which in this country would be decided by a Town Council.

28. He asked whether his colleagues wished to re-write the paper MIN/TRI/P/7. If so, paper MIN/TRI/P/13 which sprang from it would also have to be amended.

29. MR. ACHESON suggested that the Ministers should take no action on MIN/TRI/P/7, but that officials should re-write MIN/TRI/P/13, using the minutes of the present discussion for guidance. The suggestion for a redraft of MIN/TRI/P/13 was accepted and arrangement made for a drafting party of officials to meet on 13th May.

30. M. SCHUMAN suggested that the officials should take the doctrines of MIN/TRI/P/7 into account in their work.

MIN/TRI/P/12[2]

31. MR. BEVIN suggested that Ministers should consider document MIN/TRI/P/12 arising out of paragraph 4 of MIN/TRI/P/7. Were the draft terms of reference for a working party accepted?

32. M. SCHUMAN said that he accepted the draft terms of reference, but without wishing to be understood as intending to limit the freedom of conclusion of the officials who would study the questions listed in the terms of reference.

[8] See No. 8, note 4.

331

33. MR. ACHESON accepted them on the same basis and it was agreed that the working party should be set up and work in London, with a possibility of dealing with some questions in Paris if that should be more convenient.[9]

MIN/TRI/P/13

34. M. SCHUMAN suggested that in any published declaration such as the draft declaration in MIN/TRI/P/13 an expression of confidence in the High Commission should be included. This was agreed.

35. He said that he had two points to make on the draft declaration in MIN/TRI/P/13.

Prisoners of War

36. If it were decided to make a statement or a démarche (such as the draft contained in MIN/TRI/P/26)[4] about prisoners of war detained in the Soviet Union, mention must also be made of prisoners of war whose homes were in one of the countries occupied by the Germans during the war, for example, Alsace-Lorraine, Holland, Belgium and Luxembourg, who had been forcibly incorporated into the German army and were presumed still to be detained in the Soviet Union.

French Claim to Reparations

37. In paragraph (f) of the paper annexed to document MIN/TRI/P/13 he wished for reasons of internal policy to make a reservation of principle. France had never renounced in principle the right to reparations in kind agreed at Yalta but postponed at Potsdam.[10] This question could only be settled by a 4-Power agreement covering the whole of Germany.

38. MR. BEVIN asked whether this reservation was to be published in the text of the declaration.

39. M. SCHUMAN replied that he only wished it recorded in the official and unpublished minutes of the present discussion.

40. MR. ACHESON asked for an explanation on this point.

41. M. SCHUMAN referred to paragraph 19 of the Potsdam Agreement which states that reparations in kind shall not be exacted as long as the German balance of payments is unfavourable.

42. MR. BEVIN said that to his knowledge the French had never agreed to give up the claim for reparations from current production although the United Kingdom and the United States had done so. But the point did not

[9] MIN/TRI/P/12 was amended accordingly and circulated as MIN/TRI/P/12 (Final) on 22 May (*F.R.U.S. 1950*, vol. iii, p. 1050, note 7). The first meeting of the Intergovernmental Study Group on Germany (I.G.G.) set up under the terms of reference in MIN/TRI/P/12 (Final) took place in the Foreign Office on 3 July. The tripartite representatives were *U.K.* Sir D. Gainer, Permanent Under-Secretary of State for the German Section of the Foreign Office; *U.S.* Mr. Douglas; *France* M. Massigli.

[10] For the decisions on reparations at the Yalta and Potsdam conferences of 1945 see Section V of the Yalta protocol of 11 February printed in *B.F.S.P.*, vol. 148, pp. 84–5 and in Sections IIB and III of the Potsdam protocol of 2 August printed in Series I, Volume I, pp. 1267–9.

seem of much practical importance since there were unlikely to be any reparations from current production.

43. M. SCHUMAN agreed and pointed out that furthermore a 4-Power agreement would be needed.

44. MR. BEVIN said that he thought it would be helpful if the French Government, not necessarily to-day, could also agree to give up reparations from current production.

45. M. SCHUMAN replied that the French Government were agreed with their British and United States colleagues in wishing to persuade the Russians to do so.

Further discussion on MIN/TRI/P/7

46. M. SCHUMAN returned to the question of document MIN/TRI/P/7. He asked whether his colleagues were agreed that the experts should take it into account. There were important principles set out in it. For instance, in paragraph 3 the statement that the Western Occupying Powers intended to retain supreme authority in Germany, and the principles set out in paragraph 5.

47. MR. ACHESON replied that he would prefer to have no action taken on document MIN/TRI/P/7, but if experts were to take it into consideration they should ignore paragraph 4, seeing that the Ministers had already dealt with it. The last paragraph of MIN/TRI/P/7 was also confusing. The Germans had now accepted the invitation to join the Council of Europe, or were about to do so.[11] He would like to see a paper drafted in a more positive way.

48. M. SCHUMAN said that while the paper might be badly expressed he did not think that the principles set out in it were in question.

49. MR. BEVIN said that the last paragraph of the paper was intended to set out the position about Germany's entry into the Council of Europe. They must come into the Council of Europe on the basis of the existing statute without demanding modifications in the statute as a condition of their entry. Mr. Bevin's colleagues did not dissent from this statement.

50. MR. BEVIN announced that the Foreign Ministers of the Benelux countries had accepted an invitation to meet the Foreign Ministers of the three Western Occupying Powers at 3 p.m. on Saturday, 13th May.

51. The Meeting then adjourned to reassemble at 4 p.m.

---

[11] See No. 77, note 2.

No. 96

Record of Fourth Tripartite Ministerial Meeting held in Lancaster House on Friday, 12 May 1950, at 4 p.m.

[ZP 2/192]

Top secret

Present:

United Kingdom Mr. Ernest Bevin, Mr. Kenneth Younger, Sir Ivone Kirkpatrick, Lord Henderson, Mr. Ernest Davies, Gen. Sir Brian Robertson, and other Advisers.

United States Mr. Dean Acheson, Mr. Lewis Douglas, Mr. McCloy, Mr. Cooper, Dr. Jessup, Mr. Bruce, Col. Byroade, and other Advisers.

France M. Schuman, M. Massigli, M. Parodi, M. Poncet, M. Alphand, M. Lebel, and other Advisers.

Secretary-General Mr. Shuckburgh.

I German Problems
(a) Berlin (MIN/TRI/P/14),[1] paragraph 1.
(b) Declaration on Prisoners of War (MIN/TRI/P/26),[2] paragraphs, 2, 44 and Annex I.
(c) Request by German Federal Chancellor for a declaration that the territory of the Federal Republic would be defended against attack (MIN/TRI/P/10),[3] paragraphs 3, 4.
(d) Proposal for protest against Militarised Police in the Soviet Zone (MIN/TRI/P/11),[1] paragraphs 5, 6, 35–43.
(e) Level of Steel Production (MIN/TRI/P/15 and MIN/TRI/P/24),[4] paragraphs 7–13.
(f) International Authority for the Ruhr (MIN/TRI/P/18),[4] paragraph 14.
(g) Appeal to Governments by French High Commissioner on Military Government Law 75:[5] paragraphs 15–21.
(h) Removal of certain security restrictions on German trade with Soviet orbit (MIN/TRI/P/16),[4] paragraph 22.
(i) French Proposal on Nationalisation of Allied Property in Germany (MIN/TRI/P/17),[4] paragraphs 23–27.
(j) United States Proposal on German Shipbuilding for Export (MIN/TRI/P/23),[4] paragraphs 28–34.
(k) Joint Recommendation by the High Commissioners on the

---

[1] See No. 61, note 7.
[2] MIN/TRI/P/26 is not here printed. Annex I contained the final text, published in *The Times* on 13 May, for which see No. 98.i.
[3] See No. 60, note 2.   [4] See No. 76.i.   [5] See No. 8, note 6.

Establishment of a Federal Gendarmerie (MIN/TRI/P/27),[6] paragraphs 35–43.

II Migration (MIN/TRI/P/5 and MIN/TRI/P/25),[7] paragraphs 45, 46.

III Austrian Treaty (MIN/TRI/P/20),[8] paragraphs 47–49 and Annex II.

Item I German Problems
MIN/TRI/P/14[1]

MR. ACHESON suggested a redraft of paragraph 3 of the paper under consideration to bring out that the need was for deeds not words. He suggested further that when the Ministers met their Benelux colleagues they should investigate whether the Benelux could give any special help to Berlin. This was agreed.[9]

MIN/TRI/P/26[2]

2. MR. BEVIN said that M. Schuman had suggested inclusion in the draft statement on prisoners of war of a reference to prisoners of Allied nations presumed to be detained in the Soviet Union. MR. ACHESON agreed to this suggestion and for his part proposed the inclusion of Japanese prisoners of war presumed to be detained in the Soviet Union in order to make clear that there was a regular Soviet pattern of conduct. He circulated a revised draft. M. SCHUMAN agreed, but suggested that European prisoners should be mentioned first. This was agreed and the Ministers instructed a working party to prepare a further revision of the draft which was later approved and issued to the press, and is attached as Annex I[2] to this Record.

MIN/TRI/P/10[3]

3. MR. ACHESON proposed two amendments to this paper

(i) In the third paragraph the last sentence to read: ' . . . Federal Republic enjoys in effect protection under the North Atlantic Treaty.' Mr. Acheson explained that the earlier wording had not been cleared with the United States military authorities and they might perhaps find it difficult to accept.

The amendment was agreed.

(ii) The fourth paragraph to read: 'The three Allied Powers have no intention. . . .'

[6] See No. 61, note 6.   [7] See No. 40, note 4 and No. 90, note 11.
[8] See No. 59, note 3 for MIN/TRI/P/20. Annex II, not printed, contained a draft declaration on Austria, superseded by the final text at No. 98.i.
[9] The amended text of the paper on Berlin (MIN/TRI/P/14 Final) is printed in *F.R.U.S. 1950*, vol. iii, pp. 1091–2. The main points of this paper were contained in a short declaration, published in *The Times* on 13 May: see also No. 98.i.

This amendment was also agreed.

4. He asked for a clarification of the third paragraph of the proposed oral explanation. Was it the intention that the proposed answer should not be given unless Dr. Adenauer made a request in the terms described? In discussion there was some uncertainty whether or not Dr. Adenauer had already made such a request and on Mr. Bevin's proposal it was decided that the paragraph should be deleted and should be used for the guidance of the High Commissioners.[10]

MIN/TRI/P/11[1]

5. MR. BEVIN expressed some concern lest the proposed protest should lead to further fears about security in the German Federal Republic. M. SCHUMAN shared this view. MR. ACHESON replied that there were two reasons for the American proposal. First, everyone in Germany knew about the militarised police in the Soviet Zone and he did not think, therefore, that a Western *démarche* would increase fears on this score. Second, he thought it better tactics to protest first to the Soviet Union before the Soviet Union had a chance of protesting about any Federal Gendarmerie which might be established in the West. He added that for this reason the United States Delegation would propose postponing a decision on the Federal Gendarmerie (MIN/TRI/P/27)[6] until after the protest to the Soviet Union had been made. MR. BEVIN pointed out that the Gendarmerie proposed for the West was not the same kind of formation as the militarised police in the Soviet Zone. MR. ACHESON agreed, but suggested that Russian propaganda would certainly try to draw a comparison.

6. MR. BEVIN then suggested that MIN/TRI/P/11 should be considered later, together with MIN/TRI/P/27.

MIN/TRI/P/15 and MIN/TRI/P/24[4]

7. The meeting then considered the agreed tripartite paper on the level of steel production (MIN/TRI/P/15) together with the amendment proposed by the American Delegation (MIN/TRI/P/24).

8. MR. ACHESON said that the thought behind the original paper seemed to be that the High Commission should do nothing until it was forced to by the pressure of public opinion. His amendment was designed to keep the initiative for the High Commission. Instead of waiting to be goaded into action by agitation, they should tell the Germans that they would not hesitate to act if need arose. MR. BEVIN asked whether the American proposal did not amount to a suggestion for revising the Prohibited and Limited Industries Agreement. That Agreement was between Governments and was due to run until 1952. He had no present authority to undertake its modification. M. SCHUMAN agreed with Mr. Bevin.

[10] An amended text of MIN/TRI/P/10 was accordingly circulated as MIN/TRI/P/10 Final, for which see No. 104.i and *F.R.U.S. 1950*, vol. iii, pp. 1085–6.

9. MR. BEVIN continued that the United Kingdom Government had no objection to considering a revision of the permitted level of steel production if German steel production had reached the agreed limit. He thought it a mistake, however, to tell the Germans that we proposed to do this.

10. MR. ACHESON replied that, as he understood it, the Prohibited and Limited Industries Agreement could only be abrogated by common consent, but that it was open to any party to raise the question of revision.

11. M. SCHUMAN said that if the High Commission made a statement to the Germans on the lines indicated by the American draft (MIN/TRI/P/24) he thought the Germans would interpret it as an invitation to open the question at once.

12. MR. ACHESON said that he would not insist on the adoption of this amendment.

13. M. SCHUMAN agreed to drop the French proposal at paragraph (*c*) of MIN/TRI/P/15, adding that when the question came to be studied the French experts would adopt the point of view indicated in paragraph (*c*). MIN/TRI/P/15 was therefore adopted as drafted with the deletion of paragraph (*c*).[11]

MIN/TRI/P/18[4]

14. M. SCHUMAN withdrew the reservation by the French Delegation at the end of this paper and MR. ACHESON having no comment the paper was agreed without the French addition.[12]

French Appeal to Governments on Law 75.[5]

15. M. SCHUMAN said that in connexion with MIN/TRI/P/18 on the International Ruhr Authority he would like to raise the question of Law 75. Law 75 had been a bi-zonal law designed to prepare the reorganisation of the German Coal and Steel Industries. The French Government now agreed with the body of the law, but they objected to the passage in the preamble which stated that the question of ownership of these industries was to be left to a freely elected representative German Government. They opposed this passage for fundamental reasons. In the view of the French Government it was wrong in 1948 and would still be wrong in

[11] Paragraph 4(*c*), in which the French delegation stated that any study towards raising the steel level should take into account not only the state of steel production in the Western World, but also general security and political considerations, was accordingly deleted from MIN/TRI/P/15 (No. 76.i) then re-circulated as MIN/TRI/P/15 Final on 22 May (not printed). In this paper it was agreed that the High Commission should make a secret study into the steel level and should meanwhile inform the Federal Government that no change in the level was contemplated.

[12] MIN/TRI/P/18 Final was accordingly circulated on 22 May. This paper agreed that the question of transferring powers from the Allied High Commission to the I.A.R. should be referred to the study group on Germany (see No. 95, note 9). The French reservation expressing concern at the deferral of the question was deleted in MIN/TRI/P/18 Final which was otherwise the same as the text at No. 76.i.

1950 to leave this question to the German Government. No one could tell what the German Government would decide nor by what kind of a majority the decision would be carried in the German legislature. The question was how far the Bonn Government was trustworthy. The future form of Allied control over German heavy industry had not yet been decided: the Ruhr Authority was still being discussed as in paper MIN/TRI/P/18. The French Government refused to be left between two unknowns, the form of the international authority for the Ruhr and the type of ownership of German heavy industry.

16. He emphasised that the French Government was bound by a vote cast on two separate occasions and in both Houses of the French Parliament.

17. The question, moreover, was not urgent. He understood that almost a year would be necessary to complete the decartelisation of the industries concerned. The body of the law could, therefore, be applied already and a decision on the preamble postponed.

18. Moreover, the French Government considered that a decision on this point could only be taken unanimously. The question of ownership was not merely a question of applying one of the controls agreed at Washington in April 1949. It was a much more important question of the kind which was normally settled in a Peace Treaty or at least in a formal agreement between Governments. The Ministers had just agreed that the provisions of the Prohibited and Limited Industries Agreement could not be modified except by common consent. He suggested, therefore, that a decision on the future ownership of the heavy industries could not be taken by a majority vote.

19. If agreement had already been reached about the future form of Allied control, the French Government would not attach so much importance to the question of ownership, but he felt it impossible to leave the question of ownership to the Germans without having reached agreement on the form of control. He begged his colleagues to understand the French point of view on this matter. Possible German rearmament depended on the industry of the Ruhr and French public opinion therefore attached a symbolic importance to the question.

20. MR. ACHESON said that he disagreed with M. Schuman's interpretation of the Occupation Statute. If it were accepted he thought it might wreck the Occupation Statute.

21. MR. BEVIN said he agreed with Mr. Acheson. He regretted that he could not accept M. Schuman's view.[13]

[13] In the Foreign Office on 13 May, Mr. Stevens raised the question of whether this discussion should be followed up by a formal letter to M. Schuman confirming Anglo-American rejection of the French appeal on Law 75. After discussion with the U.S. delegation it was agreed that however tactfully drafted, such a letter 'far from mollifying the French might simply cause them to reaffirm their arguments . . . we should not send a letter but should let matters take their course in the High Commission tomorrow' (F.O. telegram to Wahnerheide No. 831 of 15 May on CE 2202/49/181). On 16 May the High Commission agreed by majority decision that Allied High Commission Law No. 27, superseding

MIN/TRI/P/16[4]

22. Mr. Acheson said that he could not agree at present to the proposal of the United Kingdom and French Delegations for removal of security restrictions on trade with the Soviet orbit. He was bound in this matter by instructions from his Government. Expert discussions would shortly take place, and when they had been concluded he hoped to be able to approach his Government for a decision. The matter could then be taken up in Washington.

MIN/TRI/P/17[4]

23. M. Schuman said that the three Ministers had just given the Germans the right to dispose of German sequestrated property. (This statement appeared to convey M. Schuman's acceptance of the majority vote on Law 75.) It was now proposed that the Germans should also be able to confiscate allied property. He was shocked by this proposal. There was no means of knowing what compensation would be paid, but it would probably be in non-convertible currency which the recipients would not be able to remove from Germany and might have difficulty in investing there. Even Hitler, although he sequestrated allied property in the war had not confiscated it. The question might be settled in conjunction with other related questions, but could surely not be disposed of in isolation.

24. Mr. Acheson said that no new power was being given to the German Government. The German Government was at liberty to nationalise property provided adequate compensation was paid. M. Schuman, he said, proposed preventing the German Government from exercising this power which they already had. The High Commission could certainly ensure that the Federal Government applied the principles agreed by the Inter-Governmental Working Group in awarding compensation; but this was as far as the High Commission could go.

25. Mr. Bevin said that the United Kingdom Delegation could not go beyond the principles agreed by the Inter-Governmental Working Group. Would it not be better to wait and see what the German Government proposed? The present Federal Government was unlikely to rush into measures of nationalisation.

26. M. Schuman asked if the question could not be left in suspense until a general settlement of kindred questions—reparations, pre-war duties, &c.—could be reached.

27. Mr. Bevin said that as there was no agreement the meeting should pass to the next point.

MIN/TRI/P/23[4]

28. Mr. Bevin said that he thought the question of shipping had been settled by the three Ministers at Paris in November 1949. He certainly could not agree at such short notice to the present American proposal.

Anglo-American Military Government Law No. 75, should be promulgated forthwith: *D.G.O.*, pp. 490–2.

29. MR. ACHESON said that the Americans had always made it clear that they would press this point. In Paris the Ministers had been discussing primarily ship-building for the German flag. It seemed to the United States Delegation that there were few security reasons against ship-building for export. There was much unemployment in the coastal districts which relaxation of controls would help.

30. MR. BEVIN said that he had received the American document for the first time the previous night. The United Kingdom had been near to defeat in the last war because of the German submarine campaign. German ship-building was, therefore, a most important question for the United Kingdom and he could not deal with it at the present meeting.

31. MR. ACHESON said he hoped that the question could be discussed through the diplomatic channels. He added that the principles agreed between the three Powers for dealing with Germany often seemed to break down when it came to their concrete application.

32. MR. BEVIN went on that Germany was not yet a full member of the Western Club. Much would still have to be done before she was. German shipping potential had been a danger to the United Kingdom and he did not wish the United Kingdom to be exposed to the same risk again. He was willing to discuss the matter through the diplomatic channel, but proper weight must be given to security considerations.

MIN/TRI/P/11[1] *and MIN/TRI/P/27*[6]

33. The meeting then turned to the recommendation by the High Commission for the establishment of a Federal gendarmerie and the United States proposal for a protest against the militarised police in the Soviet Zone.

34. At Mr. Bevin's request, GENERAL ROBERTSON gave a *résumé* of the Chancellor's request for a Federal gendarmerie and of the reasons which had led the High Commission to make their recommendation.

35. M. SCHUMAN said that he would like before taking a decision to have the results of further study by the High Commission. He did not like taking partial decisions which might be substantially modified later.

36. MR. ACHESON said that he had not yet been able to consult the United States Government about this paper. He would, therefore, prefer to delay a decision for some weeks. He had two reasons for this attitude. Firstly, he thought the protest to the Soviet Government against the militarised policy in the Soviet Zone should be made first and secondly, a delay would give him an opportunity to consult the American Chiefs of Staff and the President.

37. MR. BEVIN said that since the Chancellor has made no public demand in this instance he thought it would be advisable to answer his letter, otherwise we might be putting a premium on public pressure. He thought also that while the three Governments were considering their attitude it would be quite proper for the High Commission to continue their study of the question in consultation with the Federal authorities. He

suggested that these two steps should be agreed at once and the final decision considered at an early date.

38. M. SCHUMAN pointed out that the proposed Federal gendarmerie was a force of quite a different kind from the militarised police about whose formation in the Soviet Zone it was proposed to protest. After some discussion it was agreed that it would be better not to encourage the connexion of the two questions in the public mind.

39. MR. ACHESON said that Mr. McCloy suggested that if the High Commissioners could study the co-ordination of the Länder police this might reduce the numbers required for the Federal gendarmerie.

40. MR. BEVIN said that he had always supported the idea of locally controlled police as a safeguard against totalitarian abuse of power.

41. It was agreed that

(i) the protest to the Soviet Union proposed by the United States Delegation should be made by the three Powers,[14] and that

(ii) a reply should be sent to Dr. Adenauer's letter GEH 40–50 of 28th April[15] saying that the question was under study, and

(iii) the High Commissioners should continue their study of this question in consultation with the Federal authorities and report back speedily to Governments.

42. At this point the Ministers considered and approved the revised draft of the press statement on prisoners of war.[2] They directed their press officers to draw up a statement of the lines on which each delegation should brief the press about the day's business.

Item II Migration (MIN/TRI/P/5 and MIN/TRI/P/25)[7]

43. The meeting then turned to Item 2 (*b*) (ii) on the agenda—Migration.

On MR. ACHESON's proposal the paper MIN/TRI/P/25 was returned to Committee so that better account should be taken of the position of Italy.

Item III Austrian Treaty

45. The meeting then turned to Item 4 of the agenda—Austrian Treaty Problems.

46. M. SCHUMAN said that he was in general agreement with the paper submitted by the Deputies, but he must consult his Government on recommendation (*B*) and (*C*) of Part II of the paper[8] (pages 5 and 6 of the English text). After discussion M. SCHUMAN said that he hoped to get a decision by the French on these points by Thursday, 18th May.

47. MR. ACHESON circulated a draft declaration on Austria which is

---

[14] Separate notes of protest from the British, French and American governments were accordingly addressed to the Soviet government on 23 May: British text (Cmnd. 1552, pp. 130–2) was published in *The Times* on the following day.

[15] See No. 45, note 2 and further No. 104.

attached to this record as Annex II.[8] It was decided that the first sentence of the second paragraph was unclear and the United States draft was sent back to the Deputies for redrafting. The Ministers agreed on Recommendations $A(1)$ and (2) of Part II of the Deputies' paper and decided to meet on Thursday, 18th May, to learn the French Government's decision on Recommendation (B) of Part II and to consider the redraft of the declaration.

48. The Ministers then approved the lines of guidance for press briefing on the day's business drawn up by their press officers and the meeting stood adjourned until 10.30 a.m. on Saturday, 13th May.

No. 97

Minute from Mr. Bevin to Mr. Attlee

P.M./50/19 [E 1192/90]

Top secret   FOREIGN OFFICE, *12 May 1950*

Israel and the Arab States

I mentioned this question at our meeting on May 11th[1] and I now attach a record of my discussion with Mr. Acheson on this question.[2]

2. This record does not fully bring out the points at issue, which have been discussed more comprehensively between the two Delegations.[3]

3. The main points are as follows. Ever since fighting broke out in Palestine, it has been the view of all our representatives in the Middle East that the greatest contribution to a lasting settlement which could be made would be something in the nature of an Anglo-American guarantee of the final frontiers.

4. The Americans have not dissented, but in spite of constant pressure for the past two years have until now indicated that, although they recognise their share of responsibility for events, it would be impossible for them to make any statement on these lines.

5. But in the light of the problems which have arisen over the supply of arms to Israel and the Arab States we have recently brought them to modify their view. They are now willing to join with us, and with the French if the latter are willing, in making a statement on the following lines:

'The . . .[4] Governments take this opportunity of declaring their deep interest in and their desire to promote the establishment and maintenance of peace and stability in the Near East and their unalterable opposition to the use of force or threat of force between any of these States. The . . .[4] Governments, should they find that any

---

[1] No. 88.   [2] See No. 84, Item II.   [3] See No. 65, note 3.   [4] Blank as in original.

State in the area was preparing to violate existing frontiers or armistice lines, would, consistent with their obligations as members of the United Nations, immediately take action both within and outside the United Nations to prevent such violation.'

6. This is an important development of which it seems desirable to take advantage.

7. At the same time the Americans propose (and indeed regard it as a condition) that the statement should contain paragraphs about arms and war material somewhat on the following lines:

(a) 'The . . .[4] Governments recognise that Israel and the Arab States all need to maintain a certain level of armed forces for the purposes of assuring their internal security and their legitimate self-defence and to permit them to play their part in the defence of the area as a whole. All applications for arms or war material for these countries will be considered in the light of these principles. In this connexion the three Governments wish to recall and reaffirm the terms of the statements made by their representatives on the Security Council on 4th August, 1949,[5] in which they declared their opposition to the development of an arms race between Israel and the Arab States.

(b) 'The . . .[4] Governments declare that assurances have been received from all the countries of the Middle East to which they permit arms to be supplied from their countries that the purchasing country does not intend to undertake any act of aggression against any other state in the Middle East.'

8. The wording of the last paragraph above is still tentative.

9. There is the particular difficulty in our own case that specifically to make the continued supply of arms in accordance with Treaty obligations conditional upon some assurance not provided for by treaty might be contrary to our treaty obligations. We are trying to get round this by obtaining the assurances at least from Egypt, Jordan and Iraq before we make the statement, and wording the paragraph accordingly. Egypt has in fact already given an assurance somewhat on these lines but we are seeking a re-affirmation.[6]

10. If we can in fact obtain assurances of non-aggression both from the

---

[5] At the 434th meeting of the U.N. Security Council on 4 August 1949, the U.K. representative, Sir T. Shone, stated that the British Government did not 'wish anything in the nature of an arms race . . . to develop in the Middle East or anywhere else. Far from it. Any supplies of arms which we may send would be for the internal security and defence requirements of the States concerned. These are legitimate requirements for any State, and, in so far as the Middle East is concerned, are indeed essential to the normal conditions which we wish to see restored. We, for our part, would not be in favour of Middle Eastern States acquiring war *matériel* in excess of their legitimate defence requirements, and we believe the States themselves would not wish to exceed such limitations' (*U.N. Security Council: Official Records 4th Year*, No. 36, p. 21).

[6] The assurances requested of Egypt and Jordan on 11 May were given on 13 May.

Arab States and Israel, this will of course have a great advantage in itself, apart from its connexion with the supply of arms, and such assurances taken together would almost amount to an internal non-aggression pact in the Middle East.

11. The Anglo-American (and perhaps French) declaration, coupled with these assurances if we can obtain them, would also have a stabilising influence between Saudi Arabia and the Hashemite States.

12. The above declaration would not automatically oblige us to supply arms and war material to Israel, nor oblige the Americans to supply arms or war material to any Middle East State. (They are at present supplying rifles only.) But it ought to ease the position, and remove some of the difficulties about our supplying arms to Israel if we wish to do so, either immediately or a little later on.

13. The question of timing and method presents complications with which I need not trouble you in detail. They are being discussed between the two Delegations. But I should explain that on the one hand it would be preferable for the declaration to be made at the end of the Atlantic Council meeting; on the other hand, the Arab League is now meeting in Cairo, and both we and the Americans are agreed that it is undesirable for this matter to be raised there if we can avoid it. It is better to deal direct with the Governments individually, and we may therefore have to wait until the Arab League meeting is over.

14. Finally, there is the question of the association of France with such a declaration. This might be done either by making it a joint Three-Power declaration, or alternatively by the Americans and ourselves making simultaneous and, if possible, identic declarations, leaving the French to do the same if they wish. This is still under discussion between our delegations.

15. We cannot make much further progress until we hear further, as we hope to do within the next two or three days, whether Egypt and Jordan, and perhaps Iraq, are willing to give us, or to reaffirm, the necessary assurances.

16. Meanwhile, I should like to have your approval for pursuing this general line. We cannot yet be sure that we shall succeed in reaching agreement on such a declaration, but it seems well worth doing our best to get it if we can.[7]

ERNEST BEVIN

[7] On 14 May Mr. Attlee minuted: 'I agree with this line of policy'.

No. 98

Record of Fifth Tripartite Ministerial Meeting held in Lancaster House on Saturday, 13 May 1950, at 10.30 a.m.

[ZP 2/192]

Top secret

Present:

United Kingdom Mr. Ernest Bevin, Mr. Patrick Gordon-Walker, Mr. Kenneth Younger, Sir William Strang, Lord Henderson, Mr. Ernest Davies, Sir Roger Makins (Item III), Gen. Sir Brian Robertson (Item VI), Mr. Dening (Item I), Mr. Wright (Item II), and other Advisers.

United States Mr. Dean Acheson, Mr. Lewis Douglas, Mr. Cooper, Dr. Jessup, Mr. Harriman, Mr. Bruce, Mr. McCloy (Item VI), and other Advisers.

France M. Schuman, M. Massigli, M. Parodi, M. Alphand, M. de Margerie, M. Poncet (Item VI), M. Lebel, and other Advisers.

Secretary-General Mr. Shuckburgh.

    I South-East Asia (MIN/TRI/P/9).[1]
    II Colonial Question (MIN/TRI/P/21).[2]
    III Long-term development of economic relationships between Europe and the United States.
    IV N.A.T.O. (MIN/TRI/P/2, 3, 22 and 28).[3]
    V Migration (MIN/TRI/P/5 and P/25).[4]
    VI Revised declaration by Ministers on Germany (MIN/TRI/P/13).[5]

Item I South-East Asia (MIN/TRI/P/9)

1. MR. BEVIN said that the meeting had before it a paper prepared by officials to which was attached the minute setting out our common position. The French had made reservations on paragraphs 7 and 8 of this minute. He did not know whether his colleagues wished to discuss the document as a whole or whether they could accept the minute and confine discussion to the reserved paragraphs. In any case he invited an exposition of the French views on paragraphs 7 and 8.

2. M. SCHUMAN said he would like to give a brief sketch of the military position in Indo-China. The problem there was after all a common one for the West, and it was only a fitting mark of the solidarity of the three countries that he should explain the position to his colleagues.

3. France had 150,000 French troops engaged together with about 40,000 Irregulars and 60,000 local levies. The cost of the Indo-China campaign was running at 200 billion francs a year out of a total French defence budget of 500 billion francs. The rebels controlled about 90,000

---

[1] No. 56.iii. [2] See No. 68, note 1. [3] See No. 80, note 4. [4] See No. 96, Item II. [5] No. 61.ii.

troops in regular formations together with guerrilla bands, the number of which it was difficult to assess.

4. One of the chief difficulties of the French was that the native troops on their side were not particularly effective unless they were commanded by European officers and n.c.o.s. The provision of these officers and n.c.o.s. depended on the volunteer system in force in France, and the number coming forward was decreasing. It was becoming almost impossible to maintain the establishment at the requisite level. Then again arms and equipment had become worn out in the course of the last four years and it was difficult to replace these items. The rebels on the other hand seemed to be procuring large amounts of arms and their position had been particularly strengthened by the Communist control of China.

5. The French require two types of help from their Allies.

(1) Moral—they were deeply grateful for the step which their Allies had taken in recognising Bao Dai, and
(2) Military—this had to some extent been covered by Mr. Acheson's recent statement in Paris, which had made clear that supplies were to be provided with speed.

6. When the French appealed for their colleagues' help over Indo-China it was only because they considered the campaign there as being waged in the interests of the common cause. While safeguarding the interests of France, the French were also making their contribution and M. Schuman felt that the whole problem should be looked at in this framework. The collapse of the Nationalist Government in China had made the task much more difficult, and the need for help was great. He was, of course, deeply grateful for the continued encouragement and solidarity of his colleagues.

7. Mr. Acheson said that the Indo-China situation had been fully discussed in Paris between him and M. Schuman, and he felt that he understood the French position fully. With regard to the two paragraphs of the text he felt that paragraph 7 was a matter for the French to choose their own wording, and he would not have any objection to some amendment. But paragraph 8 was an interpretation of the United States attitude and if the French wished to amend this paragraph in the sense they had indicated to the American Delegation it would make it extremely embarrassing for him before Congress.

8. M. Schuman said that he accepted Mr. Acheson's statement and agreed that the two paragraphs should be left as they were.[6] He asked what his colleagues had decided about a declaration on Indo-China. The paper before them contained a British and French proposal. The French wanted a joint Tripartite declaration which would affirm the solidarity of the three countries. This solidarity not only arose from actual concrete

[6] In fact paragraph 7 was subsequently amended in the agreed text, circulated as MIN/TRI/P/9 Final and printed in *F.R.U.S. 1950*, vol. iii, pp. 1082–5.

assistance but also had a psychological side. A Tripartite declaration would have an important effect in strengthening the idea of solidarity not only in our own countries but in South-East Asia.

9. MR. BEVIN said that the question of any declaration at all was difficult. A three-Power declaration would be looked on as an attempt to interfere in South-East Asia by three Western Powers while a declaration by Governments in South-East Asia was probably not possible. In pursuance of the United Kingdom proposal we had caused enquiries to be made from our High Commissioners and Ambassadors in the area and all had reported that they thought the Governments of the area would not be prepared to take such a step.[7] Nor would such a declaration, even if we could get individual Governments to make it, necessarily have a good effect on Asian public opinion. For the moment it looked as if the Asian nations were not prepared to come out openly on the side of the West in a matter like this.

10. MR. ACHESON said that in view of what Mr. Bevin had just said and, since the Americans had made a declaration in Paris, it looked as if it was not necessary for a further Tripartite declaration to be made.

11. M. SCHUMAN said he must bow to what Mr. Bevin had said. He knew that the British Government would have liked to have helped the French as much as possible in the matter. It seemed a pity that the Asian nations were not yet ready to face facts and admit that their security was thanks to the West. He thought more action might be taken on the spot to make the Asiatics realise the danger they faced and where their best interests lay.

12. MR. BEVIN said that he appreciated M. SCHUMAN's difficulties. It might be that something further could be done after the Canberra Conference.[8] The Asian nations seemed to have a greater realisation than before of the issues with which they were faced. There was also greater appreciation in the West, including the United States of America, of the importance to be attached to South-East Asia in the common struggle. He thought that after the Canberra Conference a new stage might have been reached on which the problem of Indo-China might be examined afresh. After the Conference he thought we should pick up the threads of Asian feeling which had emerged at the Conference and pursue our course further through the diplomatic channel.

Item II Colonial Question (MIN/TRI/P/21)[2]

13. MR. BEVIN said that he was glad to give his agreement to the paper which the officials had prepared. It lifted the problem on to a new plane, from which it could be dealt with much more satisfactorily than in the past. Roughly there were two recommendations

(1) that our three countries should avoid cross purposes in the United Nations, and

---

[7] See No. 69, note 4.   [8] See No. 4, note 9, and No. 112.ii.

(2) that further conversations on the Colonial Problem were desirable soon.

With regard to Colonial matters, the United Kingdom bore a grave responsibility and its task would be made easier if the approach to the whole problem was governed by the considerations set forth in the paper.

14. M. SCHUMAN said he thought they might take note of the paper as an expression of the views of the three delegations which showed no fundamental disagreement. He thought they could also agree the conclusions of the paper.

15. MR. ACHESON said he thought the paper was a very good document. Great progress had been made in the alignment of views and he was glad to signify his agreement to the document.

16. M. SCHUMAN said that the need for close co-ordination in the United Nations had been put forward in another document which had been looked at by the Conference.[9] He thought in particular the suggestion a good one that the heads of the three delegations to the General Assembly should meet beforehand so as to co-ordinate their points of view. They could thus avoid the disappointments and frictions which had occurred in the past. It would have a great effect on the rest of the world if the three countries adopted a common attitude in the United Nations.

17. MR. BEVIN agreed with M. Schuman and said that the suggestion for a meeting before the Assembly session in the autumn had been agreed to earlier in the Conference.[9]

Item III Long Term Development of Economic Relationships between Europe and the United States

18. At Mr. Bevin's invitation, MR. ACHESON said he had a proposal to make. He thought it would be difficult to proceed with this question now. There seemed to be a certain amount of confusion and misunderstanding on the various solutions put forward. Furthermore, no progress could be made until soundings had been taken of the Canadians. He, therefore, proposed that this item should be passed over, but that each delegation should appoint a representative (who would be Dr. Jessup in the case of the Americans) to meet Mr. Pearson jointly and see whether they could not produce a joint recommendation as to what might be done by the three ministers while they were still in London. They should also recommend how to proceed after the Ministers had left. Representatives should bear in mind and make recommendations on what might be said to the press on the matter. He hoped the representatives could meet that very afternoon and first of all possibly produce some sort of line for the press, even if this was only to say that there had been a meeting between representatives of the Three Powers and Mr. Pearson of Canada, which showed that the whole problem was of joint interest and was being tackled seriously.

[9] See No. 90, Item II and note 2 *ibid.*

348

19. M. SCHUMAN said he agreed with this proposal. The French representative would be M. Alphand.

20. MR. BEVIN agreed and said that Sir Roger Makins would represent the British Delegation.[10]

Item IV N.A.T.O. (MIN/TRI/P/2, 3, 22 and 28)[3]

21. MR. ACHESON said that here, too, he proposed to postpone consideration. There had been a further French amendment since yesterday[11] and a brief discussion between Ministers this morning.[12] He thought the various drafts for the machinery to be set up should be studied by a small group over the week-end and an attempt made to reconcile the various views so that the three countries could go before the Atlantic Council with a unanimous view. The American representative to the small group would be Mr. George Perkins.

22. M. SCHUMAN agreed, and said that the French representative would be M. de Margerie. Mr. Bevin nominated Sir Gladwyn Jebb as the British representative.[13]

Item V Migration (MIN/TRI/P/5 and MIN/TRI/P/25)[4]

23. MR. BEVIN said that the revised paper on Migration, which had now been circulated, had been agreed by the three delegations except for the words in square brackets referring specifically to Germany and Italy.

24. M. SCHUMAN said that he was in agreement with the paper. He would prefer, however, that the countries chiefly interested should be mentioned by name. MR. ACHESON also agreed with the paper and with M. Schuman's suggestion.

25. MR. BEVIN agreed that the square brackets should be removed. The Ministers adopted the paper in this form and agreed that it should be issued to the press.[14]

---

[10] See further No. 107.

[11] MIN/TRI/P/29, for which see No. 80, note 4.

[12] The British record of this meeting, held immediately before the present meeting and which briefly covered the same ground as Items I, III, and IV, is not here printed. For the American record (timed at 10.45 a.m.), see *F.R.U.S. 1950*, vol. iii, pp. 1054–5.

[13] On 16 May Sir G. Jebb recorded that this sub-committee had had a successful meeting that morning: 'I developed the case for the draft we had circulated in terms which (I hope) were acceptable to my American and French colleagues, and a considerable number of delegates present said that they could accept it straight away without reservation . . . the French take the view that their agreement to support it is conditional on our supporting them as regards their "directive" to the proposed Council of Deputies. I do not think that we shall have any real difficulty in supporting their resolution to this effect, though we may have drafting proposals to make.' As regards the site of the new organization 'we can legitimately consider London to be in the bag' (minute on WU 1071/121). For discussion of these drafts by the N.A.C. and the agreed text, see No. 113 and 113.i.

[14] A text of the agreed declaration on migration, published in *The Times* on 15 May and circulated as MIN/TRI/P/25 Final, is at i below. The recommendation in the declaration for a general review by experts of the migration problem was implemented with the opening of a conference in Paris on 24 July, reported in *The Times* on the following day.

26. The revised draft declaration on Germany, prepared by a sub-committee consisting of the three Allied High Commissioners, was circulated.

27. M. SCHUMAN said that the second sentence of the second paragraph of Section 1 concerning reparations, appeared to be inconsistent with a reservation of principle which he had made the day before. He would like it to be made clear that the reference was only to items of capital equipment which were now being delivered as reparations. At MR. BEVIN's suggestion it was agreed that the experts should be asked to devise a form of words to cover this point.

28. With reference to Section 3 in which it was stated that a Study Group would be set up in London, M. SCHUMAN expressed the hope that this would not be taken as ruling out the possibility of occasional meetings in Paris, provided all three Governments were unanimously in favour of such a step. M. Schuman agreed that no specific amendment was required.

29. MR. BEVIN said that the United States delegation wished to issue with the document an Annex setting out in some detail the conditions on which the three Governments would agree to elections in Germany. The British and French delegations did not think that it was wise to do this.

30. MR. ACHESON said that, although he did not wish to insist on the publication of the Annex, he hoped that Mr. Bevin and M. Schuman would consider the point. If a declaration was made in general terms only it would merely repeat what had been said many times before. It would be made stronger if the three Governments now stated precisely and specifically the principle which would govern their actions.

31. M. SCHUMAN was not in favour of issuing the Annex for publication. He thought that a long enumeration of conditions might give the undesirable impression that the Allied Governments were multiplying their difficulties. The High Commissioners could give any necessary amplification of the declaration in oral or other statements to the Germans. MR. ACHESON said that he did not wish to press the point. But it was important that the situation should be avoided in which the Allies said that they wanted free elections, the Russians agreed and then the Allies brought out a long list of conditions. It would be better to make the conditions clear at an earlier stage. M. SCHUMAN said that it was made clear in the paper that the three Governments repeated their offer of last June; this in effect referred the Russians to the conditions which were agreed at that time. MR. BEVIN suggested that the difficulty might be overcome if the document was to end with the words 'for this purpose.' But the High Commissioners were to make clear to the press the essential conditions which would be attached to the proposal for the elections. His understanding of the proposal was that the High Commissioners should in any case communicate this declaration to the Germans and when they did so

they would have a suitable opportunity for making clear what the conditions were. MR. ACHESON agreed to this suggestion. He made the point that the conditions agreed to in Paris in June were secret and had not been published.

32. The draft declaration on Germany was adopted on these conditions, subject to the amendment of the second paragraph. On the advice of the High Commissioners it was agreed that the declaration should be telegraphed to Dr. Adenauer and should be released to the press on the evening of Sunday, 14th May, for publication in Monday mornings's newspapers. MR. BEVIN pointed out that there would be advantages in this arrangement, since few English Sunday papers gave serious treatment to news of this sort, and General Robertson had confirmed that conditions were similar in Germany.[15]

Communiqué

33. It was agreed at Mr. Shuckburgh's suggestion that the drafting committee on the communiqué should meet early in the afternoon. It would then have a draft communiqué ready for consideration by Ministers after their meeting with the representatives of the Benelux countries.

34. It was agreed that the text of a draft declaration to be issued at the end of the Atlantic Council meeting would be considered next week during the meeting of the Council itself.[16]

CALENDARS TO NO. 98

i *13 May 1950f. Published tripartite statements of the London Conference of Foreign Ministers I–VIII*

   I *Communiqué*: see note 16.
   II *Statement on Economic Problems: cooperation between Western Europe and N. America*: see No. 107, note 2.
   III *Declaration on Germany*: see note 15.
   IV *Declaration on Austria*: see No. 108, note 3.

[15] A text of the declaration on Germany, published in *The Times* on 15 May and circulated as MIN/TRI/P/13 Final (*F.R.U.S. 1950*, vol. iii, pp. 1089–91), is at calendar i. On the evening of 13 May a text of the declaration was transmitted to Wahnerheide and a copy communicated to Dr. Adenauer through American channels. The agreed statement of conditions for German unity, originally annexed to the declaration was not released to the press (see further No. 111). The text of the statement was the same as that annexed to MIN/TRI/P/13 at No. 61.ii, printed under date of 14 May in Cmnd. 1152, pp. 129–130.

[16] This meeting was continued at 5 p.m. on 13 May when the terms of the conference communiqué were agreed for release to the press that evening. A text of the communiqué, published in *The Times* on 15 May and circulated as MIN/TRI/P/30, is at calendar i. It was further agreed at this continued meeting that London conference documents should not be printed or circulated in any other form: 'M. *Schuman* said that it would give too great a weight to discussions, which had been merely discussions and not negotiations, if they were printed and circulated in this manner. To do this would consecrate them in too solemn a way' (British record on ZP 2/192).

V *Declaration on Berlin*: see No. 96, note 9.
VI *Statement on repatriation of P.O.W.s from Soviet Union*: see No. 96, note 2.
VII *Declaration on migration*: see note 14 above.
VIII *Statement on supply of arms to Israel and the Arab States*: see No. 109
[Cmd. 7977].

ii *13 May 1950 Tripartite Meeting with Benelux Foreign Ministers*, who are
informed of London discussions and decisions on Germany. Netherlands
concerned that Germany should share burdens as well as benefits of
association in Europe e.g. supply of raw materials for defence. General
concern for Benelux association with work of study group on Germany.
Belgian request for direct negotiations between Belgium and Germany
on frontier adjustments to be further considered by Tripartite Ministers
[C 3411/2514/18].

iii *13 May 1950 Tripartite Meeting with M. Stikker on S.E.A.* Problem of New
Guinea raised by M. Stikker. Mr. Acheson shares Dutch misgivings over
proposed Australian approach to Indonesia for Australian assumption of
former Dutch role in protecting New Guinea from spread of communism.
Mr. Acheson states that U.S. have told Australians that problem of New
Guinea should worked out between Netherlands/Indonesia. M. Stikker warns
that real danger of communism lies more in Indonesia than New Guinea. Mr.
Acheson takes less pessimistic view [FH 1023/1]. British concern for
maintenance of *status quo* in New Guinea explained in F.O. brief for meeting
with Stikker. 'Colonial Office stress that it is undesirable from our point of
view as a colonial power that a precedent should be created for the cession of
colonial territory to a power whose claim is based primarily on geographical
proximity' [FH 1022/45].

No. 99

*Note of an informal meeting of Ministers held at 1 Carlton Gardens on
Monday, 15 May 1950, at 9.45 a.m.*

[*PREM 8/1202*]

Secret

Present:
The Prime Minister, The Lord President of the Council, The Secretary of
State for Foreign Affairs, The Chancellor of the Exchequer.
Sir William Strang, Sir Norman Brook, Mr R.E. Barclay.

The Foreign Secretary gave his colleagues a summary of the discussions
which he had held with the United States Secretary of State and the
French Foreign Minister.

The following were among the points mentioned in the Foreign
Secretary's discussion with his colleagues.

Broad agreement had been reached on a number of miscellaneous points regarding policy towards *Germany*; and a tripartite declaration had been published in the Press that morning.[1] Publication had been delayed for a day in order that Dr. Adenauer might be given an opportunity to see the declaration before it appeared in the Press. This gesture of courtesy seemed likely to have a good effect on the attitude of the Government of Western Germany.

On the preamble to Law 75, M. Schuman could not be persuaded to agree that the German Government should be left with discretion to decide the future ownership of the Ruhr industries. The Foreign Secretary said, however, that he and Mr. Acheson were determined that the preamble should stand unaltered; and it would be made clear to M. Schuman later that day that the majority view must prevail.[2]

The paper on trade between Eastern and Western Germany had been withdrawn, as it was shortly to be discussed in Washington.[3] *The Chancellor of the Exchequer* suggested that further discussion of this question might with advantage be conducted through the North Atlantic Pact Organisation. The Pact, being a military treaty, would provide a better sanction for the conclusion of an agreement designed to prevent supplies of military value from reaching the Russians; and it seemed more likely that pressure could be successfully brought to bear on the Danes and the Dutch against the background of the North Atlantic Treaty. *The Foreign Secretary* undertook to discuss this suggestion with Mr. Acheson.

It had been agreed that further study should be given to the paper on German construction of special ships for export.[4] With a view to the protection of the ship-building industry in the United Kingdom, it was important to bring into account in this further discussion all considerations including Government subsidies to shipbuilding. The discussion should not be allowed to turn solely on the security arguments.

It was now evident that the Russians were not prepared to reach a settlement on the *Austrian Treaty*, presumably because they wished to keep their occupation troops in Austria. The question of occupation costs would be considered later in the week;[5] and *The Foreign Secretary* undertook to keep in touch with the Treasury on this point.

It had been agreed that future policy on *South East Asia* would be discussed through the diplomatic channels in the light of the results achieved at the Sydney Conference.[6] Mr. Acheson was evidently apprehensive of Congress criticism of French 'colonialism' in Indo-China; and he was anxious to secure some evidence that the French Government were prepared to adopt a more progressive constitutional policy there.

Approval had been given to a paper on our attitude towards *Colonial questions* in the United Nations;[7] and it had been agreed that the United States and Canadian representatives would keep in touch with us at the

[1] See No. 98, note 15.   [2] See No. 96, note 13.
[3] For tripartite discussion of MIN/TRI/P/16 on East/West trade (No. 76.i), see No. 96, paragraph 22.
[4] See No. 96, note 6.   [5] See No. 108.   [6] See No. 112.ii.   [7] See No. 98, Item II.

next meeting of the Assembly with a view to concerting a common line.

The Foreign Secretary said that there had also been discussions with Foreign Ministers of other European countries. The Foreign Ministers of the Benelux countries had been informed of the discussions on Germany.[8] And there had been a talk with the Netherlands Foreign Minister about South East Asia.[9] The Dutch were showing signs of anxiety about Australia's attitude towards Dutch New Guinea. They were also troubled by political developments in Indonesia, where a crypto-Communist political party seemed to be gaining ground. The Foreign Secretary had made the suggestion that assistance to Indonesia might be discussed through a conference of Ambassadors, comparable to that which had worked satisfactorily in Rangoon.

In conclusion the Foreign Secretary said that he would prepare for circulation to the Cabinet a summary account of the main features of both the bipartite and the tripartite discussions of the previous week.[10]

The Chancellor of the Exchequer said that satisfactory progress had been made in the preliminary conversations with the Americans about our revised proposals for a *European Payments Union*. It was hoped that these preliminary conversations would be concluded that afternoon. The way would then be clear to open the discussions in Paris.[11]

[8] See No. 98.ii. [9] See No. 98.iii.

[10] A summary was accordingly circulated to the Cabinet with related documents as C.P. (50)115 of 22 May (not printed from CAB 129/40).

[11] See No. 88, note 4.

No. 100

Memorandum from Sir I. Kirkpatrick to Mr. Bevin

[*C 3472/270/18*]

Top secret   FOREIGN OFFICE, *15 May 1950*

Emergency Planning in Germany

You will remember that early in April I consulted you about a difficulty that had arisen in connexion with the making of detailed plans to deal with the emergency which would arise if an attack were made upon Western Germany by forces under Soviet direction.

We have always maintained that the initiation of each of the stages of alert provided for in these plans requires political authority and that the United Kingdom High Commissioner must authorise both the initiation in the British Zone of all stages of the plan and specific actions in each stage which have political bearing.

On the other hand the French and United States High Commissioners have not been given any corresponding responsibility and the military authorities in the French and United States zones have been reluctant

354

even to discuss the military plans with their respective High Commissioners.

This situation has so far prevented the working out of properly co-ordinated emergency arrangements between the three High Commissioners. In these circumstances you authorised me to ask the United States and French Ambassadors to urge upon their Governments the necessity of their issuing the necessary instructions and authority to their High Commissioners. I spoke accordingly to Mr. Douglas and M. Baudet. They both agreed personally with our point of view and promised to put the matter to their Governments. No action appears however yet to have been taken.

Meanwhile General Robertson has been discussing the matter with the United States and French High Commissioners. Both of them say that they personally share General Robertson's views. There is, however, apparently difficulty with the military authorities, particularly on the American side, since Mr. McCloy said that he did not expect to be able to reach agreement on the subject with the United States military authorities in Germany on account of the strong differences of opinion between Departments in Washington.

In these circumstances General Robertson considers, and I agree, that it would be very useful if you could draw the attention of Mr. Acheson and M. Schuman to this problem. An opportunity for doing so would probably arise after the proposed meeting of the three Ministers on Thursday next [18 May] to discuss Austria.

If you agree to raise the matter it is suggested that the aim should be to reach agreement between the three Ministers on something like the following formula, which has been suggested by General Robertson:

'It is essential that the Allied Military Commanders in Germany in the formulation of their military plans should recognise that save in immediate emergency they must obtain political approval before taking steps which could have serious political consequences. It is appropriate that such political approval should be conveyed by the High Commissioners acting either on powers delegated to them or on instructions received from their Governments. For this purpose it is important that the High Commissioners should be informed by the Military Commanders as to their plans, and it will be the responsibility of the High Commissioners to determine what steps are likely to have important political consequences and therefore require political approval before they can be taken.'[1]

I. KIRKPATRICK

[1] Mr. Bevin minuted below: 'I agree but give them a reminder I am going to raise it.' At the ministerial meeting on 18 May (see No. 108, note 2), Mr. Bevin proposed Ministers should agree the formula cited above. '*Mr. Acheson* said that his attention had been drawn in Washington to this matter after most of the German experts in the State Department had already left to attend the present conference. He was not therefore in a position to take an

355

immediate decision. The matter was being studied inter-departmentally in Washington. As soon as he returned he would give it his attention and keep his colleagues informed. *M. Schuman* said he personally agreed with the principle of the British proposal and had no objection to it being applied within the frontiers of Germany, but he thought that the matter should also be studied in a wider framework since the Allied forces in Germany were now only a part of the total defence forces of Western Europe.'

No. 101

Memorandum from Mr. Bateman to Sir W. Strang

[*R 1074/1*]

FOREIGN OFFICE, *15 May 1950*

A meeting was held this morning which was attended by Mr. Hare (of the U.S. Delegation), Mr. Wright and myself, *inter alios*, to discuss wh⟨ ⟩her anything should be said concerning Turkey, Greece and Persia by the Secretary of State, Mr. Acheson and M. Schuman at the end of the London Conference.

2. Mr. Hare confirmed that the Turkish Ambassador at Washington had spoken at the State Department in more or less the same terms as those used by M. Acikalin in his conversation with the Minister of State.[1] Mr. Hare also drew attention to an article in yesterday's *Observer* which seemed to show that M. Schuman would not be averse from making some statement dealing with the position of Turkey.

3. I outlined the points made frequently by the Turkish Ambassador over the past six months and, after some discussion, it was agreed that something might with advantage be said by the three Foreign Ministers on the lines of the statements made by the Secretary of State and Mr. Acheson at the time of signing the North Atlantic Treaty.[2] It was agreed that although such statements would not satisfy the Turks in their present mood, they were about all that could be safely said.

4. I undertook to draw up the sort of statement which the Secretary of State might find it convenient to make. It was hoped that Mr. Acheson and M. Schuman might take similar action. I attach a draft.[3] In effect it is no more than the gist of what the Secretary of State said in Parliament on 18th May, 1949, but it strikes me as being *jejune*. A joint and more sonorous statement by the three Foreign Ministers made immediately at the end of the Conference would probably have more effect on the (new) Turkish Government[4] and the Greek Government.[5]

C.H. BATEMAN

[1] See No. 81, note 1.   [2] See No. 75, note 2.

[3] This short draft which reaffirmed Mr. Bevin's statement in the House of Commons on 18 May 1949 and stated British concern for the independence, integrity and security of Greece, Turkey and Persia, is not printed.

[4] The Republican People's government of M. S. Günaltay was defeated in the Turkish General Election on 14 May. A new Democrat government was formed by M. A. Menderes on 22 May.

[5] Sir W. Strang minuted below to Mr. Bevin: 'If nothing at all is said, the Turks (especially) will feel very much left out in the cold. Could you discuss with Mr. Acheson and M. Schuman whether to make an identic statement, or separate statements? The annexed draft is pretty thin, but there is not much more to say. W. Strang 15/3.' Following discussion with Mr. Bevin on the morning of 18 May, a longer British statement was prepared and issued on 19 May together with a separate American statement (both printed in *The Times* of 20 May, p. 4). Advance notice of the British statements was telegraphed to Athens, Ankara and Tehran at 8.55 p.m. on 18 May but the actual text was not transmitted until the following evening. Both the Greek and Turkish Ambassadors subsequently made separate representations about the lack of prior notice. In addition the Turkish Ambassador complained that no answer had been received to his note of 1 May (see No. 81, note 1). It was explained to them that the decision to issue a statement was taken at the end of the conference and the precise text had been drafted at the last minute. Mr. Acheson's statement was only finally approved by him on the train from London to Liverpool, the first stage of his return journey to America. The Turkish Ambassador was further reassured that his memorandum had been drawn to Mr. Bevin's attention and that Turkey had been discussed at the London Conference in the light of these representations (R 1074/3 and RK 1071/11).

No. 102

Note of an informal meeting held at 1 Carlton Gardens on Tuesday, 16 May 1950, at 9.45 p.m.[1]

[CAB 134/23]

Top secret

Present:
The Prime Minister, the Secretary of State for Foreign Affairs, the Secretary of State for Commonwealth Relations.
Mr. Dean Acheson.
Mr. Lester Pearson.
Sir Roger Makins, Mr. C.A.L. Cliffe.

1. *Technical Co-operation*

The Prime Minister said that he and his colleagues were anxious to know if it was possible to do anything to speed up an agreement for tripartite co-operation in atomic energy. He said that considerable progress had already been made, and the prospects of an agreement were beginning to look hopeful, when everything was upset by the Fuchs case.[2] It was now understood that, owing to the summer recess of Congress and the elections to be held in November,[3] it was unlikely that an agreement, even if reached, could come into force before the middle of next year. As a

[1] This record was circulated for information on 17 May as A.E.(M)(50)7 to the Cabinet Ministerial Committee on Atomic Energy by the Joint Secretaries, Mr. C.A. Cliffe and Mr. G.W. Penn, as 'a note of a discussion with Mr. Dean Acheson regarding the possible resumption of the tripartite talks on co-operation in atomic energy' (see No. 19, note 1).
[2] See No. 19, note 2.   [3] See No. 92, note 4.

result of this delay, the United Kingdom would be obliged to go ahead with its own atomic energy programme in full, though Ministers were extremely reluctant to duplicate any part of the work unnecessarily if there was any prospect of an agreement. Among the items on our programme on which we should be forced to go ahead were a range for testing weapons, and the third pile,[4] the construction of which had been held up when it appeared that an agreement might probably be reached. There was no doubt that Parliament and public opinion would demand that we should go ahead with our full programme if no agreement was in prospect. If, on the other hand, an agreement were to be reached, we should be spared the necessity of wasting our resources on a duplicated effort and should be able rather to concentrate on other matters which were vital to our common security. He hoped therefore that Mr. Acheson might be able to suggest some method of making early progress in this difficult matter.

In reply to a question, *Sir Roger Makins* said that, if there was no agreement and no immediate prospect of one, it would be necessary for us to go ahead with our full programme, and this would involve one or two matters on which we should need to consult the United States authorities. On our side we should in general wish to proceed, as far as possible, as if a tripartite agreement were already in force, and we would hope for the collaboration of the United States authorities. Sir Roger Makins cited by way of illustration the instance of a certain raw material (known as KEL-F) which was required for our programme. This material was in no way secret and was on sale commercially; but a licence was required before it could be exported from the United States, and there were indications that such a licence might possibly not be forthcoming. *Mr. Acheson* promised to do what he could to help in this matter, on the understanding that the material was required for the already declared United Kingdom programme.

In reply to a question from Mr. Acheson, *Sir Roger Makins* explained shortly the terms of the *modus vivendi*,[5] which dealt with two main matters,

[4] With reference to this remark, Mr. D.E. Peirson, Ministry of Supply representative on the official committee on Atomic Energy, later drew Sir R. Makins' attention (as chairman) to a meeting of the committee on 16 March at which 'I reported that "on the grounds of raw material shortage alone, it would be impossible to proceed with a third pile for several years". This statement was supported in the paper which I subsequently put into the Committee . . . As to the weapon testing range, it was agreed at the last Official Committee that, subject to the views of the Chiefs of Staff, the Prime Minister and the Minister of Defence, Lord Tedder should be asked to seek U.S. agreement in principle to our using the Eniwetok range in preference to building a range of our own' (letter of 19 May on UE 1245/76). For the background to plans for a third pile to produce plutonium at Windscale, and the question of a weapons range, see M. Gowing, *op. cit.*, vol. i, pp. 219, 286–7, 446–7 and vol. ii, pp. 379–402, 476–9.
[5] The text of the tripartite agreement on atomic energy, known at the *modus vivendi*, endorsed at a meeting of the Combined Policy Committee on 7 January 1948, is printed in M. Gowing, *op. cit.*, vol. i, pp. 266–72. This *modus vivendi* provided for very limited resumption of the Anglo-American-Canadian atomic cooperation terminated by the

the allocation of raw materials and the exchange of technical information. He said that the *modus vivendi* had expired at the end of 1949. As regards raw materials, a temporary agreement had been reached to cover the current year. The arrangements for technical co-operation, however, had never been fully implemented. A certain amount of exchange was provided for, but on too small a scale to be satisfactory.

Mr. Acheson said that he fully appreciated the anxiety of the United Kingdom to shorten the time which now appeared to be necessary before an agreement could be reached, but it was very difficult to suggest any way in which this could be achieved. There was no doubt that the Fuchs case had left public opinion in the United States in a very sensitive state. Moreover, when the tripartite talks had been suspended, though we had come fairly close together on the military side, there still remained a considerable gap to be bridged on the development aspects.

Mr. Acheson said that both the Department of Defence and the Atomic Energy Commission were convinced that they would be debarred by the MacMahon Act in its present form from doing a number of things which would become necessary if an agreement was reached. Nor was there any possibility of by-passing the MacMahon Act, since this might render individual scientists, who might be working on the type of integrated programme envisaged by the agreement, liable to prosecution. It was therefore inevitable that, before any agreement could be put into effect, legislation to amend the MacMahon Act should be introduced into Congress. He thought that in the present state of mind of Congress it would be most unwise to attempt this before they adjourned in July, even if it were possible to reach agreement in so short a time. The elections were due in November, and it was probable that the present Congress would not meet again between its July adjournment and that date. The new Congress would not meet until January, and it therefore seemed that there was very little prospect of speeding up the bringing into effect of an agreement.

Mr. Acheson thought that the proposed talks on security standards might do much to ease the situation. Once the question of security standards had been settled, he hoped that there would be a calmer atmosphere and that it would be possible to proceed in an unostentatious way to further discussions. He did not think that there should be any pre-arranged plan for these, but that events should be left to take their own course. In any event it was essential that such talks should be held with the minimum publicity, in order to avoid any possible public reaction; with this object in view, it would be best that any negotiations should be conducted by Sir Oliver Franks. Mr. Acheson undertook to review the whole position with Mr. Louis Johnson and the Atomic Energy Commission on his return to the United States.[6]

McMahon Act of 1946 (text printed in R.G. Hewlett and O.E. Anderson, *The New World 1939/1946*, vol. i – Pennsylvania, 1962 – pp. 714–22).

[6] It appears that this promised review did not take place and despite successful security

2. International Control

Mr. Pearson raised the question of resuming the talks on the international control of atomic energy. He said that Russian propaganda had been making much play with the fact that the Vyshinsky proposals for control[7] had not been accepted, and had been arguing that therefore the responsibility for failing to reach agreement lay with the other Powers and not with Russia. Owing to the suspension of the Six-Power talks,[8] it had not been possible for the Western Powers to expose the fallacies of the Vyshinsky proposals. Mr. Pearson suggested that the six Powers might perhaps now meet again for this purpose. He recognised that it would not be possible to include a Chinese representative; but the Chinese had never done much at these meetings and the Six-Power Group was in any case quite informal in its construction. Even if the Russians did not agree to take part in the resumed talks (and it was not likely that they would), a resumption of the talks would put the Western Powers in a stronger position to counter Russian propaganda on the subject. He appreciated the fears of the Foreign Office that, if it was proposed to resume the talks but to exclude China from them, both of the Chinese factions might raise objections; but he did not think that any such possibility should be allowed to stand in the way of the resumption of talks on an unofficial basis.

Mr. Acheson and *The Foreign Secretary* said that they would like to give further thought to Mr. Pearson's suggestion.

talks with the Americans in June the official committee on atomic energy was so concerned at the lack of movement on the atomic energy front, including continued difficulties over securing supplies of KEL-F, as to instruct Sir O. Franks on 6 July to raise the question again with Mr. Acheson. Sir O. Franks replied to Sir R. Makins on 7 July that he had spoken accordingly to Mr. Acheson on 6 July. 'Acheson said that it had been physically impossible for him yet to have his projected meeting with Louis Johnson, latter had recently been away in Japan and [? he] had himself had had [*sic*] to make a series of speeches. Now that Korean crises had intervened and made it impossible to find time to discuss atomic energy matters. 3. I impressed on Acheson the importance which you attached to the matter and the increasingly embarrassing situation in which you found yourselves owing to the lack of any firm indication of the American views. I am afraid however that Acheson is thinking almost entirely of Korea at the moment and that he is unlikely to interest himself very actively in atomic energy questions for the time being. We will however of course continue to keep up the pressure on the Americans' (telegram ANCAM 334 on UE 1245/100).

[7] See No. 37, note 6. [8] See No. 5, note 4.

No. 103

General Sir B. Robertson (Wahnerheide) to Mr. Bevin
(Received 17 May, 6.54 p.m.)

No. 757 Telegraphic [C 3357/2514/18]

Confidential   WAHNERHEIDE, *17 May 1950, 5.30 p.m.*

Repeated Saving to Paris, Washington, Berlin.

The High Commissioners met the Federal Chancellor on 16th May to give him further information about the London Conference.[1]

2. McCloy as Chairman opened with a long introduction designed to show how wide a field the Conference had had to cover, and how relatively small a part of that field Germany had been. Dealing with the Declaration on Germany he underlined the passages dealing with democracy and individual freedom, and emphasised that now, in the opinion of the Foreign Ministers, the presence of relatively large numbers of occupying troops in the Federal Republic was due less to the normal requirements of occupation than to the need to protect and defend the Federal Republic against external threats. The key-note of the Declaration was its re-affirmation of the intention to grant Germany progressive independence, with a disposition on the part of the Occupying Powers to interfere as little as possible and to help as much as possible.

3. He then handed to the Chancellor a set of some of the documents of the Conference,[2] the only one new to him being the terms of reference of the Study Group, showing it had been given a number of tasks beyond consideration of the Occupation Statute. McCloy said a word of explanation about each of them, and added that though the Study Group would be based on London it might at times visit Paris or Germany.

He informed the Chancellor that our Governments would shortly be protesting to the Soviet Government about the militarised police in the Russian Zone,[3] and told him that the Benelux representatives in London had agreed to increase their purchases from Berlin, and that Mr. Harriman was going to stimulate all other O.E.E.C. countries to do likewise.

4. He mentioned that M. Monnet would soon come to Germany to impart further details of M. Schuman's Plan to the High Commission and

---

[1] A verbatim record of this meeting with Dr. Adenauer, summarized below, held at 3.30 p.m. on 16 May is entered on F.O.1005/1126.

[2] These documents were (i) the declaration on Germany (No. 98.i) of which an advance text had been transmitted to Dr. Adenauer prior to publication on 15 May; (ii) terms of reference of the International Study Group on Germany (MIN/TRI/P/12 Final: No. 95, note 9); (iii) declaration on Berlin (No. 98.i); (iv) statement on repatriation of German prisoners of war from the Soviet Union (No. 98.i); (v) security guarantee for Germany (see No. 104 and 104.i); (vi) declaration on migration (No. 98.i); (vii) statement on the Schuman Plan (cf. No. 84, note 13).

[3] See No. 96, note 14.

to the Federal Government.[4] M. Francois-Poncet added that the procedure contemplated for developing the Schuman proposal was that the French Government would shortly ask the various governments concerned whether or not they wished to participate in a study group to be established in the near future to work out further details. The Federal Government would of course be invited to participate. The Study Group's task would be to make precise the general terms of the proposal, and M. Monnet's visit to Germany was a first step to this end.

5. I then said a word or two on the London Declaration, emphasising that the Chancellor should take the document as meaning precisely what it said, and as not representing in any way either propaganda or mere amiabilities. In my opinion this Declaration should be regarded as ending the era the theme of which had been concessions by the Occupying Powers to Germany, and I defined a concession as something extracted by importunacy or pressure and given grudgingly. From now on, the Foreign Ministers expected that the era of unilateral concessions would be replaced by one of co-operation.

6. The Chancellor expressed his thanks for what we had said, and his gratitude to the Foreign Ministers for having communicated the Declaration to him direct. It had been perfectly clear to him from the scope of the Conference that no concrete decisions on particular problems affecting Germany could be reached at it. He greeted in particular the establishment of the Study Group, and the news that its task was not limited to considering the Occupation Statute. Some German Papers had been complaining that the Federal Government would not be represented on the Study Group, but he himself was glad that it should not. It would be embarrassing for the Federal Government to have to participate in drawing up an Occupation Statute to be applied to the Federal Republic. From his point of view, the possibility that representatives of the Federal Government might be heard from time to time in the course of the Study Group's work, and would be allowed to furnish documentary material to it, was quite sufficient. He well understood what McCloy had said about the termination of the State of War, and hoped that practical solutions of various difficulties could be found which would not embarrass the Occupying Powers in their domestic concerns.

7. He went on to repeat his welcome for the Schuman Plan, and observed that the mention of Africa gave it particular significance, particularly for the over-populated regions of Western Europe. He added that he thought the French would agree with him that, in the preparatory stages of discussion to be devoted to elucidating the plan, the politicians should stand aside. He concluded by observing once more that he had been specially satisfied with the whole tone and form of the declaration on Germany which he regarded as ending one chapter and beginning

[4] For a report of a meeting between M. J. Monnet, Commissioner General of the Plan for the modernization and equipment of France, and the High Commissioners in Germany on 23 May, see Volume I, No. 39.

another. The Federal Government would now proceed with all its energy along the road indicated by the Foreign Ministers' Declaration.

Foreign Office please pass to Paris and Washington as my Savingrams Nos. 185 and 197 respectively.

No. 104

General Sir B. Robertson (Wahnerheide) to Mr. Bevin
(Received 17 May, 2.45 p.m.)

No. 752 Telegraphic [*C 3372/27/18*]

Priority. Top secret   WAHNERHEIDE, *17 May 1950, 11.40 a.m.*

Repeated to Bad Oeynhausen (H.Q., B.A.O.R. personal for C-in-C).

The following is brief summary of discussion between the High Commissioners and the Federal Chancellor in secret session yesterday.[1]

2. McCloy from the chair gave the Chancellor the reply to his request for a security guarantee in accordance with the instructions given by Ministers in London.[2] He handed a written text of this reply to the Chancellor and supplemented it with the oral explanations provided in our instructions. In reply the Chancellor said that he would study the text given to him carefully and hoped that it would go some way towards relieving his pre-occupations. However, he doubted whether it would satisfy entirely the fears of the German people. Reports had appeared in the press to the effect that the Western Allies intended to adopt the Rhine as their line of defence.[3] Not only did this mean abandoning most of the Federal territory but also he feared that unless the Soviet advance were checked east of the Rhine it would not be halted at all until it reached the Atlantic. After McCloy and I had made obvious rejoinders to this remark, the Chancellor said that he quite understood that military authorities could not fix their main line of defence on the line on which first contact would be made. However, he considered that it should be made clear that the Western Allies would do battle with the Soviet troops immediately they crossed the zonal border and would thereafter do their utmost to throw these troops back. The Chancellor is likely to refer to this question again at our next meeting after he has studied the text of our reply, and I feel that the High Commissioners might then make some further statement in satisfaction of his last observation.

[1] This executive session followed the general meeting recorded in No. 103. In addition to the discussion summarized below it would appear that during this session Dr. Adenauer was promised a copy of the statement of conditions for German unity, appended to but not released with the declaration on Germany (see No. 98, note 15 and further No. 111).

[2] These instructions were contained in MIN/TRI/P/10 Final approved at the fourth tripartite ministerial meeting (No. 96, paragraphs 3–4): text at i below.

[3] Cf. No. 30, paragraph 38(*c*) and No. 60.

3. McCloy then spoke of the proposal to form a Federal Police Force or Gendarmerie. He opened by saying that Ministers had come to the conclusion that a good case for the formation of such a force could be established.[4] I was glad to hear him go so far as this and to note that Francois Poncet did not demur. The following points emerged during the subsequent discussion.

(a) The Chancellor, like ourselves, does not feel that it would be appropriate to call this force a police. He seemed to be favourably attracted by the proposal that it should be called a Republican Guard.

(b) The Chancellor was not disturbed by the suggestion that the initial strength of the force should be considerably below the figure for which he had asked.

(c) The Chancellor gave it as his opinion that this force should have no powers of arrest save those which are accorded to every private citizen, namely, to intervene when a flagrant breach of the law is being committed.

(d) It was agreed to appoint a committee of four individuals representing the three High Commissioners and the Chancellor to investigate this question further and make recommendations.[5]

CALENDAR TO NO. 104

1 *22 May 1950 MIN/TRI/P/10 Final*: Security guarantee for Germany as approved on 12 May: see No. 96, note 10 [C 3139/2514/18].

[4] See No. 96, paragraphs 33–41.
[5] After prolonged investigations the Allied High Commissioners informed Dr. Adenauer in a letter of 28 July (printed in *F.R.U.S. 1950*, vol.iv, pp. 701–2) that they were unable to authorize the formation of a Federal Police Force but were prepared to lift the ban on paragraph 2 of article 91 of the Basic Law, which authorized the Federal Government to place Land Police Forces under its temporary control during an emergency, and to give approval to the setting up in each Land of a specially trained and equipped Mobile Police Force totalling 10,000 men. Discussions then began between representatives of the A.H.C. and Federal Government to work out the details of establishing Land forces.

No. 105

Memorandum from Mr. Furlonge to Mr. Bevin

[E 1023/60]

FOREIGN OFFICE, 17 May 1950

Proposed Statement on the Middle East
Approach to Israel

We have now obtained from Egypt and Jordan the necessary assurances that they will not undertake aggression against any other Middle Eastern state.[1] We are about to approach Iraq and Saudi Arabia, the only other two Arab States to which we have so far supplied arms, for similar assurances.[2]

2. The Americans have now told us that they obtained a satisfactory assurance in this sense from Israel last February. The question is whether we should now ask Israel for a similar assurance.

3. Meanwhile we have agreed with the Americans on the official level that it would be desirable for our representatives at Tel Aviv jointly to approach the Israel Government just before our proposed statement is issued, with the object of explaining its purpose and implications to them. It would be possible for H.M. Minister to request the assurance referred to above in the course of this approach.

4. On the other hand, it may be valuable for us in the future to have obtained such an assurance from Israel. Moreover if any Arab Government hesitates to give us an assurance, it would probably assist us to persuade them if we could say that Israel had given us an assurance.

5. Since we have not so far supplied arms to Israel, it is not necessary, for the purposes of the proposed statement, for us to obtain this assurance. Moreover for us to approach them now would risk giving them the impression that we were about to agree to supply arms to them.

6. Before therefore we make any approach to the Israelis in connection with our proposed statement, it is desirable to decide whether or not we intend to modify our present ban on the supply of arms to Israel.

7. Arguments in favour of relaxing the ban are:

(a) Increasing Parliamentary pressure here;
(b) the importance of eventually integrating Israel into our Middle East defence plans, for which purpose her equipment should as far as possible be British;
(c) the fact that (as submitted on other papers)[3] we may find it difficult to refrain from supplying arms to Syria and the Lebanon.

---

[1] See No. 97, note 6.
[2] Assurances were obtained from Iraq on 19 May and Saudi Arabia on 24 May.
[3] This separate submission by Mr. Furlonge on 17 May is not printed from E 1192/96.

8. Arguments against relaxing the ban are:

(1) The state of our relations with Egypt;
(2) recent indications from Syria and elsewhere that the Arab States are liable to flirt with Russia, owing to their increasing fears of Israel and opposition to fancied American support of Israel;
(3) possible adverse effect on our relations in other Arab countries, particularly Iraq, on which our representatives in the Middle East have expressed much apprehension;
(4) the possibility that if we, as well as the Americans, now begin to supply arms to Israel, the Arab States' fears of Israel will increase and the chances of inducing them to negotiate with Israel will be correspondingly reduced.

9. Rulings are therefore requested on the following points:

(a) Whether we should modify our policy on arms to Israel;
(b) whether we should endeavour to obtain an assurance of non-aggression from Israel when we inform the Israel Government of our intention of issuing a statement.[4]

G.W. Furlonge

[4] Mr. Wright supported this submission in a minute below of 17 May in favour of securing assurances from Israel but against supplying arms to Israel for the time being. Mr. Bevin minuted: 'I will decide this later E.B.'. On 19 May Mr. Furlonge recorded 'At a meeting in the Secretary of State's room on May 18, the Secretary of State stated that he did not wish us to obtain a non-aggression assurance from Israel at this stage, but that he wished Sir K. Helm, when he proceeded with his American colleague to inform the Israel Government of the contents of our proposed declaration on the Middle East, to state that we had heard from the Americans of the assurance they had given in February last to the U.S. Government and that we accepted this as being satisfactory to us'. Shortly before the issue of the Middle East statement (see No. 98.i and No. 109, note 2), Mr. Ernest Davies represented to Mr. Bevin in a minute of 23 May the 'strong feeling in the [Labour] Party over our discrimination against Israel in the supply of arms'. Mr. Davies recommended that in the event of an approach from the Israeli Government, consideration should be given to lifting the arms ban on condition that the Israeli Government gave (a) a non-aggression assurance direct to H.M.G. (b) information on their existing defence arrangements and stocks of armaments. On 26 May Mr. Davies recorded: 'I saw the Secretary of State today and he said that the Three Power statement on the Middle East has now disposed of this matter. I explained the doubts which still remain as to whether the statement definitely ends the ban on arms to Israel and the discrimination in making arms available to the Middle East. He stated that there is no ban. He said he accepted the assurance given by Israel to the United States and that country can now make its application for arms in the normal way. It is now the responsibility of the Chiefs of Staff and the Supply Departments to decide whether arms are available for Israel if she makes application. We have no objection to arms being shipped in accordance with the conditions of the statement' (E 1192/103).

No. 106

Memorandum from Mr. Furlonge to Mr. Bevin

[E 1023/93]

FOREIGN OFFICE, 17 May 1950

Proposed Statement on the Middle East
The Approach to the French

The attached draft statement[1] has now been agreed with the State Department, subject to Presidential approval.

2. It has also been cleared with the Chiefs of Staff here. The Legal Adviser, who has been consulted, is of the opinion that it does not conflict with our Treaty obligations to Egypt, Jordan and Iraq, and that the last section (as was intended) implies an obligation to act jointly with the United States and France if they are prepared to act in the event of frontier violation, but does not preclude us from taking action ourselves if either or both of them decline to act.

3. The French have not hitherto been approached pending agreement between ourselves and the Americans on the text. But the State Department, in approving the draft, have strongly urged that it should now be submitted to the French in the hopes that they will be prepared to associate themselves with it. It is suggested that the best course would be for the Secretary of State and Mr. Acheson jointly to present it to M. Schuman on Thursday, May 18.

4. The State Department are most anxious that the statement should issue as soon as possible. For this purpose it will be necessary that all the assurances required under the terms of section 2 of the statement should have previously been obtained; i.e. that the U.K. should obtain assurances from—

Egypt, Iraq, Jordan and Saudi Arabia;
The U.S. from—
Israel, Syria and Egypt;
and France from—
Syria, The Lebanon and possibly Israel.

Of these, we have obtained assurances from Egypt and Jordan and are asking for them from Iraq and Saudi Arabia.[2] The Americans have obtained them from Israel and Egypt and will require to approach Syria.

The French may wish to approach Syria, the Lebanon and perhaps Israel.

5. We and the Americans recommend that in approaching M. Schuman, the Secretary of State and Mr. Acheson should take the following general line.

[1] Not attached to filed copy. It would appear from the file that the draft statement originally attached to this minute was the final draft: published text at No. 98.i.
[2] See No. 105, note 2.

(*a*) We and the Americans are being subjected to considerable pressure, which has not so far been exerted on the French, in regard to our supplies of arms to the Arab States. We have therefore thought it desirable to indicate publicly that our policies in this respect are based on identical principles.

(*b*) We wish at the same time to make the maximum possible contribution towards the pacification of the Middle East, by expressing our opposition to any use of force either between Arab States or between the Arab States and Israel.

(*c*) In view of French interest in the Middle East, we have thought it right to give the French the opportunity of associating themselves with this statement if they so desire. If they find themselves unable to do this, they might wish to issue a statement more or less simultaneously on the same general lines as ours, which we would propose in any event to issue.

(*d*) If the French decide to participate in our statement, it will be necessary for them to obtain assurances of non-aggression from the Middle Eastern states to which they have supplied arms, as we and the Americans have already done.

6. The Americans feel strongly, and we agree, that neither they nor we should alter the text of the statement now that it has been agreed between us. It is suggested that M. Schuman should be left in no doubt on this point.[3]

G.W. FURLONGE

[3] This submission, countersigned by Mr. Wright and initialled by Mr. Bevin, was presumably discussed at the meeting in Mr. Bevin's room on 18 May: see No. 105, note 4.

No. 107

Mr. Bevin to Sir E. Hall-Patch (Paris)

No. 227 Telegraphic [*UR 1019/2*]

Immediate. Confidential   FOREIGN OFFICE, *18 May 1950, 2.20 p.m.*

Repeated to Washington, Ottawa and Saving to Brussels, The Hague, Oslo, Stockholm, Copenhagen, Lisbon, Rome.

There has been discussion in the tripartite meetings of an item originally proposed by the French on the agenda dealing with the development of long-term economic relationships between North America and Western Europe. As a result it was agreed to consult the Canadian representatives.[1]

[1] See No. 98, paragraphs 18–20, and *F.R.U.S. 1950*, vol. iii, pp. 1069–71 for the first meeting with the Canadian representative, Mr. N. Robertson, on 15 May (British record on UEE 139/8). After further meetings on 16 and 17 May, agreement was reached on an American draft which Sir R. Makins described as 'somewhat vague but it safeguards our two

2. The result is a statement by the four governments, the text of which is contained in my immediately following telegram.[2] It is being issued at 5.30 p.m. our time today.

3. The following points should be borne in mind about this statement:

(*a*) It represents a United States desire to point to work in Europe which will match the work which will be undertaken by Mr. Gordon Gray.

(*b*) It relates to the immediate future and to the group of problems which can be described briefly as 'dollar gap' problems.

(*c*) It does not prejudice in any way the development of Article 2 of the Atlantic Pact.

(*d*) It does not set up new machinery. The working relationship between O.E.E.C. (Organisation for European Economic Cooperation) and Canada and the United States will be 'on an informal basis'. Therefore the questions (1) of the form of association of Canada and the United States and Western Europe in regard to economic problems after 1952, and (2) of the possible association of other countries in some way with the Atlantic Pact organisation in the future are left entirely open.

4. For your confidential information the initiative in this matter originally came from the French who were anxious to steer the consideration of economic problems away from the Atlantic Pact, since they do not want Germany to be associated directly or indirectly with the Pact organisation though this objection is not shared either by the United States Government or His Majesty's Government. The French objective however coincided with a short-term American objective of facilitating the task of Mr. Gordon Gray. We and the Canadians were anxious not to prejudice the future in any way, especially the development of Article 2 of the Atlantic Pact, and we have therefore insisted on emphasising the short-term and provisional aspects of the proposed relationship between the O.E.E.C., Canada and the United States.[3]

essential points, namely, the development of machinery under Article 2 of the Atlantic Pact and the future organisation for associating North America and Western Europe' (minute of 17 May on UR 1019/4). In a later minute of even date Sir R. Makins informed Mr. Bevin: 'The Canadian Government have now agreed to this statement with a few minor amendments and a more extensive reference to Article 2 of the Atlantic Pact with which we can agree. If you approve also it is proposed to issue the statement at noon tomorrow.' Mr. Bevin minuted 'I agree' (UR 1019/4).

[2] Not printed. This telegram, timed at 2.35 p.m. on 18 May, contained the approved text published in *The Times* on 19 May. This text was later amended at Dr. Stikker's request to include reference to his having been consulted: final text at No. 98.i.

[3] On 20 May Sir E. Hall-Patch was instructed to pursue with the French delegation to the O.E.E.C. the question of how to set up the proposed informal working relationship between the O.E.E.C., the United States and Canada. Detailed proposals were subsequently worked out between the British and French delegations for consideration by the O.E.E.C. Council at their meeting on 2 June when it was agreed to invite Canada and the United States to become associate members. Canadian and U.S. Representatives took their places in the O.E.E.C. at the next Council meeting on 6–7 July.

No. 108

Mr. Bevin to Sir H. Caccia[1] (Vienna)

No. 211 Telegraphic [C 3413/1/3]

Immediate. Secret   FOREIGN OFFICE, 18 May 1950, 11.40 p.m.

Repeated to Washington, Moscow and Saving to Paris.

At their meeting this afternoon the three Foreign Ministers decided on course to be adopted by the Deputies in the Austrian Treaty negotiations.[2]

(a) As soon as Soviet shewed themselves ready to complete the Treaty, we should settle the unagreed Articles as quickly as possible and on best terms we can get;

(b) Until then our present position on each unagreed Article should be maintained;

(c) We should continue to place responsibility for delay on Soviet Deputy's attitude over Article 48-bis and his introduction of other pretexts, besides emphasising our own desire to settle *all* outstanding issues; and

(d) Continuity of negotiations should be maintained, but frequent meetings on present basis are undesirable and Deputies should not therefore as a rule meet more frequently than every six to eight weeks.

2. My immediately following telegram[3] contains full text of declaration on Austria which the three Ministers then approved. This will not be published until Saturday morning 20th May in order that it may first be conveyed to the Austrian Government. 'It has already been given to Austrian Minister in London.

3. The last paragraph of this declaration announces the decision of the three Governments to civilianise their High Commissioners neither the French nor the United States Government can yet say when change will be made so far as they are concerned. So far as His Majesty's Government is concerned further telegrams will be sent to you.

4. In making this decision the three Foreign Ministers agreed among themselves but *not* for publication that this change should involve no

[1] H.M. Minister in Austria.

[2] The British record of the sixth tripartite ministerial meeting at 2.30 p.m. on 18 May is not here printed from ZP 2/192. This record covered discussion on Austria, as indicated below and Germany for which see No. 100, note 1. Also discussed at this meeting, though not included in the official record was the Middle East statement (separate record at No. 109). Discussion on Austria at this meeting concerned the Western Deputies report, MIN/TRI/P/20 (See No. 59, note 3), on which a decision had been deferred at the fourth tripartite meeting on 12 May (No. 96, Item III). The recommendations in Part 1 of MIN/TRI/P/20 were approved, though recommendation C of Part II was referred for further study.

[3] Not printed. For a text of the declaration on Austria, published in *The Times* on 20 May and printed in *F.R.U.S. 1950*, vol. iii, pp. 1071–2, see No. 98.i.

break in the continuity of western representation on the Allied Council, that it would not prejudice any necessary military action and that it would in no way diminish the protection given to Austria by our military forces.

5. The three Ministers agreed that the text of the declaration should be sent to you for communication as soon as possible to the Austrian Government. Please give copies of it to your French and United States colleagues and arrange with them whether you convey it to the Austrian Government on behalf of the three Foreign Ministers or whether you all act together.

6. The Austrian Minister here expressed the view that Dr. Gruber[4] would be disappointed at the terms of the Declaration not so much as regards treaty tactics, on which he thought the decision would cause little surprise, as on lack of detail regarding concrete measures intended for lightening burden of occupation. He cited particularly occupation costs. Dr. Wimmer's attention was drawn to statement of intentions at end of second paragraph of which decision announced in third paragraph was the first fruits. If more detail was not given in the declaration of other measures intended this did not mean that other steps would not be taken they were still under study as was question of occupation costs though it would be a mistake to nourish optimistic hopes on this score so far as His Majesty's Government were concerned.

7. Dr. Coreth[5] indicated that in his view Gruber's reaction might be less unfavourable than the Minister had suggested.

8. You and your colleagues have adequate material to explain if necessary why the Ministers were regretfully unable to meet Austrian Government's wishes regarding treaty tactics. If you consider it necessary you will no doubt draw attention to the first paragraph of the declaration and to the decision announced at end of the second.[6]

[4] Austrian Foreign Minister.

[5] Austrian representative in London for the Treaty discussions.

[6] On 22 May Sir H. Caccia reported in his telegram No. 182 that the declaration on Austria 'had generally favourable reception in Austria. But the fact has not escaped the notice of the Austrian Government that we have turned down their two main requests i.e. we have rejected their proposals on treaty tactics [? and we] and the French will not pay occupation costs out of our own pockets . . . The Minister of Foreign Affairs' only comment when thanking the Western representatives for their formal communication of the declaration, took the form of two short queries about the appointment of civilian High Commissioners i.e. "can you expedite the names and dates?"' (C 3498/942/3). British announcement on 12 June of the appointment of Sir H. Caccia as civilian High Commissioner in Austria as from 1 August was followed by similar French and American appointments. As regards the treaty negotiations, the U.K. brief on Austria for the New York conference of Foreign Ministers, 12–19 September, recorded that there had been no change in the position since the London conference: 'Since then only two meetings of the Deputies have been held: no progress was made and the Soviet Deputy spent his time arguing that it would be difficult to conclude an Austrian treaty so long as the Western Powers failed to carry out the provisions of the Peace Treaty with Italy which concern Trieste' (ZP 5/40). The brief concluded that there was therefore no point in the Austrian treaty being discussed at New York.

No. 109

Record of a Tripartite Meeting of Ministers on 18 May 1950[1]

[*E 1192/116*]

Top secret

Shipments of Arms to Arab countries and Israel

1. *Mr. Acheson* informed M. Schuman that he and Mr. Bevin had had discussions together on this subject. Both the United States and British Governments had been under strong criticism in connection with the shipment of arms to the Arab states and Israel. In order to meet this situation he and Mr. Bevin had sought statements from all the Middle East countries to whom armaments were being or had been supplied, to the effect that they would not undertake aggression against any other country of the area. The United States and British Governments desired to make it clear in their turn that this was a condition on which they were supplying armaments and also that if there were any attack by one Middle East country on another they would take action both within and outside United Nations to prevent this. They accordingly proposed issuing a public declaration to that effect.

2. As France was also a country from which arms came to the Middle East they had thought it desirable to inform M. Schuman of the above and to enquire whether the French Government would care to associate itself in such a declaration.

4. *M. Schuman* said he would like to examine this suggestion which, though he could not give an immediate answer, seemed to him very sensible. Any shipments of arms from France to the Middle East had been entirely open. There had been certain shipments particularly to Syria, but Israel had been informed in each case. Certain spare parts and munitions which only France could supply were also being sent to other Middle East countries. There was however nothing hidden.

4. *Mr. Acheson* said that the two Ministers had not expected an immediate reply from M. Schuman nor indeed had their approach to him been intended in the slightest degree as a criticism of French action.

5. *Mr. Bevin* said that Syria and the Lebanon had been applying to the United Kingdom for certain arms. His Majesty's Government had not so far authorized the export of war material to Syria and the Lebanon and this was creating considerable annoyance in the countries concerned, who felt that we were discriminating against them. In the light of our general

---

[1] The discussion here recorded evidently took place at the sixth tripartite Ministerial meeting held in Lancaster House on 18 May at 2.30 p.m. (see No. 108, note 2). In a minute of 17 July Mr. A. Maclean recalled that it had been agreed after the meeting to omit the section on the Middle East statement and that the present record was prepared as an 'unofficial, strictly limited, tripartite note'. Mr. Maclean's draft record was transmitted via the American Embassy to the State Department for Mr. Acheson's clearance. The present text is as amended in July by the State Department with British and French concurrence.

understanding with the French Government that we would keep each other fully informed on matters concerning Syria and the Lebanon, we wished to inform M. Schuman of the position. We should probably now wish to allow small quantities of arms to go to Syria and the Lebanon, as France herself was already doing. He hoped that we should both be in agreement over this.

6. *M. Schuman* said he would like to examine this and would send a reply as soon as possible.

7. It was stressed that it was most undesirable that there should be any premature leakage.[2]

[2] On 20 May the Foreign Office was informed by the French Embassy that M. Schuman had agreed to participate in the statement. Arrangements were then made for the issue on 25 May of the tripartite statement (No. 98.i), published in *The Times* on the following day: also printed in *B.F.S.P.*, vol. 159, pp. 204–5. Reactions of Middle East governments were reported by the respective H.M. Representatives and later summarized by Mr. J.G. Sheringham of F.O. Eastern Department in a minute of 3 June as follows: '*Cairo* Minister for Foreign Affairs thought it would have a good effect . . . secret sources speak of almost hysterical relief in Palace and Government circles. *Beirut* Reaction of Prime Minister entirely satisfactory. *Baghdad* Prime Minister met statement with tirade against Jews. Nuri Said and others attacked it strongly in Senate. *Damascus* the Prime Minister thinks that the statement was fundamentally a good one but has been somewhat concerned about press reports that it means that spheres of influence had been allocated to the three powers . . . *Amman* Reaction generally favourable once it was realised that modification of armistice line by agreement was not precluded. *Riyadh* Ibn Saud is very pleased with statement. *Tel Aviv* General reaction . . . one of satisfaction. It has been assumed that "ban" on supply of arms to Israel has been lifted' (E 1023/104: see No. 105, note 4 for the Mr. Bevin's ruling on the 'ban'). On 6 June Mr. Furlonge drew attention to the focussing of Arab criticism on the suggestion that the statement implied the division of the Middle East by the Three Western Powers into zones of influence. H.M. Representatives were instructed, at their discretion, to give reassurances on this score. These reassurances were cited in the formal reply to the tripartite statement issued on 21 June by the Arab League and reported in *The Times* of 19 and 22 June, pp. 5 and 6 respectively. In this reply the Arab League generally welcomed the tripartite statement while making it clear that they would not accept outside interference in the determination of arms levels or maintenance of peace in the region.

No. 110

Record by Sir W. Strang of his conversation with the French Ambassador

[*WF 1071/1*]

FOREIGN OFFICE, *22 May 1950*

When the French Ambassador came to see me this afternoon for a general talk, he said that there were two developments which had occurred in connection with the recent conferences in which a greater regard might have been paid to the interests and susceptibilities of France.

The first was the proposed statement about the supply of arms to Arab countries and Israel. The Middle East had not been on the agenda of the tripartite talks. Nevertheless the French Delegation, at the last moment, had been faced with a ready-made declaration drawn up by the U.K. and U.S. Delegations, to which French concurrence was invited at short notice.[1]

I did not react to this remark. M. Massigli knows very well that we suggested that the Middle East should be on the agenda of the tripartite talks, but that the Americans preferred not to discuss the Middle East on a tripartite basis.[2]

The second was the statements issued by Mr. Bevin and Mr. Acheson about Greece, Turkey and Persia.[3] These were issued after the conference was over. The French Delegation was not consulted or even given advance notice of these statements. M. Massigli could quite understand this omission in so far as the statements referred to Greece and Persia, but France had a treaty with Turkey[4] and it would have been more in conformity with France's interests if the French Delegation had been consulted.

I said that I quite understood this. The idea of these statements had however arisen at a comparatively late stage in the discussions and the drafting took place in some haste. Both we and the Americans had felt strongly that if the North Atlantic Conference rose, with no reference made to Greece, Turkey or Persia, these countries might feel themselves left out in the cold. The Turkish Government, in particular, had repeatedly urged upon us that Turkey should not be overlooked.[5]

M. Massigli said that the French Government had been approached by the Turkish Government in the same way and that this was an additional reason why they should have been brought into the discussions. He tried to suggest that it was we rather than the Americans who had taken the initiative. I said that I really could not remember from which side the

[1] See No. 109.

[2] In a letter to Sir O. Harvey of 18 May, Mr. Wright mentioned that after the meeting recorded in No. 109, 'Massigli asked me afterwards why we had not spoken about this to the French before. I explained that I had mentioned to de Margerie last night that there might be something to put to M. Schuman today, but that it was not until the middle of this morning that the Americans and ourselves finally knew where we stood on it . . '. For your own information, we and the Americans have been discussing this for the past two weeks or so. We decided that the subject was so difficult to handle that the only hope of reaching an agreement at all was on a bipartite basis. Moreover, both we and the Americans have been under a steady fire of criticism about the supply of arms, from which the French have been happily free. It was extremely desirable to settle this matter between us as a factor in our relations, and this consideration did not apply to the French. We are only too conscious that the French may feel somewhat resentful that we had not discussed it between the three of us from the beginning. But both we and the Americans feel that, had we done so, we should almost certainly have failed to reach agreement at all, and we could very ill afford to take this risk. In any case we have now given the French an opportunity to join in if they want to' (WF 1071/1).

[3] See No. 101, note 5.

[4] The Franco-Turkish declaration of Mutual Assistance and the arrangement for territorial questions between Turkey and Syria of 23 June 1939 are printed in B.F.S.P., vol. 143, pp. 476–80.

[5] See No. 81, note 1.

initiative came. I thought that both we and the Americans had simultaneously realised that some such step was necessary. We had done no more than reaffirm statements made by us at the time of the signature of the North Atlantic Treaty.[6]

W.S.

[6] In a minute below of 24 May Mr. Wright referred to the explanation in his letter of 18 May to Sir O. Harvey (note 2) as to why the French were not approached earlier on the Middle East statement. He added that a further reason was the 'strong possibility that the French might leak . . . As regards the statements about Greece, Turkey and Persia, the Secretary of State specially directed that the French should not be brought in . . . The French are of course not concerned at all closely with Greece or Persia, and we could not handle Turkey on a separate basis.' The substance of Mr. Wright's minute was incorporated into a further letter to Sir O. Harvey of 1 June which concluded: 'I hope this will not prove to have made any lasting difficulty with the French. In bringing them into the tripartite statement about Israel and the Arab States we diminished its effectiveness in the Arab countries, who, as we feared, are reacting against the participation of France, but we took the risk deliberately to meet French susceptibilities, and further than this we really could not go' (WF 1071/1).

No. 111

Lieut-General Sir G. Macready[1] (Wahnerheide) to Mr. Bevin
(Received 23 May, 11.10 p.m.)

No. 797 Telegraphic [*C 3521/9/18*]

Immediate. Secret   WAHNERHEIDE, *23 May 1950, 8 p.m.*

Repeated to Berlin, Washington, Paris.

Our telegram No. 694 of 4th May.[2]
German Unity and all-German Elections.

At this afternoon's extraordinary session of the Council, McCloy proposed that we should agree to the immediate publication of the text of the whole statement about conditions for German unity and all-German elections recently agreed on by the Foreign Ministers in London. This text had been communicated as a secret document to the Federal Chancellor on 16th May as a result of a promise given to him by the three High Commissioners at a meeting with him in restricted session earlier that day.[3]

2. McCloy's proposal, made clear only during the meeting in a document which he circulated, was to publish this text with a brief explanatory introduction and a concluding statement which would have shown that it was the intention of the High Commission to propose to the Soviet Authorities in Germany negotiations on the subject of all-German elections at some point in the near future.

3. McCloy justified his proposal for publication by the statement that it

[1] General Macready was acting for General Robertson who was in England for staff talks.
[2] No. 53.ii.   [3] See No. 104, note 1.

had been understood in London in consequence of the agreement not to publish this statement as an appendix to the London Declaration,[4] that each High Commissioner should be free to give indications of the contents of the statement if he thought fit. He himself had been approached by several journalists recently who in the light of the last sentence of the Foreign Ministers' Declaration on Germany had asked him what were the conditions referred to. He considered however that publication while it ought to take place, ought to be tripartite.

4. We had been warned before General Robertson left that this question might arise, and he had expressed the opinion that broadly speaking we should conform to American desires about publicity on this subject, since they had taken the lead initially throughout. However the publication in the form proposed by McCloy seemed to me ill-conceived and ill-timed. I said I feared that publication now would merely put the Russians on their guard, and deprive in advance any concrete offer we might later make to them of its full effect. McCloy saw the point but said he feared the Russians might be contemplating some spectacular political announcement in Berlin over the weekend[5] and he would like to get in with our proposals first. The French representative supported my view, arguing that it would be better only to reveal our decisions when a concrete proposal had been made to the Russians.

5. It was eventually agreed that the Political Committee should meet early on Thursday to draft a letter to be addressed in identical terms by each High Commissioner to General Chuikov,[6] proposing negotiations for the holding of all-German elections on the basis agreed, these letters to be delivered if possible to General Chuikov on the evening of Thursday 25th May and released to the press in time for publication in newspapers the following morning. It was thought this news would provide an appropriate prelude to the Whitsun Rally in Berlin.

6. I agreed to this procedure subject to confirmation by you, since I am not entirely certain that you have agreed to such a proposal being put to Chuikov at this time. The communication to Chuikov would no doubt base itself, in so far as elections are concerned, mainly on the recent proposals made by the Chancellor.[7] I think it is certain that the Americans will wish also to publish, whether in the letter or as an accompanying document, the full text of the conditions for German unity agreed on in London. In para 3 of his telegram No. 673[8] General Robertson discussed the propaganda advantages and disadvantages of a full statement of these conditions: and we still feel that the political and propaganda effect of any approach to the Russians will be diminished by a full statement of the conditions we regard as essential for German unity. Nevertheless in view

---

[4] See No. 98, note 15.

[5] i.e. During the Whitsun peace rally of the Communist Free German Youth held in the Soviet sector of Berlin on 27–29 May.

[6] Chairman of the Soviet Control Commission in Germany.

[7] See No. 53, note 1.

[8] No. 53.

of the reference made in the London Declaration to the agreement reached on these conditions, I anticipate that the Americans will insist on their publication and propose, unless you instruct me to the contrary, to agree.

7. I should be grateful if any views or instructions you may have to express could reach me before the Political Committee meets at 10 am on 25th May.[9]

Foreign Office pass to Washington and Paris as my telegrams 113 and 13 respectively.

[9] On 25 May General Macready was authorized by Mr. Bevin to proceed as proposed in paragraphs 5 and 6 above. That evening he reported agreement on identical letters from each High Commissioner to General Chuikov (text printed in Cmnd. 1552, pp. 132–3). These letters, to which the London statement on German unity was appended, were delivered on the evening of 25 May and released to the press the following day. Both the identic text of the letters and statement were published in *The Times* on 27 May.

No. 112

Brief by Mr. Jackling[1]

[*UEE 4/51*]

Secret   FOREIGN OFFICE, *24 May 1950*

The Sterling Balances: E.P.C. (*50*) *58*

This memorandum by the Chancellor of the Exchequer refers to the recommendation made in E.P.C. (50) 40[2] (flag A), and approved by the Economic Policy Committee on 28th March,[2] to the effect that a two-stage settlement of the Sterling Balances problem should be sought, at first by a limited measure of funding independent of United States aid, and subsequently by cancellation of some part of the balances in return for United States assistance in the development of South-East Asia. This idea was put to Mr. Acheson by Sir Oliver Franks in April in order to obtain the U.S. Government's views on it.[3] Mr. Acheson has since made it clear that while his Government hope we will go forward with the attempt to solve the sterling balance problem, and while they are very sympathetic to our proposals for development in South-East Asia, it is essential that the latter should be represented as related to the problems and needs of the various countries considered on their merits, and not as related to the objective of dealing with sterling balances.[4]

2. While the possibility of American help both on sterling balances and

[1] This paper covering E.P.C. (50) 58 at i below was evidently prepared as a brief for Mr. Bevin at the E.P.C. meeting on 25 May (see further note 5).

[2] No. 9.i.   [3] See No. 9, note 7.

[4] Mr. Acheson's initial reactions to the British proposals were confirmed by the American delegation at a bipartite sub-committee meeting on 17 May, for which see No. 70.i(*c*).

on South-East Asian development may not be entirely ruled out by Mr. Acheson's response, it is clear that we can hold out no hope of such help to the balance holders, and that the difficulty of getting them to agree to a funding scheme is therefore increased. Nevertheless, there are strong reasons for going ahead with some attempt to tie up the balances more firmly than at present, and the Chancellor in this paper makes the following recommendations:

(a) that it would be wrong to suspend altogether further action towards a settlement of the sterling balances;

(b) that we should not at this stage commit ourselves to any particular scheme for dealing with the balances but should explore the subject generally with the Governments of India, Pakistan and Egypt, and possibly Ceylon, before finally deciding on a definitive course of action; and

(c) that the Chancellor should settle the best way of conducting the exploratory discussions, in consultation with the Secretaries of State for Foreign Affairs and for Commonwealth Relations.

Recommendation

3. That the Chancellor's proposals should be accepted.[5]

R.W. JACKLING

CALENDARS TO NO. 112

i *23 May 1950 Memo. on sterling balances: E.P.C. (50) 58* Reassesses position in light of American refusal to link the settlement of sterling balances with the question of aid for the development of South and South East Asia [CAB 134/226].

ii *16 June 1950 Account of Sydney Conference on economic development in South East Asia, 15–19 May,* by Lord Macdonald of Gwaenysgor, leader of U.K. delegation and Paymaster-General, circulated to Cabinet as C.P. (50)123. Early divisions in conference between British proposals (supported by Canada, India, Ceylon and New Zealand) and Australian proposals (supported by Pakistan) resolved satisfactorily by 'a combination of views, rather than a compromise'. Report and recommendations of conference are appended to C.P. (50)123: main recommendations are for preparation of a six year development plan and technical assistance scheme. Next meeting of Commonwealth Consultative Committee scheduled for September [CAB 129/40].

[5] Sir R. Makins noted below 'I agree'. The proposals in E.P.C. (50) 58 were approved by the Economic Policy Committee at a meeting on 25 May. 'In discussion the Chancellor of the Exchequer agreed with the Secretary of State for Commonwealth Relations that the effects of appearing publicly to have failed to reach agreement with another member of the Commonwealth on specific proposals for dealing with the sterling balances might be serious, and it was for that reason that the talks were to be purely exploratory' (E.P.C. (50) 15th meeting on CAB 134/224).

No. 113

Memorandum by the Secretary of State for Foreign Affairs[1]

C.P. *(50) 118 [CAB 129/40]*

Secret   FOREIGN OFFICE, *26 May 1950*

Meeting of the North Atlantic Council, 15–18 May

I circulate, for the information of my colleagues, the following account of the Fourth Session of the Atlantic Council, which was held at Lancaster House from 15th to 18th May. The meeting was attended by the Foreign Ministers of all twelve countries and was presided over by Mr. Dean Acheson, the United States Secretary of State.

2. The Council took the following important decisions:

(i) It established a body of Deputies.

(ii) It gave the Deputies a detailed directive on defence questions.

(iii) In a series of Resolutions [ii], it also gave directives to the Defence and the Defence Financial and Economic Committees for their future work.

(iv) It set up a North Atlantic Planning Board for Ocean Shipping.

(v) It issued a communiqué[2] setting out the principles and the objectives of the Treaty nations.

Body of Deputies

3. This body consists of Deputies of members of the Council, (i.e., Foreign Ministers) with full authority from their Governments to carry out the policies of the Council in the intervals between meetings of Ministers. The Deputies will meet regularly and will have their headquarters in London. Their chief functions will be to ensure co-ordination in the defence field, to exchange views on political matters, to co-ordinate public information activities and to consider what further action should be taken under Article 2 of the Treaty in the economic field. The Deputies will have a permanent Chairman, chosen from among their number. This Chairman will be assisted by a highly qualified staff contributed by member Governments. The full text of the Council's resolution on this subject is at Annex I [i].

4. The principal features of this new organisation are: first, that it gives continuity to the work of the Council; secondly, that it enlarges the field of its work to cover not only defence questions as hitherto, but also public

---

[1] This paper for the Cabinet, prepared under the direction of Sir G. Jebb, was preceded by a brief oral report on the N.A.C. meeting given to the Cabinet by Mr. Bevin at its meeting on the morning of 18 May (C.M. (50) 32nd Conclusions, minute 5).

[2] See i below for a text of the N.A.C. communiqué, published in *The Times* on 19 May together with the N.A.C. Resolution for the appointment of Deputies. This Resolution, appended to the present document as Annex I is reproduced in calendar i from Cmd. 7977.

information, economic and general foreign policy; thirdly, that, through the permanent Chairman of the Deputies and his staff, it provides for unified direction and vigorous leadership in the execution of the Treaty's objectives.

5. The discussion on this question at the Council meeting centred mainly on three points:

(a) Location

The French would have preferred Washington, but the Americans said from the first that they favoured Europe. The strongest argument in favour of London was that the Permanent Staffs of the Military Supply Board and the Defence Financial and Economic Committee are already here, and with full support from the two Scandinavian Delegations, there was little difficulty in reaching agreement on this point.

(b) Nature of the permanent Staff

There was general agreement that, although the Deputies would need a permanent secretariat, something more than this was necessary to provide the vigorous leadership which everyone thought necessary. The Americans took the line that this leadership could not be supplied by an international civil servant, since he would not have the backing of a member Government, and therefore proposed the device of a permanent Chairman chosen from among the Deputies. Although it was not formally agreed, it was generally understood that this Chairman would be the American Deputy. The United States Government have not yet decided whom to appoint, but they are known to attach great importance to the post and will probably choose a first-class man. It was also on American insistence that the precise nature of the proposed new permanent staff was deliberately left vague, since they thought that the organisation should be fitted round the man rather than the man into the organisation.

(c) Economic Questions

There was general agreement that future economic relations between Europe and North America after 1952 required urgent study and that in this study the position of Germany was an important factor. There was, however, some difference of view on the question where and how this study should be undertaken. The Norwegian Foreign Minister thought that the Atlantic Pact was the proper body since of all existing 'Western' organisations it alone included representatives from both sides of the Atlantic. The Netherlands Foreign Minister, on the other hand, was afraid that this would merely lead to duplication of the work of O.E.E.C., which he thought was the appropriate body to study the question. Eventually it was agreed that Article 2 (which deals with economic collaboration) was an integral and important part of the Treaty which could not be ignored and that it must be left to the Deputies to examine what further action should be taken under it, taking into account the work of other international organisations.

Directive on Defence Questions

6. The French were insistent from the start that the Council should give the Deputies a directive on the broad principles which should guide them in their examination of defence questions.[3] They wished to draw attention, in particular, to the need for making available forces for the initial battle, for adapting the composition of forces to the modern weapons they would have to use, for distributing efficiently among the member countries the production of the arms required and for dividing the cost equitably between them. In the discussion of this question several Ministers expressed doubts whether the Council was at this stage really in a position to issue such a detailed directive on technical questions. After previous consultation with the Ministry of Defence, I said that I rather shared their point of view. At the same time, I understood and sympathised with the anxiety which underlay the French proposal. I drew the Council's attention to the difficult and dangerous position of the Continental countries which would have to bear the first brunt of the battle: it would be a terrible blow to tell them that they had got to be occupied again before they could be liberated, because there were not sufficient forces to withstand the first attack. The object of the Council must be to build up such a force that the people of Europe could count on being defended and that, consequently, the enemy would be deterred from risking an attack. The views expressed by M. Schuman and myself evidently made some impression on the Americans, and at the last meeting of the Council Mr. Acheson made an important declaration in which he said that both he and his Government were in complete agreement that it was essential to create forces sufficient to resist aggression at the moment of first attack and to continue the struggle through to the end. The Council finally agreed on a modified form of the French proposal which, instead of giving specific directives, sets out certain principles and issues which it believes to be important, and asks for the advice and recommendations of the technical experts on how to give effect to them. A copy of the resolution as adopted is attached at Annex II [ii].

Resolutions on Defence

7. Attached at Annex III [ii] is the text of the six principal Resolutions passed by the Council with regard to defence matters.
The chief points in these Resolutions are:

(i) The Council asks the Defence Committee to produce as soon as possible an estimate of the cost of plans for the defence of the North Atlantic countries.

(ii) In order to fill the great gap between forces at present available and those which will be required, the Council urges Governments to ensure the progressive build up of defence forces.

[3] Cf. No. 46, note 6.

(iii) The Council also urges Governments to concentrate on the creation of balanced collective forces rather than balanced national forces.

(iv) The Council approves the Defence Committee's request to the Defence Financial and Economic Committee to examine immediately the possibility of the Treaty nations supporting additional military expenditure.

(v) The Council recognises that a sound economy is the necessary basis of the required defence effort.

(vi) The Council recognises the need for closer liaison between the various existing North Atlantic Treaty bodies.

(vii) The Council urges Governments to make their full contribution to common defence by means of mutual assistance.

8. In my opening speech to the Council I touched on most of the important points raised by these Resolutions. I said that now if ever was the time to establish some sort of balanced international forces. Not only the military burden, however, but also the economic burden of defence must be shared. The Western countries had to consider how they could build up an economy capable of carrying this burden. Against the almost religious fervour of the Communists, we must put a simple constructive industrial programme for the welfare of the people. Thus alone could we fortify the world's faith in Western civilisation and at the same time provide the means to improve our defences and deter a potential aggressor.

9. The discussion on the Resolutions themselves turned on two main points:

(a) *The Question of Balanced Collective Forces*

There was general agreement on the principle that an effective defence is impossible unless there are balanced collective forces for the whole North Atlantic area. There was some disagreement, however, on whether the establishment of balanced collective forces was compatible with the existence of balanced national forces in each country. M. Schuman thought that it was, and Mr. Acheson felt strongly that it was not. I said that I thought that our purpose was to establish forces which would satisfy national requirements in time of peace and at the same time provide the most powerful co-ordinated striking force in time of war. This view was generally accepted, and it was finally agreed that balanced collective forces must be the objective and not balanced national forces; but that in establishing the balanced collective forces, account must be taken of national requirements for internal security, commitments outside the North Atlantic area and local defence on the outbreak of hostilities.

(b) *The Relative Priority of Defence Requirements and Economic Recovery*

I explained that I could not at present accept any modification of the general principle that economic recovery enjoyed priority over defence

382

requirements. Other Ministers shared my view, and it was accordingly decided to word the relevant Resolution non-committally to say that 'while the making of additional military expenditures must be judged in the light of economic and financial conditions, adequate consideration must be given to the needs for defence.'

North Atlantic Planning Board for Ocean Shipping

10. This Board will be composed of representatives of interested member countries, and there is provision for representatives of other countries to be invited to participate in its work as appropriate. It will report directly to the Council and will work in close co-operation with the other Treaty bodies in all matters related to defence planning. At my invitation, the Board will hold its first meeting in London, probably some time in June. There was no discussion of this item at the Council, which merely approved the recommendations of the Working Group in Washington.

Statement of Principles

11. In my opening speech I expressed the hope that it would be possible for the Council to make a public declaration of faith and principles.[4] My suggestion was supported by the Danish Foreign Minister and was referred to a sub-committee. After long discussion it was eventually found impossible to reach agreement on the text of such a declaration. The Americans insisted that it should be strongly worded and show no suggestion of weakness in the prosecution of the 'cold war'. The French, on the other hand, wanted it to be moderate in tone and to contain some reference to the possibility of negotiations with the Soviet Union. Each side insisted that nothing less than a declaration on the lines they proposed would be acceptable to their public opinion. Prolonged attempts to bridge this disagreement failed, and it was therefore decided, instead, to include a brief and uncontroversial statement of principles and objectives in the final communiqué.

12. During the discussion of the communiqué I expressed some doubts about the following sentence:

> 'In formulating their directives the Council proceeded on the basis that the combined resources of the members of the North Atlantic Treaty are sufficient, if properly co-ordinated and applied, to ensure the progressive and speedy development of adequate military defence without impairing the social and economic progress of these countries.'

The Council had passed no resolution to that effect and, although I liked the passage itself, I was not certain that it was right to put it into the communiqué. Mr. Acheson said that all the statement meant was that the Treaty Powers thought that they had between them sufficient resources to

[4] For the background to this statement, see No. 84, notes 5 and 15.

look after both defence and social and economic progress, and he thought that it would be a bad look out for us all if we could not say this. On reflection, I feel that this passage is necessary.

Conclusions

13. I think the following are the main conclusions to be drawn from the Meeting:

(i) Unlike the other sessions of the Council, which were mainly concerned with the formalities of setting up the North Atlantic Treaty Organisation, this meeting was able to get down to serious discussion of the real problems of common defence on the basis of the reports from the Defence Committee. If the results were not more spectacular, that was due less to the unwillingness of Ministers to tackle the problems, than to the fact that the problems themselves are not yet ripe for solution. There was, however, a very proper sense of urgency and a realisation of the fact that unless a serious and determined start is made with rearmament now the situation will get quite out of hand in a few years' time.

(ii) We have laid down certain general principles which mark a very considerable step forward in the direction of a truly integrated defence programme. In particular, we have established the principle that narrow national interests must give way to the broader requirements of the collective defence of the whole North Atlantic area. It is now for the military experts to give practical effect to this principle.

(iii) We have also formally recognised that however much military targets may be reviewed and production rationalised, there will still be a heavy bill to foot if available resources are to be brought up to the minimum level required for an effective defence policy. It is now for Defence Ministers to say how much that bill will be and for Finance Ministers to say how far it can be met.

(iv) On the organisational side, we have taken a necessary practical step forward in establishing a body of Deputies and thus have given to the whole North Atlantic Treaty Organisation that cohesion and direction which were hitherto lacking. The effectiveness of this new organisation will largely depend on the personal attributes of the Deputies and particularly of their Chairman. It is essential that they should be of the highest calibre.

(v) The general attitude of the Americans throughout the Conference showed that they are determined to make a reality of the North Atlantic Treaty and that increasingly they regard it as the focus for the further development of the Western world. For us this means that our future relations with the United States will largely be determined by the success of our collaboration in the Atlantic Treaty. Since it is the kernel of their policy, it must also be the kernel of ours.

E.B.

I *19 May 1950* *Published Statements of the Fourth Session of the North Atlantic Council:*

    I Communiqué.
    II Resolution on N.A.T. machinery—appointment of Deputies [Cmd. 7977].

II *26 May 1950* *Annexes II–III to No. 113* : N.A.C. Resolutions on Defence principles and Reports of Defence Committee and D.F.E.C. [CAB 129/40].

No. 114

Mr. Bevin to Sir O. Franks (Washington)

No. 2771 Telegraphic [*WU 10727/17*]

Priority. Secret　　　　　　　　　　FOREIGN OFFICE, *16 June 1950, 8.50 p.m.*

Please pass following personal message from Secretary of State to Mr. Acheson.

Begins

I am much concerned about the delays over setting up the Committee of Deputies of the North Atlantic Council. When we discussed this measure in May we all felt that the need to instil vitality into the N.A.T.O. was an urgent one and the thought in our minds was that the Deputies should meet and start their work of coordination within a very few weeks. We gave the same impression to public opinion in our communiqué.[1] A month has now passed without anything happening and there is growing pressure here to know the reasons for delay. I am afraid the impression may soon gain ground that our expressions of urgency and determination last month were window-dressing only.

2. Our military authorities have been conscious for some time of the need to vitalise the Brussels Treaty Defence Organisation and to find methods of coordinating its work more closely with N.A.T. planning and in particular with the work of the other two European Groups.[2] They have worked out proposals to this end, but naturally feel that they cannot make progress until the Council of Deputies has been established and can be consulted, and the delay over this is therefore holding up their plans and having a depressing effect.

3. I entirely understand that you may be having difficulties in deciding on the nomination of your Deputy, and I do not want to rush you; but it is clear that the other countries are awaiting a lead from you and that nothing effective can be done until your Deputy is nominated and has taken up his duties. I am sure you share my view that it would be a most serious thing if the impulse which we gave to the N.A.T. at our London

[1] See No. 113.i.　　　　　　　　　　[2] See No. 24, note 8.

385

meeting were to be lost at a moment when great additional efforts by all of us are required to preserve the security of the West.[3]

[3] On 19 June Sir O. Franks replied that acting on these instructions he had handed a letter that afternoon to Mr. Dean Rusk, Assistant Under Secretary of State: 'I asked him to see that it got to Acheson as soon as possible' (WU 10727/17): see further No. 117, note 10.

No. 115

Letter from Mr. Wilson (Treasury) to Sir L. Rowan (Washington)

[*T 232/167*]

TREASURY, *16 June 1950*

Hitchman was a bit concerned after the meetings which took place in London last month of reports which appeared in the Press from time to time suggesting that we had to some extent gone back on our previously expressed intention of making viability by 1952 our principal aim, at any rate in the economic field. When we saw in the *Financial Times* of the 31st May a report that 'One result of Mr. Acheson's talks in London is thought to have been the reduction, if not removal, of what Americans considered the near fatal [British] preoccupation with viability in 1952',[1] we thought that we had better get the position straight with the Foreign Office and I accordingly wrote to Evelyn Shuckburgh. I now enclose a copy of his reply to me from which you will see how the matter was left.[2] I presume that you have access to the documents referred to in the letter.[3]

G.M. WILSON

[1] The report, published in fact on 30 May, continued: 'This aim however worthy, seemed to have been the barrier to Britain undertaking other co-ordinating action with the Continent and the North Atlantic community ... Britain's decision to embrace the European Payments Union is felt by some State Department officials to reflect a more comfortable state of mind.'

[2] In his reply of 9 June to Mr. Wilson's letter of 31 May in which Mr. Wilson asked whether there was anything in the records of the bilateral talks to confirm recent press reports as cited above, Mr. Shuckburgh stated 'As you know there was considerable discussion on this subject, but I think you are right in believing that we still stand by our original policy'. Mr. Shuckburgh cited discussion in the third bipartite official meeting (No. 34, particularly paragraphs 6, 13–14) and sub-committee meetings Nos. 1 and 4 (Nos. 34.i and 42.ii) and concluded: 'The upshot of all these discussions was that both sides largely maintained their own points of view. A joint memorandum (MIN/UKUS/P/2) was prepared, setting out these differences of approach but its intention was analytic only, and it did not attempt to make recommendations. Paragraph 5 I think makes it clear that we did not give way on any important point of principle. At the first bipartite Ministerial meeting on 10th May the joint memorandum was considered (paragraphs 1 and 2) but not discussed. It was agreed that it be adopted as a working document "setting forth the broad basis for conduct by the two countries"—and so the position was left.'

[3] On 22 June Sir L. Rowan thanked Mr. Wilson for his letter and observed 'My own view, on reading the reports of the meetings, was that there was in fact no suggestion that we had in any way revised our principal aim of viability by 1952, and I am glad to have your confirmation that my impression was correct' (T 232/167).

No. 116

Note by Sir W. Strang of an Inter-departmental Meeting

[*ZP 2/189*]

FOREIGN OFFICE, *17 June 1950*

Sir Roger Makins and I went to see Sir E. Bridges about this yesterday.[1]
Sir Norman Brook and Sir Edwin Plowden were also present.

I told Sir E. Bridges that the London Bipartite and Tripartite
Conferences were of a different character from that of those cited in the
enclosure in his letter; that their purpose was not the negotiation of
agreements but a broad exchange of views, the result of which was likely
to be no more than an adjustment of general outlook; that the agenda
comprised a long list of items, most of them of purely Foreign Office
concern; that interdepartmental consultation had, in fact, taken place on
those items of interdepartmental concern, though on an informal and *ad
hoc* basis; and that, so far as I knew, no department other than the Board
of Trade had expressed dissatisfaction. If we had made any mistake it was
perhaps in thinking that in economic matters it was sufficient to consult
Sir Edwin Plowden or his staff, and leave it to them to consult other
departments if required.

As regards the North Atlantic Council, there had been close and
continuous contact with the Treasury and the Ministry of Defence
throughout the proceedings. The upshot was, I thought, that there had in
fact been adequate consultation, though there might not appear to have
been. Both Sir R. Makins and I were firm supporters of the principle of
interdepartmental consultation, particularly in economic matters.

Sir E. Bridges and his colleagues said that while it might be true that
there had in fact been consultation, there had been a sense of uneasiness
in Whitehall at the appearance of a heavy documentation in connexion
with this much publicised conference, without any obvious signs that the
views of departments concerned were being taken into account. They
thought it would have been better if, at the start, an informal group had
been set up which could have looked at the agenda and allotted tasks in
order to make sure that all views were taken into account. There was no

---

[1] Sir W. Strang was here referring to a letter of 13 June from Sir E. Bridges, Permanent
Secretary to the Treasury, in which he followed up an earlier letter of 10 May suggesting a
post-mortem on official arrangements for the London Conference arising from a complaint
by officials at the Board of Trade on 8 May that they were not being kept sufficiently
informed. In his letter of 13 June Sir E. Bridges cited 'a feeling in some quarters that the
position of Departments other than the Foreign Office would have been easier if the
preparatory work had been focused in an official group representing all the interested
Departments. Such a group could have arranged for the preparation of briefs at the official
level, which could have been submitted to Ministers as required' (ZP 2/189). Attached to this
letter was a note of how this kind of arrangement had worked well in the past e.g. at the
Colombo Conference.

suggestion that all briefs should have passed through this group, but merely that it should be known that briefs were in fact being prepared, and whose duty it was to prepare them. The only briefs that would have needed to be passed by the group would have been briefs of wide interdepartmental concern.

The existence of such a group might also, they thought, have served to reassure ministers, some of whom had expressed concern that policies appeared to be in process of formulation without adequate ministerial consideration. The absence of the Foreign Secretary through illness had of course been a major factor in this respect.

I said that I would bear these considerations in mind on any similar occasion in future.

W.S.

No. 117

Letter from Mr. Shuckburgh to Mr. Gore-Booth (Washington)[1]

FOREIGN OFFICE, 21 June 1950

Your letter of June 5th[2] certainly asks for a good deal! However, there is always the advantage that the attempt to answer questions of this kind helps to put one's own ideas in order, so I will start in right away without preamble.

The Anglo-American Talks

The bipartite conversations between ourselves and the Americans were certainly very interesting and, I think, useful. It was particularly valuable for us to meet Jessup and Perkins and their assistants and to get to know what kind of people they are and how they are thinking. Our main impression during the preparatory official conversations was that, despite the portentous and beautifully tagged briefs which they brought with them, they had not developed very clear ideas on most of the subjects under discussion. Compared with the French, who knew exactly where they wanted to go on everything, we found the Americans somewhat plastic and therefore (since we ourselves were perhaps a little unprepared for the need to give a lead) very susceptible to the active needling of the French. When it came to the talks between the Secretary of State and Mr. Acheson, this situation was added to by the fact (which Derick Hoyer-Millar will no doubt have mentioned to you) that Acheson himself had not

[1] This letter to Mr. P.H. Gore-Booth, Director-General of the British Information Services attached to the British Embassy in Washington with an operational centre in New York, is untraced in Foreign Office archives and is here printed from a copy in the possession of the author.
[2] Untraced in Foreign Office archives.

read any of the briefs and had not had time even to be told what had been taking place during the previous weeks in the official conversations.[3]

The second main impression was this. Basing ourselves on the wording of the first five items on the bipartite Ministerial agenda, which we had been told were drafted by Acheson himself, we had been expecting, or at least some of us had been expecting, that the Americans were coming to these talks with the intention of establishing some very special and close relationship with this country as a basis on which policy in all broad fields could be built. There was a belief in certain quarters here that these talks would give us the opportunity to get back to something like the wartime relationship, in which the United States and United Kingdom would give unquestioned priority to their relations with each other and form a solid factor of leadership in all the international associations of which they are members. Frankly, some of us thought that this was expecting too much and were warned by what happened after the establishment of the famous 'continuing organisation' in Washington last year. In any event, it became quite clear early on in the official talks that the Americans were not thinking along these lines. Although of course quite willing to subscribe to the doctrine of continuous close consultation in all matters between the two countries, they made it very clear that the value of this country to the United States, apart from our Commonwealth position and our influence in the Far East and other parts of the world, lay in the leadership which we could give in Europe; and they were not prepared to encourage us to think that we could establish, through any special relationship with them, an alibi for our duties in respect of European integration, etc. This seemed a disappointment to some people here, but I confess it did not surprise or particularly distress me, since it seems quite obvious that this must be the case. The conclusion I draw is summarised in paragraph 5 of the enclosed minute which I submitted on the question of future bipartite

[3] This point was made by Sir F. Hoyer-Millar to Mr. Perkins when discussing procedures at the London Conference, as reported in Sir F. Hoyer-Millar's letter to Sir W. Strang of 2 June: 'Perkins more or less admitted the justification of what I said. He said that one of the main difficulties had been the inability of himself and the other State Department officials who had taken part in the preliminary official talks in London properly to brief Acheson when they met him in Paris on the Sunday preceding the opening of the ministerial talks. Apparently, the moment Acheson got there he had been surrounded by people like Harriman and McCloy, David Bruce, Cooper, etc., who had never stopped talking about a variety of irrelevant subjects with the result that the officials who had come over from London never had a chance of telling Acheson what had happened during the preceding fortnight . . . He admitted, however, that Acheson had been so preoccupied during the weeks before he left Washington with the Macarthy attacks, the speeches he had had to make in California and elsewhere to try and explain American foreign policy, the number of meetings he had had to have with Congress, etc., etc., that he really had had no time properly to study the agenda or to consider the major issues involved . . . In fact, Perkins said that Acheson was in very little better position than our own Secretary of State, who had come virtually straight from hospital to the meetings and had had very little time in which to brief himself about the agenda' (ZP 2/184).

and tripartite conversations.[4] A copy has also gone to Derick Hoyer-Millar.

The Tripartite Talks

The tripartite official discussions were equally valuable from the personal point of view, and I think also generally. The main difficulty which we ran up against early on was two-fold. First the French were strongly concerned to prevent the conversations appearing to be in any way aggressive in the cold war sense, and this led them to oppose our efforts to draw up a strong and positive declaration of faith in the inevitable prevalence of democratic society over dictatorial systems. The Americans in this were on our side, but in the end it proved impossible to get agreement on a worth-while declaration, and as you will have seen, all that remained was contained in the preamble to the communiqué.[5]

Secondly, the French made it very clear that they would not allow the North Atlantic Treaty to become the forum in which the economic problems affecting Europe and the American Continent should be dealt with either now or after 1952. Our idea had been to try and make the North Atlantic Treaty into the master association of the West and the umbrella under which all the various forms of cooperation should gradually be covered and even eventually merged. The French objection was based ostensibly on the absence of Germany, Sweden, Switzerland, etc. from the N.A.T. and their determination not to let the Germans be in any way associated with a military defence pact which would lead to German rearmament. This argument became rather less effective after the announcement of the Schuman Plan, and the French then concentrated (with the support of Stikker and others) on the argument that the existence and achievements of O.E.E.C. made that the natural *venue* for future economic cooperation. As you know, we eventually had to concede this important point, and arrangements are being made for the United States and Canada to be associated with O.E.E.C. for the purpose of considering the future methods of dealing with economic problems affecting the two Continents.[6] We still retain, however, in the terms of reference for the new N.A.T. Deputies Committee,[7] the principle that

[4] In this long minute of 10 June, stimulated by Sir F. Hoyer-Millar's letter of 2 June (note 3 above), Mr. Shuckburgh assessed the shortcomings of the arrangements and procedures of the London Conference. In paragraph 5 he continued: 'From the point of view of policy, it cannot be said that the bipartite talks were very successful. When it came down to it, the Americans were not prepared to go very far with the idea that they should have closer and more intimate relations with the United Kingdom than with other countries. The lesson to be drawn from this seems to be that our efforts to establish a special relationship with the U.S. should be less open and explicit, and should concentrate on particular fields (e.g. joint strategic planning and cooperation in particular areas). In other words, for this reason also we might do better next time not to have formal, bipartite conversations of so general a character' (ZP2/184). A copy of this minute was sent to Sir F. Hoyer-Millar by way of reply to his letter of 2 June.

[5] Issued by the North Atlantic Council: see No. 113, paragraph 11 and note 2 *ibid.*

[6] See No. 107, note 3.   [7] See No. 113.i.

Article 2 of the Treaty is not to be forgotten, and the post-1952 situation is therefore, in theory at any rate, not prejudiced.

The Ministerial tripartite conversations were, of course, very much affected by the announcement of the Schuman plan. That has all been so much discussed publicly and otherwise, that I need not refer at length to it. Moreover, since you wrote your letter there has been the row about the Labour Party's paper on 'European Unity'[8] and we are all rather unsettled and uncertain how our knife-edge policy in regard to Europe can be maintained. It is now clear, I think, that everything will depend on the outcome of the European Payments Scheme and of the Schuman Plan negotiations. If, as seems probable, the Payments Scheme can come into operation with our participation and if, as is much less certain, we find ourselves in a position to make proposals regarding coal and steel which will get the French out of the difficulties they are sure to encounter in their negotiations with the Germans and others, this should re-establish our position in American and European eyes; and our inability to hand over sovereign powers to the Strasbourg set-up should then be of less importance and less criticised. In any case, perhaps in the long run it will be appreciated that our action in placing our objections on the table straight away was healthier and more helpful than if we had adopted the more disingenuous tactic of throwing our caps in the air at the beginning and nibbling away at the project when it got down to details.

Our concern now is to get the N.A.T. working effectively in the field of defence. It is generally recognised in the Office that, though we may have to drag our feet in European affairs, we simply cannot afford to do so in the N.A.T. I am not saying that other Departments and other Ministers necessarily subscribe yet to this principle, but it is a principle on which the Foreign Office intends to go to bat persistently from now on. You will have noticed the following passage from the Prime Minister's statement in the House on June 13th about the Schuman Plan:[9]

> 'Now, as a result of the recent conferences in London we are, I believe, about to enter a formative and decisive phase in the organisation of the Atlantic Community. This will require, by a more effective pooling of resources, the surrender in an unprecedented degree by each country of the ability to do as it pleases. His Majesty's Government will be in the forefront of this great endeavour.'

It is for this reason that we are much perturbed about the American delay in nominating their Deputy. We want the Deputies to be a powerful coordinating factor and to get going as soon as possible, and it is of course vital that the Chairman (who will undoubtedly be the American) should be a powerful personality. There will naturally be resistances to 'coordination' from other Ministers (particularly the Ministers of Finance), but the

[8] For a text of the foreign policy statement 'European Unity' issued on 13 June by the National Executive Committee of the Labour Party, see Volume I, No. 100.i.

[9] *Parl. Debs., 5th ser., H. of C.*, vol. 476, cols. 35–7.

object of the set-up is to overcome these. We are working on proposals for re-organising the Brussels Treaty Defence Machinery and the European Regional Planning arrangements of the N.A.T. I need not outline these, as they are of course still top secret, but in brief the idea is to merge the three European Groups into one and to appoint, as the chief ginger element in the Group, a high-powered military person, who will be the agent in Europe of the Standing Group and the Principal Military Adviser of the Chairman of the Deputies. If we could persuade the Americans to put an American General in this position, our proposals would increase American participation in the responsibility for European defence planning and solve a number of problems which are now obstructing progress in the creation of balanced and effective forces for the defence of Europe. None of this, of course can be brought to point until the Deputies are in action.[10]

I think that one of the best lines you can take in general publicity in the United States is our urgent desire to make a success of the N.A.T. and to push ahead with the creation of really integrated and balanced Western forces, to which every member of the North Atlantic Treaty would make its utmost contribution, even to the extent of substantial sacrifices of sovereignty. The great advantage of the N.A.T. system from our point of view is that all members have equal status and responsibility and it is less easy for the Americans to stand on the sidelines, as they do in O.E.E.C.

I am afraid that the above, though long and windy, does not really give you much help; one gets out of the habit in this job of speculating, and anyway I am not good at it. There are to be important statements in the House of Commons next week (June 26th, I think)[11] in which an attempt will be made to set out all that we have done in taking a lead in the reorganisation of the West since the war and explaining why we are obliged to adopt what may seem to others a recalcitrant attitude towards plans for merging us irrevocably in a purely European association.[12] If the

[10] On 22 June the appointments were announced of American and British Deputies, Mr. C.M. Spofford and Sir F. Hoyer-Millar. The general surprise at the appointment of Mr. Spofford, a New York lawyer with some post-war military government experience but as yet relatively unknown, prompted assurances from Mr. Acheson on 23 June that no downgrading of the importance of the N.A.C. was intended (*The Times* of 24 June, p. 3). Mr. Bevin agreed and considered that 'the main thing now is for the Deputies to get on with their work' (message to Mr. Douglas of 28 June on WU 10727/28). The first meeting of the Council of twelve deputies took place in London on 25 July under the chairmanship of Mr. Spofford.

[11] For the debate on the Schuman Plan in the House of Commons on 26–27 June see *Parl. Debs., 5th ser., H. of C.*, vol. 476, cols 1907–2056 and 2104–2182.

[12] On 30 June this line was taken further by Mr. Bevin when, with regard to Korea, he stated in Foreign Office telegram to Washington No. 2980: 'I hope you will find means of using the prompt action of His Majesty's Government in rallying with naval forces to the support of the United States initiative under the Security Council in order to counteract United States criticism of His Majesty's Government's policy in relation to Europe and on the "foot dragging" issue generally . . . There could not be a more useful demonstration of the United Kingdom's capacity to act as a world power with the support of the

Ministers use the briefs which are being prepared for them, it should be of some help to you. Generally speaking, I feel fairly confident that, provided the theorists and armchair constitution builders do not succeed in working up too much pressure against us and too much worldwide impatience for neat solutions, we shall succeed in finding a workable and acceptable balance between the need for greater cohesion in Europe and the broader objective of creating a single Atlantic Community.

C.A.E. SHUCKBURGH

Commonwealth, and of its quickness to move when actions rather than words are necessary . . . It may also be possible to suggest that the United Kingdom would not be free to play this part if, as some circles in the United States have often suggested, the United Kingdom were to be integrated with some form of Western European federation' (AU 1075/1).

Index of Main Subjects and Persons

This straightforward index to document numbers is designed to be used in conjunction with the Summary of Contents. Subjects are principally indexed under main subject headings. Entries for persons are usually limited to a reference to the descriptive footnote. In the case of leading personalities, e.g. Mr. Bevin, items of special interest have been included.

Abbott, D.C. 11

Abdullah I., H.M. King 14

Acheson, D. 1
Anglo-American relationship 5, 15, 79, 82, 84
atomic energy 5, 102
California speeches 9, 26, 72
criticism in U.S. 3, 5, 15
empire of Charlemagne 5
Germany 5, 48, 51, 78, 95–6, 98
London: briefing inadequacies 117
objectives 5, 48, 51, 79
MIN/UKUS/P/5 'burn' 84
N.A.T. Organization 5, 51, 78, 80, 90
O.E.E.C. 48, 78, 90
visit to Paris, 78
U.S. and Europe 78, 90, 98

Achilles, T. 40.i

Açikalin, C. 81

Addison, Viscount 28

Adenauer, K. 5
Council of Europe 45, 77
Franco-German union 44
gendarmerie 45
London conference 77, 103–4
occupation statute 44, 49
Schuman Plan 77
security guarantee 60, 104

Afghanistan
MIN/UKUS/P/11 73, 84

Africa (*see also* Colonial Issues) 68
economic importance 43
MIN/TRI/P/21 & MIN/UKUS/P/10 68, 68.i

Schuman Plan 103

A.I.O.C. (Anglo-Iranian Oil Co.) 84

Alexander, Viscount 28

Allen, W.D. 12

Alphand, H. 37

America/Britain/Canada (A.B.C.) 2, 11, 88
sterling balances 9, 22
Washington (Sept. '49) 2, 11, 42

Andre, G. 37

Anglo-American relationship
economic (*see also* European Integration; U.K.: viability)
differences 1.i, 25
Financial Agreement (1945) 34
fundamentals 2, 11, 42, 54, 57, 62
London: officials 34, 34.i, 42.ii, 54, 70.i
MIN/UKUS/P/2 & 8 70
Ministers 80, 88
special 5–6, 15, 24, 27, 42–3, 67, 117
London: officials 29, 34.i(c), 54
MIN/UKUS/P/5 67
Ministers 84

Arab League 14, 97, 109

Arms supply *see* Middle East/Statement and Country headings e.g. Israel

Armstrong, W.A. 35

Aron, R. 44

Associate States (Viet Nam, Cambodia, Laos) 32

Atlantic High Council for Peace 24,

Atlantic Pact machinery *see* N.A.T. Organization

395

Atomic energy
Acheson statements   5, 102
Anglo-American-Canadian
    cooperation   19, 87, 102
France   44
Fuchs, Dr. K.   19
hydrogen bomb   5
international control   5, 102
London meeting   102
Soviet Union   5,
    abolition proposal   37, 46, 89
United Nations   5, 46

Attlee, C.R.   1
Anglo-American relations   57, 79
atomic energy   19, 102
Commonwealth   79
German rearmament/security   38, 60
Middle East statement   97
N.A.T. Organization   63

Auriol, V.   1
Germany   44

Australia
defence   43, 80, 85
London conference   7, 66
New Guinea/Indonesia   66, 98.iii, 99
sterling balances   9

Austria
Allied Commission   12.ii, 49, 59, 108
control agreement   49
Deputies   12, 59, 108
London: officials   58–9
    MIN/TRI/P/20   59
    Ministers   96, 99, 108
    declaration   98.i
occupation costs   12.ii, 59, 99, 108
peace treaty   12, 58–9, 108

Bao Dai, Emperor   4

Barclay, R.E.   3

Bateman, C.H.   34

Baudet, P.   3

Belgium
frontiers   98.ii
guarantee of neutrality in 1914   60

Benelux
economic union   20

Germany & London Conf.   17, 58,
    61.iii, 98.ii

Bérard, A.   53

Berlin (*see also* German unity)
aid,   8, 12
blockade   31
East/West trade   31
emergency planning   100
France   44
Kommandatura   58
London: officials   76
    TRI/P/24 & MIN/TRI/P/14   61
    Ministers   96, 100
Soviet Union   31
status   31.i

Berger, S.D.   34

Berthoud, E.A.   22

Bevan, A.   28

Bevin, E.   1
absences/illnesses   1, 6, 10, 17, 27, 44,
    55, 117
Acheson   78–80, 82, 84–5
Anglo-American differences   1, 3, 4
Asian sensitivities/aspirations   7, 80
Atlanticism   52, 74, 74.i, 78–9
Australia   7, 66
Berlin   49
chairman   89
China & Japan   56, 74, 80, 90
colonial policy   68, 78, 80, 98
Commonwealth   41, 78, 79
communist menace   89
defence budget   78–9
E.P.U.   3, 4, 8
European integration   52, 74.i
fundamentals   55, 57
Germany   3, 8, 18, 38, 49, 58, 74, 78,
    95–6
Harriman   4
House of Commons   18, 38, 49
Israel & arms supply   39, 82, 84, 105
London objectives   8, 41, 52, 74
M.E. statement   65, 84
N.A.C. declaration   37, 52, 84
    meeting   3–4, 7
N.A.T. Organization   41, 54, 78, 80
O.E.E.C.   78
Sadak   10, 81
Schuman   3, 4, 7

Sforza 94
South East Asia 78, 80, 98
Soviet Union 52, 74, 78
Spender 66
Stalin 4
Third Force 62
'three pillars' of foreign policy 74.i, 91
Trieste 94
viability 79
visits to Colombo 1, Paris 1, 3, 7, 10, 81,
  Strasbourg 10

Bidault, G. 24
  Atlantic High Council for Peace 24, 47

Blum, L. 44

Bohlen, C.E. 37

Borneo *see* South East Asia

Bourbon-Busset, J.L. 3

Bowker, R.J. 69

Bradley, Gen. O. 85

Bretton Woods 27, 49

Bridges, Sir E. 57
  London post-mortem 116

Brook, Sir N. 28

Bruce, D. 67

Brussels Treaty 3
  Permanent Commission 6, 30, 72
  P.U.S.C. 20, 30
  reorganization 30, 43, 74, 117

Burma
  MIN/UKUS/P/11 73, 84

Burrows, B.A. 10

Byroade, H.A. 18, 51

Cabinet Meetings & Memoranda
  Arab States & Israel 10.i, 39
  Atlanticist policy 20, 57, 62
  Austrian Treaty 12.i, 59
  China 23, 28
  German rearmament 74
  Germany 64
  London Conference 54, 74, 88
  N.A.C. meeting 113
  N.A.T. Organization 72
  Third World Power 20, 57, 62
  viability 74

Caccia, Sir H. 108

Cambodia 32

Camp, M. 33

Canada *see* A.B.C.; atomic energy;
  Commonwealth; O.E.E.C.

Canberra Conference: see Sydney

Ceylon
  defence agreement 43

Chiefs of Staff (C.O.S.)
  Austrian occupation 12
  B.A.O.R. 43
  Commonwealth defence 43, 80, 85
  defence budget 43
  German rearmament/gendarmerie 38,
    38.i
  global strategy 43, 62
  Middle East 43
  Turkey 81
  Western Europe 43

China (*see also* United Nations) 23
  Anglo-American differences 5, 23, 28,
    56, 74, 80
  aircraft in Hong Kong 23, 28, 90, 92
  Central People's Govt. 23
  communism 5, 23
  consuls in Malaya 23.i, 28, 92
  diplomatic recognition 23, 28, 56, 80
  Formosa 5, 56, 80
  Ho Chi Minh 32, 46
  Japan 50
  London: officials 29, 56, 74
    UKUS/P/8 & MIN/UKUS/P/1
    56.iii
    Ministers 80, 89, 92

Chou En-lai 23

Chuikov, Gen. V.I. 111

Churchill, W.S. 13
  German rearmament 38, 44

Chuter Ede, J. 28

Clutterbuck, Sir A. 22

Colombo Conference (Jan. 1950) 1
  Commonwealth consultative
    committee 4, 66, 112.ii
  Indo-China 4
  Japanese peace treaty 3, 50
  Middle East 10

397

Cold War Strategy (*see also* N.A.C.
Declaration)
Acheson   5, 48, 78–9
Bevin   52, 78, 89
France   41, 89
London: officials   29, 33–4, 37, 46, 54,
    74
            Ministers   78, 82, 89, 90
negotiation with Soviet Union   26, 33,
    37, 52, 54, 74, 89
    MIN/TRI/P/4   46
Scandinavia   17
Schuman   89
terminology   37, 89
world-wide objectives   15, 17, 20, 24, 43
    MIN/TRI/P/1   89

Colonial issues
Anglo/American differences   1.ii, 5, 27,
    68, 80
Anglo/French differences   32
London: officials   68
        MIN/UKUS/P/10 & MIN/TRI/P/
        21   68, 68.i
        Ministers   78, 80, 98–9

Cominform   44

Commonwealth (*see also* Sterling Balances;
South East Asia)   20, 43
Anglo-American relations   20, 22, 27,
    34, 43
Consultative Committee *see* Sydney
    conference
defence   10, 20, 43, 80, 85
European Integration   41, 79
London Conference   66
P.U.S.C.   20, 43

Communism (*see also* Cold War Strategy;
Soviet Union)   20, 37, 41, 43, 72, 74, 79,
89
Africa   26, 68.i
Bevin   89
France   41
Germany   31
S.E. Asia   26, 32.i, 43, 80, 98.iii

Continuing Organisation *see* A.B.C.

Cooper, J.S.   78

Council of Europe   3, 5, 30
Germany: invited   3
        accepts   77

Bundestag   45, 77
France   44
London:
    officials   33, 40, 61
    Ministers   78, 95
    U.K.   12, 30

Counterpart Funds   76

Cripps, Sir. S.   2
A.B.C.   88
Anglo-American relations   27, 57, 62
British Overseas Obligations   36, 43, 57
Germany   57, 62
N.A.T. Organization   35, 57, 62–3, 71
Sterling balances   42–3, 57
Third Force   62
viability   57
Western Organizations   35, 62–3
U.N.R.W.A.   88

Customs Unions   20

Dalton, H.   28

Davies, E.   72
arms supply to Israel   105
Atlanticism   72

De Gasperi, A.   94

De Margerie, R.J.   89

Defence   see North Atlantic Treaty

Defence Committee (Cabinet)   60

Defence Committee (N.A.T.)   3

De Folin, J.   37

Dening, M.E.   3

Denmark   40.i

Deputies *see* N.A.T.O.

Dollar aid *see* E.R.P.; South East Asia

Douglas, L.W.   4

Dual prices   1.i, 4

East-West trade   25.i
Berlin   31
export control/Lists 1A & 1B   84
London: officials   34
        MIN/TRI/P/16   76.i
        Ministers   78, 84, 96, 99

Economic Commission for Asia and the Far East (E.C.A.F.E.) 92

Economic Commission for Europe (E.C.E.) 30

Economic Cooperation Administration (E.C.A.) 2

Economic Development Committee (E.D.) 2

Economic Policy Committee (E.P.C.) 3,
    dollar situation (1949) 57, 62
    E.P.U. 88
    fundamentals 42, 55, 57
    isolation from U.S. 62
    sterling balances 9, 112.i

Economic & Social Council (E.C.O.S.O.C.) 92

Eden, R.A. 13

Egypt (*see also* Middle East/Statement)
    Arab League 14
    arms supply 75, 84, 97, 105–6, 109
    defence base 10, 14, 65.i, 75, 82
    financial agreement 9
    MIN/UKUS/P/6 65.i
    sterling balances 9, 42

Eritrea
    Bevin/Sforza 94.iii
    MIN/UKUS/P/7 65.ii, 84

European Coal and Steel Community (E.C.S.C.) *see* Schuman Plan

European Integration
    Atlantic alternative 20, 30, 47, 52, 72, 74.i, 91
    Commonwealth 20, 41, 79
    Third Force 57, 62, 72, 91
    U.K. 'foot dragging' 4, 71, 74, 115, 117
    London:
        officials 34, 40, 54
        MIN/UKUS/P/8 70
        Ministers 88
    U.S. relationship *see* E.R.P. & O.E.E.C.

European Payments Union (E.P.U.) 1, 3, 4, 25, 30, 54, 88, 99, 115

European Recovery Programme (E.R.P.)
    (*see also* O.E.E.C.) 2, 5, 40, 79
    after 1952:
        Acheson 5, 79, 115
        Gordon Gray 34, 78, 90, 107
        Jessup 34, 40, 71

Far East (Official) Committee 50

Far Eastern Commission 85

Formosa *see* China

France
    Customs Union with Italy 20
    Germany 41, 44, 74
    Marshall aid 79
    military strength 74
    N.A.T.: against Germany 40, 54
        inner group 41
        lukewarm towards 91
    political situation 41, 44
    reparations 95
    sensitivities:
        A.B.C./devaluation 11
        London conference 21, 24
        Middle & Near East statements 106, 109, 110
    United States 27

Franks, Sir O. 1

Fuchs, Dr. K. 19

Fundamentals *see* Anglo-American
    relationship: *economic*

Furlonge, G.W. 10

General Agreement on Tariffs and Trade (G.A.T.T.) 49

German Unity 18, 53, 64
    Adenauer 53, 103
    election proposals 53
    France 44
    London:
        officials 58, 61
        MIN/TRI/P/13 61.ii
        Ministers 95, 98–9
        Declaration 98.i
        publication of conditions 111
    Soviet Union 18

Germany, East (G.D.R.) (*see also* Berlin; Soviet Union)
    government 31
    police 31, 38, 58.i, 60
    MIN/TRI/P/11 61, 96

Germany, West (F.R.G.) (*see also* Berlin; Council of Europe; Cold War Strategy;

Germany, West (F.R.G.) *contd.*

German Unity; Schuman Plan; Soviet
Union)
Allied High Commission   5, 58, 95
allied property *MIN/TRI/P/17*   76.i, 96
B.A.O.R.   43
Benelux   17, 58, 61.iii, 90
Bizonia   49
control agreements   5, 58, 95
counterpart funds   76
declaration *see* German Unity
demilitarisation   12, 64
Denmark   40.i
debts   12, 61.i
economic problems   8, 12, 25.i, 58, 76,
    77, 78
elections *see* German Unity
emergency planning   100
E.P.U.   12
expellees (*see also* Migration)   8, 12, 76
foreign ministry   18, 49, 58
France   44
gendarmerie   12, 38, 44–5, 53, 104
    MIN/TRI/P/27   61, 96
government   5, 31, 51, 53, 58
Income tax law   8, 95
International Wheat Agreement   1.i
Land controls   95
        forces   104
Law 75   8, 96, 99
London:
    officials   40, 58, 61, 76
    Ministers   78, 95–6, 98–9, 100, 103
    Benelux   61.iii, 90, 98.ii–iii
national anthem   44
Occupation statute   5, 44, 49, 51, 61.i,
    64, 77
O.E.E.C.   74
Paris conferences (1949)   7, 18, 58
Petersberg protocol (1949)   7, 49, 51, 64
P.L.I. Agreement   12
policy towards/Western objectives   20,
    51, 58, 64, 74
    MIN/TRI/P/1   89
    TRI/P/22 & MIN/TRI/P/7   61, 61.i, 95
rearmament   27, 30, 33, 38, 40, 44, 74
reparations   95
repatriation P.O.W.s   93, 95
    MIN/TRI/P/26   93, 95–6, 98.i,
Rhine defence line   30, 60, 104

security guarantee   60, 61
    MIN/TRI/P/10   60, 96, 104.i
ship building   12, 51, 58, 77
    MIN/TRI/P/23   96, 99
status   30, 31.i, 51
steel level   12
    MIN/TRI/P/15 & 24   76.i, 96
Study Group (I.G.G.)
    MIN/TRI/P/12   61.i, 95, 103
termination state of war   12, 18, 51,
    61.i
trade   3, 76.i, 78, 84, 96, 99
United States   45, 48, 51

Gordon-Walker, P.C.   28

Gore-Booth, P.H.   117

Gray, G.   34
    U.S. aid   78, 90, 107

Greece (*see also* Near East Statement;
    N.A.T.)   16, 75, 78, 81

Griffin, R.A.   3

Griffiths, J.   28

Grotewohl, O.   31

Gruber, Dr. K.   108

Hadow, R.M.   29

Hague, The *see* N.A.T. Defence Committee

Haifa Pipeline/Refinery   10.ii
    MIN/UKUS/P/7   65

Hall, R. L.   24

Hall-Patch, Sir E.   4

Hare, R.A.   10

Harriman, W.A.   3

Harrison, G.W.   33

Harvey, Sir O.   3

Havana Charter   49

Helm, Sir K.   10

Henderson, Lord   8

Hitchman, E.A.   2

Ho Chi Minh   46

Hoffman, P.G.   4

Holmes, J.   4

Hong Kong
aircraft 23, 28, 90, 92
troops 5
Hoyer Millar, Sir F. 2, 117
House of Commons
Germany 8, 18, 38, 44
Israel/Jordan 39
Schuman Plan 95, 117
Hungary 34

Ibn Saud, H.M. King 84
India
MIN/UKUS/P/11 73, 84
sterling balances 9, 22.i, 42
trade dispute with Pakistan 9
U.S. forces in Japan 50
Indo-China 4–5, 32
London:
officials 56.i–iii
MIN/TRI/P/9 56.iii
Ministers 78, 98–9
**International Authority for the Ruhr
(I.A.R.)** 12, 44, 51
MIN/TRI/P/18 76.i, 96
International Monetary Fund 27
International Wheat Agreement 1.i
Iran (*see also* Near East Statement) 86
London: agenda 17
officials 65, 86.ii
MIN/UKUS/P/6. 65.i
Ministers 84
oil agreement 84
Iraq (*see also* Middle East Statement)
arms supply 75, 84, 97, 105–6
Kurdish question 84
Isaacs, G.A. 28
Israel (*see also* Middle East Statement) 10,
14, 39
arms supply 14, 39, 65, 75, 82, 84, 97,
105–6, 109
Jordan 10, 14
recognition 10, 39, 65
Italy
Customs Union 20

European Integration 47
London conference 94
Marshall aid 79
N.A.T. inner group 41, 94
Soviet Union 94
Trieste 94

Jackling, R.W. 25
Japan 50
Colombo Conference 3, 50
Commonwealth Group 50, 85
Control machinery 85
London:
officials 56, 56.i
MIN/UKUS/P/4 56.iii
Ministers 78, 80, 85
Peace Treaty 3, 50, 74, 80, 85
P.O.W.s
MIN/TRI/P/26 96
taxation policy 34
Truman 85
U.S. 'drift/slide' 50, 85
Jebb, Sir G. 6, 15, 24
Jessup, P.C. 3, 21, 24
Europe statements 34, 40, 71
Japan 50
Johnston, A. 28
Joint Services Mission 81
Jordan (*see also* Middle East Statement) 10,
14, 39
Arab Palestine 10, 39
arms supply 75, 84, 97, 105–6
Israel 10, 14
Jowitt, Viscount 28

Kashmir
MIN/UKUS/P/11 73
Katz, M. 4
Kirkbride, Sir A. 10
Kirkpatrick, Sir I. 3
Korean crisis 92, 117

Laos 32

Labouisse, H.R. 2, 24

Labouret, V. 37

La Tournelle, G. de 24

Laukhuff, P. 33

Lebanon
arms supply 39,84, 105–6

Lebel, C. 37

Libya
MIN/UKUS/P/7 65.ii, 84

Lie proposal *see* U.N.

Lie, T. 17, 89

Liesching, Sir P. 22

London Committee 34, 62

London Conference of Foreign Ministers
(May 1950)
origins 1, 3, 6–7
agenda 7, 12, (text) 17
arrangements/delegations 15, 21, 24
chairmen 24, 89
press 21, 78 (*MIN/TRI/P/19*) 89
records/structure 29, 34, 78, 98
information for: Benelux 17, 61.iii,
98.ii–iii; Commonwealth 66; H.M.
Opposition 13
bipartite meetings:
officials 21, 29, 33–4, 34.ii
sub committees 34.i, 42.ii, 56.i,
65.i–ii, 68, 70.i, 73
Ministers 78–80, 82, 84, 88
tripartite meetings
officials 21, 37, 40, 46, 58, 61
sub committees 56.ii, 58.i, 68, 76
Ministers 89, 90, 95–6, 98
Cabinet summaries 54, 74, 88, 99
Future coordination/consultation
MIN/TRI/P/6 40, 90
communiqué 98.i
declarations: 98.i (Austria, Berlin,
O.E.E.C. & U.S., Germany, Middle
East, migration, P.O.W.s); 101 (Near
East)
post-mortem 116–7

MacArthur, Gen D. 34

McBride, Gen. 81

Maclean, A.D. 46

Macready, Lt.-Gen. Sir G. 77

Makins, Sir R. 2

Malaya *see* South East Asia

Malenkov, G.M. 81

Mallet, W.I. 6

Mao Tse Tung 23
Soviet Union 80

Marshall Aid (*see also* E.R.P.) 2, 79

Marshall, P.H.R. 34

Martin, E.M. 80

Massigli, R. 3, 21

Matthews, W.D. 2

McCloy, J.J. 5
Stuttgart 38

McNeil, H. 1, 28

Medium Term Plan *see* N.A.T.

Merchant, L.T. 56

Middle East 10, 14
Arab weakness 14
arms supply 14, 39, 65, 75, 82, 84, 97,
105–6, 109
Commonwealth defence forces 10, 20,
43, 85
London: officials 65
MIN/UKUS/P/6 65.i
Ministers 82, 84
Pentagon talks (1947) 24
stability 10, 14, 39
strategic importance 43, 81
U.S. against regional arrangement 10,
43, 65.i

Middle East Statement (*see also* Middle East:
arms supply)
origins 10, 39, 65
assurances 75, 84, 97, 105–6, 109
London: officials 65, 75, 86.ii, 97
MIN/UKUS/P/6 65.i
Ministers 82, 84, 88, 109
text 98.i
France 65, 75, 97, 106, 109, 110
reactions 109, 110
Soviet Union 82

Migration
TRI/P/6 & MIN/TRI/P/5 40, 47.i
MIN/TRI/P/25 90, 96, 98

Military Committee 3
Military Security Board 44
Monnet, J. 103
Morrison, H.S. 28

National Advisory Council (N.A.C.) 2
Near East Statement (*see also* Middle East
    Statement) 75, 81, 84, 101
    France 110
    N.A.T. (1949) 75
Nehru, P. 4
    U.S. forces in Japan 50
New York Conference of Foreign
    Ministers (Sept. 1950) 40, 90, 108
North Atlantic Council (N.A.C.) Meeting
    (May 1950) 113
    arrangements 3, 6, 8
    agenda 6, 40
    press 84
    communiqué & resolutions 113.i–ii
N.A.C. Declaration ('grand declaration')
    Acheson 26
    Bevin 37, 52, 74, 113
    London: officials 37, 46, 54
        TRI/P/7, 23 & MIN/TRI/P/8
        46, 84.i
        Ministers 84
    rejection by N.A.C. 113
    Schuman 89, 113
North Atlantic Treaty 3
    articles II, (*see also* N.A.T.O.) 4, 6, 30,
        40
        VI 60
        IX 72
        X 30
    association of
        Austria 16, 33
        Germany 5, 16, 30, 33, 40, 47, 54,
        71, 74
        neutrals (Sweden/Switzerland) 16,
        30, 33, 40, 47, 83
        Turkey/Persia/Greece 16, 75, 81,
        84, 101
    Defence Committee 3
        report 33.i, 40, 72, 78, 113.ii

The Hague 33, 63
Medium term plan 33, 72, 89, 90, 113
military structure 3, 81
Ocean Shipping Board 113
Regional Planning groups 3, 16, 24, 30,
    117
Working Group 3, 33
N.A.T. Organisation (*see also* O.E.E.C.: U.S./
    Canada)
    as umbrella 41, 47, 117
    Ideas for: France 24, 40–1, 47, 54, 71
        U.K. 6, 12, 16, 24, 30, 33, 35, 40–1,
        57, 62–3, 71–2, 74
        U.S. 4–6, 33, 47, 51
    disagreement on economic
        functions 47, 71, 117
    defence tasks
        TRI/P/11, 16, 20 & MIN/TRI/P/2 46,
        72, 80
        MIN/TRI/P/28 & 29 80, 113
    Deputies 113, 114, 117
    inner group 27, 41
    location 16, 30, 52, 54, 80, 91, 98, 113
    London: officials 33, 40, 46, 47, 47.i,
        54
        Ministers 78, 80, 90, 98
    Netherlands 83
    Secretary-General 33, 72, 78, 80
    terms of reference
        TRI/P/8–10, 17, 19 & MIN/TRI/P/3
        46–7, 54, 62–3, 72, 74, 80
        MIN/TRI/P/22, 28–9, 80, 113.i

Oil 43
    A.B.C. 2
    Haifa refinery 10.ii
    substitution 1.i, 2, 25, 88
    Supplemental agreement 84
Organisation for European Economic
    Cooperation (O.E.E.C) 1, 3, 20
    after 1952 16, 30, 35, 41, 78, 83, 90
    Council of Europe 78
    European integration 4, 20, 47, 71
    E.P.U. 88
    French proposal (U.S./Canada) 40–1,
        47, 54, 71, 90
        London: officials 40, 47.i, 107
        TRI/P/15 71, 90
        Ministers 78, 90, 98, 107

Organisation for European Economic Cooperation (O.E.E.C) *contd.*
    U.K. objections 41, 91, 71, 117
    U.S. attitude 48, 78, 90
    Netherlands 83
    Superman 3

Pakistan
    MIN/UKUS/P/11 73, 84
    sterling balances 9, 22.i, 42–3
    Sydney conference 112.ii
    trade dispute with India 9
Palestine Relief Agency *see* U.N.R.W.A.
Paris Conferences of Foreign Ministers (1949) 7, 18, 58
Parodi, A. 7
Parrott, C.C. 33
Pau Conference (1950) 32
Pearson, L.B. 11
Penson, J.H. 12
Pentagon talks (1947) 24
Perkins, G.W. 5, 24
Permanent Under Secretary's Committee (P.U.S.C.) 6
    Anglo-American relations 27
    British Overseas Obligations 36, (text) 43
    British Policy towards communism 37
    Germany 57, 62, (text) 64.i
    U.K. membership of United Nations 20.i
    Third World Power or Western consolidation (text) 20, 24
    Western Organisations 6, 12, 16, (text) 30, 35, 57, 62
Persia *see* Iran
Petersberg Protocol *see* Germany
Philippines 5, 50, 78
Pieck, W. 31
Plowden, Sir E. 24
Portugal 73
Potsdam Conference (1945) 8, 95

Rasmussen, G. 40.i
Raynor, G.H. 29
Reber, J.Q. 29
Refugees *see* Migration; U.N.R.W.A.
Reinstein, J.J. 51
Reston, J. 40.i, 85
Rhine defence line 30, 43, 60, 104
Rickett, D.H.F. 55
Robertson, Gen. Sir B. 8
Romulo, C. 5
Rowan, Sir L. 2
Rumbold, Sir A. 34
Rusk, D. 114
Russia Committee 26

Sadak, M. 10
Safehaven 49
Sanders, W. 33
Satellite states (Soviet)
    London: officials 34, 46
        MIN/TRI/P/4 46
        Ministers 82, 90
Saudi Arabia (*see also* Middle East/ Statement) 10, 17
    arms supply 84, 105–6
    frontier dispute 65.i
    Hashemite rivalry 10, 65, 97
    London: officials 65, 86.ii
        MIN/UKUS/P/6 65.i
        Ministers 84
Scandinavia *see* Cold War; Customs Union; N.A.T.
Schuman, R. 1
    Acheson visit 78
    Bevin talks 3, 4.ii, 7
    cold war strategy 89
    Germany 44, 95–6
    Indo-China 98
    Law 75 96
    Mao Tse Tung 89–90
    Middle East Statement 109
    N.A.T. Organization 47, 90
    objections to N.A.C. meeting 7

publication of London records   98
Schuman Plan   95

Schuman Plan   77, 84, 95, 103, 117

Security Guarantee *see* Germany

Sforza, Count C.   84

Shawcross, Sir H.   28

Shepherd, Sir F.   86

Shinwell, E.   28

Shuckburgh, C.A.E.   6, 15, 24

Snyder, J.W.   2

South East Asia (*see also* Sterling Balances;
Sydney conference)
communism   26, 32.i, 43, 78, 80
economic development   2, 5, 9, 48,
112.i
London: officials   56.ii, 69
TRI/P/21 & MIN/TRI/P/
9   56.iii, 98
MIN/TRI/P/1   89
Ministers   78–9, 80, 90, 98–9
declaration rejected   69, 98
Soviet campaign   37, 78
strategic importance   5, 43, 90, 98

Soviet Union (*see also* Cold War Strategy;
Satellite States)
arms supply   82
atomic energy   5, 29, 33, 37, 44
Austrian peace treaty   59, 108
Germany   5, 18, 31, 58, 60, 78
Italy   94
London: officials   29, 33, 37, 46, 54, 74
TRI/P/13 & MIN/TRI/P/4   46
Ministers   78, 82, 89, 90
military strength   20, 29, 72, 74, 78
negotiations with
French support for   37, 44, 54, 89
MIN/TRI/P/4   46, 82, 89
U.K. objections   26, 33, 52, 54, 74,
82
U.S. public opinion   33, 37, 52
peace campaign   26, 37, 78, 89
recognition Ho Chi Minh   46
Western counter-propaganda   26, 31,
34, 46
Yugoslavia   29, 34, 46, 82, 90

Spain   17.i

Spender, P.C.   66

Stalin, J.V.   4

Standing Group   3

Stevens, R.B.   8

Steel, C.E.   58

Sterling Area   34, 80

Sterling Balances
Acheson   9, 112
Commonwealth consultation   9, 22
Egypt   9, 42
figures for   43, 43.i
India & Pakistan   9, 22.i, 43
U.K. burden   36, 43
U.K. proposals   2, 9, 42, 112.i
London: officials   34, 70.i
Ministers   80
S.E.A. development   9

Stikker, D.   3
O.E.E.C./N.A.T.O.   83
S.E. Asia   66, 98.iii

Stinebower, L.D.   29

Strang, Sir W.   1
Arab-Israeli tightrope   14
China & Japan 'black spot'   56
colonial policy   68
France & N.A.T.   91
London: chairman   24
post-mortem   116

Suez Canal   14, 43, 65.ii

Supplemental Oil Agreement   84

Sydney Conference   4, 112.ii

Sykes, B.H.C.   34

Syria
arms supply   39, 84, 105–6

Tedder, Lord   81

The Times   26

Third Force *see* European Integration

Tito, J.B.   34

Tomlinson, G.   28

Trieste   94

Trimble, W.C.   29

Trott, A.C.   10

Troutbeck, Sir J.   10

405

Truman, H.S. 85

Turkey (*see also* Near East Statement;
  N.A.T.) 81
  mediation in Middle East 10

United Kingdom (*see also* Anglo-American
  relationship)
  as world power *see* P.U.S.C.
  Atlantic bias 20, 27
  Commonwealth 20, 22, 43
  convertibility (1947) 2, 34, 57, 70
  defence expenditure 43, 78–9
  devaluation (1949) 11
  economic strategy 20, 34, 42.ii, 43, 70,
    78
  foot-dragging 4, 71, 74, 115, 117
  general election (Feb.) 1
  navy 20, 79
  relationship with Western
    Europe 34.ib
      MIN/UKUS/P/8 70, 82
  viability by 1952 2, 11, 30, 34, 54, 74,
    79, 115
      MIN/UKUS/P/2 70, 82

United Nations
  article 51 10
  arms race (1949) 97
  atomic talks 5, 46
  charter 17
  Chinese representation 5, 17, 23, 28,
    33, 46, 89, 90, 92
  Human rights 34
  Lie proposal (Security Council) 17, 23.ii,
    33, 40, 46, 89, 90
  London: officials 33, 46
      TRI/P/13 & MIN/TRI/P/4 46
      Ministers 89, 90, 92
  New York (Sept. 1950) 17, 90
  Soviet boycott 5, 17, 92
  Spain 17.i
  U.K. 20.i

United Nations Relief and Works Agency
  (U.N.R.W.A.) 10.ii
  London: agenda 17
      officials 65.i, 86.ii

      MIN/UKUS/P/6 65.i
      Ministers 84, 88

United States of America (*see also* Anglo-
  American relationship)
  army veterans 79
  Congress elections 92
  European aid *see* E.R.P. & O.E.E.C.
  France 27
  isolation 20, 27

Viet Minh 46

Viet Nam 32

Vyshinsky, A. 18

Wallner, W. 37

Washington Conferences (1947) 24
  (1949) 2, 11

Wilford, K.M. 60

Williams, T. 28

Willis, F.E. 34

Wilson, A.D. 12

Wilson, G.M. 34

Wilson, J.H. 28

Wilson-Smith, Sir H. 22

Wright, M.R. 2, 24

Yalta Declaration on Liberated Europe 33

Younger, K.G. 17
  Arab States and Israel 39
  China 92
  in charge of Foreign Office 17
  U.N. 92

Yugoslavia
  London: officials 29, 34, 46, 54
      TRI/P/13 & MIN/TRI/P/4 46
      Ministers 90
  trade agreement 34
  Trieste 94